Persuasion

Reception and Responsibility

From the Wadsworth Series in Communication Studies

Persuasion

Reception and Responsibility

ELEVENTH EDITION

CHARLES U. LARSON
Northern Illinois University, Emeritus

Australia • Brazil • Canada • Mexico • Singapore • Spain
United Kingdom • United States

Persuasion: Reception and Responsibility
Eleventh Edition
Charles U. Larson

Publisher: Holly J. Allen
Acquisitions Editor: Jaime Perkins
Senior Development Editor: Greer Lleuad
Assistant Editor: John Gahbauer
Editorial Assistant: Laura Localio
Senior Technology Project Manager: Jeanette Wiseman
Managing Marketing Manager: Kimberly Russell
Marketing Assistant: Alexandra Tran
Marketing Communications Manager: Shemika Britt
Project Manager, Editorial Production: Megan E. Hansen
Creative Director: Rob Hugel
Executive Art Director: Maria Epes

Print Buyer: Nora Massuda
Permissions Editor: Joohee Lee
Production Service: Aaron Downey, Matrix Productions Inc.
Copy Editor: Sherri Dietrich
Cover Designer: Bill Reuter
Cover Images: Large image: © Andy Williams/Getty Images.
    Insets, Left to right: © Gerard Launet/Getty Images;
    © David De Lossy/Getty Images; © Photodisc/Getty Images;
    © Royalty-Free/Corbis
Compositor: Integra
Printer: Malloy Incorporated

Library of Congress Control Number: 2005938576

ISBN 0-495-09159-6

Thomson Higher Education
10 Davis Drive
Belmont, CA 94002-3098
USA

For more information about our products, contact us at:
Thomson Learning Academic Resource Center
1-800-423-0563

For permission to use material from this text or product, submit a request online at
http://www.thomsonrights.com.
Any additional questions about permissions can be submitted by e-mail to
thomsonrights@thomson.com

For Mary, Without Whom . . .

Brief Contents

Contents

3 Traditional and Humanistic Approaches to Persuasion   52

4 Social Scientific Approaches to Persuasion   71

Preface

My first persuasion teaching assignment was to a class of 50 college juniors and seniors. I couldn't have assigned persuasive speeches—it would have taken too long and each of them would have gotten only a few opportunities to speak. Instead, I decided to teach the course from the perspective of the receiver, the consumer of persuasion who was faced with thousands of persuasive appeals every day—some of which seemed benign, others malignant. At the time, many persuasive messages distorted or invented "facts," used fallacious reasoning, and paid little heed to ethics.

Finding an appropriate textbook to use in this course was my major teaching problem. Everything on the market at the time focused on training the producers of persuasion. So I decided to write a book specifically for consumers.

The result was the first edition of *Persuasion: Reception and Responsibility*, and with the help of my friend and colleague Dick Johannesen and my editor, Becky Hayden, we discovered a huge need among teachers of persuasion for a book aimed at the consumption of persuasion. During the first convention at which the book was displayed, the *New York Times* declared it "a runaway hit." And what a history this book has seen since then. Consider the enormity of just a few events that have happened since then: AIDS infected and killed millions, terrorism is now the chief enemy, and ethics seem to have gone out the window. Technologically, we have personal computers, videotapes, and DVDs topped off by the introduction of the Internet, email, blogging, and the increasing frequency of identity theft and other forms of computer fraud. New terms that entered our vocabularies include webcast, blog, podcast, BlackBerry, cell phone, digital video and audio, iPod, satellite radio, and many others.

All these issues, and others yet to come, affect persuasion and increase the need for critical consumers of the persuasion blitz we face. In the years since that first edition, my colleagues and students have helped me revise and update the book, pointing out issues, media, and technologies that needed to be addressed. With their help and that of a series of editors and others at Thomson Wadsworth, we have arrived at an unprecedented eleventh edition that I hope will make each of your students a critical, ethical, questioning, and sometimes skeptical consumer of persuasion.

FEATURES NEW TO THIS EDITION

This edition continues to provide the successful features of earlier editions, and it has been updated with new examples and reports on recent theoretical developments. Additionally, three critical developments have occurred that I believe will affect the world of persuasion enormously. These new developments and their implications have been woven throughout all 14 chapters of this edition. What are these developments?

First, our culture is becoming increasingly varied in terms of ethnicity, race, religion, sexual preference, education, and many other areas that have direct implications for the practice and teaching of persuasion from both the producer's and the consumer's perspective. Throughout this edition you will find numerous examples, exercises, and explorations into the implications of our widely diverse culture now and in the future.

Second, our world has become astonishingly interactive, especially in terms of new media. The hundreds of new ways we have discovered to interact with one another makes each of us a journalist, editor, opinion expert, and artist with a huge potential audience for our persuasion. At the same time, new forms of interactivity have opened scores of new ways to appeal to us as consumers of persuasion. Some claim that we live in a "media age" but it is more accurate to say that we live in an interactive age. Again, the book includes examples, recent theoretical developments, and exercises involving the interactive media in our lives and how they have and will continue to change the face of persuasion—especially for receivers or consumers of this essential form of human communication.

Finally, our culture is facing a crisis in ethics. We saw the front edge of this crisis in the many recent corporate scandals and have witnessed an explosion of ethical lapses in all areas of our lives, including religion, politics, government, journalism, business practices, personal relations, and even foreign policy (e.g., ethical lapses that led to our disastrous war in Iraq). To address this crisis in ethics, Chapter 2 has been heavily revised and updated, and an Application of Ethics exercise or case study is now featured at the end of each chapter for individual or group exploration. In addition, ethical challenges and questions are raised throughout the text.

Consumers of persuasion need to continue to exercise their response-ability to investigate the persuasion coming at them. To help your students comprehend the concepts discussed in this book, each chapter begins with a list of **learning goals** and ends with a list of **key terms**. Each chapter also contains one or more **interactive boxes** that direct your students to become more aware of the impact of increasing cultural diversity and the interactive media explosion on persuasion.

Use all these features to test your students' understanding of each chapter, help them manage their roles as consumers of persuasion, and understand their responsibilities as constant receivers of a myriad of messages.

ACKNOWLEDGMENTS

This edition would not have happened without the help of my colleagues and students at Northern Illinois—especially Dick Johannesen and Joe Scudder who revised Chapters 2, 3, and 4. Thanks also to the staff at Thomson Wadsworth, beginning with Annie Mitchell, former acquisitions editor; Holly Allen, my publisher who encouraged a new edition; Greer Lleuad, senior development editor; Elisa Adams, my developmental and manuscript editor; Sherri Dietrich, my copyeditor; the many folks in the permissions, production, and marketing departments; and those colleagues who reviewed this edition and made wonderful suggestions. They were William D. Harpine, University of Akron; Claude Miller, University of Oklahoma; and Melissa Young, Texas Christian University.

And finally, I offer special thanks to the students and teachers who will use and hopefully profit from adopting, reading, and discussing the eleventh edition of *Persuasion: Reception and Responsibility*.

Charles U. Larson

PART I

Theoretical Premises

Persuasion rocks. It rocks not only our individual worlds but the whole world around us. Persuasion both changes our world and represents a way that our world changes us. Persuasion is about choice. Understanding persuasion helps us make better choices and is essential to live in our ever-changing world. It is clear that persuasion can make the world a better place just as Martin Luther King, Jr., made it clear through persuasion that society could be a better place.

Unfortunately, persuasion also has a dark side. We live in a period of reconstruction in the United States. We now face a different kind of enemy—and, perhaps, a different kind of *influence*, one that previously was unknown in this country. And persuasion is much larger than the United States and the Western world—today it is global. The more difficult task of reconstruction remains the restoration of trust in our major institutions. Trust in business leadership has also been shaken. Wall Street used persuasion to cover up years of corporate deceit, aided by one of the nation's elite accounting firms, and Enron was only the tip of the iceberg of what was to become a cascade of accounting scandals and insider trading. Trust in religious institutions was destroyed after repeated revelations of sexual improprieties by priests with minors. Ethical violations have even touched Martha Stewart and her homemaking enterprises.

Another challenge to our understanding of persuasion involves the introduction and rapid adoption of new, high-impact technologies such as personal computers and the digitization of many older technologies. And we have the ongoing development of virtual realities of all sorts. Easy and instant global communication affects us as never before. Traditional ways of doing business, conducting national and international politics, interacting with others, and even building cultures became obsolete following the globalization of virtually every aspect of human endeavor. Examples include the ability to buy, sell, trade, and bid online and to communicate continuously with a host of entities like the stock and commodities markets, airlines, friends, relatives, strangers, and even entire governments across the globe. And we do this twenty-four hours a day, seven days a week.

Underlying all of this change, however, is a constant—persuasion from all sides. In fact, persuasion has been the great common denominator in the arenas of economics, politics, religion, business, and interpersonal relations ever since humans began to interact. Never before, however, has persuasion had such potential as a tool for affecting our daily lives, as a means to many ends—both good and bad—and as a presence in every moment of our waking lives. The world we face rests on the power of persuasion.

We need to approach this profusion of persuasion in our everyday lives with an awareness that, at its core, persuasion is a symbolic act for both persuaders and receivers. We use symbols—usually words or images—in commercial interactions, interpersonal relations, family life, political endeavors, and international relations. Persuasion basically represents a democratic and humanistic attempt to influence others, to convince them to take certain actions—purchasing, voting, cooperating with one another—instead of forcing or coercing them to do so. For the most part, persuasion uses either logical or emotional means to accomplish desired ends, instead of force. Recent research and theory suggest that we process logical persuasion carefully and critically, but we process most emotional persuasion far less critically. In either case, the logical or emotional persuasion seeks to give us "good reasons" for acting. These good reasons must be delivered to the receivers via an appropriate medium, whether "one-to-one" interpersonal communication or "one-to-many" forms of communication, such as contemporary media. And the good reasons must be acceptable in terms of the norms and values of culture and society.

As you read this book, I hope that you change in important ways. We live in a world in which persuasive messages of various types continually compete for our attention, our beliefs, and our actions. What's more, the exciting times in which we live depend heavily on successful persuasion, and we spend far more time receiving persuasion than sending persuasion. We are predominantly in the role of the persuadee, receiver, or consumer of persuasive messages. So the aim of this book and class is to make you a more critical and responsible consumer of persuasion.

In some ways, you are already a critical receiver, but you can improve your reception skills. You need to identify how critical a receiver you are at the outset. How easily are you persuaded? How does persuasion work on you? What tactics are most effective with you? With others? Which are least effective?

Part I investigates these questions and establishes a perspective. Throughout Parts I, II, and III of this book you will find several tools to help you understand the concepts and theories we consider. First is a list of **Learning Goals** that precede each chapter. Second is a list of **Key Terms** at the end of each chapter. To be a successful student of persuasion, you should be able to achieve the learning goals and identify and explain the key terms. To keep our eyes on the ethics crisis described in the preceding paragraphs, each chapter also has an **Application of Ethics** exercise that you can do individually or as a class. Additionally, each chapter contains one or more interactive **boxes** that direct you to become more aware of the increasing cultural diversity we face and the impact of the interactive media explosion we are facing.

In Chapter 1, we examine how persuasion dominates our lives. We look at several definitions of persuasion, ranging from those rooted in ancient Greece to those derived from the contemporary diverse and interactivity-mediated world. Our discussion also focuses on a useful model of persuasion suggested by Hugh Rank, a scholar of persuasion, advertising, and propaganda. The model grew out of his work with the National Council of Teachers of English (NCTE) and their concern with the increase in "doublespeak"—the attempt to use words to confuse and mislead—to miscommunicate. In Chapter 2, Richard L. Johannesen discusses a variety of approaches to the ethical issues that arise whenever persuasion occurs. Keep in mind that these approaches and issues involve both persuaders and persuadees—senders and receivers. In Joe Scudder's Chapter 3, we explore the traditional humanist roots of persuasion. It is remarkable how many of the principles articulated long ago remain as good practice today. We also see the importance of understanding how persuasion is grounded in human experience and society. Scudder's Chapter 4 focuses on social science methods and what they have revealed to us about persuasion. In Chapter 5, we examine human symbolic behavior, especially as it occurs in language and in images. Finally, Chapter 6 offers several alternative ways receivers can analyze, interpret, decode, and critique persuasive language. It is not important that you find one theory or approach that you prefer, but rather that you consider the various alternatives.

1

Persuasion in Today's Changing World

LEARNING GOALS

After reading this chapter, you should be able to:

1. Identify and use interactive media.
2. Identify and explain instances of doublespeak in contemporary persuasion.
3. Explain persuasion as it is defined here and give examples of it from your life.
4. Recognize our increasing cultural diversity and make attempts to interact with persons who are culturally different than you.
5. Explain common ground and seek it in your persuasive encounters with others.
6. Explain the SMCR model of communication and its dynamics.

7. Identify persuasive messages that are processed in the central and peripheral information-processing channels.

8. Identify instances of Rank's intensifying and down playing strategies in persuasion targeted at you.

9. Develop your abilities to engage in self-protection using the Rank model.

We are engulfed in a sea of information—more than we can ever hope to process. Much of it is useless, and we can safely ignore it, but some of it is essential. This essential information should influence us to make wise and educated decisions—some easy and some difficult. Several factors that can and do influence us are the environment, our social and cultural mores, interpersonal relations, persuasion, and other factors and/or people. Our focus here is on how **persuasion** as the central form of influence in our lives is used to prompt us to vote, to purchase, to believe, and to act. We live in the age of electronic media. Mass media have been with us for a long time—since the printing press—but in a media-rich and highly technological culture, persuasion gains new power. Consider but a few new media that play important roles in our lives: the Internet, cell phones, the iPod, email, handheld computers, podcasting, blogs, and many others. All these make it easier for individuals to influence others by having their say. A soldier fighting a war in a foreign land emails his family and friends about his experiences and what is *really* happening on the front, or a person who witnessed an armed robbery describes her experiences in her blog; thus, we ordinary people become "news reporters" in exciting and individual ways, and we are being faced with ethical decisions about what to report, how reliable our sources may be, whether our biases enter in, and so on.

One theme we'll pursue throughout this book is the degree to which new **interactive media** (i.e., media in which the receiver is able to actively participate in the communication process, such as a radio talk show) persuade the public at large and individuals in particular. While these media offer us the opportunity to participate in important decision-making processes like purchasing, voting, joining, or donating, they also can "dehumanize" us. Because these media can track results (e.g., the number of "hits" on an Internet site and, in some cases, by whom) they can turn us into statistics—ratings numbers for advertisers, public opinion numbers for politicians, and return-on-investment numbers for businesses. Earlier media could track results to a certain degree (e.g., the Neilson television or Arbitron radio ratings). However, they were based on small samples and relied on viewer and listener self reports, which could be falsified. With interactive media, the "footprints" of users are recorded by actual phone calls to a given 1–800 number, hits on the Internet, the people meter combined with viewer logs, and in other ways. These new capabilities for receiver input are but a few of the challenges facing receivers (e.g., privacy issues and being invested with the power to become part of the persuasion going on). And these interactive media are not limited to cell phone or Internet uses. They include video games (which research shows can increase violent behavior), touch-sensitive screens, virtual reality, electronic payments at gas pumps that are also surrounded with persuasive ads, ATMs, and many more—all of which involve persuasion to some degree.

As the following activity box demonstrates, such interactivity can even involve physical activities such as hunting. You will be encountering such activity boxes throughout this book. They are intended to get you to do one or more of several things. First, you should consider the topics or issues being discussed and ask yourself how they relate to persuasion. Second, if there is a website mentioned, go to it and ask yourself the same question. If the issue involved interests you, go to InfoTrac® College Edition and explore it further. Finally, the boxes sometimes raise ethical questions or issues of how cultural diversity could be

---

B O X 1.1   The Age of Interactive Media: Imagine the Possibilities

One website called liveshot.com was recently developed by a Texas entrepreneur. It is an interactive hunt for big game—wild boar, antelope, deer, bear, and such. It allows persons from remote locations to interact with a robotic rifle and target the game by using a mouse that allows the "hunter" to manipulate a real rifle mounted in a real blind located in Texas where the hunt takes place. The hunter can visually inspect the hunting terrain, looking for targets using a webcam. When a target is found, the user can manipulate (i.e., aim) the robotic rifle and squeeze its trigger. One of liveshot's first users was a quadriplegic man in Indiana who hadn't hunted in 17 years and who did the aiming and shooting via a mouse operated by puffs of air he blew into a tube. By the way, he was wearing camouflage (*All Things Considered,* 2005).

Should he have had a hunting license? What other uses of this kind of interactivity can you imagine?

Imagine the implications of this level of interactive media for various persuasive attempts and how such interactions will involve receivers. The possibilities are mind-boggling, and they're on the way or are already here in competitive sports, shopping, dating, gaming, voting, and a host of other applications. For example, we have already witnessed stalking on the Internet, and in the United Kingdom sports fans can interactively tune in fan interviews and delete the commentator's interpretations. They can even manipulate camera angles, volume, and more on an individual basis, thus creating their own individualized "version" of the soccer match. What might that ability do to sports broadcasting in general?

---

involved. Try to grapple with these questions and issues and perhaps bring them up in class.

Another powerful change in our persuasion world is the degree to which our culture reflects increasing diversity. **Cultural diversity** (i.e., the increasing numbers of persons from other cultural backgrounds, races, ethnicities, sexual preferences, educations, etc.) calls for us to make adjustments in all forms of communication, including persuasion. Many times the communication results of cultural diversity are very positive. For example, in Gillette, Wyoming, the Prairie Winds organization regularly hosts a cultural festival with ethnic food, dancing, music, art, crafts, and demonstrations, and attendees can participate in them (*News Record,* 2005). Unfortunately, sometimes the results of miscommunication across diverse cultures are tragic. For example, in 2004, a Hmong deer hunter in Wisconsin killed five people because he misunderstood a persuasive attempt to convince him that the deer stand he was using belonged to someone else. He was found guilty of killing them and is now serving a life sentence without chance of parole.

As the child of Swedish immigrants, I can relate to such cultural differences in persuasion. My parents voted Democrat because their countrymen told them to; they believed in and joined certain causes, groups, churches, and bought certain brands because their fellow countrymen did; and they responded to persuasive appeals from advertisers, politicians, and ideologues for the same reasons. Today, new immigrants to America face the same kinds of appeals and respond from their own culturally diverse backgrounds, and undoubtedly they will join, vote, believe in, and donate as their countrymen do. This applies to existing subcultures as well (e.g., Latinos respond to persuasive appeals as their reference groups do, and the same applies to Blacks, Asians and Pacific Islanders, and others).

Consider the decisions you make while pursuing your degree: to enlist in ROTC , to move out and rent your own place, to vote for a certain candidate, or to join a cause. We all bring our own cultural values and psychological needs to these decisions and to others like them, and thus our decisions will be diverse. (Note: A box dealing with cultural diversity occurs in each chapter in this book. Get involved with those boxes in the same way you have been advised to get involved with the interactive media boxes.) Let's begin to explore how these various factors interact with persuasive tactics in the information age.

PERSUASION IN AN INFORMATION AGE

We live in an age in which more information is available than any person can hope to access and consider. Persuasion has changed a great deal since the days when one person could hope to reach only as many people as could assemble within reach of his or her voice. The arrival of the print medium permitted persuaders to reach many more people and allowed audiences to read and reread persuasive appeals, and even to compare them with a variety of other evidence. With radio persuaders expanded this "one-to-many" model, but the medium also brought us an enormous increase in advertising, political appeals, and increasingly sophisticated persuasive techniques. The medium also brought receivers a new kind of persuader—broadcast demagogues such as Father Coughlin and Huey Long, and more recently, Rush Limbaugh and others. Television brought us even more of these kinds of persuaders, such as Bill O'Reilly and others.

Interactive media will continue to alter the nature of persuading and the experience of being persuaded. In recent times, politicians, ideologues, and others have persuaded us to support various candidates and causes. In Minnesota, a professional wrestler named Jesse Ventura was elected governor for the most irrational and emotional reasons. His campaign's use of interactive Internet and email tactics helped Jesse "The Body" sweep away his quarrelsome opponents by convincing the public that voting for him was an individual way to protest the system. He went on to wage a running battle with the legislature and made numerous outrageous

claims. Ultimately the same interactive media that helped elect him also brought him down as chat groups, email, and Internet bulletin boards spread the news about the governor's blunders. Constant media persuasion has also convinced many of us that we need interactive items such as ATM cards, remote control devices, personal computers, home pages, the Internet, digital cameras, high-speed connectivity, cellular telephones, handheld devices like the Palm Pilot or the BlackBerry, and many others.

Do these brief examples of emotional, knee-jerk forms of persuasion mean that we need to automatically reject all the persuasive appeals coming at us from advertisers, politicians, and others? Absolutely not—in fact, it's essential that we consider many of the persuasive appeals simply to sort the wheat from the chaff. Whether as individuals, families, corporations, or governments, we need to be persuaded to do our part on a number of fronts. Take, for example, the need to preserve and restore our environment while moving toward energy independence. This means we need to decide whether to support drilling for oil in the Alaskan Wildlife Reserve or whether we should subsidize development of hydrogen energy. There are logical and emotional arguments on both sides. What are the potential costs, benefits, and alternatives?

For these and other reasons, it is more important than ever to train ourselves to become critical receivers of persuasion in an interactive information age, and providing this training is a central goal of this book and this class. As we move from chapter to chapter, you should be able to arm yourself with tools of analysis, perspectives, exercises, and examples that will allow you to become a truly critical receiver of persuasion.

Let's consider just a few of the reasons we need to become more selective receivers of persuasive messages. Researcher Jamie Beckett (1989) reported in the *San Francisco Examiner* that the average U.S. adult is exposed to 255 advertisements every day. *Advertising Age* magazine may be closer to the truth when it estimated that the average American sees, reads, or hears more than 5,000 persuasive advertising messages a day. And communications professor Arthur Asa Berger (2000) reports, "Some estimate that the total number of impressions one processes in one day is as high as 15,000" (p. 81). The 5,000 figure is probably closest to the true number of ads to which we are exposed on a daily basis. These persuasive messages appear in many formats. Take the familiar television spot advertisement, with its high-tech artistry, computer graphics, sophisticated special effects, computer animation, and digitally sweetened sound. Over 25 years ago, communications expert Neil Postman (1981) called attention to just one aspect of persuasion and its potency in shaping our values—the television commercial. By the time you're 20 years old, you're likely to have seen over a million commercials—about a thousand a week. What impressions do we get from them? Here is Postman's analysis:

> A commercial teaches a child three interesting things . . . first is that all problems are resolvable. Second that all problems are resolvable fast, . . . and third is that all problems are resolvable fast through the agency of some technology. It may be a drug. It may be a detergent. It may be an airplane or some piece of machinery. The essential message is that the problems that beset people are solvable if only we will allow ourselves to be ministered to by a technology (p. 4).

How often are we affected by this comforting belief? Did we buy a product because we subconsciously felt that it might make us more attractive, help us land a job, or impress a teacher? As these ads become more and more sophisticated, they become shorter, so the receiver must confront more of them each day, and this requires us to be alert to our need to evaluate them more critically. Instead of the staple 30-second spots of yesteryear, we now see 15- and even 10-second spots dominating TV advertising, and the 7 1/2-second spot is common in England. Product placement in television and film (e.g., a character in the story drinks a Coke) may only last a few seconds, but research shows that it persuades consumers to buy the product.

Other media also contain influential persuasive messages—newspaper and magazine advertisements, billboards and signs along the roadside, radio spots, t-shirts with product names, home pages, faxes, PR releases, and even signs in public restrooms. We find ourselves deluged with direct-marketing appeals such as catalogs, direct-mail offers, telemarketing, infomercials, Internet appeals, and more. And these persuasive appeals go beyond just building brand awareness to include persuasion that influences us in subtle ways, including messages of social and individual importance. For example, the Illinois Department of Public Health uses billboards to promote a website for people who want to quit smoking. Massive databases and sophisticated data filing and retrieval systems make it possible for persuaders to segment us into narrow groups that are vulnerable to persuasion. These examples serve to provide us with even more reasons to become critical receivers. Direct marketing uses the voluminous data about individuals that is available, and it hopes to soon be able to create market segments as small as one person. What are the implications of such deep market segmentation? How much information about ourselves should we give away? What about our right to privacy?

This is a good time for you to become familiar with your InfoTrac® College Edition subscription. Access the Web page at www.infotraccollege.com/ and type in your password. (If you don't have a password, go to the *Persuasion* book companion website at http://communication.wadsworth.com/larson11 for information about how to obtain one.) Type "persuasion" in the subject search engine and click enter. How many entries are listed? Examine one of the psychology entries and one of the rhetoric journal articles or "see also" items. (In later links, you can use the "Related Subjects" options.) Browse some interesting titles in both the academic and popular press to see the kinds of academic research being done in persuasion and see how the press approaches topics related to persuasion.

PERSUASION IN A TECHNOLOGICAL WORLD

Persuasion is essential in inducing people to try, accept, and finally adopt the many new ways of thinking, believing, and behaving that come with the global shift to a technological age. Students are urged to take more core subjects and courses in computer technology at college. Parents tell their children to reduce the volume of music systems to avoid hearing damage. The U.S. government tries to convince citizens to conserve energy by adopting energy efficient appliances or hybrid vehicles. Churches, schools, and community groups find it necessary to use sophisticated technologies (e.g., email "care lists" or "canned" fundraising direct marketing campaigns) to gain or maintain membership and financial support. Meanwhile, marketers use new technologies to convince consumers that a given product such as a cell phone camera will add excitement to their lives.

The title of this book suggests both its purpose and your job as a persuadee. *Persuasion: Reception and Responsibility* aims to make you aware of changes in the logical, emotional, and cultural persuasive appeals targeted directly at you. The book focuses on your job to engage in "**response-ability**," or your ability to wisely and critically respond to the persuasion you encounter and to make wise choices. Of course, persuasion is hardly a recent phenomenon, and it would have been good in past times for audiences to have response-ability. If they had, many tyrants might not have risen to power and wars might have been avoided. The National Council of Teachers of English (NCTE) recognized this need for people to engage their response-ability when it instituted its regular conferences on **doublespeak**, which it defined as deliberate miscommunication. The organization also announced an annual "doublespeak award" to be given to the persuader(s) whose language was most "grossly unfactual, deceptive, evasive, confusing, or self-contradictory." The award alerts persuadees to the often confusing and sometimes misleading use of words in persuasion.

DOUBLESPEAK IN A PERSUASION-FILLED WORLD

Even in a persuasion-riddled world such as ours, you would not need defensive training if all persuaders were open and honest. Too many, however, try to persuade by using doublespeak. Doublespeak comes in several guises: the half truth, the euphemism, hair-splitting, the trial balloon, bogus issues, jargon, and others. Consider the "peacekeeping" military missions engaged in around the world by our government or Bill Clinton's insistence that he had never "had sex with that woman" (referring to Monica Lewinsky). The term "ethnic cleansing" referred to mass murder in several parts of the world, and it camouflaged the existence of concentration camps and the mass slaughter of thousands by using words that sounded almost antiseptic.

If you find the words "ethnic cleansing" disturbing, access InfoTrac College Edition under the subject index option, and enter them in the search engine. You will find many articles that elaborate on the term and the genocide that followed. Which did you find most surprising?

Of course, doublespeak isn't confined to the world of politics. A real estate ad indicating that a house is "convenient to the interstate" probably means that you will hear cars whoosh by day and night. A "handyman's special" means lots of repairs. A "good work car" really means a "junker." CEOs at Enron, AIG, WorldCom, and others used doublespeak to confuse and bilk investors and employees by convincing them that "liabilities" were "assets" and that "spending" meant "earning."

For some good examples of doublespeak here and in other countries, access InfoTrac College Edition, and enter the words "euphemism" and "half truths" in the search engine. Which of the items is the most interesting? Start identifying examples of doublespeak as you encounter them. You'll be surprised how often persuaders try to miscommunicate.

B O X 1.2 **Becoming an Advertising Medium—Ethical or Unethical?**

 Viral advertising is a new form of interactive communication that turns the audience into a persuasive advertising channel, as each receiver spreads the message online like a (benign) virus. The technique resembles a chain letter. First the advertiser places an attractive or entertaining interactive message such as a game on the Web and begins to direct consumers to visit the website, which also contains a variety of advertising links from which to choose. One of these is "send this site to a friend." And the consumer does just that, because it is fun and easy to share things via the Internet. One such site at www.subservientchicken.com, is sponsored by Burger King and plays on the old "Have it Your Way!" slogan in promoting chicken offerings as opposed to the Whopper. The website features someone dressed in a chicken suit. The viewer can command the chicken to run, fly, hop, skip, and so on. There are several hundred actions programmed into the game, but If asked to perform a distasteful or obscene act, the "chicken" confronts the screen and shakes its finger at the "naughty" user. The technique persuades on at least two levels: the purchase of the product and the decision to forward the "fun" interactive site much as you might do with a chain letter. Can you think of other instances of persuasion in which this viral approach might be exploited? What about political campaigns? Religious appeals? Worthy causes? What are the ethical implications of participating in viral marketing (e.g., using "fun" media to hook consumers or urging them to spread the message)?

DEFINING PERSUASION: FROM ARISTOTLE TO ELABORATION LIKELIHOOD

Definitions of Persuasion

The ancient Greeks were among the first to systematize the use of persuasion, calling it "**rhetoric**." They studied it in their schools, applied it in their legal proceedings, and used it to build the first democracies in their city-states. Aristotle was the primary rhetorical theorist in ancient Greece, authoring more than 1,000 books and categorizing all the knowledge types in the known world for his schoolmate Alexander the Great. He defined rhetoric as "the faculty of observing in any given case, the available means of persuasion." According to Aristotle, persuasion consists of artistic and inartistic proofs. The persuader controls **artistic proof** such as the choice of evidence, the organization of the persuasion, style of delivery, and language choices. **Inartistic proof** includes things not controlled by the speaker, such as the occasion, the time allotted to the speaker, and the speaker's physical appearance. According to Aristotle, persuasion succeeds or fails based on a source's credibility, or **ethos**; the use of emotional appeals, or **pathos**; logical or rational appeals, or **logos**; or a combination of all these (Roberts, 1924). Aristotle also thought that persuasion is most effective when based on the **common ground**, which is the shared beliefs, values, and interests existing between persuaders and persuadees. This shared territory permits persuaders to make certain assumptions about the audience and its beliefs. Assuming these beliefs, persuaders use **enthymemes**—a form of argument in which the first or major premise in the proof remains unstated by the persuader and, instead, is supplied by the audience. A familiar example is "All men are mortal; Socrates is a man; therefore Socrates is mortal." The persuader needs to identify common ground or those major premises held by the audience and use them in enthymemes (see Figure 1.1).

Roman students of persuasion added specific advice on what a persuasive speech ought to include. Cicero identified five elements of persuasive speaking: (1) inventing or discovering evidence and arguments, (2) organizing them, (3) styling them artistically, (4) memorizing them, and (5) delivering them skillfully.

FIGURE 1.1 The Lincoln Financial Group establishes common ground in this advertisement between the company and any person of any race or ethnicity who is approaching retirement. Note the satisfied and happy looks on both of the faces and the healthy appearance of both persons. This resonates with the desire to have a happy, healthy retirement and helps build the common ground. Note also the examples referred to in the ad copy—"40 years building," "30 years paying off," and "20 years saving," each of which would probably resonate with any potential retiree, and the idea that "Now I want to LIVE." These words continue building common ground between the company and the potential customer.

SOURCE: Used by permission of the Lincoln Financial Group.

Both Aristotle's and Cicero's definitions focus on the sources of messages and on the persuader's skill and art in building a speech. In the communication discipline, we consider these "rhetorical" approaches to the study of persuasion because they grew out of the rhetorical traditions of the Greeks and Romans. They are still applied in current research on persuasion and its effects.

Later students of persuasion reflected the changes that accompanied the emergence of elec-

tronic media and the social sciences following World War II. Over 50 years ago, communication scholars Winston Brembeck and William Howell (1952) broke new theoretical ground when they described persuasion as "the conscious attempt to modify thought and action by manipulating the motives of men toward predetermined ends" (p. 24). In their definition, we see a notable shift from logic in persuasion toward a focus on the more "emotional" means of persuasion—those that stimulate the internal motives of the audience. Twenty years later they defined persuasion as "communication intended to influence choice" (p. 19). Wallace Fotheringham (1966), another early persuasion theorist, defined persuasion as "that body of effects in receivers" caused by a persuader's message (p. 7). Here, even unintended messages could be persuasive if they caused changes in the receivers' attitudes, beliefs, or actions. Literary critic and language theorist, Kenneth Burke (1970) defined persuasion in an intriguing way. He said that persuasion was really the artful use of the "resources of ambiguity." Burke believed that if receivers feel they are being spoken to in their "own language" and hear references to their own beliefs and values, they will develop a sense of **identification** with the persuader, believing that the persuader is like them—a concept close to Aristotle's "common ground." In Burke's theory, when persuaders try to act, believe, and talk like the audience, they create a bond with listeners, who will identify with them and will follow their advice on issues.

Taking our cues from Aristotle, Burke, and others, persuasion is defined here as "the process of **co-creation** by sources and receivers of a state of identification through the use of verbal and/or visual symbols." This definition implies that persuasion requires intellectual and emotional participation between both persuader and persuadee that leads to shared meaning and co-created identification. Communication professor and researcher Herbert Simons (2001) agrees and calls this result "coactive persuasion." Notice that like our definition, coactive persuasion is receiver-oriented and situational, relying on similarities between persuaders and persuadees and appeals to things acceptable to the persuadee, thus inducing action (p. 75).

In one sense, all persuasion consists of **self-persuasion**. We rarely act in accordance with persuasion unless we participate or interact in the process logically and/or emotionally. The words "process," "co-created," and "identification" are central in this definition.

The **elaboration likelihood model** (ELM) serves as an organizational model of persuasion and resulted in significant changes in the way theorists view persuasion. It serves as a central model throughout this book. Social psychologists Richard Petty and John Cacioppo (1986) suggested the ELM as a cognitive model in which persuasion takes one of two routes. In the **central information processing route** the receiver consciously and directly focuses on the persuasive communication while mentally elaborating on the issues and actively seeking more information. This requires significant effort on the part of the receiver. The target of the persuasive message searches out the issues, supporting evidence, alternatives, respective costs and benefits, and other potential outcomes. It usually operates in making important decisions such as purchasing a new car. Here we probably read brochures, compare prices, or go online to discover the actual amount of a dealer's profit and how the vehicle is rated by various consumer publications. Sometimes persuasion requires only a momentary period of concentration on an issue. According to the ELM, this persuasion occurs in the **peripheral information processing route**. There information may be processed almost instantly or just by the senses, without direct focusing on or researching of the decision. We decide to buy Cracker Jacks at the ball park to get the "free" prize and because they are mentioned in the song "Take Me Out to the Ball Game" that is sung at the middle of the seventh inning. At any given moment, there are millions of pieces of such trivial information available, but we consciously attend to only a few of them. The peripheral route resembles a sponge. We soak up persuasive information and may act on it, but we remain unaware of or unfocused on it in any direct or effortful way. The peripheral route usually contains shortcuts for making decisions and often includes emotional appeals.

Persuasion and Other Forms of Influence

Most communication scholars agree that persuasion usually relies on communication that attempts to change another person in some way. Many suggest that the attempt must succeed to be

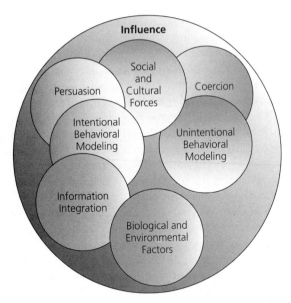

FIGURE 1.2 The relationship of persuasion to other forms of influence.

considered persuasion, and most agree that persuasion requires participation by a sender and a receiver. Persuasion usually succeeds when it adapts to the receiver's world—the situation, the context, the culture, and receivers' emotions and motivations. Figure 1.2 illustrates the relationships among various terms of influence that often confuse the new student of persuasion. The importance of each type of influence probably varies substantially from person to person and according to the context. The central point of this diagram is that many forces (including persuasion) bring change to our lives.

Those who study persuasion don't always distinguish among these forms of influence. In many discussions, "influence" and "persuasion" are interchangeable. We need to distinguish among several terms related to persuasion, including "influence," "coercion," "compliance-gaining," "acquiescence," "behavioral modeling," and "information integration."

Influence refers to a person's attitude or behavioral change. There are several ways that attitudes or behaviors may change. For example, many fans adopt the styles or behavior of their pop idols. This represents influence through behavior modeling. Similarly, many adults are embarrassed when their young child uses profanity in public—profanity that was overheard at home. This is an unintended outcome of behavioral modeling. In contrast, most parents consciously model more positive behaviors for their children, hoping to persuade them to emulate those behaviors. Persuasion always entails some degree of choice. In contrast, **coercion** uses some level of force—physical or psychological—to gain compliance, such as when peer pressure results in changes in attitude or behavior; you really don't want to go to the rock concert, but you choose to go because you know that it will please the person who invited you. So, persuasion and coercion represent two ends of a continuum ranging from free choice to forced choice. Although terrorism uses coercion, the co-creation of states of identification doesn't often result, but persuasion of a different sort can occur as an unexpected result. For example, acceptance of cultural diversity suffered after 9/11, and many people avoided air travel—especially if other passengers appeared to be of Middle Eastern extraction. Influence occurs when a person chooses a certain action in return for some future concession, as frequently happens in political favor swapping. Persuasion, as a kind of influence, occurred in making a political deal because some common ground was reached, but none of the people involved *really* changed their minds based on the merits of the actual issues. Information integration and analysis is another route to influence that doesn't involve persuasion. For example, a manager may change his or her inventory management behavior after learning that quarterly sales were up or down. Something overheard in conversation, read in the newspaper, or seen on the Internet may lead to changes in behavior, but this is not persuasion since no co-creation occurred. Co-creation is central to our definition of persuasion. Persuasive contexts extend beyond public-speaking situations but all involve some kind of co-creation. For instance, protest marches, decision-making get-togethers, staff meetings, sales presentations, and mass media events all involve the co-creation of identification between persuaders and receivers.

CRITERIA FOR RESPONSIBLE PERSUASION

How does cooperative and co-creative persuasion happen? What makes it work? Although persuasion occurs under various circumstances, three conditions seem to increase the chances that responsible receivers will make wise and knowledgeable decisions. First, responsible persuasion is most likely to occur if all parties have an equal opportunity to persuade and approximately equal access to the medium of communication. If one side imposes a gag rule on the proponents of the other side of an issue while advocates of the other side have freedom to persuade, then receivers get a one-sided and biased view of the issue. Although they are persuaded, the persuasion isn't exactly fair because of the gag rule.

Second, in an ideal world, persuaders reveal their agendas to the audience. They tell us their ultimate aims and goals and how they intend to achieve them. Unfortunately, this doesn't always happen. Political candidates need to tell us how they intend to improve the schools, how their tax proposal works, and so on. Auto manufacturers need to convince us that they are at work trying to build reliable, fuel-efficient cars. And ideologues need to warn their audience about possible negative outcomes if their ideology is implemented—the results of outlawing the "morning after" pill, for instance. Knowing the persuader's **hidden agenda** puts receivers on guard against their messages, and even just a hint of the real goals of a persuader makes us more likely to make informed choices.

Third, and most important, receivers must critically test the assertions and evidence presented to them. This means looking for information from all sides and withholding judgment until we have sufficient data. Critical receivers can still make responsible decisions even if the first two criteria for responsible persuasion are missing. In recent elections, many candidates used negative advertising and brief sound bites. As campaign critic and communication researcher Kathleen Hall Jamieson (1992) observed almost two decades ago, "All

forms of campaign discourse were becoming alike. . . . assertion was substituted for argument and attack for engagement" (p. 212). In many interviews conducted since making that observation, Jamieson confirms the continuance of this assertion versus argument and attack versus engagement pattern. Critical receivers must go beyond these sound bites and do critical research before making a voting decision.

Access InfoTrac College Edition, and enter the words "negative political advertising" in the search engine. Explore some of the articles that are referenced. Observe yourself being persuaded and how persuasion happens to you. You will be more critical and therefore more effective in rejecting messages when appropriate—and in accepting others when that is wise.

THE SMCR MODEL OF PERSUASION

The simplest model of communication, and one of the oldest and most widely referenced, is Shannon and Weaver's (1949) **SMCR model** (see Figure 1.3). The model contains these essential elements:

- A source (S) (or persuader), who or which is the encoder of the message. The code can be verbal, nonverbal, visual, or musical, or in some other modality.

- A message (M), which is meant to convey the source's meaning through any of the codes.

- A channel (C), which carries the message and which might have distracting noise.

- A receiver (R) (or persuadee), who decodes the message, trying to sift out channel noise and adding his or her own interpretation.

Suppose you tell a friend that the words used in a TV ad for the new Toyota RAV emphasize how large the car seems when it really isn't. In this case, you help your friend to make or not make a choice by explaining a source-related aspect of

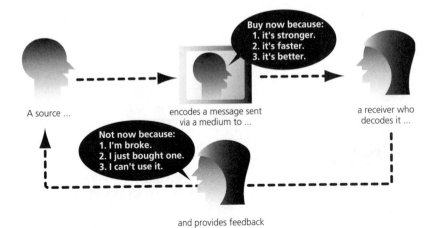

FIGURE 1.3 The SMCR model.

persuasion—in this case word choice. Then you alert your friend to the doublespeak in the ad—the product "virtually guarantees" fun times. You ask what the word "virtually" means in this advertising claim and thus focus attention on the message itself. You also point out that skillful editing and the use of special effects make the vehicle seem large. Here, you focus on the persuasive impact of the channel carrying the persuasive information. Finally, you might ask your friend what internal or unstated reason he or she has for wanting to be popular, and how they think the RAV will result in fun times. Here you focus on the receiver element of the model. Because persuasion is a process, being a critical receiver means being prepared for all four elements—the motives of the source (obvious or disguised), message elements (verbal and visual symbolic meanings), the channel or medium used to send the message, and finally what the receiver brings to the source's argument(s). Try using several tools to determine a source's motives. For example, language choice often tips us off to the source's intent. The ideas that the source thinks are persuasive to the audience almost always appear expressed in the words and metaphors used. Are they questions or exclamations? Are they short and punchy or long and soothing? For example, when Schick introduced a "cosmetic" razor called the "Personal Touch," I wondered to whom the

product was targeted and asked myself questions about the language being used. What do the words "cosmetic," "personal," and "touch" tell you about Schick's view of its potential customers? Was it aiming at a "macho" man or at women who feel they deserve special attention? The language used tells us that the target is female and the motive is to make them feel special when considering the product. Analyzing the source's message provides the receiver with two benefits. First, it alerts us to the persuasion being aimed at us. Second, it tells us things about the source that can help us when the source becomes the target of our own persuasion. Other tools also help us to analyze the intent of the message. We will look at receivers' needs and emotions, and we'll also look at the evidence contained in messages and at how it relates to the persuasive goal.

Consider the layout, graphics, and wording of an ad placed across the country by the International Fund for Animal Welfare (IFAW), opposing the harvest of baby seals in Canada—a highly emotional issue as the young seals are clubbed to death (see Figure 1.4). The copy in the ad reads:

Do you really know what can go into a simple fish sandwich? . . . Fish caught by Canadian Fishermen who also kill the baby seals. Your purchase of a McDonald's or Burger King Fish Sandwich could help buy

Do you really know what can go into a simple fish sandwich?

Fish caught by Canadian Fishermen who also kill the baby seals. Your purchase of a McDonald's or Burger King Fish Sandwich could help buy the boats, hard wooden clubs, and guns used by the seal hunters as they turn from fishing to the cruelty of killing adult and baby seals.

If you made a pledge today not to buy fish sandwiches from McDonald's or Burger King unless you were assured by the companies that no Canadian fish was used... your decision would save the seals. Canadian fishermen would have to stop sealing since they are totally dependent on their fish sales, with seal hunting a tiny sideline in comparison.

Canadian Globe and Mail of 13 March 1984, had this to say of IFAW's call for a worldwide boycott of Canadian fish: "...But what really has the officials spooked is the U.S. market. (There) The International Fund for

Animal Welfare (IFAW), which spearheads the anti-sealing protest worldwide, has started pressing U.S. purchasers not to take Canadian fish. The U.S. market is worth $1-billion a year to Canadian fishermen and the fast-food business in the United States is about a fifth of that market. Canada fears that, if one U.S. fast-food chain caves in to the protestors, all will surrender."

Over 15,000 seals, mostly babies just 2-4 weeks old, have been clubbed or shot over the last 28 days... and yet the Canadian Minister of Fisheries says there is no baby seal hunt.

You have it in your hands to save the baby seals today.

Please write or telephone one or both of the companies listed below and seek an assurance that they will not purchase Canadian fish until the Canadian Government passes a law banning the seal hunt forever.

Mr Fred L. Turner,
Chairman of the Board,
McDonald's Corporation,
McDonald's Plaza, Oak Brook, Illinois,
IL 60521
Tel: 312/887-3200

Mr J Jeffrey Campbell, Chairman,
Burger King Corporation,
7360 North Kendall Drive,
Miami,
Florida FL 33156
Tel: 305/596-7277

SAVE THE SEALS
NO
TO CANADIAN FISH

To the International Fund for Animal Welfare
I'll put animals first ... I'll do my part to help you fight the baby seal hunters.

Enclosed is my tax-exempt contribution to IFAW in the amount of:
☐ $10 ☐ $15 ☐ $25 ☐ $35 ☐ $60 ☐ $100 ☐ $500 Other $_____

We need hundreds of gifts this size to save the baby seals forever.

Name _____
(please print)
Address _____

_____
_____   Zip Code _____

International Fund for Animal Welfare
169 Main Street, Yarmouth Port,
Massachusetts 02675 U.S.A.
Our financial statement is available to contributors.

IFAW

Our boycott campaign needs your support. We cannot succeed without your funds, to carry our boycott to every community in America.

A copy of the last financial report filed with the Department of State may be obtained by writing to: N.Y. State Department of State, Office of Charities Registration, Albany, N.Y. 12231 or IFAW

FIGURE 1.4 Ad encouraging people to boycott fish sandwiches to stop the killing of harp seals.

SOURCE: Used by permission of IFAW.

the boats, hard wooden clubs, and guns used by the seal hunters as they turn from fishing to the cruelty of killing adult and baby seals.

The images and words such as "hard wooden clubs" alert you to the underlying emotional persuasion used and should prompt you to investigate more fully because emotional appeals are more likely to be biased, incomplete, or unethical. Research reveals that very few Canadian fishermen are also seal hunters; that clubbing the seals is

actually the least painful means of harvesting them; and that the furs of the seals are the object of the hunt not their flesh. It is not used in the fish sandwich as the visuals suggest. Looking carefully at the message prompts you to get the other side of the story. It also alerts you to the kinds of effects that the channel has on persuasion. An appeal on the same issue using radio would probably fail because radio lacks visual imagery. Imagine a TV ad documenting the harp seal slaughter. Would this make the message more or less effective? TV makes us more vulnerable to certain types of messages, such as humorous ones, demonstrations, exaggerations, comparisons, and before/after appeals. Video footage of the clubbing of the seals would certainly raise audience emotions.

Finally, the SMCR model suggests we need to look at ourselves to determine what kinds of motives, biases, and perspectives we bring to the persuasion. What fascinations, needs, and desires do we add in the co-creation? How do we interact with the message and the medium used? Does our cultural heritage shade the meaning of the message? Persuaders including politicians, ideologues, advertisers, propagandists, and even our coworkers, friends, and colleagues continuously seek answers to questions like these. Communication researcher Patricia Sullivan (1993) describes these steps (i.e., **tactics** flow from **strategies**, which in turn flow from overall **goals**) in her analysis of a keynote speech given by Reverend Jesse Jackson at a Democratic National Convention. Jackson's goal was to unite the party. He stressed the common ground shared among the various factions of the party; and he got the audience interacting with the message by entitling his speech "Common Ground and Common Sense," thus making the issue of unity central. He also employed a call–response (or interactive) format for parts of the speech by uttering a phrase or sentence that the audience then repeated, uniting them further.

RANK'S MODEL OF PERSUASION

Some years ago the National Council of Teachers of English (NCTE) asked for ways to teach students to become critical receivers of persuasion. Researcher Hugh Rank (1976), put the challenge this way: "These kids are growing up in a propaganda blitz unparalleled in human history.... Schools should shift their emphasis in order to train the larger segment of our population in a new kind of literacy so that more citizens can recognize the more sophisticated techniques and patterns of persuasion" (p. 5). Rank outlined a simple, easy-to-

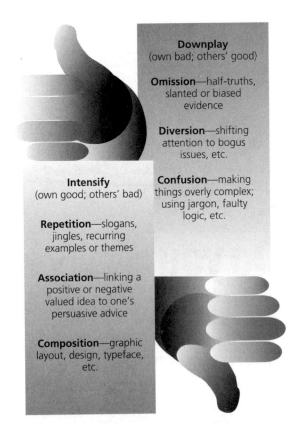

FIGURE 1.5 Rank's intensify/downplay schema.
SOURCE: Adapted by permission of Hugh Rank.

use but insightful model of persuasion, called the intensify/downplay model. It helps people to be critical receivers using a series of four strategies and six associated tactics. Rank maintains that persuaders employ these major strategies to achieve their goals. Persuaders either **intensify** certain aspects of their product, cause, or candidate, or they intensify some aspect of the competition. They also downplay certain aspects of their product or candidate, or they downplay positive aspects of the competition. Often, they do both. Figure 1.5 illustrates this model. Strategically, persuaders choose from four courses of action. They can:

1. Intensify their own good points
2. Intensify the weak points of the opposition

3. Downplay their own weak points

4. Downplay the good points of the opposition

Persuaders use tactics such as repetition, association, and composition to intensify their own good points or the bad points of the opposition, and they use omission, diversion, and confusion to downplay their own bad points or the good points of the opposition. Any one of these tactics can be used logically or emotionally using interactive or more traditional media.

Persuasive strategy, then, results from the overall step-by-step program for reaching some goal. Strategy dictates tactics or the specific kinds of arguments, evidence, or points the persuader makes. For example, a politician wants to persuade voters to support her candidacy (the goal), so she tries to make them feel good about her platform and character (the strategy of intensifying her own good). She accomplishes this by taking forthright stands on the issues. She also repeats her campaign slogan on yard signs, billboards, buttons, bumper stickers, electronic advertisements, and her website, and she uses the Capitol in the background of all her ads.

Intensification

All persuaders want to look good in the eyes of the audience—the voters, joiners, donors, or potential customers. Some tactics intensify the persuader's own good points ("He's always been a willing and honest servant for good causes."). Others intensify the bad points of the other guy, thus making the persuader look good by comparison ("He's a flim-flam man—I wouldn't trust him."). The tactics of repetition, association, and composition are all effective in implementing the strategy of intensification of our own good or others' bad points.

Repetition. One way to intensify good or bad points about a product, person, or candidate is to repeat them over and over again. That's why slogans, jingles, and logotypes work. For example, Energizer batteries "keep going and going" in TV spots, magazine ads, and even on their packages. The harp seal ad repeatedly intensifies the bad aspects of the hunt.

A fascinating discussion of repetition in advertising can be accessed on InfoTrac College Edition by entering the words "slogans" and "jingles" in the search engine. Would they be processed in the central or the peripheral route?

Association. Another tactic for intensification is association which (1) links a cause, product, or candidate (2) to something already liked or disliked (3) by the audience. Thus, the cause, product, or candidate becomes identified with the thing liked or disliked. For example, politicians know that we have fears about privacy and identity theft in cyberspace, so they tie these fears to their own causes by stating that, if elected, they intend to enact strict controls over the use of cyber-information. Advertisers associate a certain kind of athletic shoe with a well-known professional, with everyday people who exercise, or as Nike did, with a person in a wheelchair. These associations intensify the good aspects of the shoe and show that one needn't be an athlete to benefit from its features.

Composition. The third and final tactic of intensification uses physical composition of the message to emphasize one's own good points or the other guy's bad points. This usually involves the use of nonverbal or visual means and takes several forms. Altering the makeup of the printed word (as in changing "U.S.A." to "U.$.A.") sends the message that the nation is only interested in money. Altering the composition of a candidate's publicity photo often manipulates meaning. A low camera angle makes the candidate look larger than life and tells us to look up to him or her. Altering the layout of an advertisement intensifies persuasive outcomes. For example, the upper-right and lower-left corners of a magazine page or a poster are considered *fallow*, or less likely to get full reader attention. The eye only glances at them momentarily, so guess where the cigarette manufacturers usually put the health warning? These cases also exemplify the use of the peripheral route of the ELM in persuasive appeals, and we don't put much time, effort, or research into processing them.

Persuaders also use composition to compare and contrast. For example, a candidate for political office is pictured against some dramatic setting such as the Statue of Liberty. To intensify an incumbent politician's bad points, an ad superimposes his or her image on a picture of a polluted river or harbor in the home district. To emphasize the negative identification and to encourage further emotional interaction with the spot, a muted version of "America the Beautiful" might accompany a voice-over talking about the incumbent's lack of social responsibility. The polluted river or harbor, the background, the music, and the voice-over combine to "compose" the ad's meaning. Use Rank's intensification as a starting place in becoming a critical receiver.

Downplaying

Sometimes persuaders want to avoid intensifying or calling attention to something because it undermines their persuasive goal. They avoid advertising the strong points of the competition. Politicians don't tell us what a good job their opponent did recently. This strategy also can downplay the persuader's bad points while downplaying a competitor's good points. Let's now look at the tactics used in the strategy of downplaying: omission, diversion, and confusion.

Omission.   Sometimes persuaders simply leave out critical information to avoid highlighting their own shortcomings. For example, politicians leave

out the fact that the statistics supporting their position are not official. Most advertisements for foods are staged in some way. Live photographs of food are frequently unappetizing—lettuce wilts, red meat color fades, and so on. As a result, there is an occupation known as "food cosmetics" in which the expert uses a variety of techniques to make the food look better. Salads look crisper if coated with hair spray just before photographing. Photographs of floor tile adhesive look more appetizing than actual chocolate pudding. A soup manufacturer makes its chunky version look chunky by filling the bottom of the bowl with marbles so that the chunks float higher. The officials of a charitable organization omit telling the administrative costs for dispersing the charitable donations.

The Claussen pickle company intensified its own good points by advertising that its pickles are refrigerated rather than cooked. As a result, they are much crisper than competitor Vlasic pickles. They used a TV ad showing the two pickles being bent in half. The "snap!" of the Claussen pickle and the burst of juice from it really intensified Claussen's good points and demonstrated Vlasic's soggy bad point, but Claussen omitted telling consumers that the brand contains far more sodium than Vlasic pickles (their own bad point) and that refrigeration isn't necessary for Vlasic pickles (the other's good point).

It is clear that Claussen intentionally chose to omit mentioning the sodium content of its product because people need to reduce their intake of sodium for health reasons like avoiding strokes or heart attacks, so the omission has ethical implications. What would you say? What about the recent claim that Cheerios are now high in fiber? Although the claim is true, the fact that they always were high in fiber is omitted. Here the omission doesn't endanger one's health, but it is misleading and part of a marketing strategy.

Diversion. Diversion consists of shifting attention away from another's good points or one's own bad points by using substitute issues. Persuaders frequently use humor to divert attention. For instance, the Energizer "Bunny" ads use humor, and this diverts attention from the fact that all alkaline batteries have about the same life. Ford used emotional appeals to divert attention away from the poor design of its Explorer, which had a tendency to roll over, resulting in a number of deaths and injuries. Ford redirected blame to the factory-installed Firestone tires. Splitting hairs diverts attention from the major issues of the debate and siphons valuable time away from discussion and interaction between the persuader and persuadee.

Confusion. Another downplaying tactic creates confusion in the audience's mind. Using technical jargon that the receiver doesn't understand creates confusion. Weaving an intricate and rambling argument that evades the real issues results in audience confusion, as does the use of faulty logic. Consider the claim that "She's Beautiful! She's Engaged! She Uses Earth Balsam Hand Creme!" It implies a "logical progression" that, because she used the hand cream, she became beautiful, and because of that, she met and won the man of her dreams.

A METHOD OF SELF-PROTECTION

In his discussion of doublespeak, Rank (1976) offered some advice about how to detect the flaws of persuaders who use various tactics to intensify or

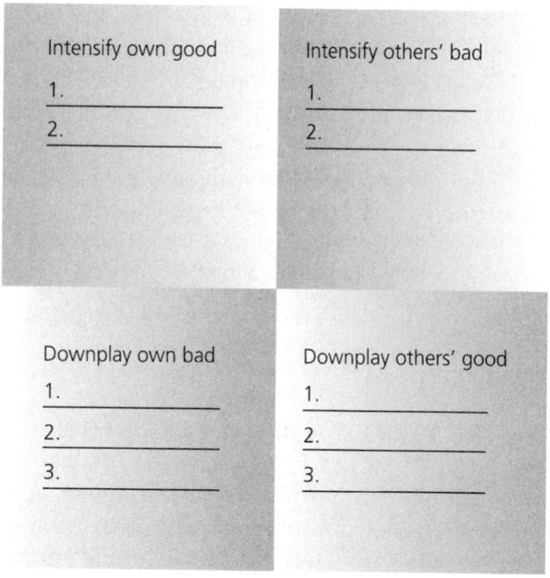

FIGURE 1.6 Intensify/downplay scorecard.
SOURCE: By permission of Hugh Rank.

downplay: "When they intensify, you downplay. When they downplay, you intensify."

Beginning in 2004, politicians exploited audience fears about retirement benefits by claiming that the Social Security System faced a crisis in funding. Supposedly, this justified setting up private investment accounts using some of the Social Security dollars regularly paid by employees and employers. The "crisis" claim was an exaggeration that backfired when opponents demonstrated that there were several alternatives to meet the shortfall, all of which involved less drastic changes. The word "crisis" caused an initial emotional reaction and thus encouraged audience interaction. However, receivers looked deeper into the issue using the central information processing route of the ELM, and the "crisis" dissipated.

A way to follow Rank's advice systematically is to divide a sheet of paper into quarters, as shown in Figure 1.6, and then enter the kinds of downplaying and intensifying going on in the message(s). Simply seeing these items makes you more alert to the kind of manipulation going on. Try using the self-protection method on an advertisement or a political speech. When the ad or speech downplays something, you intensify its shortcomings. And when it intensifies something, you downplay the intensification. We will discuss a number of other tools of analysis as we proceed, but Rank's intensify/downplay tool seems a useful general tool of analysis to employ when first faced with a persuasive blitz.

REVIEW AND CONCLUSION

If you now feel more alert to the possible ways persuaders manipulate you, congratulations! You're already on your way to becoming a more critical receiver. You now need to arm yourself with some tools of analysis that make for wise consumers. There is a bonus for learning them. Seeing what works—in what circumstances, with what kinds of people—helps you prepare to persuade others. Skillful consumers of messages learn to be more effective producers of messages. As we move ahead, apply the tools of persuasive analysis

on your own and in the study questions at the end of each chapter. Use the diversity and interactive media boxes as well as the learning goals, key terms, and applications of ethics. Also, explore the InfoTrac College Edition sites sprinkled throughout the text. Examine the ways in which persuasion operates on the interpersonal level. Every day you make decisions in nonpublic settings. Your parents may try to persuade you to avoid certain occupational fields, to seek a summer job, or to put off a purchase. You decide to heed or reject your parents' advice on the basis of your interpersonal communication with them. Rank's model helps here too. Identify what your parents intensify and downplay. Do the same thing with other interpersonal relationships— roommates, friends, colleagues, or your boss. Then try to spot the kinds of symbols that lead to or discourage identification. Critical analysis of interpersonal persuasion helps you to make informed decisions. People are persuaded daily in the public arena through advertisements, speeches, radio and TV programs, newspaper and magazine articles, and the Internet. But we need to remember that persuasion also takes place in our personal lives.

KEY TERMS

When you are finished with this chapter, you should be able to identify, explain, and give examples of the following terms or concepts.

persuasion	ethos	elaboration likelihood model	hidden agenda
interactive media	pathos		SMCR model
cultural diversity	logos	central information processing route	tactics
response-ability	common ground		strategies
doublespeak	enthymemes	peripheral information processing route	goals
rhetoric	identification		intensify
artistic proof	co-creation	influence	
inartistic proof	self-persuasion	coercion	

APPLICATION OF ETHICS

The Ethics of Omission.   A homeowner needs to sell his home but is hesitant to inform realtors or prospective buyers that there is mold in the basement that could be toxic. The homeowner has been able to get rid of the mold from time to time by spraying the basement with household bleach. What should the homeowner do? (1) Spray the basement and list the house for sale and not mention the mold problem. (2) Spray the basement and mention the problem and a solution to both buyers and realtors. (3) Hire a toxic mold expert to find out if the mold really is toxic and discover what can be done about it if is indeed toxic. (4) Don't spray the basement and simply list the house as "For Sale by Owner."

QUESTIONS FOR FURTHER THOUGHT

1. If you or someone you know recently made a major purchase (for example, an automobile, an MP3 player, or a digital camera), identify the context in which persuasion occurred. Where did the persuasion take place? In the showroom? Through a television ad? Interpersonally, such as in discussing the purchase with a friend? What kinds of appeals were made? What characteristics were intensified? Downplayed? Was the persuasion emotional or logical, or both? What did you learn from the careful examination?

2. Much persuasion occurs in interpersonal contexts. Examine one of your interpersonal relationships, such as that between you and your parents, your roommate, a teammate, or a fellow member of an organization or church. Describe how, when, and where persuasion operated in the relationship. What characteristics about yourself have you intensified? Downplayed? What about the other person's intensification? Downplaying? Which tactics worked best? Repetition? Association? Omission?

3. Beginning with the definition of persuasion offered in this chapter, create your own model of persuasion that reflects all the important elements of the definition given here.

4. Identify three types of persuasion you recently processed, and analyze each according to the definition offered in this chapter and the ELM. What verbal and/or visual symbols were used? Did you interact with the message? What did the persuader intend? Which information-processing route (peripheral or the central) operated for you? What created identification? What was intensified? Downplayed? Using which tactics? Repetition? Association? Composition? Omission? Confusion? Diversion?

5. Describe the tactics of intensification, and explain how they work. Give examples of their use on television, in print, on radio, by politicians, and by advertisers.

6. Describe the tactics of downplaying and explain how they work. Give examples of their use on television, in print, on radio, by politicians, and by advertisers.

7. Identify a current "propaganda blitz" going on in the media coverage of an event or issue. Which route in the ELM was employed? Describe current examples of the strategies of intensification and downplaying that seem central in the "war on terrorism." What tactics of intensification or downplaying are used regarding environmental issues? Are they ethical or unethical?

8. List some of the interactive media you use. How many of them came about in recent times—say since 2000? How many of them preceded the Internet?

9. Have you noticed the ways in which we are becoming a more diverse culture? How do they affect the persuasive process?

 For online activities, go to the *Persuasion* book companion website at http://communication.wadsworth.com/larson11.

2

Perspectives on Ethics in Persuasion

RICHARD L. JOHANNESEN

Northern Illinois University

LEARNING GOALS

After reading this chapter, you should be able to:

1. Discuss the importance of ethical issues and standards in the persuasion process.

2. Recognize the complexity of making ethical judgments about persuasion.

3. Apply six ethical perspectives for judging persuasion.

4. Apply specific ethical criteria for assessing political communication and commercial advertising.

5. Recognize how moral exclusion functions in unethical persuasion to harm people of diverse cultures, religions, genders, and sexual orientations.

6. Recognize how interactive and cyberspace media pose significant ethical issues for persuasion.

7. Start developing your own workable and justifiable ethical framework or code of ethics for evaluating your persuasive choices of means and ends and those of other persuaders.

S tudents enrolled in persuasion courses frequently are preparing for careers in advertising, sales, law, journalism, business, or politics. But students interested in such careers may be surprised by the extremely negative perceptions people have of the ethics and honesty of persons in such professions. The 2004 Gallup poll of perceived honesty and ethics in the professions ranked the following careers, in descending order, as lowest in perceived ethicality: television reporters; newspaper reporters; business executives; congressmen; lawyers; advertising practitioners; and, at the bottom, car salesmen (www.gallup.com; released December 7, 2004).

Evidence abounds that supports public concern over the decline of ethical behavior. According to a 2002 poll by the *Chicago Tribune* (July 28, pp. 1, 14), 66 percent of respondents believed that the ethical standards of business executives had changed for the worse in the past several decades. The 2005 Morality Meter Gallup poll indicated that 59 percent of respondents were somewhat or very dissatisfied with the moral and ethical climate in the United States (www.gallup.com; released March 8, 2005).

A national firm that conducts background checks reviewed 2.6 million job applications in 2002 and found that 44 percent contained at least some lies (*New York Times*, December 28, 2002, p. C8). Aggregated data from the Gallup Youth Survey collected between January 2003 and March 2004 revealed that 65 percent of teenagers surveyed believed that there is a fair amount or a great deal of cheating going on at their schools, and 46 percent admitted that they had cheated on a test or exam (www.gallup.com; released May 11, 2004). In his book, *The Cheating Culture*, David Callahan (2004) documents a "pattern of widespread cheating throughout U.S. society," observes that people "not only are cheating in more areas but also are feeling less guilty about it," and concludes that most of the cheating "is by people who, on the whole, view themselves as upstanding members of society" (pp. 12–14).

Access InfoTrac College Edition using Advanced Search with title. Access the item "Lying on Top: Many Are Up in Arms About the Enron Scandal—But Our Political Leaders Are Just As Disgraceful As Their Corporate Counterparts," published in *Dollars & Sense* (March 2002). How do the examples and arguments raised in the article relate to ethical issues in persuasion?

Imagine that you are an audience member listening to a speaker—call him Mr. Bronson. His aim is to persuade you to contribute money to the cancer research program of a major medical research center. Suppose that, with one exception, all the evidence, reasoning, and motivational appeals he employs are valid and above suspicion on any ethical grounds. However, at one point in his speech, Bronson knowingly uses a set of false statistics to scare you into believing that, during your lifetime, there is a much greater probability of your getting some form of cancer than is actually the case.

To help our analysis of the ethics of this hypothetical persuasive situation, consider these issues. If you, or society at large, view Bronson's persuasive goal as worthwhile, does the worth of that goal justify his use of false statistics as one means to achieve his end? Does the fact that he consciously chose to use false statistics make a difference in your evaluation? If he used the false statistics out of ignorance or a failure to check his sources, how might your ethical judgment be altered, if at all? Should Bronson be condemned as an unethical person or an unethical speaker, or, in this instance, for use of a specific unethical technique?

Carefully consider the standards you would employ to make your ethical judgment of Bronson. Are your standards purely pragmatic? (In other words, should Bronson avoid false statistics because he might get caught?) Are they societal in origin? (If he gets caught, his credibility as a representative would be weakened with this and future audiences, or his getting caught might weaken the credibility of other cancer society representatives.) Should he be criticized for violating an implied ethical agreement between you and him? (You might not expect a representative of a famous research institute to use questionable techniques, and so you would be especially vulnerable.) Finally, should his conscious use of false statistics be considered unethical because you are denied the accurate, relevant information you need to make an intelligent decision on an important public issue?

As receivers and senders of persuasion, we have the responsibility to uphold appropriate ethical standards for persuasion, to encourage freedom of inquiry and expression, and to promote public debate as crucial to democratic decision-making. To achieve these goals, we must understand their complexity and recognize the difficulty of achieving them. One purpose of this chapter is to

stimulate you to make reasoned choices among ethical options in developing your own positions or judgments.

Ethical issues focus on value judgments concerning degrees of right and wrong, virtue and vice, and ethical obligations in human conduct. Persuasion, as one type of human behavior, always contains potential ethical issues, for several reasons:

- In persuasion, one person, or a group of people, attempts to influence other people by altering their beliefs, attitudes, values, and actions.

- Persuasion requires us to make conscious choices among ends sought and rhetorical means used to achieve the ends.

- Persuasion necessarily involves a potential judge—any or all of the receivers, the persuader, or an independent observer.

As a receiver and sender of persuasion, you will evaluate the ethics of a persuasive instance based on the ethical standards you are using. You may even choose to ignore ethical judgment entirely. People often cite several justifications to avoid direct analysis and resolution of ethical issues in persuasion:

- Everyone knows the appeal or tactic is unethical, so there is nothing to talk about.

- Only success matters, so ethics are irrelevant to persuasion.

- Ethical judgments are matters of individual personal opinion, so there are no final answers.

However, potential ethical questions exist regardless of how they are answered. Whether you wish it or not, consumers of persuasion generally will judge your effort, formally or informally, in part by their own relevant ethical criteria. If for no other reason than the pragmatic motivation of enhancing your chance of success, you would do well to consider the ethical standards held by your audience.

Now we turn to the concept of ethical responsibility. What is it and what are some of its components?

ETHICAL RESPONSIBILITY

Persuaders' ethical responsibilities can stem from statuses or positions they have earned or have been granted, from commitments (promises, pledges, agreements) they have made, or from the consequences (effects) of their communication for others. **Responsibility** includes the elements of fulfilling duties and obligations, of being accountable to other individuals and groups, of adhering to agreed-upon standards, and of being accountable to one's own conscience. But an essential element of responsible communication, for both sender and receiver, is the exercise of thoughtful and deliberate judgment. That is, the responsible communicator carefully analyzes claims, soundly assesses probable consequences, and conscientiously weighs relevant values. In a sense, a responsible communicator is "response-able." She or he exercises the ability to respond (is responsive) to the needs and communications of others in sensitive, thoughtful, fitting ways (see Freund, 1960; Niebuhr, 1963; Pennock, 1960; Pincoffs, 1975).

Whether persuaders seem intentionally and knowingly to use particular content or techniques is a factor that most of us consider in judging communication ethicality. If a dubious communication behavior seems to stem more from an accident, a slip of the tongue, or even ignorance, we may be less harsh in our ethical assessment. For most of us, it is the *intentional* use of ethically questionable tactics that merits the harshest condemnation.

On the other hand, we might contend that, in argumentative and persuasive situations, communicators have an ethical obligation to double-check the soundness of their evidence and reasoning before they present it to others; sloppy preparation is no excuse for ethical lapses. A similar view might be advanced concerning elected or appointed government officials. If they use obscure or jargon-laden language that clouds the accurate and clear representation of ideas, even if it is not intended to deceive or hide, they are ethically irresponsible. Such officials, according to this view, should be obligated to communicate clearly and accurately with citizens in fulfillment of their governmental duties. As a related question, we can ask whether sincerity of intent releases persuaders from their ethical responsibility to use fair means and effects. Could we say that if Adolf Hitler's fellow Germans had judged him to be sincere they need not have assessed the ethics of his persuasion? In such cases, evaluations are probably best carried out by appraising sincerity and ethicality separately. For example, a persuader sincere in intent might use an unethical strategy.

Questions about how far persuaders should go in adapting their message to particular audiences focus on a special type of ethical responsibility. We now examine this issue.

ADAPTATION TO THE AUDIENCE

What are the ethics of adapting to the audience? Most persuaders seek to secure some kind of response from receivers. To what degree is it ethical for them to alter their ideas and proposals to adapt to the needs, capacities, values, and expectations of their audience? To secure acceptance, some persuaders adapt to an audience to the extent of so changing their own ideas that the ideas are no longer really theirs. These persuaders merely say what the audience wants to hear, regardless of their own convictions. For example, one journalist (Maraniss, 1996) observed that Bill Clinton "has been criticized throughout his career for trying to be all things to all people and saying whatever the person he is talking to wants to hear." Some persuaders go to the opposite extreme of making little or no adaptation to their audience. They do not take serious account of the nature of their audience, whether that audience is much like them or whether it reflects cultural or religious diversity. To the audience, the speaker, writer, or advertisement seems unconnected to them or unconcerned about them.

Some degree of adaptation for specific audiences in language choice, evidence, value appeals, organization, and communication medium is a crucial part of successful and ethical persuasion. No absolute rule can be set down here. Persuaders must decide the ethical intermediate point between their own idea in its pure form and that idea modified to achieve maximum impact with the audience. The search is for an appropriate point between two undesirable extremes—the extreme of saying only what the audience desires and will approve and the extreme of complete lack of concern for and understanding of the audience. Both extremes are ethically irresponsible (Booth, 2004, pp. 50–54). In this era of heightened awareness of ethnic, racial, and religious diversity, persuaders face significant practical and ethical choices concerning the appropriate degree of audience adaptation.

A frequent ethical question facing persuaders is, does the end justify the means? How should we answer that question? What are some guidelines for answering it?

THE ETHICS OF ENDS AND MEANS

In assessing the ethics of persuasion, does the end justify the means? Does the necessity of achieving a goal widely acknowledged as worthwhile justify the use of ethically questionable techniques? We must be aware that the persuasive means employed can have cumulative effects on receivers' thoughts and decision-making habits, apart from and in addition to the specific end that the communicator seeks. No matter what purpose they serve, the arguments, appeals, structure, and language we choose do shape the audience's values, thinking habits, language patterns, and level of trust.

To say that the ends do not *always* justify the means is different from saying that the ends *never* justify means. The persuader's goal probably is best considered as one of a number of potentially relevant ethical criteria from which we select the most appropriate standards. Under some circumstances, such as threats to physical survival, the goal of personal or national security may *temporarily* take precedence over other criteria. In general, however, we can best make mature ethical assessments by evaluating the ethics of persuasive techniques apart from the worth and morality of the persuader's specific goal. We can strive to judge the ethics of means and ends *separately*. In some cases, we may find ethical persuasive tactics employed to achieve an unethical goal; in other cases, unethical techniques may be used in the service of an entirely ethical goal.

Although discussed in the context of journalistic ethics, the six questions suggested by Warren Bovee (1991) can serve as useful probes to determine the degree of ethicality of almost any means–ends relationship in persuasion (see Figure 2.1).

Here are the questions in paraphrased form:

1. Are the means truly unethical/morally evil or merely distasteful, unpopular, unwise, or ineffective?

2. Is the end truly good, or does it simply appear good to us because we desire it?

3. Is it probable that the ethically bad or suspect means actually will achieve the good end?

4. Is the same good achievable using other more ethical means if we are willing to be creative, patient, determined, and skillful?

5. Is the good end clearly and overwhelmingly better than the probable bad effects of the means used to attain it? Bad means require justification whereas good means do not.

6. Will the use of unethical means to achieve a good end withstand public scrutiny? Could the use of unethical means be justified to those most affected by them or to those most capable of impartially judging them?

Perhaps now we can better answer the question, in persuasion does the end justify the means? Certainly we see more clearly some of the issues and options involved.

FIGURE 2.1 How might Bovee's questions apply for evaluating the justifications here?

THE IMPORTANCE OF ETHICS

"A society without ethics is a society doomed to extinction," argued philosopher S. Jack Odell (in Merrill & Odell, 1983). According to Odell, the "basic concepts and theories of ethics provide the framework necessary for working out one's own moral or ethical code." Odell believes that "ethical principles are necessary preconditions for the existence of a social community. Without ethical principles it would be impossible for human beings to live in harmony and without fear, despair, hopelessness, anxiety, apprehension, and uncertainty" (p. 95).

A societal or personal system of ethics is not an automatic cure-all for individual or collective ills. What can ethical theory and systematic reflection on ethics contribute? One answer is suggested by philosopher Carl Wellman (1988):

An ethical system does not solve all one's practical problems, but one cannot choose and act rationally without some explicit or implicit ethical system. An ethical theory does not tell a person what to do in any given situation, but neither is it completely silent; it tells one what to consider in making up one's mind what to do. The practical function of an ethical system is primarily to direct our attention to the relevant considerations, the reasons that determine the rightness or wrongness of any act (p. 305).

The ethics of persuasion are important both for persuaders and for receivers of persuasion. We turn now to special ethical responsibilities for audiences.

ETHICAL RESPONSIBILITIES OF RECEIVERS

What are your ethical responsibilities as a receiver of or respondent to persuasion? An answer to this question stems in part from the image we hold of the persuasion process. Receivers bear little responsibility if the persuader views them as passive and defenseless receptacles, as mindless blotters uncritically accepting ideas and arguments. If audience members actually behave as viewed by the persuader, then they have little or no responsibility to understand accurately and evaluate critically. In this view, they have minimal power of choice and almost automatically must agree with the persuader's arguments. In contrast, we can see persuasion as a transaction in which both persuaders and persuadees bear mutual responsibility to participate actively in the process. This image of persuadees as active participants suggests several responsibilities, perhaps best captured by two phrases: (1) reasoned skepticism and (2) appropriate feedback.

Reasoned skepticism includes a number of elements. It represents a balanced position between the undesirable extremes of being too open-minded or gullible, on the one hand, and being too closed-minded or dogmatic, on the other. You are not simply an unthinking blotter "soaking up" ideas and arguments. Rather, you exercise your capacities actively to search for meaning, to analyze and synthesize, and to judge soundness and worth. You do something to and with the information you receive: You process, interpret, and evaluate it. Also, you inform yourself about issues being discussed, and you tolerate, and even seek out,

divergent and controversial viewpoints, the better to assess what is being presented.

As a receiver of persuasion, you must realize that your accurate interpretation of a persuader's message may be hindered by attempts to impose your own ethical standards on the persuader. Your immediate, gut-level ethical judgments may cause you to distort the intended meaning. Only after reaching an understanding of the persuader's ideas can you reasonably evaluate the ethics of his or her persuasive strategies or purposes.

In this era of distrust of the truthfulness of public communication, reasoned skepticism also requires that you combat the automatic assumption that most public communication is untrustworthy. Just because a communication is of a certain type or comes from a certain source (for example, a government official, political candidate, news media figure, or advertiser), it must not automatically, without evaluation, be rejected as tainted or untruthful. Clearly, you must always exercise caution in acceptance and care in evaluation, as we emphasize throughout this book. Using the best evidence available, you arrive at your best judgment. However, to condemn a message as untruthful or unethical solely because it stems from a suspect source is a type of judgment that threatens the soundness of our decisions. If we reject a message, it must be after, not before, we evaluate it. Like a defendant in a courtroom, public communication must be presumed to be ethically innocent until it has been proved "guilty." However, when techniques of persuasion do weaken or undermine the confidence and trust necessary for intelligent public decision-making, we can condemn them as unethical.

As an active participant in the persuasion process, you need to provide appropriate feedback to persuaders. Otherwise, persuaders are denied the relevant and accurate information they need to make decisions. Your response, in most situations, should be an honest and accurate reflection of your true comprehension, beliefs, feelings, or judgment. It might be verbal or nonverbal, oral or written, immediate or delayed. A response of understanding, puzzlement, agreement, or disagreement could be reflected through your facial expressions, gestures, posture, inquiries, and statements during question-and-answer periods and through letters to editors or advertisers. In some cases, because of your expertise on a subject, you may even have an obligation to respond and provide feedback while other receivers remain silent. You need to decide whether the degree and type of your feedback are appropriate for the subject, audience, and occasion of the persuasion. For instance, to interrupt with questions, or even to heckle, might be appropriate in a few situations but irresponsible in many others.

Disagreement and conflict sometimes occur in intimate and informal interpersonal settings. In such situations, when at least one participant may be emotionally vulnerable, individual personalities often affect each other in direct and powerful ways. When you as a receiver in such a situation decide to respond by expressing strong disagreement, you should avoid "unfair" tactics of verbal conflict because they are irresponsible (Ross & Ross, 1982). For example, avoid monopolizing the talk with the intent of preventing others from expressing their position. Avoid entrapment, in which you lure someone into saying something that you intend to use later to embarrass or hurt him or her. Avoid verbally "hitting below the belt" by taking unfair advantage of the other person's psychological vulnerability. Avoid stockpiling or accumulating numerous grievances so that you can overwhelm others by dumping the complaints on them all at once. Finally, avoid dragging in numerous irrelevant or trivial issues and arguments in order to gain an advantage.

SOME ETHICAL PERSPECTIVES

We will briefly explain six major ethical perspectives as potential viewpoints for analyzing ethical issues in persuasion. As categories, these perspectives are not exhaustive, mutually exclusive, or given in any order of precedence. For a more extensive discussion, see Johannesen (2002).

As a receiver of persuasion, you can use one or a combination of such perspectives to evaluate the ethicality of a persuader's use of language (such as metaphors and ambiguity) or of evidence and reasoning. You can also use them to assess the ethics of psychological techniques (such as appeals to needs and values) or the appeal to widely held cultural images and myths. The persuasive tactics of campaigns and social movements can also—indeed must—be subjected to ethical scrutiny.

Religious Perspectives

Religious perspectives on communication ethics are rooted in the basic assumptions a religion makes about the relationship of the divine/eternal to humans and the world, and vice versa. In light of such assumptions, various world religions emphasize values, guidelines, and rules for evaluating the ethics of persuasion. These are the moral guidelines and the "thou shalt nots" embodied in the ideology and sacred literature of various religions. For instance, the Bible warns against lying, slander, and bearing false witness. Taoist religion stresses empathy and insight, rather than reason and logic, as roads to truth and right living. Citing facts and demonstrating logical conclusions are minimized in Taoism in favor of feeling and intuition. We can use these and other religiously derived criteria to assess the ethics of persuasion.

To explore the relation between religion and ethical persuasion, consider the following case. On two weekends in January 1987, evangelist Oral Roberts recounted on his nationally syndicated television program an encounter he had had with God the previous year. God told Roberts that he would not be allowed to live beyond March 1987 unless he raised $8 million to fund 69 scholarships for medical students at Oral Roberts University, to enable them to serve in medical clinics overseas. In an emotion-laden plea to his viewers, Roberts asked, "Will you help me extend my life?" Roberts' chief spokesperson, Jan Dargatz, defended Roberts' motives to reporters but conceded that his "methods have hit the fan." Dargatz said that

Roberts sincerely believed, "from the very core of his being," that the fund drive was a "do-or-die effort." The Reverend John Wolf, senior minister of Tulsa's All Souls Unitarian Church, condemned the appeal as "emotional blackmail" and an "act of desperation" (Buursma, 1987). Another news report revealed that in 1986 Roberts had made a similar appeal. Roberts told a Dallas audience that his "life is on the line" and that God "would take me this year" if he did not raise necessary funds to finance "holy missionary teams." "Because if I don't do it," Roberts said, "I'm going to be gone before the year is out. I'll be with the Father. I know it as much as I'm standing here." Roberts failed to raise the necessary money (*Chicago Tribune*, Feb. 26, 1987).

To assess the ethicality of Roberts' appeals, you might bring to bear an ethic for Christian evangelism developed by Emory Griffin (1976). For example, to what degree could Roberts' persuasion be condemned as that of a "rhetorical rapist" who uses psychological coercion to force a commitment? Intense emotional appeals, such as to guilt, effectively remove the receiver's conscious choice. Or was Roberts' persuasion more that of a "rhetorical seducer" who uses deception, flattery, or irrelevant appeals to success, money, duty, patriotism, popularity, or comfort to entice an audience? What other ethical standards rooted in Christian doctrine or scripture might we use to evaluate Roberts' appeals, and how might those standards be applied?

Human Nature Perspectives

Human nature perspectives probe the essence of human nature by asking what makes us fundamentally human. They identify unique characteristics of human nature that distinguish us from so-called lower forms of life, characteristics that we can then use as standards for judging the ethics of persuasion. Among them are the capacity to reason, to create and use symbols, to achieve mutual appreciative understanding, and to make value judgments. The underlying assumption is that we should protect and nurture such uniquely human

characteristics so that persons better can achieve their individual potential. We can assess the degree to which a persuader's appeals and techniques either foster or undermine the development of a fundamental human characteristic. Whatever the political, religious, or cultural context, a person would be assumed to possess certain uniquely human attributes worthy of promotion through communication. A technique that dehumanizes, that makes a person less than human, would be unethical.

In 1990 in Florida, a U.S. district court judge declared obscene the album *As Nasty As They Wanna Be* by the rap group 2 Live Crew. But in a local trial in Florida that same year, three members of the group were acquitted of obscenity charges for performing the songs. These incidents are part of a larger controversy concerning lyrics that explicitly refer to the sexual and physical abuse and debasement of women and that attack ethnic groups. For example, lyrics on the *Nasty* album vividly describe the bursting of vaginal walls, the forcing of women to have anal or oral sex or to lick feces, and such acts as urination, incest, and group sex. Similarly sexually violent lyrics can be found in songs by such individuals and groups as Judas Priest, Great White, Ice-T, and Guns n' Roses. And bigotry against immigrants, homosexuals, and African Americans surfaces in the Guns n' Roses song, "One in a Million."

Regardless of whether such lyrics are judged obscene or whether they are protected by the freedom-of-speech clause of the First Amendment, many would say that they should be condemned as unethical (Johannesen, 1997). Such lyrics treat women not as persons but as objects or body parts to be manipulated for the selfish satisfaction of males. Thus, they dehumanize, depersonalize, and trivialize women, they celebrate violence against them, and they reinforce inaccurate and unfair stereotypes of women, homosexuals, and ethnic groups. How do you believe a human nature perspective on communication ethics might be used to assess such lyrics?

Political Perspectives

The implicit or explicit values and procedures accepted as crucial to the health and growth of a particular political system are the focus of **political perspectives**. Once we have identified these essential values for a political system, we can use them to evaluate the ethics of persuasive means and ends within that system. The assumption is that public communication should foster achievement of these basic political values; persuasive techniques that retard, subvert, or circumvent the values should be condemned as unethical. Different political systems usually embody differing values leading to differing ethical judgments. Within the context of U.S. representative democracy, for example, various analysts pinpoint values and procedures they deem fundamental to the healthy functioning of our political system and, thus, values that can guide ethical scrutiny of persuasion therein. Such values and procedures include enhancement of citizens' capacity to reach rational decisions, access to channels of public communication and to relevant and accurate information about public issues, maximization of freedom of choice, tolerance of dissent, honesty in presenting motivations and consequences, and thoroughness and accuracy in presenting evidence and alternatives.

Hate speech is a broad label that includes communications that degrade, belittle, humiliate, or disrespect individuals and groups based on their race, ethnicity, nationality, religion, sex, or sexual orientation. Hate speech truly warrants our concern as an issue central to respect for diversity in our nation. In the late 1980s and early 1990s, the issue of hate speech on college and university campuses illustrated the tension between the right of freedom of speech and the ethically responsible exercise of that right. On one campus, eight Asian American students were harassed for almost an hour by a group of football players, who called them "Oriental faggots." On another campus, white fraternity members harassed a black student by chanting, "coon," "nigger," and "porch monkey." On yet another campus, a white male freshman was charged under the school's speech code with racial harassment for calling five black female students "water buffaloes."

In response to hate speech incidents, many colleges and universities instituted speech codes to punish hateful and offensive public messages. Among the forms of expression punishable at various schools are these:

- The use of derogatory names, inappropriately directed laughter, inconsiderate jokes, and conspicuous exclusion of another person from conversation

- Language that stigmatizes or victimizes individuals or that creates an intimidating or offensive environment

- Face-to-face use of epithets, obscenities, and other forms of expression that by accepted community standards degrade, victimize, stigmatize, or pejoratively depict persons based on their personal, intellectual, or cultural diversity

- Extreme or outrageous acts or communications intended to harass, intimidate, or humiliate others on the basis of race, color, or national origin, thus causing them severe emotional distress

To see the variety and intensity of hate speech websites on the Internet, go to www.stormfront.org. Read some of the hate literature of this organization, and then click on various links to websites of other hate groups and read some of their literature. What ethical issues are raised by the language used and the actions urged by these groups?

Whether hate speech is protected by the First Amendment and whether campus speech codes are constitutional, we should evaluate specific instances of hate speech for their degree of ethicality (Johannesen, 1997). We can use various ethical perspectives (such as human nature), but how might we use the values and procedures central to a U.S. democratic political perspective to judge hate speech?

Access InfoTrac College Edition using Advanced Search with title. Access the item "Hate Speech and Constitutional Protection," published in the *Journal of Social Issues*, 58 (2002). Consider how the arguments concerning the First Amendment and the Fourteenth Amendment relate to ethical judgments about hate speech.

Situational Perspectives

To make ethical judgments from a **situational perspective**, it's necessary to focus *regularly and primarily* on the elements of the specific persuasive situation at hand. Virtually all perspectives (those mentioned here and others) make some allowances, on occasion, for the modified application of ethical criteria in special circumstances. However, an extreme situational perspective routinely makes judgments only in light of *each different context*. This perspective minimizes criteria from broad political, human nature, religious, or other perspectives, and avoids absolute and universal standards (see Figure 2.2). Among the concrete contextual factors relevant to making a purely situational ethical evaluation are these:

- The role or function of the persuader for receivers

- Expectations held by receivers concerning such matters as appropriateness and reasonableness

- The degree of receivers' awareness of the persuader's techniques

- Goals and values held by receivers

- The degree of urgency for implementing the persuader's proposal

- Ethical standards for communication held by receivers

From an extreme situational perspective, for instance, we might argue that an acknowledged leader in a time of clear crisis has a responsibility to rally support and thus could employ so-called emotional appeals that circumvent human processes of rational, reflective decision making. Or a persuader might ethically use techniques such as innuendo, guilt by association, and unfounded name-calling as long as the receivers both recognize and approve of those methods.

"It's exciting to be part of a firm that's on the cutting edge of 'MORAL FLEXIBILITY.'"

FIGURE 2.2 How might situational ethics apply here?
SOURCE: © 1987 by Jim Berry, United Features Syndicate, Inc. Used with permission.

Legal Perspectives

From a **legal perspective**, illegal communication behavior also is unethical, but that which is not specifically illegal is ethical. In other words, legality and ethicality are synonymous. This approach certainly has the advantage of making ethical decisions simple: We need only measure communication techniques against current laws and regulations to determine whether a technique is ethical. We might, for example, turn for ethical guidance to the regulations governing advertising set forth by the Federal Trade Commission (FTC) or the Federal Communications Commission (FCC). Or we might use Supreme Court or state legislative criteria defining obscenity, pornography, libel, or slander to judge whether a particular message is unethical on those grounds.

However, many people are uneasy with this legalistic approach to communication ethics. They contend that obviously there are some things that are legal but ethically dubious. And some social protesters for civil rights and against the Vietnam War during the 1960s and 1970s admitted that their actions were illegal but contended that they were justifiable on ethical and moral grounds. Persons holding such views reject the idea that ethicality and legality are synonymous, view ethicality as much broader than legality, and argue that not everything that is unethical should be made illegal.

To what degree, then, can or should we enforce ethical standards for communication through laws or regulations? What degrees of soundness might there be in two old but seemingly contrary sayings: "You can't legislate morality" and "There ought to be a law"? In the United States today, very few ethical standards for communication are codified in laws or regulations. As we have indicated, FCC or FTC regulations on the content of advertising, and laws and court decisions on obscenity and libel, represent the governmental approach. But such examples are rare compared with the large number of laws and court decisions specifying the boundaries of freedom of speech and press in our society. Rather, our society applies ethical standards for communication through the indirect avenues of group consensus, social pressure, persuasion, and formal-but-voluntary codes of ethics.

Controversies surrounding computer communication on the Internet and Web illustrate not only the tension between freedom and responsibility but also the pressures to apply legalistic approaches to ethics and to create formal codes of ethics. Should you be free to say or depict anything you want, without restriction, on the Internet or Web or in email? What is your view on how ethical responsibility for computer communication on the Internet should be promoted? Through laws? Through institutional and professional codes of ethics?

University officials, perhaps on your campus, have debated whether to apply to the Internet and email activities of students existing campus speech codes that prohibit hate speech and harassment, or whether to formulate special codes of computer communication ethics to guide student use. On your campus, what official policies (set how and by whom?) govern ethically responsible communication on the Internet and Web? How adequately and appropriately do these policies speak to specific issues of communication ethics? Do these policies actually seem to address matters of legality more than of ethicality?

Dialogical Perspectives

Dialogical perspectives emerge from current scholarship on the nature of communication as dialogue rather than as monologue. From such perspectives, the attitudes participants in a communication situation have toward each other are an index of the ethical level of that communication. Some attitudes are held to be more fully human, humane, and facilitative of personal self-fulfillment than others (see Johannesen, 1971; 2002; Stewart and Zediker, 2000).

Communication as dialogue is characterized by such attitudes as honesty, concern for the welfare and improvement of others, trust, genuineness, open-mindedness, equality, mutual respect, empathy, humility, directness, lack of pretense, nonmanipulative intent, sincerity, encouragement of free expression, and acceptance of others as individuals with intrinsic worth regardless of differences of belief or behavior.

Communication as monologue, in contrast, is marked by such qualities as deception, superiority, exploitation, dogmatism, domination, insincerity, pretense, personal self-display, self-aggrandizement, judgmentalism that stifles free expression, coercion, possessiveness, condescension, self-defensiveness, and the view of others as objects to be manipulated. In the case of persuasion, then, we examine the persuader's techniques and presentation to determine the degree to which they reveal an ethical dialogical attitude or an unethical monological attitude toward receivers.

How might a dialogical ethical perspective apply to intimate interpersonal communication situations such as between friends, family members, lovers, and spouses? Earlier in the section on responsibilities of receivers, we summarized some unfair tactics of verbal conflict in interpersonal communication. How would you assess those tactics from a dialogical perspective?

Consider some of the popular interactive media such as email, chat rooms, blogs, cell phone text messaging, and Microsoft Xbox. For example, blogs (short for Web logs) facilitate extensive participation between blogger and users. One 2005 estimate indicated that 8 million American adults have created their own blogs, almost 32 million indicate they read blogs, and over 14 million say they have responded to a blog. Blog activity has been compared to a conversation or a seminar (Primer, 2005, pp. 15–16). How might we apply ethical standards rooted in a dialogical perspective to communication via blogs or other such interactive media?

With knowledge of the preceding ethical perspectives (religious, human nature, political, situational, legal, dialogical), we can confront a variety of difficult issues relevant to ethical problems in persuasion. As receivers constantly bombarded with verbal and nonverbal persuasive messages, we continually face resolution of one or another of these fundamental issues. To further help us grapple with such issues, we next consider some traditional advice on ethics which most of us have heard at one time or another—The Golden Rule.

THE GOLDEN RULE AND THE PLATINUM RULE

"Do unto others as you would have them do unto you." Most of us probably are familiar with this statement, which we have come to know as **The Golden Rule**. Persons familiar with the Christian religious tradition may think the Golden Rule is unique to that religion. In the New Testament we find: "And as ye would that men

should do to you, do ye also to them likewise" (Luke 6:31; also see Matthew 7:12). However, some version of the Golden Rule is found in the sacred literature of the major world religions, including Hinduism, Confucianism, Taoism, Zoroastrianism, and Jainism. For example, in Judaism: "What is hateful to you, do not to your fellow men." In Islam: "No one of you is a believer until he desires for his brother that which he desires for himself." In Buddhism: "Hurt not others in ways that you yourself would find hurtful" (Kane, 1994, p. 34; Samovar, Porter, and Stefani, 1998, p. 269).

One interpretation of the Golden Rule is that we should only do *specific actions* to others if we would allow them to do the same specific actions to us. Another interpretation would not require mutually specific actions but would require that the *ethical principles and standards* that we follow in relating to others are the same ethical principles we would expect others to follow in relating to us (Singer, M., 1963). Versions of the Golden Rule have been advocated not only by the major world religions but also by pagan philosophers. Thus a contemporary philosopher, Marcus Singer (1967), concludes: "The nearly universal acceptance of the Golden Rule and its promulgation by persons of considerable intelligence, though otherwise divergent outlooks, would therefore seem to provide some evidence for the claim that it is a fundamental ethical truth."

However, in the context of ethnic and religious diversity and of intercultural and multicultural communication, Milton Bennett argues that the Golden Rule best applies *within* a culture or group that has wide agreement on fundamental values, goals, institutions, and customs. In other words, the Golden Rule assumes that other people *want* to be treated in the same way we do. But this assumption is not automatically applicable in diverse intercultural and multicultural communication. Too often in such situations we may focus primarily or solely on our own values or preferences to the exclusion or minimization of values and preferences of others that differ from ours. As an alternative (or perhaps supplement) to the

Golden Rule, Bennett (1979) offers **The Platinum Rule**: "Do unto others as they themselves would have done unto them."

Certainly the Platinum Rule forces us to take into serious account the values and preferences of others, especially others unlike us, perhaps through empathy for or imagining of their experiences and worldviews. But we need to be careful that we do not interpret the Platinum Rule as requiring us automatically and unquestioningly to do what others want us to do. In making our final decision about what and how to communicate, we should carefully weigh the ethical guidance embodied in both the Golden Rule and the Platinum Rule. Then we should decide which takes precedence in our particular situation.

ETHICAL STANDARDS FOR POLITICAL PERSUASION

Directly or indirectly, we are daily exposed to political persuasion in varied forms. For example, the president appeals on national television for public support of a military campaign. A senator argues in Congress against ratification of a treaty. A government bureaucrat announces a new regulation and presents reasons to justify it. A federal official contends that information requested by a citizen action group cannot be revealed for national security reasons. A national, state, or local politician campaigns for election. A citizen protests a proposed property tax rate increase at a city council meeting. What ethical criteria should we apply to judge the many kinds of political persuasion?

During the latter half of the twentieth century, traditional American textbook discussions of the ethics of persuasion, rhetoric, and argument often included lists of standards for evaluating the ethicality of an instance of persuasion. Such criteria often are rooted, implicitly if not explicitly, in what we previously described as a political perspective for judging the ethics of persuasion. The criteria usually stem from a commitment to values and

procedures deemed essential to the health and growth of our system of representative democracy.

Of all the ethical criteria for varied types and contexts of persuasion described in this chapter, the following 11 are the most generally applicable for you to use as a persuader and persuadee. Do not look on these standards as limited only to political persuasion. They can apply to a wide variety of persuasive efforts in which you engage or to which you are exposed. Consider adopting (and modifying) these standards as your own *starting point commitment* to ethical persuasion (also see Sellers, 2004; Baker and Martinson, 2001).

What follows is my synthesis and adaptation of a number of traditional lists of ethical criteria for persuasion (Johannesen, 2002, pp. 30–32, 37–38). Within the context of our own society, the following criteria are not necessarily the only or best ones possible; they are suggested as general guidelines rather than inflexible rules, and they may stimulate discussion on the complexity of judging the ethics of persuasion. Consider, for example, under what circumstances there might be justifiable exceptions to some of these criteria. Also bear in mind that one difficulty in applying these criteria in concrete situations stems from differing standards and meanings people may have for such terms as *distort, falsify, rational, reasonable, conceal, misrepresent, irrelevant,* and *deceive.*

1. Do not use false, fabricated, misrepresented, distorted, or irrelevant evidence to support arguments or claims.

2. Do not intentionally use specious, unsupported, or illogical reasoning.

3. Do not represent yourself as informed or as an "expert" on a subject when you are not.

4. Do not use irrelevant appeals to divert attention or scrutiny from the issue at hand. Among the appeals that commonly serve such a purpose are smear attacks on an opponent's character, appeals to hatred and bigotry, innuendo, and emotionally loaded terms that cause intense but unreflective positive or negative reactions.

B O X 2.1 **Evaluating Political Persuasion**

Read the book by David Corn (2003), *The Lies of George W. Bush*. What ethical standards for judgment does Corn seem to employ? In what ways do you agree or disagree with Corn's ethical assessment of Bush's various efforts at

persuasion? In considering Corn's ethical criticisms, apply our previous discussion concerning *intention, sincerity, responsibility*, the political perspective, and suggested standards for political persuasion.

---

5. Do not ask your audience to link your idea or proposal to emotion-laden values, motives, or goals to which it actually is not related.

6. Do not deceive your audience by concealing your real purpose or self-interest, the group you represent, or your position as an advocate of a viewpoint.

7. Do not distort, hide, or misrepresent the number, scope, intensity, or undesirable features of consequences or effects.

8. Do not use emotional appeals that lack a supporting basis of evidence or reasoning or that would not be accepted if the audience had time and opportunity to examine the subject themselves.

9. Do not oversimplify complex, gradation-laden situations into simplistic two-valued, either/or, polar views or choices.

10. Do not pretend certainty where tentativeness and degrees of probability would be more accurate.

11. Do not advocate something in which you do not believe yourself.

During the 1980s, political analysts in the mass media often criticized President Ronald Reagan for misstating and misusing examples, statistics, and illustrative stories. They charged that he did this not just on rare occasions but with routine frequency in his news conferences, informal comments, and even speeches (Green & MacColl, 1987; Johannesen, 1985). The glaring misuse of facts and anecdotes in ethically suspect ways continues in national political discourse (Box 2.1).

ETHICAL STANDARDS FOR COMMERCIAL ADVERTISING

Consumers, academics, and advertisers themselves clearly do not agree on any one set of ethical standards as appropriate for assessing commercial advertising. Here we will simply survey some of the widely varied criteria that have been suggested. Among them you may find guidelines that will aid your own assessments.

Sometimes advertisers adopt what we previously called legal perspectives, in which ethicality is equated with legality. However, advertising executive Harold Williams (1974) observed:

> What is legal and what is ethical are not synonymous, and neither are what is legal and what is honest. We tend to resort to legality often as our guideline. This is in effect what happens often when we turn to the lawyers for confirmation that a course of action is an appropriate one.
>
> We must recognize that we are getting a legal opinion, but not necessarily an ethical or moral one. The public, the public advocates, and many of the legislative and administrative authorities recognize it even if we do not (pp. 285–288).

Typically, commercial advertising has been viewed as persuasion that argues a case or demonstrates a claim concerning the actual nature or merits of a product. This view is reflected in the formal codes of ethics of professional advertising associations, such as the American Advertising Federation. Many of the traditional ethical standards for truthfulness and rationality are applicable to such attempts at arguing the quality of a product. For instance, are the evidence and the reasoning supporting the claim clear, accurate, relevant, and sufficient in quantity? Are the emotional and motivational appeals directly relevant to the product?

The American Association of Advertising Agencies' code of ethics was revised in 1990. As you read the following standards, consider their level of adequacy, the degree to which they are relevant and appropriate today, the extent to which they are being followed by advertisers, and how they reflect truthfulness and rationality criteria. Association members agree to avoid intentionally producing advertising that contains the following:

- False or misleading statements or exaggerations, visual or verbal
- Testimonials that do not reflect the real choices of the individuals involved
- Price claims that are misleading
- Claims that are insufficiently supported or that distort the true meaning or practicable application of statements made by professional or scientific authority
- Statements, suggestions, or pictures offensive to public decency or to minority segments of the population

What if ethical standards of truthfulness and rationality are irrelevant to most commercial advertising? What if the primary purpose of most ads is not to prove a claim? Then the ethical standards we apply may stem from whatever alternative view of the nature and purpose of advertising we do hold. Some advertisements function primarily to capture and sustain consumer attention, to announce a product, or to create consumer awareness of the name of a product. Many advertisements aim primarily at stimulating in consumers a positive or feel-good attitude about the product through use of metaphor, humor, fantasy, and fiction (Spence and Van Heekeren, 2005, pp. 41–53). What ethical criteria are most appropriate for such attention-getting or feel-good ads?

Consider advertiser Tony Schwartz's (1974) resonance theory of electronic media persuasion, which is discussed in detail in the chapter on modern media and persuasion. Schwartz argued that, because our conceptions of truth, honesty, and clarity are products of our print-oriented culture, they are appropriate in judging the content of printed messages. In contrast, he contended, the "question of truth is largely irrelevant when dealing with electronic media content" (p. 19). In assessing the ethics of advertising by means of electronic media, Schwartz said, the FTC should focus not on truth and clarity of content but on the effects of the advertisement on receivers. He lamented, however, that "we have no generally agreed-upon social values and/or rules that can be readily applied in judging whether the effects of electronic communication are beneficial, acceptable, or harmful" (p. 22).

What ethical evaluation of effects and consequences would you make of an advertisement for Fetish perfume in *Seventeen*, a magazine whose readers include several million young teenage girls? The ad shows an attractive female teenager looking seductively at the readers. The written portion of the ad says, "Apply generously to your neck so he can smell the scent as you shake your head 'no.'" Consider that this ad exists in a larger cultural context in which acquaintance rape is a societal problem, women and girls are clearly urged to say "No!" to unwanted sexual advances, and men and boys too often still believe that "no" really means "yes."

What harmful individual and societal consequences may stem from ads that negatively stereotype persons or groups on the basis of age (old and confused), sex (women as sex objects), or culture (backward)? Our frequent exposure to such ads may indeed influence the way we perceive and treat such stereotyped persons and the way the stereotyped persons view themselves and their own abilities (Spence and Van Heekeren, 2005, pp. 54–69). "Therefore, insofar as stereotyping in advertising degrades people as persons and harms their personal dignity by degrading the societal group to which they belong, stereotyping violates people's rights to freedom and well-being and hence is unethical" (p. 68).

Commercial advertisements sometimes can be criticized for containing ambiguous or vague elements. But concern about vagueness and ambiguity in persuasion is not limited to commercial advertising. Now we examine the more general ethical implications of ambiguity and vagueness.

THE ETHICS OF INTENTIONAL AMBIGUITY AND VAGUENESS

"Language that is of doubtful or uncertain meaning" might be a typical definition of ambiguous language. **Ambiguous** language is open to two or more legitimate interpretations. **Vague** language lacks definiteness, explicitness, or preciseness of meaning. Clear communication of intended meaning usually is one major aim of the ethical communicator, whether that person seeks to enhance receivers' understanding or to influence beliefs, attitudes, or actions. Textbooks on oral and written communication typically warn against ambiguity and vagueness; often, they take the position that intentional ambiguity is an unethical communication tactic. For example, later in this book, we discuss ambiguity as a functional device of style, as a stylistic technique that is often successful while ethically questionable.

Most people agree that intentional ambiguity is unethical in situations in which accurate instruction or transmission of precise information is the acknowledged purpose. Even in most so-called persuasive communication situations, intentional ambiguity is ethically suspect. However, in some situations, communicators may believe that the intentional creation of ambiguity or vagueness is necessary, accepted, expected as normal, and even ethically justified. Such might be the case, for example, in religious discourse, in some advertising, in labor–management bargaining, in political campaigning, or in international diplomatic negotiations.

We can itemize a number of specific purposes for which communicators might believe that intentional ambiguity is ethically justified: (1) to heighten receiver attention through puzzlement, (2) to allow flexibility in interpretation of legal concepts, (3) to allow for precise understanding and agreement on the primary issue by using ambiguity on secondary issues, (4) to promote maximum receiver psychological participation in the communication transaction by letting receivers create their own relevant meanings, and (5) to promote maximum latitude for revision of a position in later dealings with opponents or with constituents by avoiding being locked into a single absolute stance.

In political communication, whether from campaigners or government officials, several circumstances might justify intentional ambiguity. First, a president or presidential candidate often communicates to multiple audiences through a single message via a mass medium such as television or radio. Different parts of the message may appeal to specific audiences, and intentional ambiguity in some message elements avoids offending any of the audiences. Second, as political scientist Lewis Froman (1966) observed, a candidate "cannot take stands on specific issues because he doesn't know what the specific choices will be until he is faced with the necessity for concrete decision. Also, specific commitments would be too binding in a political process that depends upon negotiation and compromise" (p. 9). Third, groups of voters increasingly make decisions about whether to support or oppose a candidate on the basis of that candidate's stand on a single issue of paramount importance to those groups. The candidate's position on a variety of other public issues is often ignored or dismissed. "Single-issue politics" is the phrase frequently used to characterize this trend. A candidate may be intentionally ambiguous on one emotion-packed issue in order to get a fair hearing for his or her stands on many other issues.

During the 2004 presidential campaign, George W. Bush frequently charged his opponent, John Kerry, with "flip-flopping" on significant issues. That is, Bush claimed that Kerry often changed his position on issues and thus was inconsistent or ambiguous. To what degree and in what ways do you believe that Bush's claims were fair and accurate? In addition, consider whether it is automatically unethical for a politician to change her or his position on an issue. Why or why not?

In some advertising, intentional ambiguity seems to be understood as such by consumers and even accepted by them. Consider the possible ethical implications of the Noxzema shaving cream commercial that famously urged, "Take it off. Take it all off," accompanied by the image of a beautiful woman watching a man shave to strip-tease music. Or recall the sexy woman in the aftershave commercial who says, "All my men wear English Leather, or they wear nothing at all."

Nonverbal elements of commercial advertisements sometimes invite examination of their ethicality. But scrutiny of the ethics of nonverbal communication raises broader issues, which we now consider.

THE ETHICS OF NONVERBAL COMMUNICATION

Nonverbal factors play an important role in the persuasion process. In a magazine advertisement, for example, the use of certain colors, pictures, layout patterns, and typeface influences how the words in the advertisement are received. A later chapter provides examples of "nonverbal bias" in photo selection, camera angle and movement, and editing in news presentation. In *The Importance of Lying*, Arnold Ludwig (1965) underscored the ethical implications of some dimensions of nonverbal communication:

> Lies are not only found in verbal statements. When a person nods affirmatively in response to something he does not believe or when he feigns attention to a conversation he finds boring, he is equally guilty of lying. ... A false shrug of the shoulders, the seductive batting of eyelashes, an eyewink, or a smile may all be employed as nonverbal forms of deception (p. 5).

Silence, too, may carry ethical implications. If to be responsible in fulfilling our role or position requires that we speak out on a subject, to remain silent may be judged unethical. But if the only way that we can successfully persuade others on a subject is to employ unethical communication techniques or appeals, the ethical course probably will be to remain silent.

Television coverage of the 9/11/01 terrorist attacks on the World Trade Center yielded many vivid pictures that were burned into our memories. An Associated Press photographer produced one especially emotional image—of a man plunging headfirst down the side of the still-standing North Tower. Although no captions identified the man, the photographer's telephoto lens was powerful enough that, in versions enhanced for clarity, the man's face was recognizable to persons who knew him. With regard to ethics, this photo generated criticism of the media that used the photo and praise for the media not using it. On what ethical grounds might you condemn the use of the photo? On what ethical grounds might you justify its use? Consider the likely emotional trauma for persons who knew the man. Did the ends of selling papers or crystallizing the personal dimension of the attack justify using it as a means that intensified the grief and violated the privacy of family members and friends? How does the photo feed into the public's seemingly unlimited appetite for glimpses into the intimate details of the grief of others—a process that some scholars refer to as the "pornography of grief"? (M. Cooper, 2002; and J. B. Singer, 2002.)

Persuaders sometimes use verbal and nonverbal communication to depict others, especially outsiders

---

B O X 2.3 Moral Exclusion in a Headline

The headline "An Eskimo Encounters Civilization—and Mankind" appeared in the Tempo section of the *Chicago Tribune* (May 29, 2000). Can you identify two ways in which the words in the headline reflect a process of moral exclusion? How do these words place people outside the categories where

human ethics normally apply? Hate speech, as discussed earlier in this chapter, and racist/sexist language, examined in the next section, also illustrate the process of moral exclusion. In what ways does hate speech embody the moral exclusion process?

---

and enemies, as beyond the sphere where normal ethics apply. The nature and implications of such ethical exclusion are our next topic.

THE ETHICS OF MORAL EXCLUSION

Moral exclusion, according to Susan Opotow (1990), "occurs when individuals or groups are perceived as outside the boundary in which moral values, rules, and considerations of fairness apply. Those who are morally excluded are perceived as nonentities, expendable, or undeserving; consequently, harming them appears acceptable, appropriate, or just." Persons morally excluded are denied their rights, dignity, and autonomy. Opotow isolates for analysis and discussion over two dozen symptoms or manifestations of moral exclusion. For our purposes, a noteworthy fact is that many of them directly involve communication. Although all the symptoms she presents are significant for a full understanding of the mind-set of individuals engaged in moral exclusion, the following clearly involve persuasion:

- Showing the superiority of oneself or one's group by making unflattering comparisons to other individuals or groups

- Denigrating and disparaging others by characterizing them as lower life forms (vermin) or as inferior beings (barbarians, aliens)

- Denying that others possess humanity, dignity, or sensitivity, or have a right to compassion

- Redefining as an increasingly larger category that of "legitimate" victims

- Placing the blame for any harm on the victim

- Justifying harmful acts by claiming that the morally condemnable acts committed by "the enemy" are significantly worse

- Misrepresenting cruelty and harm by masking, sanitizing, and conferring respectability on them through the use of neutral, positive, technical, or euphemistic terms to describe them

- Justifying harmful behavior by claiming that it is widely accepted (everyone is doing it) or that it was isolated and uncharacteristic (it happened just this once)

An example may clarify how language choices function to achieve moral exclusion. The category of "vermin" includes parasitic insects such as fleas, lice, mosquitoes, bedbugs, and ticks that can infest human bodies. In Nazi Germany, Adolf Hitler's speeches and writings often referred to Jews as a type of parasite infesting the pure Aryan race (non-Jewish Caucasians or people of Nordic heritage) or as a type of disease attacking the German national body. The depiction of Jews as parasites or a disease served to place them outside the moral boundary where ethical standards apply to human treatment of other humans. Jews were classified or categorized as nonhumans. As parasites, they had to be exterminated; as a cancerous disease, they had to be cut out of the national body.

Even headlines we encounter daily in newspapers or magazines may reflect (perhaps unconsciously) the process of moral exclusion. Carefully consider the headline discussed in Box 2.3.

THE ETHICS OF RACIST/SEXIST LANGUAGE

In *The Language of Oppression*, communication scholar Haig Bosmajian (1983) demonstrated how names, labels, definitions, and stereotypes traditionally have been used to degrade, dehumanize, and suppress Jews, Blacks, Native Americans, and women. Bosmajian's goal was to expose the "decadence in our language, the inhumane uses of language" that have been used "to justify the unjustifiable, to make palatable the unpalatable, to make reasonable the unreasonable, to make decent the indecent." Bosmajian reminded us: "Our identities, who and what we are, how others see us, are greatly affected by the names we are called and the words with which we are labeled. The names, labels, and phrases employed to 'identify' a people may in the end determine their survival" (pp. 5, 9).

"Every language reflects the prejudices of the society in which it evolved. Since English, through most of its history, evolved in a white, Anglo-Saxon, patriarchal society, no one should be surprised that its vocabulary and grammar frequently reflect attitudes that exclude or demean minorities and women" (Miller & Swift, 1981, pp. 2–3). Such is the fundamental position of Casey Miller and Kate Swift, authors of *The Handbook of Nonsexist Writing*. Conventional English usage, they argued, "often obscures the actions, the contributions, and sometimes the very presence of women" (p. 8). Because such language usage is misleading and inaccurate, it has ethical implications. "In this respect, continuing to use English in ways that have become misleading is no different from misusing data, whether the misuse is inadvertent or planned" (p. 8).

To what degree is the use of **racist/sexist language** unethical, and by what standards? At the least, racist/sexist terms place people in artificial and irrelevant categories. At worst, such terms intentionally demean and put down other people by embodying unfair negative value judgments of their traits, capacities, and accomplishments. What are the ethical implications, for instance, of calling a Jewish person a "kike," a Black person a "nigger" or "boy," an Italian person a "wop," an Asian person a "gook" or "slant-eye," or a thirty-year-old woman a "girl" or "chick"? Here is one possible answer:

> In the war in Southeast Asia, our military fostered a linguistic environment in which the Vietnamese people were called such names as slope, dink, slant, gook, and zip; those names made it much easier to despise, to fear, to kill them. When we call women in our own society by the names of gash, slut, dyke, bitch, or girl, we—men and women alike—have put ourselves in a position to demean and abuse them (Bailey, 1984, pp. 42–43).

From a political perspective, we might value access to the relevant and accurate information needed to make reasonable decisions on public issues. Racist/sexist language, however, by reinforcing stereotypes, conveys inaccurate depictions of people, fails to take serious account of them, or even makes them invisible for purposes of such decisions. Such language denies us access to necessary accurate information and thus is ethically suspect. From a human nature perspective, it is also ethically suspect because it dehumanizes individuals and groups by undermining and circumventing their uniquely human capacity for rational thought or for using symbols. From a dialogical perspective, racist/sexist language is ethically suspect because it reflects a superior, exploitative, inhumane attitude toward others, thus denying equal opportunity for self-fulfillment for some people.

SOME FEMINIST VIEWS ON PERSUASION

Feminism is not a concept with a single, universally accepted definition. For our purposes, elements of definitions provided by Barbara Bate (1992) and Julia Wood (1994) are helpful. **Feminism** holds that both women and men are complete and important human beings and that societal barriers (typically constructed through language processes) have prevented women from being perceived and treated as of equal worth to men. Feminism implies a commitment to equality and respect for life. It rejects oppression and domination as undesirable values and accepts that difference need not be equated with inferiority or undesirability.

Sonja Foss and Cindy Griffin (1995) develop an "invitational rhetoric" rooted in the feminist assumptions that (1) relationships of equality are usually more desirable than ones of domination and elitism, (2) every human being has value because she or he is unique and is an integral part of the pattern of the universe, and (3) individuals have a right to self-determination concerning the conditions of their lives (they are expert about their lives).

Invitational rhetoric, say Foss and Griffin, invites "the audience to enter the rhetor's world and to see it as the rhetor does." The invitational rhetor "does not judge or denigrate others' perspectives but is open to and tries to appreciate and validate those perspectives, even if they differ dramatically from the rhetor's own." The goal is to establish a "nonhierarchical, nonjudgmental, nonadversarial framework" for the interaction and to develop a "relationship of equality, respect, and appreciation" with the audience. Invitational rhetors make no assumption that their "experiences or perspectives are superior to those of audience members and refuse to impose their perspectives on them." Although change is not the intent of invitational rhetoric, it might be a result. Change can occur in the "audience or rhetor or both as a result of new understandings and insights gained in the exchange of ideas."

In the process of invitational rhetoric, Foss and Griffin contend, the rhetor offers perspectives without advocating their support or seeking their acceptance. These individual perspectives are expressed "as carefully, completely, and passionately as possible" to invite their full consideration. In offering perspectives, "rhetors tell what they currently know or understand; they present their vision of the world and how it works for them."

They also "communicate a willingness to call into question the beliefs they consider most inviolate and to relax a grip on these beliefs." Further, they strive to create the conditions of safety, value, and freedom in interactions with audience members. Safety implies "the creation of a feeling of security and freedom from danger for the audience," so that participants do not "fear rebuttal of or retribution for their most fundamental beliefs." Value involves acknowledging the intrinsic worth of audience members as human beings. In interaction, attitudes that are "distancing, depersonalizing, or paternalistic" are avoided, and "listeners do not interrupt, confront, or insert anything of their own as others tell of their experiences." Freedom includes the power to choose or decide, with no restrictions placed on the interaction. Thus, participants may introduce for consideration any and all matters; "no subject matter is off limits, and all presuppositions can be challenged." Finally, in invitational rhetoric, the "rhetor's ideas are not privileged over those of the audience." (Also see Gorsevski, 2004, pp. 75, 164.)

In concluding their explication of an invitational rhetoric, Foss and Griffin suggest that this rhetoric requires "a new scheme of ethics to fit interactional goals other than inducement of others to adherence to the rhetor's own beliefs." What might be some appropriate ethical guidelines for an invitational rhetoric? What ethical standards seem already to be implied by the dimensions or constituents of such a rhetoric?

From her stance as a feminist teacher and scholar of communication, Lana Rakow (1994) spoke to an audience of students and teachers of communication at Ohio State University. She employed the norms of "trust, mutuality, justice, and reciprocity" as touchstones for communication relationships. As part of a wide-ranging address on the mission of the field of communication study, Rakow contended that we must develop a communication ethic to guide "relations between individuals, between cultures, between organizations, between countries." She asked, "What kind of 'ground-rules' would work across multiple contexts to achieve relationships that are healthy and egalitarian and respectful?" She suggested these:

- Inclusiveness means openness to multiple perspectives on truth, an encouragement of them, and a willingness to listen. Persons are not dehumanized because of their gender, race, ethnicity, sexual orientation, country, or culture.

- Participation means ensuring that all persons must have the "means and ability ... to be heard, to speak, to have voice, to have their opinions count in public decision making." All persons "have a right to participate in naming the world, to be part of the discussion in naming and speaking our truths."

- Reciprocity means that participants are considered equal partners in a communication transaction. There should be a "reciprocity of speaking and listening, of knowing and being known as you wish to be known."

In what respects do you agree or disagree with the positions advocated by these feminist scholars? What contributions do their viewpoints make to our better understanding of the process of persuasion as it functions and as it ought to function?

A few scholars with a feminist viewpoint explore ethical issues concerning the Internet and cyberspace (for example, Adam, 2005). Our next topic examines general issues of Internet ethics from several ethical viewpoints.

ETHICAL STANDARDS IN CYBERSPACE

What ethical standards should apply to communication in cyberspace—in the realm of the Internet, the Web, email, blogs, and chat rooms? We can get guidance and suggestions from several sources (for example, Berkman and Shumway, 2003; Hamelink, 2000; Johnson, 2001; Wolf, 2003). Some of the

"Ten Commandments of Computer Ethics" formulated by the Computer Ethics Institute are particularly relevant. For example, "thou shalt not: Use a computer to harm other people; interfere with other people's computer work; snoop around in other people's computer files; use a computer to steal; use a computer to bear false witness against others; [or] plagiarize another person's intellectual output" (reprinted in Ermann, 1997, pp. 313–314).

In *Communicating Online: A Guide to the Internet*, John Courtright and Elizabeth Perse (1998) define acting ethically as simply "doing the right thing, even when no one is looking" and as "behaving properly, even when there is no chance of being caught" (p. 16). Concerning communication via email, they propose that we ask ourselves, "Would I be embarrassed or ashamed if I read my own words in tomorrow's newspaper?" It's important to never, intentionally or unintentionally, harass someone with email, or to send "flames" or messages that contain strong language and are meant to provoke or criticize. "Just like any other form of communication, don't email in anger. Give yourself a chance to cool down before you send your message" (p. 33). Whenever you use the ideas of another person from an Internet source, give that person credit by using a proper citation (p. 64). With email, listservs, and newsgroups, avoid "shouting," or routinely typing in all capitals, which generally is considered inappropriate if not rude. Also avoid "trolling," or posting messages designed simply to agitate a group to "bite back" with an extreme response (p. 82). What kind of a code of Internet ethics might you propose as appropriate, clear, and workable?

Advertising and marketing specialists increasingly capitalize on the interactive capacities of the Internet and of interactive television to create a two-way "conversation" between product and consumer. On the Internet, Java and Shockwave technologies facilitate interactive ads. Video on demand and personal video recorders (such as TiVo) afford opportunities for interactive television ads. But much of the contact, such as banner ads and pop-ups on the Internet, is not truly a

---

BOX 2.4   Ethical Implications of Cyberspace Metaphors

Some scholars argue that the dominant metaphors frequently used to describe the realm of cyberspace and the Internet actually function unethically to hinder Internet use by people who already are marginalized, neglected, and devalued by society (Adam, 2005, pp. 64, 114, 132–136; Gunkel, 2001; Kramer and Kramerae, 1997). Such metaphors for cyberspace as new world, frontier, anarchy, democracy, and community have been critiqued for their ethical implications. Consider the metaphor of cyberspace described as a community. In actuality, in what ways do cyberspace and the Internet primarily promote individualism, selfishness, intolerance of those not like us, and lack of trust through deception more than interdependence, concern and care for the less advantaged, and appreciation and tolerance of diversity within a sphere of common values and purposes? What might be some ethical issues related to metaphorically comparing the Internet to a superhighway?

---

conversation (Spence and Van Heekeren, 2005, pp. 96–107). "One-way unsolicited communications from advertisers to consumers, especially when they are conducted without the consumers' consent, are not 'interactive' and not 'conversations' even if the advertisers mislabel them as such. And insofar as they invade the consumers' privacy they are ethically unjustified" (p. 104).

How we conceptualize the Internet, what metaphors we use to describe cyberspace, actually may have ethical implications. Consider this issue as discussed in Box 2.4.

Standards, criteria, and guidelines are central to much of the earlier discussion in this chapter, and shortly we will present a framework of questions that can improve your ethical judgment. But now we discuss the often-neglected role of your formed ethical character in creating and evaluating persuasion.

ETHICS AND PERSONAL CHARACTER

Ethical persuasion is not simply a series of careful and reflective decisions, instance by instance, to persuade in ethically responsible ways. Deliberate application of ethical rules is sometimes impossible. Pressure for a decision can be so great or a deadline so near that there is insufficient time for careful deliberation. We might be unsure what ethical criteria are relevant or how they apply. The situation might seem so unusual that applicable criteria do not readily come to mind. In such times of crisis or uncertainty, our decisions concerning ethical persuasion stem less from deliberation than from our formed "character." Further, our ethical character influences what terms we use to describe a situation and whether we believe the situation contains ethical implications (Hauerwas, 1977; Klaidman & Beauchamp, 1987; Lebacqz, 1985).

Consider the nature of **moral character** as described by ethicists Richard DeGeorge and Karen Lebacqz. As human beings develop, according to DeGeorge (1999), they adopt patterns of actions and dispositions to act in certain ways.

> These dispositions, when viewed collectively, are sometimes called *character*. The character of a person is the sum of his or her virtues and vices. A person who habitually tends to act as he morally should has a good character. If he resists strong temptation, he has a strong character. If he habitually acts immorally, he has a morally bad character. If despite good intentions he frequently succumbs to temptation, he has a weak character. Because character is formed by conscious actions, in general people

are morally responsible for their characters as well as for their individual actions (p.123).

Lebacqz (1985) observes:

> ... when we act, we not only do something, we also shape our own character. Our choices about what to do are also choices about whom to be. A single lie does not necessarily make us a liar; but a series of lies may. And so each choice about what to do is also a choice about whom to be—or, more accurately, whom to become (p. 83).

In Judeo-Christian or Western cultures, good moral character is usually associated with habitual embodiment of such virtues as courage, temperance, wisdom, justice, fairness, generosity, gentleness, patience, truthfulness, and trustworthiness. Other cultures may praise additional or different virtues that they believe constitute good ethical character. Instilled in us as habitual dispositions to act, these virtues guide the ethics of our communication behavior when careful or clear deliberation is not possible.

The period from 1997 to 1999 found President Bill Clinton's character to be a primary focus of media scrutiny because of his sexual improprieties with White House intern Monica Lewinsky, because of independent counsel Kenneth Starr's investigation into alleged misdeeds by the president and his administration, because of two articles of impeachment (indictment) voted by the House of Representatives against the president (perjury to a grand jury and obstruction of justice), and because of his acquittal by the Senate on both charges. Public opinion polls during the period reflected a paradox: Clinton's job performance approval ratings ranged between 60 and 70 percent, but significant numbers of citizens doubted his personal ethical character and trustworthiness. For example, a CNN/USA Today/Gallup Poll released in mid-January 1999 (*Washington Post National Weekly Edition*, Jan. 25, 1999, p. 12) found that 69 percent of those surveyed approved of Clinton's job performance as president, and 81 percent said his presidency had been a success. In contrast, only 25 percent said he was honest and trustworthy, and only 20 percent said he provided good moral leadership. In the summer, fall, and winter of 1998–1999, Clinton gave four speeches of apology (August 16, September 11, December 11, February 12) in which he admitted engaging in sexual improprieties and lying about it and in which he progressively expressed regret, remorse, sorrow, and shame. Analyze the arguments and appeals in these four speeches to judge their degree of ethicality (see the *Weekly Compilation of Presidential Documents*).

Columnist Robert Samuelson (1998) condemned Clinton for "routine and unending deceptions"—not only about personal behavior but also about public policy: "What inhibits most people from routine lies is a sense of shame. Clinton seems to lack this" (p. 17). Other political analysts contended that the issue of personal ethical character should be of crucial importance in selecting future presidents. John Kass (1998) concluded, "Character is the only thing that matters. And we're responsible for forgetting" (p. 3). Joan Beck (1998) urged, "And next time we should pay more attention to character issues, to understand that character can't be divided into public and private sectors, and that the presidency can, indeed, be weakened by such discussions as whether oral sex counts as adultery" (p. 19). In what ways, and why, do you agree or disagree with the judgments of the various critics cited in these sections on Clinton's ethical character?

To aid in assessing the ethical character of any person in a position of responsibility or any person who seeks a position of trust, we can modify guidelines suggested by journalists. We can ask, Is it probable that the recent or current ethically suspect communication behavior will continue? Does it seem to be habitual? Even if a particular incident seems minor in itself, does it fit into some pattern of shortcomings? If the person does something inconsistent with his or her public image, is it a mere miscue or an indication of hypocrisy (Alter, 1987; Dobel, 1999; Johannesen, 1991)?

Access InfoTrac College Edition using Advanced Search with title. Access the item "Do As I Say, Not As I Did," published in *Time* (July 22, 2002). What ethical judgments could you make concerning the described comments and actions of President George W. Bush and Vice President Dick Cheney?

IMPROVING ETHICAL JUDGMENT

One purpose of this book is to make you a more discerning receiver and consumer of communication by encouraging ethical judgments of communication that are specifically focused and carefully considered. In making judgments about the ethics of your own communication and the communication to which you are exposed, you should make specific rather than vague assessments, and thoughtful rather than reflexive, "gut-level" reactions.

The following framework of questions is offered as a means of making more systematic and firmly grounded judgments of communication ethics (see, for example, Christians et al., 2005, pp. 22–24; Goodwin, 1987, pp. 14–15). Bear in mind philosopher Stephen Toulmin's (1950) observation that "moral reasoning is so complex, and has to cover such a variety of types of situations, that no one logical test . . . can be expected to meet every case" (p. 148). In underscoring the complexity of making ethical judgments, in *The Virtuous Journalist*, Klaidman and Beauchamp (1987) reject the "false premise that the world is a tidy place of truth and falsity, right and wrong, without the ragged edges of uncertainty and risk." Rather, they argue, "Making moral judgments and handling moral dilemmas require the balancing of often ill-defined competing claims, usually in untidy circumstances" (p. 20). How might you apply this framework of questions? (Also see Figure 2.3.)

FIGURE 2.3 How might the guidelines for ethical judgment help to evaluate this situation?
SOURCE: © Creative Media Services, Box 5955, Berkeley, CA 94705.

1. Can I specify exactly what ethical criteria, standards, or perspectives are being applied by me or by others? What is the concrete grounding of the ethical judgment?

2. Can I justify the reasonableness and relevancy of these standards for this particular case? Why are these the most appropriate ethical criteria among the potential ones? Why do these take priority (at least temporarily) over other relevant ones?

3. Can I indicate clearly in what respects the communication being evaluated succeeds or fails in measuring up to the standards? What judgment is justified in this case about the degree of ethicality? Is the most appropriate judgment a specifically targeted and narrowly focused one rather than a broad, generalized, and encompassing one?

4. In this case, to whom is ethical responsibility owed—to which individuals, groups,

organizations, or professions? In what ways and to what extent? Which responsibilities take precedence over others? What is the communicator's responsibility to herself or himself and to society at large?

5. How do I feel about myself after this ethical choice? Can I continue to "live with myself" in good conscience? Would I want my parents or mate or best friend to know of this choice?

6. Can the ethicality of this communication be justified as a coherent reflection of the communicator's personal character? To what degree is the choice ethically "out of character"?

7. If called upon in public to justify the ethics of my communication, how adequately could I do so? What generally accepted reasons or rationale could I appropriately offer?

8. Are there precedents or similar previous cases to which I can turn for ethical guidance? Are there significant aspects of this instance that set it apart from all others?

9. How thoroughly have alternatives been explored before settling on this particular choice? Might this choice be less ethical than some of the workable but hastily rejected or ignored alternatives?

Remember that this framework for ethical judgment is not a set of inflexible and universal rules. You must adapt the questions to varied persuasive situations to determine which questions are most applicable.

Also, this list may stimulate additional questions. The framework is a starting point, not the final word.

REVIEW AND CONCLUSION

The process of persuasion demands that you make choices about the methods and content you will use in influencing receivers to accept the alternative you advocate. These choices involve issues of desirability and of personal and societal good. What ethical standards will you use in making or judging these choices among techniques, contents, and purposes? What should be the ethical responsibility of a persuader in contemporary society? Obviously, answers to these questions have not been clearly or universally established. However, we must face the questions squarely. In this chapter, we explored some perspectives, issues, and examples useful in evaluating the ethics of persuasion. Our interest in the nature and effectiveness of persuasive techniques must not overshadow our concern for the ethical use of such techniques. We must examine not only how to but also whether to use persuasive techniques. The issue of whether to is both one of audience adaptation and one of ethics. We need to formulate meaningful ethical guidelines, not inflexible rules, for our own persuasive behavior and for use in evaluating the persuasion to which we are exposed.

KEY TERMS

When you have completed this chapter, you should be able to identify, explain, and give an example of the following key terms or concepts.

ethical issues	hate speech	The Platinum Rule	feminism
responsibility	situational perspective	ambiguous	invitational rhetoric
religious perspectives	legal perspective	vague	moral character
human nature perspectives	dialogical perspective	moral exclusion	
political perspectives	The Golden Rule	racist/sexist language	

APPLICATION OF ETHICS

Assume that you are employed in the public relations department of a large corporation. Your supervisor assigns you to present a series of speeches to community groups in a city where your company has just built a new production facility. In the speech prepared by your supervisor, you will describe the services and advantages of the plant that will benefit the community. But during a visit to the plant to familiarize yourself with its operation, you discover that the plant cannot actually deliver most of the services and advantages promised in the speech. Should you go ahead and present the speech as your supervisor prepared it? Should you refuse to give it at all? What changes might you in good conscience make in the speech? With or without your supervisor's approval? What ethical standards might you use in making your decisions? Why? What additional ethical issues might confront you in this situation? (Adapted from McCammond, 2004.)

QUESTIONS FOR FURTHER THOUGHT

1. What standards do you believe are most appropriate for judging the ethics of political persuasion?

2. What ethical standards do you think should be used to evaluate advertising?

3. When might intentional use of ambiguity be ethically justified?

4. To what degree is the use of racist/sexist language unethical? Why?

5. Do the ethical standards commonly applied to verbal persuasion apply equally appropriately to nonverbal elements in persuasion? Should there be a special ethic for nonverbal persuasion?

6. What should be the role of personal character in ethical persuasion?

7. What ethical standards do you believe should guide communication on the Internet?

8. How does hate speech illustrate the process of moral exclusion?

 For online activities, go to the *Persuasion* book companion website at http://communication.wadsworth.com/larson11.

3

Traditional and Humanistic Approaches to Persuasion

JOSEPH SCUDDER

Northern Illinois University

Aristotle's *Rhetoric*

> *Adaptation to Context and Purpose*
>
> *Audience Adaptation and a Common Universe of Ideas*
>
> *Types of Proof*
>
> *The Potency of Language*

Plato's Dialogic Approach

Scott's Epistemic Approach

Fisher's Narrative Approach

Power-Oriented Perspectives

> *The Women's Movement*
>
> *Marxist Theory*
>
> *Radical Movements*

Review and Conclusion

Key Terms

Application of Ethics

Questions for Further Thought

LEARNING GOALS

After reading this chapter, you should be able to:

1. Discuss the foundations in Aristotle's *Rhetoric* that guide contemporary persuasion and marketing.

2. Assess what Plato's dialogic approach adds to the practice of persuasion today.

3. Explain Robert Scott's epistemic approach in relationship to Aristotle's and Plato's approaches.

4. Describe Fisher's reasons for developing his narrative approach and apply Fisher's criteria of coherence and fidelity to recent persuasive narratives.

5. Identify the objections to Fisher's narrative approach.

6. Discuss the controversy among feminist rhetorical scholars regarding the value of invitational rhetoric.

7. Differentiate between those who have power in a persuasive text and those who are absent or pushed to the margins.

8. Compare and contrast Truth and truth across all the approaches in this chapter.

Unless you are an unusually motivated student, classic approaches to persuasion probably have little natural appeal to you. Several years ago, I felt that way, too. I went to graduate school to study current, cutting-edge communication principles—not ancient classics. I struggled when assigned to read the entire volume of Aristotle's *Rhetoric* in one week. It took time for me to realize that Aristotle and Plato laid the foundation for much of what we study today. Persuasion still addresses many of the same basic human motivations they addressed: the promise of a better life, the security of our homes and lives, the joy of children, the love of family and friends, the desire for justice, and the respect of others. Gaps, omissions, and blind spots, however, do exist in these early classics. They did not deal adequately with confronting powerful others—especially those in leadership positions involved in oppression. Thus, this chapter considers a wide range of persuasive approaches from the early traditional ones to more recent humanistic approaches exposing the exploitation of persons pushed to the margins of society.

ARISTOTLE'S *RHETORIC*

The formal study of persuasion has its early roots in ancient Greece where city-states valued the right of their citizens to speak on issues of the day. Greek philosophers like Aristotle tried to describe what happened when persuasion occurred. Much of what Aristotle said on the subject of persuasion has relevance today when his principles are adapted to fit contemporary society.

Aristotle was a remarkable person. Alexander the Great put Aristotle in charge of the educational system of Greece, in which job he developed schools using much that he had learned from Plato, his mentor. He established an ambitious program that we would now consider a library, where he put a thousand men to work cataloguing everything known about the world at that time. He used the findings of his researchers to write many books covering a variety of topics, including his *Rhetoric*, considered by many to be the single most important work on the study of persuasion. The next section summarizes key features from the *Rhetoric* that remain central to the practice of persuasion today.

Adaptation to Context and Purpose

Aristotle recognized that one approach to persuasion did not fit all situations. He proposed that a persuasive speaker must adapt to the context. In today's advertising and media markets, we talk about market segments and target audiences. Essentially, Aristotle recognized **segmented audiences** long ago when he saw that it is important to customize the message strategies to the specific target. Three contexts dominated his thinking: (1) **forensic discourse** considered allegations of past wrongdoing in the legal arena; (2) **epideictic discourse** treated present situations that were often ceremonial focusing on praise or blame; and (3) **deliberative discourse** dealt with future policy, with special attention to the legislative and political realms. Adaptation was not just to the place or setting but also to the purpose of the activity that would happen there.

Aristotle's three types of discourse remain relevant today, though we pursue many other contexts and market segments with our persuasion. Entertainment and media play dominant roles in our society that had limited impact in Aristotle's world,

---

B O X 3.1 Inappropriate Audience Adaptation at a Funeral Draws Fire

William F. Buckley, Jr. (2002) called attention to inappropriate politicizing at the funeral of Senator Paul Wellstone of Minnesota. Wellstone was a sworn enemy of big-money politics and a champion of the dispossessed and the environment. He died in a plane crash while campaigning for reelection to the U.S. Senate in an extremely close race; his death came just 11 days before the vote. This put the Democratic Party in a tough spot because it held only a one-seat majority in the Senate at that time.

The televised memorial service for Wellstone contained one of the most controversial eulogies in recent history. Wellstone's campaign treasurer, Rick

Kahn, was chosen by the family to eulogize Senator Wellstone. Kahn shifted from praising him to encouraging support for his legacy through the naming of the Democratic candidate to replace him. Kahn used statements such as, "We can redeem the sacrifice of his life if you help us win this election." His mixing of political purposes with a eulogy drew marked criticism. Minnesota Governor Jesse Ventura walked out after the funeral took on the tenor of a political rally. How might the situation have been different if the speaker had considered Aristotle's perspective on adaptation?

---

and persuaders today are challenged to understand the similarities and differences between each new generation and its predecessors. For example, advertisers have paid premiums in the past to reach the coveted segment of 18–39-year-olds, but persuasive strategies are changing now to follow the next age cohort of 40–59, because those in the Baby Boom represent a large and lucrative market. The important point is that Aristotle recognized that successful persuaders match appropriate persuasive tactics to the context.

Audience Adaptation and a Common Universe of Ideas

Aristotle assumed that listeners in different contexts would hold ideas in common. That is, certain types of appeals would be effective in gaining the attention of many audience members. In Book I, Chapter 5, of the *Rhetoric* (pp. 37–38), Aristotle makes one of the earliest statements about the approach–avoidance tendencies of individuals. He proposed that speakers should promote things that bring happiness and speak against those that destroy or hamper happiness. Aristotle's popular appeals included having one's independence; achieving prosperity; enjoying maximum pleasure; securing one's property; maintaining good friendships; pro-

ducing many children; enhancing one's beauty; attending to one's health; fostering one's athletic nature; and promoting one's fame, honor, and virtue. Most of these appeals remain effective today—especially appeals to a better life and the joy of friends and family (see Figure 3.1). Most elements of more modern needs approaches, such as Maslow's hierarchy of needs discussed later in the text, are found here. Aristotle clearly recognized that many of the things in this list are external and that others are internal.

In later parts of the *Rhetoric*, Aristotle provides examples of persuasive devices, such as maxims or sayings, with broad appeal to audiences. In Book II, Chapter 21, for instance, he introduces a maxim that is much like a common saying that Tony Soprano might use today: "Fool, who slayeth the father and leaveth his sons to avenge him" (p. 138). In advocating the use of maxims for listeners who love to hear universal truths in which they believe, Aristotle is advising the persuader to reinforce what the audience already knows. He says, "The orator has therefore to guess the subjects on which his hearers really hold views already, and what those views are, and then must express, as general truths, these same views on these same subjects" (p. 139). The point today is not that we need to learn the use of maxims, but that we must learn to adapt our messages to the world of our listeners. Adapting to

FIGURE 3.1 Aristotle's use of audience adaptation with appeals to the prospects for a better life and the joy of friends and family remain popular today.
SOURCE: Used by permission of Tiffany Laczkowski and Nancy Gray.

the audience's views raises ethical issues that remain today (see Box 3.2).

Types of Proof

In the *Rhetoric* Aristotle focused on what he called the artistic proofs or appeals that the persuader could create or manipulate. For example, persuaders create emotional moods by their choice of words and images and heighten the mood by varying their vocal tone, rate, and volume. Aristotle identified three major types of artistic proof—ethos, pathos, and logos—which remain remarkably current in today's world. It is useful to explore them more closely.

Ethos. Before the speaker actually makes a persuasive presentation, the audience holds an image of the persuader. Even if the persuader is totally unknown

to the audience, members will draw certain conclusions based on what they see—body type, height, complexion, movements, clothing, grooming, and so on. If the audience already knows the speaker, he or she may have a reputation for being honest, experienced, and funny. Aristotle called this image or reputation of the speaker **ethos**. A contemporary example of the use of ethos appears on eBay, one of the most profitable electronic commerce sites on the Internet. One-line reports from individuals involved in past transactions form the basis of buyers' and sellers' reputations. Users of the site earn such reputations without even seeing others or having verbal interaction. The speaker in a television program might deliberately make eye contact with various audience members and with the television cameras because eye contact can be an important element in a person's believability. Trust and credibility are salient issues today in the wake of prominent scandals from Wall Street to the White House.

What establishes a person's reputation, however, often varies from person to person. Goodwill results for many toward Bill Gates, cofounder of Microsoft, and his wife when they learn that the Gates have donated over $20,000,000 to a charitable foundation that is one of the leaders in combating AIDS and other diseases in Africa. On the other hand, many computer professionals loathe Microsoft business practices. Ethos involves many complex elements that are not always predictable. For example, former Speaker of the House Newt Gingrich was unfaithful to his wife even as he was criticizing President Clinton for being immoral. Gingrich was unable to sustain his political career after publication of the damaging information, but President Clinton survived impeachment. When a person's ethos is in question, it rarely happens without also creating an emotional reaction. This leads us to the next type of artistic proof.

Pathos. **Pathos** describes emotions that come into play as appeals are made to the things people hold dear. Persuaders assess the emotional state of the audience and design artistic appeals

---

B O X 3.2   **Effective Audience Adaptation or Pandering to the Audience?**

To illustrate a central problem that some have with Aristotle's notion of audience adaptation, let's start with a story based on a true experience. Having forgotten a hat to keep off the rain, I visited an amazing hat store in New Orleans called Meyer the Hatter. As I was trying on a reasonably priced Stetson, the salesperson said, "Boy, that hat sure looks good on you." I dismissed the comments because I thought the salesperson would say anything to make the sale. A female customer at the hat store then commented that she also liked the way the hat looked on me. I bought the hat and have had numerous compliments about it.

What was the ambivalence I faced? I considered the comments of the other customer to be genuine because that person didn't work there and had nothing to gain, but I was skeptical about whether the salesperson was being truthful or manipulative. In fact, many shoppers do not like to go shopping without a companion whose opinion can be trusted. This is also a central issue in the interpretation of Aristotle. The unresolved question is whether Aristotle was more concerned about the *appearance* of being believed than with what the audience actually believed. Thus, some see Aristotle's advice regarding the adaptation of messages as involving manipulation.

---

aimed at those states. Sometimes pathos is evident in the delivery of the message. High levels of emotion have been common in the persuasive messages of prominent religious leaders of the past and present, such as Jonathon Edwards, Martin Luther King, Jr., Minister Louis Farrakhan, and Billy Graham. Yet the danger exists that listeners will perceive the prominent use of emotion as excessive. It is clear that the passionate eulogy given by Rick Kahn at the Wellstone funeral highlighted in Box 3.1 was judged by most to be inappropriate and excessive. Howard Dean's bid to become the Democratic candidate for the presidential race in 2004 was severely hindered by his very emotional speech, deemed by some to be "over the top," given after his loss in the Iowa primary.

Pathos may involve the content of the appeal itself. Justice was one of the widely held virtues noted by Aristotle that often gives rise to emotions when it is violated. In a contemporary example, Wall Street reformers have intentionally attempted to provoke outrage toward illegal corporate actions that have cost thousands of people their jobs and caused thousands of others substantial financial losses. Emotions are easily provoked in those who suffered from the illegal actions taken by top-level executives at Enron, WorldCom, and Tyco. In the

area of politics, both major political parties attempt to evoke fear of the future if the wrong people get elected. Advocacy groups for animal rights try to produce feelings of sadness or pity for suffering animals. It is clear that the frequent use of pathos continues in the content of appeals and in the way such appeals are delivered.

In the search box of InfoTrac College Edition, using the key word option, type in the title of the article "Attorney Persuasion in the Capital Penalty Phase: A Content Analysis of Closing Arguments" by Mark Costanzo and Julie Peterson. Do you think the use of pathos is equally appropriate for the prosecution and the defense in the summation of a criminal trial?

Logos.   Appeals to the intellect, or to the rational side of humans, are represented by the Greek word **logos**. Logos relies on the audience's ability to process statistical data, examples, or testimony in logical ways and to arrive at some conclusion. The persuader must predict how the audience will do this and thus must assess their information-processing and conclusion-drawing patterns.

Aristotle and others frequently used a form of reasoning called an **enthymeme**. Aristotle describes it as following the form of what the study of logic today would call a **syllogism**. Syllogisms begin with a major premise such as:

> Young children have not developed the ability to evaluate the merits of commercial messages on television."

This major premise is then associated with a minor premise:

> Advertisers attempt to influence young children through many commercials or promotions.

This, in turn, leads to the conclusion:

> Advertisers are being unethical when they attempt to persuade young children by directing messages whose worth the children cannot evaluate.

In Book II, Chapter 22, Aristotle also recommends that the persuader be an expert on the facts in order to use such reasoning effectively:

> The first thing we have to remember is this. Whether our argument concerns public affairs or some other subject, we must know some, if not all, of the facts about the subject on which we are to speak and argue. Otherwise, we can have no materials out of which to construct arguments (p. 140).

Clearly, substance was important for Aristotle. Persuasion was not just a bag of tricks for pulling the wool over peoples' eyes. You can find logical appeals operating in your daily life. Politicians use statistics and examples to persuade you to believe a certain view or to vote in a certain way. Financial advisers use graphs and tables to persuade you that their investment options are superior to others. Often, college recruiters provide potential students and their parents with examples of jobs filled by recent graduates and their starting salaries, information regarding the reasonable costs of their institutions, as well as potential sources of financial aid. In each case, the persuader is betting that you will process the information logically and predictably.

Yet the form of the argument may not appear to you to be exactly like the one in the example. Consider a syllogism that Aristotle quotes: "Thou hast pity for thy sire, who has lost his sons: Hast none for Oeneus, whose brave son is dead?" (p. 145). Sometimes the language does not follow the format exactly. Let's consider this example again in contemporary language:

> You have pity for a father whose sons have died. (major premise)
> The brave son of Oeneus is dead. (minor premise)
> You should have pity for Oeneus. (conclusion)

So, enthymemes or syllogisms may leave out one of the premises or have parts in slightly different order. Nevertheless, the pattern of reasoning is there.

Places of Argument. Contemporary market research attempts to identify consumers' major premises. With these in mind, marketers design products, packaging, and advertising that effectively develop *common ground* and hence the co-creation of persuasive meaning. Aristotle used the term *topoi* to refer to places or topics of argument that are a good way to establish common ground. Persuaders identify these "places" and try to determine whether they will work for a particular audience. Consider a few of these topics and identify where contemporary persuasion uses them.

- *Arguments as to degree, or "more or less:"* Will candidate A be more or less trustworthy than candidate B? Are less costly Lee jeans more or less durable than Levis?

- *Past fact:* Has an event really occurred? Did a person commit the alleged crime? This tactic is very important in the courts, where a prosecutor must prove that a crime occurred and that the accused committed that crime.

- *Future likelihood:* Is something likely to occur in the future? This argument focuses on probabilities. For example, colleges attempt to recruit students by arguing that the earnings of those with a college degree are substantially higher than the earnings of those without a college degree.

Yet Aristotle recognized that it was not simply the structure of the syllogism, but the language used within it, that was persuasive. His focus on language merits attention.

The Potency of Language

Aristotle recognized that carefully chosen language is part of a successful persuasive strategy. He promoted the use of emotional expression because it makes the audience share feelings with the speaker (Book III, Chapter 7). Yet emotional language has to be appropriate to the context and situation. Moreover, Aristotle understood that when the audience shares similar feelings about the topic, the speaker can use more emotionally charged language. He emphasized the importance of **metaphor** in conveying new ideas and facts through images of the familiar: "It is from the metaphor that we can best get hold of something fresh" (p. 186). However, not just any metaphor would do for Aristotle; rather, the metaphor needed to be so lively or active that it made those hearing it actually see things. Of course, metaphors can be overdone. Like any other form of language, the metaphor must be appropriate.

Locate the article "The Arctic Persuasion" by William Powers by typing the title in the search box of InfoTrac College Edition and checking key words for the search. How are the potent powers of language emphasized by Aristotle being used by both sides of the Arctic controversy?

In sum, Aristotle's principles of persuasion are remarkably contemporary and provide the foundation for modern persuasion research. Granted, there are portions that have little relevance today and that reflect values our society does not embrace. Yet, his principle of adapting the message to the context recognizes that changes in persuasive messages should occur as the context changes. Now we turn to alternative points of view.

PLATO'S DIALOGIC APPROACH

Although the contemporary practice of persuasion owes a large debt to Aristotle, there are other perspectives on how we come to know things that guide our decision processes. Frankly, Aristotle makes some people uncomfortable. The *Rhetoric* does not give as much consideration to establishing truth as Aristotle's mentor, Plato, did. It is difficult to know whether Aristotle made a conscious break with his mentor or whether the *Rhetoric* simply should be considered in a larger context. We could interpret Aristotle's opening line, "Rhetoric is the counterpart of dialectic," to mean that his advice in the *Rhetoric* needs to be considered in conjunction with the pursuit of truth through the use of dialectics. In other places he suggests that truth typically wins the argument when it is a fair contest among equally skilled persuaders. We simply cannot know which interpretation of Aristotle is more correct.

Surprisingly, many people have more trouble with Plato's approach to truth than with Aristotle's lack of attention to it. Plato believed that as humans we do not see absolute truth directly, but only glean indirect images, glimpses, or shadows of the truth. Plato used **dialogue**, or the **dialectic method**, to pursue these truths. Dialogue is a form of discussion where the parties ask and respond to questions from the other parties involved. Plato frequently used dialogues in his writing that began with a question that defined the terms. The answers to the questions introduce the issues followed by a cross-examination from another party. In the end, some resolution results in changes, with each side of the issue demonstrating increased understanding of each position. Beyond an elitism that favored philosophers and excluded women, Plato's dialectic method promoted discovery and open public discourse. At least the value of open and public discourse was established in Greece, and dialogue began about important ideas like the practice of slavery, even though many of the issues were not ultimately resolved at that time.

Plato devoted a lot of attention to the concept of truth. In the *Gorgias*, he expressed little respect for rhetoric as it was commonly practiced because he viewed it as a skill used more to flatter, appease, disguise, or deceive than to discover truth and identify the important things in life. Plato presented the ideal speaker, in Socrates' dialogues with Phaedrus, as one who seeks the best interests of his listeners rather than advancing his own self-interests.

Plato clearly articulated that the facts of the situation do make a difference. Consider one dialogue between Socrates and Phaedrus. Socrates asked Phaedrus to assume that he had convinced Phaedrus to buy a horse and take it to war. But assume that neither Socrates nor Phaedrus really knew what a horse looked like, though Socrates did know that Phaedrus believed a horse was a tame animal with long ears. Yet a donkey also has long ears and could be very functional in a war. So imagine that someone took that donkey to war instead of a horse, and the donkey performed well. Then imagine that after the war Socrates made a speech detailing the merits of the donkey, but instead called it a horse. Socrates pointed out that merely calling a donkey a horse does not make it a horse (Plato, 1937, p. 263). So, Plato did not believe that truth was relative. There were material facts that one simply could not ignore. Beyond the factuality of these mundane details, Plato's writings present a view of **Truth** that we sometimes call *big T truth*, in which absolute and certain truths exist, but are obscured from our direct view.

SCOTT'S EPISTEMIC APPROACH

Plato's perspectives remain very important to communication ethics and dialog as presented in Chapter 2. Rhetorician Robert L. Scott (1993) bemoans the dominance of the Aristotelian tradition: "In general what may be called 'Aristotelian instrumentalism' has dominated thinking about rhetoric and the teaching of it. . . . I am suggesting that the dominant attitude . . . should be drastically altered" (p. 121). Scott objects to truth being presented as

an objective package, as if it were a possession or commodity. He suggests that truth is never certain, whether in the realm of science or public affairs, but he differs from Plato here in that he advocates *truth with a small t*. For Scott, rhetoric is a process of constant discovery in which truth is seen as moments in "human, creative processes" (p. 133). This perspective is known as **epistemic** or as a way of coming to know about things.

Although truth can be stable at times, according to Scott it cannot be static in an ever-changing world. Many discoveries come during our rhetorical encounters with others. These instances when we see something in a new way are often called *epiphanies* or *eureka moments*. Scott's perspective has many similarities to that of existential thinkers, who argue that truth is experienced in the lived moment and cannot be possessed forever. So, knowing is more than possessing facts.

Consider the game of golf. Would you invite a person who has studied the game, but never played it to give a presentation about the basics of golf? A person could read the official rules, watch the event on television, and rent some videos on playing better golf, but a person who plays the game experiences golf and knows it in a way beyond just knowing facts. Yet, even the golf game of Tiger Woods changes as he constantly learns more about it through his experiences.

Seeing persuasion as a process of constant discovery is a key principle for students of persuasion to learn. Many persuasive situations are interactive with an exchange of many questions, like bartering with the street vendor shown in Figure 3.2. It is not simply learning effective sales techniques and memorizing an effective sales script. Robert Scott's perspective clearly shows us why simply learning a set of tactics of persuasion is not enough. It seems as if this more personal approach to persuasion should have prevailed as the preferred method. Why, then, has Aristotle's influence on persuasion been greater?

That question cannot be answered with certainty, but with regard to persuasion in the modern era, many mass communication media such as television, radio, newspapers, and direct mail do not

FIGURE 3.2 A successful persuasive transaction between a street vendor and an interested buyer requires complex interaction skills involving questions from the sellers and the buyers.

permit much interaction. Aristotle's methods can be adapted more readily to marketing and advertising, which are more efficient methods for reaching consumers. Beyond the efficiency issue is the issue of certainty. It is much harder to explain or sell an approach that cannot speak with certainty. That is why sound bites are so important for the presentation of political candidates in the media. This does not mean, however, that we should ignore the lessons from Plato and Scott. Truth and trust are clearly in vogue in the aftermath of some of the biggest ethics scandals ever seen in corporate life. Sound bites will not be sufficient means to promote trust. Alternatives such as narrative theory, however, offer tangible ways to develop such trust. We look at narrative theory next.

Search for Robert L. Scott's article titled "Response to Lyne, Hariman, and Greene" by typing the author's name and the title in the search box of InfoTrac College Edition and checking key words for the search. Have his views about the epistemic nature of rhetoric changed much over the years?

FISHER'S NARRATIVE APPROACH

Communication theorist Walter Fisher (1978) shook up the dominant assumptions in the communication discipline by suggesting that humans are "as much valuing as they are reasoning animals" (p. 376). Fisher (1984; 1987) developed his ideas more formally over a decade to challenge the dominance of the **rational world paradigm**, which assumes people are essentially rational individuals basing their decisions on the quality of arguments and evidence. In his narrative theory, Fisher (1978, 1984, 1987) proposed instead that we can better understand behavior using the story, drama, or narrative as an analytical device, casting the persuasive event in narrative terms. At the core of this perspective is the belief that the drama or story is the most powerful and pervasive metaphor that humans can use to persuade and explain events. Fisher (1984) described the **narrative paradigm** as a synthesis of argumentative and aesthetic themes, challenging the notion that rhetorical (persuasive) human communication must be argumentative in form and evaluated by standards of formal logic; thus, the narrative paradigm subsumes rather than denies the rational world paradigm.

So what was it that bothered Fisher so much that he decided to take on many in the established tradition? Part of Fisher's mission appeared to be to change the trend in scholarship that was increasingly focusing on the elite rather than the common. Fisher was frustrated with the way attention had shifted to technical argument that excluded most people; in his view, it was elitist. In this respect, Fisher differs from Plato. Fisher wanted to return to the rationality of everyday argument where consideration is given to the narratives of all members of the community—not just the specialized few.

A second motivation was his desire for a more vital communication field that returned to the roots of human experience—a very existential idea. The story became such a recognized focus of Fisher's argument that those new to the study of his narrative paradigm often overlook his focus on the human experience as the generative force behind the narratives. It bothered Fisher that traditional approaches to communication often lost the soul and conviction of the human experience by dissecting the text with systems of formal logic and argument. The difference is like that between studying the human body in anatomy class by dissecting cadavers and studying it by examining living people—both approaches have value, but one misses the lived experience.

Fisher proposed that narratives succeed or fail depending on whether they have coherence and fidelity. **Coherence** refers to the way the story hangs together and thus has meaning or impact. **Fidelity** relates to whether it rings true with the hearer's experience. With a coherent story, almost everyone understands its premises or the points it tries to make. The story is told artistically, and it is believable.

Coherence relies on the degree to which the story is consistent. Consistency means that the story is logically organized or told. In other words, we generally don't know the outcome of the story or the fate of the characters until the story is complete (that is, it has a beginning, middle, and end in the most traditional cases). In consistent narratives, the characters have good reasons for doing what they do, and the impact of the situation or setting of the story also makes sense.

Fidelity in a narrative is similar to coherence but focuses more on whether the story seems realistic and is the kind of thing that really happens. It presents a rationale or *logic of good reasons* (Fisher, 1987) for the setting, plot, characters, and outcome of the narrative. Fisher presented several benchmarks of narratives demonstrating good fidelity. First, they deal with human values that seem appropriate for the point or moral of the story and for the

actions taken by the characters. Next, the values seem to lead to positive outcomes for the characters and are in synch with our own experiences. Finally, the values form a vision for our future. Persuasive narratives cut across a broad expanse of human behavior. They appeal to our native imagination and feelings.

Narratives can also form communities of identification that together lead to a common worldview. Because of this, they have been a central part of most if not all ideological movements throughout history. For example, America's founding fathers promoted a narrative of freedom and an inherent set of human rights that continues to be important for our expected conduct today.

Although many welcomed the discussion opened by the narrative paradigm, Fisher met resistance from those who had built careers on the rational world paradigm. For example, Barbara Warnick (1987) challenged Fisher's criteria as being so context-dependent that listeners would need extensive knowledge of the situation before attempting to understand a narrative. In her opinion, Fisher's standards allow so much room for interpretation that they leave the theory open to the inconsistencies of personal judgment. Others such as Rowland (1989) were not convinced that narrative encompasses as much of the communication domain as Fisher maintained.

Much territory in the narrative paradigm remains unexplored regarding bridges across differing cultures, but negotiating our different cultural narratives seems to be a good starting place to understand our differences. Whether or not the narrative paradigm is the single dominant organizing paradigm in the way communication operates is questionable, but Fisher did articulate a descriptive approach to persuasion that better captures the human experience of the average person than the more technical approach that appears to have become elitist in its assumptions. Despite the imperfections of the narrative paradigm, narratives are one of the most powerful persuasive tactics available. At times, good stories counter many facts. Fisher's narrative theory helps us understand this. The key point here is that you should never underestimate the value of a good story that resonates with its hearers.

POWER-ORIENTED PERSPECTIVES

Themes challenging the authority and power of the dominant culture run through the final group of perspectives covered in this chapter. These approaches allow us to look at a persuasive situation from the position of groups that are not in power. This group of theories has great utility in constructing defensive strategies against the abuse of power, and applications are clearly demonstrated in many social movements (see Andrews, 1980; Bowers & Ochs, 1971). These perspectives also offer reasons why some persuasive campaigns have failed with groups that are not in the majority.

Many people do not understand attacks on traditional perspectives of persuasion. These perspectives seem to function in our daily lives. After all, many of the forms of persuasion we use today have been in use for centuries. Various groups perceive, however, that the dominant culture ignores or silences them. These perspectives usually articulate some variation of the argument that traditional forms of persuasion have been the tools of the powerful to maintain control over those without power.

Superficially, there is little question that the foundations of persuasion were established among the privileged class. Aristotle was a member of the privileged class and encouraged the use of wealth. In Book I, Chapter 5, he says wealth comprised "plenty of coined money and territory; the ownership of numerous, large, and beautiful estates; also the ownership of numerous and beautiful implements, live stock, and slaves. All these kinds of property are our own, are secure, gentlemanly, and useful" (p. 39). A lifestyle such as Aristotle describes is out of the reach of many in society— and it was in his day as well. Part of the critique of traditional persuasion is that people (or groups) of privilege cannot meaningfully engage those who have been pushed to the margins of society. The

argument is that most of the elite cannot really understand what it is like to live in poverty or to suffer the humiliation that the disadvantaged feel. Despite the substantial progress resulting from civil rights legislation, it is very difficult, if not impossible, for those who are white to fully understand the constant assaults on the dignity of persons of color, for whom advantage is usually assumed to be due to preference given because of their skin color rather than their competence. Similarly, white males in positions of power find it hard to identify with the struggle of women for respect of their intelligence and competence. We now turn to several perspectives that challenge the dominant culture.

The Women's Movement

Although activism waned after the Vietnam conflict ended, it hardly disappeared. The women's movement has been very critical of the dominant culture that has suppressed women. **Feminist criticism** represents one part of the women's movement that attempts to better the lot of women. Feminist scholar Sonja Foss (1996) argues that "feminist criticism has its roots in a social and political movement, the feminist or women's liberation movement, aimed at improving conditions for women" (p. 165). So, feminist theory fits well with the prior discussion of social movements. The term *feminist* does not have one single meaning, but Foss suggests that the different varieties of feminism do share a commitment to end sexist oppression and to change the existing power relations between women and men.

A central issue for feminist theory is that traditional considerations of rhetoric and persuasion have focused on the discourse of males and been dominated by male perspectives. Feminists clearly articulate that history is "his story" and not "her story." Feminist theory questions the exclusion of the consideration of women and the issue of whether women have approached communication situations differently. Important questions are raised about how women are represented—particularly through language, but increasingly through other forms of imagery in mass media. Although feminist

---

B O X 3.3 **Culture Clash of Genders in the Salesroom**

Consider a real event that happened to one of our neighbors. She has been in the workforce for twenty years and, by all accounts, she is very competent at her job. She is married and is raising two sons, and she is no stranger to managing financial assets. One day she visited a local car dealership to buy a van to replace the family's old one. She found the salesperson to be very condescending. He did not want to negotiate price with her and suggested that her husband stop by to talk. This condescending attitude led her to purchase a vehicle from another dealership. How should females who get no respect from car salespersons address this lack of respect?

---

scholars do not all agree on the causes of and the remedies for oppression, many American feminists approach the issue as one of emancipation or liberation from male oppression, with a goal of obtaining the power necessary for women to create their own reality. Feminist scholar Karen Foss and her colleagues (1999) suggest that feminists also generally agree women's experiences are different from men's, due to differences in socialization and biology. Foss et al. claim that feminists' values of self-determination, affirmation, mutuality, care, and holism are part of a world that is superior to the traditional culture dominated by male values. Finally, says Foss, women's perspectives are not incorporated in our culture, which means that the culture has silenced women.

Sonya Foss and Cindy Griffin (1995) attack traditional notions of persuasion and propose an **invitational rhetoric** that promotes understanding rather than change. Invitational rhetoric resembles Plato's dialogical approach and is clearly not Aristotelian. It also bears a strong resemblance to Scott's proposal that rhetoric is epistemic. There are feminist activists such as rhetorical scholar Karlyn Kohrs Campbell, however, who reject the assumptions of invitational rhetoric. Whether or not such feminist values can ever become the dominant values of society, it is important to hear some of the points being made about traditional practices of persuasion.

Type the name "Karlyn Kohrs Campbell" in the search box of InfoTrac College Edition using the key word option and read her article "Inventing Women: From Amaterasu to Virginia Woolf." How does her perspective stand in contrast to invitational rhetoric?

Males in sales positions can often be very condescending to women, assuming that women know very little about items like cars and computers (see Box 3.3). Such insensitive persuasive tactics make little sense because women drive the consumer economy through their purchases much more than do men. On the bright side, we are seeing increasing use of gender-free or gender-equitable language, especially with pronouns—some organizations are getting the message. For example, many see the financial potential of professional women and are directing advertising toward them (see Figure 3.3). Those crafting persuasive messages for women must be attuned to all the possible meanings being sent. Organizational scholar Gail Fairhurst and consultant Robert Sarr's (1996) recent work on framing demonstrates how our communication can change to be more friendly to women. It is quite possible that future research will more clearly define a style of communication that women prefer. It is already evident that a chauvinistic style is not a wise choice for attempting to persuade women. Bringing about change through understanding does have one very clear implication: Understanding requires a lot of listening. Whether they fully embrace the feminist approach to change or not, persuaders can learn the valuable lesson that change begins with *listening* rather than *telling*.

Advertising has a mixed record in terms of fostering a more progressive view of women and minorities in general. Even attempts to be more inclusive are sometimes controversial and we can question the

FIGURE 3.3 Phoenix Wealth Management recognizes the importance of appealing to the intelligence of professional women.

appropriateness of many media messages (see Box 3.4). Questionable persuasive practices in the media may be fostering poor ideals for girls and women. The book *Deadly Persuasion: Why Women and Girls Must Fight the Addictive Power of Advertising,* by author and filmmaker Jean Kilbourne (2001), details the

---

B O X 3.4 Media Portrayals of Inclusiveness and Correspondence to Reality

In today's increasingly diverse society, it is desirable for most organizations to have a diverse and multicultural membership that, at a minimum, reflects the diversity of their immediate environment. Attracting potential employees and potential students to the organization from under-represented groups, however, can be a difficult task. Frequently, organizations use various media campaigns for outreach and promotion that portray a much higher percentage of diversity than is actually represented at the institution. My university's website often uses pictures that display a higher percentage of women, international students, and other persons of color than are represented by our actual student population. Do you think it is an ethical problem to portray an organization as more diverse than it really is so that those who are under-represented are persuaded to become a part of that organization? Alternatively, are such portrayals simply positive indicators signaling a more inclusive climate for persons of all backgrounds?

---

problematic influence of advertising on the development of the female image. Kilbourne calls into question many of the poor habits of our culture and the ways in which the media reinforce them. For example, she observes that only thin models are used in TV ads, and breasts are used to sell anything. She refers to an ad with a well-endowed female wearing only a bra, one side of which is held up by a string of monofilament fish line. The caption reads, "Stren—the strongest fishing line in the world." Kilbourne's earlier film, *Killing Us Softly* (1979), visually illustrates these problems in advertising.

Type "Jean Kilbourne" or "Killing Us Softly" into the InfoTrac College Edition search box using the key word option. What ethical issues with advertising are raised by her that affect females in particular?

Marxist Theory

Some feminists also embrace a form of Marxist critique because they believe structural changes must be made in society if feminist goals are to be more fully realized. A major feature of **Marxist theory** is a focus on the inequitable economic system. Marxist theorists address the issue of economic power as it exists in capitalistic countries such as the United States, Japan, and Germany. They believe that those who control the means of production (the bourgeoisie, or power elite) also control and determine the nature of society. Such elite circles were as prominent in Plato and Aristotle's time as they have been in U.S. society.

The major economic motive in capitalism is profit. Profit is naturally tied to the production and consumption of goods and services. The elite achieves production and profit by exploiting the abilities of the workers (the proletariat), dominating and oppressing them in a variety of ways. For example, the workers are enticed to produce so they can earn wages, which then permits them to purchase the essentials (and later the nonessentials) of life. This produce–earn–purchase cycle creates a never-ending and ever-increasing necessity to work in order to produce and, in turn, earn wages in order to buy products.

How does this all relate to our study of persuasion? Some ways should be fairly obvious. Because political power is needed to maintain economic power, the bourgeoisie must find members willing to run for political office and support their campaigns with money, volunteers, and other things necessary for political persuasion. Marxist critics note how the profit motive and its resulting cycle of consumption are instilled in the citizenry through subtle forms of persuasion. Belief in the value of earning money begins in childhood (i.e., having a lemonade stand and taking out the garbage to earn an allowance). As consumers and family members, we should be attuned to the persuasive

push to obtain material goods supporting this type of culture and how it can erode other values that are more important to us. The focus on earning money continues throughout adulthood (getting a well-paid job, accumulating wages to purchase a home, furnishing a home to a certain standard, and so on) and is constantly reinforced in the media. Those in power, however, largely control the economic system. Workers and citizens sometimes can exercise their own persuasive power through

nonviolent resistance like that used in protest marches (see Figure 3.4). Yet, resistance tactics sometimes escalate into violence and coercion that move beyond persuasion.

Marxist critics also identify news reporting as promoting the prevailing political and economic ideology. They argue, for instance, that the mass media depict terrorists as outlaws when a perfectly valid argument could be made that terrorists represent the proletariat and that terrorism is merely a strategy to dramatically state an opposing ideology. Moreover, it is increasingly difficult to separate the news from entertainment in current TV programming. Marxist critics of mass media note that news programs contain advertising that fosters capitalism and lends legitimacy to materialistic values. The media focus on celebrities to persuade consumers that financially successful persons (such as Michael Jordan, Serena Williams, Spike Lee, Madonna, and Donald Trump) lead the most interesting lives and that such success should be everyone's goal. The poor are rarely the focus of the news even though the world is filled with them.

Marxist critics also propose that television programming is controlled by the power elite, who make certain that the content of entertainment programming reinforces the dominant ideology (capitalism). It is therefore not surprising that the popular reality genre emphasizes glamour and money. Although news-oriented programming like *60 Minutes* sometimes exposes exploitation by the powerful, images of rampant poverty around the world are not popular even on news-oriented programming in our entertainment-dominated culture where the negative is minimized (see Figure 3.5). The Marxist critic's role is to unmask the forces of control and to reveal the dominant ideology. To Marxist critics, the mass media in general communicate a view of reality that supports the status quo. Naturally, such critiques are controversial; however, they may be useful if only to alert us to potential persuasive strategies that we as receivers may face.

Radical Movements

Although we will give social movements additional attention later in the book, we should here ask a key question, which is whether moving from verbal to physical confrontation is ever justifiable. Physical confrontation means crossing the line from persuasion to coercion. Currently, the debate continues over the ethics of physical confrontation. It is difficult to bring about change in large corporations when lax government regulations support many environmentally unsound practices. Violence and protests are two of the few avenues of influence available to groups with

few economic resources and little political clout to bring about change in problematic actions of large organizations. So, groups of radical environmentalists such as Earth First! drive spikes into trees knowing that loggers may be seriously injured when their chainsaws hit the spikes. Cut brake lines appeared on corporate vehicles of a seafood company that was not conforming to environmentally sound policies. Radicals set fire to the Two Elks Lodge in Vail to protest the actions of a company they believed to be environmentally unsound.

The question whether intimidation, harassment, force, and violence are justifiable has no easy answer. The difficulty of addressing it is reflected in the different philosophies embodied by Dr. Martin Luther King, Jr., and Malcolm X. Dr. King promoted nonviolence as the means for change, whereas Malcolm X advocated armed self-defense and revenge against the Klan and other white terrorists. It is easy to understand Malcolm X's point about not taking abuse from white people any more when we consider that over four thousand black people were lynched in the South in the decades following Reconstruction (see Burns, 1990). These violent tactics draw attention to serious issues. Although they are forms of influence, they are not persuasion.

Type the article name "Earth First Re-Evaluates Tactics After Activist's Death" in the InfoTrac College Edition search box using the key word option. Are their tactics justifiable? Are there any situations warranting violence to bring about change?

REVIEW AND CONCLUSION

Aristotle's *Rhetoric* created the dominant pattern of persuasion that held for centuries, but alternative models in the tradition of Plato view persuasion in a different way. Traditional forms of persuasion have many limitations, including the impression that those using them often do so in manipulative ways. Alternatives to the traditional approaches include processes

of discovery in which the best interests of all parties are identified. Narratives represent an alternative way of seeing the world—the persuasive nature of a good story should not be underestimated. Power also plays an important role in persuasion. For example, in social movements, persuasion is used by those who have less power in society to address those who have more power. Critical theory represents another way of thinking about the abuse of power in society. Overall, the message of these latter perspectives is that greater attention must be paid to situations in persuasion studies in which the interests of some groups are ignored by more powerful others.

KEY TERMS

When you are finished with this chapter, you should be able to identify, explain, and give examples of the following terms or concepts.

segmented audiences	logos	dialectic method	coherence
forensic discourse	enthymeme	Truth/truth	fidelity
epideictic discourse	syllogism	epistemic	feminist criticism
deliberative discourse	topoi	rational world paradigm	invitational rhetoric
ethos	metaphor		Marxist theory
pathos	dialogue	narrative paradigm	

APPLICATION OF ETHICS

Assume a major tobacco company is recruiting you to work in its advertising unit. Realizing that public perception of its products is becoming more hostile, the company wants you to create an advertising campaign that you believe violates no ethical boundaries, effectively promotes tobacco products, but improves relations with the public at the same time. Discuss which perspectives in this chapter you could use to create an ethical campaign that meets these criteria. Is such a campaign possible?

QUESTIONS FOR FURTHER THOUGHT

1. Compare President Bush to former President Clinton. In your opinion, which one rates higher on pathos? Logos? Ethos?

2. In what way are answers to question 1 dependent on the context and culture of the person answering it?

3. For today's generation in college, which of the three dimensions of credibility makes the most difference to you for evaluating someone as a parent? A professor? A boss?

4. What are Walter Fisher's big issues with communication approaches in the Aristotelian tradition? How does his approach solve or fail to solve these issues?

5. Is there more to analyzing a narrative than assessing coherence and fidelity? What?

6. Was the burning of Two Elks Lodge at Vail by radical environmentalists justified as a means to convince others of the environmental tragedies that are created

by ski resorts? When is violence justified in a protest? Why?

7. Was the violence used in the American Revolution to break away from England ethically justifiable?

8. What is your overall impression of feminists? In your world, is feminism a good or a bad thing? In your experience, when are the opinions of women typically ignored?

 For online activities, go to the *Persuasion* book companion website at http://communication.wadsworth.com/larson11.

4

Social Scientific Approaches to Persuasion

JOSEPH SCUDDER

Northern Illinois University

Dual-Process Theories

The Elaboration Likelihood Model (ELM)

The Heuristic-Systematic Model (HSM)

The Automatic Activation of Attitudes

Variable-Analytic Approaches to Persuasion

Source Effects

Message Effects

Fear and Drive Reduction

Social Judgment Theory

Alternatives to Dual-Process Models

Balance and Cognitive Consistency Theories

Accessibility and Activation of Attitudes

Perspectives on Compliance Gaining

Review and Conclusion

Key Terms

Application of Ethics

Questions for Further Thought

LEARNING GOALS

After reading this chapter, you should be able to:

1. Describe the major theories and approaches used by social scientists to study contemporary persuasion.

2. Compare and contrast the dominant dual process models: the elaboration likelihood model and the heuristic-systematic model.

3. Show what the expectancy value theories, the theory of reasoned action, and the theory of planned behavior do that the dual-process theories do not accomplish.

4. Evaluate whether Zajonc's mere exposure principle poses a fundamental problem to the major cognitive approaches.

5. Explain the connection of the memory and the activation of attitudes to persuasion.

6. Indicate which major ideas from the early Yale researchers continue to have importance and how our understanding differs in light of newer approaches.

7. Point to contemporary persuasive campaigns using fear and shock appeals and assess the merits of those approaches.

8. Discuss why compliance gaining and persuasion are not the same thing and what contemporary compliance-gaining studies do that gives a more informed view of influence practices.

Social scientific approaches to persuasion emerged only recently compared to the foundations of persuasion discussed in Chapter 3. They study persuasion using modern empirical methods. The term **empirical** refers to the practice of validating knowledge by experience or observation. Most empirical studies of persuasion use statistical methods to analyze experimental results, surveys of persuasive behaviors, or actual behaviors. Increasingly, persuasive studies also use qualitative approaches such as interviews, observations, and thematic analysis.

Changing attitudes and behaviors are typically the focus of empirical studies of persuasion. For the purposes of this chapter, attitudes are the positive, neutral, or negative evaluations a person holds of objects, activities, people, or institutions. This chapter uses current understanding of attitude change as a lens to examine the early unfolding of social scientific study of persuasion up to its most recent empirical developments. This is not intended to be a complete history of empirical studies of persuasion. Rather, the intent is to show how many of the early issues studied by persuasion researchers still are reflected in more current process-oriented theories of persuasion and how our understandings of earlier findings have changed. First, we turn to the dominant framework in persuasion research today.

DUAL-PROCESS THEORIES

According to social psychologists Shelley Chaiken and Yaacov Trope (1999), **dual-process theories** propose two qualitatively different modes of information processing that operate in making judgments and decisions. The first is a "fast, associative, information processing mode based on low-effort heuristics," and the second is a "slow, rule-based information processing mode based on high-effort systematic reasoning" (p. ix). The second route is similar to traditional understandings of persuasion we considered in Chapter 3. Dual-process theories, however, challenge the dominant rational world paradigm we met in Chapter 3, which assumed that people primarily reasoned their way to persuasion through careful consideration of arguments and evidence. Moreover, they moved persuasion to a more dynamic process orientation. We consider the two dual process theories that command the most attention: (1) the elaboration likelihood model and (2) the heuristic-systematic model. We will also consider a third mental process often discussed in conjunction with dual-process theories, the automatic activation of attitudes.

The Elaboration Likelihood Model (ELM)

We saw in Chapter 1 that social psychologists Richard Petty and John Cacioppo (1986) articulated a dual-process theory they called the **elaboration likelihood model (ELM)**. The ELM revitalized researchers' interest in persuasion. Elaboration in the ELM refers to the conscious scrutiny we use in making an evaluative judgment and requires both the motivation and the ability to process information. They place elaboration on a continuum whose ends are two different routes of information processing. The **central route** forms the high end of the continuum. It is information processing that occurs "as a result of a person's careful and thoughtful considerations of the true merits of the information present" (p. 3). It is a slower, deliberative, high-effort mode of information processing that uses systematic reasoning. When persons use the central route, it is clear that they are consciously engaged in thinking. Petty and Wegener (1999) maintain not only that the greater amount of thinking is done at the high end but also that elaboration at the high end uses a kind of thinking that adds something beyond the original information. People are making the best-reasoned judgments they can make based on their scrutiny of the information available.

Even though you possess exceptional ability to process information, that ability goes to waste if you are not motivated to process the information. This motivation may, however, happen in different ways for different people. Demonstrating relevance and importance are two key factors of motivation to centrally process a persuasive message. In other words, a persuader must be able to answer the question, *why should my target audience pay attention to this message?* Beyond importance and relevance, Petty and Cacioppo proposed that another component of cognitive motivation to process information is a general trait that some persons enjoy thinking and others do not. They called this trait the **need for cognition (NFC)**. It ranges from one extreme where persons enjoy thinking to the other where others wish to avoid cognitive effort. So, some people naturally like to think and analyze across situations whereas others

prefer not to expend any more energy thinking than is necessary.

At the low end of the elaboration continuum, people use the **peripheral route** of information processing, requiring much less cognitive effort and sometimes surveying less information than in the central route. The peripheral route may also rely on simple classical conditioning, or the use of mental shortcuts or rules of thumb. It often occurs as the result of some simple cue in the persuasion context such as an attractive or handsome source such as Angelina Jolie or Brad Pitt promoting their movie.

Persuasive messages bombard us constantly through the peripheral route, such as the brand names displayed on shoes or clothing or the sponsorship acknowledgements at events we attend. The constant reinforcement of these brands thus often happens without our conscious awareness; we take the information in like a sponge soaking up water. For example, find the repeated cue in the picture of a street café in Figure 4.1 that typically would be processed by the peripheral route. I call this the *sneaky route* to persuasion because brands and other messages often are stored in our memory outside our conscious awareness. In a recent persuasion class I asked if anyone had seen the first political commercial for an election more than two years away. One student said she had seen it, but had not paid attention to it. I asked her what she remembered. She recalled every important aspect of the commercial's message—even though she had not been carefully thinking about it. It is often harder to actively resist this type of persuasion because the tactics are not always obvious— especially to children.

Using the key word option in InfoTrac College Edition, enter "Michael Pfau" and "presidential debates" in the search box. Do you agree with Pfau about presidential debates? How do presidential race debates have different effects on your central and your peripheral processes?

Buying a computer is a complex decision. We might compare memory capacity, processor speed,

FIGURE 4.1 Find the persuasive cue in this picture of a street café that would typically be processed by the peripheral route proposed in the ELM.

software, warranty, service, size, monitor type, and other factors such as whether to buy a laptop or a less portable tower. Our thinking processes will include reasoning, scrutiny of evidence, price comparisons, and an evaluation of our computing needs, to name a few. This information will be centrally processed. Many people, however, simply do not have the ability or the motivation to evaluate which computer is best for their needs. They may call a friend or relative who knows a lot about computers for a recommendation, giving their price range and typical ways they use computers. Relying on the recommendation of others we trust or an expert requires only a small amount of central processing.

In contrast, brand preferences and our habits often lead us to process information peripherally. For instance, when asked at a fast-food restaurant what you want to drink, you may respond automatically, "Diet Coke." You do not evaluate all the choices carefully or even ask what they are. Strong brand preferences reduce the central processing necessary.

The ELM, however, does not provide much help in determining which people will rely heavily on brands and which make purchase decisions based on price. A sale price of $3.99 for a case of Diet Pepsi may lead a person with a preference for Diet Coke to change brands that week. Others may select generic diet colas because they use a different decision rule like "get the most volume for the least money." Sometimes other factors such as a strict budget, organizational regulations, or our insurance plans may influence the brands we buy.

Using the key word option in InfoTrac College Edition, in the search box find the article "The Application of Persuasion Theory to the Development of Effective Pro-environmental Public Service Announcements" by Bator and Cialdini. How do central and peripheral processing play different roles in the construction of public service announcements for environmental causes?

Peripheral processing covers a large range of behaviors. For example, the speech rate of individuals influences the way we perceive them, with some evidence suggesting that we prefer rates as fast as or faster than our own. The use of physically and socially attractive persons in advertising also reflects an appeal to peripheral processes. Sometimes, appeals to peripheral processes are more useful in drawing our attention to the message than in altering our perception of its content.

B O X 4.1 Brand Influences

What influences your choice of brands or labels? Think about purchases you made or influenced in the past month. Did you choose brand names or generic products? Do you have a brand preference for any of the following items: toothpaste, shampoo, pizza, car, gas, computer, soda, athletic shoes, clothing shops, hamburger, French fries, or ketchup? If you do have preferences, where did they originate for you?

Enter the term "speech rate" into the Info-Trac College Edition search box to see the many ways speech rate affects perceptions. In particular, read the abstract of the article on speech rate by Buller, LePoire, Aune, and Eloy. In general, how does a person's rate of speech affect perceptions?

Petty and Cacioppo's ELM rests on the assumption that people are motivated to process information because they want to hold correct attitudes, or at least those perceived as being correct in light of social comparisons and norms. Petty and Cacioppo also believe that various factors can affect the direction and number of individuals' attitudes and enhance or reduce argument strength. For instance, if an attractive or highly credible source opposes flag burning, that factor could increase or decrease the weight you might give to the Supreme Court's decision that flag burning is legal. The ELM also suggests that as people increase scrutiny through the central processing route, peripheral cues have less impact, and vice versa. This controversial proposition represents a marked difference from our other dual-process model, the heuristic-systematic model.

The Heuristic-Systematic Model (HSM)

Similarities are apparent between the ELM and the **heuristic-systematic model** or **HSM** (Chaiken, Giner-Sorolla, & Chen, 1996). The HSM proposes a **systematic processing route** that represents a comprehensive treatment of judgment-related information. It is a slow, high-effort reasoning process bearing strong resemblance to the central

processing route in the ELM. The other route, the **heuristic processing route**, is a fast, low-effort process that relies on the activation of judgmental rules or heuristics. Heuristics are mental rules of thumb that are not the most accurate procedure, but often very useful to deal with common situations; they are adaptive strategies that help us reduce the time it takes to make decisions. For example, to calculate the distance around a circle we often multiply the diameter of the circle by 3 to get a rough estimate instead of a more precise value for π of 3.14159. The HSM proposes the sufficiency principle whereby people attempt to strike a balance between minimizing cognitive effort and satisfying their goals.

We use heuristics daily. Instead of trying to remember the exact rules of right of way when two people come to a stop sign at the same time, many people simply wave the other person through the stop sign to avoid having to think too much. Some heuristics can be very misleading, like the saying that moss only grows on the north side of a tree—this simply is not true. A much better heuristic if you are lost in a forest is the fact that the sun rises in the east and sets in the west, but even this is not much help when you are lost and it is cloudy or dark.

Using the key word option in InfoTrac College Edition, search for the article "Why Sexist Language Affects Persuasion: The Role of Homophily Intended Audience, and Offense" by Falk and Mills. Do you accept their argument that sexist language leads women to ignore certain types of information? Explain how HSM would work in this situation if you buy the authors' arguments.

B O X 4.2   Graphics May Not Always Enhance a Message

Conventional wisdom suggests that a picture is worth a thousand words, but psychologists Kurt Frey and Alice Eagly (1993) provide evidence that even vivid elements in the persuasive messages may reduce the message's effectiveness when they result in low scrutiny of the message. In your experience, when do graphics aid understanding and when do they distract audiences from the point of the message?

In the HSM, systematic processing and heuristic processing operate independently and may occur simultaneously. This is probably the largest difference between the ELM and the HSM. In the ELM, there is an inverse relationship between the use of the central and the peripheral routes—as one rises, the other falls. In the HSM, we assume that people could make systematic use of some evidence at the same time they are using heuristics for other information. For example, you could make the judgment using systematic processes that a member of your work group made a good argument for doing a project a certain way, while at the same time you were making a judgment using heuristic processes about the attractiveness of that group member.

The impact of receiving too much persuasive information has not received much empirical study. It is clear, however, that people respond differently to large amounts of information. Some prefer a restaurant menu with only three choices to one that has ten pages of options. According to the ELM, the motivation of an individual to process the information is a key factor. Overloading central or systematic information processes should result in a shift to peripheral or heuristic processing. Traditional advice for creating persuasive presentations recommends the use of supporting visuals to assist understanding. After all, isn't redundancy better? We simply cannot make the blanket assertion that the use of visual aids with persuasive messages is always a recommended practice. Images in multimedia presentations may require so much attention to process that they detract from the message content rather than enhance it (see Box 4.2). Some backlash is occurring against the use of PowerPoint because viewers may pay so much attention to

writing and recording the information on the slides that they do not, or cannot, process what the information means at the same time. It may be that information overload is the reason behind the tendency some researchers have found for visual cues to override what a person is saying. Clearly, more research is needed regarding the processing of visual forms of persuasive messages and whether they enhance or detract from the oral or written persuasion that accompanies them. Simpler may be better.

The Automatic Activation of Attitudes

Psychologist Russell Fazio (1989) believes attitudes can be triggered automatically, without deliberation. This perspective has important applications in persuasive messages intended to overcome resistance to change. For example, it allows us to understand why it is difficult to change our attitudes about our addictions, health practices, and use of stereotypes.

The automatic activation perspective treats the mind as a place where a massive amount of information is stored. As in a library, some of this information is easy to access. Most pieces are connected by pathways to other pieces of information, and accessing one piece may activate others connected to it. Connections vary in strength, and those we make regularly will typically be more accessible in our memories than those we access rarely, just as places we travel frequently become easier to find.

The difficulty of changing problematic parts of our lives like a smoking habit is that it often requires changing many of these connections. Establishing new behaviors means creating new pathways in

---

BOX 4.3 Triggers That Activate Us

Think about the checkout aisles of supermarkets and the items placed there. What have you purchased in checkout aisles? What triggers do they activate for you? Why do these checkout displays frustrate parents bringing children to the market? What are some markets doing to respond to complaints resulting from this marketing practice?

---

our minds for accessing positive attitudes and behaviors that we learn to prefer to the old ones. This does not happen overnight. Understanding this process is very important in resisting persuasive attempts that automatically trigger certain processes for us. Controlling impulse buying requires understanding our triggers (see Box 4.3).

VARIABLE-ANALYTIC APPROACHES TO PERSUASION

Now that we have explored the general dual-process models that form the general framework of much of contemporary persuasion research, we return to the early years of empirical persuasion research to establish some of the long-standing specific principles of persuasion that remain important in our contemporary world. During World War II, psychologist Carl Hovland established a program of research investigating the relationship of communication to attitudes. His work carried over to one of the most extensive programs of persuasive research ever conducted, which is now known as the Yale Communication and Attitude Change Program.

Hovland considered the main persuasion variables through a number of studies focused on single issues—much like the approach used in the natural sciences (see Hovland, 1957); thus, one label for his work is the **variable-analytic approach**. The Yale group assumed that people would change their attitudes if provided with sufficient reinforcement in support of the change. In other words, people need motivation to process information that will change their existing attitudes and the actions that flow from them.

The researchers maintained that persuasion passes through a chain of steps or stages, of which *attention* was the first. Those not paying attention to the message, they believed, could not be persuaded by it. Although this assumption still holds true today for persuasion theories relying on the central or systematic route of processing, more recent dual-process theories suggest that careful attention may not be necessary for some persuasive processes in the peripheral or heuristic routes. In today's media glut, controlling the attention step has become a high priority for persuaders because media clutter makes it difficult for messages to get noticed and could block even messages intended for the peripheral or heuristic route.

For the Yale researchers, the second stage of *comprehension* was essential to persuasion because those who did not understand or comprehend a message could not be persuaded by it. Again, this assumption remains solid for central and systematic processing, but is not always required for peripheral or heuristic processing. Research has shown that **priming effects**, which occur when a cue is introduced rapidly or even at subliminal levels (below conscious awareness), can activate accessible attitudes without awareness. The *acceptance* stage was the critical point where the message was accepted or rejected, and the Yale researchers gave it the most study. As in the case of attention and comprehension, conscious acceptance of a message plays an important role in the central or systematic routes of processing. In the peripheral or systematic routes of the

---

BOX 4.4   The Stage Model and Television Commercials

Pay very close attention to each commercial during your next opportunity to watch television. Is it clear what these commercials want you to do? Which of these commercials would you tend to notice and which would you tend to bypass by changing channels? Given the short length of most commercials, do you think the stages in this Yale stage model explain whether persuasion is or is not happening for you?

---

more recent dual-process models, no conscious point of decision may exist.

The *retention* stage was important for remembering the changes made in attitudes or beliefs. Memory of attitude changes was necessary if further behavioral acts were required to complete the *action* stage of a persuasive request. Memory is also essential for the central or systematic routes in contemporary dual-process theories, but such processes often operate below conscious awareness or without much cognitive effort. *Action* was the point for the Yale researchers where the acceptance of the change in attitudes or beliefs was translated into behavior, if required to complete the persuasive request. This stage is not applicable to persuasive situations that stop with attitude change such as brand awareness.

Other stage models exist, but contemporary research generally recognizes that while stage models are useful as explanatory tools to understand these processes, true descriptions of persuasive episodes are often much more cyclic and include multiple encounters with the message—rarely is human behavior so linear as the Yale model.

Source Effects

The Yale studies particularly focused on the source's credibility or believability and the source's attractiveness to the receiver. In terms of today's dual-processing framework, source credibility usually influences attitude change through the peripheral or heuristic route, but central processing of a person's credibility could occur when a controversy erupts such as Ward Churchill's recent remarks in Colorado about 9/11.

Using the key word option in InfoTrac College Edition, search for two brief articles regarding University of Colorado professor Ward Churchill. The first is *A Windy War of Words* by Alex Kingsbury. How would you rate Professor Churchill's credibility? Now read the second article *Ward Churchill, a Cherokee Indian, was chairman of the department of ethnic studies at Boulder, Colorado,* an article from the *National Review.* Why were these remarks controversial? Are you using central or peripheral processes right now or both? What impact does the second article, mentioning that Professor Churchill is Cherokee, have on you that the first one did not? Is the fact that Professor Churchill is a Cherokee more likely to be a central or peripheral processing issue?

Research in the 1960s proposed several dimensions of credibility, but expertise, trustworthiness, and attractiveness continue to be the most widely investigated. The Yale researchers conducted credibility studies in which the same message was attributed to persuaders having various kinds of reputations. A message about smoking and lung cancer, for example, was attributed either to a college sophomore or to a doctor from the surgeon general's office. Not surprisingly, greater attitude change occurred when the audience believed the message was coming from the doctor as opposed to the student. A critical point found in these studies is that the effect of speaker credibility may decline over time if the content of the message becomes separated from the source in the hearers' memory. This is a particular problem with messages we hear only once.

Hovland and his colleagues called the decaying link between message and speaker's credibility the **sleeper effect**. It can work to a speaker's disadvantage when his or her credibility is initially high because it means that high credibility can be lost over time. However, the sleeper effect may work to the speaker's advantage when initial credibility is medium or low but very strong arguments are offered, because people may remember the strong arguments and forget about the credibility factor. Although subsequent research on the sleeper effect has yielded mixed outcomes at times, it generally provides support for the idea. The recent meta-analysis of the sleeper effect by Kumkale and Albarracin (2004) found that persuasion did increase over time for persons initially exposed to a less-credible source when the quality of the message arguments were initially judged as strong. Thus, years of research tend to support the original formulation of the sleeper effect by the Yale researchers (also see Allen & Stiff, 1998). Consistent with the more contemporary ELM, persuasion was stronger when recipients of the persuasive messages had the ability and motivation to scrutinize the message. This issue of the motivation of the listeners is one of many places where the ELM refines our understanding of past research without questioning the foundations of the original concept. Many questions remain about how it works. For instance, research is not conclusive as to whether information is even stored in memory when the credibility of the speaker is very low or the relevance of the information is low.

A recent review of five decades of credibility research (see Pornpitakpan, 2004) supports the conclusion from the Yale studies that high-credibility sources are generally more persuasive than low-credibility sources. High-credibility sources often enhance the impact of high-quality evidence. Yet, the review notes a reduction or reversal of the impact of high-credibility in some conditions. For example, high-credibility sources appear to be less effective where motivation to process the message carefully is low. Notice that the motivation of the receiver again becomes a qualifying factor of the general finding. Another consideration is the position currently held by the target audience. High-

credibility sources may be more important to use in situations where the message is advocating substantial changes from positions currently held than when attempting to get only minor changes from current positions. High-credibility sources have also been found to be more persuasive when using threats or presenting negative opinions.

A trustworthy source for one group may not carry the same weight with another group. In some contexts expertise is a better route to establish credibility, but it must appear certain and have little ambiguity. One of my family members who was experiencing back pain received conflicting recommendations from two surgeons with extensive expertise in back surgery. In this case, there was great ambiguity, it was not clear which expert had the best recommendation, and the advice from both surgeons was discounted. The two conflicting experts negated the influence of each other. The person turned to people she trusted for advice.

Another important factor in determining the credibility of a source is the degree to which the source is similar to us. Using similarity in persuasive appeals is usually attempting to appeal to peripheral processes rather than making it an explicit focus. Many organizations use visual appeals to provide evidence that other people like them are part of their organization. Examine Figure 4.2 to see how the Southern Company effectively uses this tactic.

Building unwarranted trust is a common but unethical appeal to similarity that operates through peripheral rather than central processing. Frauds often occur when persons pose as group members or enlist the help of actual group members. Such tactics are called **affinity scams** because they exploit the trust and friendship existing in groups whose members have much in common. In a Ponzi (pyramid) scheme new investor money is used to pay off earlier investors, who may make a very good return on their money and so unwittingly convince other potential investors that it is a good deal. One scam bilked $2.5 million from a group of 100 Texas senior citizens who were asked to switch safe retirement savings to securities promising a higher investment return. Consumers from close-knit groups or communities must be especially

HE'S SEEN A LOT OF CHANGES,
BUT ONE THING HAS REMAINED THE SAME.

In 1978, Anthony James began his career with Southern Company, the South's premier energy provider, as a Safety and Health Supervisor for Georgia Power. Today, he is the President and CEO of Savannah Electric. A lot has changed over the years, but Anthony can tell you one thing hasn't — Southern Company's commitment to our customers, employees and the region we serve. This dedication has helped us become one of FORTUNE® Magazine's 2002 Most Admired Companies. We will always embrace change, but Southern Company's commitment to you will remain the same. To learn more, visit us at **southerncompany.com.** | NYSE>SO

SOUTHERN COMPANY
Energy to Serve Your World™

Alabama Power   Georgia Power   Gulf Power   Mississippi Power   Savannah Electric

FIGURE 4.2 Although this Southern Company ad explicitly emphasizes to investors how it is changing to meet today's values while also maintaining its traditional values, it is probably saying something else implicitly.

SOURCE: Used by permission of Southern Company. All rights reserved.

wary of deals proposed just because several of their trusted associates participate. Offers that look too good to be true deserve more examination in the central route of processing.

The Yale studies also considered whether the height of a source leads to more or less attitude change, how the rate of delivery affects persuasion, and when eye contact produces desired effects. Taller persuaders were rated more believable and more trustworthy than shorter ones. Standards of attraction clearly vary by culture, gender, and sometimes by generation. The general assumption is that

---

BOX 4.5 The Open Discussion of Attractive Others

Ask yourself how often you openly discuss the attractiveness or unattractiveness of others with your friends or family. An analysis of private conversations among your friends will probably reveal that attraction may be more centrally processed than most people want to admit. What norms exist about discussing the attractiveness of others in public settings?

---

attraction is routinely processed in the peripheral or heuristic routes, but it may be centrally processed when explicit focus is placed on it (see Box 4.5).

Attractiveness goes beyond physical characteristics. Have you ever heard someone remark that a person is "beautiful, but too high-maintenance for my tastes"? For many, attractiveness includes prestige, social standing, and influence. The **Pelz effect** suggests that people like to be associated with those who have power and influence at high levels because it enhances their self-esteem to be associated with these people. Attractiveness also describes whether one's social style is friendly, open, and approachable.

What are some other attractiveness factors? Persuaders delivering their messages in halting or introverted ways tend to exert less effect on attitudes than those who deliver their speech in smooth and extroverted ways. Gender influences acceptance as well. Although results are mixed, attractive same-sex persuaders are often rated as less credible than attractive persuaders of the opposite sex.

Message Effects

The Yale studies considered the impacts of several message effects on persuasion, not all of which were new to researchers.

Primacy–Recency Effects. One of the oldest findings of persuasion research, presented by psychologist F. H. Lund in 1925, claimed that the most important piece of evidence should come first. We call this the **primacy effect**. The **recency effect**, that is information most recently presented, also has been found to have significant impact. Whether the primacy or the recency effect is more effective has received substantial attention. Hovland (1957) reported that the primacy–recency issue is not so straightforward. They found the first speaker did not necessarily have an advantage over the second speaker. However, the primacy of negative information has an important role in impression formation—it is particularly difficult to overcome negative information presented first.

The time frame is important in predicting whether primacy or recency effects prevail. It appears that recency effects often decay over the longer term but may be relevant in short-term situations. Research within the ELM framework suggests that listener motivation plays a large role in the processing of information and in determining the impact of primacy–recency effects. The order of the content appears to make little difference to those with high motivation to process who carefully scrutinize messages, but recency effects appear to play a greater role than primacy effects for persons less motivated (see Petty, Wegener, & Fabrigar, 1997). Again, notice that listener motivation is an important factor in the primacy–recency debate.

Message Bias and Two-Sided Arguments. Sometimes persuaders must address people who hold views that are neutral or may be contrary to their own. Should the persuader present one side or two sides of an issue? We call this aspect of persuasion, where only one side or all sides of an issue are considered, **message-sidedness**. Hovland (1957) suggested that it may be wise to first introduce the negative arguments people are already considering. Such tactics launch a preemptive strike against unfavorable information that persuaders expect the hearers may already possess. In the dual-processing framework, using two-sided arguments encourages listeners to centrally process information. Consider United Airline's ad campaign strategy dealing with its filing for bankruptcy. The campaign attempted to establish that travelers need not fear flying with United and it promoted the company's new beginning. The ad engages readers to process this information centrally rather than peripherally. It gets the lingering issue of the airline's bankruptcy out in the open.

Allen's (1998) meta-analysis of message-sidedness considered 70 studies involving over 10,000 people. It indicated that two-sided messages are more effective than one-sided messages when they refute the opposition's arguments. Even those holding similar values are likely to benefit from two-sided messages. Such messages inoculate those whose belief systems are not yet mature by forewarning them of the dangers out there. They may also generate more support against the opposition, much like a pep rally. However, it is not enough merely to mention the positions of the other side; the persuader must refute those positions. Biased information processing suggests that the need to use two-sided messages depends largely on the goals and motivation of the persuader.

Biased information processing occurs when decision-makers favor a certain position and interpret the world in light of that position. They are not giving objective or fair consideration to all possibilities. For example, an employee who has worked for Ford Motor Company for 25 years may be so loyal to Ford that she or he would never think of buying a vehicle from a competitor. Other people come from families who have been Democrats or Republicans for generations and will tend to evaluate persuasive political messages from the biases of those long-standing traditions. Some biased processing occurs because people have a lot more facts and information stored in their memories for activation of one side of an issue than others (see Petty and Wegner, 1999). If you prefer an Apple computer and have used it for years, you probably have a lot more knowledge of Apple computers than of its competitors. You can probably articulate far more features of the Apple system and why you would be most comfortable

buying another Apple computer. The same would be true if you have been a loyal user of Microsoft Windows. So, long-standing ties with products, services, and institutions often lead us to have substantially more information about them. When the quality of information accessible in our memories is very lopsided, objective processing is less likely unless we recognize and correct this deficiency.

According to psychologist Shelley Chaiken and her associates (1996), objective and biased processing originate from different motives. The HSM distinguishes among accuracy, defense, and impression motives. Two-sided messages are appropriate when the goal is to present an accurate assessment such as when making a hiring recommendation from a pool of several qualified candidates. One-sided messages, however, are perfectly fine in persuasive situations where a person is defending a position or trying to maintain an image with important others. For instance, one-sided messages are fine at a political rally that people have paid $1000 per plate to attend—those are not people who have to be convinced to support the candidate. Similarly, Petty and Cacioppo (1979) propose that biased processing is likely when the issue at hand is relevant to the target of the message and that person holds a vested interest, but objective processing is more likely when relevance is high, but the person has no vested interest in the outcome or little knowledge about the topic. Consequently, persons with large investments in a company are more likely to favor that company's products. They often do not try to do a fair comparison with the products of the competition. This biased-processing tendency is a critical problem with many boards of directors at large corporations. Biased processing appears to be more common when persuasive messages contain ambiguous information or arguments of mixed quality rather than clearly strong or weak arguments (see Petty and Wegener, 1999).

Inoculation.   Inoculation is probably the foremost strategy for helping others resist persuasion. In the persuasive context, **inoculation** is the practice of warning people of potentially damaging information or persuasive attempts that will probably happen in the future. This is typically done by giving them a weakened version of the threats and dangers in arguments, practices, or behaviors they will encounter in the future. Michael Pfau (see Pfau et al., 2001) highlights the robust nature of inoculation and demonstrates the multiple and surprising ways of accomplishing it across contexts. Increasingly, political campaigns use it to warn their supporters that attempts will be coming from opponents to turn them to "the dark side." Inoculation provides a heuristic strategy to get people to ignore persuasive attempts from the opposition without careful processing of those messages, rather like throwing away junk mail unread.

The Influence of Mood and Affect on Biased Processing.   It is fairly common for persons taking their first persuasion class during the holiday season to ask whether holiday music and holiday decorations that attempt to put people in a happy mood are an effective strategy for store sales. Although such holiday features appear to bring more shoppers to major urban centers known for such displays, such as New York City and Chicago, the exact impact of mood on specific purchases is less clear. A review of several studies of mood and its impact on the processing of information by psychologists Herbert Bless and Norbert Schwarz (1999) indicates wide agreement for the proposition that people will pay more direct attention to specific information when they are in a neutral mood or are sad. Generally, anger does not encourage objective processing. In contrast, positive moods or happy moods appear to encourage less careful analysis and greater reliance on heuristic processes or stereotypes. Thus, positive or happy moods increase the likelihood of biased rather than objective processing of information. Bless and Schwarz argue that these differences in processing may be due to the increased motivation to process information in negative situations where systematic processes are required to handle problematic situations. They suggest that persons in good moods have little motivation to expend the energy to systematically process information unless other goals require it. Moreover, they suggest that the less-efficient processing we may do when in a positive mood results from using past experiences and ways of coping with the world. Others, such as psychologists Mackie and Worth (1989), however, maintain that being in a good mood limits information processing capacity because it activates a large amount of positive material in our limited processing capacity; and thus, it is an information capacity issue. The general conclusion is that we make greater use of heuristics and stereotyping in positive moods and do more scrutiny of specific information under neutral or sad moods. Yet, several exceptions to these general conclusions have emerged (see DeSteno et al., 2004; Nabi, 2002; Mitchell et al., 2001; Petty & Wegener, 1999; Pfau et al., 2001; Wegener, Petty, and Smith, 1995).

Fear and Drive Reduction

Inducing **fear** continues to be one of the most studied tactics in persuasion research. Hovland, Janis, and Kelley laid the foundation in 1953 by proposing that the use of fear would increase the likelihood of persuasion, because compliance reduces emotional tension. The drive-reduction model is a more specialized version of the **pleasure–pain principle**— that is, people are attracted to rewarding situations and seek to eliminate uncomfortable conditions. Janis (1967) summarized the use of fear appeals and the drive-reduction model:

> Whenever fear or any other unpleasant emotion is strongly aroused, whether by verbal warning or by a direct encounter with signs of danger, the person becomes motivated to ward off the painful emotional state and his efforts in this direction will persist until the distressing cues are avoided in one way or another. Thus, if the distressing threat cues do not rapidly disappear as a result of environmental changes, the emotionally aroused person is expected to try to escape from them, either physically or psychologically (pp. 169–170).

Hovland and his associates suggested that the fear appeal is effective only if it is sufficiently intense to create a drive state that recipients believe can be effectively countered by the recommended action. This perception that the threat can be handled is now called **efficacy**. If the negative outcome seems insubstantial to the receiver, then its effectiveness is likely to be negligible. Likewise, if the credibility of the person issuing the threat or warning is low, less compliance occurs.

Controversy remains over whether using more fear is better. In the most famous fear appeal study of all time, Janis and Feshbach (1953) studied fear appeals in a dental hygiene context. They found that too much fear arousal can be less effective than more moderate fear arousal. Janis (1967) attributed these effects to an inverted U-shaped curve measuring reaction to fear appeals. That is, high levels of fear (the top of the inverted U-curve) lead to defensive avoidance but low levels of fear are not enough to induce attitude change. Thus, Janis maintained that using moderate levels of fear produces optimal results.

The superiority of moderate fear appeals has not received support from two meta-analyses by communication researchers. Paul Mongeau (1998) reviewed 28 fear appeal studies involving over 15,000 individuals. He found significant and consistent links between the use of fear appeals and attitude change; that is, more fear is more effective than less fear. Kim Witte and Mike Allen (2000) qualified Mongeau's conclusions, proposing that strong fear appeals coupled with high-efficacy messages produce the greatest behavioral change. Perhaps even more important is their conclusion that strong fear appeals with low-efficacy messages lead to **defensive avoidance** where people try to avoid, ignore, or minimize the issue if they cannot do anything about it. These results suggest that efficacy and perception of substantial fear are central to whether fear appeals succeed or fail; strong fear messages alone are not enough. Witte (1992) provides a clear articulation of these processes in her extended parallel process model (EPPM) of fear appeals.

Witte's (1992) EPPM builds on the findings and limitations of Leventhal's (1970) parallel response model and Rogers' (1975) protection motivation theory. Witte's EPPM proposes that fear appeals invoke two processes: threat appraisal and perceived coping appraisal. The first process assesses the danger presented by the threat and how urgent it is to attend to it. So, if a park ranger sees a rattlesnake ahead on the path while conducting a nature walk, she might choose to take another path or go ahead of the group and encourage the snake to go elsewhere with her walking stick. The ranger's action removes the actual danger. The second process of fear control happens when the threat is judged to be real, but it is perceived that the remedies will not be totally effective. For example, it can be a terrifying experience to be caught out on a large body of water in a sailboat during a thunderstorm producing lots of lightning when you cannot return to shore fast enough to avoid it. The tall mast on the boat makes it an attractive target. After you do all you can do to secure the boat and take as much cover as possible, coping with the fear is all you can do. Ineffective fear control in a serious situation leads to the production of anxiety and stress.

Recent research by psychologist David Roskos-Ewoldsen and his research team (2004), however, failed to support the EPPM and the conclusions of Witte and Allen (2000). They studied fear appeals in an attitude accessibility framework (see the earlier discussion of Fazio, 1989) that examines how easy it is to access information stored in our brains that fear appeals generated. They studied fear-inducing messages regarding breast cancer and messages advocating the efficacy of self-breast exams. Their results indicate that high-efficacy messages ("you can do something about the problem") produced greater accessibility to attitudes stored in the brains about the adaptive behavior (doing the exam), but high fear-inducing messages appeared to decrease the accessibility of attitudes toward the threat itself. In other words, you could make the information regarding the effectiveness of doing breast cancer self-exams more prominent and focused without creating greater perceptions of the high danger of

---

B O X 4.6   Mixed Perceptions of the Effectiveness of Using Scare Tactics

Think about campaigns using fear to reduce the use of illegal drugs, deaths from drunk driving, and infections from HIV/AIDS. Some schools show videos of the tragic consequences of mixing alcohol with driving. Others show the consequences of

unwanted teen pregnancy resulting from unprotected sex. Mixed opinions exist of the effectiveness of using scare tactics. Has persuasion using fear appeals led to change in your behavior or of anyone you know?

---

breast cancer itself. This finding revives the debate about whether producing more fear is better to change attitudes. More research is necessary to determine whether these results are limited to certain contexts or more generally challenge the conclusions of Witte's EPPM.

Why so much attention to fear appeals? Fear appeals are one of the most common persuasive devices encountered by consumers today. In a class lecture at our university, a product manager at a telecommunications giant acknowledged that one of the firm's most common sales techniques is to use fear, uncertainty, and doubt—also known as **FUD** (see FUD-counter, 2001). The origin of the term is attributed to Gene Amdahl, who claimed that salespeople at IBM tried to instill fear, uncertainty, and doubt in the minds of potential customers who were considering Amdahl computer products. Clearly, FUD tactics will not disappear any time soon, but the ethics of using them, especially in message directed to senior citizens, need more debate.

Social Judgment Theory

The book *Social Judgment* (Sherif & Hovland, 1961), the final volume of the Yale Studies in Attitude and Communication, marked the end of an era, along with Hovland's death that year. **Social judgment theory** focuses on how we form reference points, or what Sherif and Hovland called "anchors." The **anchor** is an internal reference point with which we compare other persons, issues, products, and so on that we encounter. Every issue

has an anchor at any given time. Research compares the consumer's original anchor to an anchor established later by a persuasive communication.

Perhaps the most important contribution of social judgment theory is the idea that the anchor really represents a range of positions rather than one single point. Thus, "the individual's stand on a social issue is conceived as a range or a **latitude of acceptance**" (pp. 128–129). The anchor is a range of positions acceptable to persuadees, including the most acceptable one. Yet it also includes the **latitude of rejection**, which is the range of positions that persuadees find objectionable, including the most objectionable one. Moreover, research indicates that highly ego-involved individuals have very narrow latitudes of acceptance and very broad latitudes of rejection, so that the likelihood of changing the minds of highly ego-involved people is very small. The best chance of persuasion is a message advocating a position within the hearer's latitude of acceptance and only a small distance away from the position he or she holds. One of persuaders' more important tasks is determining whether various groups of people have firmly set anchors on positions that relate to the issue at hand.

ALTERNATIVES TO DUAL-PROCESS MODELS

The theories and models that follow are alternative approaches to persuasion that do not neatly fit within a dual-processing framework. There are

---

B O X 4.7 **Ethics of Introducing Discomfort to Aid Persuasion**

Many argue that our culture is overly materialistic and manufactures desires of questionable value. Under what conditions is it ethical to introduce pain, discomfort, or disruption in people's lives to bring about conditions ripe for change? When is it ethical to create perceptions of needs that didn't exist previously? Has the attention to *cellulite* on television infomercials actually manufactured concerns over something that in previous eras was not a serious problem?

---

scholars who suggest that some of these perspectives account for changes in attitudes and behaviors better than dual-process models under certain conditions. We begin by discussing balance and consistency theories that have been very popular approaches to persuasion and attitude change over the past fifty years.

Balance and Cognitive Consistency Theories

Balance and cognitive consistency theories rest on the assumption that humans want to reduce inconsistencies because they create stress or discomfort. Social psychologists Marvin Shaw and Philip Costanzo (1970) describe **cognitive consistency theories** as "a host of proposals based upon the general proposition that inconsistent cognitions arouse an unpleasant psychological state which leads to behaviors designed to achieve consistency which is psychologically pleasant" (p. 190). A fundamental principle here is that persons who are stable and content with life are more difficult to change. Although impulse purchases and decisions are frequent and may result from other motives, some motivation like discomfort or a positive opportunity is typically necessary to move people to make major changes when they perceive life is already good. Ethical questions arise regarding the intentional creation of stress, tension, or dissonance to provoke change.

Indeed, research generally indicates that people in transition are more open to change. It is often assumed that older persons are more set in their behaviors, and in some ways they may be intransigent, but the evidence generally indicates that the attitudes of those who are stable in their midyears of life are more difficult to change than younger or older adults. Of course, middle age does not guarantee stability. Divorce, health crises, and natural disasters make people more susceptible to change at any age and make such groups prime targets for scam artists.

Cognitive inconsistencies, however, frequently arise in much less dire circumstances. For instance, when an important person in our lives makes a criticism such as mentioning that we have gained weight, we are both hurt by the criticism and hurt that a person near to us would be so inconsiderate. Perhaps this causes us to question whether that person cares for us. It may cause us to question whether anyone really loves us. Various balance or consistency approaches address situations in which our lives are conflicted.

Balance Theory. Fritz Heider's **p-o-x theory** (1946, 1958) may be old, but it still offers a simple explanation of **balance theory**. It was originally called the p-o-x theory because a person (p) was oriented toward another person (o) and an object (x) that was connected or belonged to the other person (o). It was later understood that (x) could be another person as well. It is important to recognize that one person is connected or seen as being a unit with the object or the third person. Balance happens if the two persons like each other and both hold either positive or negative evaluations of the object (or another person).

To visualize this, think of the situation as an equilateral triangle as found in Figure 4.3. In this overly simplified situation, assume that Juan and

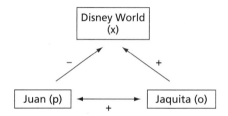

FIGURE 4.3 An unbalanced situation in Heider's p-o-x balance theory.

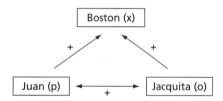

FIGURE 4.4 A balanced situation in Heider's p-o-x balance theory.

Jaquita love each other very much. They want to make their union public soon. We will label the line representing the relationship between those two persons a "+". Now assume that Juan hates Disney world. This line representing Juan's unfavorable attitude toward Disney World is noted by a "–". The line representing Jaquita's favorable attitude of Disney World is represented by a "+". The situation is unbalanced. It will cause tension if Jaquita has always dreamed of celebrating their union at Disney World.

Such disagreements are common—you probably experience this type of recurring but never-resolved argument frequently. The discomfort that arises provides the human dynamics for the Heider explanation of balance theory. When tensions arise either between or within individuals, they try to reduce these tensions. The person who does not like Disney World could reduce the importance of the issue and just go along with the other person. The couple could decide to devalue the relationship and break up, seeing that resolving conflict with their partner is going to be tough over the long run. If you would like a happy ending to the story, Jaquita could say to Juan that they both have wanted to go to Boston, persuading Juan that Boston would be a great destination to officially celebrate their new life together as a couple (see Figure 4.4).

Dissonance Reduction Theories. Dissonance reduction theories have many similarities to balance theories. Dissonance reduction theories, however, have been more prominent than balance theories in attitude change research over the past 20 years. Most have some grounding in social psychologist

Leon Festinger's (1956) theory of cognitive dissonance, which we will examine in more detail later. Festinger proposed that **cognitive dissonance** is the degree to which relationships among our cognitions about our attitudes, beliefs, feelings, environment, and actions are inconsistent with one another. Things are inconsistent when any two areas of our lives are not entirely compatible and this creates dissonance. We seek to reduce dissonance because it is unpleasant. Dissonance motivates us to change our cognitions, attitudes, or behaviors.

We may reduce dissonance in other ways than by making outright changes in our attitudes or behaviors. Festinger says we may seek new information to bolster our recent decisions that appear inconsistent with past behavior. We may also trivialize or reduce the importance of certain values, beliefs, practices, or relationships. Sometimes we reduce dissonance by avoiding a situation or particular people who make us uncomfortable. For example, when a couple divorces, other members of their social group often distance themselves from one partner while maintaining connections to the other. Dissonance reduction often proves to be most difficult for the children, who may not desire to change the relationship they have with either parent.

Dissonance reduction is not always final and may serially recur. The incompatibility of divorced parents often continues to create dissonant situations at special events and occasions—particularly weddings. Unfortunately, dissonance reduction between the parents may lead to unsatisfactory resolution of dissonance for the children. No persuasive avenue may satisfy these difficult circumstances, but temporary truces can make potentially explosive situations pleasant for important events like weddings and graduations.

Many refinements of Festinger's theory continue to emerge (for a review see Wood, 2000). Most of them recognize that a gap exists between one's current situation and a desired state. For example, dissonance may exist because a behavior we chose produced foreseeable negative consequences and may even continue to do so. Some call this guilt. Others maintain that dissonance arises when people fail to act in ways consistent with their own standards (see Stone et al., 1997). A more general proposition says that dissonance emerges when the consequences of behavior challenge existing ideas about one's self (see Prislin and Pool, 1996). A perspective-taking technique developed by Festinger wherein a person argues for a **counter-attitudinal position**—that is, a position he or she personally opposes—creates dissonance about the person's own position and makes him or her more open to arguments from the other side. Getting persons to engage in such perspective-taking exercises can be a useful persuasive tool to aid negotiations, but it is difficult to motivate people to pursue perspective taking in earnest.

Support does exists for balance and consistency theories (see Eagly & Chaiken, 1993). Psychologist Wendy Wood (2000) concludes that support for cognitive dissonance continues to be demonstrated. This group of theories clearly has utility for recognizing how persuaders may be trying to manipulate you. When persuaders try to destroy your beliefs (for example, with a message stating that joining a fraternity will likely result in a lower grade point average than living in the dorms), you ought to realize that they are creating imbalance for you. They want to change your opinion by relying on your need for psychological balance, or comfort. Of course, modern infomercials capitalize on many of our insecurities such as how being overweight or out of shape makes us less desirable to others. Providing pictures of others who are overweight or out of shape, often creates imbalance or psychological discomfort for many of us by attacking our self-concepts. The infomercials then offer remedies by providing products that they promise will resolve these conflicts for us. As consumers, we need to be armed with the awareness of how these infomercials are attempting to manipulate our level of psychological comfort.

Using the key word option in InfoTrac College Edition, find the article "The Effect of Provocation in the Form of Mild Erotica on Attitude to the Ad and Corporate Image: Differences Between Cause-related and Product-based Advertising" by Nigel K. Pope, Kevin E. Voges, and Mark R. Brown from the *Journal of Advertising*, Spring 2004. This article is one of a few that have found positive attitudes of college students toward advertising using nudity—a practice common in some European countries. What ethical, cultural, and religious issues are relevant to a corporate executive's decision to use such ads when it appears from market research that the company's customer base would be attracted to such advertising?

Disruption by Shock Tactics.   A more recent marketing tactic often intended to create dissonance is the use of messages intended to shock as a means of cutting through the clutter of the information glut. Companies such as Benetton, Abercrombie & Fitch, and Calvin Klein have come under attack for using these tactics. Advertisers and framers of campaigns widely use attempts to shock, but empirical study of these messages has been limited.

Messages intended to shock are part of the more general class of messages intended to assault the human senses or to offend sensibilities. Whereas fear appeals seek to avert future negative consequences, shock appeals are persuasive tactics that assault the senses or intentionally offend us in some way. Some fear appeals also fall in the shock category. Shock tactics typically evoke dissonance by violating our sense of appropriateness. People for the Ethical Treatment of Animals (PETA) uses shock tactics regularly to call attention to the abuse of animal rights. Their persuasive campaigns have, at times, used very graphic images, but

FIGURE 4.5 Describe the reactions you experience when viewing this persuasive message by the music group Simple Plan on behalf of PETA. Which routes do you believe process the different parts of this message?

SOURCE: Reprinted by permission of PETA.

sometimes they use pointed statements that show how major institutions violate standards of human decency, as in one campaign where they state that "IAMS tortures animals." Although using these tactics has been controversial, PETA has had several successes in getting major corporations to change their problematic animal care practices such as their campaign against fur (see Figure 4.5).

In academic research, Nabi (1998) is one of the few communication researchers to consider such messages that are not primarily focused on fear. In her consideration of disgust-eliciting messages she found that the impact of disgust could enhance or inhibit attitude change.

Although several advertising campaigns have intended to shock to promote their products, only limited empirical evidence of its impact exists. Dahl, Frankenberger, and Manchanda (2003) note the widespread use of shock appeals in public health campaigns promoting awareness of breast cancer, AIDS, domestic violence, seat belt safety, and alcohol abuse. They studied the effectiveness of shock advertising for HIV/Aids prevention. Their study suggests that offending the audience often means breaching "norms for decency, good taste, aesthetic propriety, and/or personal moral standards" (p. 269). Their results confirmed that norm violations "heightened awareness of shocking advertising content" (p. 275). Their results also indicated that the shock condition produced greater recall than the information and fear conditions. So, the violation of norms that we hold can produce dissonance that draws attention to activities violating norms.

It appears that shock appeals actually attract younger audiences because they violate traditional norms and establish individualism. Although the reasons vary, using dissonance-producing tactics such as messages intended to shock may help gain attention for a persuasive message as well as encourage cognitive processes such as message elaboration and message retention, but many ethical issues remain to be resolved. On the other hand, those using graphic images to dislodge people from their comfortable positions on important issues suggest a simple dissonance reduction strategy for those who are disgusted or repulsed—change the channel or turn the page; and, many of us do to avoid the unpleasantness.

Accessibility and Activation of Attitudes

Some of the most recent advances in persuasion recognize the importance of the site where persuasion takes place, the mental processes of the brain. Although we are likely to see great advances over the next decade in our understanding of persuasion and brain functioning, precise understanding of the connections between persuasion and centers of the brains are not well understood at this time. Nevertheless, several research programs have studied processes related to persuasion that clearly involve the importance of storage of information in memory, accessing that memory, and modifying stored attitudes in the memory. We have already discussed Fazio's line of attitude accessibility research, but at least two other notable developments are important to understand how persuasion works.

Mere Exposure and the Primacy of Affect. Psychologist Robert Zajonc's (1968) **mere exposure** hypothesis is quite simple: repeated exposure to a stimulus results in more favorable evaluation of that stimulus. In other words, the more we are exposed to something, the more we are likely to

be favorable toward it. In a classic study, Zajonc asked participants to pronounce a series of Turkish nonsense words. In varying the frequency of times of pronouncing each word, he found that more frequently pronounced words received more favorable evaluation. He reported the same pattern for different photographs of men and for Chinese-like characters. Favorability increased substantially up to about ten exposures and continued to increase at slower rates until reaching 25 repetitions. Other studies of mere exposure suggest a point of diminishing returns whereby more repetitions yield no benefit and sometimes become counterproductive, with people getting bored with overexposure.

Psychologist Robert Bornstein's (1989) meta-analysis of over 200 studies indicated that the mere exposure phenomenon appeared reliably across many different types of stimuli and objects. Moreover, Bornstein found that the mere exposure effect tended to be larger when stimuli occurred in a subliminal manner—too quickly to be consciously recognized. The very interesting finding in this analysis is that rapid exposure below the level of consciousness had greater impact than some stimuli that were consciously recognized. Given that there is much skepticism over subliminal advertising and its effectiveness, this line of research demonstrates that at least subliminal effects can be effective. Recent studies of priming behavior confirm that attitudes change in response to visual materials presented below the level of conscious awareness.

There is little doubt that mere exposure makes information very accessible simply through repetition, but there is much disagreement as to *why* it occurs. Zajonc frequently used the mere exposure findings to argue against the primacy of cognition—that is, to argue against the idea that everything—especially emotion—begins with explicit cognitive thought processes. He instead argued that affect needed no prior cognitive preferences for activation. Although Zajonc's contentions about the primacy of affect were not widely embraced when cognitive psychology was dominant, perspectives are emerging that incorporate arguments from both sides. Psychologist Icek Ajzen (2001) suggests that a multicomponent view of attitudes is becoming more popular among attitude researchers; that is, more researchers see the importance of considering the roles both affect and cognitions play in changing attitudes. Affect may be a more important influence on the development of some attitudes, and cognition in the formation of others. Some evidence suggests that we rely more on our feelings when our feelings and our beliefs do not agree (see Lavine et al., 1998). The evidence clearly supports the mere exposure principle, but there are obvious exceptions where repeated exposure may have the opposite effect, such as at my home, where the same satellite company keeps calling us even though we are on the national do not call registry.

Today's mass media regularly use mere exposure. Its application to politics is especially worth noting. Psychologists Joseph Grush, Kevin McKeough, and Robert Ahlering (1978) examined political campaigns for political newcomers and low-visibility offices. They found a significant connection between increasing the exposure of unfamiliar candidates through greater campaign spending, and winning the election. Although it is frustrating to those who want voters to base their decisions on the issues, the use of short commercials with sound bites makes sense for candidates unfamiliar to the masses.

Expectancy-Value Models. Given that the mere exposure principle and expectancy-values approaches disagree fundamentally on whether affect or cognition is more important in attitude formation, you may be surprised that expectancy-value models heavily depend on attitude accessibility. Icek Ajzen (2001), a major proponent of expectancy-value models, clearly articulates that "the expectancy-value model assumes an object's evaluative meaning arises spontaneously, without conscious effort" (p. 32). **Expectancy-value models** are built on the foundation that changes in behavior result from a rational process of assessing personal beliefs and attitudes in conjunction with the normative beliefs of important persons around us.

Persuasion researchers have had difficulty in consistently finding significant **attitude–behavior relationships**. That is, researchers have frequently found low or no relationship between attitudes and

behavioral change resulting from persuasive messages. For example, many smokers report that smoking is bad for their health and that it may eventually kill them, but if you ask them whether they intend to stop, they may say no or maybe in the future. So our attitudes may be negative toward the dangers that behaviors pose, but our attitudes toward the solutions to avert the dangers are negative, neutral, or so weakly positive that we do not start a program to change our behavior. In the **theory of reasoned action (TRA)**, psychologists Martin Fishbein and Icek Ajzen (1981) suggest that attitudes have been defined so generally that it is no surprise there are mixed results for finding the attitude–behavior relationship (see Figure 4.6). Instead, they propose that our **behavioral intentions** toward *changing* our behavior are the most important predictor of actually changing behavior, not our attitudes toward the behavior itself. In research attempting to convince people to recycle, Fishbein and Ajzen asked people to rate their intentions to actually engage in recycling and indicate how important that activity was to them, instead of asking them to rate their attitude toward recycling in general. They criticize past attitude research for not measuring specifically enough and for measuring the wrong predictors. Behavioral intentions are clearly the central feature that distinguishes this approach from all other attitude research. Many other parts of the TRA appear also in other perspectives.

As the model in Figure 4.6 indicates, the behavioral intention is a product of two assessments: (1) a person's attitude toward a behavior and its importance to him or her, and (2) the normative influence on an individual and its importance to the individual. **Normative influence** is a person's belief that important individuals or groups think it is advisable to perform or not perform certain behaviors. What we commonly call peer pressure is a form of normative influence. Normative pressure may simply be the desire to please one individual. For instance, a person in my family started flossing her teeth regularly because she did not want her dental hygienist again to tell her she was not doing a good job of flossing. Weight Watchers also uses normative pressures in its weight loss

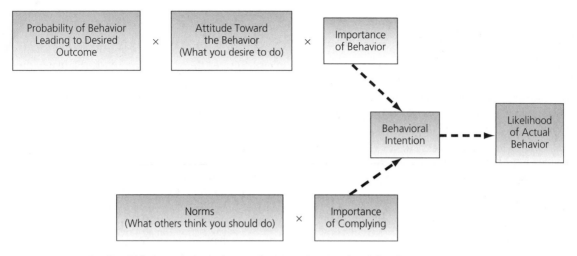

FIGURE 4.6   The Fishbein and Ajzen theory of reasoned action (TRA) for the prediction of intentions and behavior.

programs. Participants do not want the scale to go up instead of down at their weekly weigh in. In many cases, some combination of influences makes the difference. For example, many people are motivated to stop smoking or to lose weight for their own health, but also because they want to live long enough to be here to support their children and to see their grandchildren.

The same principles generally apply to an intention *not* to perform a certain behavior. It follows that, in testing the effects of a certain advertising or public relations campaign, we should test behavioral intentions, not broader attitudes. This means asking consumers, "Do you intend to try the new brand?" instead of, "How positively or negatively do you feel about the new brand?" The act of saying, "Yes, I intend to try the brand," is a symbolic commitment to actually purchase the brand.

Ajzen proposed modifications to TRA in his **theory of planned behavior (TPB)** (see Ajzen, 1991, 2001). He added a third factor, **perceived behavioral control**. The original TRA worked well in conditions where individuals perceived a strong personal sense of control over their behaviors, but it became apparent after several studies that in many situations people felt little control. This addition of perceived control better articulated

whether people really expected that a particular outcome would happen if they tried. So, you may resist your doctor's recommendation to lose weight if you have tried many diets, but never have been able to control your love of regular soda, your tendency toward binge eating, your nervous eating when you are not hungry, and your disdain for vegetables.

Overall, TRA and TRB have been strong predictors of changes in behavior (see Armitage & Christian, 2003; Ajzen, 2001). They have had broad application in health care and have had good success in predicting condom use, safe-sex behaviors, use of illegal substances, adherence to taking prescribed medications, the wearing of safety helmets, use of dental floss, and physical activity. No other theoretical perspective on persuasion and attitude change compares to the successful predictions of behavior of these two expectancy-value approaches. Of all the persuasive approaches to behavioral change, expectancy-value models appear to have the clear edge in predicting behavior, but they are far from perfect. Two large challenges remain in order to refine these approaches: (1) a better procedure for recognizing and incorporating the most relevant personal beliefs, and (2) improved ways to identify and measure relevant normative influences.

B O X 4.8   **Impact of Normative Influence and Peer Pressure**

Frequently, peer pressure is mentioned in persuasive campaigns that attempt to reduce the extremely high death rate of adolescent males in automobile accidents. Have you ever been persuaded to do something because of normative influence or peer pressure that you would not have chosen to do on your own? Have you ever purchased a particular item of clothing resulting from peer influence?

What kinds of normative pressures do family members often exert on other family members in college? When do you think normative pressure is a positive or functional force and when do you think it is a negative or dysfunctional influence? Have you ever had normative influence used to pressure you into doing something that you are really glad you did it after it was over?

Related to these models are **norms-based approaches** to behavioral change. Many persuasive campaigns use norms to demonstrate that individuals selecting the recommended behavior are in the majority. One such campaign to fight alcohol abuse is used at our university to show that the majority of students do not participate in binge drinking. Another normative approach being used at our university shows that females do succeed at calculus and actually receive higher grades than their male peers. The label *norms-based approach* is misleading because concrete facts and information are typically key components of such appeals.

Questions arise about the success of norms-based programs because it is often modest. As is often the case when the effectiveness of persuasive campaigns is assessed, success is in the eye of the beholder. Programs such as DARE and abstinence-based campaigns to reduce early sexual activity have advocates who look at the results and see success while critics look at the same numbers and see program failures.

PERSPECTIVES ON COMPLIANCE GAINING

Compliance gaining considers how one person can get another to do something. It is closely related to persuasion, but they are not synonymous. Unfortunately, many people assume that all compliance tactics are a subset of persuasion. Certainly, compliance-gaining tactics are forms of influence. Some, such as making a request of an individual, fit within the realm of persuasion, but other tactics, such as threats, sometimes fail to respect a receiver's freedom to choose and are more coercive than persuasive. We usually study compliance gaining in the interpersonal context. Gerald Marwell and David Schmitt (1967) first focused on the ways people seek to gain the compliance of others, but communication per se was not part of their agenda (see Dillard, 1990, pp. 3–5). Interestingly, they believed that compliance-gaining appeals could be made from a common set of behaviors—much like the Aristotelian idea of topoi we considered in Chapter 3. They generated a set of sixteen compliance-gaining strategies, clustered into groups of positive and negative strategies. Generating an exhaustive list of compliance-gaining strategies is difficult. Kellermann and Cole (1994) detail over sixty types of compliance-gaining messages that were identified across numerous studies, but this list is far from complete (see Kipnis, Schmidt, & Wilkinson, 1980; Rule, Bisanz, & Kohn, 1985; Wiseman & Schenk-Hamlin, 1981).

This initial phase of compliance-gaining research has been widely criticized for lacking any theoretical base, but it did identify two important dynamics. One is the situational nature of compliance gaining, as revealed in the classic study by communication researchers Gerald Miller, Franklin Boster, Michael Roloff, and David Seibold (1977) that brought compliance gaining to the attention of communication researchers. In this study, people reported using different Marwell and Schmitt compliance-gaining strategies in different interpersonal situations. This

---

B O X 4.9 Effectiveness of Abstinence Approaches

Have you ever attended a norms-based program such as DARE, an abstinence-based sexual education program, or a *Say No* or similar program to combat use of drugs, alcohol, or smoking? From your experi- ence, are such programs effective? What percentage of persons attending these programs would have to actively participate for you to consider them to be effective?

---

suggests that when planning influence messages, the persuader should ask, "What special considerations need to be made for this particular situation?"

A related dynamic is the matching of appro- priate tactics to the intended goals. Communica- tion researchers Michael Cody, Daniel Canary, and Sandi Smith (1987) reported that college students use different tactics when they believe others have some obligation, such as a landlord making repairs, than when they are asking favors of friends.

Most who still engage in compliance-gaining research have found solid theoretical bases for their research. Cognitive compliance-gaining goals are a current focus of communication researchers (see Wilson, 2002). The consideration of multiple goals is one of the most important lessons from this recent research. So, the persuader may need to consider a multilevel strategy instead of assuming that there is only one objective. Some consider- ation has been given to tactics following prior unsuccessful attempts (see Cody, Canary, & Smith, 1987). Compliance-gaining attempts appear to move from positive tactics to more negative ones as more resistance is encountered. In many of these episodes, making simple, direct requests is the pre- ferred approach. Using reasoning to make basic arguments is another popular approach. Yet the situation, the goals, and the power relationship all play a role in choosing the most effective strategy.

One of the limitations of compliance-gaining research is that it usually focuses on short-term results while many business relationships are the result of long-term efforts. Still, a unifying frame- work has not emerged to clarify whether it is best to classify compliance-gaining tactics by the message's form, the message's goals, or the message's impact experienced by the receiver. Theoretical underpin- nings for compliance-gaining studies are emerging— particularly from communication researchers. In his book *Seeking and Resisting Compliance*, Steven Wilson (2002) focuses on how people produce and resist compliance-gaining behaviors rather than just responding to them. An important new focus in this work is the understanding of a concept called **face threats**. Face threats are basically attacks on the receiver's image. We need to understand what per- suasive approaches might actually make the situation worse instead of improving it. Sometimes we dig a deeper hole for ourselves when trying to repair a relationship than we were in before we attempted to improve the situation.

Understanding Kathy Kellerman's (2004) recent goal-directed approach to gaining compliance helps us understand that some compliance-gaining beha- viors are more likely to threaten the message recei- ver's image. This more complex examination of compliance gaining involves both the consideration of the message framer's goals as well as concerns of the receiver to maintain a positive identity and image. In complex negotiations where conflicting opinions can be very heated, it is very important for all sides to maintain a positive image. It is not a desirable situation for persons to feel embarrassed to be seen by others who are important to them or to feel uncomfortable around those important others. Moreover, most of those involved in negotiations want to be able to return to the negotiating table retaining respect from the other negotiators pre- sent. So, instead of thinking of compliance gaining as a competitive situation where people win and lose, true winning strategies often provide more stable solutions where the images of all concerned

---

BOX 4.10   Fighting Fairly

What persuasive strategies do you think are acceptable when you are having a dispute with a significant other such as a spouse, partner, or good friend? Have you ever held a grudge against a person for using an unfair compliance-gaining tactic against you? What tactics would be considered fighting fairly versus fighting dirty?

---

are strengthened rather than diminished. Such solutions do not have to be revisited often because of dissatisfied parties. These face-saving strategies will typically build more positive intimate relationships with significant others and within families as well. This more recent emphasis in compliance gaining is very consistent with the idea of co-creation established in Chapter 1.

Although resistance strategies have been put forth to address the receiver's side of compliance gaining, little research has explicitly considered power relations and perceived control in the compliance-gaining situation. Another difficulty for compliance gaining from a persuasion perspective is that behavioral compliance often reflects mere acquiescence, without the development of mutual understanding. For example, all except one of the major airlines are facing major difficulties in trying to stem their economic losses. Management is fighting for survival and employees are trying to salvage a decent pension and take much smaller pay cuts than management is asking. Even though many agreements are being reached, compliance does not appear to contribute to a positive work climate. Management negotiators are using many heavy-handed compliance-gaining tactics such as threats to gain these new agreements. Polarizing compliance-gaining tactics also failed the National Hockey League in the 2004–2005 season when management locked out NHL players for the entire season.

Current compliance-gaining research as yet provides little direction for those placed in such a difficult position. Compliance-gaining research has not focused on short-term versus long-term attitudes that result from the tactics used during such difficult economic conditions where people's livelihoods are at risk. It is important to keep in mind in any dispute that the parties usually have to live together after the negotiations end. Thus, it is important to note that the outcome of a compliance-gaining attempt may achieve acquiescence and accomplish the immediate objective, but may create unfortunate long-term consequences that make long-term relationships a lot less pleasant and satisfying.

REVIEW AND CONCLUSION

There is little question that the ELM has been the superhero in the last two decades of persuasion research. Still, no single theory addresses every persuasive situation. Some, such as the ELM and HSM, address larger (macro) issues regarding overall approaches to persuasion while others address very specific (micro) persuasive situations at the tactical level, such as approaches intended to arouse fear or shock. Often we need multiple perspectives to explain fully different parts of a persuasive situation. One of my objectives of this chapter was to emphasize that the most appropriate persuasive tactics for a given situation depend heavily upon the motivation of the audience to listen and analyze carefully. The use of more statistics and evidence is unlikely to be effective when the audience is not listening. Thus, attempting to beat people into submission until they start listening is probably not the best first line of action. Another of my objectives was to make it clear that much attitude change and persuasion takes place through peripheral or heuristic processes so that as consumers of persuasion you will become more aware of what often is happening below your conscious awareness. Despite the many persuasive trends found over a number of years, it is also important to recognize that such findings

---

B O X 4.11   Impact of NHL Owners Compliance Gaining in 2004 Lockout

Although the NHL owners and players reached an agreement to play hockey again in 2005, the players are not pleased with the outcomes after losing a whole season of play. The owners have achieved much of what they wanted, but the agreement provides very few changes that benefit the players. What arguments can be made that the persuasive attempts by the owners were successful and what arguments can be made that their persuasive attempts were unsuccessful? What arguments can be made that the owners were using coercive tactics rather than persuasive ones when they scuttled the 2004–2005 season?

---

are fallible. Although research findings typically represent a greater likelihood that specific persuasive strategies or tactics will produce predictable reactions, there are often important factors like the motivation of the audience to listen and daily events that create some unpredictability in every persuasive situation.

Although others may disagree, I award the title of the most effective predictor of behavioral change to the expectancy-values approaches by Martin Fishbein and Icek Ajzen. No other approach has been as widely adopted in persuasive campaigns— particularly those that are health related. The importance of affect in the persuasive situation is gaining more respect from researchers but still needs better integration in the mainstream approaches. These theories in this chapter are representative, but not a complete consideration of the persuasion literature. We will revisit many of these perspectives throughout the remainder of the book.

KEY TERMS

When you are finished with this chapter, you should be able to identify, explain, and give examples of the following terms or concepts.

empirical

dual-process theory

elaboration likelihood model (ELM)

central route

need for cognition (NFC)

peripheral route

heuristic-systematic model (HSM)

systematic processing route

heuristic processing route

variable-analytic approach

priming effects

sleeper effect

affinity scams

Pelz effect

primacy effect

recency effect

message-sidedness

biased information processing

inoculation

fear

pleasure–pain principle

efficacy

defensive avoidance

FUD

social judgment theory

anchor

latitude of acceptance

latitude of rejection

cognitive consistency theories

p-o-x theory

balance theory

cognitive dissonance

counter-attitudinal position

mere exposure

expectancy-value models

attitude–behavior relationships

theory of reasoned action (TRA)

behavioral intentions

normative influence

theory of planned behavior (TPB)

perceived behavioral control

norms-based approaches

compliance gaining

face threats

APPLICATION OF ETHICS

Many professors intentionally introduce dissonance as a way to foster learning, change your attitudes, and provide a new lens for seeing the world in a different way. We do this at times in this book. The professor may play the devil's advocate and may not even really believe some of the outrageous things he or she says to provoke students. Are professors ethically bound to inform students that such tactics are being used to promote learning in the class? Some professors create conflict in the classroom by introducing competition where the highest-performing team receives awards—much like the dynamics on the television show *The Apprentice*. The impact of such behaviors becomes very apparent when an angry team of students storms the professor's office or a student starts crying over a poor performance. What arguments favor these practices? What arguments attack such practices? When does the behavior of a professor intentionally creating dissonance in the classroom become unethical?

QUESTIONS FOR FURTHER THOUGHT

1. An ethical issue raised by the ELM is determining when children develop the ability to centrally process persuasion at a level that allows them to make informed choices. In what situations should parents allow their children to make their own choices about purchases like cereal, toys, and clothing?

2. Discuss why females and males might process the issue of keeping abortions legal in the United States differently.

3. Given that attractiveness has proven to be a valuable factor in persuasion, what can people do in persuasive situations to make up for the fact that they are not among the beautiful people in this world?

4. Put yourself into the role of the parent of a teenager who has just obtained his or her license. What inoculation strategy might you use to try to persuade your teenager not to drink and drive?

5. Do you believe norms-based approaches can work to combat undesirable behaviors in young people? Why or why not?

6. Parking policies on campus are often hot button issues on many college campuses. Is it realistic to approach compliance with parking regulations from a persuasive rather than coercive approach? That is, could parking be regulated on campuses without the threat of fines? Does a $100 fine for parking in handicapped spaces induce greater compliance?

 For online activities, go to the *Persuasion* book companion website at http://communication.wadsworth.com/larson11.

The Making, Use, and Misuse of Symbols

LEARNING GOALS

After reading this chapter, you should be able to:

1. Identify significant human developments that were made possible via language.

2. Identify several unique facts about the English language.

3. Explain and give examples of eloquence.

4. Explain why language is symbolic action.

5. Give examples of the use and misuse of linguistic symbols.

6. Discuss Langer's theory about language use.

7. Discuss the general semanticists and their theories and goals.

8. Demonstrate how an emotion laden sentence can be defused using the extentional devices suggested by the semanticists.

9. Discuss Burke's notions of identification, substances, and the role of language as a cause of guilt.

10. Explain semiotics and its use of terms such as *text, code, signifiers,* and *signifieds.*

Author, language columnist, and critic Richard Lederer (1991) observes:

> The boundary between human and animal—between the most primitive savage and the highest ape—is the language line. The birth of language is the dawn of humanity; in our beginning was the word. We have always been endowed with language because before we had words, we were not human beings. [Words] tell us that we must never take for granted the miracle of language (p. 3).

Throughout history, the uniquely human ability to create **symbols** made possible all our major cultural advances. Symbols can be many things, such as words, pictures, art works, music, and others. The dictionary definition reads "Something that represents something else by association, resemblance or convention." (*American Heritage Dictionary*, 1985). Thus our national flag represents or stands for the 13 colonies that became the original United States and also for the present 50 United States. The most widely used type of symbol is probably language. The words stand for or represent things, ideas, feelings, and so on. Before the development of the spoken word, humans resembled the beasts. But the ability to use symbols for communication enabled us to live very differently. Tribes formed using the communicative power of symbols—especially linguistic symbols. Communication facilitated the specialization of labor, the recording of history, and allowed humans to create culture. But, like the opening of Pandora's box, the use of visual and verbal symbols to communicate also allowed humans to engage in less-constructive behaviors such as lying, teasing, breaking promises, scolding, demeaning, and propagandizing. And with the development of writing and print, people found that promises, treaties, and legal contracts could be both made and broken, and laws could be used for evil as well as good. The title of the book *Deeds Done in Words* (Campbell & Jamieson, 1990) indicates that language serves as a frequent surrogate for action. Researcher and professor Neil Postman (1992) maintains that language is an "invisible technology" or a kind of machine that can "give direction to our thoughts,

generate new ideas, venerate old ones, expose facts or hide them" (p. 127). Language theorist Kenneth Burke (1966) said it best when he noted that humans are "symbol making, symbol using, and symbol misusing" creatures.

This ability to use symbols—whether words, pictures, or art—lies at the heart of persuasion and so deserves our attention. We've seen that receivers must get to the bottom of persuasive meanings by carefully analyzing the verbal and nonverbal symbols being used or misused by persuaders. We need to ask whether the symbols prompt logical or emotional meanings and if they are centrally or peripherally processed in the Elaboration Likelihood Model (ELM). For instance, imagine a TV advertisement for a brand of beer. It probably uses verbal, visual, and musical or lyrical symbols. Together, they show that people who drink the brand enjoy a certain lifestyle and are happy-go-lucky.

Persuaders frequently use metaphors (which are a kind of symbol, such as "Marlboro Man") to emphasize their points. Two recent books on the right to privacy issues use metaphors in their titles: *No Place to Hide* by Robert O'Harrow (2005) and Daniel Solove's *The Digital Person* (2005). Both titles imply that we face two dangers—a loss of privacy and becoming mere ciphers or digits. Recent research on metaphors shows that their use increases persuader credibility, and they operate best when their theme is reiterated throughout the persuasive message and especially if used initially and in the conclusion (Sopory & Dillard, 2002).

By examining various metaphors and other symbols used in persuasion, we accomplish several things:

1. We discover the persuader's use or misuse of symbols.

2. We discover the persuader's stylistic preferences and what they reveal about his or her motives.

3. We can anticipate the kinds of messages likely to come from this source in the future.

One reason we can infer so much is that the making of symbols is a highly ego-involving and creative act. When we make a symbol, we own it—it belongs to us, and it reveals a good deal about us and our motives. The same thing occurs when others try to persuade us. They make symbols (usually language) and as a result they "own" their creations, and ownership can be revealing. Critical receivers need to know something about language and how to read it for clues regarding the persuader's motives. Let's look a little deeper into our own language.

THE POWER OF THE ENGLISH LANGUAGE

Lederer (1991) also offers many examples to help us avoid taking the English language (the common denominator for most persuasion we process) for granted. Consider just a few of them:

1. Of almost 3000 languages in existence today, only 10 are the native language of more than 100 million people, and English ranks second in the list only behind Chinese (pp. 19–20).

2. Users of English as a second language outnumber native users (p. 20).

3. English is the first language of 45 countries (p. 20).

4. Most of the world's books, newspapers, and magazines are written in English, and two thirds of all scientific publications and 80 percent of all stored computer texts are in English (p. 20).

5. English has one of the richest vocabularies—615,000 words in the *Oxford English Dictionary*—not including slang, many technical and scientific terms, newly invented words like iPod, BlackBerry, rurban, and blog). Compare that with French, which has about 100,000 words; Russian, which has about 130,000; or German, which has about 185,000 (p. 24). At the same time that it is so rich in vocabulary, English is remarkably economical. It requires far fewer syllables to translate Mark's gospel into English than into any Romance, Germanic, or Slavic language (p. 29). The King James version of the Bible uses only about 8000 words, the entire works of Homer contain about 9000, and all of Milton has only about 10,000.

6. English is now the international language of science, business, politics, diplomacy, literature, tourism, pop culture, and air travel. Japanese pilots flying Japanese airliners over Japanese air space must communicate with Japanese flight controllers using English, and the same is true of the airspace over every other country in the world (p. 30).

7. English is a hospitable language—more than 70 percent of our words come from other languages (for example, boss, kindergarten, polka, sauna, canoe, zebra, alcohol, jukebox, camel, tycoon, tundra, ketchup, pal, vodka, sugar, tattoo, and flannel, to name a few) (pp. 24).

8. Nonnative speakers report that English is the easiest second language to learn (p. 28). Lederer also demonstrates the power of a permanent aspect of the English language—its syntax. He asks students to arrange five words—"Lithuanian," "five," "scholars," "Shakespearean," and "old"—so that they make syntactical sense. Inevitably, they all come up with the same syntax or word order. Try this exercise, and discover that you and most, if not all, of your classmates come up with "five old Lithuanian Shakespearean scholars." The order of adjective strings begins with the most specific and continues to the least. There are Shakespearean scholars in countries other than Lithuania just as there other kinds of scholars. Our language use is also very sophisticated and differs in its spoken and written forms. For instance, consider the following

InwritingandreadingtheEnglishlanguage, weneedvisualcuestodeciphermessages.

There are two visual cues in that first string of words—the comma and the capital E—and both of them shout out, "Here is a word break!" We get no such help in the second string. In written

---

B O X 5.1 **Interactive English**

 Go to www.englishforum.com/00/interactive/ (or www.englishforum.com 00 interactive) and explore the many interesting and fun ways interactive media can help you improve your use of the English language. One of the many activities at the site is the daily display of a new idiom. If you don't know what an idiom is, consider this one: "As different as chalk from cheese." What do you suppose it means? At the site there is a daily famous quote and a chat group where you can leave or receive a message about the use of English. You can trade English language lessons with students from other countries. For example, Oman will trade lessons in Arabic with you. You can leave your term papers or other texts there for free critiques. Try to solve the word puzzles and learn new slang words. The site also lists good English schools in eight countries and offers students budget travel hints. And there is even an online wizard who can read your mind. You will learn much about the English language there, and you may want to invent your own words as Shakespeare did (see Figure 5.1).

English, those cues really help, but in spoken English, we lack visual cues and consequently become baffled sometimes when trying to interpret words. In spoken English, try to determine the difference between "no notion" and "known ocean," or between "buys ink" and "buys zinc," between "meteorologist" and "meaty urologist," and between "cat's skills," "cats' kills," and "Catskills," or between "tax" and "tacks." This last example resulted in a humorous student blooper. The student wrote, "The American Revolution came about because the British put tacks in their tea." So, as persuadees, we must consider whether the persuasion is coming to us in written or spoken language or via visual symbols—the channel plays an important part in our development of meaning and deciding how to react to it.

LANGUAGE, ELOQUENCE, AND SYMBOLIC ACTION

Eloquent persuasion always seems unique and fresh. It strikes us as capturing the moment, and it may even prophesy the future. The speech made by Martin Luther King, Jr., on the night before he was assassinated had elements of prophecy. King said that God had allowed him "to go up to the mountain top," that he had "seen the Promised Land," and that he doubted that he would get there with his followers. He concluded, "But, I am happy tonight! I'm not fearing any man! Mine eyes have seen the glory of the coming of the Lord!" Although the words were not wholly original (they were drawn from the Old Testament and Julia Ward Howe's "Battle Hymn of the Republic"), his use of them was prophetic in the context of the movement he was leading. They certainly were emotional and probably were processed in the peripheral channel of the ELM.

Today we find many groups using and misusing linguistic symbols in dramatic ways on buttons, badges, or bumper stickers. Consider a few: "Think Globally; Act Locally," "Guns Don't Kill; People Do," or "Da Bulls." Others use license plates as a medium to make symbolic declarations about themselves and their philosophies: "IM N RN," "REV BOB," "COACH," "I M SX C," "MR X TC," "XME OME," or "TACKY." Each of these messages symbolically makes a revealing statement about its user. Researchers know that persons displaying bumper stickers or wearing T-shirts with product or candidate labels imprinted on them will buy the products or vote for the candidate they are promoting far more often than those who don't display the labels. Making the symbolic statement means they already took action in their minds, and

FIGURE 5.1 Other words coined by Shakespeare include "amazement," "bump," "clangor," "dwindle," "fitful," "majestic," "obscene," "pious," "road," "flibbertygibbet," "slugabeat," and "useless." Can you invent some words of your own?

SOURCE: Used by permission of Wide World Photos.

their words become deeds or substitutes for action. As Burke (1966) observed, "Language is symbolic action," and we often act out what we speak.

Language can also be misused. The deaths of Afghani and Iraqi civilians became "collateral damage," in operations Rolling Thunder and Enduring Freedom (both names are also double-speak), while "surgical air strikes" made the enormous damage sound neat and clean. Market researchers decided to use the words "recipe for success," for example, to assure working women who use Crisco that they are indeed "cooks" and not merely "microwavers" who thaw and reheat meals. A great pair of words—"Budget Gourmet"—describes an inexpensive, okay, prepackaged meal, but not one of gourmet quality.

Another reason language requires careful analysis is that it tells us a lot about the persuader's motives and reveals much by its particular verbal and visual symbols. Consider the demeaning and dehumanizing language used by anti-Semitic persuaders in the past (and perhaps in the present) in referring to Jews and other minorities as "vermin," "sludge," "garbage," "lice," "sewage," "insects," and "bloodsuckers." The recent influx of immigrants from the Middle East spawned similar linguistic venom: "camel jockey," "dot head," "pak head" or "Q-tip," all of which demeaned and dehumanized others. We need to remember that "ethnic cleansing" still occurs in many places in the world, and language serves as the major weapon for instigating dehumanization and worse. In less-dramatic settings, words create emotional responses and devalue people. What do the words "lady doctor" imply? That the doctor is not as good as a male physician? That the doctor is in the business only for the fun or sport of it? Why does "lady" convey so much meaning and evoke emotional responses? Communication scholar Dan Hahn (1998) points out how language depicts males as sexual aggressors and females as stalked prey or passive entities. Consider a few examples in which the language of seduction becomes the language of stalking: the male is described as "a real animal" or unable to " keep his paws off her," while the female is "a real dish" or "a real piece of meat" to be "turned on" or "cranked." Recently we have become sensitized to the use (and misuse) of Native American references in athletics—the Braves, the Redskins, the Chiefs, the Fighting Illini, and the Seminoles.

For an interesting peek into how emotionally involved people can get over language issues, access InfoTrac College Edition, and enter the words "language style" in the search engine. Read a few of the items dealing with language and religion, language and feminism, and language and marketing and salesmanship. Report your findings back to the class.

FIGURE 5.2 As this cartoon demonstrates, language used in its spoken form can be quite different from its use in its written form.

SOURCE: Reprinted by permission of Aaron Johnson.

The world of marketing provides many examples of the persuasive power in language choice. Brand names often reveal manufacturers' attitudes toward customers. For instance, Oster Corporation markets a "food crafter" instead of a "food chopper," which tells us that Oster takes a gourmet approach. (Chopping sounds like work. Crafting? Now, that's art.) Smoking certain brands of cigarettes can make a gender statement—Eves and Virginia Slims are for her not him. At one time, the brand names of American-made automobiles suggested status, luxury, power, and speed—Roadmaster, Continental, Coupe de Ville, and Imperial. Later, new brands coming on the market suggested technology, speed, and economy—Rabbit, Colt, Fox, Jetta, and Laser. When the baby boomers started hitting midlife, auto brand names suggested wealth, quality, durability, and long lives—Sterling, Infiniti, Sable, Probe, and Escalade.

LANGER'S APPROACH TO LANGUAGE USE

We need to identify the uses and misuses of symbols, especially in the language used by politicians, advertisers, employers, and other persuaders. A useful approach to the study of language is based on the work of philosopher and language pioneer Suzanne K. Langer (1951). She recognized the power of language symbols, and like Lederer and others, she believed that the ability to create symbols distinguishes humans from nonhumans. Language lets us talk and think about feelings, events, and objects even when the actual feelings, events, or objects are not physically present. Langer associates two concepts with this capacity—signs and symbols. Signs indicate the presence of an event, feeling, or object. For instance, thunder signals lightning and usually rain. My dog goes into a panic at the sound of thunder—lightning struck close to her as a pup, so she tries to hide from it. If she could process symbols, I might talk to her about thunder and explain the futility of trying to hide from it. Only the comforting tone of my voice (another sign) seems to calm her down. We know that the red traffic light at an intersection signals potentially dangerous cross traffic. Guide dogs recognize the red light by its location on the top of the traffic signal and even learn to stop the person they are leading, but you cannot teach them to recognize the symbolic link between the red light and the words "cross traffic"—a much more complex connection. As Langer (1951) put it, "Symbols are not proxy of their objects, but are vehicles for the conception of objects" (p. 60). Because of our ability to use symbols, you and I understand the presence of danger by such things as the color red, the word "danger," or the skull and crossbones on a bottle. Using symbols seems to be a basic human need. Even persons unable to write, hear, or speak make symbols using visual signs, hand motions, and other symbolic means. Some symbols have a common meaning upon which most people agree. Langer called such symbols **concepts**, in contrast to **conceptions**, which she used to refer to any particular individual's meanings for the concept.

BOX 5.2   Brand Names: Discursive or Presentational?

Developing brand names entails more effort than you would think. It is no accident that Snuggle—a fabric softener—has a teddy bear as its logo. When you see Snuggle on the shelf, you probably do not think of actually "snuggling" up with a good book and a cup of coffee, but you might put a package of it in your shopping cart and feel good about having done so. There is no string of words to be followed when you look at the brand, its logo, or its packaging. The brand's name is a presentational symbol.

Observe the brand on your next shopping trip. Now consider another brand name—TheraFlu, a cold medicine meant to be taken as a hot drink before going to bed. There is no evidence that the brand works any better than any other nighttime cold medicine having similar ingredients. However, the brand is threatening sales of NyQuil, the first over-the-counter nighttime cold medicine on the market. Why? Perhaps there is a presentational explanation (Feig, 1997).

All human communication and hence persuasion relies on concepts and conceptions. So, naturally, the possibility of misunderstanding always presents itself.

Langer introduced three terms to be used when discussing meaning: "signification," "denotation," and "connotation." **Signification** means a sign that accompanies the thing being considered. So a skull and crossbones on a bottle signifies "Danger—Poison!" **Denotation** refers to the common and shared meaning we all have for any concept. **Connotation** refers to my or your private and emotional meaning for any concept such as "danger." The denotation of the word would be the dictionary definition of the word danger as "Exposure or vulnerability to harm or loss." (*American Heritage Dictionary*, 1985). The connotation of the word is my or your personal and individual conception of danger. Because of my Minnesota background, I find blizzards to be dangerous. Someone from Florida might not, and the obverse would be true for my connotation for the word "hurricane." And of course, we are increasingly facing culturally diverse connotations for words and concepts. For example, China thinks of itself as extraordinarily egalitarian. However, professor and marketing consultant Barry Feig (1997) reports that a flourishing trade exists there for counterfeit labels for high-priced and high-status brands of bicycles. Few persons in China own autos, but most have bicycles, and most of them are quite ordinary—

almost generic. The fake labels are symbols that communicate status in a society where status differences supposedly don't exist,

Langer also maintained that meaning is either "discursive" or "presentational." **Discursive symbols** are usually made up of sequential, smaller bits of meaning. Musically, this would be equivalent to movements in a symphony. In a drama it would be the unfolding of a plot. For our purposes, discursive symbols usually occur in the form of language. **Presentational meaning**, on the other hand, occurs all at once and the message must be experienced in its entirety, such as when one looks at a painting, architecture, or a statue, or experiences a ritual. Thus, some of the "meaning" in any advertisement is discursive (the slogans, jingles, and ad copy), and some is presentational (the graphic layout, fonts, and pictures). Similarly, some of the meaning in a political campaign occurs discursively (the speeches, press releases, and interviews), and some is presentational (the way the candidate looks, his or her "image," and the pictorial and music in spot ads).

GENERAL SEMANTICS AND LANGUAGE USE

Beginning with the landmark work *Science and Sanity* by Count Alfred Korzybski (1947), scholars known as general semanticists began a careful and systematic study of the use of language and meaning. They intended to devise tools for improving the understanding of human communication and to encourage careful and precise uses of language. Most of them were from academic departments of English or psychology, though Korzybski was originally a military intelligence officer who debriefed spies and double agents. His theory grew out of the difficulty in determining what these persons *really* meant when they communicated something. The semanticists wanted to train people to be very specific in sending and receiving words, to avoid the communication pitfalls such as stereotyping that had led to the rise of demagogues in many countries prior to WW II. For instance, the general semanticists believed people needed to learn to be aware that the appeals made by most persuaders were **maps** or inner perceptions and not **territories** or realities. A map is what exists in my or your head, but a territory is what exists in the real world. For example, you might have an image of a certain place, experience, or event. That image is only a map. That place, experience, or event may not resemble your map of it at all. With the advent of such interactive media as virtual reality, Internet gaming and dating, the home shopping network, and telemarketing, receivers face an increased blurring of map and territory. As a result, we need to heed the advice of the **semanticists** more than ever because much of the interactive world is virtual. In other words, interactive messages are maps, not territories.

Take the case of stereotyping. Stereotypes are supposedly unreliable. No member of a class or group is exactly like any other member. To counter the miscommunication that can result from stereotyping, receivers need to heed Korzybski's reminder that "the map is not the territory." In other words, our internal conceptions of other persons, ethnic groups, and ideas will differ widely from the actual persons, groups, things, and ideas. Korzybski and his colleagues recognized the difference between an event, object, or experience and any individual's conception of it. In their scheme, the word "map" equates to Langer's "conception," and the word "territory" equates to "objective reality" or close to Langer's "concept."

Our faulty maps get expressed through the language we create to convey them, and they usually miscommunicate in some way. For the general semanticists, the real problems occur when people act as if their maps accurately describe the territory, thus turning the map into the territory. Korzybski believed that we all carry thousands of maps around in our heads that represent nonexistent, incorrect, or false territories. To demonstrate this concept for yourself, write down the name of a food you have never eaten, a place you have never been, and an experience you have never had. These words serve as maps for unknown territories. You probably think that fried brains would feel slimy and gooshy in your mouth. In reality, they have the texture of well-scrambled eggs. What about your map for skydiving or for being a rock star? What about your maps for various ethnic groups? What about your map for places that you have only visited via the Internet?

Access InfoTrac College Edition, and enter the word "psycholinguistics" in the search engine. Psycholinguists are persons who try to get at what is in our heads, using our language use as their raw material. Go to the subdivisions options and select the analysis option. Examine the items referring to "Fatal Words" (which concerns the crash of ValuJet flight 592), "Words, Words, Words," "Linguistic Virtual Reality," and the language used by schizophrenics. How do the items heighten your awareness of the power of word choice?

In most cases, your maps will be very different from the territories as they really exist. Our mental, visual, and word maps present a real problem in communication, and especially in persuasion. Just as persuaders must discover the common ground of ideas so they can persuade us, they also must identify the maps we carry around in our heads. Then they must either play on those maps (using our misperceptions to their advantage) or try to get us to correct our faulty maps. Only then can they persuade us to buy, vote, join, or change our behavior. Our faulty maps are frequently expressed through language.

WAY UP NORTH, WHERE THE HUSKIES GO *BY AL O*

F I G U R E   5.3 It is clear that Bob doesn't understand the map/territory distinction.
SOURCE: Used with permission of Al Ochsner.

We create and use words to communicate and to build our maps. We react to these words as if they are true representations of the territories we imagine. To the semanticists, this **signal response** is equivalent to my dog trying to hide from lightning whenever she experiences the sign or signal of thunder. Signal responses are emotionally triggered reactions to symbolic acts (including language use), and these responses play out as if the act were actually being committed. In a recent example of the signal response, an official in the Washington, D.C., city council and aide to the African American mayor was removed from the council because he used the word "niggardly." Now, the dictionary definition of the word is "unwilling to give, spend, or share . . . stingy, scanty, or meager" (*American Heritage Dictionary*, 1985). But because the word sounds similar to a racial epithet—the "N" word—it prompted a signal response among members of the council, even after a definition of the word was given. The semanticists were accurate about the power of the signal response (National Public Radio, 1999).

The semanticists wanted to train senders and receivers to be continually alert to the difference between signals and symbols. Semanticists also try to isolate meaning in concrete terms. Let's examine a fairly inflammatory sentence and then try to defuse it using the techniques of the semanticists. Suppose I tell you, "Your generation of college students is conservative, selfish, and lazy." Your

response will probably be negative because of the connotations of some of the words used—"selfish" and "lazy" for sure, and maybe "conservative" as well. Semanticists would advise us to use what they call **extensional devices**, or techniques for neutralizing or defusing the emotional connotations that often accompany words by adding information that makes my meaning clear to you and others. One extensional device in my language use would be to identify the specific college students I have in mind. Semanticists call this **indexing**. In this case, my statement would change to something like, "Your generation of college students, who have everything paid for by their parents, is conservative, selfish, and lazy." That would calm some of you because you probably know fellow students who have everything paid for, including lots of extras that you don't get.

But I still would not be as clear as I could be, according to the semanticists. They would further urge me to use an extensional device called **dating**, or letting you know the time frame of my judgment about college students. Using dating, I might say something like, "Generation X college students who have everything paid for by their parents are conservative, selfish, and lazy." That might cool you down a little more. Here is where the extensional device semanticists call **etc.** comes into play. This device is meant to indicate that we can never tell the whole story about any person, event, place,

---

B O X 5.3   Language and Cultural Diversity

 Did you know that only four countries in all of Latin America have populations greater than the Latino population of the United States, which is now about 22.5 million? Or did you know that there are more Asians in the United States than there are in Cambodia, Laos, Hong Kong, or Singapore? Or did you know that at some point in this century, Latinos will outnumber non-Latinos? These are just a few of the many facts mentioned by Nido R. Qubein. He is an internationally known consultant, award-winning speaker, president of High Point University, and he sits on the boards of several Fortune 500 companies and is chairman of a national public

relations firm, Business Life Inc., and CEO of the Great Harvest Bread Company. He came to the United States as a teenager, with no contacts, no English language skills, and less than $50 to his name. He travels the globe and urges his audiences to remember that "people from different backgrounds send and receive messages through cultural filters" and that the same words, facial expressions, and gestures have different meanings depending on one's cultural heritage. You may want to access his home page at www. nidoqubein.com/index. There you can listen to him speak, get samples of his video and audio tapes, and get free articles written by him.

---

or thing. Using this device, I might say, "Generation X college students who have everything paid for by their parents are conservative, selfish, and lazy, among other things." Now conservatism, selfishness, and laziness aren't their only attributes. For example, they also might be "societally concerned about environmental issues," "worried about honesty," or any of a number of other positive attributes.

Finally, the semanticists would advise using an extensional device called **quotation marks**, which is a way to indicate that I am using those flag words in a particular way—my way, which isn't necessarily your way. For example, my use of the word "selfish" might relate to the students' unwillingness to help other students succeed in class. Or it could relate to their unwillingness to volunteer in the community or to do any of a number of other things that wouldn't necessarily match your meaning for the word "selfish." My sentence might now read, "Generation X college students who have everything paid for by their parents are 'conservative,' 'selfish,' and 'lazy,' among other things." Now you would probably probe for my meanings for the emotional words, or you might even agree with the sentence.

Using extensional devices in decoding persuasion helps us make sure the maps in our heads more closely resemble the territory to which we refer. Persuaders need to design specific, concrete extensional messages, especially when using emotionally

charged words or abstract words for which there can be many meanings. More important, persuadees need to consider whether they are being appealed to via the map or the territory. Abstract words such as "power," "democracy," "freedom," "morals," and "truth" are particularly vulnerable to misunderstanding. Unethical persuaders often intentionally use abstract or emotionally charged language to achieve their purposes. It is our task to remember the map/territory distinction and to use extensional devices as we attend to symbols. We must remember that receivers also have "response-ability."

To learn more about the power of words, access InfoTrac College Edition, enter the word "newspeak" in the key word option, and explore the item titled "Pomobabble" by Dennis Arrow, referring to postmodernism. Make a list of your top ten examples, make copies for your classmates, and pass them out.

BURKE'S APPROACH
TO LANGUAGE USE

Perhaps no language theorist or critic wrote as many treatises in as wide a variety of fields or with as broad a knowledge of human symbolic behavior as Kenneth

Burke did. Burke focused on language as it is used to persuade people to action. Burke (1950) defined persuasion as "the use of language as a symbolic means of inducing cooperation in beings that by nature respond to symbols" (p. 43). This active cooperation is induced by what he termed **identification**, a concept similar to Aristotle's "common ground" and our use of "co-creation," as noted in Chapter 1.

According to Burke, the development of identification occurs through the linguistic sharing of what he called **sub-stances**. He divided the word into its prefix *sub*, meaning "beneath," and *stances*, which refers to "grounding" or "places." In other words, identification rests on the beliefs, values, experiences, and views of the self that we share with others. Burke noted that these sub-stances or "places" emerge in the words we use to define things, persons, and issues. Critical receivers of persuasion need to pay particular attention to the words, images, and metaphors that persuaders use to create (or undermine) identification. Our self-concepts are made up of various kinds of symbolic and real possessions, including physical things (clothing, cars, books), experiential things (work, activities, recreations), and philosophical possessions (beliefs, attitudes, values). Identification with others develops to the degree that we symbolically share these possessions. In other words, we identify with persons who articulate a similar view of life, who enjoy the same kinds of activities, have similar physical possessions, lifestyles, beliefs, attitudes, and so on. If we identify with persuaders, we naturally tend to believe what they say and probably follow their advice. Thus, the job of persuaders is to call attention to those sub-stances that they share with receivers. The receivers' job, in turn, is to critically examine these sub-stances to see whether they truly are shared values and beliefs or whether the persuader merely makes them appear to be shared. In other words, persuadees need to decode persuaders' messages for their authenticity, and determine whether the messages reflect persuaders' real beliefs and values or are merely convenient concoctions.

The dictionary defines substance as "the essential part of a thing—its essence." The definition is especially meaningful with regard to identification. We identify with others because we share their essential beliefs, values, experiences, and so on. I am like you and you are like me to some degree; hence, I will believe you when you try to persuade me. For example, consider the Academy Award–winning film *Million Dollar Baby*. The manager character played by Clint Eastwood shares certain experiences and values with the coach character played by Morgan Freeman. Freeman relies on these shared substances to help convince Eastwood to coach and manage the aspiring young boxer played by Hillery Swank.

To Burke, most persuasion attempts to describe our "essential parts," and this description is always revealing. All words have emotional shadings and reveal the feelings, attitudes, values, and judgments of the user. Examining persuasive language can tell us about ourselves and *about* the persuaders who solicit our interest, support, and commitment. Burke also suggested that symbolic activities like the use of language inevitably cause people to have feelings of guilt. From the beginning, language automatically led to rule making and moralizing. Because we all break the rules or don't measure up to moral standards at some time, we experience some degree of guilt. Burke argued that all human cultures exhibit patterns that help explain guilt, and the development of language in each of us is foremost. For example, the word "puppy" is clearly not an actual puppy, so language that names what something is inherently leads to the idea of what something is not—**the negative**. The negative then leads to sets of "thou shalt nots," whether supernatural, parental, spousal, or societal. Inevitably, we fail to obey some of these negatives and again experience shame and guilt. "No" is one of the first things we learn as children, and we realize that it means we just displeased someone. We hear "No, no, no," over and over, and then we begin to use it ourselves. It gives us power, and we go about testing the extent of that power during the "terrible twos" and, in fact, throughout life.

The second behavioral pattern that contributes to guilt relies on the principle of hierarchy, or "pecking order." It happens in all societies and groups, and it leads to either jealousy of others or to competition. We rarely (perhaps never) reach the top of the pecking order, and we feel guilty about that as well. A third source of guilt is our innate need to achieve perfection. Unfortunately, we all fall short of our goals and so feel inadequate and ashamed for not doing our best. This shame makes us feel guilty about not living up to our own or others' expectations. How do we rid ourselves of guilt? In most religions, guilt is purged symbolically—we offer up a sacrifice or engage in self-inflicted suffering, penance, and so on. And these cures are used in our self-persuasion as well: "I'll be good, God, if only I get out of this dilemma." But the handiest and most flexible, creative, artistic, and universal means to whip guilt is through language. We usually try to get rid of guilt by talking about it—in prayer, to ourselves, to a counselor or authority figure, or to someone with whom we identify. Consider how frequently persuaders offer us symbolic ways to alleviate our guilt. The parents who feel guilty take their family on a vacation to Disney World. The imperfect child tries to do better at school by using the Internet and spending more time studying and doing extra credit assignments.

In summary, persuasion via identification works because we all share sub-stances and because we all experience guilt. In processing persuasion, try to recognize that persuaders create identification by referring to shared sub-stances—preferred beliefs, lifestyles, and values. They motivate us by appealing to our internal and inevitable feelings of inadequacy or guilt. Examine the language and images in advertisements, sermons, political appeals, and other messages, reminding yourself of the strategies being used to create identification, and also feelings of imperfection, shame, and guilt.

To see how critics have used Kenneth Burke's theories, go to InfoTrac College Edition, and select the Powertrac option. Enter the words "Kenneth Burke" in the search engine. Read the "Kenneth Burke—R.I.P." item to get a feel for the importance of his work. Access any of the items listed to learn how others have applied Burke's theories in language analysis. Report your findings to the class.

THE SEMIOTIC APPROACH TO LANGUAGE USE

Semiotics is also concerned with the generation and conveyance of meaning. A number of scholars are associated with this "science" of meaning, including Umberto Eco. Semiologists apply the tools of linguistics to a wide variety of texts. Almost anything can be a text that has one or more meanings—semioticians talk about the "meaning" of a doctor's office, a meal, a TV program, a circus, or any other verbal or nonverbal symbolic event. According to semiotic theory, all texts convey meaning through **signs** or **signifiers**. A signifier in a restaurant could be the presence or absence of a hostess. It signifies that we are to wait to be shown to our seat or that we can select our own in the case of the absent hostess. **Signifieds** are the things (events, rules, etc.) to which the signifiers refer. These signifiers interact with one another in meaningful and sophisticated, but not obvious, relationships, or sign systems, which make up the "language," or "code," of the text.

These codes can be inferred from a text. For example, consider your classroom as a text having its own signifiers and signifieds—some linguistic and some visual, some logical and some emotional. The room usually has an institutional "meaning" signified by the type of walls, lighting, boards, and so on. Blackboards and plaster walls usually signify that the building is an old one. Green or white boards and cinder block walls signify a newer building. The kinds of student desks (with or without arms), the arrangement of the room (for example, desks in rows versus groups), and the physical objects (an overhead versus a video projector) are all signifiers that tell us about what to expect when entering this "text." There may be a clock on the wall, signifying that time is important here, and it may be in view of the students or only to someone facing the back of the room (usually the teacher).

Consider several of the codes embedded in various texts. For example, a simple code is the use of black and white hats in old cowboy movies to indicate the good guy and the bad guy. Pages

aochsner@northernstar.info   ©2005Al Ochsner/All Rights Reserved

F I G U R E 5.4 Bob doesn't get the meaning of the word "euphemize."
SOURCE: Used with permission of Al Ochsner.

being blown off a calendar in a movie signify the passage of time. What meanings are conveyed by drinking out of mugs as opposed to Styrofoam cups or fine china? Each type of cup is a signifier, and each coffee drinker, consciously or unconsciously, is communicating a different message, yet words aren't necessarily involved.

In a semiotic approach to the study of meaning, we try to read each message from several perspectives: (1) the words that are or are not spoken, (2) the context in or from which they are spoken, and (3) the other signifiers in the message—visuals, colors, tone of voice, furnishings, and so on. Indeed, semioticians approach any communication event as if it were a text to be read by the receiver or analyst. More and more marketing and advertising research is being conducted from a semiological approach, according to Curt Suplee (1987) of the *Washington Post*. He quotes advertising and design celebrity George Lois as saying, "When advertising is great advertising, it fastens on the myths, signs, and symbols of our common experience and becomes, quite literally, a benefit of the product.... As a result of great advertising, food tastes better, clothes feel snugger, cars ride smoother. The stuff of semiotics becomes the magic of advertising" (p. 3).

For an excellent discussion of how semiotics can be applied and for insight into how the worlds of advertising and marketing use semiotics,

access InfoTrac College Edition, and enter the word "semiotics" in the search engine. Select the analysis option, go to the item drawn from the *Journal of Advertising Research*, and learn how agencies like Saatchi and Saatchi use the tool to market entertainment products. Now go to the research option, and select the article from *The International Journal of Market Research* to learn how Guinness beer uses semiotics in designing its advertising.

Semiotics also can help us understand where a persuader is coming from and what his or her agenda might be. What is the semiotic meaning of the following letter sent to the chair of my department?

Dear Professor Jones,

I am interested in directives as to how one may proficiency out of the speech requirement. Having been advised to seek counsel from you "specifically"—I sincerely hope you will not be displeased with my enthusiasm by asking this indulgence. There is a basis for my pursuing this inquisition as I am an adept speaker with substantiating merits. I will be overburdened with more difficult courses this fall—at least they will be concomitant with my educational objectives in the fields of Fine Arts and Languages. It would be a ludicrous exercise in futility to be

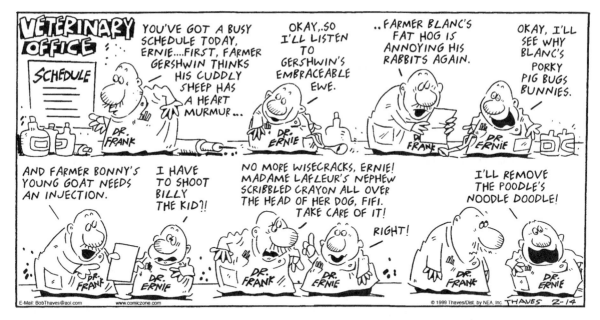

FIGURE 5.5 As this cartoon illustrates, language is fun to experiment with as well as being important in persuasion.

SOURCE: *Frank and Ernest.* ©United Feature Syndicate Inc. Used with permission.

mired in an unfecund speech course when I have already distinguished myself in that arena. I maintained an "A" average in an *elite* "advanced" speech course in High School. I am quite noted for my bursts of oratory and my verbal dexterity in the public "reality"—quite a different platform than the pseudo realism of the college environs. There is a small matter of age—I shall be twenty-two this fall. I am four years older than the average college freshman. I am afraid that I would dissipate with boredom, if confined with a bunch of *teenagers.* Surely you can advise something that would be a more palatable alternative?

Yours sincerely,

P.S. Please do not misconstrue this "inquiry" as the enterprise of an arrogant student, but one who will be so immersed in *serious* intellectual pursuits that the "speech" requirement will be too nonsensical and burdensome.

If ever a student needed to learn about communication, it was this individual. But what does the language usage here tell you about the writer of the letter? She uses sixty-four-dollar words—perhaps a code for insecurity—but she seems unsure about her choice of words, as shown by her putting words into quotation marks, which indicates that she has her own special meaning for them. She also uses italics to signify that this word has special meaning and importance. She also misuses some words. For example, she says that she is pursuing an "inquisition" when she means an "inquiry." An inquisition is a tribunal for suppressing religious heresy. She says she has "substantiating merits" when she probably means that she has "substantial reasons" for being excused from the course. These and other signifiers add up to the semiotic meaning of the letter, which is that the author is insecure and hopes to impress the recipient of the letter. As Figure 5.5 demonstrates, semiotic meanings can be toyed with for fun.

To explore the fascinating work of Berger on the semiotics of cartoons (he is a cartoonist himself), go to InfoTrac College Edition, and select the Powertrac option. Enter the words "Arthur Asa Berger" in the search engine. Then access the item titled "Scratches from a Secret Agent," and enjoy.

REVIEW AND CONCLUSION

By now, you probably have deeper appreciation for human symbol making, use, and misuse, and for the power of language as a tool of persuasion—especially the English language. You might realize how much meaning you can uncover when you critically analyze the symbols used in persuasion. It takes time and effort to decode discursive and presentational persuasion, to locate the meanings being used to create a state of identification, to determine the difference between the map and the territory, and to learn the many codes operating in various kinds of texts. To become a responsible persuadee, you need tools to assist you in analyzing the many persuasive messages targeted at you. Chapter 6 focuses on some tools for doing this.

KEY TERMS

When you have read this chapter you should be able to identify, explain, and give an example of the following words or concepts.

symbols	discursive symbols	extensional devices	sub-stances
concepts	presentational meaning	indexing	the negative
conceptions	maps	dating	semiotics
signification	territories	etc.	signs
denotation	semanticists	quotation marks	signifiers
connotation	signal response	identification	signifieds

APPLICATION OF ETHICS

Here is the situation: An interpreter arrives a few minutes before a court of law is called to order. He wants to speak to the defendant, who is a non-English speaker, to determine if using Spanish instead of English will be acceptable. The defendant lets the interpreter know that Spanish is a second language for him (his first language is an indigenous dialect), but that he understands the interpreter and proceeding in Spanish is acceptable. The interpreter has three options: (1) Tell the judge of the situation and that Spanish interpretation is acceptable to the defendant. (2) Say nothing and proceed with the interpretation in Spanish since the defendant has said it is OK with him. (3) Inform the defendant's attorney and let him decide how to proceed. Which option seems most ethical to you? Does the interpreter have any ethical obligation to inform the Judge? Is he ethically obliged to say anything?

QUESTIONS FOR FURTHER THOUGHT

1. Why is symbol making such a powerful human activity? Give several examples of how symbols create high involvement in people. Are symbols logical or emotional? Are they processed centrally or peripherally?

2. What is meant by Burke's phrase "symbol misusing"? Give some examples of the misuse of symbols.

3. Why is the English language so powerful?

4. Why is a red stoplight a sign to a leader dog, and how is that "meaning" different from the words "red stoplight" or "dangerous cross traffic"?

5. What did Suzanne Langer mean when she said that symbols are the "vehicles for the conception of objects"?

6. What is the difference between signification, denotation, and connotation?

7. What is the difference between a presentational and a discursive symbol?

8. What is the difference between a map and a territory, according to the general semanticists? Give an example of one of your food maps.

One of your geographic maps? One of your experience maps?

9. Was Bill Clinton's meaning for "sexual relations" (with Monica Lewinsky) an ethical use of language? Why or why not?

10. What is a signal response? Give several examples.

11. What are the extensional devices recommended by general semanticists? What purpose do these devices serve? Give examples.

12. What did Kenneth Burke mean by "identification"? By "sub-stance"? By the "need for hierarchy"? By "guilt"? How do these concepts explain why language is so important in persuasion and in living life?

13. What is the difference between a signifier and a signified? What is a code? Give examples of simple codes from the worlds of sports, politics, and/or advertising.

14. Is it ethical for advertisers to use guilt to get us to buy? Why or why not? Give some examples.

 For online activities, go to the *Persuasion* book companion website at http://communication.wadsworth.com/larson11.

6

Tools for Analyzing Language and Other Persuasive Symbols

LEARNING GOALS

After reading this chapter, you should be able to:

1. Identify the three dimensions of language focused on in this chapter and give examples of each that you have found or invented.

2. Discuss the powers of symbolic expression in persuasion.

3. Give examples of tools of analysis for each of the dimensions of language.

4. Explain the pentad and give examples of each term in contemporary persuasion.

5. Explain and give examples of god, devil, and charismatic terms in contemporary persuasion.

6. Explain and give examples of archetypal metaphors being used in contemporary persuasion.

7. Explain the difference between the pragmatic and unifying styles and give examples of each from contemporary persuasion.

8. Explain semiotics and discuss how texts and codes work.

Now that you have some perspective on the making, use, and misuse of symbols and an appreciation for the power of language (and the English language in particular), let's consider several ways to analyze both verbal and nonverbal persuasive symbols. Such analysis helps us to reject misguided, fallacious, and deceptive messages. We mentioned several recent examples such as the divided "official" stances on Social Security, the non-existent "W.M.D.s" in Iraq, and the lies of CEOs of corporations who bankrupted their companies while getting rich in the process. All of these used persuasive language, and we'll face many more examples in the future, so receivers need to learn about language use and how to uncover deceptive persuasion.

The cube in Figure 6.1 represents three of the many dimensions of language. They are (1) the **semantic dimension** (the meanings for a word), (2) the **functional dimension** (the jobs that words can do, such as naming), and (3) the **thematic dimension** (the feel and texture of words like "swoosh"). Following our consideration of these dimensions, you will find a discussion of several tools useful in analyzing each dimension and several example analyses. Notice that the cube consists of many smaller cubes, each representing a word or set of words having its own unique semantic, functional, and thematic dimensions. Now consider this line of ad copy: "Sudden Tan from Coppertone Tans on Touch for a Tan That Lasts for Days." On the functional dimension, the words "Sudden Tan" name a product. Semantically, much more is suggested. The word "sudden" describes an almost instantaneous tan, and, indeed, the product dyes skin "tan" on contact. The ad's headline—"Got a Minute? Get a Tan"—is superimposed over before-and-after photos of an attractive blonde who has presumably been dyed tan. On a thematic level, the words do even more. The word "sudden" sounds and feels like the word "sun," so the brand name sounds like the word "suntan."

Consider these examples of thematic language use.

- The "Kero-Sun" heater burns kerosene and warms your house like the sun.
- Have a "Soup-erb Supper" with a package of Hamburger Helper's beef-vegetable soup.

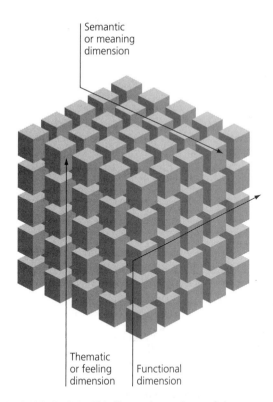

FIGURE 6.1 This figure shows three of the many dimensions of language that are at work when persuadees decode persuasive messages.

- Try My Mom's Meatloaf mix—Meat Loaf that Tastes Like Home.
- Presto named its popcorn popper "The Big Poppa," which sounds like popcorn being popped.

THE FUNCTIONAL DIMENSION: WHAT DO THE WORDS DO?

Words can do many things. They can motivate action, identify causes and effects, and lay blame. During a trial in which an abortionist and the woman who had the abortion faced charges of manslaughter, language functioned in several ways.

The defense referred to attempts to abort the fetus earlier in the pregnancy, saying, "After two unsuccessful attempts. . . ." The prosecutor used active verbs and pronouns, saying, "They tried twice, . . . they were unsuccessful," to lay blame on the woman and the doctor. In one case, the function of the words blunted the accusation—in the other, it focused blame. The functional dimension has powerful potential to simply shift our focus (Andrews, 1984). Take, for example, the function of defining, which can "frame" or set the perspective for the persuasive appeal. As communication scholar Dan Hahn (1998) observes, "Definitions are like blinders on a horse: They focus attention on some aspects while blinding us to others" (p. 53). For example, consider the quarantining of trade to a country to stop shipping into and out of its ports. You could call such an action a "blockade," which is considered an act of war. Now, call the actions "sanctions" That's what the United States did when it outlawed trade by American companies with Iran, Iraq, and North Korea, portraying these nations as part of an "axis of evil" that had sinister worldwide motives. This word choice served at least three functions. First, it signaled the three nations that the United States wasn't necessarily interested in all-out war with them (though we ultimately invaded Iraq). Second, it gave a justification for the resulting hardships being endured by their populace. Finally, it vilified the nations as "outlaws" in the world community. In another example, Hahn points out the meanings associated with the label "middle class." For some, the term means those earning between $17,000 and $64,000 per year (pp. 61– 62). To others it means a lifestyle that includes a house, two late model cars, and membership in the local YMCA. So an important dimension of persuasive language is the functions, tasks, or jobs that the words perform.

Communication researcher Robert Cialdini (2001) observes that some language functions to compensate for our personal feelings of insecurity or low self-worth. He notes that "the persistent name dropper" is a classic example (p. 173); name droppers bolster their own self-esteem by knowing important personalities. Sometimes, words create fear. Consider the underlined words in this sales pitch that functioned to instill fear in the small business owner:

> We've been talking with businesses in the area, and they tell us that they're afraid of three things. The area is growing so fast that they fear that they'll miss out on the new movers coming into the area. Research shows that twenty percent of the country is on the move at any one time, and they worry about the competition getting to these folks first. Then they tear their hair out when they hear that people who have lived in the same area for years don't even know where their business is located. And finally they're terrified that their brand loyal customers will go to the competition because of price or some other reason.

The underlined words functioned to induce fear about what might happen to the business owner's existing and potential customer base. The words interact with preexisting ideas and fears in the prospect's mind. Then he or she co-creates the possibility of loss. In another successful example, a "Got Milk?" ad claimed, "One in five osteoporosis victims is male. Luckily, fat free milk has the calcium bones need to beat it." The words create fear in the male reader who uses this new knowledge to change his behavior. So naming potential problems interacts with the reader and prompts fear and a motivation to take action—drink more milk.

Cialdini (2001) identifies several functions that language can perform other than building fear. These include the function of creating deference or blind obedience to authority (p. 182). Cialdini says that the use of titles can also function to convey authority (p. 188). Today, we hire an "administrative assistant" not a "secretary," and the new name functions to build the employee's self-worth. Another function Cialdini identifies is the power of language to create "the scarcity effect" (p. 205). Consider the words "Price Good Only While Supplies Last!" or "Act Now! Only a Few Left at this Price!" These phrases function to convince the persuadee that the product is in short supply. This creates "a sense of urgency" and prompts the prospect to take action.

THE SEMANTIC DIMENSION: WHAT DO THE WORDS MEAN?

The semantic dimension explains the various shades of meaning given to language. For example, in the abortion case discussed earlier, the defense won a ruling censoring the use of the terms "baby boy" and "human being" and allowing only the word "fetus" to be used by the prosecution. We react very differently to the word "fetus" than we do to "baby boy." Clearly, choosing words with the proper semantic meanings can be critical to the interactive co-creation of persuasive meaning.

Word choice also provides clues about the source's underlying intentions. It is not surprising that words like "questionable business practices" and "insider trading" convey different meanings than the words used by critics, which include terms like "looting" the company's pension fund, "destroying employee security," "auditing flimflams," and "corporate sharks drawn by blood." The impeachment trial of Bill Clinton produced many examples of carefully chosen language characterizing Clinton with terms such as "perjurious," "willfully corrupted," and "betrayed." They encourage certain kinds of co-created persuasive meanings. For example, receivers could infer from these words that Clinton was a habitual liar who didn't even respect the office he held or the oath of office to which he swore (Democracy Project, 1999).

Let us now turn to the thematic dimension of language to discover how words can convey feelings, sometimes even via one of the five senses.

THE THEMATIC DIMENSION: HOW DO THE WORDS FEEL?

In addition to having functional and semantic meanings, some words also have a feeling, a texture, or a theme to them. You almost physically sense them. Onomatopoeic words sound like their meaning. For example, listen to the feel of "shush," "whir," "rustle," "buzz," "hum," "ding," or "boom." Some-

what less obvious thematic examples rely on **assonance**, or the repetition of vowels or vowel sounds—for example, "the low moans of our own soldiers rolled across the battlefield like the groans of the doomed." **Alliteration** is similar except that it relies on the repetition of consonants, as in "Smoke Satin Cigarettes—Sense Their Silky Smoothness." Both alliteration and assonance are favorite tools of the advertising copywriter. They're fun to hear and repeat. Sometimes, figures of speech produce a texture or theme. For example, the use of powerful metaphors creates thematic meaning or texture. According to communication researcher Michael Osborn (1967), wartime British prime minister Winston Churchill, repeatedly used what Osborn termed archetypal (universal) metaphors of "light" to characterize the British military and citizenry and "dark" ones for the enemy. In a speech during WWII, he said,

> If we stand up to him (Hitler), all Europe may be free and the life of the world may move forward into broad, sunlit uplands. But if we fail, then the whole world, including the United States, including all that we have known and cared for, will sink into the abyss of a new Dark Age made more sinister, and perhaps protracted, by the lights of perverted science. . . . Good night then: sleep to gather strength for the morning. For the morning will come. Brightly will it shine on the brave and the true, kindly upon all who suffer for the cause, glorious upon the tombs of heroes. Thus will shine the dawn (pp. 115–126).

Archetypal metaphors usually refer to common substances or events like light and dark, birth and rite of passage, and frequently are associated with the sacred or profane. Some familiar ones include references to fire, water, and blood. President George W. Bush repeatedly used the fire metaphor to characterize the rise of democracy in the Middle East and elsewhere in the world where freedom's "flames need to be fanned." Opponents of the invasion into Iraq declared that it would take a long time to "wash the blood" from America's hands. So metaphoric language can carry a lot of persuasive cargo.

By carefully considering the functional, semantic, and thematic dimensions of any persuasive message, we exercise our response-ability as receivers. Even if our interpretation of a message doesn't match the persuader's, the analytic process we apply to persuasive messages helps ensure the responsible reception of persuasion.

THE POWER OF SYMBOLIC EXPRESSION

Symbolic expression affects emotions and/or the intellect, but it sometimes has actual physical effects. For example, the kinds of symbols people use and respond to can affect their health. People who use expressions such as "I can't stomach it," "I'm fed up," or "It's been eating away at me now for a year" are more likely to have more stomach ulcers than do others (*Chicago Daily News,* 1972). Symbolic days like birthdays have dramatic effects. In nursing homes, more persons die during the two months after birthdays than during the two months before (Lewis & Lewis, 1972). Thomas Jefferson and John Adams both died on the Fourth of July, a date of tremendous significance for both of them (Koenig, 1972). Some people die soon after the death of a loved one—and sometimes from the same disease. Symbolic sympathy pains can become real (Koenig, 1972). According to Seigel, the words we say to ourselves can also cure disease and even stop hemorrhaging (1989).

Burke (1960) makes an argument that language is symbolic action, and that may be an explanation of why words have almost magical possibilities. We know that words are central to most religious beliefs (e.g., see John 1:1, and in Genesis God speaks with each act of creation) and are usually spoken at sacramental enactments (i.e., marriage or the burial of the dead) in most if not all religions. Words are also important in law (e.g., the defendant must plead "guilty" or "not guilty" unless handicapped, and the verdict and sentence must also be spoken).

Not only do symbols deeply affect individuals, but they also serve as a kind of psychological cement for holding a society or culture together. Traditionally, a sacred hoop representing the four seasons of the earth and the four directions from which weather might come served as the central life metaphor for the Lakota Indians. The hoop's crossed thongs symbolized the sacred tree of life and the crossroads of life. A Lakota holy man named Black Elk (1971) explained the symbolic power of the circle for his people:

> You have noticed that everything an Indian does is in a circle, and that is because the Power of the World always works in circles, and everything tries to be round. In the old days when we were a strong and happy people, all our power came to us from the sacred hoop of the nation and so long as the hoop was unbroken the people flourished.... Everything the Power of the World does is done in a circle.... Even the seasons form a great circle in their changing and always come back again to where they were. The life of a man is a circle from childhood to childhood and so it is in everything where power moves. Our tipis were round like the nests of birds and these were always set in a circle, the nation's hoop, a nest of many nests where the Great Spirit meant for us to hatch our children (p. 134).

Black Elk believed that his tribe had lost all its power or "medicine" when forced out of traditional round tepees and into square reservation houses.

What symbols serve as the cultural cement for our way of life: the flag, the Constitution, the home, competition, and sports? What are the symbols that unite our diverse cultural segments? What might someone of Chinese heritage use for cultural cement? References to wisdom and age occur frequently in Chinese literature from the past to the present. What about someone of Indian extraction? East European? A good place to find the central symbols of our culture is in the language used in advertisements. Most ads promise a benefit to the consumer, elaborate on it, provide proof, and give a call to action. Benefits must reflect our wants and needs. Elaboration and proof probably reflect our need for knowledge. And we are an action-based society, as we shall see when we discuss cultural premises.

IN LOW TRACTION CONDITIONS, QUADRA-DRIVE™ FINDS AN ELIGIBLE RECEIVER AND SENDS ALL THE POWER* TO IT.

(AND YOU THOUGHT QUARTERBACKS HAD TO THINK FAST.)

FIGURE 6.2 Consider the cultural values underlying this ad for Jeep. Notice the "chalk talk" imagery and the references to football.

SOURCE: The marks JEEP® and QUADRA DRIVE™ are trademarks of DaimlerChrysler and are used with permission from DaimlerChrysler Corporation.

Now there's a revolutionary new four-wheel drive system that does the thinking, and the work, for you. Introducing Quadra-Drive, our most advanced four-wheel drive system ever. If only one wheel has traction, Quadra-Drive seeks that wheel out, then transfers all the power* to it. And, unlike some other systems, it works both front-to-rear and side-to-side. In fact, Quadra-Drive is the only system in the world that delivers maximum power all the time. So Jeep, Grand Cherokee can pull you out of situations other 4x4s just couldn't handle.

For further information about our newest, most capable sport utility ever,** please visit us online at www.jeep.com or call 1-800-925-JEEP.

Jeep

THERE'S ONLY ONE

THE ALL-NEW JEEP GRAND CHEROKEE
THE MOST CAPABLE SPORT UTILITY EVER"

*Sends 100% of the developed engine torque. **Based on AMCI overall on- and off-road performance tests using Grand Cherokee with available Quadra-Drive™ and V8 engine. †Optional. Jeep is a registered trademark of DaimlerChrysler.

To be short and concise, the ads and slogans "distill" or simplify complex ideas. This boiling down of meaning is called **synecdoche**, and politicians frequently use it. They know that concise words and phrases often become part of the evening news, thus acting as unpaid advertisements. The words also suggest a common denominator between persuader and persuadee. In an ad in *Newsweek,* the AARP used the slogan "Let's Not Stick Our Kids with the Bill!" referring to its opposition to proposed changes to the Social Security system. The phrase unified members and nonmembers of the organization to object to the proposed changes. Consider the verbal and nonverbal symbols in Figure 6.2, such as the words "Quadra-Drive™," the football "chalk talk" image, and the picture of the Jeep taking a corner. Do these words and symbols reflect any of the central values of our culture? What about AARP's use of the word "stick" in its slogan?

Political rhetoric also reflects our cultural values. Two important words used by politicians are "freedom" and "equality." As columnist David

---

BOX 6.1   Meet Mediamatic.Net

 Go to www.mediamatic.net and find numerous examples of how our new digital world is changing not only the persuasive symbols in language but in other forms of symbol making such as interactive film, virtual reality, diagramming a speech in space, mob-tagging discourse, architecture as a criminal act, video letters, and many other fascinating items on language and other symbols. Be sure to visit the Mediamatic Supermarket while you're there and learn how to get a Mediamatic t-shirt.

Broder (1984) noted, "Words are important symbols, and . . . 'freedom' and 'equality' have defined the twin guideposts of American Democracy" (p. 41). The words have the thematic qualities to stir patriotic emotions. However, they are not rated the same by all persons. As Broder notes, "Socialists rank both words high, while persons with fascist tendencies rank both low; communists rank 'equality' high but 'freedom' low, and conservatives rate 'freedom' high but 'equality' low" (p. 41).

Considerable power in linguistic symbols resides in their functional, semantic, and thematic dimensions. Not only do words reveal motives, but they also affect our self-image and express cultural ideals. Let's examine tools for analyzing these dimensions of language in persuasion.

TOOLS FOR ANALYZING PERSUASIVE SYMBOLS

Becoming aware of the three dimensions of language and nonverbal symbols helps us to become responsible receivers of persuasion. We can use various tools for the analysis of persuasion to focus our critical eyes and ears on more specific aspects of language symbols.

Tools for the Functional Dimension

Two tools for analyzing the functional dimension of language symbols in persuasion are language critic Richard Weaver's grammatical categories (especially regarding sentence and word types) and the effects of word order or syntax in sentences.

Weaver's Grammatical Categories.   Language theorist and pioneer Richard Weaver (1953) suggested that the type of sentence preferred by an individual offers clues as to that person's worldview (the way the person uses information and comes to conclusions). Weaver discussed some persuaders' preference for simple sentences, compound sentences, or complex sentences.

Simple sentences express a single complete thought or point and must contain one subject or noun and one action word or verb and an object ("He hit the ball"). Persuaders who prefer simple sentences don't see the world as a very complex place. Such a person "sees the world as a conglomerate of things . . . [and] seeks to present certain things as eminent against a background of matter uniform or flat" (p. 120). The simple sentence sets the subject off from the verb and object. There is a clear foreground and background in simple sentences, and they highlight cause and effect.

Compound sentences consist of two or more simple sentences joined by a conjunction such as "and" or "but." Weaver observed that the compound sentence sets things either in balance ("He ran, and he ran fast") or in opposition ("He ran, but she walked"). The compound sentence expresses either resolved or unresolved tension. According to Weaver, it "conveys that completeness and symmetry which the world ought to have" (p. 127). Persuaders using compound sentences see the world in terms of opposites or similarities. When you encounter compound sentences, try to identify the tension and the symmetry (or lack of it) in them.

Complex sentences also contain two or more distinct components, but not all the components stand alone as complete simple or compound sentences. Some of the elements in the sentences rely on another element in the sentence to be fully understood. Once, in speaking about word choice, Mark Twain used a complex sentence: "Whenever we come upon one of these intensely right words in a book or a newspaper, the resulting effect is physical as well as spiritual and electrically prompt" (Lederer, 1991, p. 128). The first portion of Twain's sentence ("Whenever . . . newspaper") could not stand alone; it is dependent on the last half of the sentence ("the resulting . . . prompt"), which could stand alone. The complex sentence features an intricate world with multiple causes and effects at the same time—dependency and independency or completeness and incompleteness. Weaver (1953) said it "is the utterance of a reflective mind" that tries "to express some sort of hierarchy" (p. 121). Persuaders who use complex sentences often express basic principles and relationships, with the independent clauses more important than dependent ones, as in this description by an ex-Olympic athlete:

> But after having represented the United States in five Olympic track and field teams from 1980 to 1991, I certainly have a feel for what the next class of Olympians is doing now. . . . if you are lucky enough to make it, there is the singular drama of Olympic competition (Lewis, 1999, p. 56).

Weaver (1953) also had some observations about types of words. For example, people react to **nouns** (which are defined as the name of a person, place, or thing) as if they were the things they name. Nouns "express things whose being is completed, not . . . in process, or whose being depends upon some other being" (p. 128). A persuader's noun use can reveal clues to his or her perceptions of things. When persuaders reduce persons to the level of things or objects by name calling, they do so for a reason—to deal with the people as objects, not as subjects or human beings.

According to Weaver, **adjectives** function to add to the noun, to make it special. The dictionary defines adjectives as "words that modify nouns . . . by limiting, qualifying or specifying" (*American Heritage Dictionary,* 1985). For example, "the little

blue Ford hybrid with the Alabama plates" limits, qualifies, and specifies which vehicle we mean. For Weaver, adjectives were "question begging," and showed uncertainty. If you must modify a noun, you're uncertain about it in the first place. To Weaver the only certain adjectives are dialectical (good and bad, hot and cold, light and dark). Examining a persuader's adjective use can reveal his or her uncertainty and what they see in opposition to what.

Adverbs, to Weaver, are words of judgment. The dictionary defines adverbs as "words that modify verbs, adjectives, or other adverbs" (*American Heritage Dictionary,* 1985). Adverbs represent a community judgment that helps us to agree with what the persuader thinks we believe. For example, adverbs such as "surely," "certainly," and "probably" suggest agreement. When persuaders say, "Surely we all know that thus-and-such is so," they imply that the audience agrees with them. Such adverbs encourage interactive co-creation.

Syntax. In addition to using word or sentence types to analyze persuaders' messages, we can look at the syntax used. **Syntax** is defined as "the pattern or structure of the word order in sentences or phrases." How can that have a persuasive effect? Word order can either alert or divert the reader/listener. Consider the difference between these two sentences:

- Before bombing the terrorist headquarters, we made sure the target was the right one.
- We were sure the target was the right one before bombing the terrorist headquarters.

In the first sentence, the dependent element occurs at the beginning of the sentence ("Before . . .") and alerts the reader/listener to the conditions needed before taking action. The independent element expresses the main point of the sentence. In the second sentence, the action comes first, and the dependent element focuses the attention of the listener/reader on the justification for the action.

Some persuaders place emotional or surprising words at the beginning of a sentence to reduce the impact of what follows. The audience focuses on the evidence because of the emotionality of the claim. For example, the speaker might say, "There is no greater hypocrite than the animal rights advocate who opposes the use of animals in research labs during the day and then goes home and has beef, pork, or chicken for dinner!" The reader/listener knows beforehand that the claim is about hypocrisy, and they focus on the reasons for the claim. The sentence is dramatic and creates a puzzle— "There is no greater hypocrite than whom?" we ask ourselves.

The other side of the coin is the speaker who diverts attention from the evidence by hiding the claim at the end of the sentence. This makes the audience wonder where all this evidence is leading. The speaker says, "The animal rights advocate who opposes the use of rats in the research lab and then goes home to eat beef, pork, or chicken is the kind of hypocrite we don't need in this country!" The drama of the sentence is reduced, and the power of the evidence diminished because the audience wonders about the speaker's destination.

Communication scholar L. H. Hosman (2002) notes that language variations affect one of three elements of the persuasion process: "judgment of speaker, message comprehension and recall, or attitude toward the message" (p. 372), and that these effects are crucial in information processing. This, of course, brings us back to the Elaboration Likelihood Model (ELM), and the old debate over the comparative effectiveness of emotional appeals (peripheral processing) and logical ones (central processing). Hosman also reports that active sentence structure influences perceived believability, clarity, appeal, and attractiveness in print advertisements in different ways than does passive sentence structure. "The nature of a sentence's grammatical construction or of a narrative's construction has important persuasive consequences" (p. 374). Sentence structure and word choice can reveal the persuader's motives and act as indicators of information-processing channels being used in the ELM.

To learn more about how sentence structure is used in evaluating such potentially important messages as hate letters, access InfoTrac College Edition, and enter the words "sentence structure" in the search engine. Read the article titled "More Than a Figure of Speech" by Jerrold Post. Report to the class what you discover about using sentence structure to evaluate threats. Also enter the words "hate mail" in the search engine, and examine a few of the articles listed there. What do you think about the use of language in hate mail?

Tools for the Semantic Dimension

While the functional dimension carries important verbal and nonverbal meanings, the semantic dimension of co-created interactive meaning carries the bulk of persuasion in most messages.

Strategic Uses of Ambiguity. Some think it unethical for persuaders to communicate in intentionally ambiguous ways, but they quite often do just that. They try to be unclear, vague, and general to allow for the broadest possible degree of common ground, identification, and co-creation of meaning. They want each receiver to fill in his or her own private meanings or connotations for the particular words or symbols. This strategy results in the largest number of interpretations and thus creates the largest potential audience for the persuader's brands, candidates, or causes. It also pleases as many and offends as few persons as possible. Receivers need to identify intentional ambiguity and analyze the reason(s) for the lack of clarity.

Persuaders use several methods to create strategic ambiguity. One is to choose words that can be interpreted in many (often contradictory) ways. A politician may support "responsibility in taxation and the cost of educating our youngsters." Those who think teachers are underpaid might hear this as a call for increasing funding for education. Those who hold the opposite view could as easily interpret the statement as meaning that education spending needs to be cut. The key word that increases ambiguity is "responsibility." The speaker or writer does not say what cause he or she favors. Another ambiguous word is "astronomical," as in "The budgetary implications of the war in Iraq are astronomical." Does this mean millions or billions or hundreds of billions of dollars? Depending on one's position, several meanings might result. Another way to create strategic ambiguity is to use phrases like "noted authorities on the subject seem to concur that, . . . ," which appear to lend support and credibility to the persuader's point. Communication scholar E. M. Eisenberg (1984) held that strategic uses of ambiguity can help get agreement on things like mission statements and at the same time allow individuals to interpret the statements as the persuader hopes.

In some cultures ambiguity is considered offensive. Listeners want to "cut to the chase" and stop wasting time. Persuadees in other cultures (such as Japan) value talking around the point and establishing a relationship before talking business. Still others want to mull things over and look at the issue from several perspectives.

Persuaders also create ambiguity when they juxtapose or combine words or phrases in startling ways that present issues in a new light. For example, the term "born again" is persuasive to many people. It suggests that the person's earlier religious beliefs were weak, and that their conversion caused the person to be spiritually re-created. Some born-again lobbyists labeled themselves the "Moral Majority," creating persuasive intentional ambiguity. The term was ambiguous because the group wasn't a majority but a minority, yet it had great persuasive appeal as media preachers created what political researchers Dan Nimmo and James Combs (1984) called "the Electronic Church." Another highly ambiguous term is "Moral Decay." It reminds us of "tooth decay," which nobody likes.

How can we defend ourselves against ambiguous language? The semanticists advise using increasing specificity about and concrete elaborations on any ambiguous term by using extentional devices to clarify meaning. Semioticians advise us to seek meanings in persuasive "texts" by digging into various verbal and nonverbal codes and signifiers in the text. Doing this helps determine the real thing being "signified." Advertisers use semiotics to devise global marketing and advertising strategies (Domzal & Kernan, 1993). Examining the denotations and connotations of persuasive symbols also helps us study the semantic dimension of language. Other tools address the semantic dimension of language. Among the more useful tools addressing the semantic dimension of language is the dramatistic approach suggested by Kenneth Burke.

To learn more about the uses of strategic ambiguity, access InfoTrac College Edition, and type the words "strategic ambiguity" in the search engine. Select one of the periodical references by Jim Paul, and learn how business uses strategic ambiguity.

Burke's Dramatism.   In addition to his ideas on language discussed in Chapters 1 and 5, Burke offered students of persuasion a theory and a tool for analyzing the semantic dimension of language. He called his theory **dramatism**, and his tool of analysis the **pentad**.

Dramatism maintains that the basic model used by humans to explain various situations is the narrative story or drama. Burke (1960) thought of the drama as "a philosophy of language" capable of describing and analyzing a wide variety of human symbolic acts such as language use. He focused on the differences between action (which is motivated) and motion (which is not motivated). Basic bodily functions, such as sweating or digestion, are unmotivated nonsymbolic acts. Action requires motivation and the ability to use language symbolically. We bring the action into being, and language use is thus a kind of symbolic action—it is motivated. Burke believed that we choose words because of their dramatic potential and that different individuals find certain elements in the drama more potent than others.

Burke's model, the dramatistic pentad, as its name implies, has five central elements: scene, act, agent, agency, and purpose (see Figure 6.3). **Scene** includes physical location, the situation, time, social place, occasion, and other elements. The scene could be something like "Campaign 2008," "the Oval Office," a website, or *The Oprah Winfrey Show*. Scenically oriented persons feel the scene should be a "fit container" for the action, and believe that changes in the scene will cause other changes—drilling for oil in the Arctic National

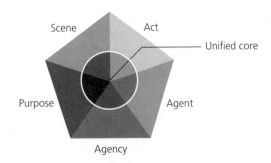

FIGURE 6.3 The five elements of dramatism ultimately affect one another, and each emerges from a common unified core—the drama itself.

Wildlife Reserve can result in a change in the ecology, perhaps a catastrophic change. They also believe that if gays are permitted to join the armed forces there will be less discrimination. The Clinton–Lewinsky scandal was distasteful because the Oval Office was the container for the act—not a fitting scene for sexual dalliance. The Lincoln Memorial was a "fit" scene for Martin Luther King, Jr.'s, "I Have a Dream" speech. The setting helped make the speech memorable.

Act refers to any motivated or purposeful action. In persuasive messages, the verb is the best indicator of the act. After all, verbs are defined as words that describe acts or actions, so looking at the verb is the best place to start applying the term *act* to your analysis. The words and actions taken by a person, and their appropriateness for the scene, ultimately affect outcomes.

Access InfoTrac College Edition, and enter the words "word choice" in the search engine. Examine the items regarding word choice in advertising from InfoTrac; the item from *ETC*, the journal of general semantics; and the item in the *Journal of Direct Marketing* entitled "The Future of 'force communication'" are especially insightful.

Agent is Burke's term for the person or group of persons who take action in the scene. They are the actors or characters who make things happen (the police officer, the corrupt politician, the

FIGURE 6.4 In Burke's terms, the agent is the focus of this ad, as you can see by the two fishermen, but other elements of the pentad are apparent also.

SOURCE: Reprinted by permission of Southern Comfort Company.

terrorist, Howard Stern, and so on). Figure 6.4 has an agent focus, as can be seen from the two youthful fishermen who are the central agents in the ad. Factors such as hatred, instinct, greed, or jealousy sometimes motivate agents. Countries and organizations (e.g., UN peacekeeping forces, the N.R.A., or pro-choice groups) also act as agents. Agent-oriented persuaders believe that strong, honest, and well-intended individuals determine the outcome of important events and even of history. And, on the other hand, they also believe that unthinking, deceitful, or dishonest agents cause bad outcomes.

Agency is the tool, method, or means used by persuaders to accomplish their ends. Some auto companies now focus on development of the fuel cell and hydrogen energy as the agencies to solve our dependence on fossil fuels. Shakespeare's

Hamlet used the play within a play as the agency to establish his uncle's guilt. Calvin Klein used nudity and prepubescent females as agencies to draw attention to Obsession Night for Men. Wheaties uses pictures of famous athletes on its packages to promote the brand as "the Breakfast of Champions." Communication strategies also act as agencies (such as intensifying one's own good points or others' bad ones).

Purpose is the reason an agent acts in a given scene using a particular agency. The persuader's true purpose can be more, or less, apparent. The U.S. Army's old recruiting slogan, "Be All That You Can Be," suggested that the purpose for enlisting was improving your skills to maximize your potential. Its new slogan, "Join the Army of One," suggests a different purpose for enlisting: you can make an individual difference and develop your skills. When the amount of aid sent by the United States to victims of a disastrous Indonesian tsunami was low compared to that sent by much smaller countries, critics in this country and abroad interpreted the action as meaning that the administration was less interested in helping others than in saving money.

These five elements can help develop a persuasive strategy in interpersonal relationships. For example, if you were trying to get a date for a rock concert, you might emphasize the scene, describing the auditorium, crowd, sounds, costumes, lighting, colors, and so on. An alternative strategy would be to focus on the act, describing the kinds of music and the interactions between performers and audience. You might also choose to focus on the agent, describing the musicians, their reputations, and their appearance. If you chose to feature agency, you might mention the new digital sound system, the unique instruments used, and special effects. Finally, you could feature purpose by telling your prospective date, "to be really 'cool,' you shouldn't miss attending the concert, and you might meet other interesting people, too."

In any given situation, all these elements of the pentad operate simultaneously to a greater or lesser degree (see Figure 6.5). Burke compared them in pairs, or "ratios," to identify a persuader's "key" term. For example, the scene can be compared with each of the other terms one at a time and we can determine which term seems most important by a process of elimination. For instance, if scene supercedes act, agent, and agency but not purpose, we can then infer that purpose is a good candidate for the persuader's key term. But purpose must be compared to act, agent, and agency to see if it supercedes those terms of the pentad.

There are ten possible ratios or pairs of terms. In *Hamlet,* for example, the dramatic tension created in the scene–act ratio comes from the fact that Hamlet's mother has married his uncle (the act) during the period of mourning (part of the scene) for Hamlet's father, the king, who has died mysteriously. His uncle inherits the throne and marries Hamlet's mother less than one month after the funeral (also part of the scene). Clearly the scene was tainted by the act. Disturbed by this imbalance, Hamlet curses his mother, saying, "She married. O, most wicked speed, to post with such dexterity to incestuous sheets!" Later, Hamlet asks Horatio whether he came to court for the funeral or the wedding, and expresses his anger in these bitter words: "Thrift, thrift, Horatio! The funeral baked meats did coldly furnish the marriage tables."

We also frequently see the persuasive power of the scene–act ratio in advertisements. For example, in Figure 6.6, the scene—the state of Alaska—offers tourists great fishing with the words "If you like your fish wild" and "twelve native species, all of them pugnacious." It notes that Alaska has "two oceans, two seas, and hundreds of bays," thereby improving the scene–act balance. After all, where but in the biggest state would you expect the biggest fight with the biggest fish?

Scene can also interact with the other elements of the pentad. In the scene–agent ratio, balance or imbalance again can indicate potent persuasion or high drama—comedy, tragedy, or melodrama. In Hitchcock's classic film *Psycho,* viewers see a scene–agent imbalance when Anthony Perkins tells Janet Leigh that he has "stuffed" all the animal specimens in the motel office. Then we see him spy on her through a secret peephole in the eye of one of the specimens. This is not the behavior of a normal motel owner. It makes the audience uneasy. This uneasiness

She goes
two blocks to
pre-school.
But college is
just around
the corner.

Your tomorrows depend on the consistent performance of your long-term investments. And that's why investors have made Kemper one of America's largest asset managers. For over forty years, the Kemper Family of Mutual Funds has been dedicated to the kind of steady, long-term performance that builds tomorrows today. To learn more, talk to your financial representative at this location.

We're Building Tomorrows Today™

Fund performance cannot be guaranteed and will fluctuate. Before you invest in a fund, carefully read the brochure and prospectus for more complete information, including management fees and expenses. ©1994 Kemper Financial Services, Inc.   219631

NAT-72B 1/94

FIGURE 6.5 This ad demonstrates the use of all the elements of Burke's pentad. The scene is a family home. The agents are father and daughter. The act is nurturing, and the purpose is planning for the future. As is often the case, the product being advertised is the agency. This ad was designed in response to another ad Kemper ran in which a father is planning for his son to go to college in response to criticisms that the company was sexist in suggesting that only males were destined for college. Knowing this, what are the purpose and agency in the current ad?

SOURCE: Used by permission of Kemper Financial Services.

implies the strong possibility of danger. The tension caused by the scene–agent imbalance is increased when we hear Perkins and his "mother" (whom he also "stuffed") arguing at the Victorian house near the motel (see Figure 6.7). We want to warn Leigh to go to another motel or at least to "lock the bathroom door." Hitchcock uses scene–agent tension throughout the rest of the film and keeps the audience on the edge of their seats.

Any of the other ten possible pairs of elements of the pentad (act–purpose, act–agency, scene–purpose, scene–agency, and so forth) might be examined to discover a persuader's key term or element. Burke believed that a persuader's key term infuses every aspect of life—home, family, job, political choices, and philosophy of life. Identifying a persuader's key terms or elements alerts us to the motives of and reasons for the persuasion and helps us predict

FIGURE 6.6 How are the scene and the act balanced in this ad?
SOURCE: Used by permission of the Alaska Division of Tourism.

FIGURE 6.7 The imbalance in the scene/act ratio in Hitchcock's film classic *Psycho* heightens dramatic tension.
SOURCE: Used with permission of Doug Walker.

future persuasive appeals. As you encounter persuasion, try to listen for the key term being used.

Tools for the Thematic Dimension

We've seen that the thematic dimension of language is that quality in certain words or sets of words that gives them a texture or "feel." While the words do have a variety of semantic meanings and syntactical functions, their most important persuasive aspect is their ability to set a mood, a feeling, or a tone or theme for the persuasion. For example, Abraham Lincoln set the theme for his famous Gettysburg Address with these words: "Fourscore and seven years ago our forefathers brought forth on this continent a new nation, conceived in liberty and dedicated to the proposition that all men are created equal." How far less stirring the speech would have been if he had said,

"Eighty-seven years ago the signers of the Declaration of Independence started a new country designed to assure us of freedom and equality." The two sentences have equivalent semantic and functional meanings, but the obvious difference between them lies in their texture.

We also noted how the repetition of consonants (alliteration) or vowels (assonance) carries thematic meaning. The advertisements for Satin cigarettes, for example, used alliteration to create a thematic meaning for the brand—"Smooth. Silky. Satin. Cigarettes." Or consider the slogan for Lexus: "The Relentless Pursuit of Perfection." It sounds unstoppable.

Sometimes parallel sentence structure communicates a thematic meaning. For example, consider the no-nonsense theme in the parallel sentences in an ad promoting MTV to advertisers. The copy accompanies a picture of a male in his twenties in an easy chair holding a TV remote, and reads,

> If this guy doesn't know about you, you're toast. He's an opinion leader. He watches MTV. Which means he knows a lot more than just what CDs to buy and what movies to see. He knows what clothes to wear, and what credit card to buy them with. And he's no loner. He heads up a pack. What he eats, his friends eat. What he wears, they wear. What he likes, they like. And what's he never heard of . . . well . . . you get the idea. MTV. A darn good way to influence the MTV Generation (*Advertising Age*, 1993, p. S-3).

Thematic meaning also can come from the use of metaphors or onomatopoeia. Let's turn now to several other tools for discovering the thematic meaning in persuasive messages. These include finding metaphorical themes; noting the use of sensory language; looking for god, devil, and charismatic terms; identifying the pragmatic and unifying styles; and use of semiotics to determine the thematic meanings of nonverbal symbols or "signifiers."

Metaphorical Style. Persuaders set the mood for persuadees by repeatedly using certain sounds, figures of speech, and images. Recent research on the effects of metaphors shows that using them increases the credibility of the persuader because they make the persuader seem more dynamic and interesting. This is especially so when the source uses only a single metaphor instead of multiple ones (Sopory & Dillard, 2002). Dan Hahn (1998) applies another archetypal metaphor—that of water as a dangerous image. Notice the positivism and the negativity of the underlined water images:

> Due to foggy thinking, the tide has been running against freedom and we are sinking in a swampland of collectivism. Therefore, despite the detractors who say don't rock the boat, the campaign we launch here will set the tide running again in the cause of freedom. The past will be submerged, and we will travel democracy's ocean highway where freedom will accompany the rising tide of prosperity (p. 115).

Hahn reminds us of other associations we have with the water metaphor. It is life giving and is also the basic element from which life emerged (p. 115). Other archetypal metaphors include references to wind and windstorms, blood and blood bonds, the locomotive as representative of the economy, and the boxing ring or the horse race as stand-ins for any of life's contests and struggles. Roads and maps also serve as metaphors for planning (e.g., "the roadmap to peace" in the Middle East).

Metaphors also help in **framing** the issue or topic to give the audience a way of seeing things. For example, imagine a persuader trying to inform the audience about the AIDS crisis in Africa, where grandparents are now raising most children due to the premature deaths of the parents. A good metaphor might be warfare, with the persuader saying, "We're in the early stages of the battle here with the veterans of past battles having to fight to the bitter end. It's not going to end with a single decisive weapon." The audience sees the fight against the disease is likely to be a long one with no real miracle cures.

To learn more about the power of metaphor, access InfoTrac College Edition, and type the word "metaphor" in the search engine. Peruse the more than fifty periodical titles, and choose some articles to read. Report your findings to your class.

Sensory Language. Courtroom communication expert Stephanie L. Swanson (1981) maintained that most effective lawyers rely on words relating to one or more of the five senses: sight, sound, touch, smell, and taste. She speculated that jurors respond to the particular sensory information channel they prefer. How could a persuader use these preferences? Suppose an attorney asks three witnesses to describe an automobile accident. The witness preferring the auditory channel might say something like, "I was walking down Oak Street, when I heard the screech of brakes, and then a sickening sound of crashing glass and metal, and someone screamed." The witness who prefers the visual channel might say, "I saw this blue Beamer coming around the corner practically on two wheels. Then he hit the brakes, and it looked like the car slid sideways toward me. Then I saw his front end make a mess of the little Geo." The witness who prefers the kinesthetic channel might say, "I had this feeling that something was about to happen, and when it did I felt frightened and helpless, and I cringed as the cars crumpled up like scrap paper." Swanson advised attorneys to "listen closely to the sensory language used by your clients...try to respond in kind—matching the sensory language of the other person" (p. 211). She suggested attending to the kinds of words used by individuals during the juror selection process—then "tailor your language to your listeners' primary sensory channel. You can 'paint a picture' for a visual person, 'orchestrate the testimony' for an auditory person, and 'touch the heart' of the

aochsner@northernstar.info ©2005 Al Ochsner/All Rights Reserved

FIGURE 6.8 It is clear that giving tickets is a god term for the evil queen, but getting a parking ticket from any of her helper dwarfs is a devil term for her.

SOURCE: Used with permission of Al Ochsner.

kinesthetic individual. Using sensory language lets the jurors feel that your discourse is directed toward them individually" (p. 211). The use of sensory language acts like an interactive medium, and it increases the likelihood for the co-creation of meaning.

Thus, in trying to identify a persuader's use of the thematic dimension of language, explore the sensory language used in the persuasion.

God, Devil, and Charismatic Terms. Another thematic or textural element of style in persuasion is the development of families of terms. Persuaders like to divide the world into tidy categories that prompt co-created meanings. Richard Weaver (1953) held that one of these category sets is made up of **god terms** and **devil terms**. Although terms or labels make up only parts of propositions, they often link with other terms or labels to shape a message or a persuasive argument. Weaver defined a god term as an expression "about which all other expressions are ranked as subordinate and serving dominations and powers . . . its force imparts to the others their lesser degree of force" (p. 211). Weaver saw a god term as an unchallenged word (or phrase) demanding sacrifice or obedience. He used three terms as examples of god terms: "progress," "fact," and "science." *Progress* still persuades, but is hampered by negative associations—pollution, for example. *Science* lost some of its credibility in recent

times also, due to negative associations such as nuclear power or genetic engineering.

Devil terms are just the opposite. They are "terms of repulsion" and express negative values. As Weaver put it, "They generate a peculiar force of repudiation" (pp. 210–215). Today's god and devil terms include "the environment," "green," "the family," "security," "terrorism," "deficit spending," "politically correct," "technology," "dittoheads," "surfing the Web," and "budget surplus." God and devil terms can vary in a diverse culture. For example, Western culture places considerable value on the term "forgiveness," considering it the correct response when one is wronged. Other cultures believe "forgiveness" is a devil term—the sissies' way out For them the god term when wronged is "revenge." Such god and devil terms alert you to potential persuasive appeals aimed at you or that you might choose to use in your own persuasion.

As we move further into the new millennium, other god and devil terms are emerging. Some of the more recent god terms include "family/family values," "low fat," "rule of law," "green vehicles," "air security," "financial security," "education," "phased retirement," "weight loss," "nutrition," "fuel cell," and "hybrid car." Try to discover others as you search for the thematic dimensions of words or terms used in advertising or political and ideological statements.

Weaver said that the connotations of certain negative terms can sometimes be reversed, making the terms neutral or even positive. Take, for example, the expression "wasted" or "getting wasted." Its use during the 1970s referred to killing Viet Cong or others perceived to be the enemy. Later, it referred to getting drunk or "stoned." Today, "wasted" has recovered its original meaning of "squandered" and refers to such topics as corporate trust, energy, and credibility.

Weaver described **charismatic terms** as "terms of considerable potency whose referents it is virtually impossible to discover. Their meaning seems inexplicable unless we accept the hypothesis that their content proceeds out of a popular will that they shall mean something" (p. 48). His examples are the words "freedom" and "democracy," which have no apparent concrete referent but still seem to have great potency and serve as god terms for U.S. foreign policy.

The terms "budget surplus" and "fanning the flames of freedom" became charismatic recently, and most agreed that a "budget surplus" was great after decades of "budget deficits" (a devil term). Nearly everyone agreed on the wisdom of "saving Social Security." Another candidate for a charismatic term is "recycling." With the growing awareness of declining natural resources, the concept of recycling applied to a host of things, such as paper, plastic, aluminum, glass. "Patriot" and "patriotic" recently became charismatic terms, but they were devil terms during the Vietnam era.

Pragmatic and Unifying Styles.   Persuaders tend to rely on one of two persuasive styles—pragmatic or unifying. **Pragmatic** persuaders want to convince neutral or opposition listeners. They want to change minds instead of reinforcing existing beliefs. Politicians speaking at a news conference rather than at a rally of their supporters tend to favor the pragmatic style. **Unifying** persuaders use a different style because they want to motivate people who already believe what they're going to say; they just reinforce beliefs to whip up enthusiasm, dedication, or encouragement. Thus, when Rush Limbaugh, Howard Stern, Bill O'Reilly, and others speak to their respective television and radio audiences, they use the tactics of the unifying speaker—their audiences already believe them. The problems for pragmatic persuaders are clear—they must change opinion before they can expect action. Unifying persuaders can be much more idealistic, and use more emotional, less objective claims and evidence than the pragmatic persuader.

What stylistic devices typify these extremes? The unifying persuader focuses on the "then-and-there"—on the past or future—when things were ideal or when they might become ideal. Because the audience fills in the blanks, abstract language choice works well for unifying persuaders; their language frequently is poetic, emotional, and filled with imagery that excites the audience's imagination. Although there is little intellectually stimulating or requiring logical examination, lots of emotional and stirring things emerge. The unifying persuader is a sounding board for the audience and provides them with the gist of the message but not the details. The audience participates with unifying persuaders in the co-creation of the message. In fact, audiences sometimes participate actively by yelling encouragement to unifying persuaders or by repeating phrases to underscore their words—"Right on" or "Amen, brother" or "Tell it like it is."

Pragmatic persuaders, because they need to win the audience, avoid appealing to abstract ideals. They use concrete words, focusing on facts instead of images and undisputed things. They avoid depicting an ideal situation in "then-and-there" terms. Rather, they focus on real aspects of immediate problems of the "here-and-now"—things that seem realistic, not idealistic. Pragmatic persuaders orient their message to the present instead of the future, and tend to focus on facts and statistics instead of imagery. Their messages pass through the central information-processing route of the ELM instead of the peripheral route, as is probably the case for unifying persuasion. Consider these words of a pragmatic persuader describing skydiving:

> When I stand in the door of an airplane in flight, I alone am responsible for the decision to jump. If the winds, clouds or any other

conditions are unfavorable, I have the option of riding down in the plane—something I have done on several occasions. Neither the pilot nor the drop zone operator forces me to jump if I choose not to. Once a skydiver exits the plane there's no going back. One person and one person only has the responsibility of deploying the parachute . . . and executing a safe landing. . . . Skydiving is not a preprogrammed carnival thrill ride with simulated risk. . . .
While the trend in American society is to find someone else to blame for your own mistakes; that is not the way it is in skydiving. To suggest otherwise indicates total misunderstanding of the sport on the part of your reporters (Kallend, 2002, p. 8).

The language is concrete and prosaic, the references are here and now, and the persuader is trying to change the audiences' mind instead of uniting them. The pragmatic and unifying styles depend on the needs of the audience and the demands of the occasion, not on the needs of the speaker.

Semiotics and Signifiers.   We referred to the field of semiotics earlier as a way to study meaning. Its most important contemporary theorist is Umberto Eco. He proposed that the process of "signification" (or the giving of meaning to a "sign") has four elements: (1) the objects or conditions that exist in the world, (2) the signs available to represent these objects or conditions, (3) the set of choices among signs, or the repertoire of responses available for use, and (4) the set of rules of correspondence that we use to encode and decode the signs we make and interpret when we communicate.

This final characteristic most directly relates to the goal of this course—the discovery of the various **codes** or sets of rules used by persuaders and understood by persuadees in the process of co-creation. We know that when a stage manager lowers the lights and asks us to turn off our cell phones and pagers, the event is about to begin; this is an example of a code. We participate in our own persuasion by "agreeing with" the code(s) the persuaders use. We become critical consumers of persuasion by continually striving to uncover and reveal these codes (Eco, 1979).

We find more subtle examples of codes in some advertisements. For example, consider the ad for Bostonian shoes in Figure 6.9. What codes operate in this ad? Some seem obvious, but others are more subtle. In fact, some codes found in the ad embed themselves within other codes. The most obvious code is that the ad tries to sell the product, although the kind of product is not so clear. But we soon discover that the product is men's shoes. Another less obvious code is that the product is an upscale one, as indicated by the composition and copy of the ad and the price of the shoes—$105. The ad is understated, with little actual ad copy. Finally, the illustration is distinctively "fine art" in its composition. Within these codes, we find a more subtle code that is only implied and never directly stated. This code signifies the lifestyle that goes with the product. The shoes merely serve as an emblem of that lifestyle. What do we see in this photograph? Clearly, it is the "morning after" a satisfying night of lovemaking (notice the coffee cups and pastries on the bed, the negligee on the well-rumpled bedding, the indentations on both pillows). The lifestyle includes a fine home (notice the expensive furniture and the framed photographs on the nightstand in the upper left corner). This lifestyle includes expensive accessories such as the Rolex watch and the Mont Blanc pen on the dresser. The stylish suspenders, the theater ticket stubs slipped into the frame of the mirror, and the picture of a beautiful wife under the tickets signify a lifestyle that values the arts, stylishness, beauty, and physical attractiveness (note the snapshot of the man, bare-chested and muscular). Clearly, this ad carries a lot of meanings, "signified" by the verbal and nonverbal symbols being used (or perhaps misused). Its persuasive message must be co-created based on agreed upon and shared semiotic codes. The signifiers, or collection of objects in the room, probably trigger emotional values that the audience holds dear.

Although analyses like this intrigue us, they are difficult to carry out without some kind of systematic methodology. The fields of theoretic semiotics and applied semiotics (for example, advertising and image/political consulting) expanded rapidly in

---

BOX 6.2   Semiotics and the Culture of Circuses

Semiotician Paul Buissac (1976) offered some fascinating examples of codes in his semiotic analysis of circus acts, illustrating this idea of an easily discernible code understood by "children of all ages" around the world:

> Wild animal, tightrope, and trapeze acts never occur back to back in the circus...they are always interspersed with clown acts, small animal acts, magic acts, or the like. If a daring act is canceled, the entire order of acts needs to be altered because of audience expectations, tension reduction, and the need to communicate that the world is alternately serious and comedic....Death-defying acts also have a code—usually a five-step sequence. First, there is the introduction of the act by the ringmaster (a godlike figure able to control not only the dangers but the chaos of the circus). This introduction, with its music, lights, and revelation of dazzling and daring costumes, is followed by the "warm-up," in which minor qualifying tests occur: The animal trainer, dressed as a big-game hunter, gets all the animals to their proper positions; the trapeze artist, with his beautiful assistants, can easily swing out and switch trapeze bars in mid-air; the tightrope walker dances across the rope with ease. Then come the major tests or tricks: getting the tiger to dance with the lion, double trapeze switches, and walking the wire blindfolded. Having passed these tests, the circus performer then attempts the 'glorifying,' or 'death-defying,' test. It is always accompanied by the ringmaster's request for absolute silence and, ironically, by the band breaking the critical silence with a nerve-tingling drum roll. Then comes the feat itself: The animal tamer puts his head into the lion's mouth; the trapeze artist holds up a pair of beautiful assistants with his teeth, demonstrating his amazing strength; and the blindfolded tightrope walker puts a passenger on his shoulders and rides a bicycle backward across the high wire. Frequently, there is a close call: An unruly tiger tries to interfere with the "head-in-the-mouth" trick, there is a near miss on the trapeze or a stumble on the high wire, and so on. Once the glorifying test is passed, the ringmaster calls for applause as the act exits and then returns for a curtain call. This sequence is a 'code' we all understand. (n. p.)

Suppose the circus tent caught fire. What would be the appropriate code for the ringmaster to use in order to reduce panic?

---

recent times, and as receivers we need a simplified way to pin down their uses (or misuses) of symbols.

This brief discussion of the semiotic approach to language and meaning gives us another tool for discovering the important first premises emerging from language preferences and the images molded from them.

To learn how semiotics is used in advertising and marketing, access InfoTrac College Edition, and enter the word "semiotics" in the search engine. Look at the article by Frank and Stark in the *Journal of Advertising Research*. Read the abstract, and then read the article and reference its footnotes through the InfoTrac College Edition system. You might also look under the related-subjects category and go to the discourse analysis option. Some fascinating titles can be found in the signs and symbols option as well.

TUNING YOUR EARS
FOR LANGUAGE CUES

Consumers of persuasion need to become vigilant when processing and responding to persuasive messages. In the course of this vigilance, one of the most important things persuaders can do is tune their ears to language for various clues to style and motives. Using some of the tools described in this chapter helps. Applying the study questions at the end of this and other chapters also helps. There are at least three specific strategies you might use to make yourself more critical of style and to "decode" persuaders:

1. *Role-play the persuader.* Assume that you are the persuader. Now, shape the persuasion you wish to present. For example, if you favor high

Perfectly fitting and proper. This day. Every day.

Every decision should be as clear-cut as your choice of Bostonian. These wingtips are trimmer, more richly detailed. And more comfortable. With cushioned innersoles and glove-soft leather linings. About $105. For nearby stores, call 1-800-444-2624.

perfectly fitting and proper
BOSTONIAN
since 1899.

F I G U R E 6.9 What messages are implied by the "code" of physical objects in this ad (theater tickets, rumpled bedclothes, articles of clothing that seem to have been hurriedly discarded, an empty cocktail glass, and so on)?

SOURCE: Reprinted by permission of the Bostonian Shoe Company.

salaries for baseball players, frame a pragmatic message for half-hearted believers, those who are neutral, or others who are only moderately opposed. Would you mention the shortness of most players' careers? After all, they receive a relatively low overall salary across a lifetime. You might compare ballplayers to entertainers, who also make several million dollars per year for relatively little actual work time. If your audience were the players' union, you might bypass the numbers and use highly emotional and abstract language to motivate them—create images of club owners as rich bloodsuckers who use up the best years of an athlete's life, use then-and-there language, and refer to new goals of the group or to past abuses by the owners.

2. *Restate a persuasive message in various ways.* Ask yourself, "What other ways could I say this?" Try to determine how these alternatives change the intent and effects of the message.

B O X 6.3   Diversity and Semiotics

 Semiotics and cultural diversity are a particularly hot topic just now, and many websites will pop up when you enter the words into any search engine. If you want to try a favorite of mine go to www.aptalaska.net/~ron/FOOD%2005/glob/irrealis.htm, which is the website for Globalization Theory. Sample the links found there (e.g., modality irealis depicts a variety of global images and contradictions such as the superimposition of Chairman Mao's face on the U.S. Capital building) and discover how many things apply to semiotics. You might also enter the words "semiotics" and "cultural studies" in any search engine and discover more.

Communication scholar Arthur Asa Berger (2005) offers a methodology for doing semiotic analysis, and he provides a fairly simple checklist. First, he advises us to consider the persuasion aimed at us as "texts" to be read, and then to start looking for clues. He has a checklist of questions to ask when trying to read persuasive texts:

1. Isolate and analyze the important signs in the text.
    a. What are the important signifiers?
    b. What do they signify?
    c. Is there a system that unifies them?
    d. What codes can be found (for example, symbols of status, colors, or music)?
    e. Are ideological or sociological issues being addressed?
    f. How are they conveyed or hinted at?

2. Identify the central structure, theme, or model of the text.
    a. What forces are in opposition?
    b. What forces are teamed with each other?
    c. Do the oppositions or teams have psychological or sociological meanings? What are they?

3. Identify the narrative structure of the text. (That is, if a "story" is being told, what are its elements?)
    a. How does the sequential arrangement of events affect the meaning? What changes in meaning would result if they were altered?
    b. Are there any "formulaic" aspects to the text (for example, hard work leads to success, justice prevails, or honesty gets its reward)?

4. Determine whether the medium being used affects the text, and how.
    a. How are shots, camera angles, editing, dissolves, and so on used?
    b. How are lighting, color, music, sound, special effects, and so on used?
    c. How do paper quality, typefaces, graphics, colors, and so on contribute?
    d. How do the speaker's words, gestures, and facial expressions affect meaning?

5. Specify how the application of semiotic theory alters the original meaning ascribed to the text.

Try using the parts of Burke's pentad. For example, take the following slogan for Grand Marnier Liqueur—"There Are Still Places on Earth Where Grand Marnier Isn't Offered After Dinner." The words appear on a photo of a deserted island. The appeal is scenic. An agent-oriented version of this slogan claims that, "People of Taste Offer Grand Marnier." A purpose-oriented version might read, "Want to Finish the Conference? Offer Grand Marnier." An agency-oriented version might say, "Grand Marnier—From a Triple-Sec-Ret Recipe." The act-oriented message emphasizes action by saying, "Make a Move—Offer Grand Marnier."

3. *Attend to language features in discourse.* Don't allow yourself to passively buy into any persuasive advice. Instead, get into the habit of looking at each message's style. Analyze messages on billboards, in TV commercials, the language used by your parents when they try to persuade you, the wording on product packages, or in the phrases used in discussions between you and friends, enemies, or salespersons. Start listening not only to ideas but to word strategies—the packaging of those ideas. Focusing on these features gives you an intriguing pastime, and helps develop an ear for stylistic tip-offs.

WHAT DO YOU CALL A WOMAN WHO'S MADE IT TO THE TOP?

Ms

She's a better prospect than ever. Because we've turned the old *Ms* upside down to reflect how women are living today. And you're going to love the results.

The new *Ms* is witty and bold, with a large-size format that's full of surprises. Whether it's money, politics, business, technology, clothing trends, humor, or late-breaking news — if it's up-to-the-minute, it's part of the new *Ms*

So if you want to reach the top women consumers in America, reach for the phone. And call Linda Lucht, Advertising Director, *Ms Magazine*, One Times Square, New York, N.Y. 10036. Tel. (212) 704-8581.

The new Ms. As impressive as the woman who reads it.

FIGURE 6.10 Using the semiotic approach in Berger's checklist, uncover the meaning of this ad. Note that the woman has "lost" items from her pockets—a passport, the keys to an Audi, credit cards, a picture of herself drawn by her child, jewelry, aspirin, a champagne cork, a $100 bill, and other signs. What do they signify? How old is this woman? Is she sentimental? Busy?

SOURCE: Reprinted by permission of Ms. Magazine, ©1992.

REVIEW AND CONCLUSION

Responsible receivers of persuasion relate to the language persuaders choose. They gain insight by looking at the semantic connotations of the words being used. They look at word order, or syntax, and at the frequency of various parts of speech. The degree of ambiguity used by the persuader is often revealing, as in the dramatistic analysis suggested by Burke. The motifs and metaphors chosen by persuaders often reveal motives. Persuadees also need to look at the god, devil, and charismatic terms used, as well as the choice of pragmatic versus unifying styles. Finally, try to apply the semiotic approach to the interpretation of persuasive messages. All these critical devices improve with role-playing, restating, and developing awareness of the words, styles, and ideas used in co-created speech, TV ads, films, political slogans, social movements, or package designs.

KEY TERMS

When you have completed this chapter, you should be able to identify, explain, and give an example of the following words or concepts.

semantic dimension	complex sentences	act	devil terms
functional dimension	nouns	agent	charismatic terms
thematic dimension	adjectives	agency	pragmatic style
assonance	adverbs	purpose	unifying style
alliteration	syntax	metaphorical style	semiotics
synecdoche	dramatism	framing	codes
simple sentences	pentad	sensory language	
compound sentences	scene	god terms	

APPLICATION OF ETHICS

Considering Richard L. Johannesen's description of ethical standards in Chapter 2, do you consider the strategic use of ambiguity ethical, unethical, or dependent on the persuader's goal and the ultimate outcome? What if ambiguity convinces you to make an unwise purchase decision? What if government reports are ambiguous about sources of intelligence to protect their sources or to protect national security? What if optimistic but incomplete research about possible cures for a disease gives the individual sufferer a reason to hope?

What might be some ethical standards for the strategic uses of ambiguity? Support your proposed standards and apply them to sample cases like those in the preceding paragraph to demonstrate how well they might work. What shortcomings, if any, did you discover in your proposal?

QUESTIONS FOR FURTHER THOUGHT

1. Transcribe the lyrics of a popular song. Now analyze them according to the functional tools presented in this chapter. Is there a preference for a certain word type? A certain sentence structure? Is the message ambiguous or concrete? Explain.

2. Describe several semantic tools. What do you think is the pentadic perspective of the president of the United States? Of your instructor?

3. Describe the tools for a thematic or textural analysis of language, and use them to analyze the persuasion occurring in a recent political campaign. What do these analyses tell you about the candidate? Try the same thing with a recent advertising campaign.

4. What god terms work for your parents? What about their devil terms? Shape a request for something from your parents expressed in their god terms. What god terms motivate the user of the interactive medium being sold on www.livehunt.com?

5. How do unifying persuaders differ from pragmatic ones? Find examples of each type of persuader in your class, in persuasive attempts

of the past, or in defenders and opponents of some issue in your community. What differences exist between these two types? Which style seems more or less likely to carry unethical persuasive appeals? Describe the differences between semantics and semiotics. Which seems more objective? When might it be appropriate to use each approach? Do you use semantics and semiotics to both analyze and create persuasive messages and, if so, how?

6. What is the difference between a text and a symbol? What is the difference between a signifier and the signified?

7. If language use serves as a medium of communication, describe its interactivity. How is it used when delivered via interactive media? Describe some cultural differences in symbolic language use within subcultures.

 For online activities, go to the *Persuasion* book companion website at http://communication.wadsworth.com/larson11.

Identifying Persuasive First Premises

Underlying all means of analytically processing the symbols of persuasion is the ancient Aristotelian concept of the enthymeme and his triad of ethos, pathos, and logos. The enthymeme serves as the analytical metaphor or organizational device for Part II. Part II is a search for the types of major premises that work in enthymemes. We identify those major premises that most audiences believe and those that audiences can be convinced of to prompt action or change.

The first category of major premise is studied in Chapter 7. It is called the process (or psychological and emotional) premise. Process premises rely on psychological factors that operate in nearly all persuadees. Persuaders tie their product, candidate, or idea to these process premises, which are then used as the major premises in enthymematic arguments that have wide appeal. In terms of the Elaboration Likelihood Model (ELM), most process or emotional premises are dealt with in the peripheral information-processing path.

Chapter 8 covers a second category of major premises called logical or content premises. Their persuasiveness lies in the audience's belief in the truth or validity of the argument, and they get processed in the central channel of the ELM. You have probably noticed that there is considerable similarity between process premises and content premises. Process premises rely on psychological or emotional needs, whereas content premises rely on logical or rational patterns. We learn these patterns of inference beginning in early childhood, and they are reinforced throughout our lives. For instance, suppose we tell two-year-old children that if they continue to cry they will have to take a "time-out" or go without television or a particular toy. What we really are using is "if...then" reasoning, or the rational pattern that actions have consequences.

Chapter 9 examines cultural premises that rely on patterns of behavior or beliefs taught to us by our society. They resemble articles of faith for audiences. For example, Americans learn that when faced with a problem they must seek a solution to it, perhaps by establishing a task force or swallowing a pill. This seems so obvious that we are dumbstruck to discover that people from some other cultures prefer simply to accept the inevitable when faced with a problem. Problem solving is a culturally transmitted pattern for us. Knowing that, persuaders motivate us to take actions by portraying the actions as solutions. Clever persuaders can create problems and then sell us a cure. Cultural premises consist of the myths and values our society holds dear. Cultural premises are probably processed in the peripheral information-processing route of the ELM.

Chapter 10 explores nonverbal premises, which are sometimes more potent than sophisticated verbal premises. Often, nonverbal premises contribute to the ultimate success or failure of persuasion. These premises are usually processed almost unconsciously following the peripheral path of the elaboration likelihood model, and they can vary widely depending on one's culture or subculture.

As you read Part II, think of yourself as searching for major premises that you and an audience hold in common. Identifying these major premise types helps you to become a more skillful persuader, but also—and more important—a better and more critical consumer of persuasion.

7

Psychological or Process Premises: The Tools of Motivation and Emotion

LEARNING GOALS

After reading this chapter, you should be able to:

1. Identify, explain, and give examples of Packard's hidden needs. Give current examples.

2. Identify, explain, and give examples of Feig's hot buttons. How do they operate in your life?

3. Identify, explain, and give examples of several positive and several negative emotions. Which are most powerful for you?

4. Explain the difference between attitudes, opinions, behavioral intentions, and behavior.

5. Explain and give examples of each of the levels in Maslow's pyramid of needs. Who do you know who seems to be self-actualizing?

6. Explain and give examples of cognitive dissonance. Where is it operating in your life?

7. Explain and give examples of consonance. Where is it operating in your life?

8. Discuss the ethics of appealing to the emotions, needs, and attitudes held by persuadees.

This chapter examines what are commonly called appeals to the emotions or the will. We will look at four kinds of emotional appeals:

1. Appeals to deeply held needs, physical or psychological

2. Appeals to positive and negative emotions

3. Appeals to attitudes and opinions

4. Appeals to psychological states of balance or consonance and imbalance or dissonance.

Some persuasion theorists distinguish between logical and emotional appeals, arguing that they represent opposite ends of a continuum and that the "better" appeals are the logical ones. This explanation assumes that persuasive appeals are either one thing or another and that the two types of appeals operate separately and independently. It is easy for us to think that both "rational" and "emotional" persuasion occur all at once as a result of some key phrases, statistics, qualities of the persuader, or other factors. While some persuasion does occur this way, far more often it occurs over time.

We've seen that most persuasion depends in part on self-persuasion, usually occurs incrementally or bit-by-bit, and often includes many kinds of communication. One "emotional" appeal might serve to capture receivers' attention. A series of "logical" arguments might reinforce the first appeal and lead to the final decision or behavior. For example, an organization called Volunteers in America asks you

to donate your car to them because the money earned from selling the car helps place neglected and abused children in safe and nurturing homes. Is the appeal emotional or logical? Well, it has elements of both. The emotional appeal is about helping kids get better treatment in a good environment. Helping others makes most of us feel good about ourselves. But there are some logical reasons for donating your car. For instance, you can get a tax deduction for the donation (something you need), and you don't even have to bring the car to them or get the car in running order—the organization has free pick-up within 48 hours and they repair it before sale. The real question is not whether this is a logical or emotional appeal, but whether you process the message centrally or peripherally. In this case, the peripheral route processes—the "feeling good" part—and the central route processes—the tax break, the 48 hour pick-up, and repair—are the emotional and logical parts of the persuasion respectively.

In this chapter, we examine several emotional appeals or premises that tap into the psychological or emotional processes operating in the peripheral route of the ELM. These appeals rely on human needs, emotions, attitudes, and the psychic comfort we feel over decisions we make. We call these appeals **process or emotional premises** or appeals because they target psychological and emotional processes that operate in most people. When we call them premises, we are referring to their uses in enthymemes. When we refer to them as appeals, we are talking about how they operate in the worlds of politics or advertising. It is probably okay to think of the words *premises* and *appeals* as nearly synonymous. Both are subtypes of persuasion that gets at our psychological processes rather than our logical or reasoning processes. For example, most of us have fear-based emotions that cause psychological tension, and we eagerly take action to relieve this tension. So, persuaders work to generate fears about our grooming and then offer us products that relieve those fears and tensions. Consider the mouthwash Listerine. Initially it was used as a powerful surgical antiseptic, a floor cleaner, and a cure for gonorrhea. It wasn't until the 1920s that it was marketed as a cure for halitosis—an obscure word for bad breath (Leavitt & Dubner, 2005). A headline in one of its early ads read, "Got halitosis? Listerine mouthwash makes your breath kissing sweet." Psychological appeals or process premises operate in business, marketing, advertising, sales promotions, politics, interpersonal communication, and ideological persuasion. Process or emotional premises operate when we buy a product because of brand loyalty, brand name, a memorable slogan, a catchy jingle, or even packaging. Recall the Snuggle fabric softener example from Chapter 5? The brand name was cuddly, as was its logo of a stuffed teddy bear. Process premises also operate in more serious situations such as enactment of homeland security laws and appeals from prison reform candidates and from advertisers trying to convince you to make major purchase decisions for a new car or home. Emotional premises appear in everyday interpersonal persuasion between neighbors, spouses, parents and children, siblings, lovers, bosses, and employees.

NEEDS: THE FIRST PROCESS PREMISE

Each of us has our own set of individual needs. Some of them are critical—we can't live without things like food, water, clothing, and shelter. Others are not critical—we can get along without

approval from others. And not everyone's needs have the same priority. Diverse cultural roots can influence the priority of our needs, but most needs resemble those of lots of other people, so various theories of motivation apply to the general population. Many appeals focus on needs, which when satisfied lead to our overall sense of well-being (for example, success on the job, being liked, or having religious faith). Without the satisfaction of these needs or some substitute, we feel frustrated, anxious, afraid, even angry, and tension results. We infer these needs from patterns of behavior that presumably satisfied and happy people exhibit. Because people seem concerned about being successful, we quickly infer a need for physical symbols of success like a Jaguar, a summer place, or a large home.

Persuasion in today's changing world usually focuses on promoting or selling symbolic ways to meet people's physiological and emotional needs. Some products, such as self-improvement courses, really can help individuals make a better impression on the boss, but what people buy, vote for, or support doesn't usually have such direct effects. They drive a BMW and enjoy what they believe to be the admiring looks they get from other drivers. Our support for a candidate may relate to a need for approval from others or a need for self-esteem—the candidate's supporters are our friends or neighbors, and they appreciate our support. And we feel good about ourselves because our support for the good candidate just might "make a difference."

If the persuader relying on the needs process premise analyzes audience needs or emotions incorrectly, persuasion sometimes boomerangs. For example, an advertiser, assuming that travelers needed tough luggage, produced an expensive TV spot in which the luggage was handled roughly while being loaded onto an airplane and then falling out of the plane in flight, plummeting down 30,000 feet, landing on some rocks, and bouncing into the air. When the luggage was opened the camera showed the undamaged contents. The ad seemed persuasive. However, sales dropped following its airing. Why? Focus group interviews revealed that most people have fears that their flight might crash, and they resented the idea that their luggage would survive when they wouldn't. The emotions of fear and resentment served as powerful motivators, as do emotions like anger, jealousy, hatred, joy, or love.

To discover why consumers respond as they do, **motivation research**—based on the social sciences and the study of marketing rather than on our traditional political, ideological, or rhetorical traditions—grew rapidly after World War II. In his best-selling book *The Hidden Persuaders* (1964), Vance Packard, author and advertising theorist, reported that a majority of the hundred largest ad firms in the country used psychoanalytic motivation research to discover deep-seated psychological needs and responses. Other persuaders such as public relations executives and fund-raisers also turned to psychological theories to discover receivers' motives, emotions, or needs, and then they tied products, candidates, and causes to those motives and needs. Packard held that much motivation research

> seeks to learn what motivations or **hidden needs** influence people in making choices. It employs techniques designed to reach the subconscious mind because preferences generally are determined by factors of which the individual is not usually aware. In most buying situations the consumer acts emotionally and compulsively, unconsciously reacting to images which they subconsciously associate with the product (p. 5).

One expert said, "The cosmetic manufacturers are not selling lanolin; they are selling hope.... We no longer buy oranges, we buy vitality. We do not buy just an auto; we buy prestige" (p. 5). Packard says that motivation researchers assume three things about people: (1) they don't always know what they want when making a purchase; (2) you can't rely on what they say they like or dislike; and (3) they don't usually act logically when they buy, vote, or join.

Motivation research reflects the symbolist tradition in psychology rather than the experimental tradition. Advertising and marketing researchers use focus group interviews to get consumers to describe the fears, pleasures, or fantasies they associate with brands and ads. Other researchers ask people to complete sentences or do word associations about the brand. This trend continues, and recent research about consumer behavior confirms many of the claims made by Packard. This kind of motivational research is still with us but now uses more sophisticated techniques that take cultural diversity into account and use interactive media to involve the receiver. N.Y.U. professor Neil Postman (Freedman, 1988) long ago observed that "Advertisers,... desperate to keep you tuned to their pitches, (are) trying some new tricks. Many of these commercials have more impact on the subconscious level" (p. 5).

Ad agencies often enlist psychologists and neurophysiologists to produce the desired effects (Freedman, 1988). For example, Amherst Incorporated, developed a research instrument called the Motivation and Attitude Profile (MAP) and used it to market goods, services, and politicians. Amherst's creative director describes the idea behind MAP this way: "People are driven by their emotions—it's not about fact or logic. Increasingly, the only button you press is an emotional one. You find out what their needs are and you discover how to reflect those needs" (Booth, 1999, p. 32). Products as varied as Haagen-Daz ice cream, Volkswagen, and life insurance rely on psychographics, which is a research technique that identifies the psychological reasons for purchase behavior. Whether we call it motivational research, lifestyle research, hidden persuaders, or psychographics, using the process amounts to the same basic idea—finding hidden or obvious needs and developing the products and ads to fulfill those needs.

To learn more about the fascinating field of motivation research, access InfoTrac College Edition, and enter the words "motivation research" in the search engine. Read several of the articles listed there. The two articles by Jerry Thomas provide a thorough description of some research techniques used. Enjoy the article "21 Meaningful Motivational Messages."

B O X 7.1   Consumer Insight—Getting Into Your Head

A Chicago-based nationwide marketing company, Claritas, used psychographics and lifestyle data to develop its PRIZM system. PRIZM is a marketing tool that identifies more than 60 market segments across the United States with names that reflect the inner psychological needs of the consumers in each. Take, for example, the segment called "Pickups and Gun Racks." Persons in "Pickups and Gun Racks" tend to live in manufactured housing or mobile homes and are heavy users of generic or house brands of sweetened soda pop. If they purchase lingerie, it tends to be from Frederick's of Hollywood. Their most recent financial transaction is the purchase of a lottery ticket. They obviously have different needs from those of the people in the segment "Town and Gowns" (you may be living there right now), and these needs, in turn,

differ from those of the people in the segment "Red, White, and Blue Collar." For persons in "Town and Gown," the most frequent financial transaction is the use of an ATM. If they purchase lingerie, it is frequently at a department store or Victoria's Secret, and most of them live in houses, apartments, dorms, or fraternity and sorority houses. PRIZM is a popular tool among many consumer marketing firms.

 Do you think marketers know too much about us? How much of this information came from government data? How much have we ourselves given away? If you want to learn more, go to www.claritas.com and view the video presentation explaining the segmentation system and other options on the company homepage.

Packard's "Compelling Needs"

One approach to the needs premise was Packard's **"compelling needs,"** which were based on his observations on the rapidly evolving advertising industry of the motivation research era. He claimed that these needs were so powerful that they *compelled* people to buy, and he identified eight such compelling needs that advertisers used to sell products. We still see them in use today, although with far more sophistication than Packard described. Marketers design ads promising that the product or service will provide real or symbolic fulfillment of these compelling needs.

Marketing consultant Barry Feig (1997) says advertisers are looking for the **hot buttons** that will motivate people and prompt purchase behavior. Feig defined hot buttons as appeals that cause receivers to become emotionally involved with a product rather than responding rationally to product reality. For example, he claims that new car purchases frequently result from the test drive and the new car smell. The purchaser becomes emotionally involved with the feel and smell of a new car and puts aside other factors like performance. Some clever persuader found a way to package that

smell in an aerosol spray can so that it can be used to sell used cars more effectively. Feig's own work in the 1990s verified Packard's hidden needs, and he found other needs not noted by Packard.

The Need for Emotional Security. Packard's first compelling need was for **emotional security**, which is defined as feelings of anxiety about the future and feelings of insecurity about our personal welfare and and safety, as seen in Figure 7.1. These feelings emerge whenever our world becomes unpredictable, and we then try to dispel them in symbolic ways. Packard attributed this need for emotional security to the Great Depression. Following W.W.II., people desperately wanted to avoid the insecurity of unemployment, the inability to make ends meet, and so on, so when they had employment, they saved regularly and bought home freezers to preserve food for the possibly uncertain future. The need still operates, but for different reasons. Terrorism seems unstoppable and is certainly unpredictable. Identity theft is mushrooming, making everyone feel insecure. AIDS threatens the economic future of the continent of Africa and elsewhere, and dangerous pollution fouls our environment hourly. The world economy

FIGURE 7.1 This ad plays on our inherent feelings of insecurity, especially in an age of identity theft and other means used to defraud people.
SOURCE: Used by permission of Sanford Corp.

seems precariously balanced. If oil prices continue to escalate, the stock market might crash, resulting in another Great Depression. With mergers, downsizing, and outsourcing, job security now concerns many people, and literacy rates have dropped to less than 70 percent from earlier highs over 90 percent, making it hard for many people to get any job other than flipping burgers.

No wonder we search for substitute symbols of security. Deodorants promise us secure social relationships. Self-improvement courses promise better job security. Retirement planning programs offer financial security. These products and services act as minor premises in enthymemes mentioned in previous chapters that have as a major first premise the belief that "security is good." Even in interpersonal relationships, the need for security causes people to search for commitment. At first, "living together" seemed to be a liberating lifestyle, but this is now questioned by some because there is no security without commitment. Author Stephanie Staal (2001) points out that the divorce rate of those who live together before marriage is 50 percent higher than the rate for those who did not. We all face unpredictable change, and that makes us vulnerable to persuasion that promises some symbol of security—a good investment program, membership in respected social groups, safety derived from security systems, owning a weapon, or interpersonal confidence stemming from trusting and reliable relationships. Feig (1997) equates this need for security with a universal hot button he calls the "desire for control." This need for security or control varies within our culture. For example, in some subcultures, security is put off until tomorrow in favor of gratification today.

The Need for Reassurance of Worth. We live in a highly competitive and impersonal world in which we often feel like mere cogs. Packard noted that people need to feel valued for what they do whether it is at a factory, a desk, a classroom, or a day-care center. Homemakers, blue-collar workers, managers, and others need to feel that they are accomplishing something of value and are appreciated by others. Packard called this the need for **reassurance of worth**, which is defined as a feeling that we are valued by others. This need forms the basis of many persuasive appeals, from ads promising to make us better parents, spouses, or friends to appeals for volunteers in good causes. A study asked managers and workers to rate ten factors in job satisfaction. Managers rated wages, fringe benefits, and working conditions at the top, but workers placed them at the bottom. They rated "appreciation for work done" at the top, followed by "my boss listens to me," and "fellow workers." Feig (1997) verified the existence of the reassurance of worth need, saying "Consumers need to feel good about themselves and fulfill their self-images—it's a basic human need" (p. 14).

Based on hundreds of interviews, sociologist Robert Bellah and colleagues (1985) concluded that most contemporary Americans see themselves in a race for material goods, prestige, power, and influence. They separate themselves from others and find self-worth in material things. Ethics author Kathleen Sibley (1997) noted the feelings of distrust felt by many employees when they learned of a company policy of monitoring employee email.

To learn more about how this perception can affect brands and businesses, access Info-Trac College Edition, enter the words "corporate ethics," and examine some of the articles there.

When we feel less and less important as individuals, we become vulnerable targets for persuasion that promises reassurance of worth. Reassurance of worth has its cultural implications also. Schiffman and Kanuk (1997) observed that Asian Americans are very brand loyal, but especially so when the brand lets it be known that they are welcome and that their patronage is appreciated by offering preferred customer cards, premiums, and so on. Other ethnic subcultures value bargaining, and still others value quality over price.

The Need for Ego Gratification. Packard found that many consumers not only needed to be reassured of their basic worth, but they also needed **ego gratification**, which he defined as feelings of self-importance and having one's ego stroked. As you can see in Figure 7.2, the traveling business woman gets special treatment from Courtyard by Marriott, including Internet access, fine furnishings, and even a cup of coffee served in a china cup instead of a plastic one. Also notice that Marriott emphasizes they cater to female business travelers and those from different ethnic groups, thus reinforcing the growing importance of females and ethnicities in the workplace. Earlier ads usually showed white male executives as customers.

Satisfaction of the need for ego gratification comes from a variety of sources—friends, co-workers, neighbors, parents, groups, institutions, and ourselves. Feig (1997) called this need the "I'm better than you" hot button, and emphasized that consumers display possessions that build their egos and meet this need. Persuaders often target groups whose members feel that they have been put down for some time, such as teachers, police officers, firefighters, and postal or social workers. After 9/11, the media brought many of these groups into a well-deserved public spotlight. They got ego gratification from being featured on TV, in newspapers and on the covers of news weeklies. Such groups can also

LOG ON AND ON.
FREE HIGH-SPEED
INTERNET ACCESS
IN EVERY ROOM.
Surf, search, chat, upload,
download, e-mail, e-conference,
live stream, podcast, webhost,
webdesign, webzine, blog . . . .
The free high-speed Internet
access in our rooms is designed to make our guests as
comfortable as possible online.
Everything else in it is designed
to make them as comfortable
as possible off.   Courtyard.®
Our rooms were made for you.℠

IT'S THE MARRIOTT WAY.℠

To reserve a room
with Free High-Speed
Internet Access,
call 1-800-MARRIOTT
or visit Marriott.com.

Marriott
REWARDS.
© 2005 Marriott International, Inc.

FIGURE 7.2 Marriott promises to fulfill the need for ego gratification by giving special attention to its business executive customer base, and thus caters to gender and ethnic diversity.

SOURCE: Used by permission of Marriott International, Inc.

now get special rates on their mortgages, grants in aid to help them buy homes, and other benefits showing national appreciation for public service. Persuaders frequently sell products, ideas, and candidates by targeting an out-group's ego needs in personal ways that appeal to self-perception.

Take family values, for example. From the late 1960s until the late 1980s the traditional family was out of style. Communal living was popular, as was living together. Those who remained committed to the ideal of the traditional family felt like outcasts. From the 1990s to the present, persuasive "pro-family" appeals succeeded in presidential campaigns, religious appeals, public relations, and the marketing of products promising a restoration of family values. Feig (1997) called this need the "family values" hot button, and noted that marketers sell a vision of the family as we all wish it would be.

If this issue interests you, go to InfoTrac College Edition, enter the words "living together" or "family values" in the search engine, and peruse some of the related articles.

Note that the ad copy in Figure 7.2 stresses the importance Marriott places on the individual—in this case, the female executive, whose needs traditionally have been largely overlooked by the hotel/motel industry. Similarly, politicians know how to stroke the egos of appropriate groups of potential voters. One Republican female candidate for governor used ego gratification with two widely differing audiences. For a GOP women's luncheon she arrived by limousine, wearing a conservative dress and scarf, and ate chicken salad for lunch. Afterwards, she changed her clothes to a black leather jacket, boots, gloves, and pants, and then drove a Harley to the Young Republicans club at a nearby college. She got rave reviews at both events (National Public Radio, 2002).

The Need for Creative Outlets.   In our modern technocracy, few products can be identified with a single artisan. This was not always the case. For example, until the Industrial Revolution craftsmen such as cabinetmakers created a piece of furniture from beginning to end—it was their unique product. The same applied to blacksmiths, craftsmen, silversmiths and others. They all could point with pride to their product. That is not often the case today, which is why we feel a need for **creative outlets**. Packard saw this need being met by offering substitute creative activities that would replace the creations previously produced by individuals. They felt less and less creative in many ways, and they needed to find ways to express their own unique creativity. Packard said persuaders targeted this need for creative outlets by promoting products and brands related to hobbies, crafts, and social activities.

FIGURE 7.3 The Fluid Milk Promotion Board strokes the ego of average citizens by making them feel special, hinting that they are sophisticated, and suggesting that they can avoid health problems by drinking three glasses of milk a day.
SOURCE: Reprinted by permission.

Today more than half the population works in the service and information industries, where most important products are intangible and not really very creative. There is no actual creation of anything, and more work is now being accomplished through technologies such as robots. People still need to demonstrate their own creativity—a need that Feig (1997) identified as the "excitement of discovery" hot button—so they engage in gardening, gourmet cooking, home decorating, collecting and restoring antiques, art, or music.

To see how the need for creativity operates today, access InfoTrac College Edition, and enter the words "need for creativity" in the search engine. Browse some of the items listed there.

FIGURE 7.4   This cartoon is based on a true incident. A wounded goose was taken in and nursed to health by an assistant to NIU's president, who was single and nearing retirement.

SOURCE: Used by permission of Al Ochsner.

The Need for Love Objects.   Packard noted that people whose children have grown up often feel a need for **love objects**. These "empty-nesters" feel lonely and unneeded when the last kid goes off to college, gets a job, or gets married. Empty-nesters fill their love needs in various ways such as doing volunteer work, devoting more time to their jobs or hobbies, or becoming a big brother or sister or a foster grandparent. Persuaders target these empty nesters in a variety of ways. For instance, many older persons get pets to serve as substitute love objects. They coddle them, spoil them, and even dress them up. The pet food industry targets "gourmet" lines to such persons who bring home Premium Cuts, Tender Vittles, Beef 'n Gravy, Tuna Surprise, or Chicken Spectacular. The food sounds and even looks like something a human might consume. Feig (1997) calls this the "revaluing" hot button, and he predicts a major increase in products that attempt to fill this need as the baby boomers approach retirement and an empty nest (see Figure 7.4).

The Need for a Sense of Power or Strength.   More than members of other cultures, most U.S. citizens seek emblems of potency or a **sense of power or strength** in symbolic ways. Packard defined this as the need for a personal extension of one's *perceived* power or strength rather than true power or strength. The bigger the car or outboard motor, the better.

Snowmobiles, ATVs, jet skis, and Harleys sell because they give the user this sense of power. Whether the brand is a double-triggered chain saw or a Hummer, an increased perception of power is the central issue. Stanley Tools sells "heavy duty" tools, not wimpy, "light duty" hammers and wrenches. Similarly, Americans seem to elect politicians who do macho things. In fact, any major candidate for the presidency must demonstrate physical strength in some way. And as males approach midlife, they often engage in macho activities like bungee jumping or bodybuilding.

The Need for Roots.   One of the predominant features of modern society is mobility. Individuals employed by any large firm will probably have to move several times during their careers, and most persons have three or more careers during their lifetime. In the decade following graduation from college, the average graduate moves a dozen times, usually crossing state lines at least once. As a result, most persons feel a **need for roots**, symbolic or real. The need for roots is defined as feelings of homesickness and a yearning for family-centered activities. When individuals move away from home, especially if it is some distance, there are some pieces of home that they can bring along with them. One is brand loyalty, which develops most strongly between the ages of 18 and 24. Recent college graduates have one of the highest levels of brand loyalty, which is why my university inked an agreement to give Pepsi exclusive "pouring rights" on campus. Only Pepsi products such as Mountain Dew, Lipton Iced Tea, or Fruitopia can be sold or served on campus. All materials used to serve the brands (cups, straws, napkins, and so on) must have the Pepsi logo imprinted on them. Pepsi gave over $8 million to the school's scholarship fund for this right, knowing that brand loyalty would develop.

The need for roots and the sense of brand loyalty also helps explain *line extensions* or the development of new products based on old and familiar brands. We feel more at home buying the new Quaker Oats Squares than another brand because of the familiar, friendly, and old-fashioned face of the Quaker Man promising "An honest taste from an honest face." He serves as an emblem of our tradition, our need for an "old-fashioned" hearty breakfast, and our need for a sense of roots. The nice thing about brand names is that they are portable—we can take them to a new home anywhere. The Lane Furniture Company appealed to the need for roots and emotional ties to home by offering newlyweds a Lane cedar chest to "take part of home" with them when they marry. We've already noted the appeal politicians make to family values. The trend toward increasingly mobile and fragmented lives is likely to continue. As a result, the need for roots remains an important motivator, and advertisers, politicians, and ideologues continue to use it in their persuasive appeals to us. Feig (1997) equates this need with his "family values" hot button and notes, "Quality time with families is still of utmost importance to Americans." Schiffman and Kanuk observe that in some subcultures (such as Asian American and Latino) family and roots stretch across several generations. In this regard, The *New York Times* noted the trend of bringing generations of family on road trips (Feig, 1997).

Brand loyalty can be further investigated in InfoTrac College Edition by typing the words "brand loyalty" in the search engine. Examine a sample of the articles listed.

The Need for Immortality. None of us wants to believe in our own mortality. The fear of growing old and dying clearly drives the healthy-living industry, which promotes such things as good nutrition, stress reduction, exercise, and a healthy lifestyle. Packard suggested that a need for immortality grew out of the need to maintain influence over the lives of family members. The breadwinner is made to feel that by purchasing life insurance he or she obtains life after death in the form of continuing financial security that will help the kids go to college even if he or she isn't there.

Other products make similar appeals to the fear of death. For instance, Promise margarine will keep you healthy longer because "Promise is at the heart of eating right." And Nivea's Visage face cream will make your skin "firmer, healthier, and younger" for only pennies a day. As the ad executive noted in an earlier quote, we aren't buying lanolin, we are buying hope—hope for a little more immortality. This need for immortality seems particularly relevant in our modern technocracy. The much-talked-about midlife crisis is an example. This occurs when people realize that "time marches on" and that they have probably passed the halfway point in their lives or when they confront some other major life event such as the death of a parent. So they get divorced, quit or lose their job, buy a sports car, run off with someone half their age, and speed away in the sports car, as if to underscore their indestructible youth. They want to be young again, or at least to enjoy some of the experiences they missed along the way. Frequently, they engage in dangerous activities such as skydiving.

There are many other persuasive appeals that succeed because they are somehow tied to the desire for immortality (Lafavore, 1995). Feig (1997) calls this the "self-nurturance and the ability to stay ageless and immortal" hot button, and noted that older persons are more willing to spend money on things that make them feel better about themselves.

If you are interested in needs and how motivational research can identify them, go to InfoTrac College Edition, and enter the words

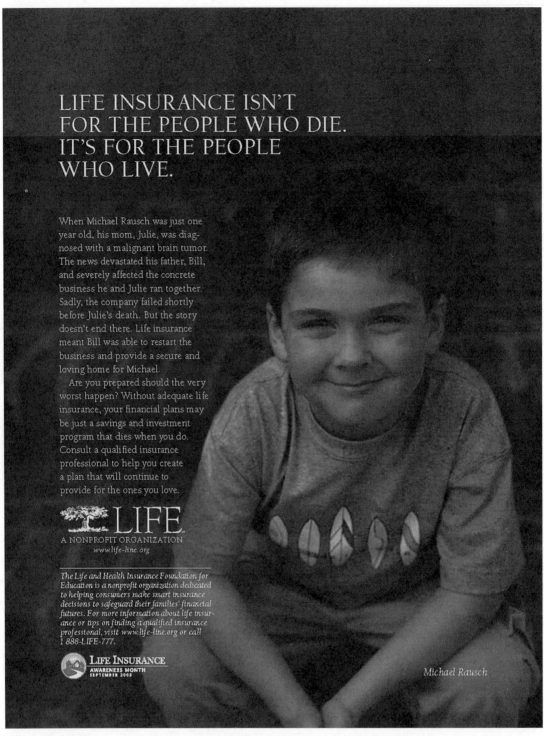

FIGURE 7.5 This ad appeals to the need for immortality by assuring readers that even if they are no longer there, they will still be able to influence the lives of their survivors.

SOURCE: Reprinted with permission of the LIFE Foundation.

"needs" and "motivation research," and explore the options there.

We now turn to perhaps one of the most well-known models of human needs. It was first described more than 50 years ago, and it is still going strong.

Maslow's Hierarchy of Needs

Abraham Maslow (1954), a well-known psychologist and pioneer in the discipline, long ago offered a simple starting point for examining people's needs. His theories about the power of human needs are judged by many to be as relevant for persuasion today as they were when he first described them. Nancy Austin (2002), a California management consultant, maintains that, though the theory may be over a half-century old, "for modern managers looking to pump up performance, it still has zing." Robert Zemke (1998), the senior editor of the journal *Training*, notes, "It's ironic that this '50s psychologist with no head for business played such a central role in the development of the psychology of management and the thoughts of modern managers." In 1998, Maslow's daughter published a revision of his work, entitled *Maslow on Management*, which was greeted with rave reviews (Rowan, 1998). And Schiffman and Kanuk (1997) say that in spite of its age, "Maslow's hierarchy is a useful tool in understanding consumer motivations and is readily adaptable to marketing strategy," (p. 100). Some of Feig's (1997) hot buttons equate to Maslow's need levels. Despite its vintage, Maslow's hierarchy still has much to teach us.

Maslow theorized that people have various kinds of needs that emerge, subside, and then reemerge. In his hierarchy of needs the lower levels of the hierarchy represent the strongest needs and the higher levels the weaker ones (see Figure 7.6). Maslow did not believe that higher needs are superior to lower needs—rather, they are less likely to emerge until the stronger lower needs have been met. The base of the pyramid represents universal needs or beliefs about which there is unanimous agreement. As we move up the pyramid, we find

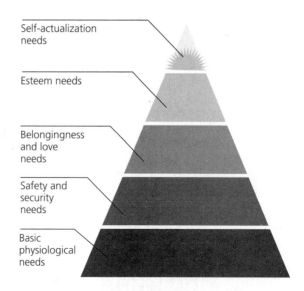

FIGURE 7.6 Maslow's hierarchy of needs.

needs or beliefs on which there may not be unanimous agreement and on which individuals place varying degrees of value. As a result, there is an upward dynamic in Maslow's hierarchy, which means that as powerful needs are met, less potent ones emerge. Maslow called this upward dynamic **prepotency**. In other words, weaker needs (such as the need for self-respect) emerge only after stronger needs (like food or shelter) have been filled. Don't try to persuade a dehydrated person to dress up before having a drink of water. The need to slake our thirst is prepotent; and until it is fulfilled, we ignore other needs. As time passes, the earlier needs also reemerge again. For example, the needs for food or water emerge and then recede as we eat or drink, but they reemerge at a later time.

Basic Needs. The bottom level of Maslow's pyramid contains the strongest needs we have—our **basic needs**, which he defined as the physiological things required to sustain life—regular access to air, food, water, shelter, sleep, and so on. Until these needs have been met, we don't usually concern ourselves with higher needs. However, basic needs can motivate behavior. For example, the person who is starving can be motivated to do all sorts of unusual things to secure food, ranging from stealing it to eating insects. And we know that the need for air can cause drowning victims to panic and drown not only themselves but also their would-be rescuers.

Security Needs. The second level of Maslow's pyramid is the **need for security**, which he defined as the ability to continue to fill the basic needs of life. We can look at these needs in several ways. If we fear losing our jobs, we have a strong need to obtain income security, and we try to find a more secure job, or we save money for hard times. Even if we have job security, we still might feel insecure about maintaining our personal safety because of the rising crime rates in our neighborhood. We might take drastic action to ward off criminals by keeping a gun on the nightstand or perhaps by moving to a gated community. Even when we feel secure in our community, we still might feel insecure because of world politics. We fear that our country is vulnerable to terrorists, who may manage to soon acquire nuclear and biological or chemical weapons. Or we fear that our leaders are considering unwise military actions against some country. Those not technically trained for the computer age have a realistic fear of being out-of-date and soon out of a job. Political analysts explained several recent election results as related to fears of economic displacement. In the interpersonal realm, we have a need for "social security," or the continuing acceptance by others. In other words, the need for security emerges and reemerges as various threats to our security become evident (see Figure 7.7).

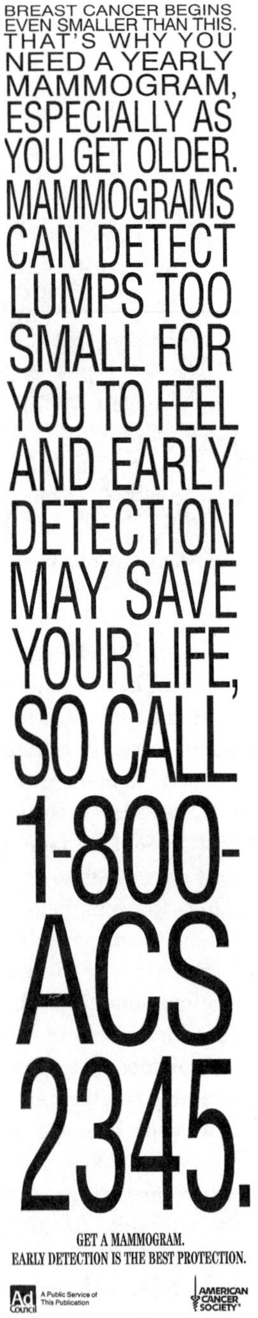
BREAST CANCER BEGINS EVEN SMALLER THAN THIS.
THAT'S WHY YOU NEED A YEARLY MAMMOGRAM, ESPECIALLY AS YOU GET OLDER. MAMMOGRAMS CAN DETECT LUMPS TOO SMALL FOR YOU TO FEEL AND EARLY DETECTION MAY SAVE YOUR LIFE, SO CALL 1-800-ACS 2345.
GET A MAMMOGRAM.
EARLY DETECTION IS THE BEST PROTECTION.
Ad Council
A Public Service of This Publication
AMERICAN CANCER SOCIETY

FIGURE 7.7 The need for security is the appeal used in this ad from the American Cancer Society.

SOURCE: Reprinted by permission of the American Cancer Society.

Today, insecurity, like change, is one of the few predictable things in life. Eight of every ten jobs being filled by tomorrow's college grads don't even exist today. It's almost impossible for you to prepare for the future because the rate and pace of change is accelerating so quickly. Computer technology now becomes obsolete in less than a year. No one can keep up with all the new (and frequently essential) information about jobs, health, communities, and a host of other personal and social issues. This need is similar to Feig's (1997) "desire to control" hot button. Feig says this need explains home-based businesses because you can become own boss and avoid layoffs.

Belongingness and Affiliation Needs. Once our security needs have been met, we become aware of needs on the third level of the pyramid—**belongingness or affiliation needs**, which are defined as the need to interact with others and to identify with some group. A number of options are open to us to meet our need for association. Usually, individuals go beyond the family and workplace and become members of groups with which they want to affiliate, such as service groups, places of worship, the PTA, bowling leagues, or golf and health clubs. Generally, we limit the number of groups we join, and we are active members in only a few. Feig (1997) identified the "need for belonging" as another of his hot buttons and noted that "Americans are the 'joiningest' people in the world." He advises doubters to examine the number of membership cards in their wallets if they don't think this is so (p. 29).

The flip side of belonging and affiliation needs is the trend toward isolation. A number of people and organizations are concerned about the tendency of people to cocoon or isolate themselves. In his article "Bowling Alone" (1995) and his follow-up book, *Bowling Alone: The Collapse and Revival of American Community* (2000), Robert Putnam observed that more and more persons join what he calls checkbook groups such as the Citizen's Utility Board, The Sierra Club, or the American Association of Retired Persons. Belonging only requires that you write a check, because the groups rarely if ever meet. Membership is down in civic and fraternal groups like the Lions, Elks, and Moose Clubs, and fewer people bowl in leagues, preferring to "bowl alone."

Like physiological and security needs, the need to belong often interacts with other needs and continues to reemerge throughout our lives. Also, what fulfills our belonging needs differs at various points in our lives and will probably change across time. It may be important to belong to a fraternity or sorority when we are in college, but after graduation, these affiliations fade and are replaced by job-related associations or other social activities. Later, when we have families, other affiliations tend to be more important to us, and we join community groups and a church or other religious organization. In this context, a recent trend is the emergence of "mega-churches" like the Mariners Church of Newport Beach, California. This church offers programming for various market segments— grief therapy, Gen X activities, and seminars on a variety of topics like twelve-step recovery, divorce dynamics, and the parenting of adolescents—all served up with cappuccino and snacks. The need to belong will always be with us because humans by nature are social beings.

Love and Esteem Needs. Once we satisfy our affiliation or belonging needs, we feel the emergence of needs in the fourth level of Maslow's model, which he called **love and esteem needs**, defined as the need to be valued by the members of the groups with which we affiliate—our families, fellow workers, friends, church congregation, and neighbors. Once we are part of a group, we want to feel that the group values us as a member and as an individual. We are happy when our families understand and admire the things we do. In her recent book *My Life So Far*, Jane Fonda quotes Oprah Winfrey as naming this need the "Please Disease" (2005) and describes it as a lifelong and unending desire to do things that will please our parent(s) and bring us love or esteem. The esteem need is also a reemerging one. That is, when we find that we are needed, loved, and esteemed by our family, our need for esteem does not fade away— instead, its focus shifts, and we now want to feel needed by our co-workers, our boss, and our friends.

Many product appeals offer a kind of symbolic substitute for esteem. For example, as Figure 7.8 shows, the kids will hold Mom in high esteem if she uses a certain brand of gas grill.

At various times, esteem seems rooted in conspicuous consumption for purposes of display. At other times (such as wartime), conspicuous consumption borders on being unpatriotic. However, important events and life experiences can change the way people satisfy esteem needs. For instance,

THE GRILLER: MARATHON MOM

No time to waste, right? So a gas grill has to perform quickly, easily. Enter MasterFlame². It's built with your schedule in mind: easy push button ignition, sturdy shelves for extra work space, a cooking system that virtually eliminates uneven heat, and multi-level cooking to prepare the main course and side dishes at one time. Give it a try... you'll find you've made a delicious dinner for your family and it wasn't a chore at all. In fact, it's our guess you'll find you even had fun.

To locate Char-Broil MasterFlame² gas grills, and find out about a free gift with purchase, just call

1-800-477-0118

THE GRILL: MasterFlame²™ FROM

Char-Broil

FIGURE 7.8 Esteem needs are the key appeal in this ad claiming a Char-Broil gas grill allows the mother to whip up a great meal for her kids, and she feels good about that.

SOURCE: Reprinted by permission of Char-Broil.

recent political, financial, and religious scandals have shaken people's faith in traditional institutions and their leadership's ability to show esteem. What kind of esteem for employees and stockholders does the crooked CEO have? Schiffman and Kanuk (1997) note that the Asian American subculture is highly motivated by esteem needs and therefore they are strivers, particularly in terms of education. People realize that working in community can help them meet their esteem needs. In fact, "community" has become a kind of God term.

Self-Actualization Needs. Maslow put **self-actualization needs** at the top of his pyramid (thereby implying that they rarely emerge). He defined self-actualization as the achievement of one's full potential or capability. At first, Maslow believed that individuals could live up to their potential only when all four of the lower needs had been met. It is hard for young people on the way up to think about self-actualization, just as it is difficult to meet love or esteem needs if individuals don't belong to some group that can offer love or esteem. But in reality, self-actualization is an integral part of everyone's life. Feig (1997) labeled this need "the desire to be the best you can be" hot button, and he identifies several examples, including the pride we all had as children when we brought home our gold-starred papers from school—they were proof of self-actualization.

FIGURE 7.9   The humor here is based on Cardinal Sicola's inability to self-actualize.

SOURCE: Used with permission of Al Ochsner.

Maslow later came to see self-actualization as occurring through what he called "peak experiences" in life. These events allowed individuals to enjoy and learn about themselves, or experience something they had only dreamed of previously. Thus, the person who ventures into the wilderness and learns to be self-reliant and not to fear isolation enjoys a peak, or self-actualizing, experience. When people take their first job after high school or college and discover that they have abilities that are of value, they probably experience a degree of self actualization. Cultural trends also affect the ways in which we seek to satisfy our self-actualization needs. Social critic T. J. Jackson Lears (1983) noted that the search for ways of identifying ourselves and our potential came about when the United States shifted from being a culture of production to a culture of consumption; that is, in moving from a secure farm existence to an unsettling urban isolation, we experienced a loss of traditional values and chaotic changes in our lifestyles. The result, Lears claimed, was the search for a "therapeutic ethos" or an identity that would let us be at ease with ourselves—that would permit us to self-actualize. To a large extent, this therapeutic ethos offers inner harmony, reduced feelings of emptiness, and hope for self-realization through patterns of consumption.

To examine the culture of consumption in which we live, access InfoTrac College Edition, and enter the words "consumption culture" in the search engine. Be sure to read the reviews of *Consuming Desires: Consumption, Culture and Happiness*, a book of essays on consumption edited by Ed Rosenblatt. They may make you want to read the entire book.

As you are exposed to various persuasive events, whether public or interpersonal, try applying Maslow's model to them. See whether it sheds light on the needs that people feel and that may motivate their actions. You may want to experiment with persuading another person using several levels of Maslow's model. If the person doesn't seem motivated by appeals to security, try appealing to basic or belongingness needs.

Uses of the Needs Process Premise

In our search for the first premises that serve as springboards for persuasion in enthymemes, human needs demonstrate one area of our vulnerability to persuasion. Whether we identify them using Packard's compelling needs, Maslow's hierarchy, Feig's hot buttons, or some other model, we all experience strongly felt needs that require some sort of satisfaction. Persuaders frequently tie minor premises to these powerful needs and allow audiences to complete the enthymematic argument by drawing the conclusion. As persuadees, we must consider the persuasive requests made of us from the perspective of our own needs. And as persuaders,

---

B O X 7.2 **Interactive Marketing and Human Needs**

 Go to www.everybodysinteractive.com and discover how marketing experts are delving into human needs using interactive media. The home page you will discover there will show you how marketers use interactive media to appeal to human needs and emotions. Explore the various options, including how The Watson Communication Group plans and executes advertising strategies for various clients such as Levi Straus, Microsoft, cosmetic dentists, skin care specialists, and others. You will see how human needs and emotions are being tapped by persuaders of all sorts.

---

we should examine the current needs of those we wish to influence. If we do that, we are more likely to succeed and to do our audience a service by giving them a way to satisfy their needs.

It is important, however, to be ethical in appealing to audience needs. As persuadees we need to ask, "Is this appeal to my needs ethical or not?" thus practicing our response-ability, and we need to ask the same questions when we take on the role of persuader. A good way to train yourself to evaluate appeals from this critical perspective—as persuadee or persuader—is to restate persuasive messages, such as TV commercials or political appeals, from the perspective of the Packard, Maslow, Feig, or other need models. As first premises on which persuasion can be built, psychological and physiological needs are powerful motivators.

EMOTIONS: THE SECOND PROCESS PREMISE

Another kind of psychological or process premise relates to our emotions. Appeals to our emotions are the second of four such process premises including needs.

What does it mean when, in the midst of a discussion, someone says, "You're just being too emotional about this"? It may mean they have noticed a physical change in your behavior. Perhaps your voice changes in timbre or volume, your face gets red, you begin to show a nervous tic, or your eyes reveal anger. Or they might be responding to the fact that you have started rattling off statistics, sounding like a courtroom attorney. Borchers (2005) refers to these two interpretations of being emotional as demonstrating the physiological and the cognitive dimensions of emotion. In the physiological dimension you feel a change in the way your body is responding to the situation. You feel your voice's change in timbre, your face flushing, and your change in facial expression. With the cognitive dimension of emotions, the changes in you are not physical responses—they are perceptual changes in the way you think about a person, an issue, or a situation. These cognitive changes are usually expressed verbally. We are probably born with the physiological dimension of emotions hardwired into our brains. However, we must *learn* the cognitive dimension and how to express what emotions we are feeling. We learn these things from experiences, parents, authority figures, friends, or role models whom we observe in films, on television, or elsewhere. In both the physiological and the cognitive dimension, there are cultural variations (Porter & Samovar, 1998), particularly when our emotions are publicly displayed. We can see this in ethnic stereotypes of the emotional, gesticulating Italian or the authority-driven German. You learn that British are very polite even when expressing anger whereas other ethnicities might be outright rude.

In both the physiological and the cognitive dimension, we are dealing with models for understanding and reacting to our feelings and beliefs. Nabi (2002) maintains that emotions have five basic components: (1) cognitive evaluation of a situation, meaning that we are aware and have thought over the situation; (2) physiological arousal, or a change in bodily functions, such as an adrenalin rush; (3) motor expression, or what we physically do about the situation; (4) motivational intentions or readiness, or what we are prepared to do and plan to do and why; and (5) a feeling state in the subject, such as when you feel happy or disappointed (p. 290). You learned to "bite your tongue" or to "count to ten" when feeling the emotion of anger, either from experience or more likely from parents or authority figures. Let's examine a few emotions that most persons feel or respond to in some way and see how persuaders use them to move us to action.

Fear

Fear is one of the most familiar emotions that we experience. Initially you learned to be afraid when you did something wrong and angered someone else—usually a parent—and were punished for the behavior. As time passed, you learned that other situations and events can also lead to negative outcomes, and you became fearful of a number of things—disease, injury, loss of property, or personal embarrassment to name a few. Nabi (2002) says that fear includes a threat to our physical or psychological self that is out of our control, and that it can change attitudes (p. 291–292).

Appeals to the emotion of fear have been one of the most researched issues in persuasion, but the conclusions of the research are often contradictory. Sometimes the fear appeal works powerfully, but at other times it boomerangs, especially if it is too strong to stomach or simply is unbelievable. Politicians have used fear appeals in negative television advertisements in campaign after campaign, and 2008 will probably not be any different. In the 2004 presidential campaign, President Bush implied that a vote for his opponent would lead to a loss of national security. Fear appeals are also common in marketing communication. For example, the insurance industry tells us to be afraid of financial loss. We are told that we need insurance for everything from floods to identity theft, the need for long-term medical care, and national disasters like

Hurricane Katrina in 2005, which made New Orleans essentially uninhabitable and resulted in billions of dollars in insurance claims. Personal grooming ads emphasize the possible loss in prestige that comes from teeth that aren't white enough, underarm odor, or bad taste in clothing. And cause-related persuasion frequently uses fear appeals in campaigns advocating family values, safe sex, and national security. In most uses of fear appeals, the persuader must first convince us of the probability of the threat before offering us a means (usually a product or practice) of avoiding it and then demonstrating that the proposed solution will work. As receivers of fear appeals, you need to carefully examine the probability of the threat, the difficulty of taking the proposed actions to dodge the threat, and the evidence that these actions will prevent the problem.

Guilt

As we observed elsewhere, guilt is a powerful motivator in persuading others to vote, purchase, donate, or join. Guilt usually comes from a realization that we have violated some rule or code of conduct but can reduce the guilt by atonement or punishment. Borchers (2005) defines guilt as "a psychological feeling of discomfort that arises when order is violated" (p. 195). Guilt frequently arises out of some kind of interpersonal situation—we have wronged our parents, children, spouse, friends, or the community, and we must set things right. For example, the politician claims that we have under-funded education, and many poor kids are left behind, doomed to failure. We can atone for the mistake by having nationwide competence tests, eliminating tenure for teachers, and getting actively involved in our children's learning. If we missed an appointment, we can send flowers or an "I'm sorry" card. If we have engaged in unsafe sex, thus endangering our partner, we can engage in preventive actions in the future. The best way to prevent drug usage by teens is for parents to ask where the teen is going, who will be there, when they expect to come home, and whether adults will be present. That

THINK HOW MUCH YOUR KIDS COULD DO IN LIFE. NOW THINK HOW DOING POT COULD STOP THEM.

Reliable evidence shows that marijuana today is more than twice as powerful on average as it was 20 years ago. It contains twice the concentration of THC, the chemical that affects the brain. Pot can turn your hopes and dreams for your kids into a nightmare of lost opportunities.

It can start with messing up in school. Kids who regularly smoke marijuana can develop symptoms of what psychologists call an "amotivational syndrome," which in plain English means:

- *decreased energy and ambition*
- *shortened attention span*
- *lack of judgment*
- *high distractibility*
- *impaired ability to communicate and relate to others*

And pot can cause a whole lot more problems than just doing badly in school. But the good news is that kids whose parents get involved with them are far less likely to do drugs.

So lay down a few laws for your kids. And the sooner the better, because the average age when teens first try marijuana is under 14 years old. To learn more, call 1-800-788-2800 or come to the web site.

PARENTS.
THE ANTI-DRUG.
theantidrug.com

OFFICE OF NATIONAL DRUG CONTROL POLICY/PARTNERSHIP FOR A DRUG-FREE AMERICA™

FIGURE 7.10   This ad by the Partnership for a Drug Free America uses the avoidance of future guilt to persuade.

advice is part of a cause related campaign sponsored by the Partnership for a Drug Free America and is about avoiding guilt in the future. Its slogan is "Parents: The Anti-Drug."

Nabi (2002) notes that the causes of guilt vary greatly across religions and cultures. In some cultures, losing face is about the worst thing a person can do. In others, dishonoring one's elders is the big guilt button. Receivers need to recognize guilt appeals for what they are and then determine what they need to do to reduce their own sense of guilt.

Anger

We usually become angry when things don't go our way. When we face some obstacle that keeps us from reaching our goal or that harms us or loved ones, we become frustrated, and we want to strike out at those who make things difficult for us. Anger is also very powerful. Nabi (2002) noted that while anger generates high levels of energy, it sometimes leads to constructive problem solving and often prompts careful analysis of messages (p. 293). Take the sentence "What did he mean by saying that I was naïve?" You might get angry over being called naïve, but you seek to get down to the actual meaning of the accusation, which is a constructive use of your anger.

We see appeals to anger in politics and cause-related persuasion and in some types of marketing and advertising. A significant proportion of the population was fearful and angry enough following 9/11 that in 2003 that they supported President Bush's call to go to war in Iraq. The justification for the action was that Iraq had caused the disasater because it harbored terrorists, and we wanted to strike back to cure the problem. In hindsight, we probably needed more careful analysis of the situation and the facts by critical receivers. The "striking back" was enormously costly in human and economic terms and didn't result in fewer terrorist attacks. In fact, it may have led to an increase in the number of suicide bombers in Iraq and elsewhere and may have been used to recruit new members of terrorist organizations. Employees, stockholders, and retirees in the late 1990s became angry with CEOs who looted their company's resources and pension funds. Some of them went on a crusade to reform the Securities and Exchange Commission, and they succeeded. They used cause-related persuasion to recruit supporters and donors by appealing to the anger felt by those who were cheated by the crooked CEOs. In my state an organization called the Citizen's Utility Board (CUB) regularly gets donations by appealing to the anger felt by consumers when utility rates are arbitrarily raised. On an intrapersonal level, some persons are angry with the way they look, even if it's their own fault. A "Fatties" organization is now bringing suit against food manufacturers for not disclosing ingredient information that might lead overweight individuals to avoid the products (see Figure 7.11). We have recently seen persons in middle age go to orthodontists to have braces put on their crooked teeth. Perhaps they were angry with their parents, who didn't take care of the problem earlier—now they are willing to pay for the improvement themselves. So anger frequently serves as a motivator in persuasion. Other negative emotions include envy, hatred, and disgust (Nabi, 2002).

Pride

On a more positive note, persuaders appeal to pride to enact legislation, sell products, and prompt joining or donating. A feeling of pride usually includes taking credit for some positive outcome in our lives. As a result, people become expressive about their accomplishments and may make announcements about the good deeds. Sometimes this causes resentment in those who haven't achieved as much, so persuaders need to be careful about using appeals to pride. And cultural differences affect the emotion of pride. Nabi (2002) reports that collectivist cultures (such as China's) "respond more favorably to pride-based appeals" (p. 296) than do cultures that are more individualistically based (such as the United States).

We can find pride appeals in many persuasive contexts. Politicians tout the accomplishments of their administrations or programs. Cause-based pride appeals are intended to make the potential donors feel proud about making a donation to the good cause. And of course many products promise to make consumers feel proud when they use the brand to improve their appearance. For example, Neutrogena Skin Clearing Tint uses a pride appeal when the ads urge consumers to "rethink makeup...now, don't cover up. Clear up." The ads give the brand credibility by using the words "Dermatologist Recommended" together with the pictures of two young females who are presumed to use the product and who appear not to have acne or blemishes.

Happiness and Joy

Happiness and joy are obviously similar. Happiness is associated with a mood, and joy indicates a positive emotional response to events. For our purposes they are synonyms. Happy persons are positive about their future, confident, sharing, and trusting, and they seem to attract other persons (Nabi, 2002). We can all think of persuasive happiness appeals made by advertisers who link use of their brand with happy outcomes and satisfied consumers. Estee Lauder's Pleasures and Pleasures for Men ran a three-page fold-out ad in the May 2005 issue of *Cosmopolitan*. It had no copy aside from the name of the brand. Instead it showed nine pictures, seven of which focused on the members of a young family. The other two pictures were of cherry blossoms and a puppy. The implied conclusion was for consumers to "Use the brand and be as happy as these folks." Politicians promise better,

Obesity:

~~"Epidemic"~~

~~"Problem"~~

~~"Threat"~~

~~"Issue"~~

"Hype"

Americans have been force-fed a steady diet of obesity myths by the "food police," trial lawyers, and even our own government.

Learn the truth about obesity at:

ConsumerFreedom.com

The Center for Consumer Freedom is a nonprofit organization dedicated to protecting consumer choices and promoting common sense.

happier, sharing, and more trusting times if we enact their policies on the economy, the environment, and education. Cause-related advertising usually implies that support for a cause such as Save the Children will bring the joiner or donor a sense of well-being, self-respect, and happiness instead of a sense of guilt for ignoring the issue. Nabi (2002) also says that appeals to happiness frequently use humor in advertising because of its ability to distract audience attention and cause laughter (p. 296).

Other positive emotions that persuaders can invoke include relief, hope, compassion, and many others.

ATTITUDES: THE THIRD PROCESS PREMISE

In Chapter 4 we looked at how researchers use a variety of theories to explain attitudes. One unifying element among these theories is that attitudes can and do serve as the unstated major premises in persuasive enthymemes. We also noted that attitudes act as predispositions to behavior, so holding an attitude or a set of attitudes makes us ready to take action. However, while attitudes are sometimes excellent predictors of behavior, at other times they are not. Psychologists Martin Fishbein and Icek Ajzen (1975) now believe that a better predictor of behavior is what they call the *intention to behave*. When the person tells you how he or she intends to act, the person is prone to act that way. By articulating their intentions, they have already acted symbolically.

Psychologists Alice H. Egley and Shelley Chaiken (1993) define an attitude as "a psychological tendency that is expressed by evaluating a particular entity with some degree of favor or disfavor" (p. 1). The important word here is "tendency," by which they mean "an internal state that lasts for at least a short time" (p. 2). Since the attitude is internal (in our heads), we must infer it using "evaluative responses." Examples of evaluative responses include expressing "approval or disapproval, favor or disfavor, liking or disliking, approach or avoidance, attraction or aversion, or similar reactions" (p. 3).

Researchers into consumer behavior identified a social function served by attitudes. For instance, they asked whether family, friends, authority figures, or celebrity figures affect our attitudes toward a brand, candidate, or ideology. They concluded that socially significant persons do influence our attitudes (Schiffman & Kanuk, 1997), and note that mass media exposure correlates highly with the formation of consumer attitudes (pp. 260–262).

Advertising researcher S. Shavitt (1990) maintained that attitudes serve both social and utilitarian functions. In researching audience reactions to advertisements, he found that the social functions of attitudes in the ads tell us what persons responding to the ads were like and in all likelihood what sorts of appeals would prompt them to action. For example, the ad might claim that discriminating people prefer high-fiber diets to high-fat, low-carb Atkins' Diets that only temporarily take off pounds. If we want to be a discriminating and slimmer person, we adopt the eating habits of other discriminating and slim persons.

Utilitarian functions of attitudes stress the features and benefits of the product. An ad might claim that the Honda Prius gets up to 60 miles per gallon, and it is extremely quiet in the electrically powered mode. Two utilitarian elements operate here—mileage and quietness. This also fits with elements of the ELM model. For example, psychologists K. G. De Bono and R. Harnish (1988), R. E. Petty and D. T. Wegener (1998), and others found that for high self-monitoring individuals, (e.g., those who were usually very aware of why they were responding to an ad), an attractive source of persuasion usually triggers elaborate processing of the message. For low self-monitoring individuals (e.g., those who were barely aware of even responding to the ad), elaborate processing is more likely to occur only if an expert rather than an attractive source conveys the message. This makes sense. If you are a high self-monitoring person, you do not want to blunder simply because a celebrity recommends the product. That makes you seem impulsive in the eyes of others. So, you do serious investigation of the product in the central processing route. Low self-monitoring persons respect expertise more than advice from a celebrity, and they avoid looking foolish by relying on the recommendation of the expert.

We usually find attitude objects in the persuader's requests for action or offers of products, ideas, candidates, beliefs, and so on. For example, recently many Americans started flying the flag and displaying patriotic bumper stickers, yard signs, and other emblems with slogans like "United We Stand" or "These Colors Won't Run." These displays are in response to political persuasion emphasizing the value of patriotism. These attitude objects serve a social function because they announce the person's attitudes. This, in turn, causes alignment or identification with others who feel the same way and helps to foster interpersonal relations and influence. The attitude object of the flag, bumper sticker, or sign serves as part of the appeal, and we follow suit if we want to identify with them. The obverse is also true: If we want to distance ourselves from jingoistic patriotism, we won't follow the requested action and may even display a "Get Out of Iraq!" sign in our yard. This reduces the possibility of forming interpersonal relationships with super-patriots.

So attitudes have an important social function in that they can either foster or discourage social networking. Nelson (2001) notes that the social function of attitudes in organizations (especially businesses) can make or break the organization. And according to D. C. Schrader (1999), the social function of interpersonal influence is largely dependent on the goal complexity of appeals. In other words, if the persuader's advice is too complicated, we judge his or her attempts to influence us as unworkable, incompetent, or inappropriate. As a result, the social function of attitudes often affects persuasive outcomes.

To learn more about the importance of interpersonal influence on getting compliance from others, access InfoTrac College Edition, enter the words "interpersonal influence" in the search engine, and review a few of the many articles listed there.

Attitudes, Beliefs, and Opinions

As noted in Chapter 4, Rokeach (1968) pointed out that individual beliefs range from primitive and strongly held to those based on authority and not as strongly held. These belief sets cluster and form attitudes which fall into two categories: (1) attitudes toward objects or issues and (2) attitudes toward situations. Both predispose us to action, but they also might confuse us when they conflict with one

another. For example, when parents protest the presence of a student with AIDS in their children's school, attitudes toward the object (the infected student) and toward the situation (the possibility of infecting my own children) can either conflict or converge. When the two attitudes conflict, the parents sympathize with the victim, but they don't want their child infected.

Opinions resemble beliefs but are far more fickle, as opinion polls demonstrate—opinions can change overnight. We have opinions about politicians, what they say in campaigns, and their actions taken after assuming office. These opinions change, especially if the politician blunders, loses to Congress on an issue, or supports a corrupt friend. Usually the politician's errors lead to low voter ratings and sometimes rejection at the polls. But opinions are fickle and unpredictable. For example, during Bill Clinton's impeachment trial, his ratings in the polls actually went to an all-time high in spite of the sordid sex scandal. Why? Rokeach's theory helps explain the riddle. People had a highly negative attitude toward Clinton's sexual dalliance (attitude toward object). But they had highly positive feelings about other issues like the economy, low unemployment, budget surpluses, and a bullish stock market (attitude toward situation). These opinions conflicted with their feelings about the scandal, and the economy won out. A similar scenario played out for President George W. Bush on his plan to institute private investment accounts as part of the Social Security system. After he campaigned for the change in over half of the states, his ratings on the issue plummeted in the public opinion polls.

To learn more about the measurement of and uses that are made of measures of public opinion, go to InfoTrac College Edition, and enter the words "public opinion" in the search engine. Check a few of the more tantalizing items listed under the periodical titles.

Social psychologist P. Zimbardo and his colleagues (1976, 1991) note that attitudes are "either mental readiness or implicit predispositions that exert some general and consistent influence on a fairly large class of evaluative responses" (p. 20). A school of advertising research known by the acronym DAGMAR suggests that ad agencies ought to Define Advertising Goals for Measured Advertising Results (Colley, 1961). In other words, establishing positive attitudes toward a brand serves as the goal of advertising, not instant purchase behavior. The idea is that if consumers have an improved image of a product, they will probably buy it sometime in the future. Therefore, if the marketer can change their attitudes, purchase eventually follows. Unfortunately, this attitude–behavior link sometimes flip flops, perhaps because of intervening variables that also affect purchase behavior such as time of day, attractiveness of the offer, a store display, price, or background music. Even in experiments with these causes filtered out, attitude and behavior do not consistently link.

The Functions of Attitudes

Attitudes can have several functions. For example, they have a cognitive or knowledge function; we aren't born with attitudes, we must learn them. Consider our attitudes about being environmentally responsible. How did they come about? Probably we first learned about air and water pollution and the dangers that they bring. Then we learned about recycling and what it can achieve. Then we learned that endangered species may act as early warnings about what might ultimately happen to humans. Only after learning all of these things do we finally form an overall attitude toward environmental responsibility. Likewise, some advertisements also persuade by teaching. A mutual fund company advertises that it is "no load" and goes on to explain what that means—customers don't have to pay commissions when they make investments. Persuadees learn the value of this and form a positive attitude toward that company, and they decide to use the company when they make investments. The same learning operates in political or cause-related campaigns. For example, since the March of Dimes no longer supports polio research (the disease has been nearly eradicated), it must teach potential donors that now it supports research into premature births—the leading cause of infant

mortality. The receiver learns about the organization and its purposes and then forms an attitude toward it and decides whether or not to send a donation.

Attitudes also influence our emotions and feelings, and thus they have what has been termed an *affective function* or an emotional outcome. For instance, our attitudes about the development of hydrogen fuels affect how we feel about this new source of energy. If we equate hydrogen energy with the hydrogen bomb, we experience fear and may actively oppose its production. Some ads target the affective dimension, or emotions. For example, how did *The Sopranos* affect viewers' attitudes and emotions toward mob figures? Chris Seay, a Christian minister, worried about his wife's response when he rushed home from church activities to watch the nudity- and profanity-filled fourth season. He ultimately convinced her that the show was about "faith, forgiveness and family values." That nifty bit of persuasion got him out of his affective dilemma (Pinsky, 2002).

Finally, attitudes have a behavioral function in that they prepare us to take certain actions. Because we hold certain attitudes toward air and water pollution, we may choose to recycle, to not buy a gas guzzler, or only use biodegradable detergents. The behavioral function of attitudes affects what we do about these issues. Some ads aim at changing attitudes in order to prompt behavior change. Two goals of advertising are to create traffic in a store or to get consumers to try a brand. The advertiser offers huge discounts or special events such as the visit of a celebrity to create traffic. They may send a free sample or offer an attractive rebate with a purchase. Few people reject anything that is free or cheaper, so they give the brand a try. The marketer's hope is that visiting the store will prompt impulse purchases or that satisfaction with the performance of the brand will lead to brand loyalty and future purchases.

Attitudes and Intention

As we noted earlier, the work of Fishbein and Ajzen (1975) added the concept of **behavioral intention** to the research on attitude and behavior change. Here, a fairly consistent set of results emerges. Attitude change usually precedes what people say they intend to do. As noted above, when people articulate what they intend to do, they have already acted symbolically. Nonverbally, when the person clips or saves a coupon, he or she has already "bought" the brand. Likewise, the person who displays a bumper sticker in favor of a certain candidate will show up at the polls to vote for that candidate on election day. Knowing this, politicians urge people to display bumper stickers, buttons, and yard signs to guarantee their votes rather than trying to persuade others who may be undecided.

Attitudes and Interpersonal Communication/Persuasion

There are several other dimensions of attitude change and the subsequent behavior puzzle. One of these is the degree to which attitudes function as tools of interpersonal communication or persuasion, or both. In other words, do expressions of attitudes have more to do with fitting ourselves into a comfortable position with others than they do with our ultimate behavior? R. J. Eiser (1987), a critic of attitude research puts it this way: "One of the main shortcomings of many attitude theories is their emphasis on individualistic, intra-psychic factors to the relative neglect of the social and communicative context within which attitudes are acquired and expressed" (p. 2). In other words, we overtly express attitudes in order to get along with and identify with others.

Attitudes and Information Processing

The focus on human information processing in the ELM which serves as a unifying model throughout this book also relates to behavioral intentions. We can't look at attitudes and behavior without also looking at how audiences process such persuasive information. One of the first questions to ask is whether the audience even comprehends the message. In the central path they usually do

comprehend the message and may even research it. In the peripheral path they probably don't. For example, "cents off" coupons as persuasive information fit with several memory networks in our minds, such as whether we already use the brand, how often, and whether the coupons are valuable enough to justify clipping them. Peripheral cues may prompt behavior. For example, people will clip more coupons if there is a dotted line around the coupon and clip even more if there is a little scissors on the dotted line. And there are diversity issues to be concerned with in deciding whether or not to offer coupons. For example, Latinos tend not to clip coupons because they associate them with food stamps, a social stigma in their subculture. So if an advertiser is targeting Latinos, that advertiser should not use coupons but may want to emphasize the warranty or quality instead.

Research into how information is stored in our long-term memory (LTM) is fairly recent, and most researchers agree that information is usually stored in networks and in the form of key words, symbols, and relationships. A good organizing device for LTM is to make one's persuasion episodic in nature, probably due to the power of the narrative or story form. For example, we all have been late for an appointment and find ourselves stuck behind the slowest driver on the road, who also misses all the green stoplights. Imagine a television commercial to promote Compoz, an over-the-counter treatment for settling people's nerves. This episode could act as a script for the commercial. The ad opens with the character realizing that he or she has nearly missed a doctor's appointment. We see them rush out to the car, get in, and speed off, only to get behind the slowpoke. They glance nervously at the clock and begin having a silent "conversation" with the slow driver. They are about to commit road rage, but instead they take a Compoz tablet. The ad closes with the slow driver turning at the next intersection and the product's slogan, "For those nerve-racking occasions try Compoz." At the behavior stage of the ELM (voting, buying, joining, or donating), the critical episode is retrieved from long-term memory and provides persuadees with good "reasons" for taking action.

To learn more about what affects our long-term memory, access InfoTrac College Edition, and type the words "long-term memory" in the search engine. Browse some of the titles.

The ELM model has prompted a multitude of research insights into the process of persuasion since its introduction. Researchers S. Booth-Butterfield and J. Welbourne (2002) suggest that the model "has been instrumental in integrating the literature on source, message, receiver and context effects in persuasion and has also been a springboard for new research in this domain" (p. 155). Although people want to have "correct" attitudes, the degree to which they will elaborate on an issue varies from individuals and situations, but the following patterns remain clear.

1. A number of variables affect attitude change and can act as persuasive arguments, peripheral cues, or attitudinal positions.

2. When motivation or ability to elaborate decreases, peripheral cues become more important and carry the persuasive load. For example, persons who are uninterested in the implications of diversity will rely on stereotyping.

3. Conversely, as motivation or ability to elaborate on a claim increases, peripheral cues lose impact. For example, if our new boss is ethnically different from us, we devalue stereotypes.

4. The persuader affects consumers' motivation by encouraging or discouraging careful examination of the argument or claim. The persuader says, "April 15 is only a week away, so bone up on the new tax laws," instead of saying, "At your income level, you might as well use the short tax form 1040EZ and file online."

5. Issues and arguments flowing from the central processing path persist, predict actual behavior best, and seem resistant to competing persuasion. Persuasion using process premises is likely to follow the peripheral path, whereas persuasion using reasoned premises is likely to be processed in the central route. Petty and Cacioppo's (1986) chart in Figure 7.12 depicts various options and routes.

Notice that the various options in the ELM depend on whether you have the motivation to process a persuasive message. You must want to investigate a given product, candidate, or cause or the elaboration process is short-circuited. If they are motivated to process an offer, appeal, or claim, persuadees must also possess the ability to complete the processing. Thereafter, the nature of the attitude change depends on which path is followed. If the peripheral path is used, the attitude change will be weak, short-lived, and less likely to yield behavior. If the central processing path is used, attitude change will be potent, long-lived, and likely to lead to behavior.

Each path has its strengths and weaknesses. Most researchers agree that attitudes have something to do with behavior, that attitudes can be altered by persuasion, and that the suggested behavior usually follows a change in attitude. What does all this mean to us as persuadees who live in a world concerned with diversity and ethics? What can we do to uncover persuaders' intentions toward and beliefs about the diverse audiences? Being aware of attitudes helps us to pinpoint what persuaders think of us and others. Identifying the attitudes that persuaders assume we have makes us more critical receivers, and so we judge persuasive attempts as ethical or unethical. We also become conscious of our attitudes, and as a result, we anticipate how persuaders use them to get us to follow their advice. However, few situations involve a single attitude. Most situations involve several attitudes, which leads to a need for consistency among those attitudes.

CONSISTENCY: THE FOURTH PROCESS PREMISE

We looked at balance theory in Chapter 4. It posits that we feel comfortable when the world lives up to (or operates consistently with) our

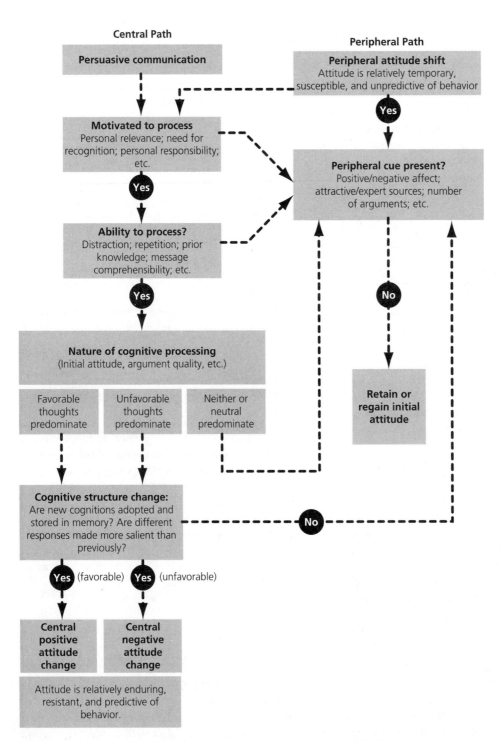

FIGURE 7.12 Decision flow in Petty and Cacioppo's elaboration likelihood model.

BOX 7.3   Ten Lenses and the Diversity Channel

In his book entitled *The Ten Lenses: Your Guide to Living and Working in a Multicultural World* (2001), Mark A. Williams, author and founder of The Diversity Channel, (a diversity training company) discusses how human emotions vary in organizations and institutions. He describes and explains ten "lenses" or perceptual filters through which most of us view our diverse world. There are the *Assimilationists* who believe that all diversities should behave like regular Americans, and then there are the *Cultural Centrists* who believe that we must not tamper with the diversity of others. The *Meritocrats* believe that if you work hard enough and pull yourself up by your bootstraps, you will achieve your goals regardless of your race, ethnicity, or other aspects of diversity. The *Victim/Caretakers* believe that bias will forever hold down persons of diverse origins. The *Colorblind* believe in ignoring cultural differences and seeking the true value of any individual whose diversity differs from the majority. The *Elitists* believe that it is their destiny and their right

to be superior to others of varying diversities. The *Integrationists* believe that the best way to break down biases and stereotypes is to merge persons of various diversities in the workplace and elsewhere. The *Multiculturalists* want to celebrate our diversity—the more diversity we have the better things will be for everyone. *Seclusionists* want to distance and protect themselves and their families from persons of diverse cultures. And *Transcendentists* believe that race, gender, and ethnicity reflect our unified humanity. Where do you fit?

 Speculate on how these lenses might apply to human needs, emotions, and attitudes. How do you look at persons of other races, nationalities, genders, sexual preference, or ethnicities? If you want to explore Williams's work further, pick up his book and take his Ten Lenses Survey or or go online to www.thediversitychannel.com and explore its home page options.

---

perceptions or our predictions of it. When this doesn't happen, we try to change either ourselves or our interpretations of events to bring about a balanced state. Persuaders offer a means (usually a product, service, or action) to return to balance and psychological comfort. If you want to change attitudes toward health care, for instance, then try to create imbalance in health care users. You might say, "With an HMO, you can't go to the best surgeon."

We all seek out psychological equilibrium, so as receivers we need to identify what puts us into states of imbalance or inconsistency, thus making us vulnerable to persuasion. If psychological equilibrium is our goal, we need to feel comfortable and look for persuasion that reinforces attitudes. As Eiser (1987) pointed out, defining the "existing frame of reference" is a critical factor in predicting attitude shifts. Once we identify the receiver's current frame of reference, we create the kind of inconsistency that prompts psychological uneasiness, that leads to attitude change.

Cognitive Dissonance Theory

A problem with balance theory is that it doesn't relate to the degree of difference between the two people or the two instances judged. Instead it looks at the kinds of differences—positive or negative—that exist in the comparisons of persons or instances. In other words, the theory accounts for *qualitative* differences between judgments but it doesn't deal with *quantitative* differences. That may seem like a minor problem, but major differences might exist between persons or concepts regarding controversial topics such as abortion, school prayer, or patriotism, so it's important to determine how far persons and their issue positions are from one another on a topic. Leon Festinger's cognitive dissonance theory (1962) addressed this problem of quantitative and qualitative differences between persons and ideas.

Unlike balance theory, **cognitive dissonance theory** predicts that when we experience psychological tension, or dissonance, we try to reduce it in some way instead of totally resolving the tension. Tension reduction has a quantitative dimension.

We can change our attitudes a little, a moderate amount, a lot, or not at all. The tension caused by dissonance grows out of our psychological belief system, whereas balance theory relies more on logical inconsistencies. Festinger defined dissonance as a feeling resulting from the existence of two nonfitting or contrasting pieces of knowledge about the world. As in balance theory, there are times when things fit or go together and times when they do not. For Festinger, the opposite of dissonance, or "consonance," exists when two pieces of information do fit together, and hence reinforce one another. Some persons change dissonant cognitions by moving their beliefs closer to one another. Others rationalize the problem away or discredit the source of the information. Others reduce dissonance by selective perception, selective retention, or selective exposure—they choose not to receive or perceive the dissonance, they forget about it, or they choose not to be exposed to conflicting information.

Recently, dissonance theory helped explain the new sense of uneasiness affecting sexually active individuals who have multiple partners. Most of us know that the main causes of infection by the AIDS virus is unsafe sex practices, the sharing of needles among drug users, and sometimes from blood transfusions or accidental exposure to the blood of AIDS carriers. What can sexually active people do to reduce the uneasiness or dissonance they feel regarding their own sexually activity? They can:

1. Devalue their beliefs about the most effective methods of birth control and use condoms
2. Devalue AIDS information, telling themselves that this is just a scare tactic to cut down on the promiscuity of the younger generation
3. Selectively perceive the information and choose to believe that *their* sex partners don't have the AIDS virus
4. Try to forget the information about AIDS through the process of selective retention
5. Try to rationalize the problem away by believing that a cure for AIDS is just around the corner
6. Become celibate or have fewer partners
7. Do more than one of these things

Although Festinger mainly dealt with the notion of dissonance, it seems clear that we seek its opposite—consonance—to reinforce our existing attitudes. We listen to the candidates of our choice and avoid listening to their opponents. Conservatives read conservative newspapers, and liberal people read liberal ones. We seek information that confirms our position and reinforces our beliefs. Several actions build consonance in this way. We can:

1. Revalue our initial beliefs, making them stronger
2. Revalue the source of the information input by giving it more credibility than it deserves
3. Perceive the information as stronger than it actually is
4. Remember the most positive parts of the information and highlight them
5. Seek out even more supporting information
6. Do several of these things

Creating consonance strengthens and reinforces attitudes, increases credibility, and probably induces action. Persuaders probably use consonance at least as frequently as dissonance. They often want to reinforce people's opinions, attitudes, beliefs, or behavior.

In many cases, dissonance theory oversimplifies the human situation. Recently, researchers in communication, psychology, and sociology have looked at a variety of other factors that affect feelings of dissonance. W. Wood (2000) points out that social factors play a role in reducing dissonance. People want to fit in with significant reference groups and engage in normative behavior to do so. Internal states determine the outcome of persuasion as much as do the source's skill at designing the dissonance or consonance producing messages.

Sources of Dissonance

What causes you to feel imbalance or dissonance? Some are unique to you, but many of them are similar for large groups of people. These more universal factors are useful for persuaders because they are potent first premises in enthymemes. Descriptions of a few common ones follow.

Loss of Group Prestige. This relates to the pride felt by members of a well-respected reference group, profession, or organization that has fallen on bad times and no longer is as highly respected. For instance, Martha Stewart was highly respected by many people who identified with her because they felt that they also had her class and good taste. They wanted to emulate her, to try her recipes, and to have a flower garden like hers. One of her fans said, "We put a copy of Martha Stewart's *Living* magazine on a coffee table. It's the prettiest thing in the living room." Another said, "We want a little of what she's got—a scant teaspoon in Marthaspeak—of her taste and talent" (Rowell, 2002, p. 16). After she suffered a financial scandal and served jail time, her sheen dimmed a bit. A former fan observed, "There's nothing in her magazine that even hints at her virtue" (Rowell, 2002, p. 16). Ultimately, however, Martha regained some of her previous sheen. The loss of group prestige affects small and large groups alike—from a fraternity or sorority to an entire profession such as lawyers or a region of the country such as the East Coast.

Economic Loss. When we feel that our economic value is in danger of being reduced, we experience dissonance. We deal with the obvious dissonance of losing a job in a number of ways. After the dot-com bubble burst, many displaced workers chose to take early retirement, others returned to school or accepted jobs with much lower salaries, and others started their own businesses.

Loss of Personal Prestige. Ads promoting hair restorers or weight reduction plans play on one's loss of personal prestige resulting from physical appearance. Being passed over for a promotion at work also leads to a loss of personal prestige. Other fears relating to loss of prestige include the loss of youth, the loss of health, and the lost of self-respect.

Uncertainty of Prediction. Whenever we move, change schools, take a new job, or break up with a spouse or significant other, we feel uncomfortable because we can no longer predict probable outcomes. Products that promise to protect us from some negative circumstance (illness, job loss, financial difficulties) use the inability to predict as a "hook" to persuade us.

Sources of Consonance

On the other side of the coin, some appeals give receivers a sense of consonance, and reinforce beliefs, attitudes, or behaviors and activate receivers.

Reassurance of Security. Today, police stations, airports, courthouses, schools, and other public buildings are protected with metal detectors and even armed guards. We want to feel secure in public places, and these preventatives provide that sense of security. Promises of job security are powerful persuaders for persons making career choices, and IRA and Keogh accounts offer retirement security.

Demonstration of Predictability. Consonance happens when the world operates in predictable ways. Manufacturers rely on the appeal to predictability by offering guarantees or warranties. And everyone likes to know what to expect at work, at home, in the community, and so on.

The Use of Rewards. Rewards or positive reinforcements increase feelings of consonance and the probability that a behavior will be repeated. Persuaders often use positive and complimentary statements to reinforce behavior. In his best-selling book *How to Win Friends and Influence People*, Dale Carnegie (1952) advised his readers to "try to figure out the other man's good points...and people will cherish your words and treasure them and repeat them over a lifetime" (p. 38). Carnegie put his finger on ways to make audiences feel good about themselves. This is still good advice for persuading audiences or influencing people. Successful supervisors seem adept at giving rewards rather than offering criticisms.

REVIEW AND CONCLUSION

We are searching for various kinds of unstated and widely held major premises that can serve in persuasive enthymemes. One of these kinds of major premises is the process or emotional premise, which appeals to our needs, emotions, attitudes, and the psychological processes of dissonance and consonance operating daily in each of us. We can see needs and wants operating in Maslow's hierarchy of needs, Packard's compelling human needs, and Feig's hot buttons. Although some of these models have been around for a long time, they still have applicability for us, as their many rejuvenations demonstrate.

A second kind of process premise involves our emotions. Persuaders target our emotional states and get at us through such things as fear, guilt, and anger or by appeals to more positive emotions such as happiness, joy, or pride. A third kind of process premise involves attitudes, beliefs, and opinions. If persuaders change our attitudes about fuel efficiency, they predispose us to buy fuel-efficient autos, furnaces, and water heaters. If persuaders want us to continue voting for a certain party, they reinforce our existing beliefs and attitudes about that party. Both of these persuasive types can be used with either attitudes toward objects and issues or attitudes toward situations. It may be important for persuaders to reinforce or change our behavioral intentions. Attitudes also impact important and not so important purchase, voting, joining, or donating decisions, as depicted in the ELM.

The fourth kind of process premise is the human desire for psychological consonance, in which we seek a world where our predictions are verified, and in which people we like approve of the same things we do. If we feel a lack of balance, or dissonance, we actively seek ways to bring our world into congruity by reducing psychological tensions. If we perceive balance or consonance to exist, we experience a sense of ease and can be easily motivated to continue to act as we have been. Persuaders try to create dissonance if they want us to change our behavior, and they create consonance if they want us to maintain our behavior. Process premises are important in the ways we persuade others and the ways in which we are persuaded.

KEY TERMS

When you have finished reading this chapter, you should be able to identify, explain, and give an example of the following words or concepts.

process or emotional premises	reassurance of worth	prepotency	attitudes
motivation research	ego gratification	basic needs	opinions
hidden needs	creative outlets	need for security	behavioral intention
compelling needs	love objects	belongingness or affiliation needs	consistency
hot buttons	sense of power or strength	love and esteem needs	cognitive dissonance theory
emotional security	need for roots	self-actualization needs	

APPLICATION OF ETHICS

It is finals week at a state university. A professor of communication gets an email from a student in one of his classes in which the student expresses a fear of failing the final exam. The two previous exams were so difficult that she was only able to get low "D" grades on them, and since the final counts double, she is in danger of failing the class. She tells the professor that she is already on probation and will be dismissed if she fails the class. Her parents have already given her an ultimatum—"get off probation or support yourself through the remaining two years of schooling!" By chance, the professor runs into the student in the library and tells her that he is not about to cater to students who don't study enough and chides her for even sending the email. She denies having sent the message and says that she suspects someone has stolen her password and sent a forgery to embarrass her. The professor convinces the manager of the university email system to track down the source of the message, and indeed it has not been sent from the student's computer but from the male teaching assistant for the class. The professor suspects that the teaching assistant wants to use the email to sexually harass the female student. There are emotional issues involved. Has the teaching assistant used a fear appeal? Is that ethical given the professor's suspicions? What should the professor do?

QUESTIONS FOR FURTHER THOUGHT

1. What is a process premise? Explain.

2. What is the difference between an attitude and a need? Give examples.

3. What did Maslow mean when he called his hierarchy of needs "prepotent"?

4. Which needs described by Packard are the most ego involving or personal in nature?

5. What is an example of the need for emotional security?

6. What is an example of how advertisers use the need for ego gratification?

7. What is an example of the need for a sense of power?

8. What emotions are being used when persuaders alert us to the possibility of job loss or identity theft?

9. What emotions are being used when a persuader tells us that we have been cheated by an auto repair shop?

10. What are three functions of an attitude?

11. What is the difference between an attitude and an opinion?

12. What is the difference between a behavior and a behavioral intention?

13. According to the ELM, which decision path will be used when purchasing ice cream?

14. According to the ELM, what happens if the audience isn't motivated to vote?

15. According to the ELM, what happens to a decision if the audience can't respond?

16. Using the elaboration likelihood model as depicted in Figure 7.12, explain the flow of information regarding a current issue.

17. What are some sources of dissonance?

18. What are some sources of consonance?

19. What ethical standards should we apply when using process or emotional appeals?

 For online activities, go to the *Persuasion* book companion website at http://communication.wadsworth.com/larson11.

8

Content or Logical Premises in Persuasion

LEARNING GOALS

After reading this chapter, you should be able to:

1. Give everyday examples such as ads or speeches that rely on logical versus emotional appeals.

2. Find everyday examples of each of the types of evidence discussed.

3. Explain the difference between the two types of analogy and when they might be appropriate.

4. Find everyday examples of the three types of syllogisms and explain them to the class.

5. Explain the three major elements and the three substantiating elements in the Toulmin model.

6. Identify examples of logical fallacies in ads, newspaper editorials, and letters to the editor in a newsweekly like *Time* or *Newsweek*.

7. Identify logical fallacies used in sensational publications like *The National Enquirer*—our nation's largest circulation "newspaper."

8. Explain the various types of reasoning (e.g., reasoning from symptoms).

Chapter 7 looked at premises based on psychological processes or emotions. Another type of premise frequently operating in enthymemes is based on people's ability to think logically or rationally. The elaboration likelihood model (ELM) suggests that this kind of persuasion uses the central information-processing route and entails considerable analysis and intellectual activity. Premises relying on logical and analytical abilities are called **content premises** because they don't rely on psychological processes and/or emotions as process premises do. Many content premises such as *causes have effects* are perceived as valid and true by large segments of the audience, so persuaders can use them as major premises in enthymemes. Some persuasion theorists call these premises **arguments** or *propositions* while marketers call them *offers*. In fact, argumentation scholars and professors Lunsford and Ruszkiewicz (2004) claim that everything is an argument, including stained glass windows, the presidential seal, and bumper stickers. Aristotle defined an argument as a statement supported by proof. The dictionary defines it as "a discussion in which disagreement is expressed for some point" (*American Heritage Dictionary*, 1985). Most theorists agree that argument contains a controversial claim which should be debatable and supported by evidence (Lunsford & Ruszkiewicz, 2004 p. 125). They make the case that an argument seeks to discover the truth in order to win conviction, while persuasion seeks to apply the known truth in order to prompt others to action. Whatever the label—premise, argument, proposition, offer or claim—this chapter looks at persuasion that uses the receiver's logical, reasoning, rational, and intellectual abilities.

For example, suppose I want to persuade you to support legalized marijuana. What would you consider good and sufficient reasons for supporting the idea? For some persons, there aren't any good (let alone sufficient) reasons for such a policy, so there would be no way to persuade those folks. For others, the policy seems so sensible on the face of it that you don't need to persuade them either. But what about those who neither approve nor disapprove—the undecided members of the audience? They require more information, evidence, discussion, and debate before taking a side. In other words, they are asking for good and sufficient reasons for supporting the proposition. You might tell them about how legalized marijuana reduced the rate of usage of stronger and more addictive drugs in Holland. You might discuss the revenues that could be generated by having the government tax marijuana just as it does with cigarettes. And you might point out that such a policy would remove criminal elements from the sale of the drug. The success or failure of any of these arguments, claims, or propositions relies on beliefs already held by the audience. They already believe that tax revenues are needed, and that criminal elements in any activity are undesirable. Those widely held beliefs serve as major or minor premises in persuasive enthymemes.

We have all encountered and learned logical patterns. Most of us believe, for example, that events have causes. When certain things occur other things invariably follow. Problems have causes but their removal resolves the problems. This pattern of rational and intellectual reasoning is called **cause–effect reasoning**. Huglen and Clark (2004) define it as "linking some cause and effect to prove their existence" (p. 23). This makes sense, because if you have no effect(s), there obviously would be no cause, and vice versa. The two have to exist together. For instance, a certain baseball team's pitching staff had experienced many training camp injuries. A logical effect of this cause would be that the team ends the season with a poor record. It's not necessary to convince anyone that injuries lead to losses. You just need to list the various injuries and rely on the cause–effect premise already at work in the audience's mind. As this example shows, the cause–effect pattern is a potent first premise in a persuasive enthymeme. Politicians and government officials, the courts, business, and advertisers all use cause–effect reasoning. Content premises persuade because they rely on widely held patterns of logical reasoning. Our goal in this chapter is to identify some of these patterns. Recognizing them will make you a more critical receiver.

WHAT IS PROOF?

Basically, content or logical premises consist of two elements—proof and reasoning. **Proof** is defined as enough evidence connected through reasoning to lead typical receivers to take or believe the persuader's advice. What may prove a point to fraternity members may not prove the same point to a university administrator. For example, one claim given to justify going to war in Iraq was that Iraq had chemical, biological, and nuclear weapons, and that these were a threat to stability in the region. What evidence would be needed to prove this claim? For some, satellite photos of supposed weapons sites sufficed. For others, physical evidence was needed—they wanted to see the actual weapons. Others required the actual weapons and evidence that Iraq intended to use them. This tells us that "proof" varies from person to person. Proof also varies from situation to situation. For example, some economists claimed that cutting the nation's budget deficit (the cause) would spur economic growth (the effect). Their evidence convinced some people but not others. When the economy improved after the deficit cuts, many of the doubters were convinced. They needed more proof than the original believers did, and the economy provided it. Other economists argued that cuts in the estate tax, taxes on dividends, and capitol gains would spur growth in the economy and thus reduce our budget deficits. The taxes were cut (the cause), but growth didn't follow (the effect).

Most contemporary theorists agree that proof is composed of two facets: **reasoning** and **evidence**. The dictionary definition of reasoning is "the use of reason especially to form conclusions, inferences, or judgments." Evidence is defined as "the data on which a conclusion or judgment may be based; something that furnishes proof" (*American Heritage Dictionary*, 1985). In the proper mix, these two elements lead persuadees to adopt or believe in the changes a persuader advocates. There are several ways to look at evidence and reasoning. First, by examining how persuaders operate, we can infer their motives and discover what they are up to. For example, suppose I want to persuade you that an unrequested kiss on the lips between a male and a female was not sexual harassment. Lunsford and Ruszkiewicz advise asking four questions: (1) Did something happen? (2) What is its nature? (3) What is its quality? and (4) What action should be taken? In this case there was an unrequested kiss on the lips, witnesses observed it, and the female objected to it. Usually, unwanted kisses on the lips are considered harassment. In this case the answer to the third question—what is its quality?—provides the proof: both participants were six years old. "Most people don't consider six year olds as sexually culpable" (p. 16–17).

Another way to look at evidence and reasoning is to investigate how specific the evidence is in relation to the reasoning it supports or the conclusion. Before the advent of electronic media, modern advertising, and contemporary propaganda, audiences were accustomed to receiving very specific and verifiable evidence. For example, if a person gave testimony to prove a point, it was critical to tell the audience why that person qualified to give the testimony. Audiences were also suspicious of some kinds of evidence such as analogies. Today, however, we accept the testimony of professional athletes when they endorse an investment plan even though they don't qualify as experts on finance. And we frequently do accept analogies as evidence, such as animated automobile tires depicted as having tigers' claws to grip the road.

Other kinds of premises and evidence convince us through the central information-processing channel. Politicians offer us evidence in support of a policy, and parents supply what they think are good reasons for not living with someone of the opposite gender unless married. Underlying these examples is the pattern of enough evidence with reasoning to result in proof.

To discover how proof operates in the law, access InfoTrac College Edition, type the word "proof" in the search engine, and select the burden of proof option(s). Read a few of the items listed.

TYPES OF EVIDENCE

Evidence varies in persuasive power depending on the context in which it is used. In some situations, for instance, statistics have a powerful effect; in other situations, pictorial evidence persuades; and in yet others, vicarious or retold experience convinces us. Experiential evidence relies on the assumption that people learn about and act on information gained indirectly, and this is why stories about the experiences of others are so persuasive. Advertisers use testimonials from both ordinary people and celebrities to endorse products, assuming that consumers vicariously absorb the experiences and buy the product. Demonstrations can also logically persuade us. This was the case in the O.J. Simpson trial when the supposed murder glove didn't fit. The defense argued, "If it does not fit, you must acquit" (Lunsford & Ruszkiewicz, p. 102).

But even when we do not learn from or become swayed by the experiences of others, our own experience is usually enough to cause us to change. The Lakota were aware of this. As a Lakota baby crawled close to the campfire, no one pulled it away with shouts of, "Hot! Stay away, baby! Hot!" as we would do in our culture. Instead, they watched the baby's progress very closely and allowed the baby to reach into the fire and touch a hot coal, burning itself mildly. They then quickly pulled the baby away and treated the burn. The experience persuaded the child to be careful with fire. Or suppose a professor explains to you her very stringent attendance policy for a television production class, but you take the policy with a grain of salt and fail the class, necessitating taking it over. You hear the same lecture on attendance on the first day of the class the next semester. If experience persuades, you won't miss a class.

There are three broad forms of evidence: (1) **direct experience**, (2) **dramatic or vicarious experience**, and (3) **rationally processed evidence**. The first two usually are processed via the peripheral information-processing route of the ELM without much forethought, whereas rationally processed evidence usually follows the central information-processing route. Direct experience demonstrates the major premise that actions have consequences. Dramatic evidence relies on the human tendency to structure our lives in narrative or story form. Rational evidence relies on our innate ability to reason using logic and evidence. In previous chapters, we looked at some theorists who present the case for dramatic evidence convincingly. Burke (1985), for example, discusses the power of dramatic or narrative evidence. Let us briefly examine these three broad categories of evidence in more depth.

Direct Experience

Most parents of more than one child tell of their one kid who always had to learn the hard way by experiencing the "actions have consequences" principle. Most of us learn the power of this principle after only a few experiences, but some seem never to catch on. Probably each of us has been in an auto accident, and as a result we have learned to call the police, family, and insurance agent, in that order. You also learned that even a minor accident can take up an inordinate amount of time, paperwork, and effort. You can probably identify some direct experiences in your life that provided a powerful form of evidence for you.

Dramatic or Vicarious Experience

All of us have learned or been persuaded by hearing about the experiences of others—that is, by vicarious experience. There are a variety of types of vicarious experience, most of them dramatic in nature.

Narratives. A good way to use dramatic evidence is through narrative. People have always been fascinated by stories, including myths, legends, and ballads, handed down in an oral/aural tradition. Literacy brought other forms of the narrative (plays, poetry, novels, and short stories). Technology has brought us still other forms such as movies, cartoons, video games, documentaries, talk shows, and broadcasts of athletic events—all having roots in storytelling. Evidence that is dramatic invites our vicarious involvement as it attempts to persuade us to a course of action. It relies on the human ability to project ourselves into the situation described by the persuader and to co-create proof. The results are powerful and long lasting.

In his book *People of the Lie: The Hope for Healing Human Evil*, noted author and psychotherapist M. Scott Peck (1983) related "The Case of Bobby and His Parents." The narrative began with Bobby, who had been admitted to the hospital emergency room the night before for depression. The admitting physician's notes read as follows:

Bobby's older brother Stuart, 16, committed suicide this past June, shooting himself in the head with his .22 caliber rifle. Bobby initially seemed to handle his sibling's death rather well. But from the beginning of school in September, his academic performance has been poor. Once a "B" student, he is now failing all his courses. By Thanksgiving he had become obviously depressed. His parents, who seem very concerned, tried to talk to him, but he has become more and more uncommunicative, particularly since Christmas. Although there is no previous record of antisocial behavior, yesterday Bobby stole a car by himself and crashed it (he had never driven before), and was apprehended by the police.... Because of his age, he was released into his parents' custody, and they were advised to seek immediate psychiatric evaluation for him (p. 48).

Peck went on to observe that, although Bobby appeared to be a typical fifteen-year-old, he stared at the floor and kept picking at several small sores on the back of his hand. When Peck asked Bobby if he felt nervous being in the hospital, he got no answer —"Bobby was really digging into that sore. Inwardly I winced at the damage he was doing to his flesh" (p. 48). After reassuring Bobby that the hospital was a safe place to be, Peck tried to draw Bobby out in conversation, but nothing seemed to work. Peck got "No reaction. Except that maybe he dug a little deeper into one of the sores on his forearm." Bobby admitted that he had hurt his parents by stealing the car; he said he knew that he had hurt them because they yelled at him. When asked what they yelled at him about, he replied, "I don't know." "Bobby was feverishly picking at his sores now and...I felt it would be best if I steered my questions to more neutral subjects" (p. 50). They discussed the family pet—a German shepherd whom Bobby took care of but didn't play with because she was his father's dog. Peck then turned the conversation to Christmas, asking what sorts of gifts Bobby had gotten.

BOBBY: Nothing much.

PECK: Your parents must have given you something.

What did they give you?

BOBBY: A gun.

PECK: A gun?

BOBBY: Yes.

PECK: What kind of a gun?

BOBBY: A twenty-two.

PECK: A twenty-two pistol.

BOBBY: No, a twenty-two rifle.

PECK: I understand that it was with a twenty-two rifle that your brother killed himself.

BOBBY: Yes.

PECK: Was that what you asked for for Christmas?

BOBBY: No.

PECK: What did you ask for?

BOBBY: A tennis racket.

PECK: But you got the gun instead?

BOBBY: Yes.

PECK: How did you feel, getting the same kind of gun that your brother had?

BOBBY: It wasn't the same kind of gun.

PECK: *(I began to feel better. Maybe I was just confused.)* I'm sorry, I thought they were the same kind of gun.

BOBBY: It wasn't the same kind of gun. It was the same gun.

PECK: You mean it was your brother's gun? *(I wanted to go home very badly now.)* You mean your parents gave you your brother's gun for Christmas—the one he shot himself with?

BOBBY: Yes.

PECK: How did it make you feel getting your brother's gun for Christmas?

BOBBY: I don't know.

PECK: *(I almost regretted the question: How could he know? How could he answer such a thing?)* No, I don't expect you could know (p. 52).

Peck then brought the parents in for counseling. However, they seemed unable to realize what message they had sent their remaining son by giving him his brother's suicide weapon. Bobby continued therapy until he was sent to live with a favorite aunt.

When I first read this dramatic example, I literally gasped as I learned about the Christmas gift, and I was totally dumbstruck to learn that it was *the* gun. When I read this dialogue aloud in class, I always hear gasps from around the room. Although the story was emotionally charged, we would be hard put to call it "illogical." In fact, it is probably totally logical to conclude that the parents' behavior was harmful, perhaps even evil. If the evidence is dramatic enough or emotional enough, persuadees will not ask for more.

Most great preachers, orators, and politicians are also great storytellers. They use the narrative to capture the audience's attention and to draw them into the topic. This effect is reinforced with other evidence, and more narratives might be worked in to keep the audience interested. Chances are, you have heard speeches or sermons in which narrative was skillfully used. Such speeches seem to have the most impact and to be remembered the longest. As a professor of mine once said, "The narrative will carry more persuasive freight than any other form of evidence."

Testimony. Testimony of a person who has seen, heard, and experienced events also is persuasive. The persuader might read aloud an eyewitness account or simply recount his or her personal experience. If the issue is unemployment, receivers might be swayed by hearing from people who are out of work. The humiliation of waiting in line for an unemployment check, the embarrassment of accepting government surplus foodstuffs, and other experiences of the unemployed will probably have dramatic persuasive power.

As receivers, we vicariously live through what the witness experienced when we hear direct testimony. Although eyewitness testimony is potent,

FIGURE 8.1 Witnesses see events or persons from their own point of view.

SOURCE: Reprinted by permission of John Jonik from *Psychology Today*.

studies have shown that it is often unreliable and even incorrect (Loftus, 1980). In many cases, as has been documented, persons have been wrongfully imprisoned on the basis of eyewitness testimony (Loftus, 1984). As Figure 8.1 illustrates, witnesses often see and hear what they want to see and hear, and give testimony from their idiosyncratic points of view.

As receivers, we need to carefully examine the testimony used to persuade us. We need to ask questions like these: Was the witness in a position to see what is claimed? Could the witness be mistaken in any way? Does the witness have a bias that might cloud his or her testimony? Might the witness have a motive for giving the testimony? Is the witness being paid for giving the testimony? What might he or she have to gain from testifying?

Anecdotes. Anecdotes are short narratives that make a point in a hurry—maybe in only a sentence or two. For example, there is the anecdote of the optimist who was asked to describe his philosophy: "That's simple. I'm nostalgic about the future." Anecdotes are often funny and are frequently hypothetical, so they are quite different from actual testimony. The key thing about anecdotes is that, unlike testimony, we rarely take them as truth. Instead, we tend to process anecdotes as if they are the exclamation points of persuasion. Consider the anecdote about Abraham Lincoln being asked why he pardoned a deserter—he quipped, "I thought he could do us more good above the ground than under it" (Moore, 1909).

Participation and Demonstration. There are several other ways in which persuaders can dramatize evidence. At an antismoking presentation, for instance, audiovisual materials can show cancerous lung tissue. Smokers can participate by exhaling cigarette smoke through a clean white tissue and observing the nicotine stains left behind. Sometimes persuaders dramatize a point by using visual aids to demonstrate the problem and solution. The demonstrations that form the core of most direct marketing on television also use participation in that the viewer is repeatedly urged to call the 1-800 number and place an order. The viewer sees the greaseless grill, the guaranteed bass bait, or the shapely persons using the Bowflex, and imagines what it would be like to use the product.

Rationally Processed Evidence

Not all evidence is dramatic. Sometimes evidence appeals to our logical processes in nondramatic and intellectually oriented ways. For instance, newspaper editorials frequently use evidence that appeals to readers' logical processes, as do other persuasive messages such as advertising. Look at Figure 8.2. The Campbell Soup Company knows that persons concerned with health and nutrition are aware of the need to increase the amount of fiber in their diet. Most of the literature on this subject has recommended eating high-fiber foods such as whole wheat bread and bran cereals. Campbell's offers similar benefits. You can get fiber by eating Manhandler soups such as Bean with Bacon or Split Pea with Ham.

As you can see from these examples, the appeal to logical processes relies on a reasoning pattern such as "the past is a guide to the future" or "the cost is less than the benefit." What are some other logical patterns that persuaders often use?

To see how many kinds of evidence exist, access InfoTrac College Edition, type the word "evidence" in the search engine, and sample the references listed.

TYPES OF REASONING

Recall our definition of proof as "enough evidence connected with reasoning to lead an audience to believe or act on a persuader's advice." We now explore the second step in the process of logical persuasion: connecting the pieces of evidence using reasoning.

Several patterns of reasoning seem to be deeply ingrained in our culture. When people violate the accepted deep structure of logical reasoning, they are often labeled "off the wall" or "out in left field." Sometimes a logical deep structure is violated and humor results. Sometimes, such violations make a potential persuader sound like a lunatic. A letter to the editor of a local newspaper discussed removing nuisance deer from public parks in the area (Scott, 1989). He pointed out what it had cost to remove such deer from other parks, the taxes hunters pay on ammunition and guns, and how removal costs were cut at another park by allowing hunting at the park. So far, so good. He begins with what appears to be an inductive line of argument using **effect-to-cause reasoning**, which is defined as citing a set of effects and then concluding by identifying their cause. We anticipate that he is about to claim something like "Therefore, hunters are positive persons and deserve to hunt nuisance deer." But what does the author conclude? Take a look.

If you were an animal, would you prefer to live ten years free, even if you died a slow death, or would you want to live it penned up, sleeping

MADE OF THE FINEST FIBER

If you're like most people who eat right, you probably give high fiber high priority.

And like most people, when you think of fiber, you probably automatically think of bran cereals.

Well, there's another good source of dietary fiber you should know about. Delicious Campbell's Bean with Bacon Soup.

In fact, Campbell's has four soups that are high in fiber.

And you can see from the chart that follows exactly how each one measures up to bran cereals.

So now when you think of fiber, you don't have to think about

FIBER IN A SUGGESTED SERVING			
CAMPBELL'S SOUP		**BRAN CEREALS**	
Bean with Bacon	9g	100% Brans	11g
Split Pea with Ham	6g	40% Brans	6g
Green Pea	5g	Raisin Brans	5g
Low Sodium Green Pea	7g	Others	5–10g
This comparison includes soluble and insoluble fiber			

having it just at breakfast.

Instead, you can do your body good any time during the day. With a hot, hearty bowl of one of these Campbell's Soups.

You just might feel better for it—right to the very fiber of your being.

CAMPBELL'S SOUP IS GOOD FOOD

Campbell's has a full line of low sodium soups for those people who are on a salt-restricted diet or have a concern about sodium.

in your own manure? I think most Americans would want to be free. That's also the way God wanted it. That's why he said it is a good thing to be a hunter. For Jesus Christ is alive and well, but Bambi never was. (n. p.)

The conclusion is wacky. It seems unrelated to the evidence.

Remember that we are looking for content premises—logical patterns that serve as the first premises in enthymemes. The deeply ingrained logical preferences serve in this way. We believe and act on what we perceive to be logical arguments backed by good and sufficient evidence and well presented to us. Fishbein and Ajzen's (1975,

1980) theory of reasoned action (TRA) is one such deeply ingrained logical structure. The theory predicts that actions are the effects of behavioral intentions. Behavioral intentions, in turn, are the results of people's attitudes on issues and on the social norms that they hold in high esteem. For example, if we were trying to persuade people to stop buying SUVs and to consider purchasing one of the new hybrid automobiles, we might compare the hybrid's performance with the poor mileage of most SUVs, note that four-wheel drive isn't really necessary for most people's needs, and back that up with a quote: "Critics claim that 95% of SUVs never venture off-road" (Lunsford & Ruszkiewicz, p. 28). This might change peoples' attitude toward SUVs. Then we could point out that the hybrid owners are opinion leaders, tend to be better educated, to have better jobs, to earn more, and to be more socially conscious. According to TRA, if our audience believes that these traits are ones to be emulated, then the shift in attitudes toward SUVs and the audience's changing respect for hybrid users will lead to a behavioral intention—the audience will consider buying a hybrid instead of an SUV. Communication scholar S. Sutton (1998) points out, however, that intentions are subject to change over time and are provisional in nature. Several researchers have found the predictive power of behavioral intentions to be either weak or negative as more and more time passes. Let us now turn to some traditional forms of reasoning.

Cause-to-Effect Reasoning

We've seen that **cause-to-effect reasoning** is powerful in our culture; even our language depends on it. For example, we rarely say, "The ball was thrown, and the window was broken." Instead, we put the cause out front and let it "create" the effect. We say, "Johnny threw the ball and broke the window." This active-voice sentence tells us that Johnny caused the ball to fly through the air, resulting in the broken window. It gives us much more information: It tells us who did what.

Persuaders frequently use cause-to-effect reasoning to identify events, trends, or facts that have resulted in certain effects. They tell us that if a cause is present we can expect certain effects to follow. If the effects are bad and we want to do something about them, we usually try to remove the cause. For instance, if you are allergic to garlic and eat some food that has garlic in it, we can predict that you are going to have an allergic reaction. Or, if you are carrying too much credit card debt, you should get rid of all but one of your credit cards. This argument assumes that cutting up all but one credit card (cause) will reduce your ability to accumulate consumer debt (effect). Both these examples make perfect sense, and that is why cause-to-effect reasoning has such persuasive power.

There are three kinds of causal reasoning: (1) A cause is identified, and you seek out its effects; (2) An effect is identified, and you try to trace it back to its cause; and (3) A series of cause–effect relationships lead to a final effect (Lunsford & Ruszkiewicz, p. 207). Advertising frequently uses the first strategy, as in an ad for a cellulite-reducing complex. It identifies the cause—a weak skin support system—and its undesirable effect—cellulite. Regular use of the product strengthens the skin support system, thus removing the cause and its effects. In the second strategy, the effect is identified. We look at the effect—global warming—and try to identify its possible causes, such as the emission of carbon dioxide from the burning of fossil fuels. Or take the case of food poisoning. The poisoning followed a buffet lunch at which only those who became ill were found to have eaten the dishes that contained mayonnaise. Conclusion? They probably were ill from *Salmonella*, a kind of food poisoning that occurs when mayonnaise is not properly refrigerated. In the third strategy, we trace a series of cause-and-effect relationships—the persuader says sulfur dioxide emissions from power plants causes acid rain, which in turn kills plant life. Conclusion? A single cause might have several effects. Acid rain also kills plankton, which are food for fish and crustaceans, and it makes soil too acidic for farming. In law courts, establishing a motive for the crime is sometimes seen as the same thing as identifying its cause. The thief needed money for his surgery and so he robbed the store (Huglen & Clark, 2004).

Communication scholar C. Hitchcock (2001) puts cause-to-effect slightly differently. He argues that there are at least two types of effect: component effect and net effect. The causes of a **net effect** are cumulative and result from a number of component effects. **Component effects** are linked to a cause but may not be the only cause of the net effect. In other words, the initial component effect contributes to the overall effect, but there might be other causes. Global warming, for instance, has several effects in addition to carbon dioxide emitted from the burning of fossil fuels. It is also caused by the release of freon gases used in refrigerators and air conditioners. Again, this kind of reasoning is usually processed in the central route of the elaboration likelihood model.

To explore how others have viewed causation, access InfoTrac College Edition, and enter the word "causation" in the search engine. Read several of the over one hundred periodical articles.

Effect-to-Cause Reasoning

Another type of reasoning that is less frequently used (and sometimes flawed) is called effect-to-cause reasoning. Sources of food poisoning, for example, are identified this way. In another example, many auto accidents are attributed to the use of a cell phone while driving. There is a problem here with the possibility of an intervening cause—who the driver is talking to and about what. Suppose that further investigation shows that in a high

percentage of these accidents the drivers were arguing with their spouses about family matters. Is the cell phone the cause of the accidents or is the discussion of family problems the intervening cause?

Reasoning from Symptoms

Persuaders sometimes identify a series of symptoms or signs and then try to conclude something from them. For example, politicians cite how much worse things are now than they were when their opponent took office. Unemployment is up, and the stock and bond markets have been ravaged. Recent polls show that people have lost faith in their ability to control their own destinies. The hope is that the voters will blame the incumbent for the troubles. Many advertisements present receivers with a set of symptoms that indicate there is a real or potential problem for them. Receivers have lost their job, can't pay the bills, and are faced with foreclosure. They need to contact Harvey's Financial Advisor Inc. Interpersonal persuasion is frequently laced with reasoning from symptoms, especially when laying blame.

Criteria-to-Application Reasoning

Sometimes persuaders establish a reasonable set of criteria for purchasing a product, voting for a candidate, or supporting a cause and then offer their product, candidate, or cause as one that fits these criteria. For example, when a credit card company makes an offer to you, you probably have several criteria in mind that the card must meet before you

FIGURE 8.3 What is the figurative analogy here?

SOURCE: Reprinted by permission of Aaron Johnson.

will take the offer. There must be no annual fee. There must be free balance transfers and an introductory rate of 0.0% and a reasonable rate thereafter. The initial 0.0% must hold for at least a year, and the company must give you frequent traveler points on any airlines plus discounts on other travel services. Unless the card meets your criteria, you reject the offer. Remember the student who cut classes and flunked because of his absences, only to have to retake the class and maintain perfect attendance, thus earning a passing grade? Reasoning from criteria to application persuaded him.

Reasoning from Analogy or by Comparison

Sometimes persuaders use a figurative or real analogy as their logical reason for some conclusion. In this form of reasoning, the persuader analyzes and describes an issue, and an analogy is made comparing this issue with an example of a similar one or a figurative one. In a real-case analogy on the war in Iraq, opponents to the war compared it to the war in Vietnam because in both cases we were fighting an indigent population that was very different from us culturally, and both sets of terrain were not conducive to traditional warfare. The conclusion is that we should not invade Iraq. In the figurative analogy, the comparison is done through a figure of speech, usually a simile or a metaphor. Consider the following figurative analogy: "War is like a boxing match in which the opponents are evenly matched and there's no referee. Rarely does anyone throw a single knockout punch. It's slugging it

out in round after round until you get the other guy on the ropes, and his managers admit defeat."

We also frequently see argument by comparison in advertising, with competing products compared in terms of cost, effectiveness, safety, and so on. For instance, the big battle over the light beer market largely relies on reasoning from comparison, with one brand claiming fewer calories and better taste than others. The same thing is seen in ads for low-tar and low-nicotine cigarettes. And the Energizer Rabbit uses comparison to make the point that the Energizer brand is much longer lasting than, say, Duracell.

Deductive Reasoning

A familiar form of appeal to logic is **deductive reasoning,** which is reasoning from the general to the specific. For example, in a legislative body a persuader might support a bill or a motion by saying something like, "The legislation before us is desperately needed to prevent the state budget from going into a deficit situation," and then providing the specifics. An editorial might begin, "Sycamore needs to pass this school bond referendum to save its extracurricular sports, its music and art programs, its newspaper, and its drama program," and then go on to describe the details. One of the problems with the deductive approach is that receivers who feel negatively about the persuader's general point may quickly lose interest and not pay attention to the specifics that are at the heart of the issue.

Inductive Reasoning

Inductive reasoning gets the specifics out on the table before bringing up the generalized conclusion. For example, in the school bond case, the persuader might begin this way:

> Many of you know that it costs over $60,000 just to run the athletic program. The budget for the marching band is over $12,000 for travel, instruction, and uniforms. I was surprised to learn that it cost over $2000 just to pay the royalties for the spring musical. We have cut and cut until there is nothing left to cut. The last referendum increase was fourteen years ago—inflation has risen over 200 percent since then. Unless we pass the referendum, the district now faces elimination of these valuable extracurricular programs.

With the specific evidence apparent, the generalization flows logically from it.

To see the variations in the use of reasoning, access InfoTrac College Edition, type the word "reasoning" in the search engine, and look at the article by Brian McGee on the argument from definition. You will see how reasoning was used to define "race" in the early twentieth century. Also check the various articles from the journal *Argumentation and Advocacy* and the item on the conditional syllogism and deductive reasoning.

MISUSES OF REASONING AND EVIDENCE

Of course, logical persuasion is vulnerable to intentional or unintentional misuse of either evidence or reasoning, or both. Let's look at some examples of the misuse of reasoning and evidence so that we can spot it when it occurs.

Statistics

One of the mainstays of logical persuasion is the use of **statistics.** We tend to believe statistics without questioning them. But we ought to ask several questions when statistical evidence is offered. First, "Is the sample from which the statistics are drawn a representative one?" In other words, is the sample selected in a way that might bias the results? Or is it a reliable representation of the larger population? We might want to know how the sample was selected. Perhaps the researchers took names from the phone directory. But not everyone has a telephone number listed, some people have several, and others only use cell phones for which there is no directory. Perhaps the subjects were approached at a shopping mall on campus and given a survey there. But, again, mall shoppers might not be representative of the population at large. Maybe the subjects were intercepted in front of the student union. Would we find any different results if we interviewed them in the morning rather than in the evening when most students are studying? These and other questions should be asked of any statistical proof used by the persuader. Another misuse of statistical evidence is the use of a single instance as an example of all instances. Thus, we hear of an enormously wealthy person who pays no taxes and are led to believe that other enormously wealthy persons pay no taxes. Still another misuse of statistics is biased sampling, which occurs when a nonrepresentative portion of the population is sampled. Responses from a sample drawn from subscribers to *Newsweek* will be very different from one drawn from subscribers to *Horticulture* or *The Organic Gardener.*

The mode of presentation can also misrepresent statistics. For example, the graph in Figure 8.4 was used to demonstrate the degree to which homosexuality exists in the general population. The shaded portion indicates persons who have had at least one homosexual encounter; the unshaded portion of the graph indicates heterosexual persons. The graph suggests that the proportion of the population that is homosexual is at least 50 percent when actual research indicates that it is far smaller—around 2 percent (Guttmacher, 1993). Clearly, the graph visually misrepresents the actual case and distorts the meaning of the statistics. What the graph fails to provide is information about the size of the sample in each segment.

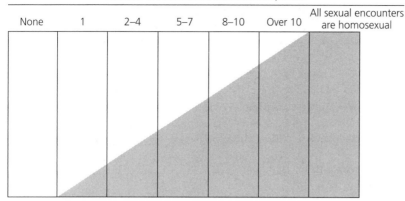

FIGURE 8.4 This graph is misleading because it implies that half the population is homosexual when the statistics being represented are much lower than that.

Testimony

One problem with the use of testimonials is that the person testifying might not be providing accurate information. Also, seemingly insignificant shifts in wording can lead witnesses to certain answers. Most of the time, we don't have the opportunity to cross-examine the person giving the testimonial. Instead, when we see or hear a person endorsing a product, a candidate, or an organization, we are forced to make up our minds right away about whether the person is qualified to give the testimonial. When testimonials are used to persuade, we need to ask whether the person giving the testimonial is an authority on the subject, and if so, how reliable he or she is. Was the person close enough to have witnessed the evidence he or she is testifying about? Is it possible that the person giving the testimonial is biased, and if so, in what direction? For example, in Chicago, a violinist was recently awarded nearly $30 million from METRA, the commuter train conglomerate. Her $500,000 violin got caught in the train doors, and when she tried to save it her leg was torn off. She testified at the trial, offering "dramatic detailed testimony...as she painfully recalled for jurors the winter day in 1995 when she became pinned against the doors of a commuter train and was dragged more than 360 feet before she fell under its wheels" (Deardorf & Finan, 1999, p. 1). Could her testimony have been biased? How much of it was used to build sympathy and thus boost the size of the award? How well could you remember what happened if you were in that situation? Was she partially responsible for putting herself at risk? These and other questions are the kinds of issues to be raised when the testimonial is being offered as evidence.

As persuadees, we need to be alert to the ways in which testimonials can be distorted or misused. We know that in many cases the testimonial is being given only because the sponsor has paid the person to give it. So, the next time you see a sports personality endorsing a product, don't assume that he or she uses it on a daily basis. By law, they only have to have tried it one time. And try to determine the degree of authority the person has about the product.

COMMON FALLACIES USED IN PERSUASION

Webster's Collegiate Dictionary defines **fallacy** as "deceptive appearance...a false or mistaken idea...an often plausible argument using false or invalid inference." It is this last definition that concerns us here: believable arguments or premises that are based on invalid reasoning. Keep in mind that a logical fallacy is not necessarily false, but its process of inference is invalid. In spite of the fact that these fallacies have been identified for centuries, they still pop up frequently in advertisements, political persuasion, interpersonal persuasion, and other arenas. Briefly, here are some of the common fallacies we encounter almost daily.

Post Hoc, Ergo Propter Hoc

Post hoc, ergo propter hoc, commonly called **the "post hoc" fallacy**, derives from the Latin meaning "after this, therefore because of this." As the translation implies, because one event follows another, the first event is assumed to be the cause of the second. We constantly run into this fallacy in the world of advertising. After using the diet pill, Jane lost 40 pounds. Maybe she just got more exercise. Citizens might charge that the reason the school system is out of money is that the superintendent and school board wasted all the money from the referendum eight years ago on unneeded frills, but it is not necessarily so.

Ad Hominem

The Latin term **ad hominem**, meaning "to or at the person," refers to any attack against an individual instead of against her or his position on the issues. The purpose is to lead the audience to take certain actions simply because of an alleged character quirk or other flaw in the person presenting the opposite viewpoint. The cartoons in Figure 8.5 are good examples of the ad hominem argument being used against the faculty president of the policy-making body on a college campus. This tactic is not usually used in advertising because products, not people, are being promoted. However, it is frequently used in ideological persuasion such as in politics. Whenever attacks are made on a person's character instead of on his or her stand on issues, be aware that the ad hominem fallacy is probably at work. If persuaders have nothing to debate, they frequently resort to attacking the personality of the opponent.

Ad Populum

As its name implies, the **ad populum** fallacy relies on whatever happens to be popular at that time. It is aimed at or to the populace. There are many historical examples of ad populum arguments—some important, some tragic, and some trivial. For example, consider just a few popular notions that justified themselves using the logic of the ad populum: Prohibition, the baby boom, rock 'n' roll, and suburbs in the 1950s. Appeals using the ad populum also abound in the worlds of fashion and popular culture—for example, wearing one's baseball cap backward or getting one's body pierced. Encouragement to "follow the crowd" clues us in to the ad populum fallacy in operation.

The Undistributed Middle

The fallacy of the **undistributed middle** can be defined as "inferring that because an individual, group, or philosophy shares some aspects or attributes with another, it shares all other aspects or attributes." It occurs in most cases of what we call "guilt by association"—for example, "Gut Malloy is a member of Tappa Kanna Bru fraternity, and fraternity boys are heavy drinkers, so he must be a heavy drinker, too." Common sense tells us that there is something missing here. The heart of the fallacy is in the phrase "fraternity boys are heavy drinkers," which is used to suggest that *all* fraternity members share *all* attributes beyond group membership. In other words, the argument assumes that heavy drinking is equally distributed among all members of fraternities when some are moderate drinkers or don't drink at all (Jensen, 1981).

Of course, this example is trivial, but persuaders use the undistributed middle principle to sway opinion and alter behavior in significant ways. For example, because someone serves on the school board, many critics assume that the person must favor all the board's decisions. This example appeared in a small-town newspaper recently:

> Consider these facts: The Japanese eat very little fat and suffer fewer heart attacks than the British or the Americans. On the other hand, the French eat a lot of fat and suffer

FIGURE 8.5 These cartoons use the ad hominem fallacy. They are aimed at the person, not the issue.

SOURCE: Reprinted by permission of Kevin Craver.

fewer heart attacks than the British or the Americans. The Italians drink excessive amounts of red wine and also suffer fewer heart attacks than the British or Americans. Therefore eat and drink what you like. It's speaking English that kills you ("Consider the Facts," 2002, p. 10).

This fallacy underlies any appeal suggesting that using a certain brand will make us like others who use it.

The Straw Man

The **straw man fallacy** sets up a weak, or "straw man," case that can be easily defeated. The persuader represents this case as the position of the other side in the debate, and then brings out key evidence and reasoning to defeat the bogus case, along with the opposition. Political persuasion is riddled with this tactic. For instance, candidate A might charge that candidate B's position on defense spending is reliance on conventional weapons. This is an easy position to demolish. Candidate A promptly shows how wrong the straw man position is by presenting impressive statistics and examples to the contrary. In the world of advertising, we occasionally see, read, or hear a straw man case. A good example is the TV ad in which the announcer says something like, "Some think this Chevy pickup truck can't climb this tough mountain carrying a Dodge pickup on its back." Then we see the Chevy climb the mountain with the Dodge on its back. Of course, if the Chevy couldn't do the job, they would never have aired the ad.

Most comparative advertising depends on the straw man fallacy. In the cola and burger wars, for instance, the opposition is often set up as a straw man waiting to be overcome by the advertiser's brand. The straw man fallacy is also commonly used in ideological arguments. Antiabortion advocates frequently argue that abortion is an inhumane form of birth control and should thus be outlawed. However, pro-choice advocates have never recommended abortion as a means of birth control—that claim is a straw man argument that will naturally be demolished by pro-life advocates.

Other Common Fallacies

Another type of fallacious reasoning uses partial or distorted facts (such as telling only one side of the story or quoting out of context). Other fallacies include substituting ridicule or humor for argument (such as depicting the opposition candidate as "a slow-dancing bureaucrat"), using prejudices or stereotypes, appealing to tradition, begging the question or evading the issue ("National health care is nothing less than socialism!"), using a *non sequitur*

(a thought that doesn't logically follow from the preceding one), or creating a false dilemma ("either outlaw deficit spending or declare the country bankrupt") (Kahane, 1992; Thompson, 1971).

LOGICAL SYLLOGISMS

A form of logical argument that goes back to the ancients is called the syllogism. **Syllogisms** are forms of reasoning with three parts: a major premise, a minor premise and a conclusion. They typify content premise persuasion and can be of three types: conditional syllogisms, disjunctive syllogisms, and categorical syllogisms.

Conditional Syllogisms

Conditional syllogisms are defined as arguments using "If/Then" reasoning. Like other syllogisms, they have a major premise, a minor premise, and a conclusion. The major premise states a logical relationship that is presumed to exist in the world and that receivers are to accept. The minor premise states the existence of one element in the relationship, and the conclusion is then drawn between the relationship and the existence of one element in it. Here is a conditional syllogism in classical form:

> If the U.S. government can't control terrorism with the present laws, then we need to give it new laws that are tough enough to stop terrorism (major premise). The World Trade Center bombings and the events of 9/11 are proof that the government can't control terrorism with the present laws (minor premise). Therefore, we need to give the government tougher laws to stop terrorism (conclusion).

The first element, or the "If" part in the major premise, is called the antecedent, and the second element is called the consequent. Affirming the antecedent, which we did in the minor premise by referring to the attacks, we can draw a valid conclusion that tougher laws are needed.

Note that the syllogism is valid, but the premises are not necessarily true. **Validity** refers to how well the syllogism conforms to the general rules of reasoning, and not to the true or false nature of the premises. The other valid way of affirming a part of the conditional syllogism is to deny the existence of the element in the major premise. Using the same example, we could state, "Since 9/11, there have been no major terrorist acts in the United States (minor premise). Therefore, there is no need for new laws (conclusion)."

Advertisers frequently make perfectly valid arguments using false premises. A good example is this statement on a package of Trilene fishing line: "If you are seeking a world record, you should use one of the pound tests coded in the chart at right." You can detect the "if . . . then . . . " format in the sentence. We all know that using the right line—Trilene—won't assure anyone of a world record fish, but receivers tend to accept it as logical and buy the line.

There are two valid ways to draw a conclusion in a conditional syllogism. First, we can affirm the "if" part of the major premise and accept the "then" part of the major premise. For example, if we affirm the first portion of the premise ("If you are seeking . . . ") we can affirm the second half about using Trilene line. The other valid combination begins by stating something about the first part of the initial premise. For example, we might say, "Smaller fish taste better," and then reject the advice on using Trilene line. A related but invalid procedure is to deny the antecedent and conclude that the consequent has also been denied. In the Trilene example we might state, "You don't want a lunker," and conclude that therefore you shouldn't use Trilene. The fallacy becomes apparent immediately—you might still want to use Trilene for another reason—perhaps because of its warranty. In a related but also invalid procedure, suppose in the terrorism example we had denied the consequent in the minor premise by saying, "We have not given enough tough new powers to the U.S. government," and then concluded, "Therefore, the U.S. government will not be able to control terrorism." The fallacy is less apparent but is still there—the lack of tough laws doesn't necessarily indicate an inability to control terrorism. Again, there could be intervening causes.

Although invalid, this form of syllogism is frequently used in advertisements. For instance, a romance is "saved" by a certain mouthwash or shampoo. Be alert to this trap. Persuaders can use a logically valid syllogism to camouflage untrue premises. Ask yourself whether the premises are true and whether the argument is valid. The conditional syllogism is similar to the cause–effect linkage described earlier.

To get a better idea of how conditional syllogisms can be used, access InfoTrac College Edition, and type the words "conditional syllogism" in the search engine. Then read the items on the various strategies for using syllogisms and on the order of information in them.

Disjunctive Syllogisms

The **disjunctive syllogism** uses an "Either/Or" format. Consider this major premise of a disjunctive syllogism: "Either we reduce the deficit or we increase taxes." The premise is usually accompanied by some proof or evidence in the minor premise, and the conclusion is then drawn. For example, a school board threatens, "Either we vote to increase property taxes or you lose all extracurricular activities." The voters would provide the minor premise of the syllogism through their votes—if they vote to increase taxes, the board denies the need to eliminate the activities. A second valid conclusion comes about if the voters vote down the tax increase and the board eliminates the activities.

This strategy works if the issue is clear-cut. However, few situations have a clear "either/or" dichotomy, even in extreme cases such as the Terry Scheivo case in 2005. She had been in a comatose state for several years, and her husband wanted to remove her feeding and water tubes, but her parents objected and the issue went into the courts. Ultimately the U.S. Congress voted on the right to life aspects of the case. The central issue revolved around the disjunctive syllogism "Either she is alive or she is dead." The real question should have been "Will she ever recover?" This argument would still exemplify a disjunctive syllogism—either she will recover or she will not—but the controversy would not have been as extreme.

BOX 8.2   **The Logic of Cultural Transformation**

In his book *Communication and Cultural Transformation: Cultural Diversity, Globalization and Cultural Convergence*, Stephan Dahl (2000) draws a distinction between "high culture" (the opera or symphony, art museums, live theatre) and mass or popular culture (MTV, sports events, newspapers), which emerged in the mid-nineteenth century. He argues that it is popular culture that really is affected by diversity issues. Some of the diversity issues he lists include social groupings, language, nonverbal communication, values, concepts of time and space, perception, and national character. For example, he maintains that in Western culture time is thought of as linear, while in Eastern cultures time is thought of as being circular in nature. Or take our nonverbal signal for "A-Okay," which is the thumb and forefinger forming the letter O. In other cultures or subcultures, the same signal has sexual implications. What kinds of differences in persuasive meaning might follow from these ways of viewing time and space? Various nonverbal gestures? Which of his other diversity issues can you see operating in your everyday life? You may want to view a copy of Dahl's book and other of his publications at www.stephweb.com/capstone/1.htm.

Strict either/or logic cannot take into account other belief systems or more than two alternatives in a situation. Examine persuasion framed in the either/or mode to search for other alternatives or belief systems under which the disjunctive model will not work.

Categorical Syllogisms

Categorical syllogisms deal with parts and wholes, or sets and subsets, of events in which the major and minor premises both involve membership or nonmembership in one of two categories. The conclusion relates the clusters of both premises into a new finding or result, as shown in the following classic categorical syllogism:

> All men are included in the class of mortal beings (major premise). Socrates is included in the class of men (minor premise). Therefore, Socrates is a mortal being (conclusion).

Although this example is frequently used to demonstrate the categorical syllogism, it is not one that you will find many opportunities to use. Its format, however, is frequently seen, read, or heard in various kinds of persuasion. Take, for example, the U.S. Marines' recruiting slogan: "We're looking for a few good men." The implied categorical syllogism is as follows: All U.S. Marines are included in the class of good men (major premise). You are a good man (minor premise). Therefore, you should become a Marine (conclusion).

Because you are a member of one category, it is assumed that you must or should be a member of another. IBM used this technique when it ran a two-page public relations ad that features two pairs of baby booties, one pink and one blue, and the question "Guess which one will grow up to be the engineer?" The question implies a cultural gender stereotype—women are poor at math and science. One underlying premise concerns engineers. It is "Persons encouraged to excel in math and science are likely to become engineers" (major premise). The next step is "Males are encouraged to excel in math and science" (minor premise). Thus we infer that "Males are likely to become engineers" (conclusion). On another level, the ad creates good public relations by implying that "Good companies encourage women to excel" (major premise); "IBM encourages women to excel" (minor premise): "IBM is therefore a good company" (conclusion). Although the first syllogism is valid (and probably true as well), the second is invalid. IBM uses the illusion of a valid syllogism to make its case that good companies encourage women to excel, but simply doing that does not necessarily guarantee that a company is "good." For other examples of cultural biases see Box 8.2, where nonverbal patterns and different ways of considering time and space are part of the cultural stereotype involved in the syllogism.

THE TOULMIN FORMAT

Most of us do not encounter persuasion that is overtly syllogistic. Instead, the syllogism often is the underlying structure in persuasive arguments. British philosopher Stephen Toulmin (1964) developed a model that identifies the kinds of logical persuasion we encounter in everyday events. According to Toulmin, any argument aimed at our logical reasoning processes is divided into three basic parts: the claim, the data, and the warrant.

Basic Elements

The **claim** is the proposition that the persuader hopes will be believed, adopted, or followed. Claims usually need to be supported by **data**, the second part of the model, which is simply evidence. Data give the receivers reasons for following the advice of the claim. The **warrant** is the reason the data support the claim; it explains the relationship between them. These three elements become clear as we examine persuasion at work. If there is reason to believe that receivers will accept the claim on its face, there is no need for the persuader to continue. However, if the persuader expects receivers to doubt the claim, then data must be presented. If the data are accepted or rejected outright, again there is no need to proceed. However, if the persuader anticipates some doubt about the claim now supported by data, then it will be necessary to present a warrant that explains the reasoning by which the data support the claim. This pattern of moving the logical argument from claim to data to warrant, and the resulting three kinds of responses (agree, disagree, and uncertain), are typical of almost every reasoned argument in the everyday marketplace of ideas. Figure 8.6 uses the claim that the United States must become a "globo-cop" to show how the flow of argument goes in the **Toulmin system**. Trace the stages of argument in the figure.

Substantiating Elements

Toulmin's system has a number of secondary terms. For example, a claim may be modified by a **qualifier**—usually a simple word or phrase such as "In most cases" or "Probably" or "It is likely that." Conceding that the claim is not necessarily universal qualifies or limits the claim. In our globo-cop example, the persuader might alter the claim to state, "In most cases, the United States should become an international peacekeeper in world crises." Qualifiers limit the claim, thus allowing for the possibility that this is not a simple case of the either/or argument.

Another minor term in the model is the **reservation**, defined as a statement that specifies the conditions under which the warrant is valid. The reservation features words like "unless" or "only if there is a reason to believe that." In the globo-cop case, suppose the warrant stated, "Except in the case of revolutions, the United States is the only remaining superpower capable of establishing and maintaining world stability." Another reservation is expressed with the word "Unless," in which case the warrant might state, "Unless the United States is not the only remaining superpower capable of establishing and maintaining world stability . . . "

Both persuaders and persuadees often overlook the use of the reservation to cite circumstances in which the claim should not be accepted. They assume that both parties begin from the same point, from the same frame of reference. We must begin at the same point or make allowances (such as reservations) to make real progress in any persuasive transaction. Coupled with the qualifier, the reservation allows for great flexibility in persuasion because both encourage dialogue; both provide the persuadee with an opportunity to object or agree to part but not all of the persuasion.

Advertisers are clever with the use of qualifiers. For example, the label on Cascade dishwasher detergent says that it will make your dishes, not spotless, but "virtually spotless." Who can say whether one spot or three spots or twelve qualifies as being "virtually spotless"? Thus, we need to be aware of two problems connected with qualifiers and reservations: (1) their absence, which can lock us into one course of action or belief; and (2) the use of vague qualifiers, which allows persuaders to wriggle out of any commitment to a product,

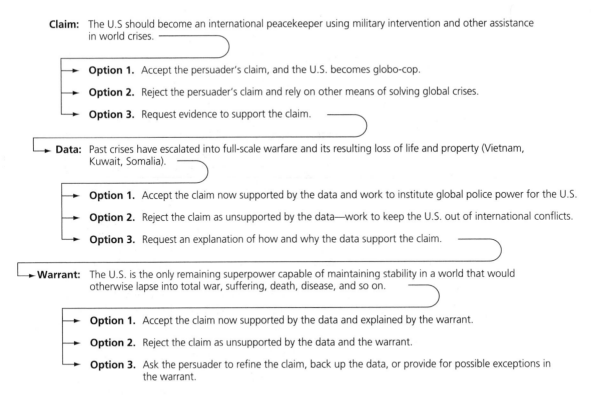

Claim: The U.S should become an international peacekeeper using military intervention and other assistance in world crises.

- **Option 1.** Accept the persuader's claim, and the U.S. becomes globo-cop.
- **Option 2.** Reject the persuader's claim and rely on other means of solving global crises.
- **Option 3.** Request evidence to support the claim.

Data: Past crises have escalated into full-scale warfare and its resulting loss of life and property (Vietnam, Kuwait, Somalia).

- **Option 1.** Accept the claim now supported by the data and work to institute global police power for the U.S.
- **Option 2.** Reject the claim as unsupported by the data—work to keep the U.S. out of international conflicts.
- **Option 3.** Request an explanation of how and why the data support the claim.

Warrant: The U.S. is the only remaining superpower capable of maintaining stability in a world that would otherwise lapse into total war, suffering, death, disease, and so on.

- **Option 1.** Accept the claim now supported by the data and explained by the warrant.
- **Option 2.** Reject the claim as unsupported by the data and the warrant.
- **Option 3.** Ask the persuader to refine the claim, back up the data, or provide for possible exceptions in the warrant.

F I G U R E 8.6 Toulmin's basic elements of an argument, applied to the example of U.S. intervention in world crises.

action, person, or idea. Persuaders may still try to interpret the qualifiers to their advantage, but it is more difficult when more details are given.

The final element in Toulmin's system for showing the tactics of argument is the **backing** for the warrant, which is information that establishes the credibility of the reasoning or connection between data and claim.

We can now see that the tactics of persuasion are not usually simple syllogisms. Instead, persuaders make claims that persuadees can respond to by (1) accepting them outright, (2) rejecting them outright, or (3) asking for proof. Persuaders then can provide data, which receivers can accept, reject, or question. If the persuadee continues to request more proof, the persuader ultimately must provide the warrant, or reason, for linking the proof to the

request. Given enough time, three other elements may enter into the persuasive appeal: the qualifier, the reservation, and the backing. What matters is that persuadees be aware, critical, and systematic as they are exposed to persuasion. Toulmin's system provides us with a simple tool that operates well with many kinds of persuasion.

Evidence on Evidence

Recently, Reynolds and Reynolds (2002) generated a list of facts we know about the uses of evidence:

1. Evidence is cognitively processed. In other words, people must process evidence in the central route of the ELM.

2. Evidence must seem legitimate in the eyes of the persuadee. In other words, the persuadee needs to view the evidence as authentic, high quality, and unbiased.

3. Evidence is evaluated by the audience. This evaluation of evidence leads to overall message evaluation, which, in turn, leads to post-message beliefs. It then follows that these post-message beliefs will lead to some sort of action.

In conclusion, evidence is probably most effective when it encourages audience participation. Earlier, we noted that persuaders are most effective in using emotionally oriented evidence when they present audiences with a dramatic scene or setting and then ask members to empathize. By using their imaginations, members of the audience co-create the proof—they incorporate the proof into their own frames of reference. In using intellectually oriented evidence, effective persuaders present claims and perhaps data to support them. They hope that warrants will be provided by the audience, but the audience members are still participating in their own persuasion when they begin to co-create a proof, even if they do not provide their own warrants. Finally, effective persuaders highlight the evidence—either as part of a narrative or in some form of analogy.

REVIEW AND CONCLUSION

Content or logical premises don't rely on the internal states of persuaders, as do process or emotional premises. Instead, they rely more on universally agreed on norms or rules. Evidence tends to be either dramatically oriented, intellectually oriented, or experiential/participative in nature. Users of dramatic evidence lead persuadees to a "logical" conclusion by creating a dramatic scene and then inviting the audience to join in the drama. Persuadees thus "prove" the validity of the premise to themselves. Users of intellectually

oriented evidence lead their persuadees to "logical" conclusions by presenting them with a set of data in support of a certain claim or content premise. The persuadees provide the connection between these data and the claim in the form of a warrant. And experiential or participative evidence may prove to be the most persuasive because of persuadees' personal involvement with the evidence. All three types of evidence rely on self-persuasion on the part of the persuadee. Persuadees participate in some way in their own persuasion, whether the evidence is intellectual, dramatic, or experiential/participative. When we engage in self-persuasion, even if it runs counter to our own beliefs, the effect of the participation is powerful.

The traditional syllogism usually forms the skeletal structure of arguments or content premises. Within this structure, the tactics or particular arguments or premises are represented by claims supported by data. Claims and data are linked through warrants.

Finally, of the types of evidence available to the persuader, several seem more important than others. Most important, probably, are those that support the three major linkages: cause–effect, symptoms, and comparisons. Also, evidence that provides a perspective for the audience is probably more effective than evidence that does not. We focused on two particularly effective methods of providing this perspective: the use of analogy, which provides a comparative perspective, and the use of narrative, which has the same ability to provide a perspective within a dramatic frame of reference. Both are also "artistic" in the sense that neither merely presents information; rather, both depict evidence in dramatic or visual formats. In sum, we are most effectively persuaded by experiences—real, vicarious, or imagined. Successful persuaders try to shape content premises—their linkages, claims, data, and warrants—in terms of the audience's experience. If persuaders invite audiences to participate in drawing conclusions, audiences will share in their own persuasion.

KEY TERMS

When you have finished reading this chapter, you should be able to identify, explain, and give an example of the following words or concepts.

content premises	participation and demonstration	deductive reasoning,	disjunctive syllogisms
arguments		inductive reasoning	categorical syllogisms
cause–effect reasoning	effect-to-cause reasoning	statistics	claim
proof	cause-to-effect reasoning	fallacy	data
reasoning		the "post hoc" fallacy	warrant
evidence	net effect	ad hominem	Toulmin system
direct experience	component effects	ad populum	qualifier
dramatic or vicarious experience	reasoning from symptoms	undistributed middle	reservation
rationally processed evidence	criteria-to-application reasoning	straw man fallacy	backing
narratives	reasoning from analogy or by comparison	syllogisms conditional syllogisms validity	

APPLICATION OF ETHICS

Two logical opposites in decision making are (1) conflict of interests and (2) compatibility of interests. In conflicts of interest, a person in a position to have inside information might be able to influence decisions so that s/he might personally benefit, as in the case of most corporate scandals. When compatibility of interests exists, persons with an inside position and information make decisions that benefit both themselves and all others with the same interests. For example, a company is having production problems that may lead to layoffs. The CEO decides to bring in efficiency experts to analyze the problem. They do so and cut costs, returning the company to profitability, and removing the layoff option. Apply both of the options to the following example: A CEO at a major automobile corporation sees the prices for energy rising at increasing rates and a resulting drop in sales of SUVs. The executive has several choices: Provide incentives for buying SUVs (e.g., "Now you can buy an SUV at employee discount rates). Another option is to develop hybrid models, which will result in higher costs of the vehicles because of the research and development needed. Another option is to "cook the books," which will jack up the stock value, at which point the CEO can sell off his stock at a profit. Which option should the CEO choose?

QUESTIONS FOR FURTHER THOUGHT

1. What are the three types of syllogisms discussed in this chapter? Give examples of each from advertisements, political speeches, or some other source of persuasion.

2. Define proof. What constitutes adequate proof for you? Does it change from issue to issue? If so, in what ways?

3. Review some magazine commentary concerning a particular issue, and attempt to identify the data offered. What kinds of evidence are they? Are they dramatic? If so, in what ways? If not, are they persuasive? Why or why not? What is the underlying syllogistic structure inherent in the discussions of the issue?

4. What is the difference between intellectually oriented evidence and emotionally oriented evidence? Give examples and explain how they differ.

5. Give examples from your own experience of (a) opinion, (b) attitudes, (c) beliefs, and (d) values that affect behavior. Give examples that do not affect behavior. How do they differ?

6. Why was "The Case of Bobby and His Parents" so persuasive? Was logic involved? Was the example an illogical one to prove the point Peck wanted to make?

7. What is the difference between a figurative and a literal analogy? Which is being used when a political campaign is compared to a horse race?

8. What are some of the ways in which statistics can be misused? Give examples.

9. What are some of the ways in which testimony can be misused? Give examples.

10. What is a post hoc fallacy? Give an example.

11. What is an ad hominem fallacy? Give an example.

12. How has the ad hominem been used in recent elections?

13. What are some contemporary examples of the ad populum being used in advertising?

14. How does the undistributed middle fallacy operate? Give examples.

15. How does the straw man fallacy operate? Give examples.

16. What is the false dilemma fallacy? How does it operate? Give examples.

17. How does the ELM help to explain the differences between content and process premises?

 For online activities, go to the *Persuasion* book companion website at http://communication.wadsworth.com/larson11.

9

Cultural Premises in Persuasion

LEARNING GOALS

After reading this chapter, you should be able to:

1. Identify and explain what cultural patterns are.

2. Recognize how you are affected by cultural training and societal pressures.

3. Recognize in persuasive messages the cultural myths of the wisdom of the rustic, the possibility of success, the coming of a messiah, conspiracy, the value of challenge, and the myth of the eternal return.

4. Identify, explain, and give examples of Reich's cultural parables in advertisements, editorials, or political speeches.

5. Identify messages that appeal to the myths of the man's man and the woman's woman.

6. Discuss image and charisma as cultural premises and explain their three central elements.

7. Identify Redding and Steele's core American values, giving contemporary examples of each.

We are all prisoners of our own culture, and as a result, we often overlook patterns of behavior that influence us and by which we are persuaded. Anyone who has visited another culture (even a similar or related culture) immediately becomes aware of significant differences between our patterns of behavior and those of the foreign culture. Not only are values, languages, and customs different, but hundreds of little things are also different, such as bus passengers lining up in orderly fashion in England, whereas Americans usually crowd around the bus door. In the United States, skiers line up in orderly fashion to wait their turn to use the lift, but in France, locals walk over others' skis to get ahead in the line. In a more significant example of cultural differences, one-third of the world's people eat using knife, fork, and spoon; another third eat with chopsticks; and the rest use their fingers

I visited several formerly communist countries in Eastern Europe in the 1990s, and quickly understood the immense difference between hard currency and soft currency. Hard currency has real worth, but soft currency is widely overvalued, so people don't want to accept it. The hotel I stayed at in Prague refused to accept soft Czech currency but was more than willing to accept hard currencies like the U.S. dollar or the German Mark. It has been that way for so many years that it has become a cultural habit in Czechoslovakia to trade currency on the black market even though trading at above the official rates has been outlawed there

for more than 50 years. I was told the best exchange rate in Czechoslovakia could be gotten from any priest. That's something that would never occur to someone from America.

In Eastern European countries at that time, most people carried a net shopping bag just in case they found something available to buy. In fact, the slang term for such a shopping bag was a "perhaps." People at that time didn't buy something because they needed it, but because it was available. Usually store shelves were nearly empty of any goods, and as a result hoarding was common—an idea that would rarely cross an American's mind.

Although many aspects of any given culture are relatively permanent, cultures are also subject to constant change. In the United States and elsewhere, for example, the constant influx of different ethnic groups and minorities is reflected in the culture in a variety of ways, and diversity and multiculturalism are apparent everywhere. For instance, in our supermarkets the shelves are always loaded, which astounds many foreigners from Eastern Europe. In addition, you will usually find ingredients for foreign dishes that weren't available just a decade ago. So increasing diversity is changing our shopping options. Many schools have sought the help of translators and interpreters to assist them in communicating with the immigrant parents of their newest students. In such small things we can see the continual changes in U.S. culture.

B O X   9.1   People of the Deer

Consider the following instance of cultural patterning. Suppose you are a member of a tribe whose sole food supply is caribou. When the animals make their fall migration south, the tribe kills enough to supply it with food until spring, when the animals migrate north to follow their food supply. The custom is to kill and preserve these deer in a period of a week or two. You have just finished the fall hunt, only to discover that you face a severe winter without having killed enough caribou to last until the spring migration north. Death is certain without sufficient supplies of protein and fat. You attend a council of elders called by the chief to address the crisis and to solicit input and ideas. What would you do? For many years, students in my persuasion classes have brainstormed solutions to this problem and come up with the following suggestions, usually in this approximate order:

- Follow the deer and kill more of them, thus increasing the supply.

- Seek an alternative food supply—we can eat berries or fish or birds.

- Send a band of the young and healthy to get help.

- Ration food to make it last longer.

- Eat all the parts of the caribou—skin, horns, everything—to increase the supply.

- Send some of the people away to another place where food is more plentiful and thus decrease demand.

- Kill some members of the tribe to decrease demand.

- Kill the most useless persons—the old first, and the very young next to decrease demand.

- Resort to cannibalism; let's eat those we kill.

The most practical solutions emerge first, and then the ideas become increasingly desperate. The actual tribe does nothing. They eat the food at their regular rates, knowing that it will not last through the winter. Then they sit and wait for death. They accept the situation, whereas Americans try to find solutions for all problems, even though some are probably insoluble. In all the years of using this example not a single one of my students has suggested doing nothing. Do you think it is good to be solution oriented? Why or why not?

To better understand the wide-reaching impact cultural diversity has on our lives, access InfoTrac College Edition, and type the words "multiculturalism" or "cultural diversity" in the search engine. Explore the many articles that address various aspects of this phenomenon.

CULTURAL PATTERNS

Cultural patterns are defined as the "socially transmitted values, beliefs, institutions, behavioral patterns, and all other products and thought patterns of a society" (*American Heritage Dictionary*, 1985). These are instilled in us from early childhood through our language, the myths and the tales we hear, and our observations of the behavior of those around us. These become cultural patterns, or the activities, beliefs, and values that typify a culture. British

passengers wait in orderly lines for a bus or subway whereas we crowd around the door. In Japan professional "packers" stuff as many persons as possible into their subways. Most persons from the U.S. would view that as unacceptable. Cultural training or patterning is the basis for some of the widely held premises we have discussed in earlier chapters.

The cultural preferences, myths, and values we embrace can all serve as major premises in enthymemes. Persuasion that builds on cultural premises occurs at a low level of awareness and is usually processed in the peripheral information-processing channel of the ELM. Thus, we often react subconsciously to various stimuli based on our cultural training. Robert Cialdini (2001) calls these reactions *fixed action patterns* or *shortcuts*, which are automatic and instantaneous. Cialdini observes that "you and I exist in an extraordinarily complicated environment, easily the most rapidly moving and complex that has ever existed on this planet. To deal with it, we need shortcuts. . . . As the stimuli saturating our lives continue to grow more intricate and variable, we will have to depend increasingly on our shortcuts to handle them all" (p. 7). And cultural patterning and cultural premises are just such shortcuts to being persuaded.

Another cultural pattern for most Americans is the value of individualism. We like the idea of pulling ourselves up by the bootstraps. There is a flip side to this individualism, as Robert Bellah and his associates (1985) pointed out in *Habits of the Heart: Individualism and Commitment in American Life*. Bellah and his colleagues did in-depth interviews with more than 200 Americans from various walks of life, and described the core American values and beliefs as "habits of the heart." Key among them was the value of the individual. Bellah and his coauthors point out:

> The central problem of our book concerned the American individualism that Tocqueville described with a mixture of admiration and anxiety. It seems to us it is individualism and not equality, as Tocqueville thought, that has marched inexorably throughout our history. We are concerned that this individualism may have grown cancerous (p. viii).

What they meant by "cancerous" is that individualism has become *me-ism*, with emphasis on the individual and not the community, thus drawing people into themselves and forgetting others. Many other observers have echoed this theme. Recall that the initial student responses to the dilemma of too few caribou are positive and action oriented, reflecting the good side of the American value of individualism. The middle responses are more reflective of a sense of community and cooperation, but the last three reflect the bad or cancerous side of American individualism. How do we identify these patterns of cultural values? Where do they come from? How do persuaders appeal to them?

To see how these premises relate to persuasion in general, we look first at how we get them— through cultural training and societal pressure. Then we look at two kinds of cultural premises: (1) **cultural images and myths**, which are defined

as real or imagined narratives that illustrate a society's values, and (2) our value system, which is defined as the hierarchical network of beliefs and values that typify a culture. Bear in mind that a value is an idea of the good or the desirable that we use as a standard for judging people's actions or motivations. Examples of American values are honesty, justice, beauty, efficiency, safety, and progress. Because our value system is a major source of persuasive leverage, you may be interested in discovering how persuaders link proposals and arguments to such values. Cultural training forms the core of our values, which then become rules for governing ourselves. Persuaders appeal to and believe these premises and expect their audiences to do so too.

CULTURAL IMAGES AND MYTHS

Every culture has its own myths and heroic figures that do things valued by the culture, and many of these myths are borrowed from other cultures, particularly European cultures. An ancient example that Greek society developed centuries ago was a series of myths surrounding the sin of pride. We have similar beliefs. You know that the overly proud student won't be elected or chosen as team captain. The more humble person will be picked. What are some of the myths or legends or images underlying American culture and society, and how do persuaders use them? Can these images be changed, and if so, how? Are they being changed at present, and if so, how? Stereotypes and proverbs are indicators of cultural myths. Let us consider a few.

The Wisdom of the Rustic

One of the legends in American lore that has great persuasive appeal is the wisdom of the rustic. No matter how devious the opposition, the simple commonsense wisdom of the backwoods hero or heroine wins out. Numerous folktales rely on this rustic image, including the Daniel Boone tales and many Abraham Lincoln stories about his humble beginnings and meager education. We believe in humble beginnings, and we believe that difficulty teaches even the most uneducated to be wise and worldly. Thus, politicians throughout American history have emphasized their humble origins. For example, Ronald Reagan emphasized his humble origin in Dixon, Illinois, and Bill Clinton let it be known that he was born in a small house in Hope, Arkansas. Neither President Bush emphasized that they came from privileged origins. If the politician cannot claim humble beginnings, he or she finds some substitute, usually hardship or suffering such as being a P.O.W. or suffering from some disability. Products are frequently marketed using a rustic as the spokesperson. Wilfred Brimley, for instance, serves as a rustic when he endorses the value of good old-fashioned Quaker Oats, and the smiling Quaker man on the package reinforces the image.

Even as we value the simple, commonsense rustic, our culture tends to devalue the intellectual or the educated. Persuaders often use this reverse side of our faith in the wisdom of the rustic: The intellectual is the brunt of jokes, and the rustic wins out over the smart guy.

Access InfoTrac College Edition, and type the words "cultural myths" in the search engine. Look at Carl Stepp's review of "Slick Spins and Fractured Facts: How Cultural Myths Distort the News," by Caryl Rivers, which deals with how cultural myths put various kinds of "spin" on news events. If you find this review interesting, you can retrieve the entire item or read Rivers' book.

The Possibility of Success

The **possibility of success** myth is best seen in the numerous novels by Horatio Alger, written for boys in the nineteenth century. The protagonist of these novels was invariably a young man who, through hard work, sincerity, honesty, law-abiding behavior, and faith in the future, was able to make good. He might even rise to the top and own his own company, have a beautiful wife, live a fine life, and be able to do good for others. The possibility of success myth appealed to immigrants, the poor, and the downtrodden. They passed it on to their

children, admonishing them to work hard to achieve success. The myth has been generalized to include women and minorities, and has great appeal for new groups of immigrants. These new immigrants, particularly those from Third World countries, often share living quarters to save money or go into business for themselves, and all members are expected to help provide for the family. The myth of possible success is as alive today as it was when immigrants came mainly from Europe. Again, this myth was observed by Tocqueville (1965):

> No Americans are devoid of a yearning desire to rise . . . . All are constantly seeking to acquire property, power, and reputation . . . . What chiefly diverts the men of democracies from lofty ambition is not the scantiness of their fortunes, but the vehemence of the exertions they daily make to improve them . . . . The same observation is applicable to the sons of such men . . . their parents were humble; they have grown up amidst feelings and notions which they cannot afterwards easily get rid of . . . " (pp. 156–158).

You may recognize your grandparents in this description if they or their parents emigrated to the United States. You may also see yourself in it.

Naturally, we are receptive to persuasion that promises the possibility of success. That's why you decided to go to college. Products and services are marketed promising success for the entire family. Politicians promise a bright future for voters who support a commonsense approach to problems. The possibility of success myth is probably what led many investors to buy Internet stocks in the late 1990s. After all, the entire human race seemed to be going online, and marketing would never be the same again. When the dot-com bubble burst in 2002, the possibility of success myth went out the window for a time. Still, whether it is a pyramid marketing scheme, the lottery, or a weight-loss club, the carrot is always the same—try and you will succeed.

To learn more about the Horatio Alger novels and the possibility of success, access InfoTrac College Edition, and type the words "Horatio

Alger" in the search engine. Explore the link to the Horatio Alger Society. Try the "Pluck and Luck," "Tattered Tom," or "Ragged Dick" novels.

The Coming of a Messiah

A cultural myth related to the possibility of success myth is the **coming of a messiah**. Whenever our society is approaching disaster or is already in a terrible mess—economic, religious, or political— or we are in a period of great uncertainty and pessimism or when things are chaotic, confusing, and frightening, we believe someone or something will save us. We want to be rescued from the chaos and danger by some great leader who projects a sense of confidence and who can turn things around. Many past leaders filled this role. For example, Abraham Lincoln emerged from semi-obscurity to save the Union. Franklin Roosevelt emerged to lead the United States out of the Great Depression and to victory in WWII. Ronald Reagan delivered us from 18 percent interest rates and unbelievable inflation. And George W. Bush was depicted as the leader who would help us win the war on terrorism. The future will no doubt bring us other problems, and you can rest assured that there will be someone who will emerge in the role of a messiah. What makes us so receptive to the messianic? First, we are action oriented, as we noted earlier, and we want our saviors to be doers. Second, we want their solutions to be simple and practical.

The Presence of Conspiracy

Another cultural premise is the belief that when we face enormous, almost overwhelming problems, the only plausible explanation is that a powerful group must be behind them. This pattern is called the **paranoid style** and is defined as using conspiracies as explanations for otherwise unanswerable dilemmas (Hofsteder, 1963). Probably the best examples are the various conspiracy theories concerning the assassination of J.F.K. Many other conspiracy arguments have recurred throughout our history such as those about the Masons and

Knights Templar, conspiracies that lent credence to the recent novel and film *The DaVinci Code* or Papal Conspiracy theories. Most recently, the conspiracy argument was used to explain the Oklahoma City bombing and the terrorism of our times. Some people believe that militia groups are presently conspiring to overthrow the government, and a few feel that the government is already in the hands of international conspirators. Many people believe there is an anti-U.S. conspiracy between Al Qaeda and rogue nations like Iran and North Korea. A conspiracy theory regarding terrorism apparently prompted the Bush administration to illegally wiretap phone calls to American citizens without obtaining a warrant, even when such warrants are granted as a matter of course. This in turn led to a conspiracy theory regarding the administration's disregard of constitutional rights

When it comes to persuasive communication, and if Hofstadter is right, we can expect to hear conspiracy offered as an explanation for problems any time three factors are operating for the audience members:

1. They have something of value to lose—power, property, or privilege.
2. They feel in danger of losing this power or property, or they have already lost some of it.
3. They see themselves as helpless to prevent the loss.

It is easy to see how belief in a conspiracy could give rise to a messiah as well. Only a messiah can defeat evil conspirators and save us. One of the dangers of this myth is that it invites mass hysteria and the rise of charismatic leaders, who seem to be heroes but who may be just the opposite.

The Value of Challenge

The myth of **the value of challenge** is fairly simple and parallels tribal tests of strength and character. It suggests that a kind of wisdom can be gained only through rigorous testing and that some rite of passage or initiation gives us power, character, and knowledge. You are probably now going through such a test in attending college. People say that going to college is more a test of endurance than training for a specific job. By graduating, you show that you can meet a challenge and handle it, that you have matured, and that you have learned how to learn. Job training comes after that. Boot camp offers another example of belief in the value of overcoming difficulty and meeting challenges. The Outward Bound program rests on the value of challenge myth. It says the most problematic children will be restored to good behavior if they get through a mountain-climbing expedition, a rafting trip down the Colorado River, or a wilderness canoe trip. Even corporate America believes in this concept and often sends its executives on such Outward Bound experiences to shape them up and build unity.

Political persuaders frequently offer voters a dramatic challenge to be met by their election. For instance, John Kennedy said that with his election a torch had been passed to a new generation and that the light from the torch would "light the world." George W. Bush promised to rise to the challenge to win the war on terrorism and return security to America. Product appeals frequently present consumers with a challenge. "Use the Soloflex machine regularly and lose 20 pounds in 30 days!" and "Get your MBA at Olivet College by attending one Saturday a month!" both rely on the value of challenge.

The value of challenge suggests that suffering could be good, or that nothing was ever accomplished without pain. Second, the myth suggests that suffering begets maturity, humility, and wisdom. Individuals learn and grow as they meet challenges and surmount them. Finally, all great leaders became so because they were tested and found equal to the challenge. Thus, defeats and failures are just tests that prepare you for the future. As you begin to catalog the persuasion aimed at you, you will find the value of challenge used frequently, whether for products, candidates, or ideologies (see Figure 9.1).

 Access InfoTrac College Edition, enter the words "meeting challenges" in the search

engine, and explore some of the ways this myth is used to persuade various constituencies.

The Eternal Return

Mercia Eliade (1971), a French professor of history, identified a historical myth persistent not only in Western culture but in other cultures as well. He called it **the myth of the eternal return**, and defined it as a rejection of concrete historical time or things that actually happened, accompanied by a yearning for and reenactment of a "periodical return to the mythical time of the beginning of things, to the 'Great Time.'" American culture embraces this myth, perhaps because our beginnings are so recent. America was conceived as a "second Eden," a chance to start anew with no historical baggage to clutter up its purpose. Many immigrants of the past and present want this chance to start over.

According to the myth of the eternal return, there was a time when things were perfect and harmonious, when events could be shaped or molded as they were meant to be. This time of creation is usually associated with a specific geographical center where things are assumed to have begun. In the United States, this center is probably Philadelphia, where the Continental Congress signed the Declaration of Independence and where the Liberty Bell is housed. Another potential symbolic center is Washington, DC, where our great historical documents are enshrined in the National Archives. At the creation there were great heroes (George Washington, Benjamin Franklin, Paul Revere, John Hancock, and others) and there were villains (King George, the colonial governors, Redcoats, and Tories). After suffering indignities, the heroes enacted some critical feat that was redemptive, and it released them and the people from their former enslavement and permitted them to create the "Great Time" or the "Golden Age." The Boston Tea Party is a familiar example.

Included in the myth is the notion that society has lost sight of its archetypal beginning and must find its way back if we are to rid ourselves of the corruption and confusion that have developed since

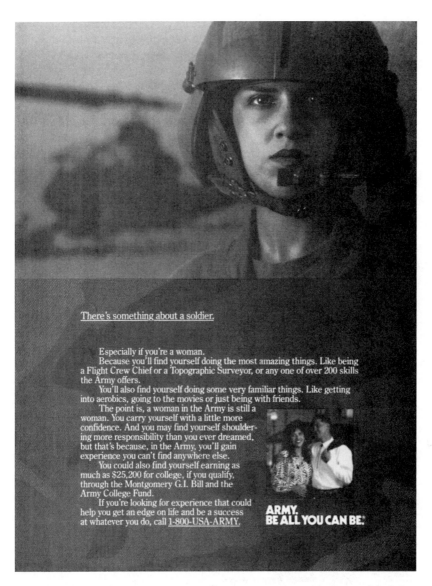

There's something about a soldier.

Especially if you're a woman.
Because you'll find yourself doing the most amazing things. Like being a Flight Crew Chief or a Topographic Surveyor, or any one of over 200 skills the Army offers.
You'll also find yourself doing some very familiar things. Like getting into aerobics, going to the movies or just being with friends.
The point is, a woman in the Army is still a woman. You carry yourself with a little more confidence. And you may find yourself shouldering more responsibility than you ever dreamed, but that's because, in the Army, you'll gain experience you can't find anywhere else.
You could also find yourself earning as much as $25,200 for college, if you qualify, through the Montgomery G.I. Bill and the Army College Fund.
If you're looking for experience that could help you get an edge on life and be a success at whatever you do, call 1-800-USA-ARMY.

**ARMY.
BE ALL YOU CAN BE.**

FIGURE 9.1 The U.S. Army's "Be All You Can Be" campaign exemplified the persuasiveness of the value of challenge myth, especially for women in this advertisement. The new slogan is "Join the Army of One," which also hints at challenge.

SOURCE: Army photograph courtesy of U.S. Government, as represented by the Secretary of the Army.

then. We usually accomplish this through reenactments of the original feat in a ritual, usually held at the center where everything began. This periodic return to the origins of our beliefs reestablishes our values for us and redeems the culture. The ritual freezes us in a mystical time that has power to transform us. As Eliade noted, "Time, too, like space is neither homogeneous nor continuous. On

This is as good a place as any to start perfecting a waterproof boot.

It was cold. It was wet. And losing your life was as easy as falling off a log.
Among early loggers in the Northwest, the boot that earned the highest praise—"Skookum tough"—was the one made by W.B. Danner. All leather, it had caulked soles to give "river pigs" a grip on shifting logs. A pair weighed about 6 lbs.
Nowadays Danner makes boots for every kind of outdoorsman. We use the same full-grain 5½ oz. leather, but we chrome tan it to repel water and reduce weight (to about 3½ lbs.).
For the inside we invented the Gore-Tex™ bootie. Water cannot penetrate its 9 billion pores per square inch, but perspiration can evaporate to the outside. The boots are guaranteed waterproof.

We use Thinsulate® Thermal Insulation. One forest ranger said the insulation was so good he couldn't tell his boots were on fire. He asked for one of our uninsulated models.
In any case, with a cushioned insole, neoprene and EVA midsoles, and Vibram® outsole, your feet are well protected from the primary source of cold, the ground.
For even lighter weight, we use Cordura® nylon in our fabric and leather boots. Originally used as tire cord, it has ten times the scuff resistance of leather, and can bring the weight of a boot down

to 24 oz. So there's a lot that's new in a Danner boot.
But it still takes 72 square feet of material to make a pair. And it still involves 250 separate operations, most of them by hand (we're about the only manufacturer that bothers with double lasting).
If you'd like a boot that's good enough to go back for resoling, we should be your bootmaker.
We got our feet wet a long time ago.

Danner
Call us for a free brochure or the name of your nearest Danner retailer: 1-800-345-0430.

CORDURA® GORE-TEX® Thinsulate

FIGURE 9.2 This ad by Danner boots appeals to the myth of the eternal return with its reference to a "Golden Age" when men were men and their boots stood the test of time.

SOURCE: Reprinted by permission of Danner Shoe Manufacturing Co.

the one hand there are the intervals of a sacred time, the time of festivals and on the other hand there is profane time, ordinary temporal duration" (Beane & Doty, 1975, p. 33). We believe in and talk about the cyclical nature of things in the two types of time. For example, when we say, "What goes around comes around," we mean, "This will come back to haunt you," "What ye sow, so shall ye reap," or "History repeats itself." We have a reverence for certain sacred times like historical holidays, ritualistic meals such as Thanksgiving or Passover, and national rites such as the inaugural address, the oath of office, or the State of the Union Address.

BOX 9.2 **Interactive Program for Anti-Drug Campaign**

 Go to www.mediacampaign.org and you will find a multi-mediated program sponsored by the National Youth Anti-drug Media Campaign. There you can search over 35 television commercials, 55 radio commercials, 80 print ads, 25 banner ads, and several screen savers all targeted at diverse audiences and ethnicities and in several languages. In addition, you can explore various news stories and informational essays about drugs, and their short-term and long-term effects, the campaign's partnership with the NFL and other sports organizations, and much more. Be sure to go to the www.freevibe.com and wwwdrugstory.org links from the main page. You will learn about how cultural values are appealed to in a number of ways by exploring the many facets of this campaign.

Commercial persuaders are aware of the importance of sacred time. They have invented special sales on historical holidays—a "Hatchet Days Sale" on Washington's birthday, an "Independence Day Sale" on the Fourth of July, and, in recent years, a "Super Bowl Sale" in mid-January. And every four years, the Olympics provides numerous instances of sacred time being celebrated. At the same time, we disdain persons who waste time, who are just passing the time, or who are "couch potatoes" living through profane time. Recessions are profane times, as are losing seasons for athletic teams. Politicians are skilled at challenging us to return to an earlier time to reestablish and renew ourselves. Not only is this apparent in their speeches, but also in the inaugural ceremonies themselves, which are acts of renewal that promise to return us to the untainted past.

In ideological campaigns and mass movements, the return-and-renewal theme is also persistent. Martin Luther King, Jr., used it in his "I Have a Dream" speech. We hear strains of the myth but referring to profane times in the pro-life, antiabortion movement. One pro-life leader said, "People are going to look back on this era the way they look back on Nazi Germany. They'll say 'Thank God there were a few sane people'" ("America's Abortion Dilemma," 1985, p. 21). This profane time was echoed by a "moral majority" leader who said of abortion, "This criminal activity . . . sets us back to the Stone Age" (p. 22).

Even in product ads we can detect appeals to the new beginnings or to the return and renewal myth. NEC Corporation says, "The new information age is built on the merging of computers and communication . . . you deserve no less. NEC, the way it will be." Mercedes-Benz reminds us, "This Year, as for Ninety-nine Years, the Automobiles of Mercedes-Benz are Like no Other Cars in the World." This myth of the eternal return is a powerful tool that persuaders use in a variety of circumstances. It is reflected in a set of cultural myths or parables described next.

REICH'S CULTURAL PARABLES

In his book *Tales of a New America*, Robert Reich (1987) contends that the future appears chaotic for a variety of reasons: rapidly advancing technology, rising expectations for prosperity throughout the world, and general confusion about where we are headed as a nation. Reich and his Harvard colleagues have identified what they call basic *cultural parables* for the United States. These parables convey

> lessons about the how and why of life through metaphor, (that) may be a basic human trait, a universal characteristic of our intermittently rational, deeply emotional, meaning-seeking species. In America the vehicles of public myth include the biographies of famous citizens, popular fiction, films, and music, feature stories about people who do good things. They anchor our political understandings. What

gives them force is their capacity to make sense of, and bring coherence to, common experience. The lessons ring true, even if the illustration is fanciful (p. 7).

Reich's work often echoes what has been emphasized earlier in our study of persuasion: Human beings are fascinated with and driven by the power of the dramatic.

Reich's parables are manifest in the following story about a man named George, the son of immigrant parents who worked hard to provide a good home. He did well in school and worked long hours to bring home a few dollars for the family. He was good in sports although he didn't have much time to participate. He never picked a fight, but on one occasion he did step in to stop the town bully and banker's son, Albert Wade, from beating up on the smallest kid in class. He let Albert have the first swing and then decked him with a single punch. George went off to fight in Europe in World War II and saved his squad by single-handedly destroying a machine gun nest, but he was too humble to wear or display the medal he received for bravery. After the war, he returned to his hometown, married his childhood sweetheart, and built a successful construction business. He gave his spare time to good causes and lived modestly. George kept to himself until his old nemesis, Albert Wade, inherited his father's bank and began to squander the depositors' savings by making shady loans to his buddies and buying himself into the office of mayor. The only person to stand up and challenge the corrupt election was George. Then Wade's bank refused to loan any money on houses built by George. In a showdown town meeting, one of Wade's corrupt councilmen finally broke down under George's accusatory gaze and spilled the beans on Wade, who ended up in jail while George went back to his modest life. It is *the* American morality play, according to Reich.

This brief story has been told over and over again in many versions, including Horatio Alger novels, and biographies of famous Americans. It contains Reich's basic cultural parables that have remained current for generations. As you read about these parables, look for the similarities between them and cultural myths.

The Mob at the Gates

The basic idea in this parable is that America stands alone as the last, best hope for a good, moral, and affluent life in a world filled with perilous possibilities and awesome problems. This parable creates an "us versus them" mentality or mind-set. The **mob at the gates** may be drug traffickers, illegal aliens, terrorists; or it may be environmental polluters, the militia movement, or foreign or slave labor that can provide goods at lower prices than American companies charge. The mob may also be the greedy corporate executives who exploit workers through insider trading, outrageous salaries and perks, and outright cheating. The mob may be secular humanists, minorities, and do-gooders. Those who see themselves as heroes may defy the mob at the gates on some issue, such as foreign competition, but on other issues, the mob may be acceptable for one side but not for the other. For instance, liberals see illegal aliens as less threatening than conservatives do.

Reich (1987) cites several persuasive events of central importance to our nation that rested on the mob at the gates parable. One is the "rotten apple" metaphor. Several rotten leaders or countries can ruin the "whole barrel" of free nations. The rotten apples at the top of corporate America have ruined the trust and confidence so essential for a healthy and growing economy. We also have seen this myth applied to George W. Bush's "rogue nations" that form an "axis of evil" that condones, supports, and even trains terrorists. Note how the language used frames the issues for us. "Rogue" nations don't play by the "rules," defined by Bush as American ways of behaving, and the "axis of evil" is reminiscent of the German, Italian, and Japanese "Axis" of World War II, thus equating those nations with fascist tyrannies.

Advertisers base many of their ads for products on this parable. Millions of germs are lying in wait to infect you, but if you use Listerine mouthwash, you'll knock them for a loop. Hordes of mosquitoes will ruin your picnic unless you are vigilant enough to spray the area with long-lasting Raid insect fog. The mob myth is a natural for ideological campaigns as well. For example, the secular humanists are supposedly tainting America's moral fiber, so it is absolutely essential to join the Born Again group. And, of course, politicians use the image in a variety of ways: The mob may be the other party, the homeless, or tax-and-spend politicians. Not to worry—the "good guys" will save the day.

The Triumphant Individual

The **triumphant individual** parable has as its subject the humble person who works hard, takes risks but has faith in him- or herself, and eventually reaches or even exceeds goals of fame, honor, and financial success. It is the story of the self-made man or woman who demonstrates what hard work and determination, combined with a gutsy approach to problems and a spunky style, can do. Usually, the individual is a loner (sometimes even a maverick) who is willing to challenge the establishment and try to do something on a shoestring.

A modern example is Bill Gates, the inventor of Microsoft, and now a major philanthropist. Another is Steven Jobs, who invented the Apple computer and built the Apple empire, beginning in his garage. Both Gates and Jobs were self-reliant and hardworking, and they believed in themselves. Another example from the fairly recent past is Lee Iacocca, the maverick at Ford who bucked the odds and the office politics, and finally persuaded the company to bring out its most successful product ever—the Mustang. He took over the nearly bankrupt Chrysler Corporation and turned the company around, paying off a $1.2-billion government bailout loan early; innovating with front wheel drive, the minivan, driver and passenger airbags, customer rebates, a 70,000-mile warranty, and the convertible.

The triumphant individual myth strikes the same chord as several cultural myths mentioned earlier, such as the wisdom of the rustic. We frequently see the triumphant individual in a variety of persuasive arenas. In politics, self-made men or women are the ones to put your money on. They made it this far on guts and a belief in themselves, and as a result, they will come out winners on election day as well. A good example is Senator John McCain who was a tortured P.O.W. during the Vietnam War and was finally returned to his home state of Arizona where he triumphed and became a senator. Some speculate that he may run for the presidency in 2008. Companies that are willing to take risks on new technologies also are a kind of triumphant individual.

The Benevolent Community

The myth or parable of **the benevolent community** reflects the essential goodness of people and their willingness to help out the other guy in time of need. An ad for Miller beer portrayed this myth in action. A small town in Wisconsin was struck by a tornado that demolished several homes, businesses, and nearby farms. But the men and women of surrounding communities joined forces and within two weeks had nearly rebuilt all that had been destroyed. Of course, at the end of a hard day of raising walls and rafters, they enjoyed drinking the sponsor's product. During devastating floods and storms, students, neighbors, and others volunteer to fill sand bags, build levies, and help out the victims. And the hurricane-ravaged Gulf states received billions of dollars in relief from donations by ordinary citizens of the "benevolent community." Though recent events have soured our trust in CEOs, corporate America regularly enhances its image after various disasters by advertising that it has donated money and products to the victims, and thus the corporation becomes part of the benevolent community. The U.S. Marines are a part of the benevolent community with their annual Toys for Tots campaign around the holidays. We find this cultural parable recurring throughout our history in struggles like abolition, women's suffrage, the civil rights movement, past and current anti-war movements, and pro-life or pro-choice demonstrations. As Reich notes, "The story celebrates America's tradition of civic improvement, philanthropy, and local boosterism" (p. 10). Persuaders will continue to use the lesson of this parable to market products, candidates, and ideologies.

Rot at the Top

The **rot at the top** parable or myth has conspiratorial aspects and revolves around a number of subthemes such as corruption, a lack of morals or ethics, decadence, greed, and the malevolence of persons in high places. Like the presence of conspiracy myth, it seems to follow a cyclical pattern, which Reich calls "cycles of righteous fulmination." First, we trust the elite, but then we find them lacking in trust or goodwill, and finally, we end up unseating them and "throwing the rascals out!" Reich traces the myth to the Founding Fathers' sensitivity to the abuse of power experienced under King George and his colonial governors. Abuses of power by elites who buy their positions of power with money and favors (as did Albert Wade) or who have been corrupted by power always exist.

Our history features numerous and varied types of rot at the top, but Reich believes that the myth usually has one of two main targets: political corruption or economic exploitation. Politically, we have seen it in Teapot Dome in the 1920s, Watergate in the 1970s, the Iran–Contra scandals of the 1980s, sex scandals in the 1990s, and, most recently, the fiscal scandals in corporate America. We often hear that big business has exploited the common man, and we still see Wall Street scandals based on insider trading by "stock market jackals" and "corporate barracudas." All of these are examples of rot at the top. The lesson of this myth is simple: Power corrupts; privilege perverts.

Writer Michael Parenti (1994) identifies several other myths that are fairly self-explanatory. "You can't fight city hall," "our leaders know best," "you can't legislate morality," and "all politicians are the same" (p. 2–13) are all examples. Communication scholar D. Hahn (1998) identified several other political myths, such as the myth of progress, the myth of youth, and the myth of love and openness (p. 128–129).

Go to InfoTrac College Edition, enter the words "corporate scandal" in either the subject or the key word search engine, and read a few of the titles listed. See if they incorporate elements of the rot-at-the-top cultural myth.

THE MAN'S MAN AND THE WOMAN'S WOMAN

Another popular cultural myth for many Americans is that for a male to be a success, he must be a macho **man's man**. Schools, family, and television tell children that important males are those who do macho things: compete in manly activities, use colognes with names like "Iron," get involved in sports, talk tough, own guns, and drive SUVs. They never show their emotions, and they die with their boots on. In contrast, the ideal **woman's woman** is soft spoken, kind, and nurturing but also practical and competent. She may work, but she is also the perfect wife and mother and is always immaculately groomed. However, she may also be vain, rarely has meaningful thoughts, and never wastes time talking about serious things.

These myths, of course, affect the way we treat our children, valuing certain things they do and devaluing others. Until recently, it was unfeminine for females to engage in any sport except tennis, golf, gymnastics, figure skating, or swimming. On the other side of the coin, it was not masculine for males to take up gourmet cooking, needlepoint, or flower gardening (vegetables were okay). Further, males weren't very nurturing or emotional, and they talked about important things like jobs, the economy, cars, and sports.

However, this myth of the distinctions between the sexes is obviously changing. High schools and colleges boast women's field hockey, basketball, boxing, and softball teams. Female executives are featured in ads for business hotels, and female pilots are shown using deodorant. At the same time, men are now expected to contribute their fair share of housework. Old myths do not die easily, however, and we still see many examples of the stereotypical macho man and the perfectly feminine woman. Beer ads feature retired athletes engaged in a man's world, bragging to one another over beers or testifying to the effectiveness of potency enhancers. One look at any current magazine shows advertisers pitching their products at people who buy into these images of men and women.

Although gender-bound and stereotypical representations of men and women are changing, these images still have persuasive power and are still used to advertise products and promote ideas. Despite reductions in gender differences in job and political candidacy and in gender-related language use, the old stereotypes are still potent persuaders. The major change in attitude toward gender-related issues has occurred in young, college-educated, upper-middle-class, nonminority populations. But the far greater proportion of our population still seems to buy into the man's man and woman's woman myths. We still see ads for SUVs, assault weapons, and chain saws, and we continue to see ads for Victoria's Secret (sort of a prudish but sexy name), *Elle* magazine, and beauty products. All of these examples continue to promote gender stereotypes. Try counting the number of features or ads in a single issue of a magazine like *Elle* or *Marie Claire* devoted to the woman's woman. Consider a few of the following feature titles from the cover of a single issue of *Cosmopolitan*: "Super Sensual Sex—Touch Him Tricks," "A Man's Body Craves Certain Strokes, Caresses and Pressure. Here's Your Hands-On Guide," or "28 Romantic Rituals to Do With Your Man," or "Try This Simple Trick and Get What You Want." They all promote gender stereotypes. The woman's woman is not only good at work and home, but she is also skilled at lovemaking. They are just a few appeals to the woman's woman myth we encounter every day.

Persuaders will adapt as Americans shift their values regarding gender and other human characteristics, such as age, single parenthood, and economic status, but their persuasion will reflect the premises that the audience believes. Persuasion is more often a reflection of a culture's values than a shaper of them (see Figures 9.3 and 9.4)

There is a broad literature on gender stereotypes. Explore it by accessing InfoTrac College Edition and entering the words "gender stereotypes" in the subject search engine. Browse the periodical selections.

IMAGE AS A CULTURAL PREMISE

Sometimes persuaders are successful because of their **image or charisma**. Somehow they seem to have a special presence, and they command the public's attention. We believe them because their presentations are convincing and dynamic, or because they have a reputation for being truthful or knowledgeable. As we noted earlier, Aristotle called this kind of credibility *ethos*, or ethical proof. More recently, researchers have worked at identifying exactly what causes or creates high ethos in some persons and low ethos in others. One research technique is to have audiences rate speakers on a variety of scales that have sets of opposing adjectives at either end. For example, the scales may have words like "fast/slow." On one end of the scale is the number 1 and on the other end is the number 5. Other word pairs include strong/weak, hot/cool, or active/inactive. Researchers see where the ratings cluster and infer that those items with positive loadings are important to credibility, image, charisma or *ethos*. The choices tend to cluster around the three traits or dimensions of source credibility: expertise, trustworthiness or sincerity, and dynamism or charisma. Together, they accounted for more persuasive success than all the rest of the dimensions. For example, the dynamism ratings were associated with words like "active," "fast," "hot," and "strong." Let us explore these dimensions of source credibility more fully.

Expertise

The **expertise** dimension of source credibility means that highly credible sources are perceived as having knowledge and experience regarding the topic they address and therefore are credible. This makes sense because we tend to put more store in ideas and advice that come from experts than in those that come from nonexperts. To whom would you go for advice on gourmet cooking—Emeril or the cook at the local cafe? The clustering of words such as "competent," "experienced," and "professional" related to the expertise dimension and have been verified by experiments in which a variety of groups listened to the same audio tape of a speaker giving the same

FIGURE 9.3 Here are examples of the myth of the "man's man" done tongue in cheek.

FIGURE 9.4 The myth of the man's man has always revolved around sexual potency, as can be seen in this Big Stinky cartoon.

SOURCE: Reprinted by permission of Nick Jeffries.

speech. The speaker was introduced to some of the groups as the surgeon general while to others the speaker was introduced as a college senior. The listeners found the "expert" much more credible than the nonexpert. Many advertisements use expert testimony from doctors, financial advisors, and scientists because they are deemed to be credible, and consumers feel that they can rely on these experts' advice. Over 35 years ago, researchers reported that three believability factors emerging from audience-generated words describing credible sources were safety, qualification, and dynamism (Berlo, Lemmert, & Davis, 1969). Qualification is similar to expertise. This dimension seems to be one of the more stable factors in determining whether we believe someone.

Trustworthiness or Sincerity

Another dimension that recurs in studies of image, credibility, or charisma is **trustworthiness** or sincerity. Early persuasion researchers at Yale first identified this factor in their studies, concluding that the credibility of any source is tied to "trust and confidence" (Hovland, Janis, & Kelley, 1953). This dimension emerged in numerous other studies over the years, and has sometimes been called "safety" or "personal integrity" (Baudhin & Davis, 1972).

An interesting indicator of trustworthiness occurs in situations in which a biased source testifies against his or her own self-interest or bias. This may give us a clue to what is really involved in the trust dimension. Psychology researchers Herbert Kelman and Carl Hovland (1953) wanted to know who would be believed in the following situation: A message promoting the need for stiffer penalties for juvenile delinquents that was attributed in one case to a juvenile court judge and in another case to a reformed drug-pushing juvenile delinquent. The audience believed the judge because of his expertise in dealing with juvenile cases, but their belief in the delinquent came from their trust that his sincere testimony was obviously against the speaker's image.

Trust or sincerity requires us to analyze speakers' motives or hidden agendas. The etymology of the word *sincerity* gives us some insights. It comes from the Latin *sincerus*, which literally means "without wax." This referred to a practice of unethical pillar carvers, who used wax to cover up blemishes in an otherwise perfect pillar that had been ruined by the carver's mistakes. Only after decades of weathering did the wax fall out and reveal the deception. So a sincere person was without wax or not camouflaged.

Audiences believe speakers who are sincere and trustworthy. These speakers maintain good

---

B O X 9.3   Diversity and Media Literacy

There is growing concern over media literacy, particularly as we enter the global community. For instance, if you don't know how to get on the Internet, are you truly literate in today's global community? How much information are you missing if you are not media literate? Do people of diverse ethnicities need different kinds of training in media literacy? Go to www.readingonline.org/[e1] which is a website that explores these and other issues. Go to the home page and explore some of the materials/articles there. From Issue 45, I particularly recommend the items on the virtual school.

---

eye contact, don't shift back and forth on their feet, and lack a tremor in their voices. Or audiences judge sincerity from speakers' reputations—offices they have held, accomplishments, and what others say about them. Trustworthiness has been repeatedly demonstrated in research studies as a key component of credibility. Although its effects vary from situation to situation, receivers believe persons they trust, whether because of their reputation, delivery, or motivation.

Dynamism

A final dimension of credibility that has been demonstrated through experimental research is not as easy to define or even describe. This factor has been labeled **dynamism**, **charisma**, or **image** by various researchers. It is the degree to which the audience admires and identifies with the source's attractiveness, power, forcefulness, and energy. The following word pairs have been used in testing for the dynamism factor: "aggressive/meek," "emphatic/hesitant," "frank/reserved," "bold/passive," "energetic/tired," and "fast/slow." The ratings clustered around the first word in each pair.

Dynamism equates with charisma, and although it is influenced by a speaker's attractiveness, unattractive persons can be charismatic or dynamic. Dynamic speakers don't necessarily move about or wave their arms to give off dynamism cues. They simply seem to take up a lot of psychological space. They enter a room and people expect them to be in charge. Their voices seem to be assured and confident. They are eloquent and

sometimes border on being poetic. They seem to know just what to say in tough or even tragic moments, and the audience lingers on their words. Dynamic persuaders populate important and crisis events across American history.

Researchers have investigated other dimensions of source credibility. A tall speaker, for example, is generally more likely to be believed than a short one. Timid or shy and reserved persons are likely to have low credibility, whereas authoritative and self-assured ones have high credibility. Bossy and egotistical persuaders lose credibility, whereas pleasant and warm persuaders do not. These and many other dimensions of source credibility interact and affect the three fundamental dimensions of credibility—trust/sincerity, expertise, and dynamism/potency.

These elements of source credibility are not shared by all cultures. In cultures in which the *baksheesh* (bribe) is the order of the day, people actually are admired for being untrustworthy. The popularity of haggling over prices in bazaars is based on insincerity, not sincerity. So credibility has cultural differences, too.

THE AMERICAN VALUE SYSTEM

The myths and parables we have examined are actually fantasy forms of deep and enduring values held by most Americans. They are expressed in myths in order to simplify them. For example, Americans have a belief or value that all persons are to be treated equally and that in the eyes of the law, they are equal. This value has been debated for more than two centuries in the context of such issues as slavery, women's suffrage, civil rights, desegregation, and affirmative action. It is acted out or dramatized in the possibility of success myth. We see the myth portrayed in print and TV ads. For example, a recent print ad for the DuPont Chemical Company featured a man who was still able to play basketball even though he had lost both legs in Vietnam. This was thanks to DuPont, who sold the raw materials for making the artificial limbs that enable the man to succeed in the world of amateur sports (see Figure 9.5).

One of the early speech communication studies that explored American core values was conducted by Edward Steele and W. Charles Redding (1962). They looked at the communication used in several presidential election campaigns and tried to extract core and secondary values. Their work has been replicated numerous times since then with very similar outcomes, suggesting that these core American values have great durability and persistence. These values are frequently articulated by the media as the values that relate to various social issues (Kosicki, 2002). You will be able to see them if you look around. The following are descriptions of the core values observed by Steele and Redding and since verified by other communication researchers.

Puritan and Pioneer Morality

The **Puritan and pioneer morality** value is our tendency to cast the world into categories of right and wrong, good and evil, ethical and unethical, and so forth. Although we tend to think of this value as outdated, it has merely been reworded. Persons on the political right and left frequently make judgments based on it. The advocates and foes of marijuana laws and of legal abortion both call on moral values such as just/unjust, right/wrong, and moral/immoral to make their cases. The injustice of terrorism, whether perpetrated against us or against others, is viewed as morally inexcusable, and the resulting loss of innocent lives

leads Americans and others to see it as having major moral dimensions. The decision by the Bush administration in 2004 not to fund new stem cell research was viewed by both sides as a morality issue. For those who favored the research, Bush's decision was bad because stem cell research might have provided cures for many diseases like diabetes and cancer. For those on the other side there was the good of not harming embryos that hypothetically could become living persons.

The Value of the Individual

This value ranks the rights and welfare of the individual above those of the government or other groups. It is encapsulated in many of our historical documents—the Declaration of Independence, the Constitution, the Emancipation Proclamation, and others. All politicians claim to be interested in the **value of the individual**, and our laws ensure and protect individual rights over all others. Further, each person has the right to succeed or fail on his or her own. Although no one is an island, no one is tied to the will of the majority either. In the world of advertising, most products are marketed with the individual in mind. Cosmetics, according to this value, are made "especially for you," and Burger King lets you "Have It Your Way." In politics and government the real power of a democracy lies within each individual. Most good causes target the individual recipient of aid and the individual donor as individuals who are "making a difference."

Achievement and Success

Achievement and success entails the accumulation of education, power, status, wealth, and property. During the anti–Vietnam War years, many young Americans rejected these values, favoring communal living and refusing to dress up for job interviews. Many of those same young people are now the upwardly mobile, achievement-oriented, and graying muppies (mature urban professionals). Many of these former renegades now evaluate others by the symbols or emblems of success they own—whether a BMW or Mercedes-Benz, a Rolex watch

For Bill Demby, the difference means getting another shot.

When Bill Demby was in Vietnam, he used to dream of coming home and playing a little basketball with the guys.

A dream that all but died when he lost both his legs to a Viet Cong rocket.

But then, a group of researchers discovered that a remarkable DuPont plastic could help make artificial limbs that were more resilient, more flexible, more like life itself.

Thanks to these efforts, Bill Demby is back. And some say, he hasn't lost a step.

At DuPont, we make the things that make a difference.

Better things for better living.

FIGURE 9.5 This ad enhances DuPont's ethos by implying that the company is responsible for Bill Demby's "getting another shot" at an active life.

SOURCE: DuPont Company photograph. Used by permission of DuPont.

or Mont Blanc pen. Persuaders frequently appeal to our need for achievement or success. Most military recruitment advertisements and slogans promise that by starting a career in the Army, Navy, Air Force, Marines, or Coast Guard you will be able to climb the ladder to success faster. If you read the *Wall Street*

Journal, success and status will be yours. First impressions count, so be sure to "dress for success" by shopping at Nordstroms, and don't wear pierced jewelry to the interview. Self-help books and programs will help you to be an achiever and will contribute to your success. The achievement and success value, like the cultural myths, seems to ebb and flow with time. Thus, self-improvement will continue to be marketed even when the values of achievement and success seem most dormant.

Change and Progress

The **change and progress** value is typified by the belief that change of almost any kind will lead to progress and that progress is inherently good for us. This is the appeal of any product that is "new" or "new and improved." Product life cycle theory, which you may have studied in a marketing class, almost dictates that change and progress in the form of improvement must recur repeatedly to delay a decline of brand sales. From a legal point, the producer of a laundry product, for example, can claim that its product is "new and improved" merely by changing the color of the "beads of bleach" in it or by slightly altering the ratio of ingredients or offering a new pouring spout. General Electric once had as its slogan "At GE, Progress Is Our Most Important Product." The word *new* is one of the most powerful words in advertising. Indeed, many changes obviously have been beneficial, such as the downsizing of the American automobile and the increase in its fuel efficiency. And few would disagree on the value of the new generations of home and business computers, or digital audio and video, or many new medical technologies. The Internet has made an enormous quantity of information on any and every topic available to almost everyone as well as making communication with people all over the globe instantaneous. At the same time, certain products and brands have built-in obsolescence. The new and improved Whirlpool dryer may just have a new coating on its tumbler. But every year manufacturers bring out new models of their product or brands that really aren't changed that much. Nonetheless, the value of change and progress continues to be a powerful first premise in many enthymemes we encounter. If you don't change and make progress, you are falling behind in life.

Ethical Equality

The **ethical equality** value reflects the belief that all persons ought to be treated equally. They should have an equal opportunity to get an education, to work and be paid a fair wage, to live where they choose, and to hold political office. But we all know that, although this value may be laudable, the reality is that not everyone is born equal, nor do they all have an equal opportunity for jobs, education, or decent housing. Nonetheless, since the nation's founding, through the abolition, women's suffrage, civil rights, and other movements, attempts to create a situation of equality have been a part of the American cultural landscape. The words from the Declaration of Independence, "All men are created equal," best illustrate the power of this value.

Effort and Optimism

The **effort and optimism** value expresses the belief that even the most unattainable goals can be reached if one just works hard enough and "keeps smilin'." The myths of the triumphant individual and the possibility of success are examples of these values in action. And in today's business world, it is important to be a "striver" or a "self-starter." Nuggets of folk wisdom such as "Every cloud must have a silver lining," "If at first you don't succeed, try, try again," "Keep on the sunny side," and "Lighten up" serve as cultural metaphors of the value we place on effort and optimism. And phrases such as "a hard worker" and "the eternal optimist" reflect how we much we believe in the value of effort and optimism. If you don't let the world get you down and keep plugging away, things will work out. This value motivates many of our life decisions.

Efficiency, Practicality, and Pragmatism

The **efficiency, practicality, and pragmatism** value is based on our need for solutions. The key question often asked of any piece of legislation is

"Will it work?" whether it be a new set of tax revisions, a new cabinet office such as the Office of Homeland Security, or new immigration statutes. This value extends to other parts of our lives, too. Years ago, my family was among the first purchasers of a microwave oven, which cost $400 then. Before making the purchase, we wanted to know whether a microwave oven would be energy efficient, practical, and handy, and not merely another fad. And of course, we now know that they are energy efficient, handy and practical, but now they are available for less than $100. On another issue, we want to be certain that an advanced education will lead to a rewarding job. We are fascinated by questions of efficiency—fuel efficiency in our cars, energy efficiency in our appliances, and efficiency of movement on the production line. And we go for practical solutions, whether it is the most efficient way to lose weight, to get in good shape, or to be able to buy one's first home. In other words, we value what is quick, workable, and practical.

Even though these values were cataloged more than 40 years ago, they still have a great deal of relevance. And the fact that they are held in high regard by liberals and conservatives speaks for their credibility and for the conviction that they are indeed "core" American values. Our culture is effective in instilling these values in nearly all its members; radicals, moderates, and reactionaries may believe in the same values, but they tend to apply them quite differently. The power of a social system or culture to train its members is immense—even though people do not often realize it, they react to the dictates deeply ingrained in them. Does this mean that values remain essentially static and cannot be changed? Not necessarily. It means only that they are so deeply ingrained in a culture that its members often forget how strong they are. They are probably processed in the peripheral channel of the ELM.

Access InfoTrac College Edition, and enter the words "American values" in the key word search engine, and examine a few of the many articles devoted to the topic. How closely do they resemble the Redding and Steele list of core values?

REVIEW AND CONCLUSION

By this time, you know that the world of the persuadee in a diverse and interactive information age is not a simple one. There are so many things to be aware of: the persuader's self-revelation in the language used and their style, the internal or process premises operating within each of us, and the interactive rules for content premises. In addition, societal and cultural predispositions for persuasion can and do act as premises in persuasive arguments. Persuaders instinctively appeal to values that rely on the societal training in the target audience. On separate levels, this training has an effect on each of us—in the cultural myths or images to which we respond, in the sets of values we consciously articulate. And in an evermore diverse world, both persuaders and receivers need to be aware that the cultural premises of today may not be the only way to see the world.

KEY TERMS

When you have finished reading this chapter, you should be able to identify, explain, and give an example of each of the following terms or concepts.

cultural patterns	the wisdom of the rustic	coming of a messiah	the value of challenge
cultural images and myths	possibility of success	presence of conspiracy	the myth of the eternal return
		paranoid style	

mob at the gates	woman's woman	image	change and progress
triumphant individual	image or charisma	Puritan and pioneer morality	ethical equality
the benevolent community	expertise	value of the individual	effort and optimism
rot at the top	trustworthiness	achievement and success	efficiency, practicality, and pragmatism
man's man	dynamism		
	charisma		

APPLICATION OF ETHICS

Dr. L. teaches a course in "Research Methods in Mass Communication" which is a difficult course for most communication majors, especially the quantitative topics like inferential statistics. A female student who is a member of a minority has been absent from classes frequently and has done poorly on all the tests. Dr. L. calls her in to discuss the problem and discovers that she is a single mother who is putting herself through school by holding down several part-time jobs. She is getting good grades in all her other communication courses and expects to graduate at the end of the semester. Furthermore, she has been promised an excellent job as an anchor newsperson and in all likelihood will never need to know statistics or research methods. The Affirmative Action Office has issued a memo stating that students who are members of a protected minority (including females) should be given special consideration and help. What should Dr. L. do? (1) Give the student a D- grade so she can graduate. (2) Give the student an Incomplete to be made up when the semester is over. (3) Give the student a failing grade. (4) Offer to give the student private tutoring in statistics—something Dr. L has not done before and is not doing for other students in a similar situation.

QUESTIONS FOR FURTHER THOUGHT

1. What are the three types of culturally or socially learned predispositions for persuasion? Give examples of each from your own experience.

2. How does a culture or society train its members? Give examples from your own experience.

3. How do you rank the core values mentioned in this chapter? How do you put them into practice? Are there other values in your value system not mentioned here? What are they? Are they restatements of the core values? If so, how? If not, how do they differ?

4. Considering today's headlines, is there a mob at the gates presently? Explain.

5. To what degree can you identify a benevolent community in your life? Explain.

6. In the popular Harrison Ford film *Patriot Games*, there clearly is rot at the top. At what critical moment does the "narrator" of the film discover the "rot"? What does he do about it?

7. Explain the ethos of the hosts of the various TV talk shows. How does each host's ethos differ from the others'—for example, does Jay Leno seem more or less sincere, expert, or dynamic than David Letterman?

8. How have the core values described by Steele and Redding operated on your campus? In your own life?

9. How have American values changed since September 11, 2001? What examples can you give?

10. The slogan "These Colors Don't Run" that appeared in many places following the events of 9/11 clearly articulate an American value. What is it?

 For online activities, go to the *Persuasion* book companion website at http://communication.wadsworth.com/larson11.

10

Nonverbal Messages
in Persuasion

LEARNING GOALS

After reading this chapter, you should be able to:

1. Differentiate and give examples of the various channels of nonverbal communication.

2. Explain what various tactics of nonverbal communication can indicate.

3. Recognize nonverbal messages in your everyday life (e.g., in interpersonal relations, advertising, entertainment, and other communication situations).

4. Alter your own nonverbal communication behaviors and determine the differences in meaning they cause (e.g., look puzzled when someone is trying to explain something to you, and see if that causes them to elaborate)

5. Identify and explain what various gestures communicate (e.g., Allstate's bowl gesture).

6. Discuss the ethical issues involved in manipulating nonverbal behavior.

Videotapes of persons shopping in stores during a devastating earthquake in San Francisco show that the first thing people did to check the environment was to see whether objects fell from shelves, windows broke, and walls cracked. The next thing they did was to check out the nonverbal behavior of the people around them. They looked for facial expressions, movement, and other cues of impending danger. During the Gulf War of the 1990s, Saddam Hussein tried to win worldwide public approval for his invasion of Kuwait by being photographed and filmed talking with young Western children who were being "detained" (or held hostage) in Iraq (see Figure 10.1). During his interviews, he touched the children in a parental way, prompting widespread criticism and even outrage, especially because armed guards stood at attention in the background and the children appeared frightened and looked past Saddam, perhaps at more armed guards behind him. Fictional hero Jason Bourne, in Robert Ludlum's best seller and popular film, *The Bourne Ultimatum*, is able to identify the disguised assassin and terrorist Carlos the Jackal by his walk. Advertising researchers now can observe and record the dilation of the pupil and the eye's path as it surveys a print advertisement.

These are a few examples of nonverbal communication that occur every day. We process thousands of nonverbal messages daily. In fact, researcher Albert Mehrabian (1971) estimated that nonverbal communication accounts for over 80 percent of the meaning transferred between people. Others agree with him (e.g., Burgoon, Bufler, and Woodall, 1996; Knapp and Hall, 2002; and Guerrero, Devito, and Hecht, 1999). Nonverbal messages also accompany most persuasive appeals we process. Do they help or do they hinder persuasion?

Nonverbal premises in persuasion resemble cultural premises in that both are taught by our cultures and learned by us. A difference between cultural and nonverbal premises is that nonverbal ones seldom are carefully analyzed. We may sense that a certain persuader seems dishonest, and that it has something to do with his or her shifty eyes. However, we rarely dissect the interaction to find out exactly what causes us to distrust the other person. Another difference is that nonverbal premises usually occur at a very low level of awareness and so aren't readily apparent. We almost certainly process them in the peripheral route of the elaboration likelihood model (ELM). We need to sensitize ourselves to some of the nonverbal factors that enter into persuasion. This sensitization serves two purposes: (1) It increases the information on which we can base our decisions, and (2) it can tip us off to persuaders' hidden agendas, favorite tactics, and ultimate goals.

Communication researcher Donald Orban (1999) points out the power of these tip-offs when he asks, "When a person glares at you, forms a fist, invades your space, [or] uses a harsh and loud voice to accompany a verbal argument demanding that you do it his way instead of your way, are you intimidated? Are you more likely to be influenced by the manner of the argument behavior or the validity of the argument?" (n.p.) Most nonverbal communication occurs almost instinctively or automatically. It is hard to fake, and even then, the persuader's intent seems to "leak" through nonverbal channels. Eckman (1999) points out that some persons such as law enforcement officers and psychologists can detect liars from their nonverbal behaviors. These liars leak nonverbal cues that indicate that they are lying.

NONVERBAL CHANNELS

There are several channels through which we can communicate nonverbal meaning. Communication researchers J. K. Burgoon, N. E. Dunbar, and C. Segrin (2002) have identified three classes of nonverbal appeals: (1) appeals to attractiveness, similarity, intimacy, and trust; (2) dominance and power displays; and (3) expectancy signaling and expectancy violations. With regard to appeals to attraction and similarity, we have long been aware that physical attractiveness is strongly correlated with persuasiveness, regardless of the expertise, sincerity, or trustworthiness of the persuader. And we have

FIGURE 10.1 What kinds of meaning do you derive from this photograph? How is the meaning communicated? Is the young boy looking at Saddam Hussein or past him? How does the presence of uniformed guards standing at attention in the background affect the kindly, concerned, and grandfatherly image that Saddam wanted to convey?

SOURCE: Photo by AFP. © 1990 Newsweek, Inc. Reprinted by permission of *Newsweek*.

also long known that the degree of similarity between persuader and persuadee is a powerful predictor of attractiveness and hence of persuasiveness. Heider's balance theory indicates that people like and believe in persons who hold opinions similar to their own and may find those individuals attractive for this reason. Since Heider's time, a variety of other persuasion theories have confirmed his predictions.

Cognitive valence theory (CVT), proposed by P. A. Andersen (1999), predicts that the nonverbal immediacy of the persuader leads to what he calls arousal, which, in turn, leads to relational nearness or closeness between the two. Another theory, proposed by H. Giles, N. Coupland, and J. Coupland (1991), is called communication accommodation theory (CAT). It predicts that people respond more positively to persuaders whose nonverbal style is similar to their own. This is particularly true when their vocal qualities are similar (tone of voice, articulation, volume, and so on) although other nonverbal channels have influence as well. Both theories link similarity and attractiveness with persuasiveness because acting and thinking like a physically attractive source is seen as socially rewarding. This accounts for various fads in clothing and communicating that are patterned after a famous or attractive person. For example, until rock music stars and film idols began piercing body parts, few thought these nonverbal messages were of much value. It turns out that piercing is a real turn-off in job interviews, so some nonverbal messages may boomerang. Both theories recognize the various channels or cues of attractiveness and similarity. They include physical movements, or **kinesics**; the use of interpersonal space, or **proxemics**; touch and texture, or **haptics**; the way one looks, or **physical appearance**; use of time, or **chronemics**; and the use of symbolic objects, or **artifactual communication**.

Communication researcher Dale G. Leathers (1986) identified seven **nonverbal channels**, including facial expression, eye behavior, bodily communication, proxemics, personal appearance, vocal factors, and haptics. Communication researchers Mark Knapp and J. Hall (2002) identified eight channels: environment (including architecture and furniture), proxemics and territoriality, physical appearance and dress, physical behavior and movement, touching another person, facial expression, eye behavior, and vocal cues. Orban (1999) identified nine channels that affect argumentation. They are eye contact, facial expression, gesture, and bodily movement (of which there are five types: emblems, illustrators, regulators, affect displays, and adaptors). Some researchers study nonverbal cues of deception and the nonverbal behavior of liars (Knapp & Comendena, 1985). We can't begin to examine all these, but we can focus on some of them, especially those that affect persuasion, beginning with Orban's and Leathers' categories.

Facial Expression and Eye Behavior

Leathers' (1986) first two nonverbal channels are **facial expression** (affect displays) and **eye behavior**. According to Leathers, the face is "the most important source of nonverbal information" (p. 19). Facial expression is familiar and readily noticed, and subtle nuances in facial expression can greatly alter perceived meaning. Orban (1999) defines eye contact as "visual interaction with the eyes of listeners" and facial expression as "variations of facial muscles that convey perceptual stimuli to listeners." He claims that these two channels can combine to "create emotional and credibility cues that can ignite or diffuse argument potential" (n. p.). Naturally, credibility is essential to persuasion, so persuaders can enhance their communication credibility via the nonverbal channel.

For more detailed information about how facial expressions and gestures affect credibility, access InfoTrac College Edition, and type "nonverbal" in the search engine. Click on the periodical option, enter the words "nonverbal communication" in the subject guide search engine, and explore the hundreds of periodical sources.

Knapp and Hall (2002) noted that people often use the face as a measure of personality, which frequently determines persuasiveness. Leathers also identified ten general classes or categories of facial expression. They are disgust, happiness, interest, sadness, bewilderment, contempt, surprise, anger, determination, and fear. Among his more specific kinds of expressions, Leathers also included rage, amazement, terror, hate, arrogance, astonishment, stupidity, amusement, pensiveness, and belligerence. Any of these could help or hinder persuasion. Leathers (1986) identified six functions that the eyes serve. One is the attention function indicated by mutual gazing. Some persons at parties or other social events continually look over your shoulder and past you as if they are looking for more interesting conversational possibilities. Would you believe persuasion coming

---

BOX 10.1 **Interactive Media and Nonverbal Communication**

 Go to www.villagehero.com/nonverbalcommunication and explore topics such as reading female body language, nonverbal communication and intimacy, how to listen with your eyes, how to be a subject in national research on nonverbal communication, how nonverbal communication operates in real estate transactions involving Asian and Indian

buyers, and other research reports on the power of nonverbal communication in the process of persuasion. Other interesting sites where you can test your ability to "read" nonverbal messages are www.nonverbal. ucsc.edu, www.natcom.org/tronline/nonverb, and members.aol.com/nonverbal.

---

from them? Other eye behavior serves a regulatory function, by indicating when a conversation is to begin or stop. When speakers look back at a person or audience, this is a signal for listeners to take their turn. Naturally, being able to express one's opinion to the source would build that source's credibility and persuasiveness, especially in interpersonal settings. Eyes can serve a power function as well, as when a leader stares at an audience. Observers noted that this was the case with Adolf Hitler and cult leader Charles Manson. The next time you see an image of either man, look at his eyes.

Eye behavior also serves an affective function by indicating positive and negative emotions. When your parents' eyes look like they are angry with you, do you listen to their persuasion? Further, eyes function in impression formation, as when persons first meet and communicate a winning image or high self-esteem. Finally, Leathers noted the persuasive function of eye behavior. We rate speakers who maintain eye contact as more credible, and we are suspicious of those whose gaze is continually shifting. If people avert their eyes when talking to us, we assume that they are either shy or hiding something. Orban (1999) puts it this way: "Through our eyes we reflect cognitive and emotional behavior. We project impressions of penetrating thought, confusion, and inattentiveness. We show our emotions of fear, anger, happiness, and sadness. We do not realize the hidden messages eye contact reveals" (n. p.).

Bodily Communication

Bodily communication has several dimensions, one of which is kinesics, or physical movements of the body, such as how a person holds her or his body (tense or relaxed), and whether the person is moving about or gesturing with the shoulders, hands, or head. Persuaders indicate power by seeming to be physically or perceptually above their audience. They demonstrate a relaxed but erect posture, dynamic gestures, good eye contact, and variations in their speaking rate and inflection. Powerless persuaders, in contrast, behave more submissively and exhibit lots of body tension, little direct eye contact, closed postures with legs and arms crossed, and use few gestures.

Knapp and Hall (2002) identified several head movements that convey meaning, including cocking, tilting, nodding, and shaking the head, as well as thrusting out the jaw. And, of course, other bodily movements convey meaning, such as clenching a fist, putting hands on hips, and standing in an open stance with legs spread apart. These movements can indicate anger, intensity, and degree of commitment or dedication, all of which can help or hinder persuasion. In some cases, gestures and bodily movements are emblematic—they stand for a particular meaning. For example, in U.S. culture, stroking the index finger while pointing it at someone indicates "shame on you," crossed fingers indicate "good luck," and the hitchhiker's closed fist and extended thumb are emblematic of wanting a ride. Orban (1999) points out several others, including the A-OK sign, (but it conveys the same meaning as "flipping the bird" to Latin Americans, so persuaders need to consider who is in the audience before using that one). Some emblems perform a regulatory function (index finger on lips means "shush"); communicate positive, negative, or neutral values (thumbs up, thumbs down, or shoulder shrugging); or provide an evaluation (as in the thumbs up or the A-OK gesture in the United States). Most obscene gestures can quickly provoke anger and usually reduce the source's credibility, depending on the cultural background of the receiver.

For some fascinating insights into how gestures and bodily communication communicate, access InfoTrac College Edition, and type the words "body talk" in the key word search engine. Explore the article by Donovin. Then enter the words "nonverbal communication" in the subject search engine. Select the eight related topics, and read about flirting, eye contact, or hugging

Proxemics

Proxemics, or the use of physical space, is the fourth nonverbal channel in Leathers' system. You have undoubtedly noticed, for example, how most people fall silent and don't look at one another when they are in crowded elevators or public restrooms. Try facing the passengers in an elevator and perhaps try to strike up a conversation. You'll be surprised at the results. Report them back to the class. Edward T. Hall identified several kinds of space in his best-selling book *The Silent Language* (1959), which and have been confirmed by numerous researchers since then.

- *Public distance.* **Public distance** is often found in public speaking settings in which speakers are 15–25 feet or more from their audiences. Informal persuasion probably will not work in these circumstances, and persuaders who try to be informal in a formal situation don't usually meet success.

- *Social or formal distance.* **Social or formal distance** is used in formal but nonpublic situations, such as job interviews or committee meetings. Persuaders in these situations are formal but not oratorical. Formal distance ranges from about 7 to 12 feet between persuader and persuadee. Persuaders never become chummy in this context, but they do not deliver a speech, either. You probably select this distance when you go to your professor's office for a conference and sit across the desk in the guest chair.

- *Personal or informal distance.* Two colleagues might use **personal or informal distance** when discussing a matter of mutual concern— such as roommates discussing a problem they share. Here, communication is less structured, and both persuader and persuadee relax and interact with one another, bringing up and questioning evidence or asking for clarification. In U.S. culture, informal distance is about 3 ½ to 4 feet—the eye-to-eye distance when sitting at the corner of a teacher's desk as opposed to the formal distance created when you sit across the desk. You probably use informal distance when you sit around a banquet table or in an informal meeting.

- *Intimate distance.* People use **intimate distance** when they whisper messages they do not want others to overhear or when they are involved in a conspiratorial, intimate, or other secret conversation. Persuasion may or may not occur in these instances. Usually, the message is one that will not be questioned by the receiver. He or she will nod in agreement, follow the suggestion given, or respond to the question asked. When two communicators are in this kind of close relationship, they probably have similar aims. The distance ranges from 6 to 18 inches and probably communicates as much to those observing the intimate pair as is communicated to the pair. When forced into intimate distance (e.g., sitting next to someone in a bus), we usually do not communicate face-to-face but instead lean away from the person while talking. In an elevator you create informal distance by speaking toward the door instead of to fellow passengers.

How do persuaders use these distance boundaries? Are we vulnerable to persuasion using proxemics? Actual examples of such persuasion often escape our notice because communication is transmitted at such a low level of awareness. Take automobile sales. When customers come into a showroom, imagine the results if the salesperson rushes over to them and, within personal or even intimate distance, asks something like, "What can I do for you folks today?" The customers will probably flee or at least escape from the salesperson, saying something like, "Well, we're just looking around." Clever salespeople stay within public distance of customers until they perceive an indication of interest or a verbal or nonverbal signal that the customers want help. Only then will they move into formal or even informal distance.

Look at the advertisements in any popular magazine, and you will notice the use of proxemics as a persuasive device (see Figure 10.2). The young adults who "go for it" in beer ads are having fun and enjoying one another in personal or intimate space. Recently, people in the real estate profession have become interested in the communicative power of the strategic use of space. Industry publications have discussed such questions as how close a real estate agent should be to prospective buyers during a tour of a home and whether the agent should lead or follow the buyers. In many other contexts—offices, hospitals, banks, prisons, and factories—serious consideration is given to the use of space as a communicative device or a communication facilitator. There are cultural differences in the use of space.

Try to be alert to the uses of space in your life. How have you arranged the furniture in your room or apartment? Does the arrangement facilitate or deter communication and persuasion? How do various people whom you know use space? Do persons from other cultures use space differently than you do? Observe how other people use space and discover how this nonverbal channel affects persuasion.

To understand how powerful communication can be, access InfoTrac College Edition, and type the words "proxemic behavior" in the subject search engine. Select the personal space option and then the periodical option, and peruse the articles listed.

Physical Appearance

It's always easy to guess what's going on toward the middle of the spring semester when my students come to class dressed to kill. It is job interview time on campus, and everyone knows that appearance sends a message to interviewers. As noted above, pierced body parts are deadly. But physical appearance involves much more than simply good grooming and proper attire. Leathers (1986) claimed that larger-than-normal facial features (nose, ears, and lips) are generally considered unattractive.

Knapp (2002) reports other findings regarding physical appearance. For instance, first-born females who are attractive are likely to sit toward the front of the class, make more comments during class, and get good grades. Attractive females are also more likely to persuade male audiences than are unattractive females. You may wonder what is meant by "attractive" in these cases. In one study, the same female subject appeared in both the attractive and unattractive conditions. In the unattractive condition, she wore loose-fitting clothes, wore no makeup, had messy hair, and was generally poorly groomed (p. 155). In the attractive condition she wore tailored clothes, used makeup, was coifed, and well groomed. The attractive condition resulted in more persuasion.

Another element in physical appearance is bodily attractiveness, according to Leathers (1986). Specifically, slenderness is considered attractive in females, whereas larger-waisted and hippier females are perceived as less attractive. A fashion trend called "heroin chic" features attractive but emaciated-appearing female models that look like they should be immediately taken to an all-you-can-eat buffet. They are neither attractive nor persuasive to the average audience member. For males, broad shoulders, a muscled body, and a tapering upper trunk result in high attractiveness ratings.

FIGURE 10.2 Which of Hall's four types of communication distance seems to be operating in this ad? Why do you suppose this distance was chosen?

SOURCE: Reprinted by permission of Hotel Intercontinental, Chicago.

ENJOY

Savor a spectacular weekend at a sensational rate.

Hotel Inter-Continental Chicago invites you to enjoy the perfect weekend getaway at an enticing weekend rate, good any Thursday through Sunday . . . up to December 30. Ideally located at 505 North Michigan Avenue, this historic landmark presides right on the "Magnificent Mile." Surrounded by splendid shops, theaters, galleries and museums, the hotel is also home to The Boulevard Restaurant, Chicago's finest new dining establishment.

Hotel Inter-Continental Chicago . . . offering elegant accommodations, incomparable dining and impeccable service. Not to mention a spectacular weekend rate **$125***
on a luxurious single or double guest room, a refreshingly low . . .

For reservations contact your travel agent or call (312) 944-4100, toll-free 800-327-0200.

HOTEL INTER·CONTINENTAL CHICAGO

505 North Michigan Avenue • Chicago, Illinois 60611

* Single or double occupancy, per night. Stay must include a Friday or Saturday night. Subject to availability and advance reservations. Not to be used in conjunction with any other program. Local taxes and gratuities not included. Not available to groups.

Leathers found that self-image also has a lot to do with ratings of attractiveness. If you feel good about yourself, you will probably practice good grooming and keep in good physical condition. Clothing and adornments such as jewelry also contribute to people's physical appearance (see Figure 10.3). With regard to jewelry, think of the different evaluations you might make of a person wearing a Rolex as opposed to a Timex or the degree to which heavy gold jewelry attracts your attention. Eastern European businessmen appeared threadbare and shabby to me when I first saw them in the 1990s, and

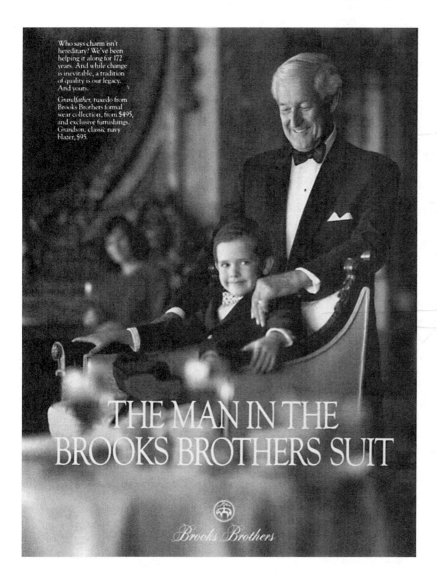

Who says charm isn't hereditary? We've been helping it along for 172 years. And while change is inevitable, a tradition of quality is our legacy. And yours.

Grandfather, tuxedo from Brooks Brothers formal wear collection, from $495, and exclusive furnishings. *Grandson,* classic navy blazer, $95.

THE MAN IN THE
BROOKS BROTHERS SUIT

Brooks Brothers

FIGURE 10.3 Clothing is used to communicate. What message is being communicated in this ad?

SOURCE: Reprinted by permission of Brooks Brothers Clothing.

I wondered what triggered my response. I later realized that they carried imitation leather attaché cases and that the quality of their suits and shoes ranked below blue-light specials at K-Mart.

Artifacts

Artifacts are physical objects that are used in construction, display, decoration, or items that are a part of one's wearing apparel. Birds feather their nests with bits of string, straw, and lint. We humans feather our nests for highly symbolic and persuasive reasons. Look at your work area or at that of a roommate or friend. You will find that it is arranged not only for work but for other reasons as well, and is usually decorated with things that symbolize the owner's sense of self, such as posters, pictures, a favorite coffee mug, and so on. **Artifactual communication**, or the messages others get from the objects we choose to display, decorate, or

FIGURE 10.4 What message(s) are sent by altering one's hair color? What about piercing parts of one's body?

SOURCE: Reprinted by permission of Nick Jeffries.

wear, is also symbolic. Culture teaches us how to react to the artifacts of others and the way they are used. These patterns of response form premises for persuasion.

A common type of artifactual communication is revealed in the objects surrounding a political persuader in a public speech—the banners, bunting, and flags all contribute to the ultimate success or failure of the persuasive attempt. Clothing is another type of artifact. What people wear sends signals about what they are like and what they believe or represent (e.g., a clerical collar or a nurse's or army officer's uniform).

Another type of artifact is exemplified in the personal objects surrounding persuaders. Consider how you feel when you go into a doctor's office that only has diplomas on the walls. What kind of person is the doctor likely to be? Will he or she be more or less persuasive? Compare that with the feeling you have when you enter a college professor's office that has posters, family photos, children's art, bowling trophies, and art reproductions. These artifacts cue the kind of persuasion you are likely to hear. In the diplomas only case, it will probably be concrete, formal, and prescriptive whereas in the posters and family photo office, it will be abstract and informal. Large objects like furniture also send signals. We expect a certain kind of persuasion when we are told to sit down at a table and the persuader sits on the opposite side. Persuaders who put a lectern between themselves and the audience will engage in formal communication. If they step out from behind the lectern or walk around while talking, they will come across as more informal. Which approach seems more

persuasive? Types of furniture can also symbolize certain characteristics. What kinds of persuasion and persons do you associate with French provincial versus early American furniture? What kind of persuasion is likely to occur in a room with metal office furniture versus one with wooden desks and leather chairs? Consider how artifactual communication is discussed by the characters in Figure 10.4. Artifactual messages vary among cultures and even subcultures. They make the difference between successful and unsuccessful persuasion. Try to identify the most effective kinds of artifacts for persuading you and for persuading others.

You will find some fascinating information about the effects of furniture and room layout in InfoTrac College Edition. Type "proxemic" in the search engine, select the personal space option, and select the related subjects option. Then select the room layout option and examine the articles listed.

Vocal Features

Each of us has had the experience of answering the phone and not being able to figure out who is calling. We listen carefully and ask innocuous questions until something the person says triggers recognition of his or her vocal features. Then we breathe a sigh of relief and carry on as if we knew who was calling all along. Leathers (1986) notes that a semantics of sound—or the meanings we deduce from the sound of a voice or other sounds like hesitation or heavy breathing—can affect the way we respond to persuaders' messages. The

F I G U R E 10.5 Here Malaprop Man demonstrates how mispronunciation can damage credibility and persuasive effectiveness.

SOURCE: *Frank and Ernest.* © United Feature Syndicate, Inc. Used with permission.

factors in each voice include volume or loudness, pitch, rate, vocal quality, clarity of pronunciation, intonation pattern, breathiness, and the use of silence. They influence whether you are persuaded by a given source, and they frequently indicate a lot about persuaders and their emotions, goals, and sincerity.

Monotonic persuaders are boring and lose most of their persuasiveness. High-pitched voices can indicate excitement while low-pitched but tense voices indicate anger; and rate of speech can indicate nervousness or confidence. Vocal quality communicates a number of things. Breathy voices in females communicate a stereotype of simple-mindedness and shallowness, whereas breathy voices in males may indicate that the speaker is effeminate. Screeching or tense voices indicate stress and concern, and nasality is often associated with arrogance. Persons who articulate poorly, mispronounce words, or have a speech impediment generally lose some of their credibility and effectiveness (see Figure 10.5).

Knapp (2002) reported on research indicating that people can fairly reliably identify certain stereotypes from vocal cues. These stereotypes include such characteristics as masculinity or femininity, age, enthusiasm or apathy, and activeness or laziness. Knapp also reported on research that identified the following correlations: (1) breathiness in males indicates youthfulness and an artistic nature; (2) a thin voice in females indicated social, physical, and emotional insecurity; (3) vocal flatness indicated sluggishness for both males and females; and (4) nasality was associated with snobbishness. Knapp noted that most listeners are sensitive to vocal cues in the communication coming from persuaders.

Tactile Communication and Haptics

Some of the more important nonverbal message carriers are the ways in which and the degree to which people touch one another. This is called

tactile communication. We know that infants need to be touched and cuddled. We also know that this need doesn't diminish as the child matures. However, in American culture the number, type, and duration of touches the growing child gets are greatly reduced as the child gets older. Children may substitute other kinds of physical contact for the touches they received from their parents, like socking or shoving someone, tickling a pal, holding hands, and so on. Leathers (1986) observes that we live in a noncontact society, with touch absent in public places, particularly between males. We probably would not accept the male vice president of the U.S. hugging and kissing the male president on his return from abroad, yet such behavior is perfectly acceptable in many cultures.

These Western norms for the use of touch, Leathers notes, usually relate to two general factors: (1) the part of the body being touched and (2) the demographic characteristics of the persons interacting, such as age, gender, social class, race, and status. The head, shoulders, and arms are the most frequently touched parts of the body, with other parts being more or less off limits to public touch. Touching is also more frequent among minorities, and persuaders who touch persuadees are the most successful (Kotulak, 1985). Persuaders who touch too much probably offend. Credibility can be drastically undermined if persuaders misread a relationship and touch or respond to touch inappropriately. Touch also conveys special kinds of emotional persuasion like empathy, warmth, and reassurance. Touching or hugging is frequent at wakes and weddings. Among firefighters, about the only acceptable touch off the job from another male is a handshake or backslap. However, firefighters on the job must sometimes calm frantic men, women, and children to save them, and they often use touch to facilitate that. So willingness to touch varies depending on the situation and the persons involved. In some religions, the laying on of hands signifies ordination and is sometimes given credit for religious conversions or faith healing.

Touch can be extremely important in facilitating certain kinds of communication. Terminal cancer patients, for example, need more touch than less ill patients. Touch expresses sympathy for someone who has been fired or who failed in some other way. In another study, strangers were asked for information by a researcher posing as an ordinary citizen. In half the cases, the researcher lightly touched the stranger on the shoulder before saying, "Excuse me, but I'm sort of lost. Can you tell me where the nearest bus stop is located?" The researcher got much more information and even conversation when using the light touch than when not using it.

Some touches are taboo, such as the touching of strangers for no reason. Other taboo touches include touching that inflicts pain (touching a wound); touching that interferes with another's activities or conversation; touching that moves others aside; playful touching that is too aggressive, as in mock wrestling, tickling, or pinching; and double-whammy touching used to emphasize a negative point, as in touching someone's belly when mentioning that they have put on weight (Kotulak, 1985).

As you continue to improve your abilities as a receiver, one of the nonverbal channels of communication to observe closely is the use of touch, whether it occurs at a first meeting with a stranger, punctuates the closing of a business deal, expresses empathic sensitivity toward another person, or provides the assurance that can help move people out of a dangerous situation. Tactile communication can say many things.

Haptics relates to touch, but not between persons. Instead it is what is communicated by the texture or the feel of objects. Velvet communicates different things than does silk, rough-hewn lumber walls communicate something different than plaster, which communicates something different than concrete.

To find more examples of the communication power of touching, access InfoTrac College Edition, and type the word "haptics" in the subject search engine. Select the periodical option, and review the articles under the touch option.

Chronemics

Chronemics is the way we use time, such as being prompt, late, or long-winded. Indeed, the use and misuse of time can communicate many messages to others. Suppose you have set a time and reserved a place for the meeting of a work group. Because you set up the meeting, you show up ten minutes early to make sure things are in order. A few minutes before the meeting is to start, two members of the group arrive and begin to chat. Right on time, to the minute, comes another group member. Now only two people are missing. You probably suggest waiting a few minutes. After five minutes, one of your missing members shows up, so you start the meeting. Nearly half an hour later, the final member arrives. What messages were sent by each member of the group? In U.S. culture, it is permissible to arrive at a meeting five minutes late, but arrive much later than that, and you'd better have a good excuse such as a flat tire, impossible traffic jam, a stalled elevator, or a speeding ticket. By coming late, you communicate to the others that you don't care about the appointment or that you are a thoughtless person and a prima donna.

However, if you are invited to a party, be sure to show up at least 15 minutes late if it is a dinner party and 45 minutes late if it is a college bash. If you arrive on time, the hosts might still be grooming themselves or putting the final touches on the place settings.

If you really want to put people in their place, make sure they have to wait to get to see you. This is a favorite trick of some police officers, corporate executives, and even college professors. And there are important cultural factors related to chronemics. One of the most familiar of these is the way time is handled by African Americans. It has come to be called "CPT," or colored people's time, even by African Americans. In a scene in the 1999 play *OO BLA DEE*, the story of an all-black women's jazz band during the 1940s, the members of the band discuss CPT. One character traces the concept to the emancipation from slavery. Before that, she says, slaves had to work from "cain't" until "cain't" six days a week, or from when you "cain't" yet see the sunrise until you "cain't" see the sunset because it's already set. Free of this grueling schedule, she goes on to say, made flexibility of time use one of the prime features of the new-found freedom. Quite naturally, the idea carried on across generations. Begin to observe how time works in your culture or subculture, but don't be surprised if it doesn't operate the same way in other cultures.

GENDER DIFFERENCES IN NONVERBAL COMMUNICATION

Recently, researchers investigated **gender differences** in nonverbal communication. For example, in a 1989 study of attitudes toward the use of touch, researchers found that women are significantly more comfortable with touch than are men, have higher levels of touch comfort than men, and that the touches are signs of a greater level of socialization (Fromme et al., 1989). Communication scholar Brenda Major (1984) noted significant gender differences in the way individuals touch others and receive such touches. While men tend to initiate touching in cross-gender encounters, they are less likely to initiate touch in same-gender encounters. Women are more comfortable about touching other women and about touching in general. Although touch often expresses warmth and intimacy, especially among women, it can also communicate power or status relationships. Men touch more frequently if they perceive themselves to be superior to the person they touch.

In terms of reactions to touch, Major noted that if the toucher is of the same status as the touchee, women react more positively and men more negatively, particularly if the toucher is a woman. Major concluded that, overall, women tend to react more positively to touch than do men and that this probably stems from the fact that girls are touched more frequently from birth on.

There are other gender-related differences in the use of touch as well. The average U.S. woman touches someone else about twelve times per day, but the average man touches someone only eight times a day (Kotulak, 1985). Touches by both males and females in the United States are more likely to involve a person of the opposite gender, which is the reverse of what occurs in some other cultures. In Western culture, touch between men generally is limited to shaking hands or backslapping with the occasional manly hug, especially in sporting events. In some cultures, it is not uncommon for males to walk down the street hand in hand.

Scholars N. Porter and F. Geis (1984) wondered if gender and nonverbal communication were related to leadership in small groups. They found that, in both all-male and all-female groups, physical placement at the head of the table is the best predictor of who gets to be the leader. But in mixed-gender groups, males emerge as the leader if they sit in the leadership position, but women do not. Researchers S. Ellyson, J. Dovidio, and B. J. Fehr (1984) investigated dominance in men and women as it relates to visual behavior. They found that dominance is usually indicated by what they called "look/speak" rather than "look/listen" behavior. Look/speak attempts to indicate dominance by speaking rather than by listening when catching the eyes of others. If women use the look/speak strategy, they are just as likely to be evaluated as dominant as are men who use the same strategy.

Communication scholar Judy Hall (1984) found that women have more expressive faces than men and smile and laugh more often than men, especially when they are in all-female groups. She speculated that smiling and laughing may be seen as unmasculine, which tends to discourage males from exhibiting these behaviors.

Regarding gaze and gaze holding, Hall found that women tend to gaze more at other persons than do men and that they are more uncomfortable than men when they cannot see the person to whom they are speaking. They also seem to be gazed at more frequently than men. Hall hinted that gaze differences between men and women exist because females are perceived as having more warmth than males. Also, males avoid the gazes of other males to avoid the potential sexual implications of such behavior.

Hall also observed that men maintain greater distances from others when in conversation and that women are approached more closely than men are. Women tend to face more directly toward the person with whom they are interacting. When given the choice of sitting adjacent to or across from others, men tend to occupy the across position, whereas women prefer the adjacent position. Finally, females are more approachable than males. She also found that women initiate touching more than men. Hall speculated that this may be due to women's appreciation for being touched more and that there may be gender-related differences for various kinds of touch, such as where on the body and how emphatic the touch is.

Hall found little research on which to base generalizations regarding body movements and positions. However, it does appear that men are more relaxed than women, more physically expansive—spreading their arms and legs and leaning back in chairs with their legs forward—and are more restless than women, fidgeting, playing with objects, and shifting their bodies in various ways. Another difference is that, while women tend to carry things in front of them, men carry things at their side.

Hall reported several gender-related differences in the use of the voice. Men are less fluent than women, make more verbal errors, and use more vocalized pauses such as "uh" or "um." Women's voices tend to have higher pitches even though their vocal mechanisms permit them to use lower ones. Women's voices have more variability in pitch, are more musical, and are more expressive than men's voices. Women's voices are also softer than men's and are judged to be more positive, pleasant, honest, meek, respectful, delicate, enthusiastic, and anxious and less confident, domineering, and awkward. Men's voices tend to be demanding, blunt, forceful, and militant (see Figure 10.6.

So there are important gender differences in nonverbal communication beyond dress and vocalic features. Successful persuaders are aware of these and use them when attempting to persuade.

FIGURE 10.6 There are some verbal gender differences in this cartoon, but notice some of the nonverbal differences, including facial expressions or affect displays, the use of touch, and the use of proxemics.

SOURCE: Reprinted by permission of Todd Michael.

To discover more about gender differences in nonverbal communication and how to use them better, access InfoTrac College Edition, and type the words "nonverbal communication and gender" in the key word search engine. Select the periodical option, and peruse some of the articles you find there.

DIALECT

Dialect, or patterns and styles of pronunciation and usage, is culture bound and often indicates an individual's socioeconomic or regional background. We learn dialect culturally. It communicates many things about us. Many of my students come from Chicago or its suburbs. South Siders get angry with me when I tell some of them to stop using factory talk. They do not hear themselves saying "dis" for "this" and "dat" for "that" and "dem" for "them." Yet they will be discriminated against if they keep their dialect. Students from the North Side and some suburbs have another dialect that may cause equal problems for them. They say "Dubbie" for "Debbie," "Shovie" for "Chevy," and "newahht" for "north." And it would be easy to document the

kind of discrimination that occurs when African American or Latino dialects are used. Be aware of your responses to various dialects, and see whether people respond to your dialect in certain ways. I have a sing-songy Minnesota dialect and get certain responses because of my frequent use of "Yup," "Don't cha know?" and "You betcha." People look for hayseeds in my hair.

THE USE OF NONVERBAL TACTICS

Nonverbal message carriers can be manipulated by persuaders in a process that scholar Ervin Goffman (1959) called "impression management." This means using powerful verbal and nonverbal signals to convince the audience that the source is a certain kind of person. One candidate for the presidential nomination wore red-and-black checked lumberjack shirts when he campaigned in New Hampshire and hip boots when his opponents began to engage in mudslinging. Bill Clinton managed our impressions of him by wearing jogging suits and other casual clothing in the White House. George W. Bush wore a pilot's uniform when he landed on an aircraft carrier, even though he was not the pilot.

BOX 10.2 Diversity and Nonverbal Communication

It is fascinating how members of diverse groups react differently to nonverbal messages. In low-context cultures like the United States and Canada, there is less emphasis on the nonverbal aspects of communication than in high-context cultures like Japan or Colombia. The nonverbal messages are there for both contexts but are not paid attention to by persons in low-context cultures. Gender is another diversity factor in expressing nonverbal behavior like facial expression. In the United States it is acceptable for women to show fear in their facial expression but not anger. The opposite is true for males. North Americans need and occupy more space than persons in Europe, who occupy more space than persons in Japan or China. And while some facial expressions are consistent across cultures, such as enjoyment, anger, fear, sadness, disgust, and surprise, there are major differences between diverse groups as to when and where it is appropriate to display such emotions. Laughter can communicate nervousness or fear in some cultures. Differences occur over how members of various cultures respond to the placement or movement of furniture. One German corporate executive working in the United States became so upset about visitors to his office moving the "guest chair" that he had it bolted down. Some mediators in conflict resolution meetings spend more time getting the furniture arrangement just right than they do in preparing for the agenda.

 To learn more about these examples and many others, go to www.beyondintractibility.org/m/cross_ cultural_communicatiion and scroll down to the section on nonverbal communication. Be sure to visit some of the links there and learn how nonverbal communication works in such diverse groups as Jewish and Arab Israelis, Angolans, and blacks and whites and in Islamic cultures. Listen to participants in Beyond Intractibility experiments.

The use of clothing to communicate nonverbally in impression management is a popular topic in the corporate world. In her book *The Power of Dress*, Jacqueline Murray (1989) provides a number of case studies to demonstrate the persuasive use of dress. For example, at Electronic Data Systems, everyone has a military look, with clean-shaven faces, shiny, black, plain-toed shoes, white shirts, dark suits, and army-style haircuts for men. Murray identifies three categories of business dress: (1) "corporate dress," which is used by bankers, attorneys, and executives; (2) "communication dress," which is used by persons in sales, marketing, education, personnel, and high-tech industries; and (3) "creative dress," which is used by interior decorators, commercial artists, persons in advertising, boutique owners, and entrepreneurs. Corporate dress is simple in line, shape, and design, tends to be tailored, and features gray and blue colors for suits, and off-white or light blue for shirts and blouses. Corporate dress also uses fabrics such as silks, herringbones, tweeds, and flannels in suits or dresses, and plain cottons, wools, or linens in shirts and blouses. Communication dress features suits and dresses that are practical, relaxed, and semi-traditional, and includes blazers and sports coats. Communication dress includes a mix of colors for the blouses and shirts, featuring stripes or relaxed prints, and fabrics such as knits and loose or bulky weaves. Creative dress tends to be loose-fitting, with elongated lines and exaggerated design in both suits and dresses and blouses and shirts. The preferred colors in this category are striking, dramatic hues, as well as understated taupes, peaches, and basics. Although some may question Murray's conclusions, few would argue with her premise that dress is important as a nonverbal channel of communication.

OTHER NONVERBAL MESSAGES

Eye movements and other movements of the head can also communicate. We are all aware of the negative impression we have of persons whose eyes

Top view

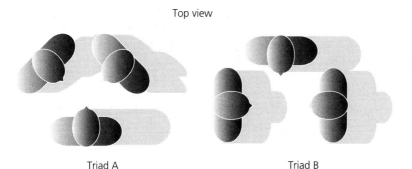

Triad A   Triad B

FIGURE 10.7 Notice the difference between the body positions of the persons in each triad. Which is involved in "blocking" behavior?

are continuously darting about or who can't look us in the eye for more than a brief moment. Completely different meaning can come from what is called "gaze holding," or maintaining eye contact with another person. Usually, this conveys sexual interest. Even the rate of eye blinks can communicate. Vance Packard (1964) reported that grocery shoppers' eye blink rates slow down as they proceed up and down the aisles to the point that they are almost mesmerized.

Albert Scheflen (1973) found that when a psychiatrist uses the "bowl gesture" patients often open up and reveal more about themselves and their problems. This gesture in used in persuasion and is the logo for the Allstate company.

People use their bodies to invite or inhibit communication. This is termed **blocking behavior**. Notice the two configurations in Figure 10.7. In triad A, the body positions of the three persons would inhibit a fourth person from joining in the conversation, whereas in triad B, the body positions invite participation.

Another way to block or invite communication is using objects such as furniture or piles of books on a library table to block communication. Research shows that lifting or lowering the chin at the ends of sentences serves as a signal that the person intends to continue to speak or that he or she is done speaking and someone else can join in. And, of course, we are all aware of the communicative power of head nodding, winking, and various obscene gestures, which varies in meaning from culture to culture. Orban (1999) and others

call these nonverbal indicators "regulators." Among the regulators are those that involve turn taking, turn requesting, and turn yielding or "back channeling," where the listener encourages the speaker to continue instead of taking his or her turn. Orban says back channeling indicates a listener's full attention and interest, which means back-channeled persuaders will advocate longer and with more enthusiasm.

As you begin to observe the nonverbal messages occurring around you, you will discover an almost infinite number of potential nonverbal message carriers. Who reaches for the check at a restaurant first? What do nervous gestures or twitches, volume, tone, and pauses communicate? How do you interpret curious habits such as cracking one's knuckles or doodling, which could communicate subconscious tensions?

Even the sense of smell seems to be an important carrier of information. We are all aware, for example, of the person who uses too much perfume, cologne, or after-shave lotion or of the person with body odor. Apparently, we can detect more subtle odors as well. For instance, some persons claim to be able to smell hostility or tension in the air upon entering a room. Many homes have unique and characteristic odors caused by the kinds of food cooked in them, the kinds of cleaning solutions used, the presence of pets, or the kinds of wood used in their construction or furnishings. The fragrance of a new car is now available in aerosol cans to spray in used cars, thus making them seem newer and "fresher."

REVIEW AND CONCLUSION

By this time, you know that the world of the persuadee in an information age is not an easy one. You need to be aware of so many things: the persuader's self-revelation via language choices and the internal or process premises operating for each of us. The responsible receiver recognizes the variety of nonverbal channels, including facial expression, eye behavior, and bodily communication. You need to be aware of the ways in which gestures and posture, proxemics, physical appearance, and artifacts can communicate. You also need to realize that vocal communication, tactile communication, haptics, chronemics, and gender all send messages. These premises do not make receivers' tasks any easier, given that they operate at particularly low levels of awareness, and we often overlook them as we analyze persuasion. That's probably because they are processed in the peripheral channel of the ELM where we don't really do much analysis. You will have to train yourself to be more sensitive to nonverbal elements in the persuasive process, so you can skillfully use these channels in your own communication, but, more importantly, so you can accurately decode the real meaning of the messages aimed at you every day.

KEY TERMS

When you have read this chapter you should be able to identify, explain, and give an example of the following words or concepts.

kinesics	nonverbal channels	social or formal distance	vocal features
proxemics	facial expression	personal or informal distance	tactile communication
haptics	eye behavior		gender differences
physical appearance	bodily communication	intimate distance	dialect
chronemics	proxemics	artifactual communication	blocking behavior
artifactual communication	public distance		

APPLICATION OF ETHICS

You are in charge of nurse/patient relations at a small town hospital, and recently you have hired nurses from other cultures. You are just beginning to realize that there are great cultural differences in the way nurses view their work and interact with patients. For example, in the United States nurses value individualism and reliance, while 70 percent of the rest of the world's nurses value collectivism over individualism. This is exemplified by two philosophies regarding health care: (1) to each person according to what is available in a free market versus (2) to each patient according to their need. Your hospital has limited resources and diverse patients, nurses, doctors, and staff working together, often on the same patients. How will you go about training the various diversities to cooperate, especially when their philosophies on health care are so different? Your options are (1) have an open free-for-all discussion of the issues; (2) conduct individual counseling with nurses, doctors, and staff who must work together but disagree about the two opposing philosophies; (3) hire a professional consulting group specializing in diversity and nursing to con-duct a series of diversity seminars; or (4) handle the conflicts on a case-by-case basis.

QUESTIONS FOR FURTHER THOUGHT

1. What are some of the facial expressions you find easiest to identify? Which is most difficult?

2. What is kinesics? Give some examples, and explain how and what they communicate.

3. Which of your friends uses gestures most effectively? What does he or she do that makes the gestures so effective?

4. What are some examples of how physical appearance sends messages in your world? What are some examples of the way physical appearance identifies a contemporary musical artist or group?

5. With what artifacts do you surround yourself? What do they mean to you? (Some students have reported that the first thing they do after unpacking for dormitory living is to purchase "conversation pieces" or artifacts that symbolize themselves.) What about your roommate? What artifacts does he or she use? What do they symbolize about him or her? What about your family members' artifacts?

6. How often do you touch others? Try to increase the number of touches you use, and observe the responses of others. Does the increase have any effect? If so, what?

7. What are some examples of how chronemics operates in your life—on campus, in the dorm, in the classroom, and at home?

8. What are some of the gender differences in nonverbal communication as they appear in contemporary advertising?

9. What is the predominant dialect where you live? Are there any other dialects that you can identify in your community? What effects do they have on people's attitudes and behaviors?

10. What is "blocking" behavior? Give examples from your everyday life.

11. What are some ways you respond to texture or haptics?

12. What are some cultural differences in nonverbal communication?

13. Would it be ethical to manipulate your nonverbal behavior to affect persuasive outcomes?

 For online activities, go to the *Persuasion* book companion website at http://communication.wadsworth.com/larson11

PART III

Applications of Persuasive Premises

Part III studies persuasion in a variety of contexts. We ask how our analyses of these contexts help us to make critical judgments about whether to buy, elect, join, quit, give, or believe. Chapter 11 explores a familiar application, the persuasive campaign or movement—a series of messages designed to lead receivers to specific ends. Chapter 12 focuses on how to become a persuader. In addition to helping you persuade others, what you learn will help you to become a more critical consumer of persuasive messages aimed at you. In Chapter 13 we explore mass media. Mass-mediated messages range from the brief but influential TV or radio commercial to more extensive advertisements, speeches, documentaries, and news reports. We will discover that the media of our time, especially the interactive media, may be the determining factor in deciding which problems our culture should concentrate on. Finally, Chapter 14 investigates print and electronic advertising—and discusses how they have come to dominate contemporary American society.

11

The Persuasive Campaign
or Movement

LEARNING GOALS

After reading this chapter, you should be able to:

1. Compare and contrast campaigns and single-shot persuasion.

2. Explain why campaigns are communication systems.

3. Differentiate among the three types of campaigns and give examples of each.

4. Demonstrate how campaign goals, strategies, and tactics are used in campaigns.

5. Identify and explain the five stages of the Yale campaign model.

6. Explain the hierarchy of effects model.

7. Differentiate between social movements and other types of campaigns.

8. Discuss symbolic convergence and show how it is used in persuasive campaigns for products, persons, and ideas.

For many years, the study of persuasion focused mainly on the public speech and "single-shot" or "hypodermic needle" perspective on persuasive communication. This model placed a receiver at a certain position on an issue prior to an injection or "shot" of persuasion. Following the persuasion, the researcher either speculated about or tried to statistically measure any changes that might have occurred in the receiver. This approach makes for simple models for persuasion, but it hardly matches reality. After all, instances in which a single persuasive message changed the outcome of events are rare indeed. Most persuasion is incremental and cumulative instead. For instance, if you were considering whether to buy a digital camcorder, vote for a candidate for office, give money to a charity, or join a cause, your decision would not be instantaneous. Rather, it would be the result of a series of messages. Some would be processed in the peripheral path of the elaboration likelihood model (ELM), such as the ads for the camcorder, the candidate's appearance, your history with the charity, or the stirring words of the leader of the movement or cause. Other elements in your persuasion would be processed via the central route. These might include what *Consumer Reports* had to say about the camcorder or what editorials say about the candidate or statistics on how much of a donation is dedicated to administrative costs.

Until the 1990s, marketing, advertising, and public relations campaigns were dominated by the single-shot approach. Ad and public relations campaigns were both seen as periods of time during which many messages were being sent, but it was still assumed that a single ad or news release could sell a product, candidate, or cause. Then a new term came into vogue—**integrated marketing communication** (IMC)—which refers to more carefully coordinated activities of marketing, advertising, public relations, sales promotion, packaging, personal selling, websites, branding, brand contacts, and event staging. Each element works with the others and leads to synergies that make the whole far greater than the sum of the parts.

For a long time, political scientists also ignored the communication dimensions of political campaigns, with the possible exception of research on campaign financing and public opinion polling. They remained focused on the nature and structure of government and ignored "mere politics." Meanwhile, most of the research done on campaigns occurred in advertising or marketing departments and was proprietary, meaning that it belonged to the client, candidate, or cause leader, who paid for it, and they seldom made it public. The fact that candidates used focus groups to determine their dress or hairstyle was the best kept secret in town. Remember the politician who changed her style of dress and mode of transportation when she shifted from a GOP women's luncheon audience to a college campus? No doubt her campaign committee wished the revelation hadn't become public.

Campaign and movement theory has come a long way, and this is appropriate, given that the persuasive campaign is probably the most prevalent form of persuasion today. In this chapter, we look at three general types of persuasive campaigns: **product-oriented**, **person or candidate-oriented**, and **idea- or ideologically oriented**.

We shouldn't underestimate the impact of advancing technology on persuasion. The Internet, interactive media, digital audio, video, and graphics all can convey powerfully persuasive messages. Consider what a changed world we face in the near future. The number and sophistication of persuasive campaigns will increase. Market segmentation will be much easier to accomplish. Experts predict that soon campaigns will be aimed at a segment of one—you.

To learn more about how sophisticated market segmentation has become, access Info-Trac College Edition, and enter the words "market segmentation" in the subject search engine. Browse a few of the periodical items, and then go to the related subjects listing and select "students as consumers." Finally, go to the related subjects option, where you will find research about yourself under "college students as consumers."

CAMPAIGNS AS SYSTEMATIC COMMUNICATION

Campaigns and mass movements are classic examples of communication systems at work. The first communication system discussed in this text was Shannon and Weaver's SMCR model, which includes a feedback loop (see Figure 1.3). Any communication system produces a predictable flow of information and a means of soliciting feedback. In campaigns, the flow of persuasive information includes all the verbal and nonverbal auditory and visual symbols such as words printed on a sign, page, or screen; graphics, typeface, pictures, and auditory pictures created by music, words, and sound effects. Campaigns thus represent complex and challenging sets of messages for persuadees to process. A nonverbal visual symbol in a campaign might be a picture of a Ford Mustang in a magazine and a nonverbal auditory symbol might be the sound of audience applause or booing of the candidate.

In most integrated campaigns, experts research their target audience, and then plan press releases, print and electronic ads, and webpages, testing them at each stage in their development. Audience research helps to schedule media time or space in appropriate magazines, newspapers, and radio and TV networks. Evaluations of the results are then used to make mid-flight corrections. Generally, it used to take at least three exposures to an ad to create **brand awareness**. The first exposure passes by almost unnoticed by consumers. The second exposure alerts consumers to the existence of the product and creates curiosity about it. The third exposure either prompts a pre-existing need for the product or begins to create a new need for it. Today, more exposures are probably needed due to advertising clutter caused by increased media options, more brands, and so on. The consumer finally acts by purchasing, voting, or donating once enough exposures have been processed.

CAMPAIGNS VERSUS SINGLE-SHOT PERSUASIVE MESSAGES

Campaigns are not merely series of messages sent to audiences, though they once were thought of that way. Political campaigns used to start on Labor Day and end on the day of the election. Now they might begin years in advance and will surely encompass much more than just debates over specific issues. Campaigns differ from single shots of persuasion or from collections of persuasive messages delivered over time in several ways.

1. Campaigns create "positions" in the audience's minds for the product, candidate, or idea.
2. Campaigns are intentionally designed to develop over time. They have stages for getting the audience's attention, preparing them to act, and, finally calling the audience to action.
3. Campaigns dramatize the product, candidate, idea, or ideology for the audience, inviting members to participate with the campaign and its goal(s) in real or symbolic ways.
4. Campaigns use sophisticated communication technologies to reach target prospects.

Starting in the late 1980s, computers began to store large amounts of information about potential voters, customers, donors, and joiners. These technological advances led to what is called "data-based marketing" where the persuader gathers information about prospective voters, customers, donors, or joiners to be used in future campaigns long before they are actually put to use.

To learn more about IMC, access InfoTrac College Edition, and enter "integrated marketing" in the search engine. Look at some of the articles included in the *Journal of Advertising Research*.

Following movements or campaigns is like watching a TV series. Although the episodes can stand alone (each has its own beginning, middle, and end), together they form a collage of messages that meld together until an entire image or picture of the campaign is perceived and stored. If it is well designed, large segments of the population will have been exposed to enough "episodes" that most will come away with a similar image of the product, candidate, or idea.

SIMILARITIES AMONG THE TYPES OF CAMPAIGNS

The three campaign types (product, person, and idea or ideology) share some similarities. All of them occur over time. Most are targeted and use mass media to accomplish their goals. Several high-profile individuals are usually present in person and idea campaigns, but not necessarily in product-oriented campaigns. The person-oriented political campaign centers on an individual's name. The focus of such campaigns may be on electing someone to office, freeing someone from prison, or raising enough money to pay for someone's organ transplant. The slogan might feature a candidate's name—"Be Sure to Vote for John Countryman"—or it may feature a person needing financial support—"Dollars for Jimmy, Our County's Liver Transplant Candidate." In issue- or cause-oriented campaigns the slogan or theme usually features the cause—"Think Globally; Act Locally" or "Stop Smoking Now." Political campaigns might focus on a cause or issue such as stem cell research policy, terrorism, or school vouchers. There are also some differences among the three types of campaign, which we'll discuss later in this chapter.

GOALS, STRATEGIES, AND TACTICS IN CAMPAIGNS

Campaigns don't sell anything, but they do deliver a prospective consumer, voter, donor, or joiner to the point of sale, donation, voting, headquarters, or website of the good cause. The successful campaign must also educate and prepare the consumer, voter, or joiner to take action. To accomplish this task,

campaigns must (1) zero in on well-defined **goals**, (2) create appropriate **strategies** to accomplish the goals, and then (3) use various **tactics** to put the strategy into action. This pattern of goals leading to strategies, which in turn lead to tactics, applies to all three types of campaigns.

The *goal* for a Claussen's pickles campaign might be to increase sales in specified test markets by 10 percent. The campaign staff then works out a promising strategy. For Claussen's, the *strategy* was to use TV spots to show the unique features and benefits of the brand. The product is refrigerated rather than cooked, so the pickles are crisper and crunchier than the competition. Previously, Claussen's had only used print ads, which can't show crispy and crunchy very well. To implement the TV *strategy*, Claussen's used the tactic of comparative advertising, matching Claussen's against Vlasic's in the TV spots. The *tactic* was to show Vlasic's cooked pickle being bent in half without breaking, whereas Claussen's pickle couldn't be bent without snapping in two, giving off a spray of brine accompanied by a crunchy sound effect.

In a political example, the *goal* in primary election campaigns is to win the party's nomination from opposing candidates. *Strategies* for achieving this include ignoring the opposition, taking the high road on the issues, and simply letting the candidates attack one another. A *tactic* for implementing the strategy might be to stage a debate against several empty chairs, each labeled with the name of one of the opponents. The campaign models highlighted in the following discussion demonstrate similarities and differences among campaign types. Your task is to use the models to help you make decisions about purchasing, voting, joining, or supporting causes.

DEVELOPMENTAL STAGES IN CAMPAIGNS

All three types of campaigns pass through a series of predictable stages as they grow and mature and adapt to audience feedback, the competition, the issues, and the demands of the persuasive situation.

FIGURE 11.1 Many devices are used to establish product, person, or idea identification in campaigns. Logos such as this are one kind of identification device. Why is the winged foot of Mercury used? What does it communicate? Why put it between "GOOD" and "YEAR"? Answers to these questions help explain how product image or identification develops.

SOURCE: Used by permission of the Goodyear Tire and Rubber Company.

One campaign *goal* of a new product, candidate, or idea is to establish itself in the audience's consciousness. A variety of *strategies* can accomplish this identification. For instance, a company might give out free samples, a candidate announces his or her candidacy, or a group stages a dramatic protest. This initial message helps the campaigner learn about the audience. Perhaps prospects buy the brand because of its warranty and not its price. Maybe the voters don't favor increasing taxes on gasoline but do respond to the issue of deficit reduction. Animal rights supporters may respond to some issues but not others. So, in all three types of campaigns, strategies are tried and kept, altered, or dropped as the campaign develops, beginning with its goals and moving to its strategies and tactics.

The Yale Five-Stage Developmental Model

Most campaigns include one or more of the stages of a model developed by researchers at Yale University (Binder, 1971). The model is highly applicable to product, person, and ideological campaigns and has been used to analyze hundreds of campaigns. The five functional stages noted by the researchers are identification, legitimacy, participation, penetration, and distribution.

Identification. **Identification** is defined as establishing a position in the minds of consumers, voters, and potential converts. Many products and causes use logos to create audience identification. The well-established logo of the Goodyear Tire and Rubber Company, shown in Figure 11.1, has the winged foot of Mercury inserted between the two syllables of Goodyear, to suggest that the company's products are swift and safe. The lower case "e" used to identify the environmental movement was inserted inside the capital letter "C" to create the logo of the Commonwealth Edison electric company, suggesting that the company is environmentally conscientious—a good position for an energy monopoly. A series of arrows in a triangle with the point of each arrow bent to point at the next arrow is the logo for any kind of recycling. The name associated with the product, candidate, or cause is critical and closely related to the logo.

The name *Newsweek* suggests that it contains the news of the past week, and the name of Cadillac's "Escalade" SUV is meant to suggest good taste, classiness, and European distinction since the brand's name is similar to the French term for a walking path. Candidates for office may label themselves the "people's candidate" or a similar term to create identification. In the abortion controversy, anti-abortion advocates chose "pro-life" for their cause. It "framed" the issue by suggesting that advocates are in favor of life. Who would disagree? It also implies that opponents of the movement are either anti-life or pro-death. Upstaged by the "pro-life" framing label, abortion rights advocates had to settle for the far less effective "pro-choice."

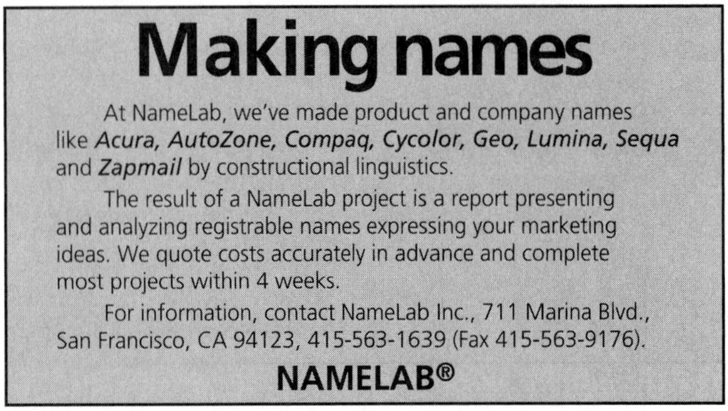

FIGURE 11.2 The name of a product, political entity, or cause is part of the mix of factors that create identification for the brand.

SOURCE: Used by permission of NameLab.

To demonstrate the potency of a good name, ask a sample of people to name three brands of turkey. Butterball will be on everyone's list while many competitors' names will not. Then ask what the key benefit of a Butterball turkey is, and they will tell you that it is the moistest brand. Figure 11.2 shows an ad for NameLab, a company that designs and tests various names to help organizations establish an identity for a product, political entity, or cause.

Another device that helps create identification is consistent color coding and typefaces. The campaigner picks a color code and uses it in packaging, advertising, letterheads, and perhaps uniforms. For instance, U.P.S. carriers wear dark brown uniforms, and their trucks are painted dark brown. Political candidates usually select some combination of red, white, and blue. The successful Stop ERA movement to defeat the Equal Rights Amendment adopted the color red, used signs shaped like stop signs, and had movement supporters wear red and white clothes when they demonstrated.

Slogans also promote identification, "Folgers— The Mountain Grown Coffee," "When You Care Enough to Send the Very Best," "You're in Good Hands with Allstate," and "Smart. Very Smart" are all successful examples. Consider how coordinated and successful the campaign for State Farm Insurance Company has been over the years. The slogan and jingle "Like a Good Neighbor, State Farm Is There" is the central theme, as is the red and white color code. Agents are urged to live in the community they serve, to join civic organizations there,

and to be visible and active in their communities. All advertisements must include the slogan, colors, and the agent's pictures. Agents are advised to send congratulatory cards to customers and their families on important days. National advertising usually includes a feature on a specific agent who was there when needed.

Finally, jingles, uniforms, salutes, and all sorts of campaign paraphernalia like balloons or buttons help establish name and purpose identification in all three types of campaigns.

Legitimacy. The second stage in the Yale model is the establishment of **legitimacy**, which is defined as being considered a worthy and believable brand, candidate, or cause. Candidates usually achieve legitimacy by gaining endorsements or by winning primaries. Legitimacy can also serve as a power base. Candidates demonstrate their power by holding rallies, appearing with well-known supporters or celebrities, or being photographed with symbols of legitimacy, such as the U.S. Capitol building, the Lincoln Memorial, or the White House. For incumbents, legitimacy derives from holding office. A favorite tactic for both incumbents and challengers is getting endorsed by local newspapers, politicians, and well-known and respected citizens. Another is to list experience in government or community groups, church affiliations, family accomplishments, and so on. Expertise, sincerity, and dynamism or charisma are also elements in establishing candidate legitimacy.

Product campaigns sometimes gain legitimacy by demonstrating the product in use—a favorite tactic in the television marketing of exercise machines and kitchen gadgets. Professional athletes wear Nikes to demonstrate the legitimacy of the shoes and may offer a testimonial for the product. Established endorsers like the Underwriter's Laboratory and Good Housekeeping seals of approval also create legitimacy. Brands also develop legitimacy by associating themselves with good causes, or by sponsoring sports events such as the Virginia Slims Tennis Tournament.

In ideological campaigns, large numbers of participants and heavy funding both demonstrate legitimacy. Newspaper ads with the names of known supporters who endorse the movement also help establish legitimacy. Large numbers of angry citizens show up at council meetings, and these events turn up on the evening news. In one high school, students protested their school lunch program and showed their legitimacy using nonviolent protest tactics. One day, hundreds of students boycotted the hot lunch, leaving the school with tons of leftovers. The next day, all students bought the hot lunch, leaving the school short of supplies. The following day, everyone paid with a large bill, running the cashiers out of change. The next day, they paid in pennies, creating havoc in the checkout lines as cashiers had to count pennies. On the fifth day, the school met with students about improving the lunches.

Participation.   The legitimacy stage of campaigns usually blends so smoothly with the **participation** stage that it is almost impossible to tell when one ends and the next begins. The participation stage is defined as the recruitment and involvement of previously uncommitted persons. In the legitimacy stage, the participants are known supporters. In the participation stage, the leaders seek to show their clout. There are many techniques for doing this. Some require effort by participants, such as marching at a protest, while others require minimal or only symbolic participation, such as signing a petition or wearing a button. Customer rebates are another form of participation. The customer fills

out the rebate form and mails it in to get money. All these items encourage real and symbolic participation with the brand. Customers even advertise the brand by wearing clothing imprinted with the brand logo. Coupon offers are another way to promote participation.

A movement may urge participation in real or symbolic ways. People wear armbands or badges, yell slogans at rallies, put signs on their lawns, or distribute leaflets. Candidates running for student body president may ask others to canvass dormitory floors or student groups. These kinds of activity get people involved in the campaign or movement and guarantee further active support. Sometimes new technologies are used to encourage participation. Examples include holograms and scratch and sniff perfume strips, or free music downloads. We see participation also in the uses of interactive media on the Internet.

During the nominating process and primaries of the presidential campaign of 2004, Governor Howard Dean used the participative interactivity of the Internet to generate previously unheard of donations to his candidacy. Following the election, he was named head of the Democratic Party. We can anticipate that both parties will be replicating his efforts for the 2008 campaign. If you are taking this class during an election year, visit the websites of some of the candidates looking for new uses of interactivity to generate candidate support—financial or other kinds of help. All these participative devices are designed to get the audience involved with the product, candidate, or cause, and even symbolic behavior represents both commitment and participation. Participation fits nicely with the idea of persuasion as a process of co-creation, as discussed in Chapter 1 and elsewhere. As Figure 11.4 demonstrates on page 252, participation can include interacting with an advertisement.

Penetration.   The **penetration** stage can be defined as the point at which a person, product, or idea has earned a meaningful share of the market, electorate, or other constituency. For products, gaining a significant market share is enough to achieve the penetration stage. Chrysler's various

She makes it look effortless.

Reflecting the thousands of hours she's practiced and honed her skills, until every muscle responds in unison

to the command for perfection. It is this dedication, this courage to face competition boldly and without compromise, that has inspired Phillips Petroleum to proudly sponsor United States Swimming since 1973.

And we'll be national sponsor for years to come. Because we believe that with every leap of grace and form, we are watching the future of our nation take shape.

PHILLIPS PETROLEUM COMPANY *Phillips 66*

FIGURE 11.3 Phillips Petroleum established its legitimacy by sponsoring U.S. Olympic teams.

SOURCE: Reprinted by permission of the Phillips Petroleum Company.

B O X 11.1 Interactive Media and Campaign Participation

 Mitsubishi recently launched an interactive Internet campaign in which an Eclipse drives from one Mitsubishi banner ad on the screen to another. Then the viewer can take over the car and drive it around the screen. Following the test drive, viewers are invited to play the "Thrill Ride Challenge" game and drive around one of four race courses. Depending on their score, they could win a Mitsubishi flat screen TV or an Apple iPod. The company hopes to harvest 20,000 dealer leads from the campaign. Viewers are also directed to a link where they can build their own Eclipse—including options, color, and so forth—and get a price quote (Morrissey, 2005). To see how interactive media can be used to sell products go to www.modemmedia.co.uk.

---

innovations, including front-wheel drive, the mini-van, and the 7-year/70,000-mile warranty enabled it to penetrate the auto market. The market share that these captured forced the competition to follow suit. That is a sure sign that a campaign has reached the penetration stage.

A successful penetration stage in campaigns for products usually prompts a response from the competition. Early in the primary campaign season, candidates don't have to win the most delegates to establish penetration. Running third might be enough. Other indications of political penetration include higher ratings in opinion polls, increases in financial contributions, increases in the number of persons volunteering to help, and larger crowds showing up for campaign events. Communication scholar T. A. Borchers (2001, 2005) reports that one of the keys to Jesse Ventura's becoming Minnesota's governor in 1998 was his use of email and his website to turn out large crowds on short notice—seven hundred people in the small town of Willmar within an hour.

In ideology-oriented campaigns, penetration is achieved when those in power find that they are barraged by mail or have to repeatedly answer questions about the campaign topic. Other indicators of penetration in these campaigns include large rally crowds that inconvenience supporters of the status quo and increased financial and volunteer support.

Distribution. The fifth and final stage of development, **distribution**, is defined as the campaign or movement's succeeding and rewarding supporters in some way. The candidates now live up to their promises. They signal their supporters that social change is going to occur. Patronage or government jobs help distribute the rewards won by the campaign. In movement campaigns persons on the campaign staff or in leadership are appointed to positions of power. One problem with ideological and political campaigns is that sometimes the persuaders don't live up to their promises

Distributors and users of products participate in the distribution stage by sharing some of the profits from the products. Stores are paid slotting allowances for devoting some of their shelf space for special offers. They can get an extra discount for pushing certain products. Dealers also are urged to participate in contests to win prizes and luxury vacation trips by increasing monthly sales. The retailers are given dealer loaders or valuable display containers like wheelbarrows or garden carts in which to display the brand and which are theirs to keep or offer as sweepstake prizes. And both dealers and customers can earn prized items such as an NBA Championship warm-up jacket. Devices such as rebates, money-back coupons, and other purchase incentives act as kinds of distribution to customers.

Product-Focused Models

Some campaign models help to describe all three types of campaign, and other models focus on one type of campaign. Let's examine models that are

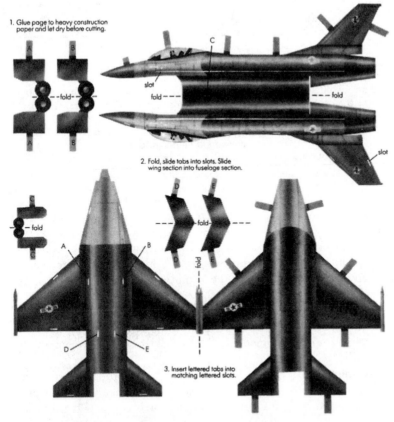

1. Glue page to heavy construction paper and let dry before cutting.

C

slot

fold

fold

fold

A B

A B

fold

2. Fold, slide tabs into slots. Slide wing section into fuselage section.

slot

C

fold

D E

fold

D E

A B

fold

D E

D E

3. Insert lettered tabs into matching lettered slots.

FIGURE 11.4 This ad for the Air National Guard encourages real, not symbolic, participation by cutting out the model F-16 and gluing it together, or by joining the Air National Guard.

SOURCE: Courtesy Air National Guard.

One of two ways to get your hands on an F-16.

If you think you're too young to fly, cut it out.

Fold. Assemble. And prepare for take-off.

While your paper airplane may not quite reach the speed of sound, use it as a reminder of just how fast the Air National Guard can help you get your future off the ground.

And we're not just talking about a military career. Air Guard training can prepare you for a civilian career in over 200 fields of technical expertise. Every-

thing from meteorology to security. Telecommunications to computer technology.

We'll even pay part of your college tuition. What's more, you'll have the chance to take part in exciting adventures that can lead you around the world.

All you have to do is serve as little as two days a month and two weeks a year.

Want to learn more? Call your local recruiter. And find out if you're cut out for the Air National Guard.

AIR NATIONAL GUARD

Americans At Their Best.

88-501

appropriate for and focused on product-oriented campaigns.

The Hierarchy of Effects Model. Advertising and marketing experts Robert Lavidge and Gary Steiner (1961) suggested a model that for many decades has set goals in marketing and advertising agencies. This model assumes that potential customers must pass through a series of stages beginning with initial lack of brand awareness and ending with ultimate purchase. The **hierarchy of effects model** remains as valid today as it was when first suggested (Schultz and Barnes, 1991).

The model has seven distinct stages and employs various communication, advertising, research, and promotional strategies and techniques at each stage. In the first stage, consumers are completely unaware of the product, brand, or service being promoted or of the promised benefits. So the persuader's first task is to identify current patterns of use of similar products, brands, or services using focus groups, surveys, and other research methods. For example, suppose the makers of Oreo cookies want to add a new product to the Oreo and Double Stuffs line. They do research using focus groups and observing people eating the regular Oreos and the Double Stuffs. Most people start eating the cookies by splitting the cookie layers in two, licking off the filling, then eating the cookie portion—behavior that had originally inspired Double Stuffs (Fortini-Campbell, 1992). Consumers rate the filling as the best part of Oreos/Double Stuffs and say that a cookie with a different flavored filling would sell. Voilà! Now we have the Double Chocolate Stuff by Oreo.

With a consumer-driven product like cookies, the hierarchy of effects model suggests creating consumer awareness of the product and then developing consumer knowledge about it. The brand gets a name, a slogan, and a jingle, and public relations sends invitations to the media for the premiere taste-testing press conference. Then teaser ads communicate that "Double Chocolate Stuffs are coming soon!" Various promotional devices are used, such as free samples, events, and coupons. As the awareness stage merges with the developing knowledge stage, the advertiser teaches consumers about the brand. Researchers then test consumers' knowledge level using surveys, mall intercepts, and unaided and aided recall.

In the fourth and fifth steps—liking and preferring—the advertiser uses image ads that communicate that status and glamour are associated with the brand by using celebrity testimonials. If the brand has competition, the advertiser might use comparative ads with taste tests that demonstrate that Double Chocolate Stuffs are better than the competition's single lemon filled cookies. Consumers are now aware of the brand and have reason to like and even prefer it. The only task remaining is to convince them to try it. A goal of many persuasive campaigns is to induce trial, and this occurs in the final two stages of the hierarchy or the conviction and purchase stages, where consumers are convinced that the brand deserves a try and then go out and purchase it.

Lavidge and Steiner's hierarchy of effects model is but one model that helps us understand the goals, strategies, and tactics of product-oriented campaigns. Let's continue with some others.

The Positioning Model. In their best-selling books *Positioning: The Battle for Your Mind* (Trout and Ries, 1986) and *The New Positioning* (Trout, 1995), marketing experts Jack Trout and Al Ries offer their **positioning model** as a way to attract prospects. The definition of positioning is to get the brand, candidate, or idea/ideology into top of mind awareness (TOMA) among consumers, voters, or joiners. Having top of mind awareness is defined as being in the consumer's top five to nine identifiable brands, depending on the complexity of the product. Trout and Ries advise searching for unoccupied niches in the marketplace and then positioning the brand in that psychological space. These niches and appeals to them are almost always processed in the peripheral channel of the ELM. Here are some ways to position a brand in the marketplace.

- *Be the First.* The first brand to appear in a product class has the natural advantage of being the pioneer in that product class. Lunchables by Oscar Mayer, now a 15 year success story, are such a brand and were initially positioned in the "first" niche in 1990 throughout their introductory and subsequent campaigns. Other snack-pack brands followed, but none could claim pioneer status. Lunchables were subsequently able to offer *line extensions*, or new and improved versions of the product/brand such as Lunchables with a Dijon mustard packet and a chocolate mint dessert.

- *Be the Best.* Consumers shop for quality and are usually willing to pay a reasonable price for high-quality brands. This niche is filled by the brand that can claim to be the best in the product category. Swift's Butterball turkey, noted earlier, is one of the most expensive brands, and claims to be best because a full pound of butter is injected into each turkey, resulting in butter-basting leading to the benefits of moistness and good taste. Research shows that Butterball consumers spend more time in the supermarket and buy more premium condiments and desserts, like cranberry relishes or bakery pies, than other brand consumers. Retailers are glad to prominently display the brand. Over the years, several imported car brands have tried to claim the best position. At one time, Mercedes-Benz seemed to be the permanent occupant of the position. Later, other brands such as Jaguar and BMW also claimed to be best, resulting in a crowded niche.

- *Be the Least Expensive.* Besides shopping for quality, consumers often shop for price, so being able to claim that one's brand is the least expensive is a definite advantage. A good example is the burger and cola wars. Another is Wal-Mart's Every-Day Low Pricing. Even with high-ticket items such as cars, computers, and camcorders, price wars proliferate. The Geo, Hyundai, and other brands compete to offer the best value. The airline industry goes through regular cycles of fare wars. Various

bank and credit cards engage in price wars related to annual fees and low initial finance rates. And the same is true for mortgage rates.

- *Be the Most Expensive.* Status is sometimes critical to buyers, and they demonstrate status by buying the most expensive brand on the market such as a BMW. Coco Chanel, the renowned French clothing designer and perfumer, insisted on marketing only the most expensive brand.

- *Tell What You're Not.* Another position for gaining TOMA is telling consumers what the brand is not. On the brink of bankruptcy, 7-Up was saved by claiming that the soft drink was the "Uncola." Dr. Pepper imitated this strategy and also captured a portion of the cola market. Given recent interest in various health issues, numerous brands claim to be fat free or to have no carbs.

- *Position by Gender.* Many brands target only one gender, by positioning themselves as the woman's brand or the man's brand. Virginia Slims and Eve cigarettes are examples. After learning that pro football players and many outdoor workers wear pantyhose in cold weather for warmth, one company considered marketing a male version. Among its strategies were naming the brand Mach-Hose, getting testimonials from outdoor construction workers and firemen, offering it in camouflage colors, and selling six packs of the hose. Calvin Klein's Obsession for Men and the magazine *Gentleman's Quarterly* are obviously positioned by gender, as is the ad for Lincoln Financing Company shown in Figure 11.5 on page 256. Communication researcher A. N. Valdivia (1997) analyzed product advertising for women's lingerie and discovered that both gender and class positioning of competing brands. After looking at catalogs for Victoria's Secret and Frederick's of Hollywood, she concluded that Victoria's is targeted at the female upper middle class while Frederick's is targeted at the male and female lower middle class. Victoria's Secret sounds discreet and Victorian, whereas Frederick's of

Hollywood sounds male dominated, voyeuristic, and glitzy. Victoria's address is "London" and a prerecorded English voice answers when you place a telephone order. Frederick's models are unknowns and usually are photographed against simple fabric backdrops. Victoria's models are well-known and usually are photographed in indoor and old-world settings suggesting elegance and class.

- *Position by Age.* Advertisers often target a given cohort as the most likely prospect for a product or brand. Cohorts can be defined either as those born in the same year or those born in a certain set of years, like Baby Boomers or Generation Xers. Targeting a specific set of potential consumers has many advantages because you can custom tailor all aspects of advertising and other appeals for that specific cohort. For example, one of the most targeted and fastest growing cohorts is the Baby Boom generation, born between 1946 and 1964. The American Association of Retired Persons (AARP) chose a brilliant name and marketed itself based on benefits like lobbying efforts on behalf of retirees, discounts on certain products, group activities like low rates on travel, and information about topics like retirement planning, inexpensive health insurance, and exercise equipment. People are invited to join AARP at age 45 instead of 65, and they receive a subscription to *Modern Maturity* magazine (an aptly named title). It has the largest circulation in the country, making it an ideal magazine for targeting this affluent and growing cohort. Imagine how the targeting of cohorts affects packaging, slogans, message strategies, and media buys.

Politically Oriented Campaign Models

Although they share some characteristics with product-oriented campaigns, politically oriented campaigns differ in many ways from the marketing of products or brands. For example, there is only limited research data available to candidates, and politically oriented campaigns usually must communicate much more sophisticated information than product/brand campaigns. The complex information will be processed in the central route of the ELM. Let us now turn to developmental models that help explain political campaigns.

The Communicative Functions Model. Communication researchers Judith Trent and Robert Friedenberg (2000) describe four stages that a political campaign must achieve if it is to be successful. They call their approach the **communicative functions model**.

In the first stage, the candidate makes a formal announcement of candidacy and lays some groundwork by mapping out the district, organizing financial committees, developing contacts in key areas of the district, and so on. This stage is called the "surfacing" stage. The main campaign themes are floated and focused, and the candidate's image is tested and promoted. Issues are addressed, position papers are issued, and, with luck, adequate funds are raised. In presidential politics, this process may begin as early as the day after the most recent presidential election.

In stage 2 of this model, the "winnowing" stage, the primary election campaigns serve to narrow or winnow the field of candidates and to focus issues. More people get involved, as in the participation stage of the Yale model. These persons may pass out leaflets, attend rallies, sponsor fund-raisers, or perform some activity that gets them involved. In presidential politics, this stage is extremely expensive, even with the matching funds the government gives to candidates. As much as $50 million or more can be spent in pursuing a presidential nomination (National Public Radio, 1999). Of course, the costs are smaller with lower offices, but even senate primaries cost several million dollars. This is a dangerous stage for candidates because they might make promises that they later can't fulfill or they might reveal plans that come back to haunt them. They also might make mistakes, misstatements, or "gaffes" that undermine their legitimacy.

During stage 3, the "nomination" stage, the candidate is legitimized in the eyes of the media

I have a MOTHER.

I have a FATHER.

I even have a BIG BROTHER.

I DON'T need someone else looking out for me.

I NEED someone who can help me look out for myself.

Lincoln
Financial Group

At Lincoln Financial Group, our goal is to make the financial world clear and understandable so you can make informed decisions. *Clear solutions in a complex world*
1-877-ASK-LINCOLN

www.lfg.com © 1998 Lincoln National Corporation SMR 98-0690

FIGURE 11.5 In this ad, Lincoln Financial promotes its product by appealing to the independent woman, thus positioning Lincoln's services by gender. Considering the increased number of women in the labor force and in various kinds of investment plans, the strategy seems to be a good one.

SOURCE: Used by permission of the Lincoln Financial Group.

and potential voters, as are the party's platform and themes. The final stage, the "election stage," is that period between nomination and election day when candidates hectically go from state to state and crowd to crowd saying basically the same thing, over and over again. Here, the use of the press is critical in paid-for political promotions like billboards, signs, bumper stickers, buttons, TV ads, radio spots, or newspaper ads. Unpaid media coverage such as interview programs or short sound bites on the evening news can be critical. Candidates also use purchased media spots aimed at the right target audience at the right time, in the right way, and in a cost-efficient manner.

The advent of the Internet in national politics during the 1996 presidential primaries means that future candidates at all levels must use this method of communicating with their constituencies. This interactive and highly personal medium will only increase in importance in campaigns in the future.

Both candidates for mayor of my small town (population 12,000) had web pages with multiple links back in 2000. As we will see in Chapter 13, this use of media is sophisticated and complex. Political campaign messages are probably processed in both the central and the peripheral information-processing routes of the ELM. Issue-oriented messages probably follow the central path and require rational thinking and preparation. Image-oriented messages, though they may be rationally thought out, are probably processed peripherally.

In the third edition of *Political Communication in America*, Robert Denton and Gary Woodward (1998) focus on the strategies and tactics used in political campaigns. They say that strategies are the various plans a campaigner forms in hopes of achieving the campaign goal or goals; tactics are the means used to implement the strategies or to put them into action. In political campaigns, of course, there is but one goal—to win election to office—but several strategies could be used to meet that goal, such as winning the primary, raising money, or getting favorable voters registered. Referring to R. Faucheux (1998), Denton and Woodward identify four strategy types that occur in any political campaign. The first is a "message sequence strategy" that addresses the order in which various campaign messages should be sent out. These could be messages about issues, the candidate or the opponent, qualifications for office, and personal beliefs. Second, a "timing and intensity strategy" suggests when messages should go out, and how much effort, money, and other resources should be dedicated to that phase of the campaign. Third, a "mobilization and persuasion strategy" focuses on reaching and convincing groups of voters who might be favorable to the candidate, such as first-time voters, homeowners, minority voters, and the party faithful. Finally, an "opportunity strategy" allows the campaign to respond to the unexpected events, opportunities, or threats that inevitably arise. Examples include revelation of the amount of money being spent or the source of the funding, negative advertising, or a scandal involving the candidate or his or her opponent.

Several message sequence strategies are possible. The "ignore the opposition" strategy usually means being positive in speeches, news releases, interviews, and comments from the beginning of the campaign until election day and rarely or never referring to the opponent. The "aggressive message sequence" strategy begins the campaign on a positive note but then quickly turns to negative campaigning focused on the opponent's shortcomings. In the final days of the campaign, this strategy is implemented by using a dual-track approach with both positive and negative or comparative appeals. With the "frontal attack strategy," the candidate begins with negative and comparative ads focusing on the opponent's shortcomings, turns positive in the middle portions of the campaign, and then closes using the same dual-track approach as in the "aggressive" strategy.

Several message timing and intensity strategies are available as well. With the "tortoise strategy," the candidate begins slowly, communicating and spending only modestly, and then builds momentum until election day, when a message and spending blitz happens. The "bookend strategy" uses a big, flashy, and expensive opening with a steady buildup and the same blitz strategy used to close the campaign the day before election day. With the "Pearl Harbor strategy," the candidate starts very slowly and is barely noticeable. This is intended to lull the opposition into underestimating the candidate's strength, which then allows him or her to sneak attack the opponent at an opportune moment.

Opportunity strategies might include "setting a trap," whereby the candidate attacks the opponent over a minor shortfall to set the opponent up to respond in such a way as to lead to a much larger criticism. For instance, the candidate might accuse the opponent of being financed by an enormously rich father who is trying to buy the election for his spoiled son or daughter. The opponent responds by saying that it is no sin to be successful and to spend money on what one truly believes. Then the candidate springs the trap by revealing that dear old Dad amassed his fortune by exploiting slave labor in China. The "technological advantage strategy" was used in the 1996 presidential campaign by numerous candidates who were aware of the newly emerging Internet and put up sophisticated web pages, which surprised their uninformed opponents. "Three's a crowd" is a strategy that takes advantage of a crowded field by financing a minor third or fourth opponent who will siphon off votes from the real opponent. The "lightning rod strategy" gets a controversial person to endorse the opponent or introduces a controversial issue to which the opponent can only respond in a negative, controversial, and highly visible way.

Persuasion and mobilization strategies relate to how the candidate deals with voter groups—the party faithful, undecided voters, and those favoring the opponent. Candidates identify their voter base and the undecided voters and then reinforce them with messages and turn them out to vote.

To learn more about political campaign communication, access InfoTrac College Edition, and enter the word "campaign" in the search engine. Select the political campaigns in mass media option, and browse the selections.

Idea/Ideological Campaigns

In the idea or ideological campaign, neither a product nor a person nor candidate is promoted. Instead, the persuader wants the audience to engage in or change some behavior or to embrace some religion or other ideology. In the change of behavior option, campaigns might promote preventive measures that individuals might take to avoid contracting STDs. Other campaigns solicit donations to various not-for-profit churches, charities, or other good causes. Idea campaigns urge people to help the environment by recycling aluminum, glass, tin cans, and plastic containers. A protest campaign might persuade people to wear black armbands on a certain day to indicate their displeasure with a policy or law. In early 2003, the group Women Against Military Madness (WAMM) protested the saber-rattling rhetoric of various members of the second Bush administration directed toward Iraq. They held rallies, sold yard signs and bumper stickers reading "Say No! to War with Iraq," and used other tactics to implement their strategies for avoiding a U.S. invasion of Iraq,

which we now know happened despite their efforts. Any of the elements in the Yale model help explain the strategies of such campaigns, and some elements of the product/person campaign models can also apply. But other models specifically explain idea/ideological campaigns or social movements.

The Social Movements Model. Communication researchers Charles J. Stewart, Craig A. Smith, and Robert E. Denton, Jr., (2001) define and describe the social movement model of idea/ideological campaigns. They maintain that social movements have seven unique characteristics that set them apart from product- or person-oriented campaigns. First, social movements are organized groups of people, with leaders who usually act as spokespersons for the movement. Second, although they are organized, social movements are not institutionalized or recognized by those in power. Third, they attract large numbers of persons and are large in scope either geographically or historically. Thus, pro-lifers would qualify as a social movement, whereas promoting radon-free drinking water probably wouldn't because of its limited scope.

Fourth, social movements either promote or oppose social change. There are three subtypes of groups promoting or opposing change. The "innovative movement" wants to totally replace existing social values and norms, and includes movements like gay liberation or radical feminism. The "revivalistic movement" seeks only partial change in society and a return to past values. The "resistance movement" seeks to block instead of favor change. For example, the pro-choice movement wants to keep *Roe v. Wade* in effect, and the NRA opposes limitations on the right to own handguns. Fifth, social movements are moralistic, preaching about good versus evil, right versus wrong, or patriotism versus treason. Sixth, social movements encounter opposition from those in power. The power may be held by formal groups such as the military, police, or a regulatory body. This opposition often leads to symbolic and then real violence, as has happened in a number of dramatic cases.

For their part, those promoting change might begin by shouting slogans, then move to violence against property, and ultimately against people. Finally, persuasion is the essential tool for attracting new converts, changing people's minds, and ultimately motivating members to take action. The persuasion may be verbal or nonverbal, it may attempt to use mass media, and it usually includes a call to action on the part of the persuadee.

Social movements also have their own set of developmental stages. Stewart, Smith, and Denton's model of a social movement outlines five stages: "genesis," "social unrest," "enthusiastic mobilization," "maintenance," and "termination" stages. In the "genesis stage," ideologues preach about perceived shortcomings or injustices. These early prophets might go unheard for a long time, but finally, like-minded persons are drawn to these prophets, and the first stage creates a core of devoted supporters. Then, usually, a dramatic event catapults the issue into the public spotlight.

In the "social unrest" stage, growing numbers of people identify with the movement and now are agitated by the identification of the devils and gods of the movement. This leads to the third stage of "enthusiastic mobilization" when the true believers begin to convert more and more people and continue to encounter opposition from those in power. These converts are now activists, not merely persons who identify with the movement. Fourth, in the "maintenance" stage the movement adopts a lower profile as the media attention turns to other events, and some success is perceived by converts. These successes dull enthusiasm for and drain energy from the movement, so it must bide its time until a significant event occurs to rekindle enthusiasm. In some cases, the movement achieves its goal(s), or it may merely wither and die in the "termination" stage. Perhaps supporters lose faith and patience, or the movement becomes outmoded, or its leaders are assimilated into the establishment, or it becomes irrelevant.

The Agitation and Control Model. In their book *The Rhetoric of Agitation and Control*, John Bowers, Donovan Ochs, and R. J. Jensen (1993) describe several stages in ideological movements that must occur before the movements ultimately fail or succeed. In the first stage—the "petition stage," agitators petition the sources of power such as the government, a corporation, or a school district, making demands or "requests" that slightly exceed what the power source will give up. The power source thus appears unreasonable. The agitators now initiate the "promulgation stage" or the marketing of the movement. Using handbills, leaflets, and rallies, the agitators develop their movement by informing outsiders of the unreasonableness of the power source. At this stage, the movement leaders hope to gain recruits and get publicity that will attract even more recruits, as was the case in 2005 when the American Civil Liberties Union and other free speech groups objected to illegal surveillance of American citizens by the Bush administration and a nationally publicized social movement was born.

If promulgation succeeds, the movement moves into the "solidification stage." Now the newly recruited members are hyped up through rallies, marches, and protest songs like "We Shall Overcome" or "We Shall Not Be Moved." They may use salutes and symbols or uniforms. In the "polarization stage," the movement leaders target the uncommitted population. They do this by focusing on a flag issue or person. The reason they are called flag issues or persons is that they epitomize the ultimate enemy or are the most easily recognized symbol of what the movement or ideology objects to or hates. Past flag issues have been the aborting of fetuses, the use of napalm on civilians, the mistreatment of refugees, illegal surveillance of citizens, and the bombing of civilian targets. Flag persons personify the issue. Past flag persons have included President Lyndon Johnson, Saddam Hussein, and President George W. Bush. In local politics, flag persons might include mayors, councilpersons, senators, representatives, or others depicted as the root of the problem. The polarization stage forces the onlookers to choose between us and them.

In the fifth stage, the "nonviolent resistance stage," such tactics as name calling or rent strikes are used. For instance, police call in sick with the "blue flu," or students occupy a building and claim that they have liberated it. These and other devices call attention to the movement and usually bring some sort of response from the power source, such as calling out the army or police. Usually, the media will cover the confrontation. Then agitators claim repression or Gestapo tactics. Usually, this leads to the "escalation stage," which increases tensions in the power source. Perhaps threats are made, such as rumors of planted bombs or public displays of weapons. Perhaps some violent act occurs, such as a strike with billy clubs and fist-fights, a killing or kidnapping, or the bombing of an important building or landmark like the Twin Towers. If the power source represses the movement at this time, there usually is a split within the movement between those who favor violence and those who favor nonviolence. Bowers, Ochs, and Jensen call this the "Gandhi versus guerrilla stage." Usually, the nonviolent segment goes to the power source and argues that, unless they give in, the guerrillas will take over. Violence will escalate as was the case in Operation Iraqi Freedom when the numbers of bombings by insurgents increased radically as the occupation wore on.

Depending on the power source's response, the final stage may or may not emerge. This last stage—the "revolution stage" rarely happens, but social movements using the rhetoric of agitation and control have led to revolutions in a variety of places in recent decades. With the world focused on global terrorism and the United States engaged in a costly war, we will very likely continue to see such agitation and control tactics used as objection to the actions of various governments increase. The ability of the agitation and control model to describe, explain, and even predict stages in movements across time testifies to both its validity and its reliability.

The Diffusion of Innovation Model.   Some idea campaigns hope to induce people to adopt new practices or change their behaviors, such as following safer procedures in a factory, reducing their intake of red meats and fats, or conserving energy.

Everett Rogers (1962) studied the stages through which people approach the adoption of any new technology such as computers, cell phones, email, the Internet, or BlackBerries. The stages also occur with adopting new practices such as recycling or changing values such as favoring the hybrid auto-mobile. Rogers' diffusion of innovation model also has some applicability to product- and person-oriented campaigns. He outlined four stages on the way to adopting change.

In the first stage—the "information/knowl-edge stage"—the potential adopter acquires or actively seeks information about the innovation. How does it work? What are its features and ben-efits? How much will it cost? How have other adopters rated it? When people first became aware of the practice of recycling, which was a time-consuming activity with little direct payoff, few persons rushed out and got containers for alumi-num, glass, tin cans, newspaper, and mixed paper. However, being made aware of recycling drew people's attention to various pieces of information like the life expectancy of local landfills and the effects of deforestation on the climate.

In the second stage— the "persuasion stage"— the potential adopter processes informa-tion aimed at inducing him or her to actually try the new product or practice. Those advocating the change might use testimonials from well-known persons who have adopted the new product or practice.

In the third stage—the "decision, adoption, and trial stage" —the potential adopters decide to try the new practice. They get the recycling containers, or they order prescriptions, groceries, books, or other items via the Internet. Then they use the new technology, product, or practice. Sometimes, marketers request that new users respond to the product/brand/practice by completing a rating survey. This technique moves potential adopters into the "confirmation and evaluation stage, in which they reconsider the adoption and measure its performance against their expectations. They ask if it delivered what it promised and was it worth the costs. If they continue usage, they then search for information that confirms the adoption.

BOX 11.2 Cultural Diversity in Campaigns

In 2005, three media and advertising professional organizations sponsored the first National Expo of Ethnic Media to identify how best to target campaigns to the over 50 million ethnic Americans. Soon the number of ethnic consumers, voters, joiners, and donors will outnumber nonethnic ones, thus representing an enormously powerful market segment. Take just one part of this huge segment—Hispanics and/or Latinos. They presently represent an advertising expenditure of $3.5 billion per year, but they are changing. Why? Because by 2020, only 34 percent of Hispanics/Latinos in the United States will be from the first born generation. The newer generations will be more acculturated, be better educated, will speak English, and probably will be more affluent, according to the Pew Hispanic Center. Today, 88 percent of Hispanics/Latinos under the age of 18 are foreign born. When you combine the Hispanic/Latino minorities with other culturally diverse groups, you get a "New American Mainstream," according to Guy Garcia (2005) in his best-selling book of the same title. What are the implications for politicians, advertisers, and idea/ideological persuaders? What do these numbers imply for other culturally diverse minorities?

If the diffusion model interests you, access InfoTrac College Edition, and "diffusion of innovation" in the search engine. Browse some of the periodical selections.

The Rogers model is helpful in considering campaigns that offer new and innovative practices to consumers. With the rate of change accelerating in our information age, we will undoubtedly go through these stages repeatedly. Knowing what is happening in such situations helps put decisions to adopt new practices into a clearer perspective, resulting in wiser choices.

Besides these developmental models of campaigns, several other theories help explain the success or failure of a given product-oriented, person-oriented, or idea/ideological campaign.

Symbolic Convergence Theory

Most of us like to affiliate with people with whom we agree and who are like us in Burke's "substantial" ways, and we seek to find communities of agreement or groups of people who share our basic values and lifestyles. This requires the merging of my meanings for events and values with your meanings for those same things. Having similar values and lifestyles identifies us as a particular audience to whom advertisers, politicians, and ideologues try to appeal. How do such "communities of agreement" develop?

The first clues to the power inherent in the social creation of meaning came from the work of Robert F. Bales (1970), a professor of sociology at Harvard. His initial interest was in identifying the kinds of verbal interactions in small, task-oriented groups. He noticed that in one category of interaction, group tension was released through the telling of stories. Bales called this category "dramatizes." He began to describe the way these stories or mini-dramas seemed to develop or, as he put it, **chain out** in the group, resulting in what he called **fantasy themes**.

At this point, Bales' work caught the attention of E. G. Bormann and his students and colleagues. They also noticed fantasy sharing in small groups and thought that the process of small group building of reality had a wider application. This wider application of fantasy sharing was ultimately developed by Bormann (1985), his students, and other researchers, and it helps explain how shared meanings begin, develop, continue, and finally motivate us to action. The theory is known as "**symbolic convergence theory**," and its technique of analysis is called **fantasy theme analysis**. This theory was initially applied to small-group communication. After witnessing the power of the theory and methodology in the analysis and explanation of group communication, Bormann and his followers applied them to interpersonal, corporate, institutional, and organizational communication. For our purposes as students of persuasion, the theory and methodology are ideal for doing audience analysis for product, idea, and political campaigns. When combined with focus group interviews and research techniques like surveys and Q-sort analysis, the theory and method have great power for analyzing the kinds of dramas to which specified groups of consumers and voters respond (Cragan and Shields, 1994, 1995).

A basic premise of symbolic convergence theory is that reality is socially based and symbolically constructed. That means that each of us perceives the world as a result of our interactions with others and our adoption of and addition to the meanings of these interactions using symbols. Second, many of these interactions include stories or narratives, a pattern we have noted in earlier chapters. As we initially hear these stories or fantasies, we ignore them, embrace them, or participate in them. It is in the participative behavior that we create social reality and come together in symbolic convergence. That is, we share common symbols, meanings, and cues to them.

A brief example might help here. At the halftime show of the 2005 Super Bowl, Janet Jackson intentionally or unintentionally exposed her naked breast. The incident got instant and widespread media coverage and triggered thousands of group discussions among the massive audience. One person says, "Well that family's been messed up since they were kids." Another person chimes in, "Right, just look at her bleached brother molesting kids." A third says, "His goofiness started with that moon walk thing." The story or fantasy is beginning to chain out or become a shared version of reality. Media reports added to the fire, and when brother Michael was acquitted of ten molestation charges, another set of "reality links" and **"fantasy links"** probably chained out. When aided by media coverage, enough of these group fantasies resemble one another and symbolic convergence has occurred.

It doesn't matter what the truth or reality about the event is, it is what people participate in and come to believe that forms our social reality.

Because we share our inputs and interpretations with others in our social groups, we come to believe them even more devotedly than if we got them from a respected authority. If the story becomes widely believed, we have a national **rhetorical vision** that can powerfully motivate.

In thousands of studies, Bormann, his students, colleagues, and followers identified the operation of symbolic convergence in political and other campaigns. (Bormann, 1985). This pattern replicated itself in studies of purchasing and joining behavior. The technique was used to generate plot ideas for a popular prime time comedy series.

In political campaigns fantasy types, or favorite topics, themes, or images, emerge. Reporters cover the campaigns and develop their own rhetorical vision in which they "dig out the real truth." One fantasy theme is that of the "frontrunner," or the candidate with the early legitimacy who is focused on by the media, which covers such issues as whether the candidate is showing signs of stumbling, is hiding something, or is acting as a stalking horse for other candidates. Another political campaign fantasy theme is that of the baseball game, with the candidates being in the "early or final innings" or unable to "get to first base" with the electorate. Another theme makes use of boxing images, with candidates being "on the ropes" or "delivering knockout blows" to the opposition, who is just a "lightweight" and not a real "contender."

In political and product-oriented advertising, the ad agency puts "spin" on the product by issuing press releases about it, by getting press coverage for giving the product away to some worthy group, or by emphasizing the product's astounding benefits. Bert Metter (1990), chairman of the J. Walter Thompson USA advertising agency, puts it this way:

> We are in the age of spin. The art and science of creating images is out of the closet.... As spin becomes more common...we've got to deliver more effectiveness.... The agencies with the answers will succeed. Others will have a lot of spinning to do (p. 36).

In product-related campaigns, Cragan and Shields (1995) found various types of individuals who have differing principles and beliefs. Their symbolic convergence tends to happen on one of three "planes" or philosophies. They are the **"pragmatic (or practical) plane;" "the righteous (or highly principled) plane;"** and the **"social (or interactive) plane."** Suppose you want to sell growth-enhancing ingredients to cattle growers, and you want to reach those growers on each plane. For the pragmatic cattle growers, you would stress the practical statistics on cost, effectiveness, and increased yield and profits. For the righteous cattle growers, you would stress that the enhancer is totally natural and does not violate any USDA regulations. For the social cattle growers, you would want to use testimonials from other cattle growers to the effect that just about everybody in the know is using the enhancer. Cragan and Shields have used this model to help sell agricultural products and drugs, increase enrollment in private schools, and train firefighters. (If you are interested in which plane or philosophy you fit, go to the website for this book and take a brief survey about the kinds of activities and beliefs you like or hold dear and discover whether you are a pragmatic, righteous, or social type consumer. Cragan and Shields also related how such spin operated in idea or ideological campaigns. Symbolic convergence "spin" was used to convince the Iowa legislature to permit riverboat casinos, to recruit physicians to small towns, and to help train firefighter instructors.

We shouldn't forget that symbolic convergence is not limited to political campaigns. Following the train, bus, and subway bombings in London and Spain in 2005, the public meaning of the word "terrorism" took on new dimensions. Terrorism was associated with a series of small cells of individuals around the world, which meant no country was safe, not even neutral ones. And perhaps the cells were coordinated by Osama Bin Laden and the leadership of other "rogue nations" that formed an "axis of evil," which justified a "War on Terrorism." Those key words got picked up by the press

and soon by the public also, and ultimately emerged into a global rhetorical vision.

REVIEW AND CONCLUSION

All persuasion involves self-persuasion. We must agree to be persuaded and then find good reasons for deciding. Many of these good reasons are already embedded in our conscious or subconscious memory. Clever persuaders identify ways to cue these memories and connect them to a product, candidate, or idea or ideology. Persuaders tune persuadees' ears to the kinds of messages that will be communicated in campaigns seeking new buyers, new voters, or new joiners. The formal and functional characteristics of campaigns that we have explored seem to persist over time, forming permanent patterns. The ever-shifting issues and increasingly sophisticated technologies of product testing, public opinion polling, media production, and direct marketing are a few of the elements of change.

Among the recurring aspects of campaigns are the systematic flow of communication from persuader to audience and back to the persuader via a feedback loop (something that typifies all communication systems). Another is the establishment of formal goals, strategies, and tactics and the creation of a position or niche in the audience's mind. There are also stages through which most campaigns must pass, which usually involve a participatory dramatization of the product, candidate, or idea/ideology in which the audience is involved in real or symbolic ways. Then there are the kinds of appeals that unify and recruit zealots for the mass movement and the "chaining out" of rhetorical visions in campaigns/social movements that ultimately involve mass audiences.

You need to become a critical receiver who makes responsible decisions about which product to buy, which candidate to vote for, and which ideas or ideologies to endorse. These decisions are appropriate only after thorough analysis of the campaigns. Ask yourself how the campaign responds to feedback and what its objectives, strategies, and tactics are. Ask how the campaign positions the product, person, or idea and what developmental stages emerge during the campaign and in what kind of drama you are being invited to participate. When you have answered these questions, you will be ready to make a responsible decision.

KEY TERMS

By the time you have read this chapter you should be able to identify, explain, and give an example of the following key terms or concepts.

integrated marketing communication	Yale five-stage developmental model	communicative functions model	symbolic convergence theory
product-oriented	Identification	social movements model	fantasy theme analysis
person or candidate-oriented	legitimacy	agitation and control model	fantasy links
idea- or ideologically oriented	participation	diffusion of innovation model	rhetorical vision
brand awareness	penetration		pragmatic (or practical) plane
goals	distribution	chain out	the righteous (or highly principled) plane
strategies	hierarchy of effects model	fantasy themes	social (or interactive) plane
tactics	positioning model		

APPLICATION OF ETHICS

A rapidly growing approach to campaign persuasion, whether for product, person, or idea/ideological campaigns is known as "stealth marketing" or "buzz marketing." It is based on the old adage that the best kind of advertising is word of mouth and is a response to increasing consumer, voter, and joiner skepticism about traditional advertising and to the increasing use of Tivo technology to zap television ads. Buzz marketing hires people to engage in "word of mouth advertising without informing the potential consumer that they are being paid for telling the consumer positive things about the product/brand, person, or cause being promoted (Ahuja, 2005). One of the most vulnerable market segments for this approach is teens, and the "buzz agents" being hired are usually between the ages of 13 and 19. In addition to promoting the brand or service, these agents also do consumer research by asking those they buzz about the competition, their preferences, and so on. Sometimes they give out free samples. Tremor Inc., which is a subsidiary of Proctor and Gamble, employs over 280,000 such agents. The parents are informed prior to recruitment that their lucky child has been selected to influence family and friends by joining the "Tremor Crew" and get paid at the same time. This gets around the parental consent issue. Tremor Inc. has been very successful in marketing the Toyota Matrix, Coca Cola, Cover Girl makeup, and movies like *My Big Fat Greek Wedding*. What are the ethical implications of this type of "honest deception" marketing (Ahuja, 2005)? What are some of the critical issues? Is the practice fair if the consumer doesn't know the word of mouth is paid for? If you were asked to become a part of a Tremor Crew, would you? Why or why not?

QUESTIONS FOR FURTHER THOUGHT

1. Choose a current campaign for a product, person, or idea/ideology. What appear to be its objectives, strategies, and tactics?

2. Define each of the Yale developmental terms. Can you identify examples of the first three stages in a magazine or newspaper campaign?

3. In the agitation/control model, what stage of a campaign or movement is represented when we vote for or against a particular candidate or proposition? Why?

4. What are some ways now being used to position products you use? Candidates running for office? Idea campaigns requesting your active or financial support? Mass movements seeking converts?

5. Identify a social movement that is either going on or seems to be developing. Use the social movements model and agitation/control model to trace its development. Which most accurately describes what is happening?

6. Using Bormann's symbolic convergence theory, explain the same social movement identified in question 5. Which of the methodologies seems most message oriented? Which is most audience related?

7. Which plane or philosophy fits with you—pragmatic, righteous, or social? How do you know?

8. Identify several fantasy types in a campaign for a product made popular in the previous decade. Are they similar to those for today's products?

9. Using the diffusion of innovation model, study the development of a new product in the marketplace.

For online activities, go to the *Persuasion* book companion website at http://communication.wadsworth.com/larson11.

12

Becoming a Persuader

LEARNING GOALS

After reading this chapter, you should be able to:

1. Conduct an analysis of a hypothetical audience using demographics and identifying their needs.

2. Organize the same speech via the three formats of space, topic, and chronology.

3. Identify, explain, and give examples of stock issues used in considering a policy issue such as randomly assigned registration dates being debated on campus.

4. Give a speech using the motivated sequence format and exhibiting good delivery techniques and persuasive language.

5. Explain how you can improve your own credibility.

6. Identify various forms of proof statement in the mass media.

7. Explain the critical effects that the choice of channel can have on persuasion.

Thus far, we have focused on receiver skills: how to be a critical, responsible, and ethical consumer of persuasion. However, sometimes, we must become persuaders. Luckily, we can apply the knowledge we gained in our role as persuadee to our occasional role as persuader. We can use tactics of intensification/downplaying; we can mold our persuasion using process, content, cultural, and nonverbal premises; and we can apply our knowledge of what is ethical in persuasion.

As a persuader, you'll take your first steps in preparing your message by learning about your audience and shaping your message. Here, considerations such as patterns of organization, kinds of proof, and styling of messages will be important. Also, you must choose how to go about delivering your message, which includes choosing the channel as well as thinking about your voice and posture, making eye contact, and so on. Finally, you want to be aware of some common persuasive tactics. Throughout this entire process, you need to ask whether what you are doing is ethical in terms of the models presented by Richard Johannesen in Chapter 2. Sometimes, you need to ask questions about the lasting, larger issues in life. One such question is, "Is what I am being persuasive about likely to have a more negative or more positive effect on my listener's lives? For that matter, will it make for a better or worse world?" Being an ethical persuader means being part of a community in which your persuasion has a positive

effect on relationships in that community. Your persuasion must not undermine the idea of community.

AUDIENCE ANALYSIS: KNOWING YOUR AUDIENCE

It is easy to assert that persuaders should know as much as possible about their audience, but it is not always so easy to prescribe specific ways you can get to know them. One of the best ways is to listen to them when they persuade, because they will likely use tactics that would be persuasive to them. For example, I often use narratives and examples to get you to take my advice. If you want to persuade me, fill your message with narratives and examples. I also look at my audience's patterns of processing information in terms of the elaboration likelihood model (ELM). I want to use the central information-processing route when that is appropriate, and I want to allow the audience to use the peripheral information-processing route when that is called for.

In other words, you will need to do some **audience analysis**, which is defined as learning as much as possible about your projected audience— their ages, their majors, the gender split in the

FIGURE 12.1 If you were preparing to speak in an informal situation such as this, how would you do your audience analysis?

audience, and many other things. Study audience members, observe them, listen to them, and analyze what they say and how they say it. When your parents try to persuade, how do they go about it? What kinds of evidence do they use? Some people, for example, are most easily persuaded when they think they are the ones who came up with the idea for change. It is best to give such persons several alternatives and let them make the choice. Then they "own" the idea or innovation. Others are most satisfied with a decision if they see that significant others have made or are making the same or similar decisions. Best-selling author Robert Cialdini (2001) calls this tool of influence "social proof," which means viewing a behavior or decision as correct "to the degree that we see others performing it" (p. 100).

But is it ethical for the persuader to use social proof to win the day? It depends on the issue, the costs, and the potential benefits of following the decision or action. It is far more important for us as persuadees (sensing that a persuader is using social proof to convince us) to ask ourselves whether we should decide or act simply because others have acted in a certain way. Sometimes the masses are wrong, and we need to forge a different path. Thus, the ethical issue reverts back to where it should be— with receivers of persuasion. It is certainly true that

persuaders *ought* to be ethical, but unfortunately that is not always the case. We need to be on guard and not be fooled by affinity appeals such that we follow the advice of persons who only seem to be like us. Recognizing ethical and unethical appeals aimed at us as persuadees also helps us to practice ethical persuasion when we are in the persuader's role.

To learn how important knowing your audience is, access InfoTrac College Edition, and type the words "social proof" in the subject search engine. Examine the items published in *Direct Marketing*. Then type in the words "audience analysis" in the key word search engine. Explore the many ways being used to analyze the invisible audience going to locations on the Web.

AUDIENCE DEMOGRAPHICS

When persuasion is aimed at larger audiences, persuaders can use demographics to analyze the audience. **Demographics** describes people in quantifiable terms of their shared attributes—their likes, dislikes, and habits, as well as age, gender, education, religious beliefs (if any), and income.

If you subscribe to *Outdoor Life, Field and Stream,* and *Sports Illustrated,* you likely differ from the person who subscribes to *The Atlantic Monthly, Horticulture, Organic Gardening,* and *Bon Appétit.* Both of you would be good bets for catalogs featuring outdoor clothing. Probably neither of you is interested in rock music or MTV. Your affiliations (church, fraternal, or community groups) are another demographic index.

Some marketing firms specialize in doing demographic research. Between their databases, census data, state government records such as driver's and fishing licenses, returned warranty cards, and many other sources, all of us have been identified demographically. What do you think about having all that information about you available to anybody wanting to sell you something? Is it ethical for the government, publishers, and others to sell that information?

Most of us don't do this kind of in-depth and elaborate analysis of a potential audience, but we can do a lot even with limited time and resources. For example, suppose you plan to make a presentation to the athletic board of your college or university. You want the board to ban smoking in the football stadium during home games. This will be a controversial proposal, and it could have unintended effects such as a campus-wide ban on smoking. You need to find out who the board members are, what they do for a living, and where they live. How have they voted or acted in the past? What kinds of past funding have they used? What kinds of alternatives have they allowed? Why? Most of that kind of information will be a part of the public record and easily found in their minutes, quotes in the student newspaper, and so forth. What demographic factors should you look at in preparing a formal persuasive presentation?

Audience factors that make a critical difference vary with the goal of your presentation. Age is important if you are discussing tax planning for retirement, but not if your topic is recycling. Gender is important for discussing screening for cervical cancer but not for a presentation about flu shots. Level of income, political affiliations, and many other factors may be more relevant in some situations than others. The board has both male and female students, faculty, athletes, administrators, and alumni on it; they vary in background, and one of them is the athletic director. Which of the following will you want to explore about your audience?

- *Average age.* Will it matter how many are over fifty or under eighteen? Probably. The older ones may see the proposal as just another "do-gooder" idea. The younger ones could see it as another infringement on student rights.

- *Income.* Will it matter if they are well-to-do or struggling to get by? Probably not, but smoking has become an expensive habit. So it could.

- *Gender.* The board is made up of both genders, so that will probably not be an important factor.

- *Religion.* This factor is one you can probably ignore. However, if your proposal was to have board approval for pregnancy counseling, it clearly would be important.

- *Family size.* Will it matter if your audience members have two or five children? Probably, because most parents discourage their children from smoking.

- *Political party.* In this case, political affiliation would have little bearing, unless the state has been aggressively pursuing no-smoking regulations.

- *Occupation.* Will the board members' occupations affect their willingness to consider the proposal? Probably. If the nonstudent board members are white-collar workers, they might know how smoking regulations are resented by some in the workplace. Some persons are well aware of the dangers of secondhand smoke, so knowing how many board members are nonsmokers will be important.

- *How many of them smoke or smoked at one time?* This will be a key factor. Smokers usually resent being told when and where they can indulge. Former smokers usually know how repulsive the smell and mess caused by smokers are and usually object to smoking in their presence.

BOX 12.1   Interactive Audience Analysis

We are all aware of the presence of email spam. Why do you think some spammers pick on you and others don't? How do they know to what you might respond? To get an idea of how detailed audience analysis has become in the interactive age, type the words "audience analysis" into the search engine at www.imediaconnection.com/consumer. How might you use sites like these when you need to do audience analysis?

How will you find out this information? Perhaps you could distribute a questionnaire designed to get other demographic information and include a question about their smoking and drinking habits. This will of course require that you allow enough time before the presentation for you to gather data. Do you think the athletic director will be concerned about loss of ticket and concession income if smokers boycott the games? After all, the stadium seats are often filled by townspeople and other adults who are more likely to be smokers.

Once you know the key demographic factors for your group/topic/context, the next stage is to explore them. The public relations people at your school can provide information about where board members live, and this can cue you as to their income and age. For example, some students live in fraternity or sorority houses while others live in dorms or apartments, and many live at home and have families of their own. Nonstudent members could live in town or commute from the suburbs. If the board has turned down past requests from students versus faculty versus administrators, you need to know why. Sometimes, merely talking to one or two typical members of a group before you attempt to persuade can be helpful in getting to know the audience. Any characteristics they share as a group can be useful in shaping your message for that audience. Would it be ethical for you to do demographic research for your presentation? Why or why not?

Determining Audience Needs

Some audience touchstones are emotional, some logical, some cultural, and some nonverbal. We can do some fairly sophisticated analysis of our target to determine **audience needs**. We might focus on the responsibility of the university to protect the health of students, faculty, and visitors to sell our idea. Or we could talk about the need of university decision makers to constantly keep up to date with social and environmental issues. Most of the "hot buttons" that help persuade others can be traced back to emotions, memories, and experiences that are common to large percentages of the population.

All audiences have some sets of shared experiences. Everyone remembers taking their first test to get a driver's license. Most of you remember your first visit to the campus where you now go to school and not knowing where the various buildings were located. Stored memories can be persuasive building blocks. What might be some of these stored experiences for the members of the governing board? Those who smoke or have smoked may remember their first cigarette. Former smokers will remember how difficult it was to finally quit. Some board members may remember not being particularly bothered by smoking when outdoors. Others will recall moving to a different seat to avoid smokers. The next time you need to persuade someone, try to list the experiences he or she likely has had and determine whether any can be tied into your message.

Tony Schwartz (1973) identified what he called the "task-oriented" approach to persuading, which is also useful for audience analysis. To use it, ask yourself whether your goal fits with the athletic board's authority to enact your proposal. Try to find out the state of mind of your audience—the board, the sales force, or the job interviewer. What is their likely mood? Will they be relaxed? Will they have doubts? Take these things into account, and design your message accordingly.

Once you know something about your target group and how its members feel about your topic, you can shape the message. People are more likely to recall messages that are well organized, so you need to consider the various forms of organization available to you.

FORMS OF ORGANIZATION

There are a number of ways to organize messages to make sure they are memorable and persuasive. We will look at five such formats here: (1) the **topic format**, (2) the **space format**, (3) the **chronological format**, (4) the **stock-issues format**, and (5) the **motivated sequence format**. For the first three of these formats, we will use the following example: A student group on my campus wanted to bring a highly successful filmmaker (a former student) back to school as a guest speaker to discuss the challenges of film production. The speaker was willing to donate his honorarium to the sponsoring student group to be used for field trips, travel to national conferences, and funding for a career day.

Organization by Topic

Organizing by topic is most useful when the message you want to convey covers several topics or issues. Here is a list of topics the student group might present in the filmmaker example:

- His fame and success as a reason to bring him to campus
- The kind of role model he would provide
- The special opportunity to preview his latest film
- The degree to which he is in demand on the speaking circuit
- His generosity in donating his fee to the student group in the department
- The other benefits to be derived from his presence on campus: publicity for the school,

the added programming made possible by his donation, and the career counseling he might be able to give to aspiring student filmmakers

By presenting these topics with supporting evidence, you give the student government a variety of good reasons to fund the speaker. The topic format is a good choice when presenting specific reasons for some suggested action.

Organization by Space

Organizing by space is a good choice when you want to compare your topic to some larger picture. In the filmmaker example, you might compare the relative cost of the desired speaker to that of speakers invited by other groups. The filmmaker's fee might be only a quarter of that asked by another student group for a less well-known speaker. Further, his fee might represent only 5 percent of the total guest speaker budget for the semester. And your student group may be only one of more than 20 similar groups in the university, so the fee is not out of line. In the spatial format, you might draw several pie graphs. In one, you could visually depict your speaker's fee as one-twentieth of the pie and label the remainder "Other Speaker Fees." Another graph might show your five percent share as only a fraction of the funds allocated to other student groups. In all these examples, you are using space as an organizing principle.

Organization by Chronology

Sometimes, the essential message in persuasive communication is best relayed by taking the audience through the issues in historical sequence or organizing by chronology. You might relate the filmmaker's career as follows:

1. In 1975, he became a major in our department and took his first media classes there.
2. Two years later, he transferred to the USC film school. But he still values the basics of filmmaking he learned while he was with us.
3. He made his first picture as an independent writer/producer a year later.

4. It was released the next June, and as a minor summer hit, it recaptured the initial investment plus a small profit.

5. Later that year, the film got several "honorable mentions" at film festivals, and he then signed a contract to make pictures for one of the largest film studios.

6. In the next few years, he turned out several moneymakers and prize winners.

7. Then, in 1982, he made his first blockbuster, *and* went on to win the Oscar for directing.

8. He is now one of the best-known writer/producers in Hollywood.

As a result of these facts, the committee backed the proposal and provided funding.

Organization by Stock Issues

The **stock–issues** organizational format is most useful for persuaders who are proposing a change in policy. The name "stock issues" refers to the fact that there are three universal (stock) issues that must be addressed when major policy changes are considered. They are sort of like the stock characters in melodrama: the villain, the hero, the heroine, the hero's helper, and so on. Any time there is a policy change under consideration the stock issues will be discussed. These stock issues are the **need for change**, a **plan to solve the need**, and your proof statements showing that the **plan meets the need** or removes the problem(s) you have raised and recognized. We frequently see stock issues used as content premises in the world of politics and business, and in other policy-making forums as well.

As a persuader attempting to bring about a change in policy, you need to begin by demonstrating a strong need for altering the status quo. You have the **burden of proof**. (As a receiver, you should also be aware of the stock issues. Any time you are the target of persuasion focused on policy change, identify which side of the debate is suggesting change. That will tell you who has the burden of proof.) Establish the need for change by citing symptoms of the problem. You should

research specific instances that demonstrate to the audience that they are suffering something, are losing something, or are in danger of losing it. In terms of the FUD model mentioned in Chapter 4, you need to create fear, uncertainty, and/or doubt. Tie the symptoms to a cause that, if removed and replaced, will solve the problem. For instance, you might state that there is a need to protect fans at university athletic events from the unpleasantness and health hazards of secondhand smoke. Next present a reasonable alternative to the status quo—the plan or the new policy. You are suggesting a ban on cigarette smoking within all the campus stadiums. Finally, show how that "plan meets need." One way to do this is to show that the plan has been successful in other places. Perhaps a no-smoking policy has been adopted at a neighboring venue with great success. Another way is to point to relevant historical events that prove your point, such as the repeal of Prohibition and the resulting positive effects on the economy in the Great Depression. This is arguing from precedent. Still another way is to use expert testimony to the effect that the plan for change has a reasonable chance of succeeding.

At each stage in the stock-issues organization, expect a rebuttal. In some cases, it will be openly stated, as in a policy debate within your student government. If you are giving a speech covering all three stock issues—need, plan, and plan meets need—anticipate such rebuttals and be ready to counter them. You might also short-circuit anticipated rebuttals by presenting a two-sided message stating the anticipated rebuttals and answering them then and there, depriving the opposition of an opportunity to impress the audience with its rebuttal.

Organization by the Motivated Sequence

Another organizational pattern, one that resembles the stock-issues approach, is the motivated sequence format, suggested by communication scholars Alan Monroe, Douglas Ehninger, and Bruce Gronbeck (1982). This format uses five steps to get persuadees to attend to the message, to feel a need to follow the persuader's advice, and, most importantly, to take action related to the advice. The motivated sequence is a good pattern to use in sales, recruitment, politics, and many other contexts.

The first step—the attention step—aims at capturing the attention of the audience. You could begin your message with a question, a startling statistic, or a fear appeal. Or you could use a quotation, a joke, or an anecdote—a brief incident or cliché that makes the point. A good example of the anecdote relates to the umpire who was asked if he called strikes and balls the way he saw them or the way they were. He responded, "They ain't nothing until I calls 'em." Other approaches are to make an important announcement in the first few moments of the message, begin with a narrative or story, or use a visual aid. The audience may process the attention gaining emotionally or in the peripheral channel of the ELM, but you want listeners to process more of your claims centrally.

In the second step of the motivated sequence, you try to convince the audience that they are losing something, are about to lose something, or could be gaining something but aren't. This is the need step (as in the stock issues approach), and it can be tied to the attention-getter.

Steps 3 and 4 are the visualization and satisfaction steps. Here you give examples, data, testimony, or some other form of proof to induce the audience to visualize what life will be like for them if they follow your advice—for instance, if they invest part of their student loan in student housing to build up a nest egg for the future. Or you might take the opposite tack pointing out what life will be like if they don't invest in the rooming house and instead graduate with the burden of student loans at government imposed high rates of interest. And they will graduate without the experience of having been in business for themselves, and, most importantly, without a nest egg to build their future on. Following this visualization step, you can then offer some way to satisfy the positive need or to avoid some negative consequences—for example, showing them how easy getting a student loan is and how little is needed for a down payment on income property.

Finally, the persuader needs to give a definite, specific, and realistic action step. It probably will do little to no good to ask audience members to alter their attitudes on the topic. Asking for change is different from providing good reasons for changing an attitude. And attitudes are fickle, and it is hard to know whether an audience has really changed. It is far better to give the audience specific things to do, such as flossing to avoid tooth decay, saving energy by turning down the thermostat, making real estate a wise investment, graduating with no debt and a handsome nest egg, or earning good grades. In one research study, people given a booklet with specific action steps to cut electricity consumption registered less use of electricity on their meters in the following two weeks than did those not given the specific action steps (Cantola, Syme, and Campbell, 1985). If you want the audience to write to their elected representative, it is a good idea to have a petition on hand that members can sign or to announce the phone number and email address of the legislator's local office and perhaps a sample email or note. After all, phoning or emailing is much easier than writing a letter, especially if you have to start by finding an address.

A related model for making a persuasive appeal is called the **AIDA** approach—short for attention, interest, desire, action. In this model, as in the motivated sequence, the first step is to capture the audience's attention using any of the tactics cited earlier. In the second step, the persuader's goal is to heighten the audience's interest in his or her topic or proposal. This might be done using a satisfaction or a visualization process, as in the motivated sequence. Or the persuader might tell how many persons have already tried the product or procedure and found it to be useful, or point out unforeseen problems with continuing the present practice.

Once attention and interest have been gained, the next task is to create a desire in persuadees to purchase the product or service, vote for the candidate, or follow the advice. In product-related persuasion, this usually is done by providing some product benefit or product promise. For example, Chrysler advertised built-in air bags for the front seat and side doors. The obvious benefit of this feature was that it could save lives in an accident. In its action step, Chrysler asked the customer to go to the nearest Chrysler dealer to learn more about the air bag and to take a test drive.

Rank's Desire-Stimulating Model

Hugh Rank (1982), whose intensify/downplay model was introduced in Chapter 1, has offered a simple four-part model for creating desire. His techniques are not a method of organizing a presentation. Instead, his techniques and examples relate to product promotion, but they can be used in other kinds of persuasion and in all of the forms of organization discussed in the preceding section. Rank says that persuaders can use four kinds of desire-stimulating tactics with this model (see Figure 12.2). First, they can promise the audience's security or protection by demonstrating that their advice will allow the audience to **keep a good** they already have but might be in danger of losing. He calls the opposite **getting a good**. Politicians frequently point out all the funding they have brought to their districts and then claim that their reelection will mean keeping this good. The other approach to motivating persons via various kinds of "good" is to point out that, although they are not going to lose something they already have, they are not taking advantage of an available good. It might be an inexpensive online account for buying and selling stocks and mutual funds or something as simple as Jell-O's no-bake cheesecake. If audience members have not tried the new good, telling them about it might motivate them to acquire it.

A third desire-stimulating tactic relates to **avoiding a bad** or preventing an uncomfortable symptoms or feelings. Persuaders promise that by following their advice people can either avoid a bad, get rid of a bad, or experience relief from it. A fourth approach is **getting rid of a bad**. For example, you probably would consider reducing credit card debt a good thing to do. Rank called these approaches the "prevention" and "relief" appeals. Advertisers often promise that their

FIGURE 12.2 Rank's model for ways to create desire in audiences.

products will prevent the embarrassments of bad breath, body odor, or dandruff or will provide relief from headaches, heartburn, flyaway hair, or acne. Such "scare and sell" approaches can also be used in non-product persuasion. For example, a persuader can promise that by passing the school bond referendum we can "avoid" losing athletic and music programs and other extracurricular activities. More recently, school districts have been reassuring students and parents that their school buildings are safe because of the presence of security devices and personnel. The idea is that these precautions will prevent killings such as occurred in Littleton, Colorado, in 1999 and demonstrate that the school board is responsible and credible.

FORMS OF PROOF

People want good reasons for changing their attitudes, beliefs, and decisions. The proofs required for taking action steps, even good ones, are even more demanding. Let's look at the forms of proof available to persuaders and discuss how you can use them to prompt audiences to change attitudes or take action.

Statistical Evidence

Sometimes the most effective proof or support is **statistical evidence**. For instance, an important goal of some car buyers is to get good gas mileage. In this case, EPA data will probably persuade them to choose a car model more effectively than will a salesperson's reassurances that the car is a real gas saver. Statistics persuade best when they are simple and easy to understand. When you decide to use statistics, make them clear, and provide a reference point for the numbers. For instance, if you are warning persuaders about the severity of the national debt, make it real to them. Tell them that interest on the debt amounts to $1800 per year for every man, woman, and child in the country and that the average family has to pay taxes from January 1 until March 15 to work off its share of the interest on the debt.

Narratives and Anecdotes

Earlier, we noted the power of drama, stories, and jokes. **Narratives** make examples come alive and make them easy to recall and relate to. The story of a person rising from rags to riches probably persuades more people than any set of statistics does. An effective narrative I use tells about the success of the Cabela family and its widely distributed outdoors catalog and several retail outlets. Mr. Cabela began in the 1950s by purchasing hand-tied trout flies from Japan at a fraction of a penny each. He advertised them in newspapers in trout country using an initial offer of "Five Hand-Tied Trout Flies— Only $.25!!! Free Shipping and Handling," and he got some orders. But the venture didn't really take off until he changed his ad to read, "Five Hand-tied Trout Flies—Absolutely Free!!! Shipping and Handling—Only $.25." The example persuaded several advertising clients to include the word "Free!!" in their ads. Earlier we gave an example of an anecdote with the umpire.

To discover the power of the narrative and statistical evidence, access InfoTrac College Edition, and type the word "persuasion" in the search engine. Select the persuasion/rhetoric periodicals option, and find the article titled "Persuasive Effects of Story and Statistical Evidence." There you will find the details of an interesting research study on the topic implied by the title.

Testimony

We usually suspect people who attempt to persuade us using only their own feelings or opinions. This is why the testimony of another person is valuable. Of course expert testimony is the best kind, but even unqualified testimony has influence. Testimonials act as a kind of social proof, to use Cialdini's term.

Visual Evidence

Walk into a department store where a salesperson or a videotape is demonstrating a food processor or a pasta machine, and you will see the power of visual evidence. The many television offers for various cooking gadgets also testify to the power of the demonstration. Ron Popeil has made millions of dollars using the technique, beginning with his Pocket Fisherman and continuing with his Ronco glass and bottle cutter and various other unlikely kitchen devices. Much of the information offered in the demonstration is processed in the peripheral channel of the ELM. Visual persuasion also can be used—and misused—in political news coverage and advertising (Simons, 2001). You probably have presentational skills that can use computerized visual aids like PowerPoint.

Of course, actual demonstrations of products are not always feasible, but persuaders can develop various kinds of visual evidence (such as graphs or charts) to help the audience understand the problem. Visuals should be large enough that everyone can see them. They should also be simple, because complex charts will only confuse the audience. For example, a student promoting a trip to Jamaica sponsored by the student association effectively used travel posters, large pictures of local cuisine, easily seen cutouts of sandy beaches, and other images of tropical life to motivate her audience.

Keep visual evidence unobtrusive. For instance, it may be better to use drawings of how to fend off an attacking dog than to bring your dog to class and have it pretend to attack you while you demonstrate how to fend it off. Plan to use graphs, charts, and informational handouts in your presentation, but hold the handouts until the end or they will get all of the audience's attention.

You will find three very interesting articles about the use of visual evidence by accessing InfoTrac College Edition and typing "persuasion" in the search engine. Select the persuasion/rhetoric periodicals option, and explore the articles you find there, as well as related subjects. Then enter the words "visual evidence" in the key word search engine. There you will find some fascinating articles on the uses and power of visual evidence.

Comparison and Contrast

Sometimes it is difficult to put problems in perspective. People tend to see issues from single viewpoints and judge them inaccurately. For instance, how big is the problem of disposing of your old cell phone batteries in landfills? How does it compare with the problem of the disposal of auto or flashlight batteries? It is a little hard to know, so persuaders should provide something with which to compare or contrast their point about cell phone battery disposal, like comparing the quantity of pollution from one discarded cell phone battery compared with one discarded flashlight battery. As another example, it doesn't help the audience much to know that OPEC decided to increase crude oil production by 550,000 barrels per day. It will be more meaningful to mention that this is an increase of 20 percent over previous production levels. Or tell your audience that the increased production will reduce the price of a gallon of gas by as much as 25¢—that will mean even more to them than the number of barrels of oil. Or compare the gas mileage of the new gasoline/electric-powered hybrids with that of other fuel-efficient car models.

BUILDING YOUR CREDIBILITY

All the evidence in the world, organized perfectly and delivered well, will not persuade if listeners do not trust the persuader. In matters such as persuading the boss to give us a raise, **credibility** is a key factor. What makes some people credible and others not? How can we build our own credibility before and during persuasion?

In Chapter 1 and elsewhere, we discussed the idea of credibility using Aristotle's ideas about the reputation of the speaker, the speaker's delivery during the speech, and the audience's response to the speaker's image. In more modern times, ethos or credibility has translated into several dimensions. We roughly equate reputation with the known expertise of the speaker. For example, when in research studies an identical speech is attributed to experts in some cases and to novices in others, the "expert's" speech is always rated as more persuasive than the "novice's." Effective delivery is related to sincerity, dynamism, and charisma. We don't believe speakers who cannot maintain eye contact, and tall speakers have more persuasive potential than do short ones. Further, speakers with an animated delivery persuade more effectively than do speakers who are frozen at the podium. Exciting language usually helps make the speech more credible, and a well-groomed speaker is more credible than an unkempt one. Most of these points seem obvious, yet they are overlooked daily by sales reps, politicians, spouses, teachers, students, and parents. Here are some examples from everyday life in which the elements of credibility can be used.

Trust

We trust people for many reasons. We trust them because they have been trustworthy in the past, because they have made direct eye contact, and because they have a calm voice. We also try to give off **trust** cues. We look at our persuadees directly; we try to sound sincere; we remind our audience of our past record for trust; and we refer to times when it would have been easy to break that trust. You might, for example, remind your boss of the many times when she was out of town and you could have slacked off but didn't. Or you might remind your parents of the many opportunities you had to party but studied instead. All these devices help build credibility.

Expertise

How do we know whether someone is a true expert on something? Generally, we look for **expertise** in past success at a task. If a person was a good treasurer for the fraternity or sorority, he or she will probably be a good treasurer for the student government. You can also signal expertise by being well prepared and by demonstrating knowledge about the topic. Being willing to engage in Q and A sessions when you have finished speaking communicates expertise. Even if you do not have direct expertise on a given topic, you can "borrow" it by referring to known experts in your presentation. It is always useful and ethical to refer to your sources' background so receivers can judge the credibility of their testimony.

Dynamism

Dynamism is an elusive quality. It is sometimes related to physical appearance, in that attractive people tend to hold attention better than less attractive persons. Attractiveness or charisma probably cannot be developed much. However, many people who aren't particularly attractive are nonetheless persuasive and dynamic. Dynamic speakers seem to take up a lot of psychic space—they have stage presence. You can project a dynamic image in several ways. One is to speak with authority—project your voice, maintain appropriate volume, and choose words that indicate certainty. Try speaking a little more rapidly than you do in normal conversations. Good posture and good grooming also signal dynamism, as do appropriate gestures, facial expressions, and eye contact.

WORDING YOUR MESSAGE

Stylistic speeches and exciting language choices persuade better than dull speeches. How do persuaders develop style in their presentations? What kinds of factors make some speeches, advertisements, or other persuasion memorable while other presentations are quickly forgotten or even ignored?

Varied Vocabulary

Most of us need to improve our vocabularies. You should try to rewrite your speeches using word variety to make them livelier, flashier, more dramatic, or more humorous. It helps to develop an interest in puns and other wordplay, as they can help you get the attention and earn the goodwill of your audience. Study the eloquence of great speakers from the past. Pay attention to the language used in government news releases, by politicians, and in advertisements. Try to learn a new word a day and use the thesaurus feature on your computer.

Figures of Speech, Alliteration, and Assonance

Enhance your style by using appropriate **figures of speech** at the right time. We discussed several in Chapters 5 and 6. Metaphors and similes help your audience visualize a point. The audience ties the information to the metaphorical structure and then remembers the information better as a result. Alliteration—the repetition of consonant sounds—and assonance—the repetition of vowel sounds—also enliven style. Both create a kind of internal rhythm in the message, which makes it more lively and memorable. We see both alliteration and assonance in "A portable phone system? Gee! No, GTE." Both devices help improve your style.

Vivid Language

Choose **vivid language** to catch your audience's interest. Although vividness can be overdone, it is more frequently overlooked in favor of dull and uninteresting language. Which of the following is more vivid?

> I'm offended by your representation of lutefisk. It is not rubbery!

Lutefisk may be "a rubbery and repulsive ethnic dish" to the socially deprived, but to the properly initiated, it is the nearest thing to ambrosia this earth has ever produced.

Vivid and colorful language helps make a persuasive presentation memorable and effective. Developing your vocabulary arms you with more vivid and persuasive language. Familiarize yourself with famous quotations, which you can find by a subject search on any Internet search engine. Just enter the words "famous quotations" and you will find what you're looking for. There are also websites dedicated to listing quotations by category.

Concise Language

Go over your presentation and pretend you are paying 50 cents per word to send it by telegraph. Then see how much excess baggage you can cut. You can come up with more **concise language** that way. Straightforward statements are usually most effective. Make your major point as a concise assertion or frame it in a provoking question. Then follow up with elaboration. If you try to say everything in the opening sentence, you will confuse your audience. The use of concise language also will help build your credibility and will improve the organization of your presentation.

Parallel Structure

Parallel structure uses similar or even identical wording or sentence structure to make a presentation memorable. For example, in a speech to the American Legion, former president Bill Clinton once said, "I am not the only American whose life has been made better by your continuing service here at home. From baseball to Boy Scouts; from keeping veterans hospitals open to keeping kids off drugs; from addressing homelessness to preventing child abuse to instilling a deep sense of patriotism

into still another generation of Americans, a grateful nation owes you a debt of gratitude." His repeated use of the "from . . . to . . ." format provides parallel structure and symmetry in the speech. The idea behind parallel structure is to build audience expectations. For example Cicero once said, "Ask not what your country can do for you: rather ask what you can do for your country." President John Kennedy used almost exactly the same words in his inaugural speech in 1960.

Imagery

Imagery appeals to our senses. Perhaps you can't bring the smell, taste, touch, sight, or sound of something to the audience, but you can use words that conjure up sensuous memories. It might be of a "tall, cool glass of chilled beer dripping with beads of perspiration" or the "fragrant smell of Mom's pot roast, ready to fall apart, with its juices making a savory gravy that starts your mouth watering." A famous salesman once said "Don't try to sell the steak; sell the sizzle." Think about the sensory experiences your audience has had that you can evoke. A good way to develop this skill is to take a given product and try to restate its appeals in terms of the various senses. For instance, Campbell's soups are "Mmm, Mmm, Good." How might they be described using the other senses?

Humor

The use of **humor** in persuasion is an obvious stylistic asset if handled properly, and can build credibility as well. But a word of warning is necessary here: If a persuader uses humor that is inappropriate, in bad taste, or just plain unfunny, it will likely backfire. If you are going to use humor in your persuasion, test it out with friends and relatives. How can you develop humorous examples, comparisons, anecdotes, and stories? People who regularly engage in public speaking usually have a ready supply of humorous material with which to embellish their speeches. They develop the humorous aspects as they work up other materials for their speeches. Humor sometimes relies on the breaking

FIGURE 12.3 The trapeze artists seen in the cartoon face broken expectation, which accounts for the humor in the cartoon, together with the surprised looks on their faces.
SOURCE: Used with permission of Doug Walker.

of expectations as can be seen in Figure 12.3. If you can never remember a story or joke, keep a file of stories or jokes or just punch lines. When you need the material, the file will trigger your memory. Late night television can provide you with humorous examples, as can your daily newspaper, *Reader's Digest*, and friends who frequently tell jokes. Don't forget the Internet. Just enter your subject and the word "humor," and have some fun while building a successful and entertaining presentation. You can also use visual humor such as cartoons, perhaps by using PowerPoint.

DELIVERING YOUR MESSAGE

Usually, we think of delivery as relating just to the source or speaker. But other factors can affect the delivery of your message, including the channel and the means of audience involvement. Persuaders often overlook these. In the following section, we will look at all these factors.

The Persuader

Among the factors that persuaders adjust before and during delivery are their posture, eye contact, body movement and gesture, articulation, dress, grooming, and vocal quality. Other factors under the speaker's control are the use of visual aids and other nonverbal cues. Some persuaders are so nervous that they cannot stop pacing back and forth. And when they do stop, they stand ramrod stiff, looking

as if they might freeze into statues. Other speakers are so relaxed that they seem uninterested in their own messages. They slouch over the podium or slide down into their chairs during a meeting. What does the posture of the speaker in Figure 12.4 suggest?

Clearly, posture can signal the audience that you are either nervous or too relaxed. Observe persuaders in differing contexts—interviews, speeches, arguments—and you will see that the effective ones avoid both extremes. The ideal posture lies somewhere in between. You should be alert and erect, and your shoulders should not tense or slump. Your posture should communicate confidence.

You will be more believable if you maintain eye contact with your audience. You don't need to look at everyone individually (unless you are speaking to only one person). Instead, look at various areas in the room. Politicians look directly into the TV camera and so seem to make eye contact with each viewer. In meetings, establish eye contact with as many participants as possible.

Body movement and gestures liven up a speech, as long as they don't distract. Using gestures during a speech keeps audience attention. However, it is a mistake to over-rehearse gestures, body movements, and facial expressions. These nonverbal elements in delivery must appear natural, not staged, to have a positive effect. We all use gestures every day without thinking about them. Let your natural impulses guide you in your use of gestures in formal and interpersonal exchanges. Nothing can add more to your message than a

FIGURE 12.4 Posture is important in giving a persuasive message. Is this speaker's posture appropriate for the formal situation seen here?

natural gesture, movement, or facial expression (Scheflen, 1964).

Articulation and vocal quality also affect your delivery. Everyone has heard people who pronounce words incorrectly; as a result, the audience focuses on the error and not on the message. Successful persuaders work on articulation, pronunciation, and vocal quality. Listening to yourself on tape will help you pinpoint your mistakes and focus on your vocal quality. Some persons, especially females, think that a breathy or "thin" voice makes them sound sexier, but just the opposite is true. If you are interested in persuading others, spend some time working on your voice and your articulation.

The Channel

Choosing the correct channel for sending your message is another key element in delivery. In one rural political campaign for the U.S. House of Representatives on which I worked, the candidates put most of their money into billboard space—which was rather surprising in this media age. In this case, however, the candidate's district was large, stretching nearly half the length of the state, and no single TV network reached all of it. Using

TV would have meant having to pay a triple load to get a single message across. But because the district was so large, all residents had to drive to shop, do business, socialize, worship, and farm. Thus, the billboard was the one channel that could touch nearly all voters in the district.

Recent presidents have returned to using radio for regular weekly persuasive talks. Why is radio such an appropriate channel for political persuasion? It is estimated that Americans listen to the radio an average of four hours a day, and more than half listen at work, especially females (Russell & Lane, 1999). People also listen to the radio while they are doing something else—driving, reading, commuting, exercising, and so on. By choosing the relatively inexpensive medium of daytime radio, politicians can reach people they otherwise might not, and at a reasonable price. Cable television has some of the same advantages of reach and low cost.

On a more personal level, ask yourself what is the best way to inform your boss that you will look for another job if you don't get a raise or promotion. Perhaps tapping the grapevine might be best, or sending a straightforward memo, or asking her to be a reference so she will not get an

---

B O X 12.2 **Honoring Diversity in Public Speaking**

Lenora Billings-Harris is an internationally known public speaker working on diversity issues with Fortune 500 companies, and she offers the following advice for public speakers wanting to be diversity conscious. First, select your language carefully. One ill-chosen word can undo you in an instant. For example, saying "Hey guys…" in a mixed gender group can offend some. Pointing to your "flip chart" can offend any Filipinos in the audience—refer to your easel instead. Research your audience first—who will be there? Be careful about using humor even if it is self-deprecating. Whenever possible use people's names, especially during question and answer sessions; and don't refer to someone as "the tall guy in the back." If you do refer to ethnicity make sure that you've got the right word. Some Latinos resent being referred to as "Hispanic" since that term groups together persons from Cuba, Mexico, Latin and South America, and Puerto Rico. (The word was invented by the U.S. Census Bureau more than 35 years ago to categorize people who spoke only Spanish.) One way around this potential trap is to use the words "Americans of (blank) heritage." The same goes for the word "Oriental," which refers to rugs, a certain cusine, and certain styles of furniture. When speaking of people, use the adjective "Asian." If a member of the audience uses a potentially insensitive word, don't call attention to it in public unless it is truly offensive; instead talk to the person privately after the presentation. If the word is truly offensive, point that out by saying something like, "Most persons consider that usage offensive and using it reduces your credibility." Billings-Harris notes some potentially offensive usages and offers acceptable alternatives. Use "outcasts" instead of "black sheep." Refer to occupations in nongendered ways—"postal workers" not "postmen." Can you think of other examples of embracing diversity in your public speaking? For further study, go to @www.sideroad.com/PublicSpeaking/politicalcorrectness, and explore not only the work of Billings-Harris but the many interesting links on public speaking.

---

out-of-the-blue inquiry about you from another firm. In general, start by listing all the potential channels that could be used to send your message. Then try to match them with your audience. If your audience uses a particular channel over others, then that is probably a good one to use.

Sometimes, persuaders encourage audience participation, which can increase audience energy and activity. Get your audience involved by asking direct questions and addressing people by name. Or leave a sentence incomplete and let listeners finish it. One speaker got audience involvement right away by asking everyone to stand up before he even began his speech. He then asked them to become aware of the muscles they were using in their feet, ankles, calves, and thighs at that moment and tied this awareness to his topic—the need to develop communication awareness on the job. One word of caution: Don't distribute any printed material until the end of the speech. Audiences start reading right away, and you will lose them.

COMMON TACTICS OF PERSUASION

There are some persuasive tactics that are used frequently and even are emphasized in public speaking and sales short courses. Let's consider some of the more common ones.

The Foot in the Door or Door in the Face

Robert Cialdini (2001) describes several persuasive tactics, including the foot-in-the-door and the door-in-the face techniques. The **foot-in-the-door** technique relies on getting a potential customer, joiner, donor, or convert to make a small initial commitment that starts what will become a long-term relationship resulting in ever larger sales, contributions, and commitments. To illustrate, some time ago I signed a protest petition from the Citizens' Utility Board (CUB), which promised to use the petition to prevent price increases by Illinois utilities—Commonwealth Edison, Ameritech phone services, and the gas company, for example. Soon after, I received a newsletter explaining that CUB had stopped one of the utilities from instituting a 15 percent price increase. But the battle was not over, because the utility was appealing. Could I donate $50, $25, or even $10 to help carry on the fight. I donated $10. Next, a letter from CUB informed me of another victory, but warned that the other utilities were suing CUB, and asked that I become a full-fledged dues-paying member of the organization for only $25. My signature on the petition was merely a foot in the door, and I continue to receive requests for donations.

In the retail field, this technique might mean getting a prospective retailer to agree to carry one item in a product line. That commitment becomes the foot in the door to the retailer's finally agreeing to carry the entire product line. As Cialdini puts it, "You can use small commitments to manipulate a person's self-image; you can turn citizens into 'public servants,' prospects into 'customers,' prisoners into 'collaborators'" (p. 67). Cialdini relates how the same technique is used by the highly successful Amway Corporation. Staff members are asked to set specific sales goals and then write them down: "There is something magical about writing things down. So set a goal and write it down. When you reach that goal, set another and write that down. You'll be off and running" (p. 71). The written commitment somehow translates into motivation and action.

The **door-in-the-face** tactic is what a persuader uses when turned down on a request for a significant commitment, and then settles for an initial small commitment or engages in what Cialdini calls the **rejection-then-retreat** strategy. In other words, if a salesperson tries to get the prospect to go for the top-of-the-line or "loaded" version of the brand but is rejected, he or she can always retreat by offering a stripped-down version of the brand. Cialdini attributes the effectiveness of this strategy to feelings of responsibility and satisfaction on the part of customers, joiners, or donors. By agreeing to the lower commitment, they can feel as if they are in control of the

situation and have "dictated" the deal. This satisfaction makes them happier with their decisions. A related persuasive approach is to "sell up" after retreating to a position of concession. Thus, once you've signed the contract to buy the new car, a good salesperson will offer you the extras—the undercoating and soundproofing, the extended warranty, the upholstery fabric protection, and so on.

Others have suggested similar tactics using somewhat different terms. The following are some tactics suggested by Drs. William Howell and Ernest Bormann (1988). They may overlap with some of the other techniques discussed previously. Examine your world of persuasion for examples of these tactics in action.

The Yes-Yes Technique

A common tactic in sales and other persuasive appeals is called **yes-yes**. The source attempts to get the target group or person to respond positively to several parts of the appeal, withholding the key request until last. Having agreed to most parts of the appeal, the persuadee is likely to say yes to the key and final request. For example, suppose you are trying to sell a lawn service. You might ask the homeowner, "You would like to have a beautiful lawn, wouldn't you?" The answer is going to be yes. Then you ask, "And you'd like to get rid of the weeds?" Another yes is likely. "And wouldn't it be nice if these things could be effort free?" A yes answer is likely again. Now that the homeowner has accepted all your points in favor of the service, it is nearly impossible to respond with a no to "Then you'll want to sign up for our lawn service, won't you?" By accepting the yes pattern, the buyer accedes to your final request.

The same technique is useful in a meeting in which a persuader gets the participants to agree to all but the final point in favor of, say, a change in work schedules. They agree that flexibility is good, that more free time for workers is good, and so on. They are then likely to agree that the change is a good one.

The Tactic of Asking Not "If" but "Which"

It is easier to make a choice between two alternatives than from among many. This is the strategy behind the **"don't ask if, ask which"** persuasive tactic. I learned as a parent of young children that the worst thing to ask on Saturday mornings was, "What would you like Dad to make for breakfast today?" It was better to say, "Which would you like for breakfast today—Dad's blueberry pancakes or Dad's blueberry coffee-cake?" The same thing applies in persuasion. Don't ask your audience to choose from too many options; ask them to choose from only a few or only two—"Would you rather have us undercoat your new car, or do you want to take it elsewhere?" or "Would you rather meet on your promotion this week or next?" or "Do you want guns or butter?" Although this tactic can be manipulative, and hence can be used unethically, it has the distinct advantage and value of forcing some decision or action when buyers, voters, or others are stubbornly trying to avoid it.

A Question for a Question

A tactic some people use to throw others off guard is to respond to a request with a question. For example, if asked, "Wouldn't you like to sign up for our lawn service," they say, "Why do you think I would want to do that?" or "What gave you that idea?" You can use this tactic, too. Responding with a question, or asking the person to repeat or elaborate on the question, also gives you time to think. **Answering a question with a question** puts the ball back in the other person's court. People who question you sometimes are trying to discredit or annoy you. Turn the tables—answer with another question. Suppose a prospect for advertising services asks, "Who else has used your services? Maybe I could check with them before deciding to go with your agency." A good response is, "I can bring you written testimonials about how successful we are in generating qualified leads. Or I can give you names and phone numbers for local businesses that might be slightly different than yours, and you can call. Or I can do both. Which would you prefer?"

The Partial Commitment

The **partial commitment** tactic resembles the door-in-the-face or rejection-then-retreat strategy but uses acts instead of words to lead the prospect to the final request. Once you are partially committed, you are a good prospect for full commitment. Evangelists often close their pitches by asking people in the tent or auditorium to bow their heads and close their eyes for prayer. This gets a partial commitment from the audience. The preacher then asks the Lord to enter the hearts of all and asks those who want God to come into their lives to raise their hands. The final request may then be, "Those of you with your hands up come to the front and be saved."

We see this tactic elsewhere, too. Trying a sample of a product represents a partial commitment, as does clipping a coupon. The smart auto salesperson won't ask you to sign a sales agreement right off the bat. Instead, he or she will suggest that you look around and see whether you find anything that appeals to you and then suggests that you take it for a test drive. Merely by looking around, you are partially committing to the sales pitch, and the test drive is usually the clincher.

Of course, other kinds of commitment are used to persuade. When a politician asks you to sign a petition to put his or her name on the ballot, your signature is a form of partial commitment to that politician. A favorite way to generate "qualified leads" in the marketing of some products is to run a sweepstakes. Anyone who submits an entry for the free version of the product has already made a partial commitment to buy it and thus is a good sales lead to follow up.

Planting

Memory responds best, it seems, to messages that have sensory data as raw material. The tactic of **planting** uses one or more of the five senses to open a channel to the audience's memory of how they experienced the product, idea, or candidate. This kind of memory is almost certainly processed in the peripheral information-processing channel.

Restaurant ads often appeal to several senses, and not just the sense of taste. They describe the "crisp and crunchy garden salad" to appeal to the sense of touch. They offer "sizzling hot steaks seared on a grill" to appeal to the sense of hearing. They describe the "thick red tomato sauce" to appeal to the sense of vision and use the words "a steaming fragrance of garlic and spices" to appeal to the sense of smell.

In a classic case of invoking the sense of touch in an ad campaign, Charmin was successfully marketed as an uncommonly soft toilet tissue in TV ads because the grocer, a Mr. Whipple, was always caught squeezing the packages when he thought no one was looking. An ad for an automobile may have someone slam the door so audience members hear the solid "thunk" and mentally compare it with experiential memories of the rattles of their own five-year-old cars. Tie persuasion to senses via planting, and the audience will recall your message better and longer.

The IOU

Sometimes called the reciprocity tactic, the **IOU technique** gets listeners to feel they owe you something. For instance, the insurance salesperson spends several hours doing a complex assets-and-debts analysis to prove to the prospect that he or she needs more insurance. The sales rep then spends several more hours explaining the figures to the spouse, perhaps taking the couple out to lunch or dinner. By the end of all the special treatment, the couple may feel that they really ought to buy something even though they may not need it or cannot afford it. They respond to the obligation—the IOU—that was created by the salesperson's effort.

After observing how reciprocity works in various cultures, Cialdini (2001) notes that the need to reciprocate—the IOU—transcends "great cultural differences, long distances, acute famine, many years, and self interest" (p. 21). Persuaders find this tactic useful when it is hard to make a first contact with buyers, voters, or joiners. You can place your audience in your debt by giving them free samples or offers of help. As a listener, you may want to remember that "There's no such thing as a free lunch."

REVIEW AND CONCLUSION

We all have to persuade at some point. To be effective, we need to analyze the audience before planning how our format will affect the message. We must develop our forms of support and our use of language as we think about which will be most persuasive. We must also control factors in delivery. We need to use source factors, such as posture, eye contact, and dress. Channel factors are subject to our control as well. Receiver factors can be used to get the target group involved in its own persuasion. As you are called on to persuade, use these skills in preparing. Rely on the audience analysis and demographics that the receiver-oriented approach teaches—listen to your audience. Get messages out of them, not into them.

KEY TERMS

After reading this chapter you should be able to identify, explain, and give an example of the following key terms.

audience analysis	topic format	stock-issues format	stock-issues
demographics	space format	motivated sequence format	need for change
audience needs	chronological format		plan to solve the need

plan meets the need

burden of proof

motivated sequence format

AIDA

keep a good

get a good

avoid a bad

get rid of a bad

statistical evidence

narratives

testimony

visual evidence

comparison and contrast

credibility

trust

expertise

dynamism

figures of speech

vivid language

concise language

parallel structure

imagery

humor

foot-in-the-door

door-in-the-face

rejection-then-retreat

yes-yes

"don't ask if, ask which"

answering a question with a question

partial commitment

planting

IOU technique

APPLICATION OF ETHICS

A fellow student in your public speaking class gives a speech on the dangers to freedom of speech posed by renewing The Patriot Act. After listening to the speech, you realize that your classmate has made inaccurate claims based on inadequate research. Apparently the rest of your classmates are enthusiastic about her speech. You also know that she has stage fright and just getting through the speech has been a victory for her. There is a question and answer period where you could point out her inaccuracies. Should you remain silent, hoping that no harm will come to the class from hearing the speech? Or should you approach her privately and tell her that her claims are inaccurate and her research is inadequate? Or should you inform the instructor about the inaccuracies and research shortcomings?

QUESTIONS FOR FURTHER THOUGHT

1. What demographic clusters can you identify for the people in your class? In your dorm? In a club? Elsewhere?

2. What is a task-oriented message? Give examples from ads in which persuaders used this technique effectively. Give other examples from ads in which they failed.

3. What are the forms of organization? How do they differ from the forms of support? What might be other ways to organize a message?

4. What is AIDA, and how does it differ from the motivated sequence?

5. What are Rank's desire-building tactics? How do they work?

6. What are the factors that make up a speaker's credibility? Give examples of people who have them. Find ads that rely on each factor.

7. Where does humor fit into the persuasion process? Give examples of sources that use humor. Does it relate to the audience? How?

8. How can a persuader get his or her audience more involved? What are some examples you have seen or heard recently?

9. What is the difference between the forms of proof discussed here and those discussed in Chapter 8?

10. How does "planting" work? What about "getting an IOU"?

 For online activities, go to the *Persuasion* book companion website at http://communication.wadsworth.com/larson11.

13

Modern Media and Persuasion

LEARNING GOALS

After reading this chapter, you should be able to:

1. Appreciate societal changes that followed the introduction of the spoken, written, printed, electronic, and interactive words.

2. Show how the interactive word has already begun to change global society.

3. Explain the resonance principle and how it relates to Schwartz's theory of evoked recall.

4. Explain and give examples of what Schwartz means by "experiential meaning."

5. Explain Marshall McLuhan's concepts of hot and cool media.

6. Explain and give examples of the various reasons people use media, as discussed in uses and gratifications theory.

7. Demonstrate familiarity with the wide variety of information available on the Internet.

8. Apply ethical standards to Internet communication.

Since the development of spoken language, other media of communication have developed, and each of them has made communication and hence persuasion easier and more far reaching. Each of these media innovations has changed the scale and pace of human life.

MEDIA INNOVATIONS

Five major communication innovations, each tied to the development of a new medium or technology, have shaped and changed the world and the way we see it. These innovations or technologies are: (1) the spoken word, (2) the written word, (3) the printed word, (4) the electronic word, and (5) the interactive word.

The Spoken Word

The first communication innovation in human history was the ability to speak and to symbolize. As Lederer pointed out in Chapter 5, prior to language we were not truly human beings. We sense the reverence for the spoken word in many avenues of human activity. In religion, for instance, the Judeo-Christian story of the creation in the book of Genesis indicates that each creative act was accomplished by God speaking (e.g., "And God said 'Let there be light, and there was light—the

first night and the first day.'" In our daily social life, this reverent attitude toward the **spoken word** continues. We must be sworn in to testify, or to address the court, and the judge must speak the sentence before the convicted person can be taken to prison. We rely "on a person's word," actions "speak for themselves," and we look for "the final word" on various issues. We swear in political officials with the spoken word, and we require new citizens to take a spoken oath of loyalty.

The spoken word permitted humans to become social animals and to work together for the common good. It allowed one generation to pass down the history and knowledge of the tribe in myths, ballads, or legends, and thus progress could occur. The wheel didn't have to be reinvented each generation. The spoken word led to the organization of information that could be shared by everyone. In oral/aural cultures, information or knowledge is most fully held by the old; thus, age is valued and honored. Among the Lakota, every newly married couple was given an Old One to live in the couple's tepee for tending fires, comforting the babies, and giving advice. This helped the couple, and provided the Old One with a home. There were no bag ladies among the Lakota.

The spoken word still exists, of course, but not in the same way it did in an oral/aural world (Ong, 1982). In the oral/aural culture—and even after—the spoken word was an experience, an event. It occupied time, not space. It was ephemeral—the beginning of the word was gone before its end was uttered. Its only permanence was in the human mind and memory, and people re-experienced it only by re-uttering it.

The Written Word

The next major communication innovation was the development of the phonetic alphabet, which unlike pictographs is tied to speech sounds. With this alphabet, people could collect knowledge and store it. Advances of various kinds could be based on these stored records of what others had tried to do and how. The **written word** allowed societies to develop complex legal systems and to assign or deed land and other possessions. Unlike knowledge stored in the spoken word, information in writing can be recalled precisely.

For centuries, however, few people could read or write, and only the rich could afford scribes. Knowledge was power and could be obtained and centralized by those who controlled the written word—kings, emperors, feudal lords, and church leaders. Information became individual property that could be owned and not necessarily shared. The great ancient libraries were the repositories of society's knowledge and information, but they didn't loan out books. That would have to wait until Benjamin Franklin invented the lending library. So, not everyone had access to the gathered knowledge or information, and without it the average person remained ignorant and at the bottom of the social order.

Once writing made the ownership of knowledge possible in Europe, Asia, and elsewhere, the concept of ownership was applied to other property—land, cattle, horses, jewelry, and buildings. No such concept existed in the oral/aural cultures of Native Americans, to whom written claims to land treaties were "worthless scraps of paper." Where the spoken word took up time, the written word took up space, was not ephemeral, and lasted across generations (Ong, 1967). This permanence made people rely on written records for the "last word" on an issue. Indeed, the written word came

to be thought of as more trustworthy than the spoken word, and even those who couldn't read wanted to see things in writing before they would believe them. As Ong (1967) observed:

> Ancient Hebrews and Christians knew not only the spoken word but the alphabet as well.... But for them and all men of early times, the word, even when written, was much closer to the spoken word than it normally is for . . . technological man. Today we have often to labor to regain the awareness that the word is still always at root the spoken word. Early man had no such problem: he felt the word, even when written, as primarily an event in sound." (p. ix)

The Printed Word

The third communication innovation was Johannes Gutenberg's moveable type and the printing press in the late 1400s. This made knowledge less expensive, more portable, and available to more persons. The effects of spreading the power of the **printed word** to average people were immense, beginning with more widespread literacy and eventually making possible such intellectual revolutions in Europe as the Renaissance and the Reformation. Because information could be spread and shared fairly inexpensively, the "New Science" developed rapidly. Scientists could read about one another's work and experiments and build on what others had done. The same phenomenon occurred in other areas such as music, philosophy, commerce, and religion. People could read the writings of Martin Luther, and his objections to the Church, and they were printed and distributed widely. The notions of serfdom were superseded by the idea of individual ownership of land or a business.

Governments weren't unaware of this diffusion of knowledge. Soon most of them set up censorship policies to help them control the spread of information. Not until John Peter Zenger was tried for sedition for printing a tract criticizing a British colonial governor did the notion of freedom of the press come into being. Curiously, Zenger was

I TAPE TV SHOWS AND WATCH THEM ON FAST-FORWARD----IT'S A FORM OF TRASH COMPACTING.

THAVES 10-13

FIGURE 13.1 Certain aspects of modern electronic media are causes of concern, as this cartoon demonstrates.

SOURCE: *Frank and Ernest.* © United Feature Syndicate, Inc. Used with permission.

tried not for *writing* the criticism but for *printing* it. The British government held all printers responsible for what they published, in effect making every printer an unofficial censor.

Like the power of the spoken word, the power of the printed word has diminished. Although the number of newspapers published in the United States has risen since the advent of television, readership of newspapers and newsmagazines is down. More than 30 percent of the U.S. population is functionally illiterate, meaning that they can't read such simple things as menus, directions for operating appliances, labels, and street signs; in the nineteenth century the literacy rate was 90 percent (Kaplan, Wingert, and Chideya, 1993). Some estimates indicate that even those who do read newspapers devote only about eight minutes a day to them. The rate of book reading in the United States is less than one-third of a book per year per person, and that includes students.

Still, the printed word brought about a revolution in many areas of human accomplishment. Musical scores, scientific theories, and artistic images could be printed cheaply and exchanged among scientists, composers, and artists across national boundaries, and those who read or saw these items learned from one another's works. In terms of persuasion, the printed word gave us widespread literacy, which greatly influenced the way people formulated and shared their thoughts. Literacy in the Western world led to a new view of humans as unique individuals and led to great discoveries, and inventions in Europe and America also resulted from shared knowledge via print. Literacy even extended childhood by making protracted formal education both necessary and possible. Prior to the printed word, children were considered to be just like adults and were sent to work in the coal mines, city streets, or farm fields to work like the grown-ups.

The Electronic Word

The **electronic word** came into being in 1844 with the invention of the telegraph. Then, in 1876, came the telephone, transforming the spoken word into electronic impulses, and the radio, which transformed spoken words into electronically produced sound waves using Morse code to spell out words.

It is possible to get a glimmering of the effect these inventions had. While the Pony Express got a message across the country in just ten days, people could telegraph the message in minutes. In a sense, the electronic word wiped out not only space but time as well. People now could learn almost immediately of election results, sports events, catastrophes, stock prices, and joyous and sad family events. Other channels of the electronic word—television, computers, video games, cell phones, VCRs, DVDs, and CDs—are now bringing and undergoing change. Some critics claim the explosion of electronic media adversely affects us, and will soon make us incapable of interacting with others on any level. People are also concerned about the amount of television watched by the average U.S. child—and adult (see Figure 13.1).

We live in a world in which electronic and print messages literally surround us—on billboards and in newsletters, magazines, catalogs, signs on shopping carts, Internet banners, unwanted spam and pop-ups, telemarketing, electronic kiosks in airport terminals, demonstration videos in supermarkets, and so on. Despite even newer technologies like TiVo or iPod that allow viewers to bypass ads, electronic mass media are still the most effective channels to persuade us to buy products, to vote, and to take up causes. One reason is that they are inherently oral/aural in nature. That is, in the same way that spoken words are ephemeral or fleeting, electronic signals or images are also fleeting (unless we choose to record them). We experience them more than we logically think them through, and we probably process them in the peripheral channel of the ELM and fail to critically investigate them.

The Interactive Electronic Word

With interactive electronic media, the receiver gets into the act much more than with earlier media. We are just beginning to deal with this channel. To date, the electronic word has affected us mostly as receivers—we consume more of these media than we produce. Few of us produce television messages, but all of us consume them. With interactive electronic media, however, we become both producers and consumers of messages—the **interactive word**. Consider virtual reality technology, for example. Surgeons now conduct virtual operations for training purposes. Then robotic laser scalpels are programmed, using the virtual operation, to perform the actual one. Virtual reality might replace the showroom floor or retail outlet. Charles Madigan (1993), describes a hypothetical virtual purchase this way:

> A customer in his or her own living room facing a bigger-than-life fully digitized television screen will say, 'Shop Ralph Lauren.' After a pause of only a few seconds, the image of Ralph Lauren will come, smiling to life on the screen.... Ralph will ask for some particulars.... Perhaps price will be discussed.... It won't really be Ralph Lauren.... More accurately, it will be virtual Ralph having a virtual conversation (p. 14).

Already you can try on items of clothing virtually and alter their color schemes. Other possible uses for virtual reality technology include virtual golf lessons taught by a virtual Tiger Woods or virtual warfare. Most of the air sorties flown in operations Desert Storm and Iraqi Freedom were rehearsed using virtual reality technology. The military is particularly interested in this interactive media, as is the pornography industry.

If you think these examples of the potential of virtual reality technology seem farfetched, go to InfoTrac College Edition, and type the words "virtual reality" in the subject search engine. Explore just a few of the nearly one thousand periodical titles listed there. Also go to some of the commercial applications listed there. The listings will give you locations where you can actually experience it. Report back to your class what you have discovered.

According to Stewart Brand's (1987) description, the print, film, and computer industries realized 20 years ago that phenomenal changes in communication technology were imminent and that the ability to develop them effectively and prudently was far improved by pooling their resources. So the Media Lab at MIT sought out the brightest and best media researchers and asked them to literally invent the future in the various communications industries. The three industries were already beginning to converge before The Media Lab was instituted, as shown in Figure 13.2. Some examples of this convergence or overlapping of media include print that is computer typeset and enhanced visually by digital video technology, or computer-generated and produced video graphics and electronic mail, faxes, and digital audio. Even some print ads contain a chip that plays music. Some observers foresee a much broader convergence of the three technologies, which will look more like Figure 13.3.

Already the predicted changes exceed the wildest dreams of even a decade ago. A brief example demonstrates this point. Brand predicted, "Twenty years from now your TV set will probably

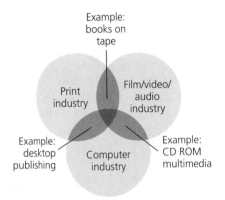

FIGURE 13.2 The convergence of the print, film/video/audio, and computer industries and technology in the 1990s.

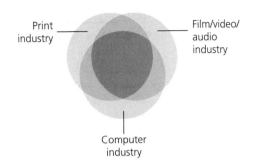

FIGURE 13.3 The convergence of the print, film/video/audio, and computer industries and technology today and in the future.

have 50 megabytes of random access memory and run at 40 to 50 MIPS [millions of information pieces per second]. It'll basically be a Cray computer" (Brand, 1987, pp. 77–78). While we're not there yet, we have come very far and are closing in on Brand's predictions.

The work of two important media theorists, Tony Schwartz and Marshall McLuhan, can help us understand the experiential nature of the current electronic and interactive technology and can begin to prepare us for the developments we will encounter in the coming decades.

To find out how Hollywood is taking to the new interactive electronic word, access InfoTrac College Edition, and enter the words "media innovations" in the search engine. Find the article titled "Traffic Jam" by Laura Stevens.

SCHWARTZ'S PERSPECTIVES ON MEDIA USE

The ideas in Tony Schwartz's book *The Responsive Chord* (1973) have been used by sources ranging from presidential media staff to firms and ad agencies selling everything from baby powder to booze.

Since its publication, Schwartz has consulted and still consults with politicians, industry, the mass media, and the government. Schwartz offers two competing models for explaining the way media work to persuade: (1) the **evoked recall**, or resonance, model and (2) the transportation, or teaching, model. Schwartz favors the first approach and offers reasons.

Resonance and Experiential Meaning

The evoked recall model rests on the **resonance principle**, which is defined as using messages or message elements that cue out meanings that receivers already have in their conscious or unconscious minds. This leads to a harmony or resonance between source, message, and receiver. The basic idea is that it is better to get a message out of receivers than to try to put one into them. In other words, it relies on the set of experiences and memories that people already have stored inside their heads. This set of past experiences can be cued to produce what Schwartz called **experiential meaning** or the resonance principle. It's as if the receiver says, "I've been there," after getting the message, and thus the reference to the stored experience resonates with the audience in the same way that notes of music resonate or harmonize with one another.

Using this approach, persuaders might address the problems people have, such as a stalled car.

BOX 13.1 Interactive Media and Shopping

 Most of us already shop for some things online, such as books and clothing, but what about an interactive site with a mega-menu that tops most major department stores? Go to www.shopping.com and surf through the multitude of options there, ranging from 11,000 baseball cards with price comparisons from over 20 sources or an online college degree in interactive media or interactive branding. Enter whatever you are shopping for at the top of the page and select from the categories in the next space. Click the "find" button and explore the interactive mega-market, which could run to thousands of options. What might sites like this do to traditional in-store, television, and catalog shopping? How might a political candidate use a similar site to compare positions on various issues, to solicit voter input, or to raise money?

The potential buyer of a AAA membership knows what a stalled auto is like, and the source can use that experience to build a persuasive message around those feelings. Actors in the ad might show frustration, signaling the anxiety motorists have felt when they knew a stall would make them miss the commuter train and prevent them from accomplishing important things at work. The music or score can heighten those fears. The voice-over might then say soothingly, "When you've got to be there, Triple A gets you there." Schwartz observed that most experiential meaning is not cued symbolically (with words) because it is not stored in words. Instead, it is stored as a physiological feeling or a sense of ease or uneasiness. We all know what it feels like to be embarrassed, and our recollection of that can be cued out of us. The same is true for other emotions, such as those discussed in Chapter 7. The surest way to cue feelings out of receivers is via dramatic enactment. The source's message dramatizes the feeling in the receiver's head through music, color, sound effects, the actors' facial expressions or tone of voice, the acoustics, or some other nonverbal and usually visual or auditory image or message.

What are some stored experiences and emotions that are common to large numbers of people and how can media cue a recall of them? We've looked at the stalled car example already. Some others are: (1) forgetting an important anniversary or event, (2) a plugged toilet or sink, (3) missing out on a great sale, losing one's wallet or car keys, and so on. Any event or situation to which people respond with something like "You're getting awfully close to home" probably is evoking experiential meaning. Mass media persuaders, especially advertisers, cue out these resonating experiences using media. As you examine the media persuasion aimed at you in magazine ads, TV and radio spots, billboards, or the Internet, try to identify the common experiences being targeted.

In all likelihood, we process experiential meanings in the peripheral channel of the ELM without much intellectual evaluation. Instead, they simply feel right. In Schwartz's words, they are resonating in a **responsive chord**. There are several scripts that can cue out these meanings, thus implementing Schwartz's resonance principle and evoked recall. They are the verbal script, the visual script, and the auditory script. Depending on future technological developments, other scripts may emerge. They will probably relate to one of the five senses.

The Verbal Script

Schwartz's ideas run counter to what many ad agencies practice and to much persuasion theory, which emphasizes specificity, logic, and word choice. In this opposing view, the **verbal script** is the message in words that we see or hear and the information they evoke. When ad agencies test their ads, they usually ask people to look at various ads and then to recall the words, images, statistics, and names in the ad. Rarely are respondents asked about their feelings or experiences, or about relating to the characters in the ads. However, if the verbal script resonates and cues experiences from the audience, powerful results usually occur. For example, a recent radio ad for a brokerage firm cued the experience of being trapped by an automated telephone answering system and its menu. The ad said, "If you want to check your balance, press 1 now. If you want to get a quote, press 2 now. If you want to talk to a real financial advisor, press 8 now and start over. Or try calling Financial Expertise at 1-800-MONEYAID." This message is probably processed in the peripheral channel of the ELM because of its experiential nature. We all listen to similar irritating automated menus and despise them.

The Auditory Script

The typical TV spot also has an **auditory or sound script**, which are the things you hear that are not words. The "language" of sound—sizzles, pops, grinds, klunks, plops, and buzzes—can often cue powerful, unconscious emotions. For instance, good feelings about parties are cued by the sounds of beer being poured. Then the advertiser simply adds words: "We've got beer in a can that's as good as beer from a keg—Hamm's draft in the new aluminum can." This auditory script is then reinforced by the musical score and sound effects such as laughing or beer-gulping sounds.

We have all had experiences cued out of our collective storehouses of audio memories. For example, take a classic ad for Diet Coke targeted at working women ages 18 to 34, who are the typical drinkers of diet cola. We see a group of attractive women gathered at the drinking fountain at break time and looking out the window. One says something like, "Okay, it's time," (the verbal script), and a muscular male construction worker across the street peels off his T-shirt (the visual script). The women sigh (the auditory script) as he pops a Diet Coke and swigs it down. The words are practically irrelevant because it is the sights and sounds that make the ad work. These act as cues for the experience of voyeuristic lusting in the mind

experienced by everyone. There is nothing logical about the ad or the response it cues from viewers. The same kinds of experiences can be cued out of receivers in an entertainment program, a radio spot ad, or a print ad containing a musical chip playing a holiday tune while advertising the ideal Christmas gift. They all rely on stored experiential memories associated with a particular cue like a sound effect or a musical score.

The Sight or Visual Script

The **sight or visual script** also serves as an important source of cues. We see (and hear) Liquid Plumber clearing the plugged kitchen sink as the yucky water whirlpools out with a slurping sound. Another way the sight script cues feelings is via camera angles and movement and visual editing. A low angle distorts size somewhat and says that this person is someone to be looked up to or is a cut above most people. Quick-cut edits convey a sense of action. A snowmobile cuts through a huge snowdrift, suggesting action and excitement. The view then cuts quickly to downhill racers carving their way through a tough slalom course, and a final quick cut shows ice-boat racers zooming across a frozen lake. Not until the end of the ad does the verbal script say, "Warm Up Winter This Year. Come to the Winter Wonderland of Lake Geneva." The ad then closes by showing an attractive couple snuggling in front of the fireplace in the ski lodge. The visual script does most of the work here. It builds the excitement and cues experiential meaning from the audience's subconscious. The verbal script merely tells viewers that Lake Geneva is where the memories can be brought to life.

Other aspects of the sight script, such as the set, costumes, or props, continue the job of evoking responses from us. Many newscasts convey a "newsroom atmosphere" using a visual script. Printers churn out copy, people rush around the set carrying pieces of paper meant to be news flashes, and so it looks like the anchorperson is in a functional newsroom. The actual anchors who read the news stories are in another room in front of a blue screen, which is superimposed on the newsroom set to give the visual impression that they are in the middle of the hustle and bustle. Similarly, the background shots for political candidates can cue nuances of meaning. If candidates are standing in front of the Lincoln Memorial with the president, they must be devoted to issues of equality and justice.

The title of Schwartz's book, *The Responsive Chord*, reflects the relationship between the audience and the message cued out by the advertisement, the articles printed in magazines, the banners on the Internet, or the programs seen on TV. Schwartz noted that the issue of truth is irrelevant in examining this kind of persuasion. Today, we see print ads with little or no copy but that present a potential dramatic script that could be brought to life on a television screen. A good example of the resonance principle being used by advertisers can be seen in the storyboard of an Acura Integra ad, shown in Figure 13.4. The ad aims at graying baby-boomers who recall the experience of playing with Hot Wheels when they were kids. The script resonates with these experiences stored in the target's conscious or unconscious mind. Persuaders identify such common experiences and then design print or electronic ads that prompt audiences to recall the experience while also mentioning the brand, candidate, or cause.

What if the audience doesn't have such a stored experience? Schwartz recommended **planting** the experience in early campaign ads and then cueing it out at the point of purchase. For example, show macho guys in whitewater rafts being bounced up and down as they navigate the Colorado River. Then they reach a slack pool, paddle to shore, and open their coolers to enjoy a cold can of Bud. The person who has never whitewater rafted now has the experience planted in his or her mind. The next step is to reinforce that experience in print ads, focusing on the final scene, and with shorter TV and perhaps radio ads. Then, at the point of purchase, voting, or joining, some cue such as a rafting picture on the packaging prompts the recall and hopefully the purchase.

As it is used in contemporary advertising, Schwartz's resonance principle presents receivers of persuasion with several challenges. They need to identify common experiences that the persuasion aims to prompt out of them. They may need to analyze persuasive messages that plant experiences to be triggered later at the point of purchase, voting, or donating. They also need to be aware of relationships between the verbal, auditory, and visual elements in any persuasion.

To learn more about Tony Schwartz, access InfoTrac College Edition, and type the words "Tony Schwartz" in the search engine. Read Kostelanetz's interview with Schwartz, and see what else you can learn about this media master.

McLUHAN'S PERSPECTIVES ON MEDIA USE

The Modern Media Revolution

Marshall McLuhan (1963) was the author of 36 widely acclaimed books on electronic media. He was also remarkably accurate in anticipating media effects, and his 40-year-old predictions such as the **development of a "global village"** are just now coming to pass. We saw the global village in action when nearly 100 countries around the world sent help to the victims of Hurricane Katrina in late 2005. A recent book by one of his critics is entitled *The Virtual McLuhan* (Theall, 2002), and his popularity is experiencing an enormous rebirth. Once again he is being labeled the "guru of new media," and most of his works are being reissued due to the relevance of his work. His work is being examined from the perspective of the new media, including interactive ones. For example, 40 years ago, he predicted virtual reality, cyberspace, the Internet, and that information would become the crucial commodity of the future. He thought that most people were looking at the present through a rearview mirror, viewing the past instead of the

MUSIC AND SFX THROUGHOUT

30 Second Television Commercial
COMMERCIAL TITLE: "Hot Wheels"
COMMERCIAL NO: HAAI 3358
PRODUCT: 1994 Acura Integra
                  Sports Coupe & Sedan

Introducing the new 1994
Acura Integra.

Not since Hot Wheels®...

have cars been this much
fun.

© 1993 Acura Division of American Honda Motor Co. Inc. Acura and Integra are registered trademarks of Honda Motor Co., Ltd. VTEC is a trademark of Honda Motor Co. Ltd. Make an intelligent decision. Buckle up.

Track sold separately.

FIGURE 13.4 This ad for the Acura Integra taps into the experience of having played with a Hot Wheels racetrack, thus resonating with the experiences of its target audience—male baby boomers and others who enjoyed the toy.

SOURCE: (Reprinted by permission of American Honda Motor Co.)

future as a guide to decisions and actions. That's probably how we are looking at the mushrooming of terrorist organizations and their actions—we assume their past actions will be repeated and then we go about taking actions and enacting laws designed to prevent similar actions in the future. In reality, the past actions will probably not be repeated and new (and perhaps deadlier) tactics will be employed.

Type the words "Marshall McLuhan" into any search engine and you will find that his work has taken on new relevancy in an interactive media age. I found over 50,000 entries. McLuhan's most often quoted idea was that "The medium is the message" (1964), by which he meant that the effect a new medium has on culture is much greater than the actual messages it carries. The invention of print is a good example. The Renaissance was much more important than the books that were printed at the time. It became a whole new way of thinking, acting, and organizing. Television as a medium was much more important for its impact on modern life than any television programming has been. We were entertained by *I Love Lucy*, but we were not really informed by her program. Instead, we were introduced to a new way of life. We got live news on TV instead of yesterday's news in today's newspaper. The live news was much less in depth but much more interesting. To work an extra timeout into professional football and thus squeeze in more commercials, television producers introduced the two-minute warning. This led to the two-minute drill which changed football from a running game to a passing game. So TV gave us some things but also cost us others.

McLuhan's ideas resemble Schwartz's in many ways, and the two worked together for a short time. McLuhan believed that we relate to media in two ways. First, he said that every medium is an extension of one of our senses or body parts. For example, print is an extension of our eyes—it allows us to see much more than we could prior to its invention. Television is an extension of our eyes and our ears, so we can see and hear more than we could without television. And the computer is an extension of our brain. It allows us to think of much more than we could prior to its presence.

Media also can change our way of thinking about our world. For example, when the telegraph gave people the ability to communicate quickly across great distances, thus destroying space, we began to think of our country as much smaller than we had before. We could now predict the future better. We could know the price of wheat at the Chicago markets in seconds, even way off in Kansas where it was grown. In fact, the power to predict may have led to what we now call the "futures market," in which we buy and sell wheat

that hasn't yet been planted. TV also gave us new ways of organizing our lives around its programming, such as the six o'clock or ten o'clock news at night, *The Today Show* and its clones in the morning, and *Sesame Street* in the afternoon for school kids. In fact, most people schedule their lives to some degree around TV programming.

Television has surely altered our sense of community and belonging as well. Following the devastating submerging of New Orleans and other parts of the Gulf coast, millions of people altered their views about a variety of things like donating aid, and what it was like to be black and poor. They also probably altered their viewing habits by watching 24/7 news channels and the Weather Channel. And with TVs on more than seven hours a day in the average American home, there simply is not enough time for the socializing and family life that occurred prior to its existence. Sixty-five percent of children above the age of eight have a television set in their bedrooms, further fracturing family relations (Kaiser Family Foundation, 1999). This has created what one critic labeled "the lonely crowd," in which people in neighborhoods and apartment complexes rarely know one another. In contrast, in some Third World countries the television set is owned by the entire village or community and brings people together to interact— which may or may not be useful.

Television also has an easy **access code**, which means we don't have to learn to watch it in the same way we had to learn to read. As a result, living in contemporary times can be facilitated by what we learn via TV. MTV clearly altered American pop culture, and many believe it provided new and disturbing role models for actions such as violence against women. Research verifies this. In fact, MTV was so concerned about the possibility that the network partnered with the American Psychological Association to develop a warning system that gave indications of the link. Go to www.apa.org/practice/mtvpreview.html to learn more about this disturbing possibility.

T A B L E 13.1   Hot and Cool Media

Medium	Source of Information	Definition	Participation	Type of Medium
Television	Lighted dots	Low	High	Cool
Books	Completed letters	High	Low	Hot
Cartoons	Dots on paper	Low	High	Cool
Photographs	Image on film	High	Low	Hot
Telephone	Low-fidelity sound wave	Low	High	Cool
Movies	Moving image on film	High	Low	Hot
Telegraph	Dots and dashes in sound	Low	High	Cool
Digital audio	High-fidelity sound wave	High	Low	Hot
Personal computer and Internet	Lighted dots	Low	High	Cool

McLuhan distinguished the difference to be between the signal used by a medium and the messages it conveyed. The **signal** is what stimulates our information-processing receptors; print stimulates our eyes, radio stimulates our ears, and television stimulates both. The message is the meaning intended and conveyed by the signal. Some signals come to us in what McLuhan called a complete or high- fidelity form, while others come to us in an incomplete, or low-fidelity, form. **High-fidelity forms**, such as radio with its complete words, sentences, and music, require little from our information-processing receptors like our eyes or ears. They only require us to assemble the signal's elements into complete messages. **Low-fidelity forms** include the telegraph, whose electronic impulses or dots and dashes had to be translated into letters and then into words. Low-fidelity media require us to stretch our senses and convert incomplete signals into complete messages. According to McLuhan, the same message sent via the two forms would have somewhat different meanings. The high-fidelity form results in little physiological or **sensory involvement**, and it doesn't take much physiological effort to process the message. The low-fidelity form requires much more participation and results in high physiological or **sensory participation**. McLuhan called the high-fidelity

or complete message signals hot media and the low-fidelity or incomplete ones cool media (see Table 13.1).

Hot Media

Hot media rely on signals having high fidelity, completeness, or **definition** as McLuhan called it. Hot media include film (but not TV), digital music (but not analog music), photos (but not cartoons), and books (but not comic books). McLuhan considered them hot because, unlike cool media such as television, they do not require much work from our sensory receptors to communicate a message. Hot media have complete or fully finished signals. For example, films are made up of sequential photographs filling the whole screen and are separated by a brief blackout to create the illusion of motion. Television pictures are quite incomplete, in comparison, and not all pixels on the half-lit lines of resolution on the screen are themselves glowing, so there is an even more incomplete signal.

Cool Media

The signals we perceive and process in **cool media** have low fidelity, definition, or completeness, so we must work harder to physiologically process them. Cool media include television, the telephone, and the computer screen. Consider the telephone. It does not have a high fidelity speaker in the earpiece. In fact if you really want to know what the fidelity of its speaker is, just hold it away from your ear by a foot or two. That is why it is sometimes difficult to determine who is calling us. We had to imagine a lot of sound quality with the old wind-up phonograph. To be decoded, these cool media require physiological and mental work on our part. A cartoon's signal consists of line drawings that are far less complete than a photograph.

What kinds of messages are best for cool media? McLuhan said that cool media breed cool messages. In 1964, he predicted that someday a movie star would be elected president and 16 years later, that's what happened. Today, the politicians who catch on are easy-going and cool, like Bill Clinton and George W. Bush. They both are informal and ambiguous in their style and messages. They differed widely on policy but were very similar in communication style. Likewise, we see more and more TV commercials relying less on words or scripts and more on creation of a mood or feeling. Viewers add to or subtract from such commercials and arrive at their own final meaning. Think of the spots that create a sense of anticipation through the use of music, sets, or lighting. We hear the sounds of a love ballad. Then we see a well-dressed couple slowly walking down the stairs of the fancy restaurant. The man gives the valet the keys to get his car. Up drives a Volkswagen Passat. Only then does the voice-over tell us that the Passat is in good taste anywhere. The specific content of the message is incomplete, and so the message matches the cool quality of the TV signal.

It is interesting to apply some of McLuhan's ideas about hot and cool media to recent communication technologies that have become widespread only since his death. As cellular technology increases, for instance, we will be processing more and more cool signals such as photographic and televised images. When cell phone reception breaks up, we experience the further cooling of an already cool medium. It may get so cool that both parties agree to hang up and try again later. McLuhan

also accurately predicted a great increase in the use of cool media, resulting in increased audience participation. And he predicted that when coupled with satellite transmission of TV, radio, telephone, and computer messages, these cool media would lead to his global village, in which everybody would be interested in everybody else's business. We are now beginning to experience just that in the form of the Internet, chat groups, blogs, and email, all of which are highly participative and involving, as his theory would predict.

Here, the theories of McLuhan and Schwartz overlap and enhance one another. The involving and participatory trend, coupled with the notion of identifying experiences that can be prompted by mini-cues and allow people to add their own meanings, provides a powerful set of tools in the hands of creative and insightful persuaders.

To discover how much impact Marshall McLuhan's ideas have had on the information age, access InfoTrac College Edition, and enter the words "Marshall McLuhan" in the search engine. Read a few of the articles listed there.

USES AND GRATIFICATION THEORY

Uses and gratification theory is another approach to studying the effects of mass media, which focuses on how receivers use media to gratify their individual needs. It assumes that we all have differing needs for various types of information and hence must use various media at different times (Blumler, 1979; Rubin, 2002). This theory maintains that there are four basic needs for which we turn to mass media. The first need is **surveillance**, or the need to keep track of our environment. We fulfill this need with information messages that include the weather, news, stock market quotes, sports results, the price of gasoline, or the garage sales section of the want ads. There is too much happening for us to keep track of all of the events and persons affecting our daily lives, so we usually turn to the media to keep up to date.

The second need is **curiosity**, or the need to discover and learn about previously unknown information that is not critical to our interests and daily lives. Topics about which we are curious might include the upcoming TV season, celebrity gossip, new technologies, or the details of a direct mail or direct television sales offer. News tabloids trade on this need. No one really believes in Elvis sightings, or 40-pound babies being born, but they buy the tabloids that publicize these unlikely instances. In fact, *The National Enquirer* is the largest selling "newspaper" in the world. Our curiosity is piqued by the sensationalist headlines and the paper regularly sells out.

The third need we use media to gratify is **diversion**, or relief from boredom. For example, we watch movies or sporting events on TV. We read books or magazines, or we listen to our favorite CD. We might play video games to divert ourselves. Media are used in this case to fill time but not really to gather information that we believe we must know.

The fourth need is for **personal identity**. We are uncertain about our identities in a changing world, so we turn to media to help us discover who we are and what we stand for. To fill this need we might read about places we have never visited. We might watch The Learning Channel or learn what we believe about politics and government by listening to radio talk shows. We learn what we are not by watching "trash TV" talk shows such as the *Jerry Springer Show*. Interestingly enough, persons who are more self-assured and outgoing fill personal identity needs by reading whereas less self-assured and outgoing persons rely on television to fill this need.

Other lesser needs such as nostalgia are also filled by media airing such things as old movies, oldies radio stations, and purchases of CDs of *Patsy Kline's Greatest Hits*. The need for mastery and control is served, for example, by watching game shows to see if we know more than the contestants, or playing video games and entering chat groups to compare accomplishments. All these needs serve as

attention-getting devices in persuasion and as first premises in enthymemes.

Knowing how people are using media to gratify needs can help us plan targeted persuasion. As receivers, we need to monitor our own uses of media and what are we turning to media in hopes of gratifying.

AGENDA SETTING

Another explanation of the ways mass media persuade us relates to their **agenda-setting** function (McCombs and Shaw, 1972). According to this theory, the public agenda includes the kinds of issues people discuss, think, and worry about. This agenda is powerfully shaped and directed by what the news media choose to highlight and what they choose to ignore and downplay. This is especially important since the concentration of media ownership has increased with mega-media giants like Rupert Murdoch or the Wrigley company owning and controlling much of what we read, see, and hear. The main point about agenda setting is that mass media do not tell us what to think; but they do tell us what to think about (see Figure 13.5). How many would have stayed glued to their TVs during the O. J. Simpson trial if the media hadn't reported on it daily? Would we be thinking about the war on terrorism if the media hadn't run stories about various bombings around the world involving persons affiliated with Al Quaida? We probably wouldn't even recognize the name of the network's leader.

Deciding what to focus on and, equally important, what not to focus on in reporting the day's events falls to a small number of "gatekeepers" such as reporters for the wire services, editors, news photographers, and others. They have access to more news than they can possibly report and so must choose what stories to run, which way to point their cameras, and whom to interview. How do they make program decisions, and by what criteria? Not much is known about this process, but there are some hints as to how and why the decisions are made. Media scholar J. Meyrowitz (1985) refers to one criterion called

FIGURE 13.5 Although media may not tell us what to think, they can tell us what to think about.

SOURCE: *Berry's World.* © United Feature Syndicate, Inc. Used with permission.

people whom advertisers want to reach, such as upscale spenders, gourmet cooks, or sports fans.

One criteria for determining what news to present is the nature of the audience. Persons who read *U.S. News & World Report* or who watch *The O'Reilly Factor* will be more conservative than those who read *Newsweek* or who watch Jim Lehrer on PBS. Gatekeepers frequently select stories that put a conservative slant on an issue, thus setting a different agenda for the conservative readers than for the liberal ones. Another criterion for deciding what is to be broadcast or printed is whether it can be delivered as a 20- to 30-second sound bite or told simply and quickly to answer the journalist's five key questions—who, what, when, where, and why. Communication scholars Hall Jamieson and Kohrs-Campbell (1996) define a **news bite** as a piece of news less than 35 seconds long, delivered by a credible source in an energetic way (see Figure 13.6). If the first story in the broadcast is a news bite, then it hasn't been an important news day. However, if the first story is of a national tragedy or a breaking scandal, viewers know that an in-depth report will follow.

Because they provide us with yesterday's news tomorrow, newspapers are practically compelled to run stories that TV news programmers chose the day before. Both the newspaper and the news weekly can do in-depth coverage of issues, but fewer and fewer people are reading them and for less and less time.

Another criterion used by gatekeepers to determine what gets reported and what does not is the expressiveness or dramatic quality of both the audio and video in the story (Meyrowitz, 1985). The old chestnut about "man bites dog!" being more interesting and newsworthy than if the dog bit the man applies here. Newsworthy stories include the instantaneous reactions of parents who just heard that their children have been killed in an auto accident. The camera zooms up to their faces, and the audience supposedly experiences how they must feel.

Critical receivers of persuasion need to diversify their reading of, listening to, and viewing of news and information to expose themselves to as many divergent sources as possible. Try listening to

least objectionable programming. "The key is to design a program that is least likely to be turned off, rather than a program viewers will actively seek out" (p. 73). Some media critics note that, although media advertisements purportedly sell products to viewers, the economic design of the mass media industry is to sell audiences to advertisers. With TV, for example, we think of programs as products for which we pay a price in that we have to watch ads from the programs' sponsors. In reality, we are the products, and we are being sold to the advertisers. That's why Sweeps Week is so critical. So, the media's agenda-setting goal is to design programming that will capture and hold the attention of the largest number of people or segment of

Berry's World

© 1988 by NEA, Inc.   J-D

"You're talking in 30-second bites again."

FIGURE 13.6 The 30-second news bite is one criterion that affects gatekeepers' decisions about what is newsworthy and what is not. As this cartoon implies, the news bite might even be affecting our conversational styles.

SOURCE: *Berry's World.* © United Feature Syndicate, Inc. Used with permission.

the news as reported on public television stations or National Public Radio. Above all, don't let one medium so dominate your awareness of the world that you overlook other sources of news and information. Even if you watch as much television as others, vary your sources of information.

To see how gatekeepers can promote their advertisers through news selection, access InfoTrac College Edition, and enter the word "gatekeeper" in the search engine. Find the selection titled

"Now the Editor as Marketer," and speculate how you been affected by editorial selection.

NEWS MANIPULATION AND PERSUASION

The news industry is a business, and the media stand to profit from the success of their clients and customers. Do the media manipulate the news, as some critics suggest, or not? If so, we ought to acquaint ourselves with the possible tactics that can make or unmake the news. That knowledge will allow us an extra safeguard against possible "hidden persuasion" in news programs.

Key News Sources

Three major wire services (AP, UPI, and Reuters) supply most of the news we see, hear, and read. There is nothing wrong with that small number of sources, as long as the news is accurate and as long as the key news items get printed or broadcast. But the key items don't always get prominent coverage, and it can't all be blamed on the gatekeepers. Even half-hour TV news programs contain only 22 minutes of news or about 3000 total words. The average 400-words-per-minute reader can cover that in only 7 to 8 minutes, and that, in fact, is about the average time spent per day by newspaper subscribers on reading their newspapers. So we miss a lot of important information if we rely only on electronic media for news. When you are trying to gain a certain segment of the market, which is what news broadcasts must do to earn profits for the corporate networks and their shareholders, the temptation is to manipulate the news to make it more interesting, sexier, sensational, and entertaining. As Edward R. Murrow put it: "One of the basic troubles with radio and television news is that both instruments have grown up as an incompatible combination of show business, advertising, and news. Each of the three is a rather bizarre and demanding profession, and when you get all three under one tent, the dust never settles"

(Matusow, 1983, p. 304). The show-business aspects of today's news distort electronic news just as yellow journalism distorted print news. Here are some specific ways news can be manipulated.

Methods of Manipulation

Ignoring. One way gatekeepers distort the news is by simply ignoring it. Officials ignored the danger of buildings containing asbestos until one school district in Virginia finally brought suit. Asbestos without a lawsuit apparently wasn't an interesting story. Until recently, few persons in the United States could say where Afghanistan was located, and fewer knew who Osama Bin Laden was and why he mattered to them in any way. Most political scandals are initially ignored because they don't seem interesting or sensational enough. This was the case for a recent governor of Illinois and a scam involving bribes for truck driver licenses that happened on his watch. Not until one of the drivers with a license purchased by a bribe hit a school bus killing a dozen or more children, did the media pay attention to what had probably been suspected all along.

Favoring the Sponsor. Because every commercial news program has sponsors, news reporters and editors may soft-pedal any negative news about these sponsors. For example, it took years to pass a law forcing broadcasters to refuse advertising from cigarette manufacturers, and there is an ongoing campaign to keep beer and wine ads from being banned. It is always wise to ask who the sponsor is for a newscast. Getting news from several sources helps us to avoid sponsor-favoring editing, but this is getting even harder as a few large corporations buy up many communication outlets. Sometimes, broadcasters preview the news for advertisers. There is a practice of distancing advertisers from what could result in negative publicity. And as we noted earlier, there is a greater and greater concentration of media ownership, which in itself might favor the sponsor. For example, General Electric owns NBC, Westinghouse owns CBS, and Disney owns ABC.

The Pseudoevent. Although there is an overabundance of news each day, not all of it is interesting or entertaining, so news reporters are often drawn to highly dramatic or bizarre events. Historian Daniel Boorstin (1961) called these **pseudoevents** or "planned news." Such stories fall somewhere between public relations and soft news, such as reporting on a celebrity like Michael Jordan coming out of retirement. Various mass movements hold marches, rallies, or vigils or use violent tactics such as bomb scares to get media attention. A bomb scare is not a natural or ordinary event. It had to be planned and executed, hence the prefix in *pseudo* in pseudoevent, denoting an unreal event. If workers announce ahead of time that they are going to go on strike tomorrow, it guarantees news coverage of the walkout.

Bias: Verbal and Nonverbal. A skillful interviewer can make an interviewee seem to be quite different from his or her real self. News reporters can make a candidate seem controversial by dubbing an audio track of booing on a video track showing people cheering and then having the announcer say, with a frown on his or her face, that the candidate faces opposition from left and right. Or editors might superimpose two or more conflicting images such as angry farmers and grain dealers, or angry college students and college loan officers. They select who is featured, choosing only pro or only con advocates. You can't look at and listen to all the print and electronic news available to combat this sort of bias, but you can diversify your exposure. Let us now turn to the newest entrant in not only the news industry but the advertising and related persuasion industries—the Internet.

THE INTERNET AND PERSUASION

A recent editorial in the *Chicago Tribune* noted that early in its life (i.e., the 1980s), the Internet was unregulated and reliant upon the good will of its "Netizens," or citizens of the net. But there was a dark side. "Then came the hackers, the viruses,

---

B O X 13.2   Diversity and the Media

 The Freeman Institute is an educational resource that celebrates cultural diversity in a number of ways, such as training in dealing with diversity and books and videos on the topic and many other issues. Their slogan is "Dealing with People Who Drive You Crazy." Go to their web page at www.freemaninstitute.com/cultures and explore the links that direct you to a number of diverse communities. Select from among the options that deal with the diversity group and media and explore their

content. For example, regarding Latinos, you might want to select the "Electric Mercado" link and discover how media are now advertising to the $331 billion global retail and the $3.2 trillion business-to-business markets. Or you might want to try some of the Black, Native American, or Asian American sites. You can watch a preview of Dr. Freeman's course and book on *The Value of Mutual Respect* as well as many other interesting links.

---

the worms, spyware, phishing and spam . . . . a handful of groups are now looking into whether the entire Internet needs an overhaul. . . . With more than a billion Internet users . . . a structural overhaul is not an outlandish idea" (*Chicago Tribune*, July 4, 2005).

With the bursting of the dot-com bubble and falling Internet advertising revenue, many dismiss the importance of the Internet as a persuasive channel. And while we can trace the number of hits a certain site gets, we don't know whether people read what is there, let alone if it persuades them. Yet those in the know point to the sweeping effects the Internet continues to have on the global economy. The Internet is changing the structure of persuasion as no other medium has since television. It is a major technological revolution that is changing the structure of our communication practices. There are now new ways for persuasion to be delivered, such as the viral persuasion mentioned earlier at www.subservientchicken.com sponsored by Burger King to market its chicken offerings. The Internet is also changing the persuasive process by altering the power structure of the participants. Let's review how the Internet is changing the way we persuade and are persuaded.

Changes in the Information Power Structure

When we considered the massive changes resulting from the printed word, we noted that the biggest change was the redistribution of information as

power. Perhaps the most significant contribution of the Internet is the redistribution of the control of information. Automobile salespersons do not like the Internet because dealer costs for vehicles are available online to potential customers, who can then solicit competitive bids from various dealers knowing what they stand to make on the sale. What a great tool for the persuadee! Travel agents were previously the major source of information for long-distance trips, but no longer. Now, they are closing their doors due to competition from the Internet. Reservations can be made without direct human assistance, and some carriers provide additional incentives for using the Internet, such as special fares online. Southwest Airlines, the most profitable airline over the past decade, uses the Internet as its primary source of booking trips and no longer pays commissions to travel agents. Its new discount service called DING at www.southwest.com/ding/ might interest those of you interested in saving money on travel. Companies such as Priceline.com and Travelocity.com enable consumers to find bargain fares. The Internet is changing the lodging industry as well. Travelers can stay in luxury hotels such as the Hotel Inter-Continental or Swisshotel for prices as low as one would pay at a Hampton Inn. The Internet is a boon to bed-and-breakfasts as well, enabling them to publicize their presence very inexpensively. The challenge for persuaders is to frame persuasion in ways that draws visitors to their sites, and not their competitors.

Information on Demand

A major selling point of the Internet is its ability to deliver information immediately around the clock. Traditional businesses struggle to find hours to accommodate customers across time zones, but the Internet provides and collects information worldwide regardless of the hour. Of course, in complex situations that involve many issues, it's still preferable to deal with a person, but many routine transactions are well suited to the Internet, just as automatic teller machines can handle most of our banking needs. The task for persuaders promoting such products is how to attract potential customers to their site. We are only in the first stages of experimenting with that challenge, and when that challenge is answered, persuadees will have another issue to contend with. In the meantime, the Internet allows persuadees to easily research available information on candidates, brands, donating, or joining a particular organization.

Direct-to-Consumer Markets Without Geographic Boundaries

The Internet also provides direct market access to people around the globe. Farmers growing crops find the best markets most easily using the Internet. Small, independent coffee growers possess the means to sell their crops internationally for better prices by cutting out the middleman—a process called disintermediation. This is another way to persuade via the Internet. Many fine artists now use the Internet's direct-to-consumer capability to sell their art and avoid paying commissions. Art dealers often take a 40 to 50 percent commission when items are sold through galleries. People use eBay to buy and sell across national boundaries to avoid taxes and regulations. Their challenge is to write a persuasive message that convinces prospects to place a bid. For persuadees, the Internet can make price, quality, quantity, and selection available before they have to make a purchase decision.

Increased Access and Convenience

The Internet offers convenience for those limited by geography, time, or special requirements, providing remote parts of the world with access to many of the amenities available to those living in or near cities. For example, many consumers report that their most precious commodity is time—time to spend with families, on hobbies, in community involvement, and on other diversions. Consumers may now choose online purchase opportunities such as peapod.com and can consider more choices than are generally available locally. This option is changing the retail industry in favor of persuadees. Or take the marketing tactic known as niche marketing. For example, people with very narrow or very wide feet have more shoe options via the Internet than at the shoe store in the mall. Persuaders who wish to focus on niche or specialty markets can now do so. The Internet is also a great source for parts to repair discontinued items. OfficeMax.com advertises that it can delivere toner cartridges for a discontinued printer model on the next business day and at a cheaper price. That kind of offer can be very useful to persuadees who own such a printer.

The Immediate Transfer of Information and Financial Resources

Many customers need information and financial transfers immediately, and companies and banks can use the Internet to provide this capability, thus giving them a competitive edge. The use of email attachments simplifies the immediate transmission of information. Many types of financial payments are now available on the Internet, and the seller is paid immediately, which is a distinct advantage given the cost of borrowing money to maintain cash flow. Electronic deposits and withdrawals are made to our banks and we can purchase online through systems being marketed to consumers such as PayPal. So in the contest to get and keep more customers, the ability to provide information and financial services is a persuasive benefit to many consumers. Obviously, making it more convenient

It's where leading businesses find the leading technology.

CDW.com 888.239.7315

CDW has everything you need to find the right technology for your business. Like more than 50,000 products in stock. And hundreds of brands. And account managers who are free to recommend the best technology out there—not just the best from any one manufacturer. So you get objective advice and plenty of choices. Which may be why so many businesses nationwide turn to CDW. To find out what we can do for you, call or visit our Web site.

FIGURE 13.7 CDW combines a massive physical inventory with efficient Internet technology to serve 69,000 Web customers daily.

SOURCE: (All rights reserved. Visit www.cdw.com.)

to handle such transactions is a boon to most persuadees.

Ethical Behavior on the Internet

Ethical use of the Internet is a big issue. Its unseemly underbelly brings opportunities to exploit others. Children are particularly vulnerable to adult predators, and stalking online is not uncommon. As with mail-order houses, consumers must always question whether a persuader is trustworthy. So a key issue for persuaders on the Internet involves establishing their credibility, and for persuadees the task is to search out credible sources. Many merchants and persons doing business on the Internet are forming associations that provide some level of assurance of trustworthiness. Privacy issues continue to arise regarding the protection of customers' personal information by businesses on the Internet.

REVIEW AND CONCLUSION

The average college freshman has watched tens of thousands of hours of television and hundreds of thousands of commercials by the time he or she comes to school. And TV is just one media channel being used for persuasion. Billboards, films, magazines, and newspapers affect most of us. Labels, bumper stickers, T-shirts, and other paraphernalia persuade us. All in all, we live in a highly persuasive, media-rich environment, and we need to be aware of how media affect us, especially in regard to persuasion. New media have effected great changes in how we were persuaded in the past and how we are being persuaded in the present. We have looked at the major communication innovations over time and how they changed persuasion and society forever after their introduction. We need to be persuaded about some things, and media persuasion is sometimes the best way to get information about alternatives.

You can protect yourself from persuasive attempts made by various media by looking beneath the surface. Look for the responsive chords being plucked via the verbal, visual, and auditory scripts, and whether the messages that elicit them are hot or cool. Examine how the introduction of a new medium extends one of your senses or body parts. Consider whether "the medium is the message" and what the implications of that concept are as you are targeted by persuaders. In public affairs, look for the agenda being set and what you are being forced to think about and how that affects you as a persuadee. You also need to examine your own patterns of behavior in media use. Why do you turn to media, and to which media do you turn? What needs do they meet for you? Also consider the immense changes we are facing because of the development of new communications media (Gumpert and Drucker, 2002; Larson, 2002; Postman, 1996; Zettl, 1996). Establishing trustworthiness remains important across all of these media innovations, but it is particularly important with regard to the Internet.

KEY TERMS

By the time you have finished this chapter, you should be able to identify, explain, and give examples of the following words or concepts.

spoken word	auditory or sound script	sensory involvement	personal identity
written word		sensory participation	agenda-setting
printed word	sight or visual script	hot media	news bite
electronic word	planting	definition	ignoring
interactive word	development of a "global village"	cool media	favoring the sponsor
evoked recall		uses and gratification theory	pseudoevents
experiential meaning	access code		verbal and nonverbal bias
responsive chord	signal	surveillance	
verbal script	high-fidelity forms	curiosity	
	low-fidelity forms	diversion	

APPLICATION OF ETHICS

On April 2, 2004, editors at two newspapers decided to publish a controversial front-page picture of the dismembered and charred remains of four American civilian contractors with their body parts hanging from a bridge. A crowd of Iraqis were cheering the sight in the foreground. The editors had to consider a number of ethical issues before deciding to publish the photo. Here are a few of those issues to consider. Should the picture have been published at all? From the "Letters to the Editor" in the days following, publication opinion ran from "outlandish" to "necessary for the public to see" to one suggesting the papers get a Pulitzer Prize for poor taste. What if the bodies were of soldiers? What if the bodies were Iraqi? What if they hadn't been dismembered or charred? What if they had been of women and/or children? Could running the photo affect public opinion about the war? Would you run the picture on the front page? Inside? Would you warn readers of the graphic nature of the photos? Why or why not?

QUESTIONS FOR FURTHER THOUGHT

1. What are some similarities between primitive oral/aural cultures and the electronic culture in which we now live?

2. Why is information associated with power? Give examples.

3. How was the concept of ownership associated with the development of writing?

4. What changes in society resulted from the development of print?

5. How did literacy both free us and enslave us?

6. What are some of the developments at the Media Lab at MIT? How will they affect us in the future?

7. Which media type—hot or cool—dominates our times?

8. What are some examples of the criteria gatekeepers may be using to determine what to put on the evening news?

9. What are the implications of an unregulated Internet?

10. What should the ethics of Internet communication include?

11. What are the implications of the exploding presence of interactive media?

12. How does cultural diversity affect the many media of our times?

13. What are the implications of the many persuasive appeals made on the Internet?

 For online activities, go to the *Persuasion* book companion website at http://communication.wadsworth.com/larson11.

14

The Use of Persuasive Premises in Advertising and IMC

Key Terms   Questions for Further Thought

Application of Ethics

LEARNING GOALS

After reading this chapter, you should be able to:

1. Explain the difference between advertising and integrated marketing communication.

2. Differentiate among the various elements of integrated marketing communication, such as sales promotion, PR, advertising, event planning, and others.

3. Explain the functions of demographic, socio-graphic, and psychographic advertising research.

4. Identify and explain various techniques for positioning a brand.

5. Explain the VALS model's major and minor categories of consumers.

6. Recognize weasel words used in print advertising.

7. Apply Rank's 30-second-spot quiz to several television spots.

8. Differentiate between obvious, sophisticated, and subliminal sexual appeals in advertising.

Advertising is a fascinating kind of persuasion to study. Product ads have a dramatic impact on our purchasing and other behaviors, such as our identifying with brands, forming attitudes toward them, and choosing our preferred lifestyle. In previous chapters, we discussed various approaches to direct and interactive marketing, Internet ads, market segmentation, and data-based marketing. **Integrated marketing communication** (IMC) is a new and unique way to promote brands using more than traditional advertising and persuasion. A major goal of IMC is to build a one-to-one dialogue or relationship with consumers using various kinds of communication including persuasion. It includes direct marketing, public relations, event planning, sales promotion, packaging, and personal selling. All of these operate together to create a unified message with unique appeal. In this case, the whole is greater than the sum of its parts. This chapter focuses on advertising as the key (but not the only) element in successful IMC. And there are other emerging trends in advertising. For example, advertising aimed at Latinos in the United States continues to grow. At 13 percent of the U.S. population they are the largest ethnic minority. McDonald's devotes 10 percent of its general-market ads to Spanish-language spots (Wentz and Cuneo, 2002). The fastest growing minority is Asians from a variety of countries, while the fastest growing market segment is consumers aged 50+ years.

The Internet is another force changing the face of advertising, and it will play a major role in the future (Cuneo, 2002). "All Things Considered" reported early in 2006 that more and more traditional advertising efforts (e.g., television spots, etc.) are being replaced with Internet ads and banners (N.P.R., January 3, 2006). The Internet also is being used for what is called "permission advertising" where the consumer asks to receive an extended ad on behalf of the brand. And more and more people are going online. ("All Things Considered," January 3, 2006). Research shows that 92 percent of teens are online. Hoping to tap into this teen market, Frito-Lay devotes 9 percent of its marketing budget to Internet ads (Thompson, 2002). A Frito-Lay promotion with Microsoft's Xbox prompted 700,000 new customer registrations at http://Doritos.com, where you can also get a form to enter a sweepstakes.

 To gain an appreciation for the many facets of Internet advertising, access InfoTrac

College Edition, and enter the words "Internet advertising" in the search engine. Select the "advertising campaigns" option and then the case studies. Read and report on any of them.

Americans are the world's biggest and best producers and consumers of advertising. Consider the following:

- The average per capita expenditure on advertising in the United States is now over $1,000/year.

- The average American sees or hears almost 2,000 advertisements per day. No wonder there is what the industry calls "clutter."

Compare those numbers with what the reset of the world spends, including the Western democracies such as the United Kingdom, Canada, and the rest of "old" Europe. They spend less than $50/year on a per capita basis. No wonder the many newcomers to the United States from a variety of countries cannot believe that anyone can process all that advertising. And the fact is that no one can. Nonetheless, the rate of U.S. spending on ads is increasing. That's reason enough for persuadees to learn about this form of communication (Larson, 2001).

Some advertising ranks as pop art and is creative and entertaining, and some of it is simply awful. Our goal in this chapter, however, is not to evaluate the creative side of the industry but to learn how advertising affects human society and behavior and where it is likely to go in the future here and throughout the global economy. We need to discover whether those effects are bad or good for humanity in general, and how understanding advertising can help us understand ourselves as consumers. Marxist critics see advertising as a tool of the upper classes used to exploit the lower classes because it creates wants for unneeded goods and tempts people to waste their money on them. Advertising executives see ads as a way to beat the competition. Consumers see them as either just so much clutter or as a kind of entertainment. Marketers often intend advertisements not just to persuade but also to inform, and that is one of their

values. We need product, political, and idea/ideological information to make purchase, voting, and joining decisions.

ADVERTISING, SALES PROMOTION, AND POSITIONING

We all are targets of advertising, and we ought to be aware of the kinds of appeals targeted at us in order to make wise purchase, voting, joining, and donating decisions. Let's begin with some basic principles of modern advertising.

Branding, Brand Names, Slogans, Jingles, and Logos

Contemporary advertising grew out of the development of packaged goods in the late nineteenth and the early twentieth centuries. Producers needed to differentiate their version of a product type from the competition to promote brand recognition in consumers' eyes. Earlier consumers bought generic and unbranded products from barrels, sacks, and other containers at a general store. One way to differentiate your kind of coffee was to give it a name or brand. **Brands** are the names given to a certain manufacturer's version of a product type. Different brands of coffees compete with one another, but they also compete with teas, cocoa, and spiced ciders in the "hot drink" product category and with soft drinks, juice, bottled water, and others in the "beverage" category. So brands compete within and across product categories. We need to differentiate between a brand and a product category.

Advertising **slogans** and **jingles** became part of the popular culture with the advent of radio and radio advertising in the 1920s and 1930s. Slogans are defined as catch phrases that express a brand name, its benefits, and its personality. Gatorade has a different personality than Gulp, which is different from Snapple or Blast. Jingles are usually a musical version of the slogan with lyrics. Television emerged in the 1950s and permitted advertisers to not only talk and write about the brand, but also to demonstrate it using print, visuals, special effects, animation, mood music, sound effects, and various other audio and video techniques.

Several strategies to market the brand more effectively emerged in those early years of modern advertising. For instance, the name of the brand made a big difference in the way it was perceived and embedded in consumers' minds. Lifesavers was a good brand name because it described how the brand looked, and it was the first hard candy to be branded so it needed to look different from generic hard candies. One of the earliest facial soaps to be marketed was called "Palm Olive," suggesting that the product contained a combination of coconut and olive oils. Another way to differentiate a brand from the competition is to make an attractive offer. Consider Cracker Jacks, which came up with a novel offer in the 1880s to differentiate itself from other popcorn snacks. Each package offered consumers a "Free Prize" inside. Netflix differentiates itself from the competition by offering a free trial period in addition to no late fees.

Another way to differentiate a brand is by its packaging. Coors and Coors Light now come in unbreakable 16 ounce plastic bottles rather than glass ones or aluminum cans. Consider other brand names to see whether they differentiate the brand. In the frozen turkey market, one brand excels as we observed earlier. Ask people to name a brand of frozen turkey, and most will say "Butterball," the brand with the greatest name recognition. The name is memorable and says something about the brand's attributes and benefits. Butterball turkeys have the reputation of being the moistest brand because they are basted with a pound of butter (Dollas, 1986). Consider a few other brand names that demonstrate the brand's benefits, such as DieHard batteries, Easy Off oven cleaner, No Pest Strip insect repellant, Jiffy Lube oil changes, Taster's Choice instant coffee, Fruitopia fruit drinks, and others. A good brand name describes product benefits, fits with company image, and is memorable. It should also be easy to pronounce

and promote, suited to the product packaging, contemporary, and persuasive. Research on shopping lists shows that consumers often list brands and not product types to aid their shopping (Rothschild, 1987).

Closely related to the brand name are the brand's slogan and **logo** or its corporate emblem. Which coffee is "good to the last drop"? Maxwell House wins with its slogan and logo of a coffee cup with the last drop about to fall out of the cup. Starbuck's name doesn't communicate much about the brand or its benefits, but it has an identity as an upscale young person's coffee house specialty brand.

Go to InfoTrac College Edition, and enter the words "slogan" and "logo" in the key word search engine. Review any of the case studies cited there, and report back to the class. The one titled "Branded!" talks about branding yourself.

Packaging

Packaging is the container or wrapping that protects and identifies the product, reinforces the brand name, and builds **brand equity** (or the brand's recognizability), and it can have value as a promotional device. By law, packaging must provide information about the brand's contents and should inform consumers about its functions, features, benefits, and methods of use. The package should also make the brand attractive, recognizable, and easy to see and stock on store shelves and displays. Showing the package in ads helps consumers recall the product's advertised characteristics and benefits at the **point of purchase** (POP). The POP is defined as the place where the consumer can purchase the brand. This is usually in the retail store, but there are other ways to purchase goods nowadays, such as by phone, from a catalog, or online. The package can also carry a sales promotion, such as a coupon, and it can seem valuable in and of itself. For example, Grolsch beer bottles have a ceramic stopper and can be used to store other liquids once the beer is gone. Nabisco Saltines originally used a handy tin box that could be used to store nuts, bolts, thread, and many other things, and the L'Eggs plastic "egg" containers were used for storage, crafts, and containers for jelly beans in Easter baskets, as well as serving as the package for hosiery.

Packages also make a brand impression, especially when used in the strategy of package/placement placement in movies and television programming. There, characters make conspicuous use of familiar brands like Coke, Sweet Success Foods, Toyota, Proctor and Gamble, and G.M., to name a few. Is it effective? Communication scholar T. Borchers (2002) reports that sales of Red Stripe beer jumped 50 percent after Tom Cruise sipped from a can of the brew in a popular film. As a critical consumer, try to identify the effects of branding, packaging, and labeling and how they interact with brand advertising. For example, look at the packaging of Mrs. Butterworth's and Log Cabin syrup.

Sales Promotion

Sales promotions are defined as temporary inducements to encourage immediate purchase. Consumer-targeted sales promotions include special sale pricing like "two for the price of one" and short-term price reductions like "special six hour sales." They also include coupons, rebates, extra product in the package, contests, premiums, sweepstakes, recipes, and bonus packs. All sales promotional offers are designed to increase demand. They try to "pull" the brand through the supply pipeline using artificially pumped-up consumer demand for the brand as the carrot, and short-term limits such as expiration dates or limited supplies as the stick to prompt purchase. If the demand increases sufficiently, the store manager is forced to stock the brand. The manager has been pulled into moving the brand and in turn uses "push" tactics like special pricing, discounts, and store displays to move the brand off store shelves. All these sales promotions work hand-in-hand with brand advertising, brand naming, packaging, and other practices to form the IMC that persuades us to buy certain brands.

Positioning

We live in a world filled with too many products and brands to remember. Research shows that we can only recall a finite number of brands in each product category. Some theorists speculate that this top of mind awareness **(TOMA)** is limited to between five and nine brands. For complex product categories such as computers, most consumers recall only about five brands, whereas they recall as many as nine brands in less complex categories such as beer or breakfast foods. As a result, a brand needs to stand out so it will be remembered at the point of purchase when TOMA most significantly affects purchase behavior. TOMA is most likely created through information processed in the peripheral channel of the ELM—things like slogans, jingles, mood music, and packaging.

Most contemporary professionals in the field agree that advertising is a tool of marketing. In other words, companies don't come up with a product and then try to sell it to consumers using advertising messages. That strategy is known as an "inside out" approach. Rather, the successful marketer begins with the minds of consumers, tries to identify potentially unmet or unsolved needs or problems, and then designs a brand or redefines an existing brand to fill the need or solve the problem. That is an "outside-in" strategy. This approach of beginning with consumers was made popular by Al Ries and Jack Trout. In their best-selling books *Positioning: The Battle for Your Mind* (Ries and Trout, 1986), *The New Positioning* (Trout, 1995), and *Focus: The Future of Your Company Depends on It* (Reis, 1996), they deal with the concepts of **positioning** and **repositioning**, which are strategies for finding an empty niche in the consumer's minds that a given brand might fill and then targeting that niche. For example, the designers of a snack food asked consumers to open bags of potato chips, pour them into serving dishes, eat a few, and tell what each of their five senses processed. Customers then were asked to comment on the chips and tell what they liked and disliked about them, and how they would use them in entertaining. They said the chips were hard to

BOX 14.1   Interactive Media and Kids

Over 16 million children had Internet access in 2000, and the number increases every year. Most of the time parents don't monitor their children's online activity except to block pornographic sites using the V-chip. A proposal is now under consideration to turn the V-chip into an A-chip that would block interactive advertising as well as pornographic websites. In its spring 2005 issue, *ChildrenNow* raised a number of questions regarding interactive advertising and how it might be used in the coming digital age. It said that soon the Internet will be accessible from your digital television set, and kids will be able to make purchases using a remote control. The most advertised product types aimed at children today are breakfast cereals, soda pop, and fast foods. Critics attribute the 300% increase in childhood obesity in part to advertising. Some predict an average shortening of the life expectancy of today's children of about five years as a result. Many companies also create websites (and soon TV sites) that attract children in to them by making video games available for free and then promoting the brand via the game. Examples include the Kool-Aid Mad Scientists "Mix it Up" game, Kraft's "TooMuchFun.com" and "Chips Ahoy! Cookie Guys' Housewarming Party" on the http://NabiscoWorld.com website. This strategy of offering free games laced with advertising for the brand is called "advergaming" and is a part of "T-commerce," or television commerce, and is defined as the ability to purchase goods using your digital television and its remote control. It is now in operation in the United Kingdom, and Domino's Pizza is using it very successfully there to take orders (Espejo and Romano, 2005). To explore the implications of these innovations, go to www.childrennow.org/. Then go to the issues link, followed by the interactive advertising link. Go to the link to read how interactive media is used to sell to kids. You can also go to www.stayfreemagazine.org/archives/13/ and learn more about how companies are advertising to children via interactive media. Do these tactics seem ethical? Why or why not?

store, and sometimes they were burned or had parts of the green peel on them—can't serve those to guests. They also smelled and felt greasy, and broke easily, leaving small pieces that no one wanted to serve or take. In response, the company designed an alternative—which was, of course, Pringles. They were easy to store, never burned, weren't greasy because they were baked, not fried, were all the same size and shape, and rarely broke because of their protective packaging. Pringles were positioned as the easiest chip to store and serve.

Once a position has been established for a product, advertising prepares customers for trial and ultimate purchase. Advertising lays the groundwork for sales by increasing brand awareness using repeated slogans or jingles and by communicating and improving the brand's attributes and benefits. What is needed is advertising that makes an attractive offer that will move consumers to the point of purchase. Once consumers are at the POP, sales promotion and personal selling close the deal.

PROBLEMS OF AN OVER-COMMUNICATED SOCIETY

One of Ries and Trout's (1986; Trout, 1995; Reis, 1996) main points is that we live in an **over-communicated society**. There is simply too much communication for the average person to even hope to process. They claim that, in response, the average consumer develops an oversimplified mind, which largely ignores most of the information to which it is exposed. People select the brands they think are good and then stick with those preferences because it makes shopping easier. We call these preferences **brand loyalty**. Brand loyalty makes it easier to live in an over-communicated society because you never have to change your mind, and you can easily ignore all the ads for competing brands. Interestingly, brand loyalty is most strongly developed in consumers like yourselves who are between the ages of 18 and 24. Brands are portable. You can take them with you wherever you go. Pizza Huts are found across the country, and you can get Coca-Cola anywhere in the world. Also, brand loyalty helps consumers predict quality and value from place to place. This is appealing to those in the early years of their careers and those who face frequent job or location changes.

Advertising agencies often face the criticism that they sell people unnecessary products or brands that might even be harmful, like tobacco, alcohol, and foods high in sodium or fat. As Michael Schudson notes (1984), they defend themselves by claiming that their aim is "not to change people's product choices but to change their brand choices. Advertising... is a competitive war against commercial rivals for a share of a market" (p. 54). To break through the cluttered media landscape and get into oversimplified minds, advertisers must find something that is already in the audience's mind and then tie it to their brand. This is similar to Schwartz's evoked recall model, which gets messages out of audiences, not into them. Ries and Trout (1986; Trout, 1995; Reis 1996) suggest that the best way to do so is to use an oversimplified message. They report the results of a name recognition survey in which only 44 % of persons recognized a photo of then Vice President George Bush while 93 % of them recognized Mr. Clean—he was a much simpler message than Bush.

The over-communication problem is exacerbated by what Ries and Trout call the media explosion, which we looked at in Chapter 13. It includes TV, cable, satellite, radio, newspapers, news weeklies, magazines, catalogs, direct mail, billboards, bus signs, interactive media, and even signs in public restrooms. But there are other message carriers at work as well (see Figure 14.1). So not only do we have too many messages coming at us, but now they are everywhere. Even the human body carries trademarks like Calvin Klein, Gucci, Benetton, and Guess. Retailers like McDonald's and Subway insist that their staff members wear the brand at work on their uniforms.

Ries and Trout also call attention to the "product explosion." For example, there are mega-supermarkets, mainly in Europe and the United States, that contain more than 60,000 items from which to choose, compared to the 12,000 to 20,000

we find in the usual supermarket. And each year 25,000 new trademarks are registered at the U.S. Patent Office, with "hundreds of thousands of products and brands being sold without trademarks" (Ries and Trout, 1986, p. 14; Trout, 1995; Reis, 1996). Not only is there an increase in the volume of brand advertising, but ads also are used to promote professionals and non-profits like lawyers, doctors, universities, pharmaceutical companies, and hospitals—institutions that rarely if ever felt the need to advertise to potential clients. No wonder brand loyalty develops early and persists for many years.

Breaking Through the Clutter

How do advertisers overcome the triple whammy of exploding media, products, and advertisements? In other words, how do they break through the clutter? The techniques of positioning provide one way to do so. We encountered some of these tactics in Chapter 11, which covered market segmentation in persuasive campaigns. Here are some of them: "being first" helped products such as Jell-O, Kleenex, and Xerox copiers break the clutter and become imprinted in consumers' minds. These brand names are now virtually generic terms for the product category and are known as **master brands**. Not only was the Apple Personal Computer the first in the PC market, but it was also the first user-friendly PC. This let them get the jump on IBM, but later, Apple lost its competitive edge to a variety of other brands that offered new, better, and more universally adopted, user-friendly software such as Windows by Microsoft.

For brands not first in the market, positioning becomes even more important. They don't want to be "me too" brands. In earlier advertising eras—the brand benefit or the unique selling proposition and the brand image eras—the competition wasn't nearly as fierce as it is today. With more and more "me too" versions on the market, neither product benefits nor image ads work well. Brands have to be unique in the marketplace, and usually advertisers rely on simple but distinctive ad copy to communicate this.

The poetry of product benefits can still work, though, as can be seen by the many enduring

F I G U R E 14.1 One of the major problems for advertisers today is what Ries and Trout call the "advertising explosion," by which they mean not only the increased volume of advertising but also the new advertising vehicles, surfaces, or places where advertising can appear.

SOURCE: Used with permission of Al Ochsner.

brands that have been around for 75 years or more. For example, the Ivory Soap slogan "99 and 44/100% Pure—It Floats" was among the earliest product benefit ads, and the "It Floats" benefit was the result of a factory worker who accidentally pumped too much air into the soap. Not long after that, consumers asked for the floating version of Ivory because it was easier to find in the bathtub. It has now dropped from the leader in the product category to the number 6 selling soap. Why? Not because of poor advertising but because more people now take showers and finding the soap isn't a problem anymore (Parente, 2004). Other examples of convincing ad benefit copy include "At Ford, Quality Is Job #1," "Introducing the Smell of Luxury," and "Dermatologist Recommended." We still encounter colorful poetic ad copy, as Figure 14.2 demonstrates.

A variety of techniques can make a product seem to be the only brand in the category that has a certain benefit. There aren't many niches in a given product category, so, if competitors are firmly entrenched in the audience's mind, what can be done? One possibility is to go up against one of them with comparative advertising. Ries and Trout give an example of this approach in the Avis Rent-a-Car campaign, whose slogan was, "Avis is Number 2 in Rent-a-cars, so We Try Harder." After 13 years of losing money, Avis made $1.2 million the first year after admitting to being second, $2.6 million the second year, and $5 million the third year. Then ITT, the parent company, ditched the number-two idea and promptly lost money. Interestingly, the ads didn't hurt the market leader, Hertz. The campaign took business away from other brands in the market like National and Budget.

Another way a brand can break through clutter is to reposition itself (Trout, 1995) by telling consumers "what we're not." Seven-Up was near bankruptcy when its advertising agency came up with one of the most successful brand turnarounds in advertising history with the invention of the word "Un-cola," which they then used in very creative ways. The campaign positioned Seven-Up as the third soft drink, behind Coke and Pepsi. Dr. Pepper used the same tactic later by claiming to be not like a cola.

Another approach takes advantage of existing brand image or reputation. For example, Arm & Hammer produces baking soda, but more recently it began to make and sell the stuff in bulk to cattle farms to aid digestion and resulting increases in

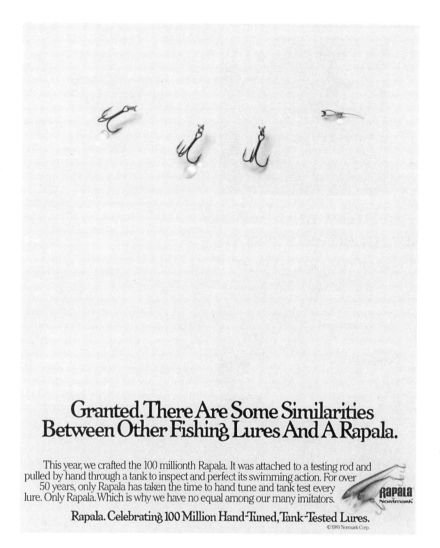

FIGURE 14.2 How did this hard-hitting product ad by Rapala break through the clutter?

SOURCE: Reprinted by permission of Normark Corp.

weight gain. This practice of bringing new brand products to market is called **line extension**, and relies on one's reputation or brand equity to break through the clutter. Inventing new uses for a brand also helps to reposition it. Again Arm and Hammer baking soda provides a great example. The brand has an unaided recognition of 97 percent, so there was no need to increase brand awareness. In 1972, the company decided to advertise a previously mentioned but not promoted new use—as a deodorant in the refrigerator. Clever ads used supposed visual odors coming out of the refrigerator which were then "absorbed" by the Arm and Hammer. Sales increased 72 percent in less than two years (Honomichl, 1984). Another strategy used by many "me too" brands is the claim to be better than old standbys to break clutter. The problem is that it's hard to convince consumers that a brand is better. Price can be another clutter breaker. A product can find a low-priced niche, such as that filled by the Hyundai or Focus, or it can find a high-priced niche like Jaguars and BMWs (see Figure 14.3).

The Purdey firearm. Created by James Purdey and Sons, the fabled London firm that has been gunmaker to the royal family since Queen Victoria's reign.

Today, the company's impeccable traditions are scrupulously maintained under the direction of The Honourable Richard Beaumont, son of the Second Viscount Allendale.

For more than 170 years, Purdey has produced sporting guns so distinctive, no two are exactly alike. The barrel of one cannot be interchanged with the stock of any other.

Purdey and Rolex: The most refined expressions of their respective arts.

So meticulous is their construction, only 70 are produced in a year. So artful is

Hand-engraving is a hallmark of Purdey guns.

their workmanship, every one is signed by the craftsman who made it. And so enduring is their precision, Purdey guns are traditionally passed down from generation to generation.

Under Richard Beaumont's chairmanship, the most rigid traditions of bespoke gunmaking prevail. Every part of

every Purdey is custom-made. Distances between the owner's eye, cheek, shoulder and trigger finger are calibrated. The measurements are designed into the stock to ensure that each gun is precisely fitted to its owner.

Richard Beaumont is a man who maintains standards of craftsmanship that speak of a more civilized time. Which makes his choice of a Rolex understandable.

Purdey utilizes the finest craftsmen in the world.

ROLEX

Datejust Oyster Perpetual Chronometer in stainless steel and 18kt gold with Jubilee bracelet. Write for brochure: Rolex Watch U.S.A., Inc., Dept. 435, Rolex Building, 665 Fifth Avenue, New York, New York 10022-5484. World headquarters in Geneva. Other offices in Canada and major countries around the world.

FIGURE 14.3 This product image ad breaks through the clutter using a copy-heavy strategy to tell Rolex's product story. The comparison between Rolex watches and Purdey shotguns relies on both the price and quality niches.

SOURCE: Reprinted by permission of Rolex Watch U.S.A., Inc.

Other clutter breakers are "positioning by gender or age." One product occupying the age niche is *Modern Maturity* magazine, which has the leading magazine circulation. Brands such as high-fiber or low-sodium foods, cholesterol and arthritis remedies, and retirement planning advertise there. Or consider the marketing of such products and services as iPods, Zappos, the BlackBerry, Nads hair remover, or resume' writing companies, all of which position themselves by age to reach the younger consumer.

Distribution and packaging can break clutter, too. L'Eggs was the first hosiery to be distributed in supermarkets. That fact and its packaging gave it a unique position in the hosiery market (Ries & Trout, 1986). In contrast to ordinary envelope hosiery packaging that needs to be folded and packed by hand, the L'Eggs hosiery could simply be stuffed into the container by machine, thus eliminating labor costs and reducing price. The egg-shaped container also was used by consumers to make craft items or for storage (Dollas, 1986).

Advertisers can also break through the clutter by repositioning an existing brand, as was the earlier case with 7-Up. A more recent repositioning is the changing of Cheerios from a children's brand to an adult one by stressing its high-fiber content (see Trout, 1995). The brand always had high fiber, but ads never mentioned that until recently, and Cheerios was losing its children segment to sweetened brands like Fruit Loops or Pebbles. Choosing the right name for a brand not only cuts through the clutter but can create a position for the brand. A powerful bathroom cleaner named itself "The Works," which fits with the idea of trying the ultimate—consumers were urged to "Give It The Works!"

All these clutter-breaking techniques grow out of various ad research on ways to get into consumers' heads and create ads that will "resonate," to use Schwartz's term (1973). Let's explore some research targeting specific markets.

GETTING INTO THE CONSUMER'S HEAD: ADVERTISING RESEARCH

Four kinds of advertising or integrated marketing research can be used to get consumer data. They are (1) demographics, (2) psychographics, (3) geographics or sociographics, and (4) ethnography (O'Guinn, Allen, & Semenik, 2006) Sometimes one, two, or all four kinds are used. Specific ways of conducting these kinds of research include gathering information that comes from census data, surveys, questionnaires, warranty cards, state and local governments, focus group interviews, the pupilometer (which tracks the eye as it scans a printed ad), and the tachistoscope. All attempt to identify Feig's (1997) consumer hot buttons and cold buttons.

Demographics

Demographics identify specific market segments on the basis of data like annual income, religious affiliation, political preferences, age, family size, gender, purchase patterns, or any combination of such factors (O'Guinn, Allen, and Semenik, 2006). Based on these data, advertisers design ads that feature certain kinds of characters or have certain settings, props, and so on. One demographic pattern involves the growing number of DINKs or folks with double-incomes and no-kids (see Figure 14.4). DINKs comprise two subgroups: (1) those who intentionally have no children and are largely self-indulgent, and (2) those whose children have left home and are now independent. The first group tends to be younger, have discretionary income, and likes to spend on themselves. The second group is the now-aging front edge of the baby boom, who also have discretionary income but who spend it in different ways—on travel, grandchildren, etc. And aging boomers are increasing at the rate of more than 2 million new consumers a year.

Advertisers need to appeal to these subgroups in very different ways, and demographic data help advertisers know a lot about these folks. For example, there are about 157 women for every 102 men in this age group, and their rate of divorce is three times the national rate. They tend to get up earlier in the day and retire earlier at night. They spend lots on grandchildren and on travel. Now, *you* play advertising executive with these data and tell when, where, and how you would appeal to this market segments for what

Berry's World

"WOW! We're DINKS — a double-income, no-kids couple!"

FIGURE 14.4 Demographics identified one segment of DINKs as older couples with no dependent children or couples who never had children and in which both persons had jobs. Advertisers appeal to this group in different ways than they advertise to other groups with other needs.

SOURCE: *Berry's World*. © United Feature Syndicate, Inc. Used with permission.

have a much smaller reach but greater frequency and are less expensive? How about using the History Channel? Or would you use direct mail to persons over the age of 60 in the states where many older citizens retire? Whom would you pick to be your spokesperson—Angela Lansbury, Burt Reynolds, Mike Ditka, Tina Turner, or someone under the age of 30? Demographics help target segments, and can also help design effective ad copy and make wise media choices.

To learn how demographics can predict such diverse things as trends in purchasing products online and immigration patterns, access InfoTrac College Edition, and enter the word "demographics" in the search engine. Select the "Demographics 2005" article, and you will discover what children as consumers in 2010 will be like. Report back to the class.

Psychographics

Psychographics is the study of consumers' lifestyles and how they feel about a product or brand (Amft, 2004). It provides data about how consumers spend their time and money, what activities they engage in, what interests them, and what their opinions are on issues (O'Guinn, Allen, & Semenik, 2006, pp. 221–224).

Activities, Interests, and Opinions. These three terms form the central focus of a segmentation system called VALS or values and lifestyles. Examples of activities are work, social events, vacations, hobbies, entertainment, club memberships, and community activities. The subcategory of good-life activities includes cultural events, gourmet cooking, investing, travel, or wine tasting. Advertisers could look at outdoor activities like skeet shooting, fishing, RVing, or motorcycling. In each of these subcategories, advertising needs to be tailored. The golfer interested in gourmet cooking, skeet shooting, and digital photography is different from the bowler who is interested in the same things. Each needs to receive personalized advertising messages.

kinds of brands. Your product is a nationwide network of health clubs that can be used anywhere in the country while traveling. Would you advertise in *Modern Maturity,* with the world's largest subscription base with lots of **reach**, defined as the number of persons who see or hear the ad, but not much **frequency**, defined as how often they see the ad? Or would you make your appeal during local evening news shows, which

Examples of interests include the family and home, achievements, recreation, fashion, technology, food, and media. Opinions relate to oneself, international, social, and political issues (e.g., global terrorism or global warming), business and economics (e.g., the price of oil), religion and culture, education, and the future (e.g., interactive television).

Psychographics ask people to respond to questions about their activities, interests, and opinions in relation to a particular brand. Advertisers then infer the respondents' lifestyles and how they are likely to respond to a brand. For example, a study determined what type of consumer would bring a malpractice suit against their doctor. Items in the survey included:

- I have a great deal of confidence in my own doctor.
- Many physicians are out of date.
- Physicians are overpaid.
- Malpractice is hard to prove.
- You are your own best doctor.

Responses ranged from "strongly agree" to "strongly disagree." Trends in responses are then correlated to persons actually bringing malpractice suits.

Persons strongly agreeing with the following items are highly likely to use Listerine mouthwash rather than Listermint mouthwash:

- I do not feel clean without a daily bath.
- Everyone should use a deodorant.
- A house should be dusted three times a week.
- Odors in the house embarrass me.
- The kind of dirt you can't see is worse than the kind you can see.
- I am a very neat person.
- Dirty dishes should be washed after every meal.
- It is very important for people to wash their hands before eating each meal.
- I use one or more household disinfectants.

Effective ads based on this trend included appeals to the germ-killing and antiseptic qualities in the brand, such as "Clean Doesn't Mean 'Good Tasting' in Mouthwashes—Use Listerine Today!"

The psychographic model most widely used in advertising and marketing is the VALS system, which can be studied at www.kellog. northwestern.edu/faculty/sterntha/module2. It describes three general lifestyles and then breaks them down into subcategories (Borchers, 2004). The general categories are (1) persons who are need-driven, (2) persons who are outer-directed, and (3) persons who are inner-directed (see Table 14.1).

Need-Driven Consumers. These consumers live in the midst of poverty. They represent only 11 percent of the population and have little discretionary income. They are forced to use their income to buy essentials. There are two subcategories of need-drivens: survivors (4 percent of the population) and sustainers (7 percent). Survivors struggle to buy the daily necessities, tend to mistrust people and brands, and are usually social misfits. They live in slums, have limited education and meager incomes, and most likely are from a minority. Sustainers' buying patterns are dominated by price and daily needs. They are a little better off, are very concerned with security and safety, and really want to get ahead and think they can because they are street wise. They have limited educations, low incomes, and aren't necessarily from a minority. Price is important to them, but they also are cautious and want warranties. Their want to get ahead and are targets for get-rich-quick schemes such as multilevel marketing, the lottery, or dealing drugs.

Outer-Directed Consumers. They make up 67 percent of the marketplace and are crucial targets for all advertisers. Outer-directeds include belongers (35 percent), who are conventional, traditional, rarely experiment with new products or services, and tend to be blue-collar workers with low to middle levels of education. They are family oriented, like products with domestic

Table 14.1 VALS Segmentation

Percentage of Population (age 18 & over)	Consumer Type	Values and Lifestyles	Demographics	Buying Patterns
NEED-DRIVEN CONSUMERS 4%	Survivors	Struggle for survival Distrustful Socially misfitted Ruled by appetites	Poverty-level income Little education Many minority members Many live in city slums	Price dominant Focused on basics Buying for immediate needs
7	Sustainers	Concern with safety, security Insecure, compulsive Dependent, following Streetwise, determined to get ahead	Low income Low education Much unemployment Live in country as well as cities	Price important Want warranty Cautious buyers
OUTER-DIRECTED CONSUMERS 35%	Belongers	Conforming, conventional Unexperimental Traditional, formal Nostalgic	Low to middle income Low to average education Blue-collar jobs Tend toward noncity living	Family Home Fads Middle and lower mass markets
10	Emulators	Ambitious, show-off Status conscious Upwardly mobile Macho, competitive	Good to excellent income Youngish Highly urban Traditionally male, but changing	Conspicuous consumption "In" items Imitative Popular fashion
22	Achievers	Achievement, success, fame Materialism Leadership, efficiency Comfort	Excellent income Leaders in business, politics, etc. Suburban and city living	Give evidence of success Top of the line Luxury and gift markets "New and improved" products
INNER-DIRECTED CONSUMERS 5%	I-am-me	Fiercely individualistic Dramatic, impulsive Experimental Volatile	Young Many single Student or starting job Affluent background	Display one's taste Experimental fads Source of far-out fads Clique buying

Table 14.1   VALS Segmentation (Continued)

Percentage of Population (age 18 & over)	Consumer Type	Values and Lifestyles	Demographics	Buying Patterns
7	Experiential	Drive to direct experience Active, participative Person-centered Artistic	Bimodal income Most under 40 Many young families Good education	Process over product Vigorous outdoor sports "Making" home pursuits Crafts and introspection
8	Socially conscious	Societal responsibility Simple living Smallness of scale Inner growth	Bimodal low and high incomes Excellent education Diverse ages and places of residence Largely white	Conservation emphasis Simplicity Frugality Environmental concerns
2	Integrated	Psychological maturity Sense of fittingness Tolerant, self-actualizing World perspective	Good to excellent incomes Bimodal in age Excellent education Diverse jobs and residential patterns	Varied self-expression Esthetically oriented Ecologically aware One-of-a-kind items

SOURCE: Reprinted with permission of Macmillan Publishing Company from Arnold Mitchell, *Nine American Lifestyles: Who We Are and Where We Are Going* (New York: Macmillan, 1983). Copyright © 1983 by Arnold Mitchell.

appeals, are nostalgic, and are good targets for direct-response television ads such as those for "Great Music of the 80s," and are affected by fads. Emulators (10 percent) are upwardly mobile, ambitious, status conscious, and competitive. They have good incomes, tend to be young, and live in urban areas. Emulators are into conspicuous consumption, purchase "in" products, and are good targets for the newest, most expensive styles in clothing, automobiles, and activities. Achievers (22 percent) have "made it" and are interested in efficiency, leadership, achievement, success, fame, comfort, and conspicuous consumption. They have high incomes and levels of education, and live in suburbs and trendy parts of large cities. They tend to be leaders in politics, business, and community activities, buy top-of-the-line brands

and new products, and are good targets for luxury items.

Inner-Directed Consumers.   Inner-directed consumers (22 percent) are divided into four subcategories. "I am me" consumers (5 percent) are individualistic, experimental, impulsive, dramatic, and volatile, come from affluent backgrounds, reject traditional possessions or ways, but may not have much discretionary income. They are students or are just starting on the occupational ladder.

Experientials (7 percent) want to have many and varied experiences and participate in many activities. They are introspective, frequently artistic, and have high or low incomes depending on their life choices. They have good educations, support the arts, are likely to have families, and to be under

40 years old. Experientials' buying habits focus on vigorous outdoor sports like mountain climbing, and they are also into do-it-yourself projects related to the home, and are good targets for products from L. L. Bean or Eddie Bauer.

Societally conscious consumers (8 percent) want simple living and are concerned with the environment. They have a sense of societal responsibility and may join the Sierra Club, Greenpeace, the Nuclear Freeze Movement, or the Green Party. They seek smallness of scale and inner growth. They are mainly white and have excellent educations but bimodal incomes. These consumers live in large cities, small towns, or on farms. They have a conservation orientation, and focus on simplicity and frugality. They are good targets for energy-saving devices, good gas mileage hybrids, organic gardening, and wine making.

Integrated consumers (2 percent) feel good about themselves, are tolerant, and have a sense of psychological maturity. They self-actualize and take a broad view of the world, and are concerned over issues like acid rain and products that pollute. They have good-to-excellent incomes, vary in age, work in diverse occupations, and are good targets for products that allow for self-expression, such as restoring historic homes or collecting unique things. They are good targets for art, music, or drama. This market segment is growing, while need-driven consumers are declining, and the proportion of outer-directed consumers remains stable. Advertisers use these patterns to design brands and the ads for promoting them, and targeted offers that appeal to the patterns of each group.

To better understand how psychographics can help segment markets, access InfoTrac College Edition, and enter the words "psychographics" in the search engine. Read some of the articles.

Sociographics/Geographics

Sociographics or **geographics** is the study of how, why, and where people live. Its basic assumption is that "birds of a feather flock together." People choose to live with or near persons similar to themselves. Sociographics/geographics is a combination of the places people live, demographics (the clusterings of variables associated with them), and psychographics (O'Guinn, Allen, and Semenik, 2006). Research on these data is done by sampling persons from a zip code area that resembles the kind of neighborhood the advertiser believes will be attracted to the brand. Then the researchers invite residents to participate in focus groups and answer a survey about the brand and its competitors. Researchers look for patterns in the survey responses and words used repeatedly in focus group comments. The ad agency's creative staff designs messages around the consumer-generated copy points. Sociographics also show media-use patterns and program preferences.

A related system is PRIZM, which is marketed by the Claritas Corporation. The system has identified 62 distinct psychographic and sociographic neighborhood types. It uses catchy names that suggest what the neighborhood is like. For example, one is called "two more rungs," for the young emulators on their way up. "Shotguns and pickups" are high-school-educated, blue-collar workers who live in mobile homes, have a large-screen TV, a dusty pickup, and drink generic brands of sugared soft drinks. They are frequently overweight and usually go to fast food or all-you-can-eat buffet restaurants. Claritas knows an amazing amount about "towns and gowns," or typical college towns like the one where you might be. They are populated largely by white singles who are college students or recent grads, vote Republican, and jog. They use ATM machines, bounce checks frequently, and are unlikely to have a van, a toy-sized dog, mutual funds, or burglar alarm systems. However, they do have personal loans, like to water and snow ski, read *Modern Bride* or *Gentleman's Quarterly*, and drive Subaru DL4s, Toyota Tercels, Hundai Excels, or Volkswagen Jettas. They like *David Letterman* but hate Sunday morning interview programs.

 As critical consumers of persuasion, you need to be alert to the degree to which advertisers have psychographically designed ads aimed at you or your market segment. For more details go to http://www.clusterbigip1.claritas.com.

Ethnographics

A research technique called **ethnographics** depends on the researcher going out into the field and observing how consumers select and use brands. Then they interview users and probe for details. For example, they might watch shoppers in the bread department and see if and how many shoppers examine the expiration date on the packages. Or if they are interested in how consumers use and consume food, they might go to the consumers' homes and ask to see and photograph their refrigerator, freezer, pantry, and cookbooks. Then they ask questions about which ingredients are used most frequently, how long things have been in the freezer, and what the homemaker's favorite recipes are. Based on the results, the researchers go to the R & D department and develop a new brand or reposition an old one (e.g., Cheerios) to fit the consumers' reported habits and needs.

A good recent example was the development of Gillette's Sensor 3 disposable razor. It is specifically designed for women (Parente, 2004) and was based on the differences between the ways men and women shave. Researchers noted that when men cut themselves while shaving, they blamed the shaver. When women cut themselves when shaving their legs, they blame themselves. When interviewed, men said they wanted a sharper razor whereas women wanted a duller one. After asking more probing questions, researchers found that women used a razor with the handle pointing up while men shaved with the handle pointing down. This makes sense since men usually shave their face at a sink, while women usually shave their legs while showering. The women got upset when they dropped the razor, which meant bending down to pick it up and getting water and soap or shampoo in their eyes. Women reported that a thicker, nonslippery handle would be preferred. Armed with this research, designers created the Sensor 3 for women with three spring-loaded blades, protective microfins, and an ergonomically styled, thicker, rubber-coated handle with grip-holding ridges. The men's Sensor had two razor blades with a similar handle but with a smaller head to shave hard-to-reach places around the nose and mouth. Both razors got high marks, and Gillette launched a successful nationwide rollout in 2002.

Go to InfoTrac College Edition, and enter the words "demographics," "sociographics," "psychographics," and "ethnography" one at a time in the search engines. Which of the three yields the most entries? Why do you think that is the case?

FROM RESEARCH TO COPY: THE LANGUAGES OF ADVERTISING

Research results go to the agency's creative staff for conversion into attention-getting and memorable ad and PR copy. It must be believable but should also sell the brand amidst the clutter. John O'Toole (1985), the former CEO of a major ad agency and past president of the American Association of Advertising Agencies, made some interesting observations about reaching the audience. He believes the consumer should be at the center of the process, and that the only kind of language—verbal and nonverbal—that effectively persuades targets the consumer as an individual. The first task with a new brand is to develop a personal profile of the consumer and then use personal language and copy, such as, "Aren't you glad you use Dial? Don't you wish everyone did?" or the Sears DieHard battery ad copy that follows a demonstration of the battery in action: "The DieHard. Starts Your Car When Most Other Batteries Won't." These copy lines aim at an individual and not the masses. Consumers recognize their experiences in the words and visuals of the ad.

WEASEL WORDS IN ADVERTISING

We need to examine how clever persuaders use words in ads to mislead us. Carl Wrighter's classic book *I Can Sell You Anything* (1972) focuses on some of the key words used to deceive us. He calls them **weasel words** because they allow persuaders to seem to say something without really saying anything. These words let sources weasel their way out of a promise. They are key tip-offs to the kind of pitch to guard against. Though Wrighter first identified them over 30 years ago, you will discover that they are still frequently used in today's advertisements.

Helps

The word "helps" seems to offer aid, relief, or perhaps a solution but promises nothing. For example, take the slogan "Listerine mouthwash helps prevent colds." What is the promise here? Can you expect that you will feel better in a few days if you use Listerine? If you did, was your improvement the from the help Listerine gave? When you really think about it, drinking lots of liquids and getting enough rest is what really helps.

Like

Another weasel is the word "like." A tennis star says, "Driving a Nissan Maxima is like driving an expensive European model." The house brand is "just like" the expensive name brands. You can easily see the deception with a word that has as many loopholes as "like." It only means that something resembles something else—and that resemblance may be a stretch. Cindy Crawford is supposed to be like women all over the world. A prepared food tastes just like homemade. A jug wine tastes like the expensive French brands. Fruitopia will make you feel like you are an athletic champion.

Virtually

The weasel word "virtually" resembles "like," except that it seems to promise even more. The new cotton chamois shirts are "virtually indestructible." Leatherette feels "virtually" like cowhide. Cascade leaves your dishes and glassware "virtually spotless." The promises seem so specific, and there is only a tiny loophole. But that loophole widens when the customer says that the leatherette wore out after several months or finds spots on the dishes just washed with Cascade. If the product did the job, the word "virtually" would be irrelevant.

Faster

Some products need to be fast acting, such as over-the-counter medication or products related to personal safety. The brands in this product category frequently use the weasel word **"faster"** to sell the brand. Goodyear tires stop faster. Faster than what? Another brand? Than a donut? They give no basis for comparison. When you encounter this weasel, start making comparisons with the competition.

As Much As

This weasel word seems to offer high performance but only to a point. "You can save as much as 50 percent with a Good Health Club prescription membership." You may save nothing, a little, or maybe 50 percent, but there are no guarantees on the 50 percent savings. When you see the words **"as much as"** or "up to," let the buyer beware.

DECEPTIVE CLAIMS IN ADVERTISING

Another kind of deception in ads is in the claims that they make. Clever promoters use claims to attract our attention and to prompt us to buy, to vote for candidates, or to adopt certain practices, but they promise little. Let us look at several kinds of claims identified by Wrighter (1972).

The Irrelevant Claim

Some ads make claims that sound impressive but are irrelevant if you look at them closely. The basic tactic is to make a truthful claim that has little to do with the benefits of the brand. Then the claim is dramatized in such a way as to link the claim with the product, candidate, or movement. J&B scotch claims to be "rare" and "natural." Are other scotch whiskeys unnatural? If you can't find an answer to your question, you have identified an irrelevant claim. Wrigley's new "Green Apple Extra" chewing gum has a scratch and sniff feature, but that's irrelevant. You chew gum for its flavor, not its aroma. The Ford Escape is "built for the road." Well, so are all brands and models.

The Question Claim

Wrighter noted a kind of claim that asks a question. "If you can't trust Prestone, who can you trust?", "Why not buy the original?", "Would a bunch of guys really go at it this hard just for a Michelob?", and "Why not catch a lunker—with Stren monofilament?" are all examples of the question claim. Notice that the product advantage is only implied. Trusting one's antifreeze is okay, but the question implies that dependability is to be found only in Prestone. Why buy the overpriced original? Maybe the Michelob is just an afterthought. Will using Stren guarantee that you'll get a big one? Not likely. When you see a question mark, ask for details and guarantees.

The Advantage Claim

Wrighter noted some claims that seem to offer a unique advantage for the brand. For example, Mother's noodles are made with 100 percent semolina wheat, but so are all the other brands, including the generics. Compare the levels of vitamins in several types of breakfast cereal. They are all about the same, and most of the protein comes from the milk you add. These are advantages that aren't advantages. Politicians often claim to have humble origins, which is supposed to be an advantage. It may be a real disadvantage. People who had humble beginnings might be very insecure. They might have limited educations, social skills, and abilities to

FIGURE 14.5 The hazy claims about longevity and yogurt may confuse the persuadee enough to try the product, just to be on the safe side.

SOURCE: Used by permission of Dannon Milk Products.

communicate with leaders in higher social strata. Whenever you are faced with a person, product, or idea that claims some significant advantage, ask if it is real and if it is exclusive to that brand, candidate, or cause.

The Hazy Claim

The hazy claim confuses the buyer or voter. The Dannon yogurt ad in Figure 14.5 implies that Dannon yogurt eaters live longer. As you read the ad copy, you see that the only health claim Dannon truly makes is that its yogurt has active cultures. But is it good to eat Dannon yogurt,

yogurt of any kind, or no yogurt? Dannon persuades us through its hazy slogan: "If you don't always eat right, Dannon yogurt is the right thing to eat." Why is it right? Who says? With what proof?" Again, we can see hazy claims widely used in the world of politics. For example, a politician says that she supports both global economic policies and tariffs. These are 180 degrees apart.

The Mysterious or Magic Ingredient Claim

Wrighter says that some claims refer to a magical or mysterious ingredient that makes their brand better. Noxzema sells a brand called Acne 12, which they say contains a secret ingredient dermatologists prescribe most. Oxy-Clean contains "a powerful yet gentle medication no ordinary cleanser has." Zantrex-3 claims to have an ingredient—bifurcated compounds—that can increase weight loss by 546 percent when compared to pills having ephedrine. That mysterious or magic ingredient claim would be difficult to track down. Chlorets succeeded by claiming that each one had a magic drip of "retsyn" in it which accounted for the brand's superiority. Retsyn is another word for salad oil which was used as a binder in the manufacture of Chlorets. You will discover many other kinds of claims made through the mass media. The important thing is to maintain a critical attitude.

Rank's 30-Second-Spot Quiz

Hugh Rank, at www.webserve.govst.edu/users/ghrank/advertising, outlined an easy-to-apply set of key questions to ask about advertising appeals. His system, the 30-second-spot quiz, is in his book *The Pitch* (1991). Rank began by pointing out that any advertisements, but especially TV spots, are a synthesis of complex variables like research, scripts, settings, camera angles, acting, props, costumes, colors, and so on. Responsible consumers need to look at the spots in a sequential way. Rank suggested listing the shots or visual frames that make up a

TV spot in sequence. There might be up to 40 quick-cut edited shots in a 30-second spot, and most have an establishing shot, which sets the stage for the ad. Various versions of a spot for a new brand of beer used images of familiar sights in the cities in which the advertising was tested. The San Francisco version used the Golden Gate Bridge, and the Chicago version used the Sears Tower. Other shots further the story of the ad. A medium shot showing a couple from the waist up involved in an argument tells us that conflict is central to the story. The audio comes up, and we discover that they are arguing about whether to buy an American or a foreign-made automobile. The camera moves in for a close-up shot of the man's face, and we hear musical tension increasing as we see and hear the tension in his face and voice. Then the close-up shot shifts to the woman's face, and we hear her say, "You know, you're cute when you're serious like this." Then we hear a giggle and see them nuzzle with one another as they look at a Hundai ad. The shots tell the story. Your job as a receiver is to list the shots in order until the ad is completely described. Then try to identify the underlying structure of the spot. For example, the underlying structure of the ad just described is conflict resolution, but a surface variation could have used two males for the argument. This would alter the dialogue, tension, drama, and meaning of the ad. Rank also suggests recognizing the audience's involvement in the spot. What benefits are being promised by the brand? For example, the Ford Escort initially advertised that it had aerodynamic styling, independent wheel suspension, and rack and pinion steering. These are features of the Escort not benefits. Features should offer some benefit to the consumer. For instance, aerodynamic styling offers better handling, less wind resistance, better gas mileage, and a quieter interior. Once these preparatory steps are taken, Rank suggests asking five basic analytical questions:

1. *What attention-getting techniques are being used?* Most ads appeal to one or more of the five senses (see Figure 14.6). Most also appeal to consumers' emotions and use the unexpected, the interesting, and the noticeable to capture

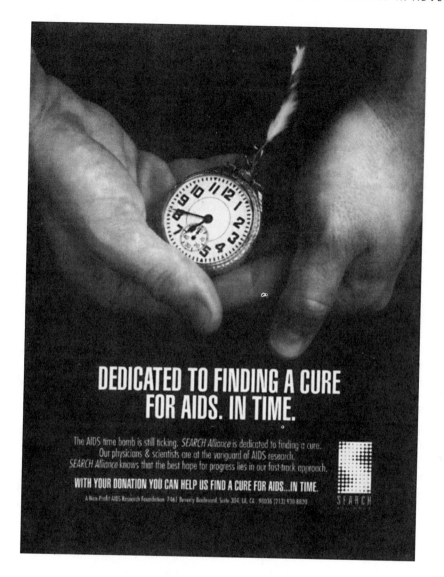

DEDICATED TO FINDING A CURE FOR AIDS. IN TIME.

The AIDS time bomb is still ticking. *SEARCH Alliance* is dedicated to finding a cure. Our physicians & scientists are at the vanguard of AIDS research. *SEARCH Alliance* knows that the best hope for progress lies in our fast-track approach.

WITH YOUR DONATION YOU CAN HELP US FIND A CURE FOR AIDS...IN TIME.

A Non-Profit AIDS Research Foundation 7461 Beverly Boulevard, Suite 304, LA, CA. 90036 (213) 930-8820

SEARCH

FIGURE 14.6 Using Rank's 30-second-spot quiz, explain how this ad gets consumer attention.

SOURCE: By permission of Search Alliance.

consumer attention and often keep the consumer wondering until the end what brand the ad is trying to sell.

2. *What confidence-building techniques are being used to convince consumers that they can trust the brand?* Authority figures, repetition, references to the number of years the brand has been successful, and appeals to trust and sincerity all inspire trust. The use of expert testimony from a doctor or lawyer, guarantees, and warranties all build consumer trust and confidence.

3. *What desire-stimulating techniques are being used to motivate consumers to try the brand?* Rank said identifying the benefits is a good way to discover these techniques. He noted that most ads offer one or more of the following as desire-stimulating reasons to try the brand: Preventing

or avoiding some bad thing (discomfort or embarrassment), protecting or keeping some good thing (status, appearance, or wealth), gaining relief or getting rid of some bad thing (dandruff or financial worry), and acquiring or getting some good thing (a new economical car that gets great mileage or a good interest rate on a home loan).

4. *What urgency-stressing techniques are being used to get consumers to "act now"?* Examples include expiration dates or language warning that the price is only good "while supplies last."

5. *What response-seeking techniques are being used to tell consumers what kind of action is being sought?* Examples include "try" the brand, "purchase it," "join," or "call" the 1-800 number.

CHANGES IN OUR WORLD: IMPLICATIONS FOR ADVERTISING

Recall the trends noted at the beginning of this chapter. Markets are becoming more global, fragmented, and diverse. More families than ever now rely on two or more incomes per household and are often strapped for time. Who are the targets of ads promising convenience and the saving of time? Working spouses? Widows and widowers? Single persons? Divorced persons? To some extent all of these, because of busy two-income families and kids who have increased activities. As a result, meals are no longer the traditional family around the dinner table. Families are dining out, bringing home meals, or having home delivery of dinner. Americans now eat more than half of their meals out.

Another change has been the emphasis on convenience for these same consumers. Since the introduction of 1-800 dialing, it is easier to purchase anything from clothing to baseball tickets. Time is a commodity for most two-income families and should be spent carefully, and so mail-order and online purchasing not only saves time but allows you to avoid the inconvenience of finding a parking spot, walking to the store, and waiting in line to check out. Many strip malls and even megamalls now have "space for lease" because we now face a very competitive marketplace, especially given the amount of income spent using catalogs, the Internet, shopping channels, and other direct-marketed outlets. Today we see pre-Christmas sales right after Halloween as well as the traditional post-Christmas sales. We start selling back to school stuff right after the Fourth of July. Retailers want to get a jump on the competition. Large discount chains have increased as well, and so advertising had to increase to beat the competition. In the years to come, there will be still more clutter for us to try to sift through, and we are only on the front edge of interactive and Internet advertising.

Creating Interest, Desire, and Conviction

Advertising consultants Vestergaard and Schroeder advise getting attention for an ad by asking a question that consumers cannot answer. This provokes curiosity and leads the audience to interact with the ad. Examples include scratch 'n' sniff ads, recipes, and ads including a true/false quiz for the reader to answer. An ad by General Motors asks, "Do you know where your next fender is coming from?" Then they satisfy the reader's curiosity by answering, "America's body shops are being flooded with imitation parts. Look-alike doors. Copycat hoods. Imitation bumpers, grills, fenders and more.... Insist on genuine GM parts." This ad copy not only answers the attention-getting question in the headline, but it also creates interest, desire, and conviction in the consumer via product benefits. Notice the frequent use of sentence fragments—"look-alike doors and copycat hoods." These give the advertiser extra shots at the reader.

Advertisers also need to avoid looking like "me too" imitations of the original. All dog food looks pretty much the same—either like gravel if it is dry or like glop if it is canned. But look at what Gaines Burger did. In the first place, the name sounds like and the product looks like hamburger—the all-American food. Of course, its redness is not natural. It's just iron oxide and won't hurt your dog, but it will cause your mind to make a link with hamburgers on the grill. Another tactic used to create interest, desire, and conviction for a "me too" brand is to stress its high quality. For example, a face powder named Solar Power SPF—20 is marketed by a company named Physicians Formula. Now if a physician formulated the powder, it must be good. Its slogan is "Your eyes won't believe your face." If they claim that the brand has the best quality for the price, they are not likely to be asked to prove the claim. Another approach is to appeal to anything scientific by including some scientific-sounding ingredient such as got2b, DZM-21, or Aididas' "aluminum free deodorant with cotton TECH that absorbs wetness." An advertiser can also make a scientific claim like "Contains the pain reliever recommended most by doctors and hospitals." Of course that ingredient is aspirin. Or someone wearing a white lab smock tells us about the features and benefits of the brand.

Getting Action

The hardest thing to do in sales is to close the sale or to **get action**. "Buy now!" would seem to be the most direct call to action, but there are other ways to say "buy" without using the word "buy," which can turn many prospects off. For example, "act now," "phone now," and 'send now" say the same thing but avoid the potentially negative word "buy." Other urgency-stressing words stress Cialdini's scarcity principle to prompt action, as in "offer good until," "24-hour sale," or "only a few left at this price." Of the many ads studied by Vestergaard and Schroeder, 32 percent used directive language. Directive language falls into one of several categories.

1. *The imperative clause*, which gives an order. "Get one today" is one example. Another example is in an ad for a fishing lure supposedly in short supply—the Shadrap. The ad copy for

it implied that the company was only able to send a limited quantity to the United States and then added, "That's enough for every serious fisherman ... as long as they take only one—if you see one, grab it!" I bought six, and they were only available to rent in Ely, Minnesota, gateway to the Boundery Waters Canoe Wilderness Area.

2. *Other less directive and more suggestive language encouraging purchase*, like "Isn't it time you tried Dial?" or "Why not try Dial?" or "Dial is Worth a Try."

3. *Directive language invites the reader/viewer to send for details, use the trial sample, or remember the product*. These appeals might get a sale, but more often, they create what are called "qualified leads" that can be followed up on later. For example, if consumers send in for a free pamphlet on energy saving, they are probably good prospects for storm windows, aluminum siding, insulation, or solar panels. Vestergaard and Schroeder recommend seventeen verbs other than the word "buy." They are "try," "ask for," "take," "send for," "call," "make," "come on," "hurry," "come," "see," "give," "remember," "discover," "serve," "introduce," "choose," and "look for."

SEXUAL APPEALS AND SUBLIMINAL PERSUASION IN ADVERTISING

The use of sexual appeals and subliminal persuasion in advertising is not new, but it is very controversial. For example, feminists are concerned about advertising's exploitation of the female body. Others, like parents, school officials, and physicians are concerned about increases in STDs in today's youth and teenage pregnancy. They question the ethics of subliminal appeals. Sexual appeals in ads range from the blatant ones promising sexual success (e.g., Viagra) to more sophisticated and symbolic ones that only suggest sexual

---

B O X 14.2 Cultural Diversity and Advertising

 The fastest growing and most fascinating segments of the ad industry are the multicultural and diversity markets. A variety of agencies specializing in diverse and multicultural advertising have mushroomed in the past decade. A prime example is the Allied Media Corporation located online at www. allied-media.com/. Just consider a few of the services it offers for advertisers to target various cultures and ethnic segments: public relations, media planning, direct marketing, media design and placement, event planning, Web design, multimedia productions, mailing lists, ethnic radio and television, and translation. It specializes in all the kinds of segments that come to mind first, such as Latinos, African Americans, women, and Asian Americans, but it also places ads aimed at less well-known market segments, such as Arabic newspapers, Arabic-language electronic media, Arabic targeted direct mail, and others. It provides the same services for the Russian, South Asian, Middle Eastern, Polish, Portuguese, Gay/Lesbian, and Native American markets. Visit its website, and you will be amazed at the depth and breath of the kinds of skills and services now emerging to address the advertising needs of our increasingly diverse and multicultural country and world.

---

success if the brand is used (e.g., Victoria's Secret). And there are also subliminal ads that suggest sexual success but target the unconscious or subliminal level.

Freud maintained that sexual and procreative urges are among the most powerful motivators of human action. They frequently lead to some symbolic behaviors such as fathers passing out cigars on the birth of a new child. These symbolic actions often give sexual meanings to objects and actions. Freud saw cylindrical objects such as pens, cigarettes, and guns as symbols of male genitalia and round or open objects such as goblets or open windows and doors as symbols of female genitalia. To him all sorts of ordinary everyday activities such as smoking a cigarette, cupping the hands, or fiddling with one's pen unconsciously symbolized sexual activities. His work was ridiculed by many, but it was taken very seriously by many people in the field of advertising. Simple observation makes it clear that sexual appeals abound in ads. Let's examine some obvious, some more sophisticated and not so obvious, and some possibly subliminal uses of sexual appeals in print and electronic ads. These kinds of appeals are likely to be processed in the peripheral channel of the ELM.

Researcher A. N. Valdivia (1997) deconstructed two very different kinds of sexual appeals in lingerie catalogs. The merchandise was priced almost the same but the quality was very different, and the ad appeals were not nearly equivalent. For example, the name of one company, Victoria's Secret, connotes an old-world class that seems almost prudish. The other catalog, Frederick's of Hollywood, connotes a kind of leering glitziness. The settings in Victoria's Secret ads connote wealth, leisure, class, and an English country house atmosphere. In Frederick's of Hollywood, the photos are mostly shot against fabric backdrops, and the only items of furniture in them are beds, couches, and poolside lounge chairs. Victoria's Secret models appear demure and look away from the camera. Frederick's of Hollywood models leer at the camera, hands on hips, eyes closed, and jaws clenched. The Victoria's Secret catalog is published every month and costs $3 (though no one really pays for it), the company's home address is in London, their telephone operators speak with an English accent, and the catalog is mailed from England.

To learn more about the use of sexual appeals in advertising, enter the term "sexual social marketing" in InfoTrac College Edition to find the article on sexual social marketing by Reichert, Heckler, and Jackson. What conclusions are drawn there about the impact of sexual appeals on processing?

FIGURE 14.7 Blatant uses of sexual appeals promise sexual success to the user of the product.

SOURCE: Reprinted by permission of Tsumura International.

Blatant Sexual Appeals

Blatant sexual appeals usually promise sexual success or satisfaction to the user in both the verbal and the nonverbal channels. In the ad for Royal Copenhagen Cologne for Men (Figure 14.7), the appeal is quite obvious—use the brand, and you will experience sexual success. The words "Some of the wildest storms occur below deck" trigger the readers' minds and the inset picture of the naked couple kissing tells the rest of the story. The reader would have to be slow not to get the meaning here.

Some more subtle sexual appeals are at work in the ad, such as the phallic prow of the ship and the bottles of cologne. The two bottles, one boxed and one opened, might suggest sex. The photo inset seen in a "secret" window makes all of us voyeurs.

More Sophisticated Sexual Appeals

More **sophisticated sexual appeals** only hint at sexual satisfaction with use of the brand. Such appeals contain subtle cues to indicate sexual prowess. For example, in an ad by Tiffany for a sterling silver flask named Pendant, a close-up photo shows the Pendant flask, dripping water, and resting in the cleavage of a well-endowed, wet, and apparently nude woman. The stem of an orchid is inserted into the flask on which a praying mantis is perched. The ad contains the brand name but no words or promise of sexual success, prowess, or satisfaction. Yet the ad clearly uses a sexual appeal. Freud would probably note the symbolism of the phallic orchid stem inserted into the vaginally shaped flask, and the abundance of water as symbolic of completed intercourse. But why the praying mantis?

Subliminal Appeals

Subliminal appeals are a highly controversial topic (Phillips and Goodkin, 1983). In fact, many people doubt their very existence. Why should this topic stir up so much controversy? It does so because it runs counter to the idea that human beings are by nature logical, not emotional, and are certainly not totally preoccupied by sex. Then, too, subliminal persuasion smacks of sensationalism. Let us examine the arguments of those who claim that subliminal messages exist and the controversy over whether the technique works.

Support for the Existence of Subliminal Messages. The basic premise underlying **subliminal persuasion** rests on the notion of the unconscious mind and that its impulses are so powerful that they must be enacted in conscious life, even if in only symbolic ways. Freud believed that the unconscious mind is constantly at work processing information that the conscious mind simply ignores. Those who believe in the existence of subliminal appeals maintain that such appeals are sometimes so short-lived and disguised that the conscious mind ignores them, yet at the subconscious level, they are extremely powerful and highly motivating.

Go to www.subliminal-message.info/age_of_subliminal_communication/html for a recent evaluation of the topic.

The technique was dismissed when first publicized in the 1950s, but it was and still is barred from use in the electronic media by the FCC. However, their ruling did not cover the print and film media. Over a dozen commercial research firms in Chicago and New York still offer services in producing subliminal messages for advertisers. The issue reemerged in the presidential campaign of 2000. A negative television ad was commissioned by the Republican National Committee criticizing Al Gore's prescription drug proposal. It had the word "RATS" flashed over the images and spelled the word "Democrats this way "Democ-RATS." The CIA has an ongoing interest in subliminal persuasion in intelligence work, espionage, and counterespionage (Goodkin & Phillips, 1983).

Researcher and professor of advertising, Wilson Bryan Key popularized the issue of subliminal sexual appeals in his books *Subliminal Seduction* (1973), *Media Sexploitation* (1977), and *Clambake Orgy* (1980). All the books claimed that subliminal erotic cues were embedded in magazine ads appealing to subconscious and repressed sex drives. These **embeds** were faintly airbrushed into ads in the final stages of production and were subconsciously remembered later when cued by a store display to buy the brand. Key was originally struck by the need to retouch photos in most liquor ads by airbrushing in images of ice cubes in the glasses—real ice cubes melted under the hot lights needed for magazine-quality photos. Since the persuaders were airbrushing in the ice cubes, he reasoned that they might consider airbrushing in a subtle message such as the words "buy" or "good" in the cubes. Key showed 1,000 persons such an ad and asked them to describe the feelings they had while looking at them. Although 38 percent didn't respond, 62 percent reported that the ad made them feel sensual, aroused, romantic, sexy, and even horny. Key reports having replicated the test with several ads and other audiences with similar results.

More recently, Kevin Hogan (2005) observed that subliminal perception has been back on the front burner since 1990. His research and that of others show that while subliminal audio messages do not work—with the exception of priming and stealth marketing discussed earlier—the story is much different with visual or video subliminal messages. Hogan contends that the visual cortex responds to stimuli not in conscious awareness and takes unseen information and shares it with other parts of the brain, causing actions to be taken. He reports an experiment on paying for drinking water conducted by Piotr Winkleman, a psychology professor at the University of California at San Diego in 2004. Testing undergraduate students there, Winkelman used thirst, amount of consumption, and the price one was willing to pay for a glass of water as variables. Subjects would be offered a glass of water in two conditions—one after seeing a happy face and the other after having seen an angry face. Thirsty subjects drank twice as much after being exposed to a happy face versus an angry one and were willing to pay $0.38 versus only $0.10 after the angry face.

Some Possible Subliminal Ads. Let's explore some advertisements that may indeed use subliminal or near-subliminal persuasion. In all cases, their appeals seem to promise sexual prowess, success, and satisfaction. Consider the two perfume ads in Figures 14.8 and 14.9. The first ad is called "The Promise Made," and the second is "The Promise Kept." They were run side by side or on consecutive pages. Observe what has changed between "The Promise Made" and "The Promise Kept." For instance, in "The Promise Kept," the champagne bottle is empty, the phone is off the hook, the fire has died down, the woman's shoes and perfume atomizer are on the dais, the flowers on the left seem to have blossomed and opened in the heat, and the woman's earrings are off, as is her stole. What subtle sexual messages do you find in the difference between the two ads? Do the headlines imply any dual meanings?

Now turn your attention to Figures 14.10, 14.11, and 14.12. They were part of an ongoing series of ads for Seagram's gin called the "Hidden Pleasure" campaign. The ads use embeds, but instead of hiding them, Seagram's points them out to readers. The appeals in them are not directly sexual but rather are only benignly romantic. In the ad in Figure 14.10, the key words turn out to be "HIDDEN PLEASURES," "Serve One," and "It's a hit," because embedded in hidden images in the ice cubes and drops of moisture on the glasses are two tennis players. The male at the left has his racquet lifted as if serving a tennis ball; the female on the right has her racquet in the ready position. In Figure 14.11, the ad designers have once again given a clue for finding the embed: The words "Hint. It's as smooth as a moonlit waltz" are at the left of the goblet where an arrow points to a waltzing couple emerging out of the air bubbles in the martini glass. In Figure 14.12, we see a couple embedded in the ice cubes sitting next to one another on a swing, holding hands.

Are Subliminals Effective? If subliminal messages are used, can they be effective in persuasion? The past president of the American Psychology Association's Division of Consumer Psychology says, "Absolutely.... The controversy has always been over changing people's attitudes. That you can't do. What you can do is trigger a prior attitude or predisposition" (Lander, 1981, p. 45). That statement reflects what we have been talking about all along—the most effective persuasion taps information that receivers already possess. As we have repeatedly observed, effective persuaders get messages *out of* their audiences, not *into* them.

While the ad people deny using the technique, subliminal self-help tapes have become a multibillion-dollar business, and many users are true believers in the method. Of course, certain ads that use sex aren't at all subliminal about their messages. The Calvin Klein ads promoting Obsession for Men are good examples. Others border on the subliminal. The message is hazy but clear enough to give you the idea the advertiser wants you to get. A good example is the

"The Promise Made"

FIGURE 14.8 What kind of promise is being made?

SOURCE: Courtesy Lanvin Parfums Co., New York.

campaign to promote Travel Fox sneakers using ads that contained little ad copy. The visuals showed various permutations of a man and a woman wearing the shoes and posing in various suggestive positions, as shown in Figure 14.13. Did it work? Sales in the New York market tripled in the year following publication of this and partner ads.

For a good analysis of whether subliminal persuasion exists and works, access InfoTrac College Edition, and enter the words

FIGURE 14.9 What differences imply that the promise was kept?

SOURCE: Courtesy Lanvin Parfums Co., New York.

"subliminal advertising" in the search engine. Go to the subliminal projection option, and select the "view periodicals" option. Explore a few of the articles reviewed there. Of special interest is the article by Stuart Rogers titled "How a Publicity Blitz created the Myth of Subliminal Advertising."

REVIEW AND CONCLUSION

As noted earlier, we live in a world exploding with new products, brands, and media that are even more cluttered with ads for those products and brands. Yet advertisers catch our attention and

HERE'S TO ANOTHER SUMMER OF HIDDEN PLEASURES FROM SEAGRAM'S GIN.

Serve one. It's a hit.

Seagram's Extra Dry Gin

FIGURE 14.10 Can you see the "hidden" image?

SOURCE: Reprinted with permission from Ogilvy & Mather.

try to educate us about their brands' features, benefits, and advantages. They use clever cues and sales promotions to prompt us to buy at the point of purchase. These ads and sales promotions are but two elements in what is now termed integrated marketing communication. IMC integrates several elements with advertising to make impressions or brand contacts on consumers. These elements include public relations, packaging, imprinted items (such as clothing, napkins, wrapping paper, and cups), and special events that feature the brand (such as the Pepsi Challenge or the Virginia Slims Tennis Tournament), consumer trade sales promotions, and direct marketing. IMC specialists use sophisticated kinds of research, including demographics, sociographics, psychographics, and ethnographics to target narrow segments of the general audience. Based on this research, they develop products (e.g., Pringles and the Sensor 3 disposable razors), ad copy, layouts, and scripts to appeal to various needs and desires. Ads often use misleading and even deceptive weasel words and misleading claims. And advertisers sometimes use blatant, sophisticated,

Hint. It's as smooth as a moonlit waltz.

CAN YOU FIND THE HIDDEN PLEASURE*
IN REFRESHING SEAGRAM'S GIN?

FIGURE 14.11 What hidden picture can you find in this ad?

SOURCE: Reprinted with permission from Ogilvy & Mather.

and subliminal sexual appeals to hype their brands. As consumers, we need to be on guard, for there is an ethical dimension to advertising, and ads can easily be detrimental instead of being informative.

According to John Chaffee (1998), the positive side of advertising is that it provides consumers with valuable information about brand benefits in important areas like safety, health, nutrition, and cleanliness, as well as about more mundane issues like being attractive, sexy, and successful. He also argues that advertising as a tool of competition inevitably leads to lower prices, which is inherently advantageous for consumers. At the same time, author Russ Baker (1997) points to such questionable practices as brand manufacturers trying to manipulate the editorial content of the media in which their advertising appears. They

FIGURE 14.12 Obvious enough for you?

SOURCE: Reprinted with permission from Ogilvy & Mather.

warn media executives that they intend to withhold advertising if editorial content is critical of the brand or even of the product category. They have been successful in censoring programming and articles to their benefit, and in some cases, they have managed to spike certain programs or articles. Recently, the Bush White House was discovered paying media personalities to slant news stories in favor of the president's words and actions. You might want to take a look at advocates on both sides of the issues in A. Alexander and J. Hanson's (2003) provocative book *Taking Sides: Clashing Views on Controversial Issues in Mass Media and Society*.

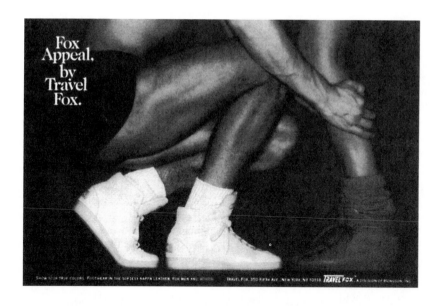

FIGURE 14.13 In this ad for Travel Fox sneakers, the words "Fox" and "appeal" tell you what is going on as we see a man and woman obviously in a sexual position.

SOURCE: Used by permission of Hall & Cederquist Advertising, Inc.

KEY TERMS

When you have finished reading this chapter, you should be able to identify, explain, and give an example of the following words or concepts.

integrated marketing communication	TOMA	frequency	weasel words
brands	positioning	psychographics	faster
slogans	repositioning	need-driven consumers	as much as
jingles	over-communicated society	outer-directed consumers	get action
logo	brand loyalty	inner-directed consumers	blatant sexual appeals
packaging	master brands	sociographics	sophisticated sexual appeals
brand equity	line extension	geographics	subliminal appeals
point of purchase	demographics	ethnographics	subliminal persuasion
sales promotion	reach		embeds

APPLICATION OF ETHICS

You work for East/West Medical Corporation, which performs medical testing. It has purchased ad time on television news programs to announce that consumers can get a free test kit for melanoma screening at the local Kroger supermarket. The ads masquerade as informational news items using the same anchorperson as the news program uses. A question concerning the ads has been raised. Critics ask, "Is it ethical to make an ad appear to be a news item?" The screening kit is free, and the consumer simply sends it in to East/West and gets results back in a week or so for a small processing fee. The fee is mentioned in the directions for use of the kit but not in the ad. Some say that if it saves lives, it can not be unethical. Others say that society relies on news journalists to present the truth, the whole truth, and nothing but the truth, and the "ad as news" violates the social contract between viewers and journalists. There are several options open to East/West. They could label the TV spot as an advertisement at the outset of the spot, thus alerting the viewer. They could label it at the end of the ad after it has been processed by viewers. They could change their appeal by not emphasizing the "free" aspect of the offer and telling the viewer that there will be a processing charge. They could stop using the news program as an envelope for the ad. Which option would you choose and why?

QUESTIONS FOR FURTHER THOUGHT

1. How much money is spent for advertising in the United States per person compared with that spent in other countries?

2. How might advertising reflect the values and norms of a culture?

3. What might a Marxist critic say about the purpose of advertising?

4. What is "positioning," and how does it relate to the niche?

5. What product features can serve as niches?

6. What are some of the problems of an "over-communicated society"?

7. What is the "product explosion," and how does it affect us?

8. What does "breaking through the clutter" mean?

9. Why is "American-made" an example of positioning?

10. What are the difference between demographics, sociographics, and psychographics?

11. What is a DINK?

12. What is VALS, and how does it work?

13. What are focus groups, and what is their purpose?

14. What are some of the languages of advertising? Give examples.

15. How does advertising research lead to advertising copy? Give examples.

16. What are weasel words? Give examples.

17. What are some deceptive claims? Give examples.

18. What is meant when we say that a product has become semanticized? Give examples.

19. What differentiates blatant sexual appeals in advertising from sophisticated ones? Give examples.

20. How are subliminals used in advertising? How effective do you think they are?

 For online activities, go to the *Persuasion* book companion website at http://communication.wadsworth.com/larson11.

Epilogue

One recurring phenomenon that I have noted while revising *Persuasion: Reception and Responsibility* is the continually increasing rate of change. Not only have we seen the rise of terrorist networks across the globe, but many of them seek to destroy the American economy and our sense of security. After the events of 9/11, no one can travel by air with the same sense of confidence that this is the safest mode of transport. New technologies emerge practically weekly. Another ongoing change involves the "boomer" effect. The baby boomer generation that opposed the Vietnam War as "hippies" and "yippies" have moved beyond their trend-setting (and frequently greedy) years as "yuppies" (young urban professionals). Some are now past their highest-earning years as "muppies" (mature urban professionals) and well into their "ruppie" (retired urban professionals) stage of life. They continue to impact our society enormously. Since the last edition of this book, we have seen the dot-com bubble burst and the economy go from boom to bust, and now we are running an enormous budget deficit with no end in sight. And following the corporate scandals and bankruptcies of the late 1990s and early millennium years, our faith in the integrity of CEOs of major corporations and large accounting firms is shot. We have become an incredibly diverse nation as compared to just a few years ago, and this diversity will have sweeping effects in the new millennium.

Technology continues to affect us in unexpected ways. For example, the wreckage of the space shuttle *Columbia* recovered by mountain hunters and fishermen using inexpensive but sophisticated GPS (global positioning satellite) devices. They simply recorded the coordinates of the wreckage and reported that to the authorities. And, of course, use of the Internet, email, e-commerce, and so on has grown exponentially. When I revised the ninth edition of this book, the Internet contained about 10,000 pornographic sites; it now carries millions. And there are other technologies and sophisticated techniques of persuasion yet to be introduced. As all of these and other changes unfold, the number and sophistication of persuasive messages continues to mushroom. The increase in persuasion is almost becoming exponential. Thus, it's more important than ever for us to become critical receivers of persuasion. My feelings are reinforced by Rod Hart (1999), a noted communication researcher and professor of communication at the University of Texas at Austin. He describes the dramatic appeal he makes to his students each term:

> On the first day of class, I observe to my students that all persuaders ask is to borrow just a bit of their minds just for a little while. . . . I tell my students that my course will return their minds to them. I tell them that the cups-full of themselves they willingly loan out to teachers and preachers and cheerleaders in the bleachers can lead to an empty cupboard. I tell them that if they keep giving portions of themselves away that there will be nothing left when they need themselves most—when confused, when frightened, when pressed for a decision. I tell them that persuasion is a science that moves in increments, that it happens most powerfully when it least seems to happen at all. . . . I try to instill a kind of arrogant humility in my students, a mindset that gives them the courage to disassemble rhetoric but also the wisdom never to underestimate it. . . . The persuasion course is the most important course they will take in college (n. p.).

As you conclude this course, I hope you will not cease practicing the critical reception skills discussed here. I hope you will try to expand your efforts, skills, and abilities to critically disassemble rhetoric. I hope you will continue to recognize the complexities of the world in which we live and the many persuasive messages we receive. I trust in your instinctive suspicion of persuasive appeals. Together with Professor Hart, I "trust, mostly, in the critical mind's wondrous capacity to call a spade a spade and a rhetoric a rhetoric, to depuff puffery and to make mortals of gods and to maintain a tenacious resolve that we shall not all fall, lemming-like into the sea."

References

Chapter 1

All Things Considered, April 11, 2005.

Alter, J. (2002). "The Body": So Jesse's act is suddenly very old. We've learned that wrestlers can govern until government has to wrestle with something truly important. *Newsweek*, July 1, p. 37.

Beckett, J. (1989). Ad pitches popping up in unusual places. *San Francisco Examiner*, July 17.

Berger, A. A. (2000). *Ads, fads, and consumer culture: Advertising's impact on American character and culture*. Oxford: Rowan & Littlefield.

Berkowitz, L. (Ed.). *Advances in experimental social psychology* (*Vol. 19*, pp. 123–205). Orlando, FL: Academic Press.

Brembeck, W., & Howell, W. S. (1952). *Persuasion: A means of social control*. Englewood Cliffs, NJ: Prentice-Hall.

Brembeck, W., & Howell, W. S. (1976). *Persuasion: A means of social control* (2nd ed.). Englewood Cliffs, NJ: Prentice-Hall.

Burke, K. (1970). *A grammar of motives*. Berkeley: University of California Press.

Fotheringham, W. (1966). *Perspectives on persuasion*. Boston: Allyn & Bacon.

Gearhart, S. M. (1979). The womanization of rhetoric. *Women's Studies International Quarterly*, 2, 195–201.

Hall Jamieson, K. (1992). *Dirty politics: Deception, distraction and democracy*. New York: Oxford University Press.

Marwell, G., & Schmitt, D. R. (1990). An introduction. In J. P. Dillard (Ed.), *Seeking compliance: The production of interpersonal influence messages* (pp. 3–5). Scottsdale, AZ: Gorsuch Scarisbrick.

McLuhan, M. (1964). *Understanding media: The extensions of man*. New York: Signet.

News Record, Gillette, Wyoming, May 10, 2005.

Petty, R. E., & Cacioppo, J. T. (1986). The elaboration likelihood model of persuasion. In L. Berkowitz (Ed.), *Advances in experimental social psychology* (Vol. 19, pp. 123–205).

Postman, N. (1981). Interview. *U.S. News & World Report*, Jan. 19, p. 43.

Postman, N. (1985). *Amusing ourselves to death: Public discourse in the age of show business*. New York: Penguin Books.

Rank, H. (1976). Teaching about public persuasion. In D. Dieterich (Ed.), *Teaching and doublespeak*. Urbana, IL: National Council of Teachers of English.

Roberts, R. (1924). *The works of Aristotle*. Oxford: Clarendon.

Shannon, C. E., & Weaver, W. (1949). *The mathematical theory of communication*. Urbana: University of Illinois Press.

Simons, H. W. (1976). *Persuasion: Understanding, practice, and analysis*. Reading, MA: Addison-Wesley.

Sullivan, P. A. (1993). Signification and Afro-American rhetoric: A case study of Jesse Jackson's "Common ground and common sense" speech. *Communication Quarterly*, *41*, 1–15.

Toffler, A. (1980). *The third wave*. New York: Bantam Books.

Chapter 2

Adam, A. (2005). *Gender, ethics, and information technology.* New York: Palgrave Macmillan.

Alter, J. (1987). The search for personal flaws. *Newsweek,* Oct. 19, p. 79.

Bailey, R. W. (1984). George Orwell and the English language. In E. J. Jensen (Ed.), *The future of nineteen eighty-four* (pp. 23–46). Ann Arbor: University of Michigan Press.

Baker, S., & Martinson, D. L. (2001). The TARES test: Five principles for ethical persuasion. *Journal of Mass Media Ethics, 16,* 148–175.

Bate, B. (1992). *Communication and the sexes.* (Reissue). Prospect Heights, IL: Waveland Press.

Beck, J. (1998). Clinton's character under siege once again. *Chicago Tribune,* Jan. 25, sec. 1, p. 19.

Berkman, R. I., & Shumway, C. A. (2003). *Digital dilemmas: Ethical issues for online media professionals.* Ames, IA: Blackwell Publishing.

Bennett, M. J. (1979). Overcoming the golden rule: Sympathy and empathy. In D. Nimmo (Ed.), *Communication yearbook 3* (pp. 407–422). New Brunswick, NJ: Transaction Books.

Booth, W. C. (2004). *The rhetoric of RHETORIC: The quest for effective communication.* Malden, MA: Blackwell Publishing.

Bosmajian, H. (1983). *The language of oppression* (rpt. ed.). Lanham, MD: University Press of America.

Bovee, W. G. (1991). The end can justify the means—but rarely. *Journal of Mass Media Ethics, 6,* 135–145.

Buursma, B. (1987). Do-or-die deadline rallies Roberts' flock. *Chicago Tribune,* Jan. 17, pp. 1, 10.

Callahan, D. (2004). *The cheating culture: Why more Americans are doing wrong to get ahead.* New York: Harcourt.

Christians, C., et al.(2005). *Media ethics* (7th ed.). Boston: Pearson/Allyn & Bacon.

Cooper, M. (2002). Covering tragedy: Media ethics and TWA flight 800. In R. L. Johannesen (Ed.), *Ethics in human communication* (5th ed.) (pp. 319–331). Prospect Heights, IL: Waveland Press.

Cooper, T. W. (1998). New technology inventory: Forty leading ethical issues. *Journal of Mass Media Ethics, 13,* 71–92.

Corn, D. (2003). *The lies of George W. Bush: Mastering the politics of deception.* New York: Crown.

Courtright, J. A., & Perse, E. M. (1998). *Communicating online: A guide to the Internet.* Mountain View, CA: Mayfield.

DeGeorge, R. (1999). *Business ethics* (5th ed.). New York: Prentice-Hall.

Dobel, J. P. (1999). *Public integrity.* Baltimore, MD: Johns Hopkins University Press.

Ermann, D. M., Williams, M. B., & Shauf, M. S. (1997). *Computers, ethics, and society* (2nd ed.). New York: Oxford University Press.

Foss, S. K., & Griffin, C. (1995). Beyond persuasion: A proposal for an invitational rhetoric. *Communication Monographs, 62,* 2–18.

Freund, L. (1960). Responsibility: Definitions, distinctions, and applications. In J. Friedrich (Ed.), *Nomos III: Responsibility* (pp. 28–42). New York: Liberal Arts Press.

Froman, L. A. (1966). A realistic approach to campaign strategies and tactics. In M. K. Jennings & L. H. Ziegler (Eds.), *The electoral process.* Englewood Cliffs, NJ: Prentice-Hall.

Goodwin, H. E. (1987). *Groping for ethics in journalism* (2nd ed.). Ames: Iowa State University Press.

Gorsevski, E. W. (2004). *Peaceful persuasion: The geopolitics of nonviolent rhetoric.* Albany: The State University of New York Press.

Green, M., & MacColl, G. (1987). *There he goes again: Ronald Reagan's reign of error* (rev. ed.). New York: Pantheon Books.

Griffin, E. A. (1976). *The mind changers: The art of Christian persuasion.* Wheaton, IL: Tyndale House.

Gunkel, D. J. (2001). *Hacking cyberspace.* Boulder, CO: Westview.

Hamelink, C. J. (2000). *The ethics of cyberspace.* London: Sage.

Hauerwas, S. (1977). *Truthfulness and tragedy.* Notre Dame, IN: University of Notre Dame Press.

Johannesen, R. L. (1971). The emerging concept of communication as dialogue. *Quarterly Journal of Speech, 57,* 373–382.

Johannesen, R. L. (1985). An ethical assessment of the Reagan rhetoric: 1981–1982. In K. R. Sanders, L. L. Kaid, & D. Nimmo (Eds.), *Political communication yearbook 1984* (pp. 226–241). Carbondale: Southern Illinois University Press.

Johannesen, R. L. (1991). Virtue, ethics, character, and political communication. In R. E. Denton, Jr. (Ed.), *Ethical dimensions of political communication* (pp. 69–90). New York: Praeger.

Johannesen, R. L. (1997). Diversity, freedom, and responsibility. In J. Makau & R. C. Arnett (Eds.), *Communication ethics in an age of diversity* (pp. 155–186). Champaign: University of Illinois Press.

Johannesen, R. L. (2000). Nel Noddings' uses of Martin Buber's philosophy of dialogue. *Southern Communication Journal, 65*, 151–160.

Johannesen, R. L. (2002). *Ethics in human communication* (5th ed.). Prospect Heights, IL: Waveland Press.

Johnson, D. G. (2001). *Computer ethics* (3rd ed.). Upper Saddle River, NJ: Prentice-Hall.

Kane, R. (1994). *Through the moral maze: Searching for absolute values in a pluralistic world.* New York: Paragon.

Kass, J. (1998). Blame for crisis lies not in the stars but in our apathy. *Chicago Tribune,* Jan. 16, sec. 1, p. 3.

Klaidman, S., & Beauchamp, T. L. (1987). *The virtuous journalist.* New York: Oxford University Press.

Kramer, J., & Kramerae, C. (1997). Gendered ethics on the Internet. In J. M. Makau and R. C. Arnett (Eds.), *Communication in an age of diversity* (pp. 226–243). Urbana: University of Illinois Press.

Lebacqz, K. (1985). *Professional ethics.* Nashville, TN: Abingdon.

Lester, P. M. (1991). *Photojournalism: An ethical approach.* Hillsdale, NJ: Erlbaum.

Lester, P. M. (2003). *Visual communication* (3rd ed.). Belmont, CA: Wadsworth.

Ludwig, A. (1965). *The importance of lying.* Springfield, IL: Thomas.

Maraniss, D. (1996). The comeback kid's last return. *Washington Post National Weekly Edition,* September 2–8, pp. 8–9.

McCammond, D. B. (2004). Critical incidents: The practical side of ethics. In D. Lattimore et al., *Public relations: The profession and the practice* (5th ed.) (pp. 84–85). New York: McGraw Hill.

Merrill, J. C., & Odell, S. J. (1983). *Philosophy and journalism.* New York: Longman.

Miller, C., & Swift, K. (1981). *The handbook of nonsexist writing.* New York: Barnes & Noble.

Niebuhr, H. R. (1963). *The responsible self.* New York: Harper & Row.

Opotow, S. (1990). Moral exclusion and injustice: An introduction. *Journal of Social Issues, 46,* 1–20.

Pennock, J. R. (1960). The problem of responsibility. In C. J. Friedrich (Ed.), *Nomos III: Responsibility* (pp. 3–27). New York: Liberal Arts Press.

Perelman, C., & Olbrechts-Tyteca, L. (1969). *The new rhetoric.* Notre Dame, IN: University of Notre Dame Press.

Pincoffs, E. L. (1975). On being responsible for what one says. Paper presented at Speech Communication Association convention, Houston, TX, Dec.

Primer: Blogs and blogging. (2005). *Media Ethics* (Spring), *16,* pp. 14–16.

Rakow, L. (1994). The future of the field: Finding our mission. Address presented at Ohio State University, May 13.

Ross, R. S., & Ross, M. G. (1982). *Relating and interacting.* Englewood Cliffs, NJ: Prentice-Hall.

Samovar, L. A, Porter, R. E., & Stefani, L. A. (1998). *Communication between cultures* (3rd ed.). Belmont, CA: Wadsworth.

Samuelson, R. (1998). Clinton's problems with the other L word. *Chicago Tribune,* Jan. 30, sec. 1, p. 17.

Schwartz, T. (1974). *The responsive chord.* Garden City, NY: Anchor.

Sellers, M. (2004). Ideals of public discourse. In C. T. Sistare (Ed.), *Civility and its discontents* (Ch. 1). Lawrence: University Press of Kansas.

Singer, J. B. (2002). The unforgiving truth in the unforgivable photo. *Media Ethics, 13,* 30–31.

Singer, M. G. (1963). The golden rule. *Philosophy, 38,* 293–314.

Singer, M. G. (1967). The golden rule. In P. Edwards (Ed.), *Encyclopedia of philosophy,* Vol. 3 (pp. 365–366). New York: MacMillan.

Spence, E. H., & Van Heekeren, B. (2005). *Advertising ethics.* Upper Saddle River, NJ: Pearson/Prentice-Hall.

Stewart, J., & Zediker, K. (2000). Dialogue as tensional, ethical practice. *Southern Communication Journal, 65,* 224–242.

Toulmin, S. (1950). *An examination of the place of reason in ethics.* Cambridge: Cambridge University Press.

Wellman, C. (1988). *Morals and ethics* (2nd ed.). Englewood Cliffs, NJ: Prentice-Hall.

Wheeler, T. H. (2002). *Phototruth or photofiction? Ethics and media imagery in the digital age.* Mahwah, NJ: Erlbaum.

Williams, H. M. (1974). What do we do now, boss? Marketing and advertising. *Vital Speeches of the Day, 40,* 285–288.

Wolf, M. J. P. (Ed.). (2003). *Virtual morality: Morals, ethics, and the new media.* New York: Peter Lang.

Wood, J. T. (1994). *Gendered lives: Communication, gender, and culture.* Belmont, CA: Wadsworth.

Chapter 3

Andrews, J. (1980). History and theory in the study of the rhetoric of social movements. *Central States Speech Journal, 31,* 274–281.

Aristotle. (1984). *Rhetoric.* (W. R. Roberts, Trans.). New York: Modern Library.

Bowers, J. W., & Ochs, D. J. (1971). *The rhetoric of agitation and control.* Reading, MA: Addison-Wesley.

Buckley, W. F., Jr. (2002). Burying Wellstone. *National Review Online,* Nov. 1. Accessed Dec. 19, 2002, at http://www.nationalreview.com/buckley/buckley110102.asp.

Burns, S. (1990). *Social movements of the 1960s: Searching for democracy.* Boston: Twayne.

Campbell, K. K. (1998). Inventing women: From Amaterasu to Virginia Woolf. *Women's Studies in Communication, 21,* 111–126.

Fairhurst, G. T., & Sarr, R. A. (1996). *The art of framing: Managing the language of leadership.* San Francisco: Jossey-Bass.

Fisher, W. R. (1978). Toward a logic of good reasons. *Quarterly Journal of Speech, 64,* 376–384.

Fisher, W. R. (1984). Narration as a human communication paradigm: The case of public moral argument. *Communication Monographs, 51,* 1–22.

Fisher, W. R. (1987). *Human communication as narration: Toward a philosophy of reason, value, and action.* Columbia: University of South Carolina Press.

Foss, K. A., Foss, S. K., & Griffin, C. L. (1999). *Feminist rhetorical theories.* Thousand Oaks, CA: Sage.

Foss, S. K., & Griffin, C. L. (1995). Beyond persuasion: A proposal for an invitational rhetoric. *Communication Monographs, 62,* 2–18.

Foss, S. K. (1996). *Rhetorical criticism: Exploration and practice* (2nd ed.). Prospect Heights, IL: Waveland Press.

Griffin, L. M. (1952). The rhetoric of historical movements. *The Quarterly Journal of Speech, 38,* 184–188.

Kilbourne, J. (1979). *Killing us softly.* Cambridge, MA: Cambridge Documentary Films.

Kilbourne, J. (2001). *Deadly persuasion: Why women and girls must fight the addictive power of advertising.* New York: Free Press.

McGee, M. C. (1980). The ideograph: A link between rhetoric and ideology. *Quarterly Journal of Speech, 66,* 1–16.

Plato. (1937). *The dialogues of Plato* (Vol. 1). (B. Jowett, Trans.). New York: Random House.

Rowland, R. C. (1989). On limiting the narrative paradigm: Three case studies. *Communication Monographs, 56,* 39–54.

Scott, R. L. (1993). Rhetoric is epistemic: What difference does that make? In T. Enos & S. C. Brown (Eds.), *Defining the new rhetoric* (pp. 120–136). Mahwah, NJ: Erlbaum.

Warnick, Barbara (1987). The narrative paradigm: Another story. *Quarterly Journal of Speech, 73,* 172–182.

Chapter 4

Ajzen, I. (1991). The theory of planned behavior. *Organizational Behavior and Human Decision Processes, 50,* 179–211.

Ajzen, I. (2001). Nature and operation of attitudes. *Annual Review of Psychology, 52,* 27–58.

Allen, M. (1998). Comparing the persuasive effectiveness of one- and two-sided messages. In M. Allen & R. W. Preiss (Eds.), *Persuasion: Advances through meta-analysis* (pp. 87–98). Cresskill, NJ: Hampton Press.

Allen, M., & Stiff, J. (1998). The sleeper effect. In M. Allen & R. W. Preiss (Eds.), *Persuasion: Advances through meta-analysis* (pp. 175–188). Cresskill, NJ: Hampton Press.

Armitage, C. J., & Christian, J. (2003). From attitudes to behavior: Basic and applied research on the theory of planned behavior. *Current Psychology, 22,* 187–195.

Bless, H., & Schwarz, N. (1999). Sufficient and necessary conditions in dual-process models. In

S. Chaiken & Y. Trope (Eds.), *Dual-process theories in social psychology* (pp. 423–440). New York: Guilford Press.

Bornstein, R. F. (1989). Exposure and affect: Overview and meta-analysis of research, 1968–1987. *Psychological Bulletin, 106,* 265–289.

Chaiken, S., & Eagly, A. H. (1976). Communication modality as a determinant of message persuasiveness and message comprehensibility. *Journal of Personality and Social Psychology, 34,* 605–614.

Chaiken, S., Giner-Sorolla, R., & Chen, S. (1996). Beyond accuracy: Defense and impression motives in heuristic and systematic information processing. In P. M. Gollwitzer & J. A. Bargh (Eds.), *The psychology of action: Linking cognitions and motivation to behavior* (pp. 553–578). New York: Guilford Press.

Chaiken, S., & Trope, Y. (Eds.). (1999). *Dual process theories in social psychology.* New York: Guilford Press.

Cody, M. J., Canary, D., & Smith, S. (1987). Compliance-gaining strategy selection: Episodes and goals. In J. Daly & J. Wiemann (Eds.), *Communicating strategically.* Hillsdale, NJ: Erlbaum.

Dahl, D. W., Frankenberger, K. D., & Manchanda, R. V. (2003). Does it pay to shock? Reactions to shocking and nonshocking advertising content among university students. *Journal of Advertising Research,* 268–280.

DeSteno, D., Petty, R. E., Rucker, D. D., Wegener, D. T., & Braverman, J. (2004). Discrete emotions and persuasion: The role of emotion-induced expectancies. *Journal of Personality and Social Psychology, 86,* 43–56.

Dillard, J. P. (Ed.). (1990). *Seeking compliance: The production of interpersonal influence messages.* Scottsdale, AZ: Gorsuch Scarisbrick.

Eagly, A. H., & Chaiken, S. (1993). *The psychology of attitudes.* Fort Worth, TX: Harcourt Brace Jovanovich.

Falk, E., & Mills, J. (1996). Why sexist language affects persuasion: The role of homophily, intended audience, and offense. *Women and Language, 19,* 36–43.

Fazio, R. H. (1989). On the power and functionality of attitudes: The role of attitude accessibility. In A. R. Pratkanis, S. J. Breckler, & A. G. Greenwald (Eds.), Attitude structure and function (pp. 153–179). Hillsdale, NJ: Erlbaum.

Fazio, R. H., & Towles-Schwen (1999). The MODE model of attitude-behavior processes. In S. Chaiken & Y. Trope (Eds.), *Dual-process theories in social psychology* (pp. 97–116). New York: Guilford Press.

Festinger, L. (1956). *A theory of cognitive dissonance.* Stanford, CA: Stanford University Press.

Festinger, L. (1962). *A theory of cognitive dissonance.* Stanford, CA: Stanford University Press.

Fishbein, M., & Ajzen, I. (1975). Belief, attitude, intention, and behavior. Reading, MA: Addison-Wesley.

Fishbein, M., & Ajzen, I. (1981). Acceptance, yielding and impact: Cognitive processes in persuasion. In R. E. Petty, T. M. Ostrom, & T. C. Brock (Eds.), *Cognitive responses in persuasion* (pp. 339–359). Hillsdale, NJ: Erlbaum.

Frey, K. P., & Eagly, A. (1993). Vividness can undermine the persuasiveness of messages. *Journal of Personality & Social Psychology, 65,* 32–44.

FUD-Counter. (2001). How does FUD relate to Linux? Nov. 1. Accessed Dec. 17, 2002, at http://fud-counter.nl.linux.org/rationale.html.

Giner-Sorolla, R. (1999). Affect in attitude. In S. Chaiken & Y. Trope (Eds.), *Dual-process theories in social psychology* (pp. 441–461). New York: Guilford Press.

Grush, J. E., McKeough, K. L., & Ahlering, R. F. (1978). Extrapolating laboratory exposure research to actual political elections. *Journal of Personality and Social Psychology, 36,* 257–270.

Heider, F. (1946). Attitudes and cognitive organization. *Journal of Psychology, 21,* 107–112.

Heider, F. (1958). *The psychology of interpersonal relations.* New York: Wiley.

Hovland, C. I. (1957). *The order of presentation in persuasion.* New Haven, CT: Yale University Press.

Hovland, C. I., Janis, I. L., & Kelley, H. H. (1953). *Communication and persuasion.* New Haven, CT: Yale University Press.

Janis, I. L. (1967). Effects of fear arousal on attitude change: Recent developments in theory and experimental research. In L. Berkowitz (Ed.), *Advances in experimental social psychology* (Vol. 3, pp. 166–224). New York: Academic Press.

Janis, I. R., & Feshbach, S. (1953). Effects of fear arousing communications. *Journal of Abnormal Social Psychology, 48,* 78–92.

Kellermann, K. (2004). A goal-directed approach to gaining compliance. *Communication Research, 31*, 397–446.

Kellermann, K., & Cole, T. (1994). Classifying compliance-gaining messages: Taxonomic disorder and strategic confusion. *Communication Theory, 4*, 3–60.

Kipnis, D., Schmidt, S. M., & Wilkinson, I. (1980). Intraorganizational influence tactics: Explorations in getting one's way. *Journal of Applied Psychology, 65*, 440–452.

Kumkale, G. T., & Albarracin, D. (2004). The sleeper effect in persuasion: A meta-analytic review. *Psychological Bulletin, 130*, 143–171.

Lavine, H., Thomsen, C. J., Zanna, M. P., & Borgida, E. (1998). On the primacy of affect in the determination of attitudes and behavior: The moderating role of affective-cognitive ambivalence. *Journal of Experimental Social Psychology, 34*, 398–421.

Leventhal, H. (1970). Findings and theory in the study of fear communications. In L. Berkowitz (Ed.), *Advances in experimental social psychology* (Vol. 5, pp. 119–186). New York: Academic Press.

Lund, F. H. (1925). The psychology of belief, IV: The law of primacy in persuasion. *Journal of Abnormal Social Psychology, 20*, 183–191.

Mackie, D. L., & Worth, L. T. (1989). Cognitive deficits and the mediation of positive affect in persuasion. *Journal of Personality and Social Psychology, 57*, 27–40.

Martin, P. Y., Laing, J., Martin, R., & Mitchell, M. (2005). Caffeine, cognition, and persuasion: Evidence for caffeine increasing the systematic process of persuasive messages. *Journal of Applied Social Psychology, 35*, 160–183.

Marwell, G., & Schmitt, D. R. (1967). Dimensions of compliance-gaining behavior: An empirical analysis. *Sociometry, 30*, 350–364.

Miller, G. R., Boster, F. J., Roloff, M. E., & Seibold, D. R. (1977). Compliance-gaining message strategies: A typology and some findings concerning effects of situational differences. *Communication Monographs, 44*, 37–51.

Mitchell, M. M. (2000). Able but not motivated? The relative effects of happy and sad mood on persuasive message processing. *Communication Monographs, 67*, 215–226.

Mitchell, M. M., Brown, K. M., Morris-Villagran, M., & Villagran, P. D. (2001). The effects of anger, sadness, and happiness on persuasive message processing: A test of the negative state relief model. *Communication Monographs, 68*, 347–359.

Mongeau, P. A. (1998). Another look at fear arousing persuasive appeals. In M. Allen & R. W. Preiss (Eds.), *Persuasion: Advances through meta-analysis* (pp. 53–68). Cresskill, NJ: Hampton Press.

Nabi, R. L. (1998). The effect of disgust-eliciting visuals on attitudes toward animal experimentation. *Communication Quarterly, 46*, 472–484.

Nabi, R. L. (2002). Anger, fear, uncertainty, and attitudes: A test of the cognitive-functional model. *Communication Monographs, 69*, 204–216.

Nabi, R. L. (2003). Exploring the framing effects of emotion. *Communication Research, 30*, 224–247.

Petty, R. E., & Cacioppo, J. T. (1979). Effects of forewarning of persuasive intent and involvement on cognitive responses and persuasion. *Journal of Personality and Social Psychology, 37*, 1915–1926.

Petty, R. E., & Cacioppo, J. T. (1986). *Communication and persuasion: Central and peripheral routes to attitude change.* New York: Springer-Verlag.

Petty, R. E., Wegener, D. T., & Fabrigar, L. R. (1997). Attitudes and attitude change. *Annual Review of Psychology, 48*, 609–647.

Petty, R. E., & Wegener, D .T. (1999). The elaboration likelihood model: Current status and controversies. In S. Chaiken & Y. Trope (Eds.), *Dual-process theories in social psychology* (pp. 41–72). New York: Guilford Press.

Pfau, M., Szabo, E. A., Anderson, J., Norrill, J., Zubric, J. C., & Wan, H. (2001). The role and impact of affect in the process of resistance to persuasion. *Human Communication Research, 27*, 216–252.

Pornpitakpan, C. (2004). The persuasiveness of source credibility: A critical review of five decades' evidence. *Journal of Applied Social Psychology, 34*, 243–281.

Prislin, R., & Pool, G. L. (1996). Behavior, consequences, and the self: Is all well that ends well? *Personality and Social Psychology Bulletin, 22*, 933–948.

Rogers, R. W. (1975). A protection motivation theory of fear appeals and attitude change. *Journal of Psychology, 91*, 93–114.

Roskos-Ewoldsen, D. R. (2004). Fear appeal messages affect accessibility of attitudes toward the threat and adaptive behaviors. *Communication Monographs, 71*, 49–69.

Rule, B. G., Bisanz, G. L., & Kohn, M. (1985). Anatomy of a persuasion schema: Targets, goals, and strategies. *Journal of Personality and Social Psychology*, *48*, 1127–1140.

Shaw, M. E., & Costanzo, P. R. (1970). *Theories of social psychology*. New York: McGraw-Hill.

Sherif, M., & Hovland, C. I. (1961). *Social judgment: Assimilation and contrast effects in communication and attitude change*. New Haven, CT: Yale University Press.

Smith, S. M., & Petty, R. E. (1996). Message framing and persuasion: A message processing analysis. *Personality and Social Psychology Bulletin*, *22*, 257–268.

Stone, J., Wiegand, A.W., Cooper, J., & Aronson, E. (1997). When exemplification fails: Hypocrisy and the motive for self-integrity. *Journal of Personality and Social Psychology*, *72*, 54–65.

Wegener, D. T., Petty, R. E., & Smith, S. M. (1995). Positive mood can increase or decrease message scrutiny: The hedonic contingency view of mood and message processing. *Journal of Personality and Social Psychology*, *69*, 5–15.

Wilson, S. R. (2000) Identity implications of influence goals. *Journal of Language & Social Psychology*, *19*, 195–222.

Wilson, S. R. (2002). *Seeking and resisting compliance: Why people say what they do when trying to influence others*. Thousand Oaks, CA: Sage.

Wiseman, R. L., & Schenk-Hamlin, W. (1981). A multidimensional scaling validation of an inductively-derived set of compliance-gaining strategies. *Communication Monographs*, *48*, 251–270.

Witte, K. (1992). Putting the fear back into fear appeals: The extended parallel process model. *Communication Monographs*, *59*, 329–349.

Witte, K., & Allen, M. (2000). A meta-analysis of fear appeals: Implications for effective public health campaigns. *Health Education & Behavior*, *27*, 591–615.

Wood, W. (2000). Attitude change. Persuasion and social influence. *Annual Review of Psychology*, *51*, 539–570.

Zajonc, R. B. (1968). Attitudinal effects of mere exposure. *Journal of Personality and Social Psychology*, *9*, 1–27.

Chapter 5

American Heritage Dictionary. (1985). Boston: Houghton Mifflin.

Berger, A. A. (1989). *Signs in contemporary society: An introduction to semiotics*. Salem, WI: Sheffield.

Burke, K. (1950). *A rhetoric of motives*. Berkeley: University of California Press.

Burke, K. (1966). *Language as symbolic action: Essays on life, literature, and method*. Berkeley: University of California Press.

Burke, K. (1986). *Language as symbolic action*. Berkeley: University of California Press.

Feig, B. (1997). *Marketing straight to the heart: From product to positioning to advertising*. Chicago: American Management Association.

Hahn, D. (1998). *Political communication: Rhetoric, government and citizens*. State College, PA: Strata.

Korzybski, A. (1947). *Science and sanity*. Lakeville, CT: Non-Aristotelian Library.

Langer, S. K. (1951). *Philosophy in a new key*. New York: New American Library.

Lederer, R. (1991). *The miracle of language*. New York: Pocket Books.

National Public Radio. (1999). *Morning Edition*, Feb. 3.

Postman, N. (1992). *Technopoly: The surrender of culture to technology*. New York: Vintage Books.

Suplee, K. (1987). Semiotics: In search of more perfect persuasion. *Washington Post*, Jan. 18, Outposts sec., pp. 1–3.

Sopory, P., & Dillard, J. (2002). Figurative language and persuasion. In Dillard and Pfau (Eds.), *The persuasion handbook: Developments in theory and practice*. Thousand Oaks, CA: Sage.

Chapter 6

American Heritage Dictionary. (1985). Boston: Houghton Mifflin.

Andrews, L. A. (1984). Exhibit A: Language. *Psychology Today*, Feb., p. 30.

Barol, B. (1988). The 80s are over. *Newsweek*, Jan. 4, pp. 40–48.

Berger, A. (1984). *Signs in contemporary culture*. New York: Longman.

Black Elk. (1971). *Touch the earth*. New York: Outerbridge & Dienstfrey.

Broder, D. (1984). The great American values test. *Psychology Today*, Nov., p. 41.

Buissac, P. (1976). *Circus and culture: A semiotic approach*. Bloomington: Indiana University Press.

Burke, K. (1960). *A grammar of motives*. Berkeley: University of California Press.

Chicago Daily News. November 24, 1972. "Fed up? It may lead to an ulcer."

Cialdini, R. (2001). *Influence: Science and practice*. Boston: Allyn & Bacon.

Democracy Project (1999). www.ipa.udel.edu/democracy.

Dillard, J. P., & Pfau, M. (2002). *The persuasion handbook: Developments in theory and practice*. Thousand Oaks, CA: Sage.

Domzal, T., & Kernan, J. (1993). Mirror, mirror: Some postmodern reflections on global marketing. *Journal of Advertising*, Dec., p. 20.

Eco, U. (1979). *The role of the reader*. Bloomington: Indiana University Press.

Eco, U. (1984). *Semiotics and the philosophy of language*. London: Macmillan.

Eisenberg, E. M. (1984). Ambiguity as a strategy in organizational communication. *Communication monographs, 51*, 227–242.

Farrell, W. (1974). *The liberated male*. New York: Random House.

Hahn, D. (1998). *Political communication: Rhetoric, government and citizens*. State College, PA: Strata.

Hosman, L. H. (2002). Language and persuasion. In J. P. Dillard & M. Pfau (Eds.), *The persuasion handbook: Developments in theory and practice*. Thousand Oaks, CA: Sage.

Kallend, J. S. (2002). Skydiving responsibility lies solely with jumper. *Chicago Tribune*, Aug. 11, sec. 2, p 8.

Kittredge, W. (1996). The war for Montana's soul. *Newsweek*, April 15, p. 43.

Koenig, P. (1972). Death doth defer. *Psychology Today*, Nov., p. 83.

Lederer, R. (1991). *The miracle of language*. New York: Pocket Books.

Lewis, C. (1999). The athletes are the games. *Newsweek*, Feb. 15, p. 56.

Lewis, H., & Lewis, M. (1972). *Psychosomatics: How your emotions can damage your health*. New York: Viking Press.

Marshall, D. (1999). An Olympic-size problem. *Newsweek*, Feb. 15, p. 20.

Messner, M. R. (1998). *Politics and masculinity: Men in movements*. Thousand Oaks, CA: Sage.

Nimmo, D., & Combs, J. (1984). *Mediated political realities*. New York: Longman.

Osborn, M. (1967). Archetypal metaphors in rhetoric: The light-dark family. *Quarterly Journal of Speech*, April, 115–126.

Seigel, B. (1989). *The healing power of communicating with your body*. New York: Weider.

Swanson, S. L. (1981). Sensory language in the courtroom. *Trial Diplomacy Journal*, Winter, pp. 37–43.

Tannen, D. (1990). *You just don't understand: Men and women in conversation*. New York: Morrow.

Weaver, R. (1953). *The ethics of rhetoric*. Chicago: Regnery.

Yates, S. J. (2001). Gender, language and CMC for education. *Learning and instruction, 11*, 23–34.

Chapter 7

Austin, N. (2002). The power of the pyramid: The foundation of human psychology, and thereby motivation; Maslow's hierarchy is one powerful pyramid. *Incentive*, July, p. 10.

Bellah, R. N., Madsen, R., Sullivan, W. M., Swoder, A., & Tipton, S. M. (1985). *Habits of the heart: Individualism and commitment in American life*. New York: Harper & Row.

Booth, E. (1999). Getting inside a shopper's mind: Direct marketers are working out how and why consumers arrive at decisions, in order to satisfy their needs. *Marketing*, June 3, p. 32.

Booth-Butterfield, S., & Welbourne, J. (2002). The elaboration likelihood model: Its impact on persuasion theory and research. In J. P. Dillard & M. Pfau (Eds.), *The persuasion handbook: Developments in theory and practice* (pp. 155–173). Thousand Oaks, CA: Sage.

Borchers, T. A. (2005). *Persuasion in the media age*. (2nd ed.). Boston: McGraw-Hill.

Burke, K. (1961). *The rhetoric of religion: Studies in logology*. Boston: Beacon Press.

Carnegie, D. (1952). *How to win friends and influence people*. New York: Simon & Schuster.

Colley, R. H. (1961). *Defining advertising goals for measured attitude results*. New York: Association of National Advertisers.

De Bono, K. G., & Harnish, R. (1988). Source expertise, source attractiveness, and the processing of persuasive information. *Journal of Personality and Social Psychology, 55*, 541–546.

Egley, A. H., & Chaiken, S. (1993). *The psychology of attitudes*. New York: Harcourt Brace Jovanovich.

Eiser, R. J. (1987). *The expression of attitude*. New York: Springer-Verlag.

Feig, B. (1997). *Marketing straight to the heart: From product to positioning to advertising—how smart companies use the power of emotion to win loyal customers.* New York: American Marketing Association.

Festinger, L. (1962). *A theory of cognitive dissonance.* Stanford, CA: Stanford University Press.

Fishbein, M., & Ajzen, I. (1975). *Belief, attitude, intention, and behavior: An introduction to theory and research.* Reading, MA: Addison-Wesley.

Fonda, J. (2005). *My life so far.* New York: Random House.

Frankl, V. (1962). *Man's search for meaning: An introduction to logotherapy.* New York: Washington Square.

Freedman, D. H. (1988). Why you watch some commercials—whether you want to or not. *TV Guide,* Feb. 20.

Friedman, J. L., & Dagnoli, J. (1988). Brand name spreading: Line extensions are marketers' lifeline. *Advertising Age,* Feb. 22.

Lafavore, R. (1995). From here to eternity: Men's desire for immortality. *Men's Health,* Nov., p. 74.

Lane, W. R., King, K. W., & Russell, J. T. (2005), *Kleppner's advertising procedure* (16th ed.). Upper Saddle River, NJ: Pearson Education.

Larson, C. U., & Sanders, R. (1975). Faith, mystery, and data: An analysis of "scientific" studies of persuasion. *Quarterly Journal of Speech, 61,* 178–194.

Lears, T. J. J. (1983). From salvation to self realization: Advertising and the therapeutic roots of the consumer culture. In *The culture of consumption: Critical essays in American culture, 1880–1980.* New York: Pantheon Books.

Levitt, S., & Dubner, S. (2005). *Freakonomics: A rogue economist explores the hidden side of everything.* New York: Harper Collins.

Maslow, A. (1954). *Motivation and personality.* New York: Harper & Row.

Nabi, R.L. (2002). Discrete emotions and persuasion. In J. P. Dillard & M. Pfau (Eds.), *The persuasion handbook: Developments in theory and practice.* (pp. 289–309). Thousand Oaks, CA: Sage.

National Public Radio. (2002). *All things considered,* Aug. 30.

Naughton, R. (2002). More headwind for Martha: As investigators run out of patience, the diva of domesticity may be ordered to testify in Washington. *Newsweek,* Sept. 2, p. 45.

Nelson, R. (2001). On the shape of verbal networks in organizations. *Organization Studies,* Sept.–Oct., 797.

Osgood, C. E., & Tannenbaum, P. H. (1955). The principle of congruity in the prediction of attitude change. *Psychological Review, 62,* 43.

Packard, V. (1964). *The hidden persuaders.* New York: Pocket Books.

Petty, R., & Cacioppo, J. (1986). *Communication and persuasion.* New York: Springer-Verlag.

Petty, R. E., & Wegener, D. T. (1998). Attitude change: Multiple roles for persuasion variables. In D. T. Gilbert, S. T. Fiske, & G. Lindsay (Eds.), *Handbook of social psychology.* Boston: McGraw-Hill.

Pinsky, M. S. (2002). Houston minister views Gospel according to the Sopranos. *Orlando Sentinel,* Sept. 4, 2000.

Porter, R., & Samovar, L. (1998). *Intercultural communication: A reader.* Belmont, CA: Wadsworth Publishing Co.

Putnam, R. (1995). Bowling alone: America's declining social capital. *Journal of Democracy 6,* 65–68.

Putnam, R. D. (2000). *Bowling alone: The collapse and revival of American community.* New York: Simon & Schuster.

Rokeach, M. (1968). *Beliefs, attitudes, and values: A theory of organization and change.* San Francisco: Jossey-Bass.

Rowan, J. (1998). Maslow amended. *The Journal of Humanistic Psychology,* Winter, 84.

Rowell, R. (2002). Martha's taste, not her ethics lures fans. Knight Rider/*Business News,* Oct. 2.

Schiffman, L., & Kanuk, L. (1997). *Consumer behavior.* Upper Saddle River, NJ: Prentice Hall.

Schrader, D. C. (1999). Goal complexity and the perceived competence of interpersonal influence messages. *Communication Studies,* Fall, 188.

Shavitt, S. (1990). The role of attitude objects in attitude functions. *Journal of Experimental Psychology, 26,* 124–148.

Sibley, K. (1997). The e-mail dilemma: To spy or not to spy. *Computing Canada,* March 31, p. 14.

Staal, S. (2001). Warning: living together may ruin your relationship. *Cosmopolitan,* Sept., p. 286.

Williams, M.A. (2001). *The ten lenses: Your guide to living and working in a multicultural world.* Herndon, VA: Capitol Books.

Wood, W. (2000). Attitude change: Persuasion and social influence. *Annual Review of Psychology*, 539.

Zemke, R. (1998). Maslow for a new millennium. *Training*, Dec., 54.

Zimbardo, P. G., Ebbesen, E. E., & Maslach, C. (1976). *Influencing attitudes and changing behavior*. Reading, MA: Addison-Wesley.

Zimbardo, P. G., & Leippe, M. R. (1991). *The psychology of attitude change and social influence*. New York: McGraw-Hill.

Chapter 8

American Heritage Dictionary. (1985). Boston: Houghton Mifflin.

Burke, K. (1985). Dramatism and logology. *Communication Quarterly*, *33*, 89–93.

Butler, L. D., Koopman, C., and Zimbardo, P. (1995). The psychological impact of watching the film *JFK*: Emotions, beliefs and political intensions. *Political Psychology*, *16*, 237–257.

Clark, H. H. (1969). Linguistic processes in deductive reasoning. *Psychological Review*, *76*, 387–404.

Consider the facts. (2002). *Pine County Courier*, July 25, p. 10.

Dahl, S. (2000) *Communications and cultural transformation: Cultural diversity, globalization, and cultural convergence*. London: E.C.E.

Deardorf, J., & Finan, E. (1999). Barton wins $29.6 million. *Chicago Tribune*, March 2, p. 1.

Fishbein, M., & Ajzen, I. (1975). *Beliefs, attitude, intention and behavior: An introduction to theory and research*. Reading, MA: Addison-Wesley.

Fishbein, M., & Ajzen, I. (1980). Predicting and understanding consumer behavior: Attitude behavior correspondence. In I. Ajzen & M. Fishbein (Eds.), *Understanding attitudes and predicting social behavior*. Englewood Cliffs, NJ: Prentice-Hall.

Fisher, W. R. (1987). *Human communication as narration: Toward a philosophy of reason, value, and action*. Colombia: University of South Carolina Press.

Garfield, B. (1988). Ad review: Good commercials finally outnumber the bad ones on TV. *Advertising Age*, March 14, p. 86.

Guttmacher, A. (1993). Social science and the citizen. *Society*, July–Aug., p. 2.

Huglen, M, & Clark, N. (2004). *Argument strategies from Aristotle*. Belmont: Thomson Learning.

Jensen, J. V. (1981). *Argumentation: Reasoning in communication*. New York: Van Nostrand.

Kahane, H. (1992). *Logic and contemporary rhetoric: The use of reason in everyday life*. Belmont, CA: Wadsworth.

Loftus, E. F. (1980). *Eyewitness testimony*. Cambridge, MA: Harvard University Press.

Loftus, E. F. (1984). Eyewitness testimony. *Psychology Today*, Feb., p. 25.

Lunsford, A., & Ruszkiewicz, J. (2004). *Everything's an argument*. Boston: Bedford/St. Martins Press.

Moore, C. (1909). *A short life of Abraham Lincoln*. Chicago: Houghton Mifflin.

The payoffs for preschooling. 1984, *Chicago Tribune*, Dec. 25, p. 25.

Peck, M. S. (1983). *People of the lie: The hope for healing human evil*. New York: Simon & Schuster.

Reinard, J. C. (1988). The empirical study of evidence: The status after fifty years of research. *Human Communication Research*, Fall, pp. 25–36.

Reynolds, R., & Burgoon, M. (1983). Belief processing, reasoning and evidence. *Communication Yearbook*, 7, 83–104.

Reynolds, R., & Reynolds, J. L. (2002). Evidence. In J. P. Dillard & M. Pfau (Eds.), *The persuasion handbook: Developments in theory and practice* (pp. 427–444). Thousand Oaks, CA: Sage.

Santos, M. (1961). *These were the Souix*. New York: Dell books, p. 148.

Scott, B. (1989). *Rockford Register Star*, Nov. 8, editorial page.

Thompson, W. N. (1971). *Modern argumentation and debate: Principles and practices*. New York: Harper & Row.

Toulmin, S. (1964). *The uses of argument*. Cambridge: Cambridge University Press.

Zorn, E. (2002). Season to kill enriches some, repulses many. *Chicago Tribune*, Nov. 11, sec. 2.

Chapter 9

American Heritage Dictionary. (1985). Boston: Houghton Mifflin.

America's abortion dilemma. (1985). *Newsweek*, Jan. 14, pp. 20–23.

Baudhin, S., & Davis, M. (1972). Scales for the measurement of ethos: Another attempt. *Speech Monographs, 39,* 296–301.

Beane, W. C., & Doty, W. G. (1975). *Myths, rites, and symbols: A Mercia Eliade reader.* New York: Harper Colophon.

Bellah, R. N., Madsen, R., Sullivan, W. M., Swidler, A., & Tipton, S. M. (1985). *Habits of the heart: Individualism and commitment in American life.* New York: Harper & Row.

Berlo, D., Lemmert, J., & Davis, M. (1969). Dimensions for evaluating the acceptability of message sources. *Public Opinion Quarterly, 33,* 563–576.

Cialdini, R. (2001). *Influence: Science and practice* (4th ed.). Needham Heights, MA: Allyn & Bacon.

Edelman, M. (1967). Myths, metaphors and political conformity. *Psychiatry, 30,* 217–228.

Eliade, M. (1971). *The myth of the eternal return: Of cosmos and history.* Princeton, NJ: Princeton University Press.

Hahn, D. (1998). *Political communication: Rhetoric, government, and citizens.* State College, PA: Strata.

Hofstadter, R. (1963). *Anti-intellectualism in America.* New York: Knopf.

Hofstadter, R. (1967). *The paranoid style in American politics and other essays.* New York: Vintage Books.

Hovland, C., Janis, I., & Kelley, H. (1953). *Communication and persuasion.* New Haven, CT: Yale University Press.

Kelman, H., & Hovland, C. (1953). Reinstatement of the communicator: Delayed measurement of opinion changes. *Journal of Abnormal and Social Psychology, 48,* 327–335.

Kosicki, G. M. (2002). The media priming effect: News media and considerations affecting political judgments. In J. P. Dillard & M. Pfau (Eds.), *The persuasion handbook: Developments in theory and practice* (pp. 63–82). Thousand Oaks, CA: Sage.

Parenti, M. (1994). *Land of idols: Political mythology in America.* New York: St. Martin's Press.

Reich, R. (1987). *Tales of a new America.* New York: Times Books.

Santos, M. (1961). *These were the Sioux.* New York: Dell.

Steele, E. D., & Redding, W. C. (1962). The American value system: Premises for persuasion. *Western Speech, 26,* 83–91.

Tocqueville, A. de. (1965). *Democracy in America.* New York: Mentor.

Chapter 10

Andersen, P. A. (1985). Nonverbal immediacy in interpersonal communication. In A. W. Seligman & S. Feldstein (Eds.), *Multichannel integrations of nonverbal behavior* (pp. 1–36). Hillsdale NJ: Erlbaum.

Andersen, P. A. (1999). *Nonverbal communication: Forms and functions.* Mountain View, CA: Mayfield.

Burgoon, J., Bufler, D., & Woodall, W. (1996). *Nonverbal communication: The unspoken dialog* (2nd ed.). New York: McGraw Hill.

Burgoon, J. K., Dunbar, N. E., & Segrin, C. (2002). Nonverbal influences. In J. P. Dillard & M. Pfau (Eds.) *The persuasion handbook: Developments in theory and practice* (pp. 445–473). Thousand Oaks, CA: Sage.

Ekman, P. (1999). A few can catch a liar. *Psychological Science, 10,* 3.

Ekman, P. (2004). *Emotions revealed.* New York: Times Books.

Ekman, P., & Friesen, W. V. (1975). *Unmasking the face: A guide to recognizing emotions from facial expression.* Englewood Cliffs, NJ: Prentice-Hall.

Ellyson, S., Dovidio, J., & Fehr, B. J. (1984). Visual behavior and dominance in men and women. In C. Mayo & N. Henley (Eds.), *Gender and nonverbal behavior.* New York: Springer-Verlag.

Fornoff, S. (2005). Money talks, so builders listen to the experts. *The San Francisco Chronicle.* June 4, 2005.

Fromme, D., Jaynes, W., Taylor, D., Hanhold, E., Daniell, J., Rountree, R., & Fromme, M. (1989). Nonverbal behavior and attitude toward touch. *Journal of Nonverbal Behavior, 13,* 3–13.

Giles, H., Coupland, N., & Coupland, J. (1991). Accommodation theory: Communication, context, and consequence. In H. Giles, J. Coupland, & N. Coupland (Eds.), *Contexts of accommodation: Developments in applied sociolinguistics* (pp. 1–68). Cambridge: Cambridge University Press.

Goffman, E. (1959). *The presentation of self in everyday life.* New York: Doubleday.

Guerrero, L., DeVito, J., & Hecht, M. (1999). *The nonverbal communication reader: Classic and contemporary readings.* Mt. Prospect, IL: Waveland Press.

Hall, E. T. (1959). *The silent language.* Garden City, NY: Doubleday.

Hall, J. A. (1984). *Nonverbal sexual differences: Communication accuracy and expressive style.* Baltimore, MD: Johns Hopkins University Press.

Knapp, M. L., & Comendena, M. E. (1985). Telling it like it isn't: A review of theory and research on deceptive communication. *Human Communication Research, 5,* 270–285.

Knapp, M. L., & Hall, J. (2002). *Nonverbal communication in human interaction* (5th ed.). Belmont, CA: Wadsworth.

Kotulak, R. (1985). Researchers decipher a powerful "language." *Chicago Tribune,* April 7, sec. 6.

Leathers, D. (1986). *Successful nonverbal communication: Principles and applications.* New York: Macmillan.

Major, B. (1984). Gender patterns in touching behavior. In C. Mayo & N. Henley (Eds.), *Gender and nonverbal behavior.* New York: Springer-Verlag.

Mehrabian, A. (1971). *Silent messages.* Belmont, CA: Wadsworth.

Murray, J. (1989). *The power of dress.* Minneapolis, MN: Semiotics.

Orban, D. K. (1999). The integrative nature of argument and non-verbal communication in different communication contexts. Unpublished paper delivered to Midwest Basic Course Directors Conference, Feb. 4–6.

Packard, V. (1964). *The hidden persuaders.* New York: Pocket Books.

Porter, N., & Geis, F. (1984). Women and nonverbal leadership cues: When seeing is not believing. In C. Mayo & N. Henley (Eds.), *Gender and nonverbal behavior.* New York: Springer-Verlag.

Scheflen, A. (1973). *Communicational structure: Analysis of a psychotherapy session.* Bloomington: Indiana University Press.

Siennicki, J. (2000). Gender Differences in Nonverbal Communication. www.colostate.edu/Depts/Speech/recs/theory20.

Umiker-Sebeok, J. (1984). The seven ages of women: A view from American magazine advertisements. In C. Mayo & N. Henley (Eds.), *Gender and nonverbal behavior.* New York: Springer-Verlag.

Chapter 11

Ahuja, B. (2005). *Buzz marketing: Honest deception.* www.commercialfreechildhood.org/articles/4thsummit/ahuja.

Bales, R. F. (1970). *Personality and interpersonal behavior.* New York: Holt, Rinehart & Winston.

Binder, L. (1971). *Crisis and sequence in political development.* Princeton, NJ: Princeton University Press.

Borchers, T. A. (2005). *Persuasion in the media age* (2nd ed.). Boston: McGraw-Hill.

Bormann, E. G. (1985). *The force of fantasy.* Carbondale and Edwardsville: Southern Illinois University Press.

Bowers, J. W., Ochs, D. J., & Jensen, R. J. (1993). *The rhetoric of agitation and control.* Prospect Heights, IL: Waveland Press.

Cragan, J. F., & Shields, D. C. (1994). *Applied communication research: A dramatistic approach.* Annandale, VA: Speech Communication Association and Creskill, NJ: Hampton Press.

Cragan, J. F., & Shields, D. C. (1995). *Symbolic theories in applied communication research: Bormann, Burke, and Fisher.* Cresskill, NJ: Hampton Press.

Denton, R., & Woodward, D. (1998). *Political communication in America* (3rd ed.). Westport, CT: Praeger.

Faucheux, R. (1998). Strategies that win! *Campaigns and Elections,* Jan., pp. 24–32.

Fortini-Campbell, K. (1992). *The consumer insight book.* Chicago: Copy Workshop.

Garcia, G. (2005). *American mainstream: How the multicultural consumer is transforming American business.* New York: Harper Collins/Rayo.

Lavidge, R. J., & Steiner, G. A. (1961). A model for predictive measurements of advertising effectiveness. *Journal of Marketing, 24,* 59–62.

Metter, B. (1990). Advertising in the age of spin. *Advertising Age*, Sept. 17, p. 36.

Morrissey, B. (2005). Mitsubishi issues web "Thrill ride challenge." *Adweek*, June 8, 2005.

National Public Radio. (1999). *All things considered*, April 2.

Rogers, E. (1962). *The diffusion of innovation*. New York: Free Press.

Schultz, D. E., & Barnes, B. (1999). *Strategic advertising campaigns* (4th ed.). Lincolnwood, IL: N.T.C. Business Books.

Schwartz, T. (1973). *The responsive chord*. New York: Anchor/Doubleday.

Stewart, C. J., Smith, C. A., & Denton, R. E., Jr. (2001). *Persuasion and social movements* (4th ed.). Prospect Heights, IL: Waveland Press.

Trent, J. S., & Friedenberg, R. V. (2000). *Political campaign communication* (4th ed.). New York and London: Praeger.

Trout, J. (1995). *The new positioning: The latest on the world's # 1 business strategy*. New York: McGraw Hill.

Trout, J. & Ries, A. (1986). *Positioning: The battle for your mind*. New York: Harper & Row.

Valdivia, A. N. (1997). The secret of my desire: Gender, class, and sexuality in lingerie catalogs. In K. T. Frith (Ed.), *Undressing the ad: Reading culture in advertising*. New York: Peter Lang.

Chapter 12

Cantola, S. J., Syme, G. I., & Campbell, N. A. (1985). Creating conflict to conserve energy. *Psychology Today*, Feb., p. 14.

Carnegie, D. (1952). *How to win friends and influence people*. New York: Simon & Schuster.

Cialdini, R. (2001). *Influence: Science and practice*. Boston: Allyn & Bacon.

German, K. Gronbeck, B, Ehninger, D., & Monroe, A. (2004). *Principles of public speaking*. New York: Allyn & Bacon.

Howell, W. S., & Bormann, E. G. (1988). *The process of presentational speaking*. New York: Harper & Row.

Molloy, J. T. (1977). *The dress for success book*. Chicago: Reardon & Walsh.

Monroe, A., Ehninger, D., & Gronbeck, B. (1982). *Principles and types of speech communication*. Chicago: Scott, Foresman.

Rank, H. (1982). *The pitch*. Park Forest, IL: Counter Propaganda Press.

Russell, J. T., & Lane, W. R. (2005). *Kleppner's advertising procedure* (16th ed.). Upper Saddle River, NJ: Prentice-Hall.

Scheflen, A. E. (1964). The significance of posture in communication systems. *Psychiatry, 27*, 316–331.

Schwartz, T. (1973). *The responsive chord*. Garden City, NY: Anchor.

Selby, P. (1902). *Lincoln's life story and speeches*. Chicago: Thompson & Thomas.

Simons, H. (2001). *Persuasion in society*. Thousand Oaks, CA: Sage.

Woods, M. (1993). Toothbrush tips for wellness. *Chicago Tribune*, Sept. 12, sec. 5, p. 3.

Chapter 13

Blumler, J. (1979). The role of theory in uses and gratifications studies. *Communicationo Studies, 6*, pp. 9–34.

Boorstin, D. (1961). *The image: A guide to pseudo-events in America*. New York: Harper & Row.

Brand, S. (1987). *The media lab: Inventing the future at M.I.T.* New York: Viking Penguin Books.

Chicago Tribune. (2005). Time to explode the Internet? July 4, 2005, editorial page.

Cirino, R. (1971). *Don't blame the people*. Los Angeles: Diversity.

Gumpert, G., & Drucker, S. J. (2002). From locomotion to telecommunication, or paths of safety, streets of gore. In L. Strate, R. Jacobson, & S. J. Gibson (Eds.), *Communication in cyberspace: Social interaction in an electronic environment* (2nd ed.). Cresskill, NJ: Hampton Press.

Hall Jamieson, K., & Kohrs-Campbell, K. (1996). *The interplay of influence* (4th ed.). Belmont, CA: Wadsworth.

Kaiser Family Foundation. (1999). *Kids and media at the new millennium*. Menlo Park, CA: Author.

Kaplan, D., Wingert, P., & Chideya, F. (1993). Dumber than we thought. *Newsweek*, Sept. 20, pp. 44–45.

Larson, C. U. (2002). Dramatism and virtual reality: Implications and predictions. In L. Strate,

R. Jacobson, & S. J. Gibson (Eds.), *Communication and cyberspace: Social interaction in an electronic environment* (2nd ed.). Cresskill, NJ: Hampton Press.

Lederer, R. (1991). *The miracle of language.* New York: Pocket Books.

Levin, D. (1998). *Remote control childhood?* Washington, DC: National Association for the Education of Young Children.

Madigan, C. M. (1993). Going with the flow. *Chicago Tribune Magazine,* May 2, pp. 14–26.

Matusow, B. (1983). *The evening stars: The making of a network news anchor.* New York: Ballantine Books.

McCombs, M., & Shaw, D. (1972). The agenda setting function of the media. *Public Opinion Quarterly, 36,* 176–187.

McLuhan, M. (1963). *Understanding media: The extensions of man.* New York: Signet.

Meyrowitz, J. (1985). *No sense of place: The impact of electronic media on social behavior.* New York: Oxford University Press.

Ong, W. S. (1967). *The presence of the word.* New Haven, CT: Yale University Press.

Ong, W. S. (1977). *Interfaces of the word.* Ithaca, NY: Cornell University Press.

Ong, W. S. (1982). *Orality and literacy: The technologizing of the word.* London: Metheun.

Postman, N. (1996). Cyberspace, schmyberspace. In L. Strate, R. Jacobson, & S. J. Gibson (Eds.), *Communication and cyberspace: Social interaction in an electronic environment.* Cresskill, NJ: Hampton Press.

Powers, R. (1978). *The newscasters: The news business as show business.* New York: St. Martin's Press.

Ramhoff, R. (1990). Bart's not as bad as he seems: Simpsons as positive as other family. *Rockford Register Star,* Oct. 18, sec. 2, p. 1.

Rubin, A. (2002). The uses and gratifications perspective of media effects. In J. Bryant & D. Zillman (Eds.), *Media effects: Advances in theory and research.* Mahwah, NJ: Erlbaum.

Schwartz, T. (1973). *The responsive chord.* Garden City, NY: Anchor/Doubleday.

Theall, D. (2002). *The Virtual McLuhan.* Toronto: McGill-Queens University Press.

Victory, V. B. (1988). Pocket veto. *Advertising Age,* April 25, p. 20.

Zettl, H. (1996). Back to Plato's cave: Virtual reality. In L. Strate, R. Jacobson, & S. J. Gibson (Eds.), *Communication and cyberspace: Social interaction in an electronic environment.* Cresskill, NJ: Hampton Press.

Chapter 14

Ajmone, T. (2004). *The Age of Subliminal Communication.* www.subliminal-message.info/age_of_subliminal_communication/html.

Alexander, A., & Hanson, J. (2003). *Taking sides: Clashing views on controversial issues in mass media and society.* Burr Ridge, IL: McGraw-Hill/Dushkin.

Amft, J. (2004). Psychographics: A Primer. www.psychographics.net.

Baker, R. (1997). The squeeze. *Columbia Journalism Review,* Sept.–Oct.

Becker, H., & Glanzer, N. (1978). *Subliminal communication: Advances in audiovisual engineering applications. Proceedings of the 1978 Institute of Electronical and Electronics Engineers: Region 3.* Atlanta: Institute of Electronical and Electronics Engineers.

Berger, A. (2000). *Ads, fads, and consumer culture: Advertising's impact on American character and society.* Lanham, MD: Rowan & Littlefield.

Borchers, T. (2002). *Persuasion in the media age.* Burr Ridge, IL: McGraw-Hill.

Chaffee, J. (1998). How advertising informs to our benefit. *Consumers' Research,* April.

Chicago Tribune (2005). Time to explode the Internet? July 12, p. 12.

Cuneo, A. (2002). Creative execs stress the importance of the Internet. Accessed Nov. 13, 2002, at www.adage.com using QuickFind Id: AAO20F.

Diamond, E., & Bates, S. (1984). *The spot: The rise of political advertising on television.* Cambridge, MA: M.I.T. Press.

Dollas, C. (1986). Butterball turkeys: An examination of advertising theory and practice. Unpublished starred paper, Department of Journalism, Northern Illinois University, De Kalb.

Engel, J., Blackwell, D., & Miniard, P. (1993). *Consumer behavior.* Chicago: Dryden.

Espejo, E., & Romano, C. (2005). Children and media policy brief. *Children Now,* Spring, pp. 1–8.

Gallonoy, T. (1970). *Down the tube: Or making television commercials is such a dog-eat-dog business, it's no wonder they're called spots.* Chicago: Regenery.

Global marketers spend $71 billion. (2002). *Advertising Age*, Nov. 11, pp. 1–18.

Goodkin, O., & Phillips, M. (1983). The subconscious taken captive. *Southern California Law Review, 54*, 1077–1140.

Happy 65th birthday to 5,500 Americans—daily. (1988). *Chicago Tribune*, April 20, sec. 8, p. 10.

Hogan, K. (2005) Covert subliminal persuasion: 7 facts that will change the way you influence forever. *The Science of Influence Library*. Eagan MN: Network 3000 Publishing, Forthcoming.

Honomichl, J. (1984). *Marketing research people: Their behind-the-scenes-stories*. Chicago: Crain Books.

Key, W. B. (1973). *Subliminal seduction: Ad media's manipulation of a not so innocent America*. New York: Signet.

Lander, A. (1981). In through the out door. *OMNI*, Feb., p. 45.

Larson, C. (2001). *Persuasion: Reception and responsibility* (9th ed.). Belmont, CA: Wadsworth Publishing Company.

Mitchell, A. (1983). *Nine American lifestyles: Who we are and where we are going*. New York: Macmillan.

National Public Radio. (2006). *All things considered*. January 3.

O' Guinn, T., Allen, C., & Semenik, R. (2006). *Advertising and integrated brand promotion*. Mason, OH: Thomson-Southwestern.

O'Toole, J. (1985). *The trouble with advertising*. New York: Times Books/Random House.

Parente, M. (2004). *Advertising Campaign Strategy* (4th ed.). Mason, OH: Thomson-Southwestern.

Phillips, M., & Goodkin, O. (1983). The subconscious taken captive: A social, ethical, and legal analysis of subliminal communication technology. *Southern California Law Review, 54*, 1077–1140.

Postman, N. (1987). *Amusing ourselves to death: Public discourse in the age of show business*. New York: Penguin Books.

Rank, H. (1991). *The pitch*. Park Forest, IL: Counter Propaganda Press.

Reis, A. (1996). *Focus: The future of your company depends on it*. New York: Harper Collins.

Ries, A., & Trout, J. (1986). *Positioning: The battle for your mind*. New York: McGraw-Hill.

Rogers, S. (1992). How a publicity blitz created the myth of subliminal advertising. *Public Relations Quarterly*, Winter, pp. 12–18.

Rothschild, M. (1987). *Advertising: From fundamentals to strategies*. Lexington, MA: Health.

Schudson, M. (1984). *Advertising, the uneasy persuasion: Its dubious impact on American society*. New York: Basic Books.

Schwartz, T. (1973). *The responsive chord*. New York: Anchor Doubleday.

Segmentation and targeting. (2004). At www.kellog.northwestern.edu/sterntha/htm/module2/1. Evanston, IL: Kellog School of Business.

Storch, C. (1988). Humble grocery cart now a video ad vehicle. *Chicago Tribune*, May 1, Tempo sec., pp. 1, 5.

Subliminals used to fight smoking. (1987). *De Kalb Daily Chronicle*, Nov. 18.

Thompson, S. (2002). Frito-Lay reports Doritos online ad success. Accessed Nov. 18, 2002, at www.adage.com using QuickFind Id: AAO21A.

Trout, J. (1995). *The new positioning: The latest on the world's # 1 business strategy*. New York: McGraw Hill.

Valdivia, A. H. (1997). The secret of my desire: Gender, class, and sexuality in lingerie catalogs. In K. T. Frith (Ed.), *Undressing the ad: Reading culture in advertising*. New York: Peter Lang.

Vestergaard, T., & Schroeder, K. (1985). *The language of advertising*. London: Basil Blackwell.

Weiss, M. J. (1989). *The clustering of America: A vivid portrait of the nation's 40 neighborhood types —Their values, lifestyles, and eccentricities*. New York: Harper & Row.

Wentz, L., & Cuneo, A. (2002). Double-digit Hispanic ad growth continues. Accessed Sept. 16, 2002, at www.adage.com using QuickFind Id: AAN95S.

Williamson, J. (1977). *Decoding advertising: Meaning and ideology in advertising*. London: Marion Boyers.

Winkelman, P. (2004). *Emotion and consciousness*. Eagan, MN: Network 3000 Publishing, Forthcoming.

Wrighter, C. (1972). *I can sell you anything*. New York: Ballantine Books.

Epilogue

Hart, R. P. (1999). Teaching the undergraduate persuasion course: Why? In A. Vangelesti, A. Daly, & G. Friedrich (Eds.), *Teaching communication: Theory, research, and methods* (2nd ed.). Hillsdale, NJ: Erlbaum.

Index